The Best Book
of

MS-DOS 5

The Best Book of

MS-DOS 5

Alan Simpson

SAMS

A Division of Macmillan Computer Publishing

11711 North College, Carmel, Indiana 46032 USA

To Susan and Ashley, as always.

International Standard Book Number: 0-672-48499-4

Library of Congress Catalog Card Number: 91-60444-4

Development Editor: *Dan Derrick*

Manuscript Editors: *Katherine Stuart Ewing and Jodi Jensen*

Production Editor: *Katherine Stuart Ewing*

Technical Editor: *Rob Caserotti*

Illustrator: *Don Clemons*

Production Assistance: *Jeff Baker, Scott Cook, Sandy Grieshop, Bob LaRoche, Michele Laseau, Tad Ringo, Johnna VanHoose*

Indexer: *Jeanne Clark*

Printed in the United States of America

Trademarks

All terms mentioned in this book that are known to be trademarks or service marks are listed below. In addition, terms suspected of being trademarks or service marks have been appropriately capitalized. SAMS cannot attest to the accuracy of this information. Use of a term in this book should not be regarded as affecting the validity of any trademark or service mark.

Above Board is a trademark of Intel Corporation.

The Brooklyn Bridge is a trademark of White Crane Systems.

Carbon Copy and Carbon Copy Plus are trademarks of Meridian Technology, Inc.

Certus is a trademark of Foundation Ware.

COMPAQ is a registered trademark of COMPAQ Computer Corporation.

Concurrent DOS/386 is a trademark of Digital Research, Inc.

Connection CoProcessor is a trademark of Intel PCEO.

COPY AT2PC is a trademark of Microbridge Computers International.

Crosstalk Mark IV and Crosstalk XVI are trademarks of Crosstalk Communications.

DESQview is a trademark of Quarterdeck Office Systems.

dBASE is a registered trademark of Ashton-Tate Corporation.

Disk Optimizer is a trademark of SoftLogic Solutions, Inc.

DNA Networks is a trademark of DNA Networks, Inc.

EasyLAN is a trademark of Server Technology, Inc.

ELS Netware II is a trademark of Novell, Inc.

Epson is a registered trademark of Epson America, Inc.

Fastback Plus is registered trademark and The Logical Connection is a trademark of Fifth Generation Systems, Inc.

FastTrax is a trademark of Bridgeway Publishing Co.

Fastwire II is a trademark of the Rupp Brothers.

FaxMail 96 is a trademark of Brook Trout Technology, Inc.

Flu-Shot + is a trademark of Software Concepts Design.

IBM is a registered trademark and PS/1 and PS/2 are trademarks of International Business Machines Corporation.

JT-FAX 9600 is a trademark of Quadram Limited Partnership.

LAN Smart is a trademark of Localnet Communications, Inc.

LANtastic is a trademark of Artisoft Inc.

Lap-Link is a trademark of Traveling Software, Inc.

Lotus and 1-2-3 are registered trademarks of Lotus Development Corporation.

Mace Utilities and Mace Vaccine are trademarks of Paul Mace Software.

Manzana Third Internal Plus and Manzana Host Powered Plus are trademarks of Manzana Microsystems Inc.

ManyLink and ManyLink for Work Groups are trademarks of Netline.

Microsoft, BASIC, and MS-DOS are registered trademarks of Microsoft Corporation.

Norton Utilities is a registered trademark of Peter Norton Computing.

Paradox is a trademark of Ansa Corporation.

Paranet Turbo is a trademark of Nicat Marketing Corp.

PC Anywhere is a trademark of Dynamic Microprocessor Associates, Inc.

PC Connection is a trademark of PC Connection.

PC-MOS/386 is a trademark of The Software Link.

PC Tools Deluxe is a trademark of Central Point Software.

ProComm Plus is a registered trademark of Datastorm Technologies, Inc.

Prodigy is a trademark of Prodigy Services Corp.

R-Doc/X is a trademark of Advanced Computer Innovations.

RAMpage is a registered trademark of AST Research, Inc.

SideKick is a registered trademark of Borland International, Inc.

Software Bridge is a trademark of Systems Compatibility Corp.

Speedstor is a trademark of Storage Dimensions, Inc.

SpinRite is a trademark of Gibson Research Corporation.

Sysgen Bridge-File is a trademark of Sysgen, Inc.

Word for Word is a trademark of Design Software Inc.

WordPerfect is a registered trademark of WordPerfect Corporation.

WordStar is a registered trademark of MicroPro International Corporation.

Overview

Contents

P A R T

DOS Essentials

P A R T

Managing Programs and Files

P A R T

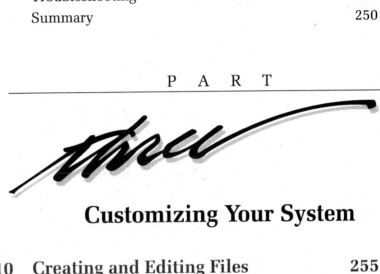

Customizing Your System

PART

Programming DOS

P A R T

Advanced DOS Techniques

Introduction

DOS 5, the latest version of Microsoft's disk operating system, offers the most significant changes and improvements since the change from DOS 1 to DOS 2. For the beginner and casual user, DOS 5 offers a new DOS Shell that provides a greatly simplified, graphic interface, as well as on-line help—features sorely missing from or weak in earlier versions of DOS.

For the more power-hungry user, DOS 5 offers macros, much improved memory control, a vastly improved text editor, and much more.

Who This Book Is For

You might be wondering if this book is the correct one for you or your particular computer. The answer is "yes" if your equipment and experience level match any of these:

- ❏ You use or own an IBM or IBM-compatible microcomputer (such as COMPAQ, Epson, Sharp, or any of the other "clones"). All of these computers use DOS.

- ❏ You have no computer experience whatsoever and are not even sure what DOS is.

- ❏ You have some experience and are familiar with DOS, but want to expand your knowledge of DOS in general, or DOS 5 specifically, to gain more power in using your computer.

Probably the only person this book is not designed for is the DOS programmer whose main concern is learning or using assembly language. That topic, though related to DOS, is generally covered in books devoted to assembly language programming.

Versions of DOS Supported

I know you have Versions 1 through 5 to contend with—not to mention several subversions in between like 3.1, 3.2, 3.3, and so forth. For the most part, this book focuses on version 5, particularly in the more tutorial-based chapters.

However I'm aware that not all users will have DOS 5, and some users who work with multiple machines need to change from one version to another. Hence, in the reference section of this book (Appendix B), I provide more version-specific information, as well as an indication of which version introduced a particular command.

How Much Do You Need To Know About DOS?

One of the most common questions I hear, even from somewhat experienced users of word processing and spreadsheet programs, is "What is DOS?" I'll answer that question right off the bat in Chapter 1.

A second common question is "How much do I need to know about DOS?" The answer to that question varies, but a good general answer is "The more, the better." Certainly the basics of running programs, copying, moving, deleting, and renaming files are practically essential to everyone who ever sits down at the keyboard. These are the topics I cover first in this book.

If you want to be a true power user and learn how to configure your system for maximum speed and performance, you'll want to learn about batch files, memory management, macros, system configuration, and so forth; more advanced topics that are discussed in later chapters of this book.

This book is designed to take you from the most important "need to know" information, and then to more advanced, though to some extent, "nice to know" information. Therefore, you can read as far as you wish to learn what you want to learn and then keep the book around for future reference to find information on an "as needed" basis. Here's a summary of the contents of the book:

Part 1: DOS Essentials

Part 1 teaches you about the important role that DOS plays on your computer, and how to explore and see what's currently available to you. These are truly the essentials because you need the skills presented here to locate and run programs — which is what using a computer is all about.

Part 2: Managing Programs and Files

This part focuses on important skills in managing diskettes, your hard disk, and general file management such as copying, moving, renaming, deleting, "undeleting," and searching for files. These techniques are certain to make your day-to-day computer use simpler and more efficient.

Part 3: Customizing Your System

These chapters take you deeper into DOS and show you techniques for tailoring your equipment to your needs and simplifying its use. Also in this part, you'll gain more control of your screen, printer, and keyboard.

Part 4: Programming DOS

Part 4 moves you into the realm of "programming" DOS, where you'll learn to create your own DOS commands to further simplify your work. The type of programming described here is the relatively easy creation of batch files and macros, so you don't need a background or education in computer science to use these powerful techniques.

Part 5: Advanced DOS Techniques

Part 5 takes you "inside" your computer and DOS, where you'll learn about the various types of memory and storage on your machine, solutions to common problems, and other techniques that add more power and flexibility to your computer prowess.

Appendixes

Appendix A presents instructions for installing DOS 5 on your computer. Appendix B is a quick and extraordinarily thorough reference to all DOS commands; including useful information on version differences among commands.

Features of the Book

Icons

The icons in this book identify sections that are dedicated to DOS 5 users, DOS 4 and 5 Shell users, command prompt users, or mouse device users, as follows:

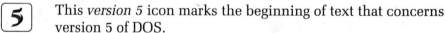 This *version 5* icon marks the beginning of text that concerns version 5 of DOS.

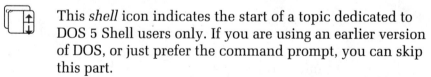 This *shell* icon indicates the start of a topic dedicated to DOS 5 Shell users only. If you are using an earlier version of DOS, or just prefer the command prompt, you can skip this part.

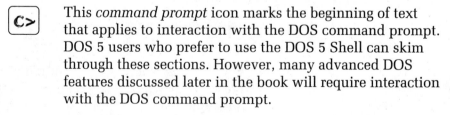 This *command prompt* icon marks the beginning of text that applies to interaction with the DOS command prompt. DOS 5 users who prefer to use the DOS 5 Shell can skim through these sections. However, many advanced DOS features discussed later in the book will require interaction with the DOS command prompt.

This *mouse* icon designates text that explains procedures for using the mouse to accomplish tasks with the DOS 5 Shell.

Endpapers

Inside the front cover, you'll find a quick reference to common DOS operations; applicable to all versions of DOS. DOS 5 users can find a quick reference to using the DOS 5 Shell inside the back cover of this book.

Acknowledgments

Even though only a single author's name appears on the cover of a book, every book is a team project. I'd like to give credit where due and thank the following people:

Gary Masters was instrumental in the development of the initial creation of this book; his careful editing and boundless knowledge of DOS vastly improved the original manuscript.

Cliff Phillip also contributed to many sections of this book, particularly the references in Appendix B.

Many thanks to my agent, Bill Gladstone of Waterside Productions, for keeping my writing career busy and productive.

Thanks to all the people at SAMS who supported and produced this book and brought it from the "idea" stage into your hands.

And of course, many thanks to my wife Susan and daughter Ashley for being patience and supportive through yet another demanding "Daddy project."

DOS Essentials

Chapters 1 through 5 provide a framework for understanding your computer and DOS. Because you will use the techniques presented in these chapters every time you use your computer, the time you invest in learning this essential information will certainly be time well spent.

These chapters discuss the following essential topics:

❏ The role of DOS with your computer, and why you must know about DOS.

❏ How to start your computer with DOS, and why you can't start your computer without DOS.

❏ How information is organized on a computer and how to find the information you need.

❏ How to run programs on your computer.

These chapters are written so that even a beginner can follow at a comfortable pace. If you read each chapter thoroughly, you'll find that you are well on your way to understanding your computer, and that will help you use it more effectively.

Your Computer and DOS

All computers are designed to perform one basic task: read instructions. In this sense, a computer is similar to a stereo or cassette player. If you turn on a cassette player without music (stored on a cassette tape) in it, the cassette deck does nothing. When you put in a recorded cassette tape and press the Play button, the stereo plays whatever music the tape "tells" it to play, be it Beethoven, the Beatles, or Bon Jovi.

Similarly, if you turn on a computer without a *program* (instructions) in it, the computer does nothing. However, when you "play" a program (which is usually stored on a magnetic *disk* rather than on a cassette tape), the computer does whatever the program's instructions tell it to do, such as manage your business, create graphics, or help you write a book.

If you work around people who use computers, you've probably heard the word DOS (pronounced *dawss*) mentioned repeatedly. Why are "computer people" always talking about DOS? Because DOS is a very special program that makes many things possible on the computer. Furthermore, every time you work with a computer, you are certain to use DOS.

Before you learn the specifics of DOS, I'll discuss computers in general and define some common computer terms like *hardware*, *software*, *RAM*, and *DOS*. This will make the computer (and the strange language that people use when talking about it) less mysterious and intimidating.

Computer Hardware

Computer *hardware* is the stuff you can see and touch and would probably break if you dropped it on the floor. A microcomputer *system* usually consists of the computer itself and several *peripheral devices* (or simply *devices*) such as the video monitor, printer, keyboard, and perhaps others. For example, Figure 1.1 shows a computer system that uses several peripheral devices.

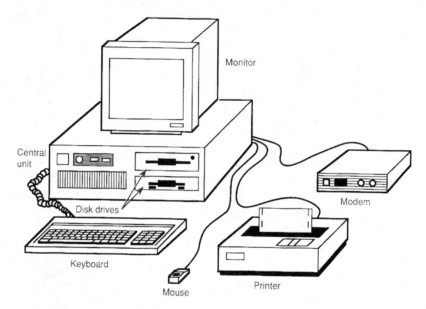

Figure 1.1. A microcomputer system that includes several devices.

Virtually all microcomputer systems consist of a central unit (also called the system unit), a keyboard, and a video monitor. Most microcomputers also have at least one disk drive for storing programs and information.

Other useful devices that you can attach to your computer include a printer, which provides *hard* (printed) copies of information from the computer; a *modem* (short for modulator/demodulator) for communicating with other computers via telephone lines; and a *mouse*, an optional device that lets you interact with the computer without having to type on the keyboard.

A discussion of the functions of these peripherals follows.

The Keyboard

You use the keyboard to type information into the computer. The primary section of the keyboard is similar to a standard typewriter, except that the carriage return key is replaced by a key labeled Enter, Return, or with the symbol ⏎. (As you'll see later, the Enter key is an important one on computers.)

In addition to the standard "typewriter" keys, most computer keyboards also include a numeric keypad (similar to that on an adding machine), cursor control (arrow) keys, and function keys. Look at Figure 1.2 and identify the keyboard that most resembles your own. Note the location of the various special keys.

L Is Not One, O Is Not Zero

If you are accustomed to using a typewriter, you may have developed a habit of typing the letter *l* for the number *1* and the letter *O* for the number *0*. You need to break this habit when you start using a computer. Even though *1* and *l* and *0* and *O* may look the same on paper, they definitely are not the same to a computer. When you need to type the numbers 0 or 1, use the number keys above the keyboard or those on the numeric keypad.

The Video Monitor

The video monitor (also called the *screen,* the *monitor,* the *display,* or the *VDT)* shows what you type at the keyboard and what the computer's response is. Like a TV screen, the monitor usually has an on-off switch. Note, however, that on many monitors, the off position is marked with a 0 (zero), and the on position is marked with a 1 (one).

In addition to the on/off switch, your monitor might also include a knob to control brightness (sometimes identified with a "sunburst" symbol) and another knob to control contrast (sometimes identified by a circle divided into a dark half and a light half). Use these to adjust the brightness and contrast on your screen to make text more legible and background colors easier on your eyes.

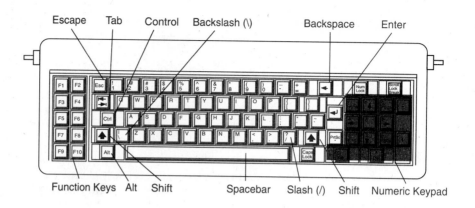

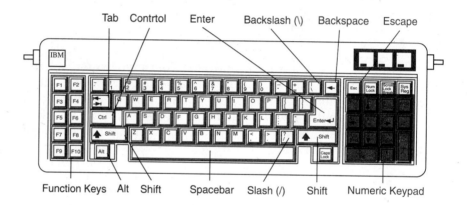

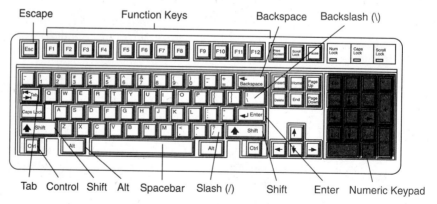

Figure 1.2. Examples of various computer keyboards.

The Printer

Although a printer is an optional device, most computers have a printer attached in order to make *hard copies* (copies printed on paper rather than on the monitor) of information. If your computer has a printer attached, DOS (and this book) will help you use it to its fullest potential.

Various types of printers are available for modern microcomputers, such as the fast *dot matrix* printer, the slower *daisy-wheel* printer, and the powerful and versatile *laser* printer. These various printers, and techniques for using them, are discussed in Chapter 12.

Disk Drives

The disk drive (or drives) on your computer play a role similar to that of a turntable or cassette player on a stereo. Computer programs are stored magnetically on diskettes, in much the same way that music is stored magnetically on cassette tapes. As the drive spins the diskette within its casing, the computer reads information from and records information on the diskettes.

Microcomputer diskettes come in two basic sizes—5.25-inch floppy diskettes (or minidiskettes) and 3.5-inch microfloppies (or microdiskettes). Your computer probably has at least one disk drive that is capable of handling one of these diskette sizes.

The larger of the two, the 5.25-inch diskette, is the "older model," but it is still used on most microcomputers. The smaller, sturdier 3.5-inch diskette is a newer model, used primarily on IBM PS/1, PS/2, and similar computers and on most portable computers. Figure 1.3 shows both types of disks.

Notice that the 5.25-inch diskette has a *write-protect* notch, and the 3.25-inch diskette has a write-protect slide. You use these to prevent information from accidentally being erased from the diskette. I'll discuss this write-protection feature in more detail in Chapter 6.

General Care of Diskettes

Always handle diskettes with the label side up and your thumb on the label. This helps prevent your touching the magnetic media (particularly on 5.25-inch disks where the magnetic media is exposed in a large oblong cut-out section). This procedure also ensures that you insert the diskette into the drive correctly.

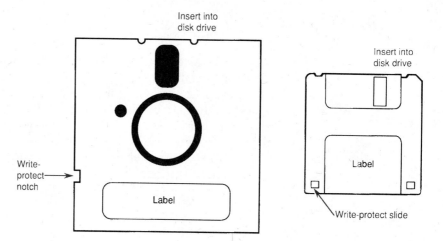

Figure 1.3. Two types of diskettes.

> NOTE: The diskette drive "in-use" light is on only when the computer is actually reading from or writing to the diskette. Simply inserting a diskette does not make the light go on.

When you remove diskettes from your computer, keep them away from extreme temperatures, dust, dirt, coffee spills, pets or young children, and—most importantly—magnets. If you use 5.25-inch diskettes, be sure to place the diskette back in its paper sleeve to keep dust and dirt off the exposed magnetic media.

The procedures for inserting and removing 3.5-inch and 5.25-inch diskettes are somewhat different, as discussed in the following text.

Inserting and Removing 5.25-Inch Diskettes

If your computer uses 5.25-inch disk drives, the front of the drive probably resembles either Figure 1.4 (a full-height drive), or Figure 1.5 (a half-height drive).

Before you can insert a diskette into a 5.25-inch drive, you must first open the latch. To open the latch on a full-height drive, place your thumb near the top of the latch, your forefinger near the bottom of the latch, and gently push in with your thumb while pulling out with your finger.

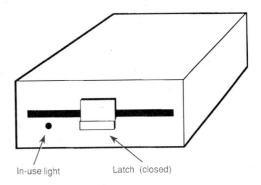

Figure 1.4. A full-height 5.25-inch disk drive.

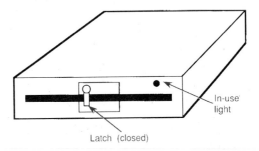

Figure 1.5. A half-height 5.25-inch disk drive.

To open the latch on a half-height drive, simply swing the latch so that it is in a horizontal position.

To insert a diskette into the drive, hold the diskette so that the label is up and toward you (the oblong hole will be facing toward the drive). Gently push the diskette all the way into the drive.

If you are using a full-height drive, close the latch by pressing it downward. To close the latch on a half-height drive, swing the lever down until it is in the vertical position. The diskette is now fully inserted and ready for use.

To remove a diskette from a full-height drive, simply open the latch and pull the diskette out. To remove a diskette from a half-height drive, first swing the latch to the open (horizontal) position. The diskette will partially pop out. Gently pull the diskette the rest of the way.

Remember to return the 5.25-inch diskette to its protective paper sleeve when you remove it from the disk drive.

Inserting and Removing 3.5-Inch Diskettes

Most 3.5-inch disk drives do not use levers or doors, and they look something like the drawing in Figure 1.6. To put a 3.5-inch diskette into a drive, hold the diskette with the label up and toward you (the metal shutter will be facing the drive). Gently push the diskette into the drive slot until you feel a slight click; that locks the diskette in the drive.

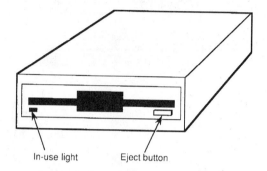

In-use light   Eject button

Figure 1.6. A 3.5-inch diskette drive.

To remove the 3.5-inch diskette, push the eject button on the drive. The diskette will partially pop out. Gently pull the diskette the rest of the way.

Fixed Disks

In addition to diskette drives, many computers also have a fixed disk (or *hard disk*, as it is often called). Unlike the drives that use diskettes, a fixed disk uses magnetic media that cannot be removed; it stays inside the fixed disk unit at all times.

A single hard disk can store as many programs as dozens, or even hundreds, of diskettes can. Whenever you buy a new software product (a program), you copy it onto your hard disk and then store the original diskette in some safe place. In the future, when you want to use a program, such as an inventory manager or a form-letter generator, you don't need to bother with diskettes. Just select (or type) the name of your program, and it's immediately available for use.

In addition to its great storage capacity, a hard disk drive operates at a much higher speed than diskette drives do, which in turn increases your productivity.

Even though the hard disk is usually optional, some software products require your computer to have one. If you work with very large volumes of data, such as a mailing list with thousands of names and addresses, a hard disk is almost a must. I discuss this topic in more detail later in this chapter.

Disk Drive Names

Each disk drive is assigned a "name," which consists of a single letter followed by a colon. The diskette drives are always named A: and B: (if your computer has only one drive, it is named A:). The hard disk is always named C:. Note, however, that some computers might have additional hard disks named D:, E:, F:, and so on.

Figure 1.7 shows the locations and names of various disk drives on several computers. If your computer has two diskette drives, drive A: is usually above, or to the left of, drive B:.

Random Access Memory

At the very heart of every computer is the Random Access Memory, abbreviated RAM. (RAM is often called *main memory* or just *memory*.) RAM is composed of small electrical components called *chips*. These chips are mounted inside the main system unit and need never be removed.

When you first turn on your computer, most of RAM is empty. When you tell your computer to perform a particular job, it copies the program (instructions) required to perform that job from the disk into RAM. Once the program is in RAM, the computer reads the program's instructions and behaves accordingly. Figure 1.8 shows an example, where a program to manage accounts receivable is currently in RAM.

Some people find this arrangement of disk drives and RAM a bit perplexing. After all, if a program is already stored on disk, why can't the computer just read the instructions directly from the disk without first copying them into RAM? There are actually a few reasons for this, but the most important is speed. Basically, RAM operates at a much higher rate of speed than the disk drives. The computer copies a program into RAM before executing its instructions to ensure that everything goes at top speed so that your work gets done as quickly and efficiently as possible.

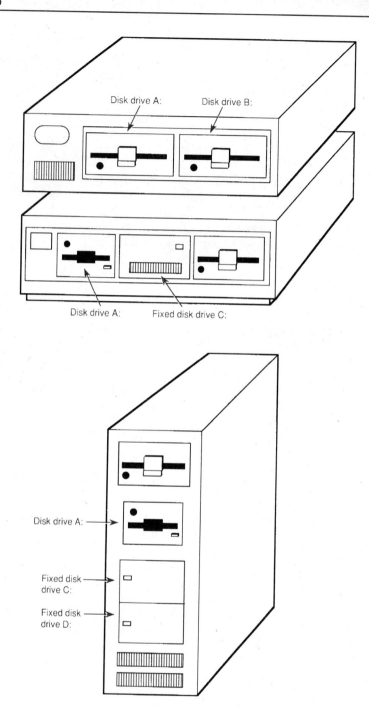

Figure 1.7. Names of disk drives on various computers.

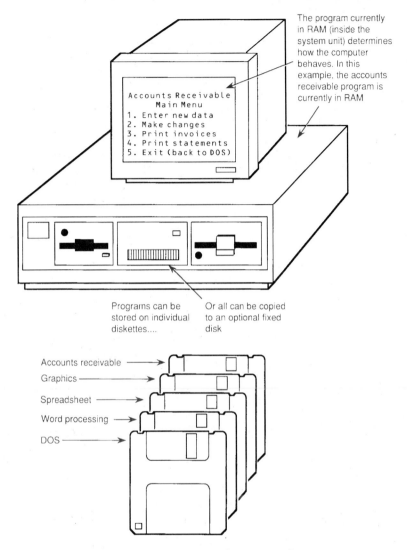

The program currently in RAM (inside the system unit) determines how the computer behaves. In this example, the accounts receivable program is currently in RAM

```
Accounts Receivable
     Main Menu
1. Enter new data
2. Make changes
3. Print invoices
4. Print statements
5. Exit (back to DOS)
```

Programs can be stored on individual diskettes....

Or all can be copied to an optional fixed disk

Accounts receivable
Graphics
Spreadsheet
Word processing
DOS

Figure 1.8. The program currently in RAM determines how the computer behaves.

If RAM is so much faster than the disk drives, why not just store everything in RAM and forget about the disk drives? Well, there are several reasons for this, too. The most important being that, although disks store information *magnetically*, RAM stores information *electronically*. As soon as you turn off the computer, or the electricity goes off, everything in RAM vanishes instantly! For this reason, RAM is said to be *volatile*.

The fact that RAM is so volatile is a bit unnerving to some beginning computerists and is the basis for many computer "horror stories" about power outages causing huge losses of computer information. These stories are often exaggerated, however, because RAM only loads a *copy* of information from the disks. Even if a sudden power outage causes RAM to go blank, everything on disk remains unharmed and intact.

If all this business about loading programs into RAM and executing instructions and so forth sounds a bit intimidating to you, don't worry. As you will see in coming chapters, DOS takes care of all the details for you. When you want to use a program on your computer, all you have to do is type a *command* (usually one word) or press a button. DOS takes care of the rest.

Computer Software

I've already talked about how *software* provides instructions that tell the computer how to behave. When you buy a piece of software (a program), it is stored on a diskette. To use the software, you enter a command that tells the computer to load that program into RAM and to execute its instructions.

There are literally thousands of software products available for modern microcomputers—everything from video games to accounting packages. The following sections briefly discuss the major categories of software.

Word Processing

Word processing programs turn your computer into a sort of super-sophisticated typewriter. In fact, word processing programs have virtually replaced the typewriter because they offer features that no typewriter can provide. With a word processor, you can easily move, copy, or delete words, sentences, paragraphs, or entire groups of paragraphs. You can even reformat an entire document (such as changing the margins or line spacing) with the press of a key.

Some word processors can check and correct your spelling and even suggest changes in your grammar. Most also provide capabilities for printing form letters, mailing labels, and envelopes.

Desktop Publishing

Desktop publishing programs turn your computer into a powerful typesetting machine that can produce printed pages with various print sizes and fonts, margin notes, embedded graphs, and other advanced printing features (such as those you see in this book).

Spreadsheets

If you've ever used a ledger sheet to work with financial data and have had to change an entry and recalculate the entire ledger sheet with your calculator, pencil, and eraser, you're sure to love spreadsheet programs. A spreadsheet program acts much like a ledger sheet, except that when you change any individual piece of information on the ledger sheet, all the calculated values on the sheet are instantly updated for you.

Many spreadsheet programs also provide a graphics capability that lets you instantly plot ledger information on a graph. Spreadsheets are great for projecting "what-if" scenarios, because you can experiment with any piece of information, such as interest rates or potential sales forecasts, and immediately see the results of your experiments.

Database Management Systems

Database management systems are designed to manage large volumes of information, such as mailing lists, customer lists, inventories, financial transactions, and scientific data. These programs let you store, change, delete, sort, search, and print large volumes of information.

Most database management systems (abbreviated DBMS) also let you develop very specific *applications* that are tailored to your own business needs. For example, a single database management system could be used to manage your company's accounting, inventory management, personnel information, sales prospects, and customer lists.

Some database management systems also provide graphics capabilities that let you see information in the form of graphs, pie charts, and other types of graphs.

Accounting Packages

Accounting packages are programs specifically designed to aid in bookkeeping and accounting. Most accounting packages are modularized so that you can buy and use only what your company requires. Accounting packages usually consist of the following modules: General Ledger, Accounts Payable, Accounts Receivable, Time and Billing, Payroll, Job Costing, Inventory Control, and Manufacturing Planning.

Operating Systems

Regardless of which types of software you use with your computer, you must have an *operating system*. This program starts your computer and manages the flow of information to and from the various components, such as the diskettes, the hard disk, the printer, and so on.

DOS, an acronym for Disk Operating System, is such an operating system. As you'll learn in coming chapters, DOS provides many services that are absolutely essential to your computer.

Computer Capacities

Suppose that a friend or a computer salesman shows you a computer, pats it gently atop the monitor, and says "This baby has an 80386 microprocessor running at 20 megahertz, with 640K RAM, and a 30-meg hard disk." Unless you are already familiar with computer terminology, you might wonder if this person is even speaking English. Yes, this person is speaking English and is describing how "big" and how fast the computer is. I will define these often-used computer buzzwords.

Kilobytes

A single character of information occupies one *byte* of storage on a computer. Hence, the word "cat" occupies three bytes, and the word "Banana" occupies six bytes. Most diskettes can store many thousands of bytes, and hence their capacities are often expressed in *kilobytes* (often abbreviated *K* or *KB*). You can think of a kilobyte as 1,000 bytes (though, actually, it's 2^8, or 1,024 bytes). Hence, a 720K diskette can store 737,280 characters of information. Because the average typed, double-spaced page contains 2,000 characters, a 720K diskette can store approximately 360 typed pages (that is, 720,000/2,000 equals 360).

Megabytes

> NOTE: In case you insist on absolute accuracy, I should mention that a megabyte is actually 1,024 kilobytes, or 1,048,576 bytes).

Some diskettes, and certainly all hard disks, can store millions of bytes, and their capacities are measured in *megabytes* (often abbreviated as *M* or *MB* when written or the word *meg* when spoken). A megabyte is equal to a thousand kilobytes, or approximately one million bytes. Therefore, a 30MB (that is, 30 mg) hard disk can hold about 30,000,000 characters, or about 15,000 typewritten pages.

RAM also stores information, but rarely as much as is on a hard disk or even on diskettes. Remember, RAM stores a copy only of the program that you are using at the moment. Therefore, you need only as much RAM as your computer's largest program requires.

"People" Bytes

To demonstrate how kilobytes and megabytes relate to everyday work requirements, look at a practical example. Suppose that you want to buy a computer to manage a mailing list of 100,000 customers. By "manage," you mean that you need to be able to add and delete customers, sort them into zip code order (for bulk mailing), isolate certain customers (such as those that are delinquent in payments), print form letters and mailing labels, and perhaps perform other jobs.

Your best starting point would be to select *software* that can handle such a big job—even before you start looking at computers. For the sake of this example, assume that you decide to use a large, powerful database management system to help you manage the customer list, because it can do everything you need to do.

> NOTE: Most software products list their minimum computer requirements on the box that the program is packaged in; that way, you know what's involved before you buy the program—or a computer.

Of course, you also need an operating system, because the computer can't run without it, so you select DOS as your operating system. To determine how much RAM and disk storage capacity your computer will need, look at the minimum requirements of each software product. Suppose that DOS specifies the following minimum requirements:

System Requirements:

256KB RAM (minimum)

One 720KB 3.5-inch diskette drive
or
One 360KB 5.25-inch diskette drive

Now suppose that your database management program states the following minimum requirements:

System Requirements:

640KB RAM (minimum)

A fixed disk with at least 4MB of space available

One 3.5-inch or one 5.25-inch floppy disk drive

Here it's easy to see that the computer you buy will need at least 640K RAM because the larger of two programs requires that much. You need at least one floppy disk (diskette) drive: either a 3.5-inch drive that can handle at least 720KB or a 5.25-inch drive that can handle at least 360KB.

You will also need a hard disk for the database management system, one that has at least 4MB of space available on it. The word *available* is important because it refers to the amount of space that remains on the hard disk after you store all your other programs there.

Right off the bat, you should plan on DOS and other miscellaneous programs occupying at least two megabytes. The database management program needs at least 4MB, so that brings the total up to 6MB so far.

Don't forget, however, that you also need to store your 100,000 names and addresses on the disk. How much space does that require? Well, look at an exceptionally large name and address and determine how many bytes it requires:

Mr. Thadeus P. Tabacopolous
University of California at Cucamonga
Department of Medicine
17047 Ocean View Drive, Bldg. C-0433
Cucamonga, CA 92011-0433

Counting all the characters (including blank spaces between words) gives you 135 bytes. If you allot as much space for all 100,000 names and addresses, you'll need 13,500,000 bytes (13.5MB) for the names and addresses. Adding that to the 6MB required by DOS and the database management system brings the total hard disk storage requirements up to 19.5MB.

You could get by with a computer that has about a 20MB hard disk. However, it's a good idea to buy at least double the capacity of hard disk storage that you think you need, because one way or another, you'll eventually grow into it. The increase in the cost of purchasing a 40MB hard disk as opposed to a 20MB hard disk is fairly small, so you should probably spend a little extra money to buy a lot of growth potential.

You might be wondering why you need at least 20MB (20,000,000 bytes) of disk storage, but only 640KB (640,000) bytes of RAM in this example. Because RAM only stores one program at a time, you only need as much RAM as the largest single *program* that your computer uses. In this example, the database management program, which requires 640K of RAM, is the largest. Therefore, the computer will need at least 640K RAM. The names and addresses are *data* (information), not a program (instructions), so they have no bearing on the amount of RAM required. When the database management program is in RAM, it will "know" that the names and addresses (all 13,500,000 characters worth) are stored on disk, and it will manipulate and print them without bringing them all into RAM.

I should point out that this example is something of an oversimplification, designed mainly to help clarify how computer buzzwords translate to work requirements. In truth, many programs, particularly spreadsheets, store data in RAM. Furthermore, it is possible to store several programs in RAM, and useful to do so in many situations. Therefore, your best bet is to define your needs in terms of the work you want the computer to perform and then consult an expert before you invest in a computer.

Megahertz

Besides the storage capacity of a computer, *clock speed* is an important factor. All computers operate with an internal *clock*. Each time the clock "ticks," the computer does a tiny bit of work. The speed at which the clock ticks is measured in *megahertz* (abbreviated *Mhz*). One megahertz equals one million ticks per second.

The maximum clock speed of a computer is closely related to the model number of the *microprocessor* that the computer uses. (The microprocessor, also called the Central Processing Unit or CPU, consists of components that execute instructions stored in RAM and perform operations, but I do not need to go into detail about that just now). The five microprocessors used in most modern IBM-compatible microcomputers are the 8086, the 8088, the 80286, the 80386, and the 80486 models.

NOTE: Often, the first two digits of the model number are dropped when discussing microprocessor models. For example, a "386 machine" is a computer that uses the 80386 microprocessor.

The first-generation microprocessor (for IBM-compatible microcomputers) was the 8088, which ran at a clock speed of 4.77 Mhz. The next-generation microprocessor was the 8086, which can operate at a top speed of about 8 Mhz. The next-generation microprocessor is the 80286, which can operate at speeds up to about 20 Mhz. The newer 80386 and 80486 models can operate at speeds in excess of 30 Mhz.

To give you an idea of the differences in speed of these various microprocessors, Table 1.1 shows examples of the time required to calculate the sum of 10,000 large numbers on three different computers using various microprocessors.

Table 1.1. Time required to add 10,000 large numbers.

Microprocessor Model	Clock Speed	Time Required
8086	8 Mhz	128 seconds
80286	12 Mhz	32 seconds
80386	20 Mhz	8 seconds

NOTE: Even though programs do not require a specific clock speed, some programs run only on computers that use an 80286, 80386, or 80486 microprocessor.

When purchasing software, you will never see any "minimum speed" requirements listed on the package because any program can run at any clock speed. However, a faster computer is a more productive computer, so any investment in speed is a worthwhile investment.

So Where Does DOS Fit In?

I've already mentioned that DOS is an operating system—a specialized set of programs that you use to start and operate your computer. It is DOS that actually coordinates all the components of your computer, even to the point of getting other programs into RAM and starting them running.

Much of what DOS does actually occurs automatically, "behind the scenes" where you do not have to be concerned with it. But DOS definitely lets you perform important and useful tasks, including those in the following list:

❏ Run applications programs, such as business programs, graphics programs, word processors, spreadsheets, and any other program you want to use.

❏ Organize large amounts of information for quick and easy retrieval.

❏ Format diskettes and copy information to them to share with co-workers or for use on other computers.

❏ Make backup (copies) of information on your hard disk so that if you ever accidentally erase information, you can always get it back.

❏ Add new components—such as a mouse, a modem, or a laser printer—as your system grows.

❏ Internationalize your computer for printing in foreign-language alphabets.

Before you do any of these tasks, however, you need to get DOS "up and running." That's exactly what you will learn to do in the next chapter.

Summary

This chapter examined the basic components of a computer system and discussed the purpose of each element. This chapter also defined several computer "buzzwords" which you might have heard (or eventually will encounter) in your work with computers.

❏ Computer hardware consists of the physical components of your computer, such as the central processing unit, the keyboard, the monitor, and other optional devices.

❏ Programs, which tell the computer how to behave, are stored magnetically on hard disks and diskettes.

❏ Floppy disk drives allow the computer to read information from and record information on diskettes.

❏ A fixed disk (or hard disk) is an optional device that can store copies of programs and information from many dozens, or even hundreds, of diskettes.

❏ RAM (Random Access Memory) is the part of the computer that stores whatever program you happen to be using at the moment.

❏ Software is the name given to programs (that is, instructions) used in RAM and stored magnetically on disks.

❏ The amount of software that a diskette, hard disk, or RAM can store is measured in bytes (a single character, such as the letter *A*), kilobytes (about 1,000 bytes), and megabytes (about 1,000,000 bytes).

❏ The speed at which a computer operates is measured in megahertz, abbreviated Mhz.

❏ DOS (an acronym for Disk Operating System) is a special set of programs that your computer needs to get started and to use all other types of programs.

Starting Your Computer and DOS

As mentioned in Chapter 1, without DOS (or some other operating system), you can start a computer, but you can't do anything. That's because when you turn on the computer, it immediately searches the diskette in drive A: (or the hard disk, if one is available) for an operating system. If the computer cannot find DOS or some other operating system, it has no operating instructions, so it simply does nothing.

The procedure DOS and your computer go through when you turn on the computer is sometimes called *booting up*. This term comes from the expression "picking yourself up by the bootstraps," which is a good analogy to how a computer starts. That is, first the computer gets power; then it automatically starts searching the disk for the operating system (DOS) that actually gives the computer the instructions it needs to do work.

> NOTE: If you already know how to start your computer and what version of DOS is installed on it, you can proceed directly to Chapter 3.

Because there are so many different types of computers and different versions of DOS, the exact start-up procedures for your particular computer cannot be specified here. However, this chapter explains general start-up procedures and shows you how to determine the version of DOS that is installed on your computer.

Installing DOS

> NOTE: If you experience a problem during the start-up procedure, see the Troubleshooting section near the end of this chapter for advice.

Before you can use DOS, you need to install it on your computer. Note that DOS only needs to be installed once—not every time you want to use it. If you are sure DOS is already installed on your computer, you can read either the section titled "Starting DOS With a Hard Disk" or the section "Starting DOS Without a Hard Disk," as appropriate for your own computer.

> NOTE: If you are learning DOS on a microcomputer that's also used by students in a class or by co-workers, you can safely assume that DOS is already installed.

If you are certain that DOS is not already installed on your computer, you need to install it before reading any further in this book. Appendix A provides basic installation guidelines, using DOS Version 5.0 and an IBM computer as the example. If you are using an earlier version of DOS or a non-IBM computer, you should first read the installation instructions that came with your version of DOS.

Hands-On: Starting DOS with a Hard Disk

If your computer has a hard disk and DOS has been installed to start from the hard disk, the steps for starting DOS are simple:

1. Be sure that any `floppy disk drives` are empty. If the disk drive has a latch (or door), put it in the "open" position.

2. Turn on the `computer` (as well as the `monitor` and `printer`) by turning on all the appropriate knobs and switches. (If your switches are labeled 0 and 1 rather than off and on, switch them from 0 to 1.)

3. Wait until the computer finishes its power-on tests (most computers sound a "beep" at this point).

4. Skip to the section titled "Entering the Date and Time."

Hands-On: Starting DOS Without a Hard Disk

If your computer has no hard disk (or if DOS is installed so that it must be started from a floppy disk), the following steps start DOS:

> NOTE: Chapter 1 shows you the location of drive A: and explains the proper way to insert a diskette.

1. Insert the `DOS Startup disk` in drive A:.

2. Turn on the `computer` (as well as the monitor and printer) by turning on all the appropriate switches.

3. Wait until the computer finishes its power-on tests and sounds a "beep."

4. Proceed with the next section.

Entering the Date and Time

Depending on the setup of your computer and the version of DOS you are using, your screen might show a request that asks you to enter the current date and time before proceeding. If your computer does not have a battery-driven clock to keep track of the date and time when the computer is off, DOS will probably ask for the current date by displaying a message similar to

```
Current date is Tue 1-01-1980
Enter new date (mm-dd-yy):
```

> NOTE: If you make a typing mistake, use the Backspace key to erase the error; then make the correction.

The blinking cursor to the right of the colon (:) indicates that DOS is waiting for you to enter the current date. Type the current date using the format mm-dd-yy (e.g., 6-1-91 for June 1, 1991). Press the Enter key (labeled as ↵, Enter, or Return) on your keyboard.

Next, DOS probably displays a message similar to

```
Current time is 1:04:43.47p
Enter new time:
```

Again, the blinking cursor indicates that DOS is waiting for you to enter the time. Even though DOS displays the time down to a hundredth of a second, you can just type the hour and minute, using a *p* to indicate *PM*. For example, type 9:30 for 9:30 AM, or 4:30p for 4:30 in the afternoon. Press Enter after typing the time.

Note that versions of DOS prior to DOS 5 expect you to enter the time in 24-hour (military) format, where morning hours up to noon are expressed as usual (that is, 1:00 a.m. to 12:00 noon), but after noon, each hour has 12 added to it. For example, the hour for 1:00 p.m. is 13, for 2:00 p.m. the hour is 14, and so on until 11:00 p.m., which is hour 23. Midnight is expressed as hour zero (0).

For example, if the current time is 3:30 in the afternoon, you would enter the current time by typing 15:30 and then pressing the Enter key. (You can enter the time in military format in DOS 5 as well, but DOS 5 immediately converts that to standard meridian, that is, AM/PM time.)

What happens next depends on the version of DOS that is currently installed on your computer, as well as how DOS is installed. If you are using a version of DOS prior to Version 4, you will see the DOS *command prompt*, which usually appears as a single letter followed by a greater-than sign, such as A> or C>. (See Figure 2.1.) Your screen might also show additional information, such as the version of DOS in use and copyright notices.

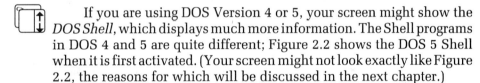

```
C:\>date
Current date is Tue 01-01-1980
Enter new date (mm-dd-yy): 6-1-91

C:\>time
Current time is 12:00:40.91a
Enter new time: 4:30p

C:\>
```

Figure 2.1. The DOS command prompt.

If you are using DOS Version 4 or 5, your screen might show the *DOS Shell*, which displays much more information. The Shell programs in DOS 4 and 5 are quite different; Figure 2.2 shows the DOS 5 Shell when it is first activated. (Your screen might not look exactly like Figure 2.2, the reasons for which will be discussed in the next chapter.)

For the time being, however, assume that your computer is displaying the DOS prompt. The next section shows you how to determine which version of DOS is currently installed on your computer (in case it is not already displayed on your screen).

Determining Your Version of DOS

Although the newest version of DOS (Version 5) is the focus of this book, it also can be used with earlier versions. If your screen is now displaying the DOS prompt (for example, A> or C>) with a blinking cursor to the right, you can easily determine what version of DOS is in control by following these simple steps:

1. Type VER

2. Press Enter

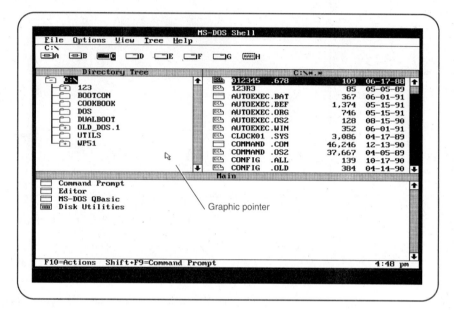

Figure 2.2. The DOS Shell when it is first activated.

NOTE: When typing DOS *commands*, such as VER, you can use uppercase, lowercase, or a combination of upper- and lowercase letters.

The screen now displays a brief message similar to the one that follows:

MS-DOS Version 5.xx

Don't be concerned if the message you see is worded differently; the important fact is that the correct version number appears.

What you do now depends on which version of DOS you are using. Note that the version number is displayed as a whole number followed by a decimal number (such as *Version 3.30* or *Version 5.00*). The numbers to the right of the decimal point represent minor changes within a particular major revision of DOS.

NOTE: If you are currently using Version 2 or 3 of DOS, you can skip to the section titled *Getting It Down Pat.*

If you are using Version 4 or 5 of DOS, continue with the next section.

The DOS Version 4 and 5 Shells

If you are using Version 4 or 5 of DOS, the DOS Shell is probably already displayed on your screen. (If it is not, don't worry, you can display it at any time.) Look again at Figure 2.2 to see how the DOS 5 Shell looks on your screen when it is first activated (although your particular screen might look slightly different).

The DOS Shell provides a more convenient method for interacting with DOS, and it is available in only Versions 4 and 5. It is called a "shell" because, in a sense, it surrounds the complicated inner workings of DOS and lets you interact with DOS in a simplified, *graphical* manner.

As mentioned earlier, the new DOS 5 Shell is significantly different from the old DOS 4 Shell: The new shell is faster, smaller, and more powerful; it contains more features; and it is generally easier to modify and use. Whenever I refer to "the DOS Shell," without specifically referring to the DOS 4 Shell, I mean the DOS 5 Shell. You'll learn how to use the DOS 5 Shell in the next chapter.

NOTE: If you are using DOS 4, you should seriously think about upgrading to DOS 5—both the operating system and the Shell have been greatly enhanced.

Determining Your DOS Version from the Shell

> NOTE: Here is a quick way to determine which version of DOS you are using, even if the Shell is currently displayed on your screen:
>
> 1. Press Shift+F9 (hold down the Shift key and press the F9 key, then release both keys) to leave the Shell.
>
> 2. Type VER and press Enter. Note the DOS version number on your screen.
>
> 3. Type EXIT and press Enter to return to the shell.

If the DOS Shell is not on your screen and you are certain that DOS Version 5 is installed on your computer, refer to the following appropriate section to activate the DOS Shell.

Starting the DOS Shell from a Hard Disk

If your computer has a hard disk and you are certain that you are using Version 4 or 5 of DOS, start the DOS Shell by typing DOSSHELL and pressing Enter. The DOS Shell that appears on your screen resembles Figure 2.2, although it may look slightly different for reasons discussed in the next chapter.

Starting the DOS Shell on a Computer with No Hard Disk

If you are certain that your computer has no hard disk and that DOS Version 4 or 5 is installed on your computer, use the following steps to start the DOS Shell:

1. Remove the Startup diskette from drive A:.

2. Insert the DOS Shell diskette in drive A: and close the drive latch or door, if the drive has one.

3. Type DOSSHELL.

4. Press Enter.

The DOS Shell appears on your screen.

An Alternative Startup Procedure for DOS Version 5 Users

5 If your computer is not equipped with a hard disk, but you are sure that DOS Version 5 is installed on your computer and your computer uses 3.5-inch diskettes (as opposed to 5.25-inch diskettes), you can use the following alternative procedure to start DOS and the DOS Shell simultaneously:

1. Remove any `diskette` in drive A:.

2. Insert the `DOS Shell/Help diskette` in drive A:.

3. Turn on the `computer` (as well as the monitor) by turning all switches to on (or from 0 to 1).

The DOS Shell (similar to the one in Figure 2.2) then appears on your screen.

Getting It Down Pat

The fact that different computers and different versions of DOS require different startup procedures can be a bit confusing at first. If your startup procedure is more complicated than merely flipping on a switch, you might want to repeat this chapter while jotting down notes about the different steps for starting your computer.

Keep these notes near the computer so that you (and anyone else who uses your computer) can refer to them as necessary. You might also want to jot down the exact version number of DOS that is installed on your computer, as you may need to know this from time to time as you read this book.

Turning Off the Computer

You can turn off your computer any time that the DOS command prompt or the DOS Shell is displayed. However, it's good practice first to remove any diskettes from their drives before you turn off the computer.

Feel free to turn off your computer to take a break at any time as you read through this book. Now that you know how to start DOS, you should be able to pick up where you left off easily.

Troubleshooting

If your computer does not start, determine which of the following descriptions most accurately represents your problem and then try the suggested solution.

- ❏ If the screen displays the message `Non-System disk or disk error Replace and press any key when ready`, you have inserted the wrong diskette in drive A:, the disk is not inserted properly, or your hard disk does not have DOS installed on it. Remove any diskette that is in drive A:. Place the correct Startup disk in drive A: (even if your computer has a hard disk). If you've installed DOS Version 4 or 5, insert the copy labeled Startup. If you use DOS Version 3.3, insert the disk labeled Startup or Startup/Operating. If you are using an earlier version of DOS, use the disk labeled DOS—not the one labeled DOS Supplemental Programs. After you insert the disk and close the drive latch (if the drive has a latch), press any key to try starting DOS again.

- ❏ If the computer seems to start, but nothing appears on the screen, be sure your monitor is turned on and then turn the brightness knob clockwise to illuminate the screen. If this does not help, turn off the computer and monitor and be sure all the wires are properly plugged into the back of the computer and into the wall socket. Then turn on the computer and monitor again.

- ❏ If nothing happens when you turn the power switch on the computer (for example, you cannot even hear the fan running), return the switch to the off position, and be sure everything is plugged in according to the directions in your computer's operation manual. Then try again.

- ❏ If all else fails, refer to your computer's operation manual and the DOS manual for additional startup procedures.

Summary

This chapter showed you how to start your computer with DOS and how to find out which version of DOS is installed on it. The main points of this chapter are summarized in the following list:

❏ If your computer has a fixed (hard) disk on which DOS is installed, your basic startup procedure is to remove any diskettes from the floppy disk drives, leave the drive latches (if any) in the open position, and turn the on/off switch to on (or 1).

❏ If your computer does not have a hard disk or if DOS is not installed to start from the hard disk, you must first insert a DOS startup diskette into disk drive A: and then turn on the computer and the monitor.

❏ The DOS Shell is available only in Versions 4 and 5 of DOS. Although these two shell programs have similarities, this book focuses only on the newer—and greatly superior—DOS 5 Shell.

❏ The DOS command prompt, which typically appears as a single letter followed by a > symbol and a blinking cursor, is available in all versions of DOS (although it might not immediately appear in Versions 4 and 5).

❏ A blinking cursor next to the command prompt indicates that DOS is waiting for you to type a command and then press the Enter key.

Exploring the Shell and Command Prompt

5 This chapter offers an opportunity to learn the basics of using the DOS 5 Shell (if you are a DOS 5 user) and the command prompt. The command prompt is applicable to all versions of DOS.

Keep in mind that this chapter presents an overview of all basic techniques available to you for interacting with DOS, and that's a lot of information for a beginner. There is no need to memorize every technique presented in this chapter. In later chapters, you'll gain plenty of experience using DOS. Nonetheless, do read on to get a basic overview of interacting with DOS, and use this chapter for future reference when you need a reminder about a particular technique.

Even if you are not currently using DOS 5, you might also want to read about the DOS 5 Shell here. Chances are, once you see how easy it makes your work with DOS, you'll want to switch to version 5. The section titled "Upgrading to DOS 5" near the end of this chapter gives you some tips on doing so.

About the DOS Shell

In Chapter 2, you got your computer, DOS, and the DOS Shell (if you're using DOS 4 or 5) "up and running." Figure 3.1 shows how the DOS Shell looks on a high-resolution graphics screen (such as on a computer equipped with a VGA, MCGA, or EGA display). Note that some of the information, such as specific drives, directories, and file names shown, will probably be different on your screen.

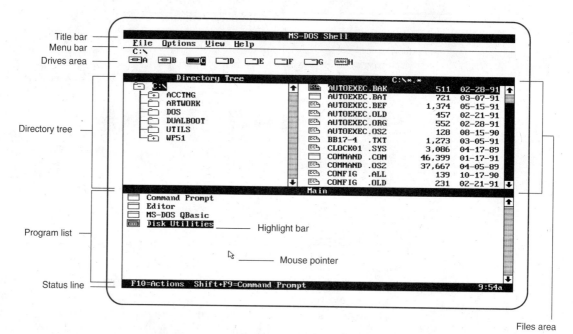

Figure 3.1. The DOS Shell on a high-resolution graphics screen.

NOTE: Figures 3.1 and 3.2 show the default Program/Files Lists view, which you can select from the View pull-down menu (see "Changing the View" later in this chapter).

NOTE: Figure 3.2 shows how the DOS Shell looks on a text screen, such as a monochrome or CGA display, which cannot display icons. Notice also that some of the information presented on the two screens is different, because the figures were taken from two different computers. Nonetheless, the basic structural appearance of the two screens remains the same.

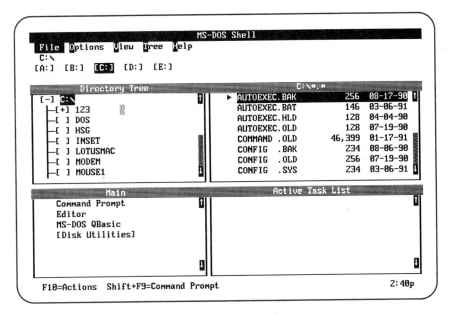

Figure 3.2. The DOS Shell on a text screen.

Most of the figures in this book depict the DOS Shell on a high-resolution graphics screen. However, only the icons are different, so you shouldn't have any problems following the examples presented in the book.

The main elements of the DOS Shell are labeled in Figure 3.1 and are also summarized in the following list:

Title Bar: shows the name of the current screen or window.

Menu Bar: shows the names of available pull-down menus (File, Options, View, Tree, and Help).

Drives Area: displays the names of disk drives available on your computer.

Directory Tree: lists the directory structure of the current disk drive.

Files Area: lists the files in the currently selected directory.

Program List: displays the contents of the Main program group, which includes programs, such as QBASIC and the Editor (discussed later), and program groups, such as Disk Utilities (also discussed later).

Highlight Bar: indicates the currently selected option. You move this about the screen to make selections.

Status Line: shows helpful keys available at the moment.

Mouse Pointer: appears if you have a mouse installed and moves in whatever direction you move the mouse.

You can easily move from one area of the Shell to another using either your mouse or keyboard. Before I go into specifics about how to do that, I'll discuss some general mouse concepts and terminology, just in case you prefer using a mouse.

About Mice

 If your computer is equipped with a mouse (and the mouse is properly installed), you'll see the mouse pointer on your screen. As you roll your mouse about your desktop or mouse pad, the mouse pointer moves in the same direction that you move the mouse.

Your mouse has two or three buttons on it. When you are using the Shell, only one button is active. This is generally the one that your index finger naturally rests on when you place your hand on the mouse. In most cases, this is the left mouse button, because mouse manufacturers assume that you'll use your right hand to roll the mouse.

However, if you've installed your mouse as a left-hand mouse, the right button will most likely be the active one. You may have to experiment a bit to determine which is the active button on your mouse.

Throughout this book, the following terms are used to discuss how to operate your mouse:

Click: Roll the mouse pointer to the option you want and then press and release the active mouse button once.

Double-Click: Roll the mouse pointer to the option you want and then press and release the active mouse button twice in rapid succession (as quickly as possible).

Drag: Roll the mouse pointer to the option you want and then hold down the active mouse button while rolling the mouse.

You'll get a chance to practice some basic mouse maneuvers in a moment.

About the Keyboard

Many operations in the Shell require combination keystrokes. Whenever you see two keystrokes separated by a plus (+) sign, that means "Hold down the first key while you press the second key." For example, the keystroke combination Shift+Tab means "Hold down the Shift key and press the Tab key." You can then release both keys. (You can also hold down the Shift key and press Tab repeatedly to type multiple Shift+Tab keystrokes).

Navigating the DOS Shell

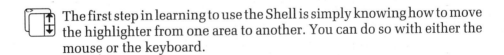 The first step in learning to use the Shell is simply knowing how to move the highlighter from one area to another. You can do so with either the mouse or the keyboard.

Hands-On: Navigating with a Mouse

 To move to any area of the Shell with a mouse

1. Roll the `mouse pointer` to the general area to which you want to move the highlighter.

2. Click `once`.

The Highlight bar moves to the selected area. You can also move directly to a given option within an area by clicking that option once.

In some cases, a single click only moves the highlighter to an option. To actually select an option, you may need to double-click it, as you see later. Note, however, that some options, such as directories in the Directory Tree area and disk drives in the Drives area, are selected even when you just click them once.

Throughout the book, I'll point out when double-clicking is not required. On the other hand, when working on your own, if you click an item and nothing happens (other than the item becoming highlighted), try double-clicking that item.

Hands-On: Navigating with a Keyboard

You can easily use the keyboard to move the Highlight Bar to any area of the Shell as well:

❑ Move ahead to the next area by pressing the Tab key.

❑ Move backward to the previous area by pressing Shift+Tab.

❑ Within any area, press the ↑, ↓, ←, or → keys to move the Highlight Bar from one option to the next.

These options only move the highlight bar from one area to the next or from one specific option to the next. To actually select the currently highlighted option, you must press Enter. You'll get some experience with this shortly.

Using Scroll Bars

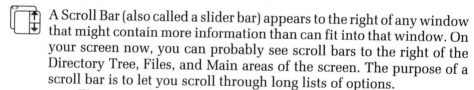 A Scroll Bar (also called a slider bar) appears to the right of any window that might contain more information than can fit into that window. On your screen now, you can probably see scroll bars to the right of the Directory Tree, Files, and Main areas of the screen. The purpose of a scroll bar is to let you scroll through long lists of options.

Figure 3.3 shows an example Files List window, with the Scroll Bar on the right. (The figure also summarizes general techniques for using the scroll bar).

Notice in the figure how the Scroll Bar is partially black, partially white. The white part, called the Slider Box, shows (proportionally) how many file names are currently displayed in the window, whereas the black portion shows (proportionally) how many files are not displayed in the window.

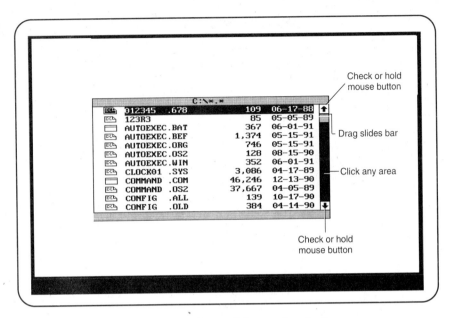

Figure 3.3. Sample scroll bar and techniques.

The general techniques for using a mouse with a Scroll Bar are

❏ Scroll up or down one line by clicking one of the `Scroll Bar arrows`.

❏ Scroll continuously by pointing the `mouse pointer` at one of the Scroll Bar arrows and holding down the `mouse button`.

❏ Scroll to a specific area by dragging the `Slider Box` to wherever you want it to be within the Scroll Bar (for example, three-fourths of the way down to view the options that are three-fourths of the way down from the top).

You can also use the following keys to operate the Scroll Bar whenever the highlighter is within a window that contains a Scroll Bar:

❏ Scroll up or down one line by pressing the ↑ or ↓ key when the Highlight Bar is at the top or bottom of the window.

❑ Scroll continuously by holding down the ↓ or ↑ arrow key.

❑ Scroll a page ("screenful") at a time by pressing the Page Up (PgUp) or Page Down (PgDn) keys.

❑ Jump to the beginning of the list by pressing Home.

❑ Jump to the end of the list by pressing End.

If the Files Area of your Shell screen appears to contain more files than are currently in the window, you might want to take a couple of minutes to try these techniques. You'll see that Scroll Bars are used in quite a few places throughout the DOS Shell.

Using the Menu Bar

 Near the top of the Shell, you'll see the *Menu Bar* (sometimes called the *Action Bar*). The Menu Bar provides access to commands (options) that tell DOS what to do for you. You can use either the keyboard or the mouse to access the menu bar.

Accessing Menus with a Mouse

 To access the pull-down menus with a mouse

Click any option in the Menu Bar to view its pull-down menu.

If you want to leave the menu without making a selection

Click any neutral area outside the menu, such as the Title Bar at the top of the screen.

Accessing Menus with a Keyboard

If you prefer to use the keyboard, you can use the keys listed in Table 3.1 to access the pull-down menus.

Table 3.1. Keys used with the Menu Bar.

Key(s)	Effect
F10 or Alt	Highlights an option on the Menu Bar
← →	Scrolls to the left or right across Menu Bar options.
Enter	Selects the currently highlighted Menu Bar option or the currently highlighted pull-down menu option.
↑ ↓	Moves the highlight up and down through pull-down menu options.
Esc	Cancels the most recent selection or leaves the Menu Bar if no pull-down menus are displayed.

You can also select items from menus by typing the underlined letter that appears in the option. For example, as soon as you press Alt or F10 to activate the menu bar, notice that (on a graphics screen) one letter in each option is underlined. (On a text screen, the letter may be highlighted or brightened).

To select the option without scrolling to it with the arrow keys, you can just type the underlined letter. If you inadvertently select an option you don't understand, press Escape to "back out" of that selection.

About Menu Options

 Figure 3.4 shows the Files pull-down menu on the Shell screen. DOS uses several conventions in menus to provide additional information about each option at a glance:

Dimmed: A menu option that is dimmed is currently unavailable (usually because it makes no sense in the current situation). The option automatically brightens and becomes available when the current situation warrants.

Ellipsis . . .: An option that has an ellipsis after it will take you to a *dialog box* (described later) when selected.

Diamond: Some menu options act as "toggles" that can be turned on and off by selecting the option. A diamond next to an option indicates that option is currently turned "on." (You'll see examples later.)

Keystrokes: A keystroke or keystroke combination such as F7 or Ctrl+\ to the right of an option indicates that you can press that key (or keys) as an alternative to selecting the menu option. Keystroke alternatives such as these are often called *shortcuts*.

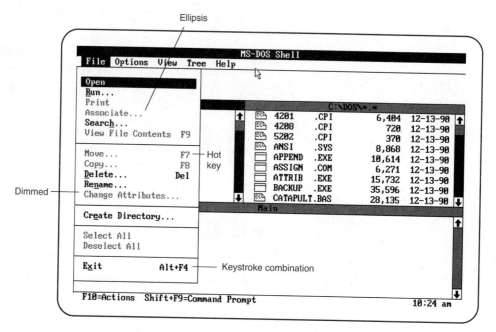

Figure 3.4. Summary of menu navigation techniques.

Changing The View

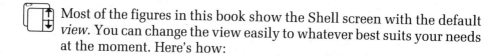 Most of the figures in this book show the Shell screen with the default *view*. You can change the view easily to whatever best suits your needs at the moment. Here's how:

1. Select View from the Menu Bar (either by clicking that option or by pressing Alt-V.

2. Select any of the five views:

Single File List: Removes the program area from the screen. Use when you want to be able to see a longer Directory Tree and Files List.

Dual File Lists: Presents two independent drive, directory, and files areas. Useful for moving and copying files across drives and directories (covered in Chapter 8).

All Files: Displays all files on the drive as though they were all one directory. The name, size, directory location, and other information about the currently highlighted file is displayed to the left. Useful for operations that involve files from multiple directories.

Program/File Lists: The default setting shows the Drives, Directory Tree, Files, and Program Areas.

Program List: Displays the Program List area.

Another window that may appear on your screen is the Active Task List. Turn this window on and off by selecting Enable Task Swapper from the Options pull-down menu.

I talk about all these features in more detail in later chapters. For now, just being able to select the view you want is sufficient.

About Dialog Boxes

Another tool for communicating with DOS is the dialog box, so named because the box (or window) requests information, which you provide. For example, if you select File Display Options from the Options pull-down menu, you'll see the dialog box shown in Figure 3.5. The figure also points out some items that often appear in dialog boxes.

Navigating a Dialog Box

Moving the cursor or highlighter through a dialog box is pretty much the same as doing so on the main Shell screen. With the keyboard:

❏ Press Tab to move forward; Shift+Tab to move backward.

❏ Within a group of options, press ↑, ↓, ←, → to move from option to option.

❏ Press Enter to select the currently highlighted option.

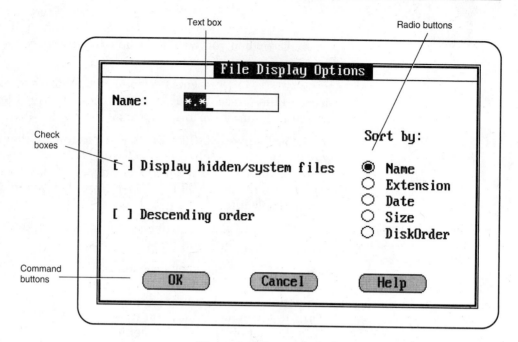

Figure 3.5. A sample dialog box.

 With a mouse, just click the area or specific option to which you want to move.

Using Text Boxes

A *text box* requires that you type some text. In some cases, the text box already contains some suggested text, such as *.* in the sample dialog box showing in Figure 3.5. To use a text box with a mouse

❑ Click `wherever` you want to start typing within the text box.

❑ Type `text`.

If you are using a keyboard rather than the mouse

❑ Press `Tab` or `Shift+Tab` until the cursor gets to the text box.

❑ If you want to replace all the text in the box, type the new `text`.

❏ If you want to insert text into the box, position the cursor where you want to insert text (using the ← and → keys) and type the new text.

Table 3.2 lists keys that you can use to make changes to text in a text box.

Table 3.2. Keys used with text boxes.

Key(s)	Effect
← →	Scrolls to the left or right through existing text
Delete (Del)	Deletes the character over the cursor
Backspace	Deletes the character to the left of the cursor
Tab (or Shift+Tab)	Moves to the next/previous item in the box, if any

Using Radio Buttons

Some dialog boxes contain a set of mutually exclusive options, such as the Sort by: options in the sample dialog box in Figure 3.5. The buttons you use to select from such options are called *radio buttons* because, like a push-button car radio, pressing one button automatically "unpresses" another.

> NOTE: Because the cursor does not actually appear in the radio buttons, you need to watch the cursor as you press Tab or Shift+Tab to see when it moves to the radio button area.

To use radio buttons with a mouse, click the button you want. If you are using a keyboard:

❏ Press Tab or Shift+Tab until you get to the radio button area.

❏ Press ↑ or ↓ to move to the option you want.

❏ Press Tab or Shift+Tab to move to the next area (if you wish).

Using Check Boxes

Some dialog boxes also offer *check boxes*, where you can either turn the option on, by placing an X in its check box, or off, by removing the X from its check box. The check box itself is simply a pair of brackets, like this [ ].

To use check boxes with a mouse, click anywhere on the option or the box to place or remove the X.

With a keyboard

❏ Press Tab or Shift+Tab until the cursor gets to the check box.

❏ Press the Spacebar to place or remove the X.

Using the Command Buttons

A list of *command buttons* appears at the bottom of most dialog boxes. To select a button with a mouse, click it once. With a keyboard, you need to press Tab or Shift+Tab until the button you want is selected (a small underline appears in the button). Then press Enter to select that button. Here, in a nutshell, is what the command buttons do:

OK: Activates any changes or selections you've made, and returns to the shell.

Cancel: Escapes the dialog box without activating any changes or selections.

Help: Provides help with the current dialog box (covered later in this chapter).

If you are using a keyboard, here are some shortcuts keys you can use to "press" the command buttons:

❏ Press Enter to select OK

❏ Press Escape to select Cancel

❏ Press F1 to select Help

One of the best features of the shell is that you can get instant on-screen help at any time; whether you're in a menu, a dialog box, or just on the screen. The next section talks about general techniques for using the help system.

Using the DOS Shell Help System

The Shell has a built-in *help system* to provide immediate answers to questions and solutions to problems. There are three ways to access the help system:

❏ Press the F1 key (at anytime when you're in the shell).

❏ Select the `Help command button` from the current dialog box (if any).

❏ Select `Help` from the Menu Bar to access the Help pull-down menu.

The first two methods generally provide *context-sensitive* help, which means that the help that appears on your screen is relevant to whatever you are doing at the moment or whatever option is currently highlighted on your screen. The third option, using the Help menu, provides access to the same help screens, but through a more general means. Both types of help are described in the following sections.

Context-Sensitive Help

If a dialog box is displayed, or you've highlighted an option and want some help with it before actually selecting it, you can press the F1 key or click the Help button (if one is available). For example, if you select Confirmation from the Options pull-down menu, then select Help (or press F1) from the dialog box that appears, the help window shown in Figure 3.6 appears on your screen.

Like a dialog box, help windows have command buttons at the bottom, and you use the same techniques to select those buttons. The help text appears in the center of the box, and a Scroll Bar to the right of the help text lets you scroll up and down through additional text (if any).

Here are some features that are common to all help windows:

Related Topics: Related topics appear in the help text in different colored or reversed text. For help with any related topic, double-click the topic with your mouse or press Tab until the highlighter gets to that topic and then press Enter.

Close: Select the Close button (or just press Enter) when you've finished with the help window and want to return to what you were doing before.

Back: Select the Back button to *back up* to the previous help window (if any).

Keys: Provides help with the keyboard.

Index: Takes you to the help index, where help topics are organized in general categories.

Help: Offers help on using the help system in general.

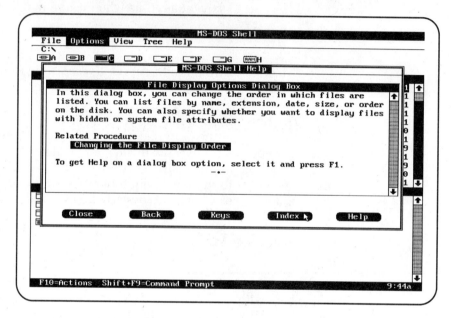

Figure 3.6. An example help window.

Using the Help Menu

In addition to the context-sensitive help, you can get general help from the Help pull-down menu. If you're using a mouse, click Help in the Menu Bar. If you are using the keyboard, press F10 or Alt and then press H to select Help. A menu with the following options appears:

Index: Takes you to the help index, where topics are presented in alphabetical order (like the index in a book).

Keyboard: Provides information on keys used with the Shell. After selecting Keys, use Tab and Shift+Tab to highlight any

option and then press Enter to select it, or double-click any
option with your mouse.

Shell Basics: Lets you read many helpful screens about the
organization of the Shell and its various features.

Commands: Provides help with menu commands (options)
organized in the same manner that they are on the menus.

Procedures: Offers step-by-step instructions about how to
perform many common DOS procedures.

Using Help: Offers information on using the Help system.

About Shell: Shows the current version and copyright
information.

As with all help windows, those that you get to from the Help
menu provide command buttons, and in some cases, uniquely colored
text that you can select to get instant help on that topic.

Hands On: Practicing with Help Screens

The best way to learn the help system is to start using it. To get started,
I recommend you try the Using Help option on the Help menu first. You
might also want to explore the Shell Basics help screens, which will
reinforce some of what you've learned in this chapter.

Of course, there's no need to memorize all the information,
because you can simply "pop back" to the help system whenever you
feel like it.

The Great Escape

With such an array of choices, features, and help tools available, it's not
uncommon for a beginner to start feeling a bit lost from time to time. In
fact, two of the most common questions uttered by beginners are
"Where am I?" and "How do I get back to...?"

If you keep in mind the following two points, you should be able
to answer at least one of those questions in most situations:

❏ When you are in unknown territory, press Escape or select the
   Cancel button (if any) to try "backing out" to more familiar
   territory.

❏ Get more help by pressing the F1 key or click the Help button (if any).

Please be forewarned: Although pressing Esc or clicking Cancel can get you out of unfamiliar situations, it cannot always "undo" an action that you've already performed. Therefore, do not proceed with an unfamiliar command under the assumption that you can just cancel it later. The proper way to back out of unfamiliar territory is to do so before making selections. As the saying goes: If in doubt, Escape key out or press F1 for help.

Hands-On: Changing the Shell Colors

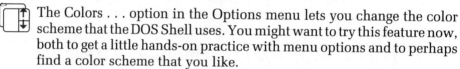 The Colors . . . option in the Options menu lets you change the color scheme that the DOS Shell uses. You might want to try this feature now, both to get a little hands-on practice with menu options and to perhaps find a color scheme that you like.

If you want to try it from the keyboard, start at the Shell (press Esc if any help windows are displayed) then

1. Press Alt or F10 to activate the Menu Bar.

2. Press Enter to pull down a menu.

3. Press the → or ← until Options pull-down menu appears.

4. Press ↑ or ↓ until the Highlight Bar is on the Colors . . . option.

5. Press Enter to select Colors . . ..

The Color Scheme dialog box displays examples of various color schemes, as shown in Figure 3.7.

6. To try one of the color schemes, first press Tab or Shift+Tab until the Highlight Bar gets into the list of Color Scheme options.

7. Press ↓ and/or ↑ until the color scheme you want to try is highlighted.

8. Press Enter.

9. Repeat steps 7 through 9 to try various other color schemes.

10. Notice that the cursor is in the OK box. When you find a color scheme you like, press `Enter` to select OK and leave the dialog box.

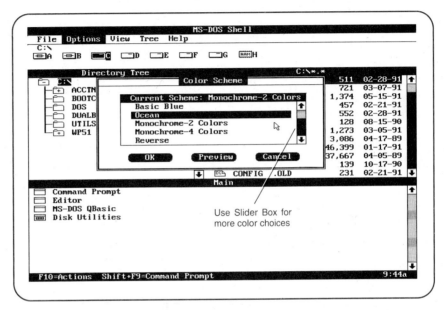

Figure 3.7. Dialog box of available color schemes

 If you're using a mouse, you can follow these steps to try out other color schemes:

1. Click the `Options` selection in the Menu Bar.

2. Click the `Colors . . .` option.

3. Double-click whatever `color scheme` you'd like to see.

4. Repeat step 3 until you find a color scheme that you like.

5. When you are happy with your color scheme, click `OK` to leave the dialog box.

Later in the book, you'll learn how to create your own custom color schemes. For the remainder of this chapter, I discuss the basics of using the other means of interacting with DOS, the command prompt.

The Command Prompt

 As an alternative to using the Shell, you can use the command prompt to interact with DOS. In earlier versions of DOS (prior to 4) the command prompt was the only way to interact with DOS. If you are experienced with earlier versions, therefore, you can certainly continue to use the command prompt. However, if you are a beginner, chances are you'll find the Shell an easier and more supportive means of interacting with your computer.

Exiting the DOS Shell

 First of all, if you are using DOS 5 and want to switch to the command prompt, you need to exit the Shell. There are two ways to exit the Shell and get to the command prompt:

> **Full Exit:** The Shell is removed from memory, and any current temporary settings are lost. You have access to all memory when the command prompt appears.

> **Partial Exit:** The shell and all its current (temporary) settings remain in memory. The command prompt appears and all commands are acceptable, but available memory is limited.

Making a Full Exit

Unless the shell is doing something, such as running several programs (as discussed in the next chapter), you'll probably want to make a full exit to DOS when you need to get to the command prompt. That way, you'll have full access to all your computer's memory.

NOTE: You cannot make a full exit from the Shell if tasks are running, as described in Chapter 5.

To make a full exit

❏ Pull down the F i l e menu from the Menu Bar.

❏ Select E x i t.

❏ As a shortcut, press the F 3 key.

NOTE: Once you leave the Shell, pressing Escape does not bring you back, nor does F1 offer any help. Those are only available within the Shell!

Returning from a Full Exit

To return to the Shell after making a complete exit, you need to start from scratch, following these simple steps:

❏ Type D O S S H E L L

❏ Press E n t e r

Making a Temporary Exit

If you need to make a temporary exit from the Shell to access the command prompt (for example, when several tasks are running, as described in Chapter 5), use one of the following steps:

❏ Select C o m m a n d   P r o m p t from the Program List

❏ Press S h i f t + F 9

The command prompt appears, and you can enter any valid DOS command. However, the Shell and any other programs you had running remain at least partially in memory.

Returning from a Partial Exit

To return to the Shell after making a partial exit

❑ Type EXIT

❑ Press Enter

Note that if a copy of the Shell is in memory, and you try to access the Shell with the DOSSHELL command, you load yet another copy of the Shell into memory instead of coming back to the original Shell.

Therefore, if you ever find yourself at the command prompt, and don't remember which method you used to exit the Shell, I suggest you first type EXIT (and press Enter) to return to the Shell. If a copy of the Shell is not already in memory, nothing happens—no big deal. Now you can just type DOSSHELL and press Enter to load a new copy of the Shell without wondering whether this is the first or second copy of the Shell in memory.

Basic Command Prompt Usage

 The DOS command prompt typically shows the current drive and directory, followed by a greater-than sign (>) and a blinking cursor. For example, if your computer does not have a hard disk, the command prompt might appear as follows when you are using floppy disk drive A:

    A:\>_

On hard disk drive C:, the command prompt might look like

    C:\>_

or . . .

    C:\DOS>_

if \DOS is the current directory.

Entering a command at the command prompt is a two step process:

❑ Type the complete command (you can use the Backspace key to back up and make corrections).

❑ Press Enter to "send" the completed command to the computer.

It's important to remember to press Enter after typing a command, otherwise the computer just sits. Hence, when I say "Enter the command..." in this book, I mean that you should type the command and then press Enter.

About Commands

Every DOS command has its own *syntax*, which consists of a verb (or command name); perhaps one or more required *parameters*, which are things the command verb operates on; and perhaps some optional *switches*, which refine or alter the way the command operates.

When entering a command, you type the command verb first, followed by a blank space and the parameter(s) if any, followed by another blank space, and any optional switches. I'll use the DIR command (which shows the names of files in a directory) as an example of a command, because it can be used with or without parameters and switches.

In its simplest form, DIR can be entered by itself at the command prompt

        DIR

NOTE: Remember that just *typing* a command isn't enough, you have to press Enter after typing the entire command.

That command tells DOS to show the names of all the files on the current drive and directory. You can add a parameter to that if you wish. For example, if there is a floppy disk in drive B: and you want to see the names of files on the disk, you could enter the command:

        DIR B:

Notice that there's a blank space between the verb (DIR) and the parameter (B:).

DIR also accepts several switches. For example, the /p switch tells DIR to display its information one "page" (screenful) at a time. To add the /p switch to the previous example, you would type

        DIR B: /p

Notice that there is a blank space between the parameter and the switch.

Upper- and Lowercase Letters in Commands

DOS is oblivious to the difference between upper- and lowercase letters, so you can use them interchangeably. That is, as far as DOS is concerned, *DIR*, *dir*, and *Dir* are exactly the same thing.

Don't forget, however, that as mentioned in Chapter 1, you cannot use the letter *l* for the number *1*, nor the letter *O* for *0*. If you need to type numbers, use the numbers along the top of the keyboard, or if you have one, the numeric keypad with the Num Lock key activated.

NOTE: You'll learn more about DIR in the next chapter. For now, I'm using it as a general example of a command.

Help with Commands

DOS 5 offers some limited on-screen help with commands (earlier versions of DOS offered none). If you know what command you want to use, but cannot remember its exact syntax or optional switches, you can get a quick reminder by typing the command followed by a space and /?. For example, to get help with the DIR command, you would enter

```
DIR /?
```

The screen displays a description of the command and its syntax. A brief description of any switches is provided. For example, Figure 3.8 shows the help screen for the DIR command after entering DIR /? at the command prompt.

On the syntax screen, items in square brackets ([ ]) are optional. Hence, for the DIR command, the [pathname] parameter and all the switches are optional. Note, however, that if you want to use an optional parameter or switch, you don't type the brackets. For example, `DIR /p` is a valid command; `DIR [/p]` is not. (If you try to enter the `DIR [/p]` command, DOS just informs you `Parameter format not correct - [`, which means that the `[` character is not acceptable in the command.)

If you are an experienced user, you might find these small helps useful as reminders. If you're a beginner, the information provided is undoubtedly too brief to be of any value, but you can always refer to Appendix B near the back of this book for a complete reference to every DOS command.

```
Displays a list of files and subdirectories in a directory.

DIR [drive:][path][filename] [/P] [/W] [/A[[:]attributes]]
  [/O[[:]sortorder]] [/S] [/B] [/L]

  [drive:][path][filename]
              Specifies drive, directory, and/or files to list.
  /P          Pauses after each screenful of information.
  /W          Uses wide list format.
  /A          Displays files with specified attributes.
  attributes  D  Directories              R  Read-only files
              H  Hidden files             A  Files ready for archiving
              S  System files             -  Prefix meaning "not"
  /O          List by files in sorted order.
  sortorder   N  By name (alphabetic)     S  By size (smallest first)
              E  By extension (alphabetic) D  By date & time (earliest first)
              G  Group directories first   -  Prefix to reverse order
  /S          Displays files in specified directory and all subdirectories.
  /B          Uses bare format (no heading information or summary).
  /L          Uses lowercase.

Switches may be preset in the DIRCMD environment variable.  Override
preset switches by prefixing any switch with - (hyphen)--for example, /-W.

C:\>
```

Figure 3.8. DOS 5 help for the DIR command.

Command Shortcuts

If you don't have DOS 5 or just prefer the command prompt to the Shell, you should also be aware of some shortcut keys that can help you enter the same or similar commands repeatedly or make a correction to a faulty command that produced an error message. Those keys are listed in Table 3.3.

Hands-On Example: Entering a Command

You have already entered some DOS commands, such as VER, DOSSHELL, and/or EXIT, by this point, but for a quick hands-on exercise in using the editing keys, follow these steps:

1. At the command prompt, type DIR /p.

2. Press Enter.

3. If you see the Press any key to continue... prompt, press any key (such as the Spacebar). Do so until you get back to the command prompt.

4. To reenter that command, but with the /w switch, first press F3 to retype the entire command.

5. Press ← or Backspace.

6. Type w (so the command reads DIR /w).

7. Press Enter to enter this new command.

Admittedly, this is a simple example. Chances are, you won't find the correction keys useful until you start entering lengthy, repetitive commands. Nonetheless, keep these keys in mind as a useful shortcut if you work at the command prompt often.

Table 3.3. Editing keys used with commands.

Key(s)	Effect
F1 or →	Retypes one character from the previously entered command.
F2	Retypes all the characters up to the character you type next.
F3	Retypes the entire previous command, from the right of the current cursor position.
F4	Moves up to the next character you type without copying any characters.
Backspace or ←	Deletes the character to the left of the cursor.
Insert (Ins)	Inserts the next characters typed into the previous command (you can then press F3 to bring back the rest of the previous command).
Esc	Cancels all characters up to the point at which you press Esc, places a backslash at that point, and advances the cursor one line. You can start over and then type your corrected command. When you press Enter, the \ and all characters to the left of it are ignored.

Repeating Groups of Commands

Normally, DOS only lets you repeat the last command entered. But DOS 5 includes a new feature, named DOSKEY, that lets DOS "remember" a long series of commands.

Pausing and Canceling Commands

> NOTE: For information on sending command output to the printer or a file, see Chapter 12.

Some commands produce several pages (screens) of commands. You can halt screen scrolling by pressing Ctrl+S or Pause. Pressing any key (or Ctrl+S) then resumes scrolling.

If you want to terminate a command altogether while it's displaying text on the screen, press Ctrl+Break or Ctrl+C. These keys, however, only stop a command in its tracks; they cannot "undo" a command that has already completed its job.

Internal and External Commands

Some DOS commands are *internal*, which means they are stored in memory and always accessible. Other commands are *external*, which means they are stored as small programs on disk. To use an external command, DOS needs to be able to find it on disk.

We won't go into detail on this matter right now, but suffice it to say that the PATH command (covered in Chapter 11) is the simplest way to ensure that DOS can always find its own external commands, and therefore you can ensure that the external commands are always available to you.

Upgrading to Version 5

5 If you are using an earlier version of DOS, yet you like what Version 5 has to offer, you can upgrade to Version 5 easily and inexpensively. Contact your computer dealer, software store, or any mail-order house (many of whom advertise regularly in computer magazines) for pricing information. Then refer to Appendix A in this book (or to the DOS Version 5 manual) for quick-and-easy instructions about upgrading your computer to DOS Version 5.

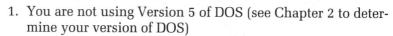 Along these same lines, if your computer is not equipped with a mouse, but you like the point-and-click interface that the mouse offers, you can probably add a mouse to your current computer inexpensively. Contact your computer dealer for details; then refer to the mouse's operation or to Appendix A in this book for instructions about installing the mouse for use with DOS Version 5.

5 Incidentally, if you already have a large investment in software programs that you use with an earlier version of DOS, you do not need to worry about "losing" those programs when you upgrade to Version 5 of DOS. You can easily upgrade without having to upgrade or change existing programs. In fact, you don't even need to reformat your hard disk or copy any files to floppies and back after the upgrade. The DOS Version 5 installation procedure lets you easily replace an earlier version of DOS without any of the complications you might expect (though a quick backup of your hard disk is recommended and provided for during the installation—just as a safety precaution).

Troubleshooting

If you experience problems during this chapter, try to locate the exact problem in the following sections and then follow suggested solutions.

❑ If you cannot get the DOS Shell running, one of three things is wrong:

5 1. You are not using Version 5 of DOS (see Chapter 2 to determine your version of DOS)

2. The wrong diskette is in drive A: (see the section titled "An Alternative Startup Procedure for DOS Version 5 Users" in Chapter 2)

3. If your computer has a hard disk, type CD\DOS (be sure to use a backslash [\ ] rather than a forward slash [/]) at the command prompt and press Enter. Then type DOSSHELL and press Enter.

❏ If none of the arrow keys, nor the PgUp or PgDn keys, work on your keyboard, press the key labeled Num Lock once (to "unlock" the numbers on the numeric keypad); then try the arrow keys again.

❏ If you cannot get your mouse to work in the DOS Shell, be sure it is properly connected, as per instructions that came with the mouse.

❏ When you exit the DOS Shell and try to get back into it, the message Bad command or file name appears. In this case, you might simply have misspelled the command. (For example, you typed DOSHHEL instead of DOSSHELL.) Retype the command (using the proper spelling) and try again.

❏ If your valid DOS command still produces the Bad command or file name message, chances are that DOS cannot find the external command on your disk. Read about the PATH command in Chapter 11.

Summary

This chapter has provided general techniques for using DOS. Again, there is no need to memorize every technique now, because you'll be given plenty of hands-on exercises in future chapters. You can refer to this chapter for reminders as needed. To summarize the most important techniques covered in this chapter:

❏ To move the Highlight Bar through the Shell from your keyboard, use the Tab, Shift+Tab, ↑, ↓, ←, and ↑ arrow keys.

❏ If you have a mouse, you can select a Shell option by moving the mouse pointer to it and clicking.

❏ To select an option in the Shell, double-click it, or move the highlighter to it and press Enter.

❏ To access the DOS Shell Menu Bar, press the F10 or the Alt key and then press the Enter key or just click the menu option you want.

❏ When the Menu Bar pull-down menus are displayed, you can move the Highlight Bar using the ↑, ↓, ←, and → keys or you can click any option.

❏ To leave the Menu Bar—or an accidental selection from a Menu Bar pull-down menu—press the Esc key.

❏ If in doubt, Escape key out or press F1 for help!

❏ To scroll through lengthy displays that have Scroll Bars to the right, ↓, PgDn, ↑, or PgUp keys or click the up- and down-pointing arrows in the help window or drag the Scroll Box to where you want to be in the list.

❏ To change the colors on your screen, select Colors . . . from the Options pull-down menu. Select the color scheme you want and press Enter.

❏ To leave the Shell and get to the command prompt, select Exit from the File pull-down menu, press F3, press Shift+F9, or select Command Prompt from the Program List.

C>

❏ To enter commands at the command prompt, type the complete command and then press Enter. (When I say "Enter the command..." in this book, that means "Type the command and then press Enter".)

❏ To return to the DOS 5 Shell from the command prompt, enter the command EXIT. If that doesn't work, enter DOSSHELL (and don't forget to press Enter!).

Exploring Your Computer

Most computer work consists of running programs to manage data (information). As this chapter explains, programs and data are stored on computer disks as files, and DOS is the tool that you use to locate programs and run them.

The exact files stored on a computer vary from system to system and user to user. However, if your computer is brand new, and the only program you've installed is DOS, the files that comprise DOS are probably the only files on your computer. If you share a computer with others in a company or a classroom, many more files might exist, because each computer user can create and save his or her own files.

This chapter focuses on specific techniques you can use to see the names of all the files stored on any computer that uses DOS. At first, the techniques presented in this chapter might seem abstract because they don't directly help you solve a particular problem, such as managing an inventory. However, be assured that you will use these basic techniques in all your future computer work, every time that you use the computer.

Disk Files

Any program or collection of data stored on a computer disk is saved in a *file*. The name is actually quite appropriate: Just as a filing cabinet contains many different files (typically stored in manila folders), a computer disk also stores many different files. Figure 4.1 illustrates this simple analogy.

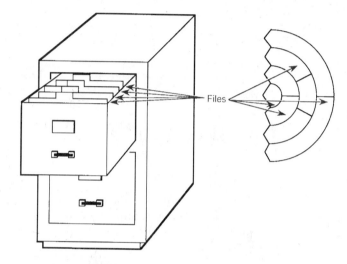

Files

Figure 4.1. Like filing cabinets, computer disks store files.

Unlike filing cabinets, which typically contain only printed information, computer disks can store two different types of files:

❏ *Program files* (or *programs*) contain instructions that tell the computer what to do and how to do it.

❏ *Data files* (or *text files*) contain data (information), such as names, addresses, letters, and inventory or bookkeeping data.

Every file on a disk, whether program or data, has a name that consists of two parts—*base name* followed by *extension*. The base name can be one to eight characters long. The optional extension always starts with a period (.) and can contain as many as three additional characters. File names cannot contain blank spaces. Following are some examples of legal file names:

```
APPEND.EXE          IBMDOS.COM
LETTER_1.TXT        9.WKS
SALES.DAT           GRAPH
```

In the first example file name, APPEND is the base name, and .EXE is the extension. When talking about file names, experienced computer users often refer to the period that separates the base name from the extension as "dot." Hence, when spoken, the file name MYLETTER.BAK would be pronounced *my-letter-dot-back*.

As a rule of thumb, the file's base name usually describes the contents of the file, and the extension usually describes the type of information in the file. You'll learn these details later; for now, merely remember that file names consist of two parts—the base name and the extension.

Disk Directories

NOTE: As mentioned in Chapter 1, a hard disk cannot be removed from the hard disk drive, so you never actually see the disk itself.

A hard disk can store many hundreds, or even thousands, of files. To make it easier to manage a large number of files, you can use DOS to divide the hard disk into *directories*, each of which contains its own set of related files. You might think of directories as the drawers of a file cabinet, as illustrated in Figure 4.2.

Like file names, directory names can only have as many as eight characters (which is why in Figure 4.2. the directory that stores files for the Marketing department must be abbreviated). Like file names, directory names may not contain blank spaces. A directory name can have a three-character extension, but to prevent directory names from being confused with file names, people rarely use extensions with directory names.

Individual directories can be further divided into subdirectories. You might think of subdirectories as areas within a drawer (or directory) that are marked off with dividers. The example in Figure 4.3 shows that the Sales department's file drawer contains two sections (subdirectories), one for Bob's records and one for Carol's.

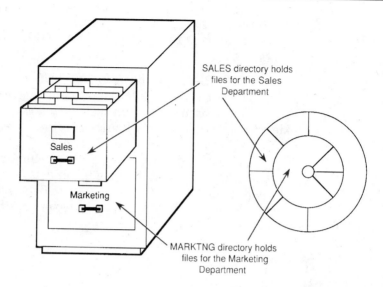

Figure 4.2. Each directory on disk has its own set of files.

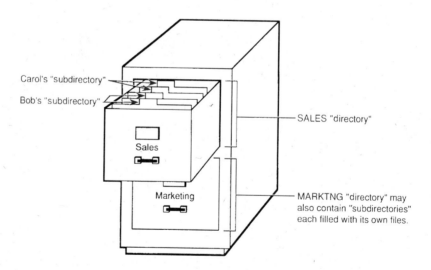

Figure 4.3. Directories can be further divided into subdirectories.

Subdirectory names follow the same conventions as directory names. That is, they can be as many as eight characters long, cannot contain spaces, and generally do not include an extension.

Locating a file in an office that doesn't use computers involves a simple, obvious series of steps:

1. Go to the correct filing cabinet.

2. Open the correct drawer.

3. Read through the file labels until you locate the file you want.

The process for locating a file on a computer is very similar, except that the terminology is a little different (and obviously, no paper is involved):

1. Insert the correct `diskette` into the disk drive or access the correct hard disk drive (like going to the correct filing cabinet).

2. Access the correct `directory` or `subdirectory` (like going to the correct drawer in the file cabinet).

3. Glance through the file names on the display screen to find the right `file` (like thumbing through the labels on top of manila file folders).

Part of learning to use your computer properly involves keeping track of where you've stored files and also being able to "look around" through disk drives, directories, and file name lists to access files whose locations you might have forgotten.

The Directory Tree

NOTE: Chapter 8 discusses the best techniques for organizing the information on your computer's hard disk into directories.

The *structure* of directories and subdirectories on a disk is often referred to as the *directory tree*. Every hard disk and diskette contains an initial directory called the *root* directory. DOS automatically assigns the simple name \ to this root directory. Any additional directories (and subdirectories) that you create are considered to be "below" the root directory.

To illustrate this concept, let's suppose you are using a company's computer whose hard disk contains files organized into three directories—one for the Sales department, one for the Marketing department, and one for the Shipping department. Furthermore, individual employees in each department have divided these directories into separate, "personal" subdirectories, in which they store their own files. Each employee has used his or her first name as the name of his or her subdirectory.

The directory tree for such an organization appears in Figure 4.4. (Note that the root directory, as mentioned earlier, is always shown at the top of the hierarchy).

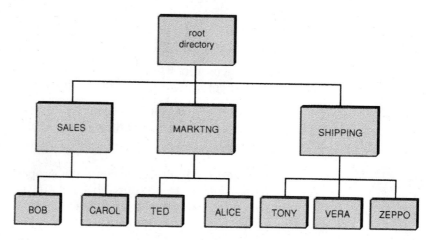

Figure 4.4. A directory tree divided into departments and further divided into employees within each department.

Now before we move to other topics, take a minute to review the following important information:

❏ A disk drive contains a disk and usually has a letter name (such as A: or C:).

❏ To organize information on a disk, you can subdivide the disk into directories and subdirectories.

❏ Every directory contains its own unique set of files.

As you'll see, it's pretty easy to explore the disk drives (usually called simply *drives*), directories, and files on any computer system.

Using the DOS 5 File List

The DOS 5 Shell provides graphic information about, and access to, the drives, directories and files on your computer system. (If you are using an earlier version of DOS, proceed directly to the section in this chapter titled "Managing Files and Directories From the Command Prompt."

> NOTE: Drives, directories, and file names shown in Figures 4.5 and 4.6 include examples that do not appear on your screen.

The top portion of the Single File List Shell is composed of three parts titled the *Drives Area*, the *Directory Tree Area*, and the *Files Area*, as shown in Figure 4.5. In that example, the computer has floppy disk drives A and B and hard disk drives C through F. Users have already created quite a few directories on disk drive C, as you can see in the Directory Tree area.

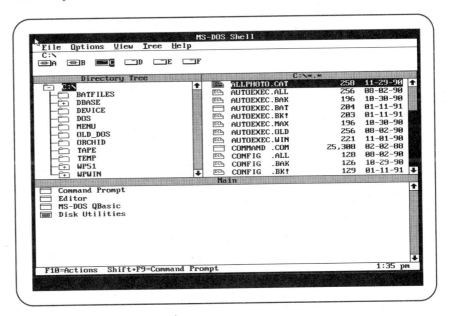

Figure 4.5. A sample Shell display.

As another example, Figure 4.6 shows how the Shell would appear on a new computer that has only floppy drives A and B, a single hard disk, C, and only one directory beneath the root, named DOS, on it.

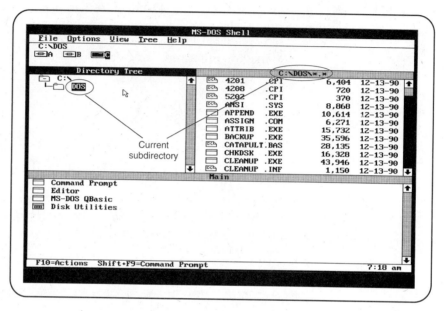

Figure 4.6. Another sample Shell display.

The Disk Drives

The names of the disk drives available on your computer appear beneath the Menu Bar. If you have a graphics monitor, you see an icon for each drive and perhaps notice that the icon for hard drives (C and higher) look a little different than the icon for floppy drives.

The information displayed in the Directory Tree pertains only to the current drive. The icon for the current drive is highlighted in the Drives area, and its name also appears at the top of the Directory Tree (for example, C: in Figure 4.6).

Selecting a Drive

To select a drive (thereby making it the current drive), you can use either of the following techniques

Click the name or icon of the drive you want

or...

1. Press Tab or Shift+Tab until the highlight bar gets to the Drives area.

2. Move the Highlight Bar to the drive you want by pressing ← or →.

3. Press Enter to select the currently highlighted drive.

As an alternative to using the arrow keys and Enter, you can also hold down the Ctrl key and press the letter name of the drive you want to select. For example, press Ctrl+C to select drive C.

When you select a different drive, the directory tree and files list change immediately to show information about the currently selected drive.

If you attempt to select a floppy disk drive that does not contain a usable disk, you see in a dialog box the error message Drive not ready. You can either insert a disk into that drive and select OK (or press Enter) to try again, or you can select cancel (or press Escape) to access the empty drive.

Updating the Drive Selection

If a floppy disk drive is current, and you change the disk in that drive, you'll notice that the Shell is not updated automatically. Whenever you change a floppy disk, you need to reselect its name (or icon) from the Drives area to update your screen. (If you're using a mouse, double-click the drive icon).

The Directory Tree

Beneath the current drive indicator is a graphical representation of the directory tree on the current drive. Notice that DOS displays the directory tree in a vertical *line* format rather than the horizontal hierarchical format shown in Figure 4.3. DOS uses this format simply because it fits on the vertically oriented screen better.

The topmost directory in the tree is always the root directory, which DOS always names simply \. The current drive and its root directory name are always displayed at the top of the Directory Tree; for example C:\.

The name of the current directory always appears in the title bar at the top of the Files area, preceded with a \. For example, in Figure 4.6 the C:\DOS*.* indicates that the Files windows is currently showing all the files in the DOS directory of disk drive C. (I explain *.* in a moment.)

If the directory tree contains more directory names than can fit in the window, use the Scroll Bar at the right of the window to view other parts of the tree. (Basic Scroll Bar techniques were covered in Chapter 3.)

Selecting a Directory

To select a directory so that you can see what files it contains
Click the name of the directory you want to select

or...

1. Press Tab or Shift+Tab until the highlighter gets to the directory tree area.

2. Use the ↑ or ↓ key to move the highlighter to the directory you want to select. (As a shortcut, you can press Home to jump to the top or End to jump to the bottom, of the tree.)

The Files list to the right of the Directory Tree immediately changes to show the names of files on the currently selected directory.

Expanding and Collapsing Branches

Each directory beneath the root directory is sometimes referred to as a *branch* in the tree. To avoid cluttering the Directory Tree area with too much information, *subdirectories* (directories that branch off directories other than root) are not intially displayed in the Directory Tree area. Instead, if a branch leads to still other branches, its icon contains a plus sign (+).

If a branch is already expanded, its icon contains a minus sign (–) as a reminder that you can collapse that branch if you wish. If there are no subdirectories beneath the particular directory, its icon is empty.

There are several ways to expand and collapse directory tree branches to view more or fewer directory levels.

Expanding One Level

> NOTE: You might find it easiest to use the + and – keys on the numeric keypad.

❏ To expand a branch one level, click the + icon next to the directory name or highlight the directory name and then press + or select Expand One Level from the Tree menu.

❏ To collapse an expanded branch, click the – icon next to the branch name or highlight the branch name and then press – or select Collapse Branch from the Tree menu.

When a branch is expanded, you can select any subdirectory name that appears to view the names of files on that subdirectory simply by selecting the subdirectory name. Either move the highlighter with the ↓ and ↑ keys, or click the name of the subdirectory.

Fully Expanding a Branch

Rather than just viewing one additional level of subdirectories, you can fully expand a branch to see all levels. To do so

1. Highlight the name of the directory you want to expand.

2. Press * or select Expand Branch from the Tree menu.

Fully Expanding All Branches

If you want to fully expand all the branches in the directory tree

Select Expand All from the Tree menu.

Even though there is no "Collapse All" option to return to the one-level view of the tree, you can quickly return to that level by collapsing and then expanding the root directory.

If you have several directories on a disk drive, you might want to select that drive and practice some of the techniques we just described, just to get a feel for it.

The Files Area

 The right half of the File List screen displays the names of the individual files on the current drive and directory. On a graphics screen, *program files* (that is, files that contain instructions for the computer) are indicated by a rectangular icon. *Data* (or *Text*) files, which contain information rather than instructions, are marked by an icon that has its upper right corner folded down. (These icons do not appear on a text screen, but you can still identify *program* files by their file name extensions, which usually are .BAT, .COM, or .EXE).

The Files Area also displays the size of each file (in bytes) and the date that the file was created or last changed.

If the current directory contains more file names than can fit into the window, you can use the Scroll Bar (as described in Chapter 3) to view other file names.

Initially, the Files window displays the names of all the files in the current directory in alphabetical order. You can, however, reduce the list to fewer file names, change the sort order, and do a few other tricky things, described in the following sections.

Selecting File Names to View

One way to avoid scrolling through long lists of file names is to limit the list to file names that match a particular pattern. To do that, you first need to know about two DOS *wildcard characters*:

? Matches any single character
* Matches any group of characters

When you combine a wildcard character with "regular" characters, you create an *ambiguous file name*. For example, the ambiguous file name J*.* isolates file names that begin with the letter J, because J* matches any file name that starts with J and is followed by any other characters, and .* matches any extension.

The ambiguous file name *.LET isolates file names that have extension .LET. The ambiguous file name QTR*.DAT isolates file names that start with the letters QTR, that are followed by any other characters, and that have the extension .DAT (for example, QTR1.DAT, QTRLY.DAT, QTR31989.DAT, and others that contain a similar pattern of letters).

The ? wildcard matches any single character. For example, the ambiguous file name QTR?.DAT isolates file names that begin with the letters QTR, that are followed by any *single* character, and that have the extension .DAT. For example, QTR?.DAT matches QTR1.DAT, QTR2.DAT, and QTRJ.DAT, but not QTR31989.DAT. The ambiguous file name JAN19??.EXP isolates file names such as JAN1987.EXP, JAN1988.EXP, JAN1989.EXP, and so on.

To limit the list of file names to a particular file name pattern

1. Select File Display Options from the Options menu. You should see the Display Options dialog box shown in Figure 4.7.

2. Type the new file name pattern or use the ←,→, Delete, and Backspace keys to help change the existing one.

3. You can then press Tab or Shift+Tab or use your mouse to select other items in the dialog box (described in the sections that follow).

4. Select OK or press Enter when done.

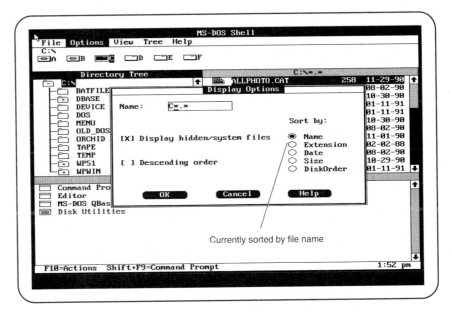

Figure 4.7. The Display Options dialog box, C*.*.

Only file names that match the pattern you entered in step 2 appear in the Files area. Notice also that the new file name pattern replaces the *.* in the Title Bar of the Files window.

This simple technique can come in handy when you are looking for a business letter stored in a file, but don't know what floppy disk (or directory) it's on. However, you're pretty sure you gave it the extension .LET, because that's the extension you use for all your letters.

> NOTE: We'll discuss many more ways to search for files, and viewing the contents of files, in Chapter 8.

One way to start looking for the file would be to first change the file name display option pattern to *.LET. Then select one directory after another, or one floppy disk after another, to quickly view only the files with the .LET extension, until you find the file you're looking for, as in the example shown in Figure 4.8.

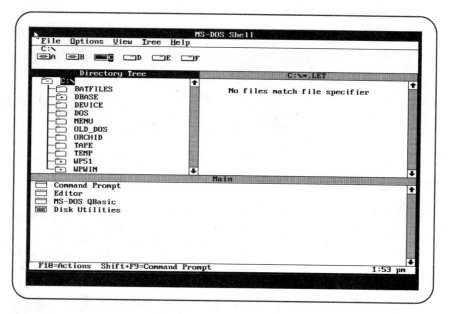

Figure 4.8. Only file names with the .LET extension are listed.

If the current floppy disk or directory does not have any files with the .LET extension, the Files area shows simply *No files match file specifier* (the file specifier being the drive, directory, and file name pattern in the Window Bar at the top of the Files window, for example *.LET in Figure 4.8.).

Redisplaying All File Names

Don't forget that once you change the file name pattern, the new pattern stays in effect until you change it again. To redisplay all file names, you need to change the pattern back to *.*.

The Optional Command Prompt

C> For DOS 4 and 5 users, the command prompt (discussed in the sections that follow) is simply an alternative method of using DOS. Whether or not you use it is simply a matter of personal preference. You probably should try some of the alternative techniques presented in the following sections, so if you ever need to use a computer that has an earlier version of DOS, you will know what to do. First, you must leave the Shell and activate the command prompt by pressing the F3 key.

Remember, if at any time you decide that you would prefer using the Shell rather than the command prompt, you need only type the command DOSSHELL at the command prompt and then press Enter. This reactivates the DOS Shell.

Managing Files and Directories from the Command Prompt

C> If you are using DOS 3, you need to use DOS commands to move among disk drives and directories and to view file names. Although you can't see the "graphical" presentation of disk drives, directories, and file names that the DOS 5 Shell offers, you still can find your way around the computer.

Changing Disk Drives

When the DOS command prompt appears, it usually displays the name of the current drive (without a colon) followed by a greater-than (>) sign. For example, if your screen is displaying the prompt

    A>

you are currently accessing disk drive A:. If your screen displays

    C>

you are accessing hard disk drive C:.

You can change your current drive to another drive name by typing the new drive name (including the colon) and pressing Enter. Note, however, that accessing an empty floppy disk drive does not work. If you attempt to do so, DOS displays an error message, such as Not ready reading drive A, and then presents the options Abort, Retry, Ignore (early versions of DOS) or Abort, Retry, Fail? (Versions 3.3, 4, and 5).

To correct the error, insert a diskette into the drive and press R to retry the command or press A to abort (cancel) accessing the new drive. (If you have problems accessing drives, see the Troubleshooting section at the end of this chapter.)

Suppose that your computer has two floppy disk drives but no hard disk. You would follow these steps to access disk drive B:

1. Insert a diskette (perhaps a DOS diskette other than the one currently in drive A:) into disk drive B:.

2. If the disk drive has a latch or door, be sure it is completely closed.

3. Specify disk drive B: by typing B:.

4. Press Enter to access the new drive.

The command prompt now displays the name of the current drive, B>. To again access disk drive A:, type A: and press Enter.

Suppose that your computer has a hard disk and one floppy disk drive named A:. To log onto drive A: (which of course, must contain a diskette), type A: and press Enter. To again access the hard disk drive C:, type C: and press Enter.

Viewing Directory Names

The DOS TREE command shows the names of directories and subdirectories on the current hard disk or floppy diskette. You can use this command to check your hard disk, or any diskette, to see whether it has already been divided into directories and subdirectories. You use the TREE command like any other DOS command; type its name at the command prompt and then press Enter.

The results of the TREE command vary slightly from one version of DOS to the next. In general though, versions prior to 4 display only subdirectory names that are beneath the current directory. Therefore, to view all the directory names on a disk, you would want to start from the highest-level directory—the root directory. To do so, you need to use the CHDIR or CD (for Change Directory) command to switch to the root directory (I'll discuss this command in detail in a later section in this chapter).

Assume that your computer has a hard disk named C:. Use the following steps to change to the root directory of drive C: and view the names of all directories on that disk:

> WARNING: The backslash (\) and the slash, or forward slash, (/) are not the same characters. Be sure to press the backslash (\) character as indicated in these steps.

1. Type `C:` and press `Enter` to access the hard disk.

2. Type `CD\` and press `Enter` to change the current directory to the root directory.

3. Type `TREE` and press `Enter`.

If entering the TREE command produces the error message `Bad Command or File Name`, see the Troubleshooting section near the end of this chapter.

If there are no directories (or subdirectories) on the hard disk, the screen displays a message, such as `No subdirectories exist`. If there are directories (and subdirectories) on the hard disk, DOS lists their names on the screen. In versions of DOS prior to Version 4, the listing resembles the following example (with different names, of course):

```
DIRECTORY PATH LISTING FOR VOLUME

Path: \DOS
Sub-directories: None

Path: \SALES
Sub-directories: \BOB
                 \CAROL

Path: \MARKTNG
Sub-directories: \TED
                 \ALICE

Path: \SHIPPING
Sub-directories: \TONY
                 \VERA
                 \ZEPPO
```

If you are using DOS Version 5, the TREE command displays the directory in the following format:

```
C:\
├──── DOS
├──── SALES
│      ├──── BOB
│      └──── CAROL
├──── MARKTNG
│      ├──── TED
│      └──── ALICE
└──── SHIPPING
       ├──── TONY
       ├──── VERA
       └──── ZEPPO
```

Printing the Results of a Command

If the TREE display whizzes by too quickly on your screen, you can send its output to the printer. Chapter 12 covers many techniques for using your printer effectively. For the time being, however, you just need to know that you can send the output from any command to the printer by following the command with a blank space and the symbol > PRN. Just think of PRN as an abbreviation for the PRiNter and the > as an arrow pointing to the printer.

> NOTE: If you have a laser printer, you may need to eject the page to see the printout. See Chapter 12 for details.

Therefore, if you type the command TREE >PRN and press Enter now, the directory tree will be displayed on your printer. (You can think of the plain-English translation for TREE >PRN as being "Show me the directory tree and send the results to the printer.")

Determining the Current Directory

On some computers, you can tell which directory is current by looking at the command prompt. For example, if the current directory is named DOS, the command prompt shows C:\DOS>. If the current directory is the root directory of drive A:, the command prompt shows A:\> (because the root directory is named \).

If your command prompt does not show the name of the current directory, there are two techniques you can use to see the name of the current directory. One is to enter the CHDIR or CD command with no additional directory name. That is, type `CD` and press Enter. The names of the current drive and directory appear on your screen and then the command prompt reappears.

Another way to view the name of the current drive and directory is to use the DOS PROMPT command to customize the command prompt. Chapter 12 discusses the PROMPT command in detail, but for the time being, suffice it to say that entering the command PROMPT PG changes the command prompt so that it displays both the current drive and directory. To try this yourself, type `PROMPT $P$G` and press Enter.

The command prompt continues to display the current drive and directory for the remainder of your current session (that is, until you turn off the computer). That way, you can see which directory is current at any time by glancing at the command prompt.

Accessing a Different Directory

To access a different directory on a disk, use the CHDIR (usually abbreviated as CD) command. (Both are actually abbreviations for CHange DIRectory). When you use the commands, precede the name of the directory that you want to access with a backslash (\). The TREE command that you used earlier listed the names of directories (if any) available on your computer.

The following simple steps demonstrate how to change to the directory named DOS. If your computer does not contain a directory named DOS, substitute one of the directory names from your directory tree (use a directory name rather than a subdirectory name). The steps also assume that you are currently using hard disk C:.

1. If your computer has a hard disk, first type `C:` and press `Enter` to make drive C: current.

2. Type `CD \DOS` (or substitute the name of another directory in place of DOS).

3. Press `Enter`.

Your command prompt displays the name of the new current directory. For example, after switching to the directory named DOS in the previous steps, your command prompt would display

```
C:\DOS>
```

If you do not have a hard disk, chances are that most of your floppy disks will have all of their files stored on the root directory. If you can find a diskette with multiple directories, however, you'll be able to use the CHDIR or CD command to change directories on that diskette.

Accessing Subdirectories

To access a subdirectory, you must specify the entire *path* in the CHDIR or CD command. The "path" is the series of directory names that leads from the current directory name (or root) to the final subdirectory. Separate each directory name with a backslash (\).

For example, suppose that your disk has a subdirectory named BOB beneath the SALES directory. The TREE command would display this fact in the following format in Version 3 of DOS:

```
Path: \SALES
Sub-directories: \BOB
```

or in Version 4 . . .

```
    └── SALES
          └──BOB
```

or in Version 4 or 5, in a format that resembles the Tree display in the Shell.

To access the BOB subdirectory, you must include both the SALES and BOB names—separated by backslashes—in the CHDIR or CD command, as in the following example. (Again, you can substitute names that are relevant to your own directory tree in place of \SALES\BOB.) First, type `CD \SALES\BOB` and then press Enter.

When you use the CHDIR or CD command to change to a different directory or subdirectory, you can move "down" one level by excluding the backslashes. For example, assuming that BOB is a subdirectory beneath the SALES directory, and SALES is the current directory, you can enter the command CD BOB to move "down" to the BOB directory. The command prompt would then show `C:\SALES|BOB>`.

Note that this technique, however, works only when you are moving down one level in the tree. To access the SALES\BOB subdirectory from any directory other than SALES, you would need to type the complete path to get to the subdirectory. That is, you need to enter the command `CD \SALES\BOB`, which tells DOS that in order to get to the BOB subdirectory, it needs to take a path starting at the root (\), down to the SALES directory, and then down another level to the BOB subdirectory.

If your disk is already divided into directories and subdirectories, you may want to practice using the CD command on your own to switch among the various directories. (Chapter 9 displays some handy shortcut techniques.) In a moment, you'll learn how to view the names of all the files on the current directory.

Accessing the Root Directory

As you might recall, the root directory is always named \. Therefore, to change to the root directory, you type only CD \ and then press Enter. The command prompt displays C : \ to indicate that the current directory is root.

Viewing File Names

The DOS DIR command displays the names of all files on the current directory, as well as the names of subdirectories (if any) beneath the current directory. In general, you will probably use this command to check a floppy disk or directory to see what files it contains.

You use the DIR command just as any other DOS command; type it at the command prompt and press Enter. You can try it right now, regardless of what disk or directory is current, by typing DIR and pressing Enter.

NOTE: The DIR command also displays other information, such as the number of files in the current directory and the amount of storage space remaining on the current disk.

The DIR command displays a list of file names, extensions, sizes, and the dates and times that files were created or last modified. For example, your screen might show the following file names and information:

```
UTILS                <DIR> 03-01-91    9:40a
COMMAND    COM       37637 06-17-91   12:00p
DISKCOPY   COM       10428 06-17-91   12:00p
FIND       EXE        5983 06-17-91   12:00p
```

The first item is actually a directory named UTILS, as indicated by the <DIR> label. The directory was created on March 1, 1991, at 9:40 a.m. The remaining items are program files. You know this because programs files usually have one of the following extensions: .COM (for command), .EXE (for executable, or .BAT (for batch). (You learn more about file name extensions in Chapter 7.)

The DIR command does not show the period that normally separates a file name from its extension. Instead, it aligns the file name extensions in a column to improve readability. Hence, the files displayed are actually named COMMAND.COM, DISKCOPY.COM, and FIND.EXE. Each of these was created or last edited on June 17, 1991 at 12:00 noon. The largest of the three files contains 37,637 bytes of instructions, the smallest contains 5,983 bytes.

Slowing Down the DIR Display

If there are many files on the current directory, DOS displays them too quickly for you to see. You can use the /P *switch* to make DOS pause after it lists one screenful of file names. Be sure to use a forward slash (/) rather than the backslash (\) character. For example, type the command DIR /P and then press Enter.

If the directory contains more than one screenful of file names, the screen displays only one "page" of file names and the prompt Press any key to continue... When you are ready to view the next screenful of file names, simply press a key. Continue paging through the file names until the DOS command prompt reappears.

Displaying File Names on a Different Drive

You need not actually change to a new disk drive to see what files are on it. Instead, specify the disk drive name (preceded by a space) after the DIR command. For example, suppose that your current drive is hard disk drive C:, but you want to see the names of the files on a diskette in drive A:. To do so, type the command DIR A: and press Enter.

Displaying File Names in a Different Directory

You also can view the names of files on any directory without changing your current directory. Include the complete directory name in the DIR command. Be sure to precede all directory (and subdirectory) names with a backslash. For example, if you are currently accessing the DOS directory, but you want to see the names of files in the \SALES directory, you would type the command DIR \SALES and press Enter.

As you know, the root directory is always named \. Therefore, to view the names of the files that are stored on the root directory, you would type the command **DIR** \ and press Enter.

Viewing Specific Groups of Files

You don't need to view all the file names on a particular diskette or directory; you can limit the display to files that match some *pattern* of characters. This is similar to using an alphabetically arranged Rolodex file, which lets you "flip to" a smaller group of cards to narrow your search for a particular card.

To search for (isolate) file names that match a pattern, use the following DOS wildcard characters:

    ?   Matches any single character
    *   Matches any group of characters

NOTE: Wildcard characters can be used only with file names, never with drive, directory, or subdirectory names.

When you combine the wildcard characters with "regular" characters, you create an *ambiguous file name*. For example, the ambiguous file name M*.* isolates all file names that begin with the letter M, because M* matches file names that begin with M followed by any characters, and .* matches any extension.

The ambiguous file name, *.LET isolates only those file names that have the extension .LET. The ambiguous file name QTR*.DAT isolates file names that start with the letters QTR, that are followed by any other characters, and that have the extension .DAT (for example, QTR1.DAT, QTRLY.DAT, QTR31989.DAT, and so on).

The ? wildcard matches any single character. For example, the ambiguous file name QTR?.DAT isolates file names that begin with the letters QTR, that are followed by any single character, and that have the extension .DAT. For example, QTR?.DAT matches QTR1.DAT, QTR2.DAT, QTRJ.DAT, but not QTR31989.DAT. The ambiguous file name JAN19??.EXP isolates file names such as JAN1987.EXT, JAN1988.EXT, JAN1989.EXP, and so on.

Try using these wildcards yourself. Suppose that you are looking for a file whose full name and extension you do not recall, but you do know it begins with the letter C. To display only those file names that begin with the letter C (on the current drive and directory), type **DIR** **C*.*** and then press Enter.

Your screen might display a list that resembles the one in Figure 4.9. If no file names on the current drive and directory start with the letter C, DOS displays a message, such as `File not found` and then redisplays the command prompt so that you can enter another command.

```
C:\>DIR C*.*

 Volume in drive C has no label
 Directory of C:\

COMMAND  COM    25308 02-02-88  12:00a
CONFIG   MAX      126 10-29-90   5:12p
CONFIG   WIN      143 11-01-90   4:05p
CONFIG   BAK      126 10-29-90   5:12p
CONFIG   PDX      126 11-15-90   6:10a
CONFIG   ALL      128 08-02-90   9:29a
CONFIG   SYS      130 01-11-91   3:10p
CONFIG   OLD      157 06-15-90  11:02a
CPANEL   COM    19858 09-28-87  12:00p
CONFIG   BK!      129 01-11-91   2:44p
        10 file(s)      46231 bytes
                     11464704 bytes free

C:\>
```

Figure 4.9. Sample display from the command DIR C*.*.

Suppose that you want to see only the names of files that have the extension .BAT. In that case, you type the command `DIR *.BAT` and press Enter. If you want to see only the names of files that begin with the letters BASIC and that have the extension .COM, type the command `DIR BASIC*.COM` and press Enter.

Note that if the current drive and directory does not contain any files that match the ambiguous file name, DOS displays the message `File not found`; then it redisplays the command prompt and awaits your next command.

Keep in mind also that DIR displays only the names of files in the current directory (or subdirectory). Therefore, after you use CHDIR or CD to change to a new directory or subdirectory, entering another DIR command displays only the names of files on the new directory or subdirectory.

In the next chapter, you'll begin to see that ambiguous file names can be very powerful tools for managing your computer files. For the time being, however, remember that ? represents any single character and that * represents any group of characters in an ambiguous file name.

Displaying Only File Names

> NOTE: Appendix B contains additional information about all DOS commands, including the important DIR command.

If you want to display only the names of files and subdirectories—without sizes, dates, and times—use the /W switch with the DIR command. The W stands for *wide*, because this switch lists the file names in a horizontal format. For example, to view a wide display of the files on your current directory, type the command DIR /W and then press Enter.

Printing File Names

To list file names on the printer rather than on the screen, add > PRN (*redirection symbol* and a *device name*) next to the DIR command. For example, if your printer is connected and ready to accept output, type the command DIR >PRN and press Enter. This produces a printed copy of file names on the current disk drive and directory.

> If you are using a laser printer, you might need to eject the page from the printer manually. See Chapter 12 for details.

Troubleshooting

This section discusses common problems that you might encounter while exploring disk drives and directories. If you need additional information, refer to Appendix B, which discusses all DOS commands in more detail.

❏ DOS displays the message `Bad command or file name.` This error occurs in two situations: either you misspelled a command or program name, or you attempted to run a program that is not available on the current disk drive or directory.

    1. If you simply misspelled a command (such as typing DOR rather than DIR), type the command again and press Enter.

    2. If you are certain that you typed the command properly and you still see the error message `Bad command or file name,` you are attempting to run a program that is not available on the current disk drive or directory. Be sure the file name is in the current directory on the current drive. For example, the TREE command is actually a DOS program that DOS must find on the disk. In DOS 3, the TREE program is usually found in the root directory. To run the TREE command, first access the root directory by typing CD \ and then pressing Enter. Then type TREE and press Enter.

❏ DOS displays the message `Abort, Retry, Ignore` or `Abort, Retry, Fail.` This error occurs when you type a command that the computer cannot carry out, such as when you attempt to access an empty floppy disk drive.

    1. If you can determine the cause of the problem based on the brief message that appears above the `Abort, Retry, Ignore` or `Abort, Retry, Fail` options, do so and then press R to retry the command.

    2. If you cannot correct the situation, type the letter I to select Ignore, or F to select Fail (whichever is displayed on your screen as an option). The command prompt will display `Current drive is no longer valid.` You must then switch to a valid drive. For example, if you have a hard disk named C:, type C: and press Enter. If your disk drive A: contains a diskette, type A: and press Enter. The command prompt will redisplay the current drive name.

❏ DOS displays the message `General failure reading drive` followed by a drive name (such as A). In this case, the diskette in the drive is not *formatted* and therefore cannot be accessed yet. Try a different diskette or see Chapter 6 for formatting techniques.

❏ You type a command, but DOS does nothing. This occurs when you type a command and forget to press Enter. Typing a command merely displays it on the screen. You must press Enter to "send" the command to the computer's processor. If you forget, DOS waits indefinitely, until you press Enter.

Summary

This chapter discussed the way in which information is organized into directories and files on a computer. It also discussed techniques and commands for accessing disk drives, directories, and subdirectories and for viewing the names of available files. These are the most fundamental (and perhaps most important) techniques for using your computer, as they permit you to use any program to manage any information contained in your computer. The following summary lists these important techniques:

❏ DOS provides two handy wildcards to help you manage computer files. ?, which stands for any single character, and *, which stands for any group of characters.

❏ You must enter commands to access different drives and directories and to view file names.

❏ To change the current drive from the command prompt, type the new drive name (including the colon) and then press Enter.

❏ To display the name of the current directory and drive in the DOS command prompt, type the command PROMPT PG and press Enter.

❏ To display the names of directories and subdirectories on the current drive, change to the root directory, type the command TREE, and press Enter.

❏ To access a directory or subdirectory, use the CHDIR—or CD—command, followed by the directory name (or path), and then press Enter.

❏ DOS Version 5 offers the File List, which presents a graphical summary of the drives, directories, and file names available on the computer.

❏ To access the DOS 5 File List from the initial DOS Shell screen, select the Single File List option from the View menu.

❏ Keys and techniques that you use in the File List are summarized inside the front cover of this book.

Running Programs

So far, you've learned that your computer stores programs (instructions) and data (information) in files and that these files can be better organized by storing them in separate directories and subdirectories. You have also learned how to access disk drives, directories, and subdirectories and how to view the names of files stored in the current directory or subdirectory.

Now that you know the basics of how to search for specific files, you need to learn how to use those techniques to find and run programs that put the computer to work. This chapter demonstrates techniques for running two types of programs: 1) programs that came with your DOS package (DOS programs) and 2) optional programs that you purchase separately (*application* programs).

DOS Programs

Although DOS, in itself, is a program, it also includes additional programs that help you perform common tasks. In this chapter, you'll use one of the simpler of these DOS programs, named CHKDSK (short for CHecK DiSK). CHKDSK checks the storage capacity of your disk (or diskette), reports on how much RAM is available, and can even fix minor disk problems.

Application Programs

Whether you bought your computer for personal use or are using a computer owned by a company or a school, you probably have programs other than DOS available on your computer. As mentioned in Chapter 1, a computer is like a tape player, and programs are like cassette tapes. After you buy a tape player, you need to purchase tapes to play on it. After you buy a computer, you must purchase programs to run on it.

Your computer might already have several programs installed on it, particularly if you are sharing it with co-workers or fellow students. For example, the hard disk on a business computer might already contain the popular WordPerfect word processing program, the Lotus 1-2-3 spreadsheet program, and the dBASE IV database management program. Because these application programs are purchased and installed separately from DOS, I have no way of knowing which particular application programs are currently installed on your computer. However, I can give general pointers to help you locate and use any program that is available on your computer.

This chapter uses the Lotus 1-2-3 spreadsheet program in examples that demonstrate how to run an application program. Of course, I cannot possibly go into detail about actually using the 1-2-3 program; this is a book about DOS, and to fully discuss 1-2-3 would require hundreds of additional pages.

> NOTE: Although application programs often require you to learn different techniques for effective use, most programs provide instant help when you press the F1 key.

To effectively use an application program, such as Lotus 1-2-3, WordPerfect, dBASE IV, or any other, you need to read either the printed documentation that came with the program or a separate book that focuses on that program. Also, if you are sharing a computer with others in a company or school, you can use a simple, nontechnical technique to find out which application programs are currently installed on your computer and how to run those programs: Ask someone who knows.

> WARNING: Do not run the DOS FORMAT.COM program until you've thoroughly read Chapter 6 of this book.

NOTE: Please be forewarned: Although the techniques you will learn in this chapter will help you find and run any program on your computer, you should run only those programs mentioned in this chapter or those that you know something about. If you arbitrarily run programs that you know nothing about, you might inadvertently erase important information from your disk!

Running Programs from Files List

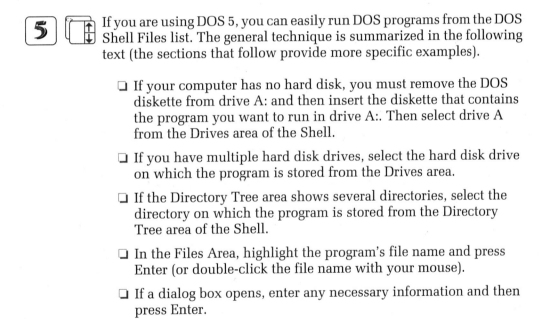 If you are using DOS 5, you can easily run DOS programs from the DOS Shell Files list. The general technique is summarized in the following text (the sections that follow provide more specific examples).

❏ If your computer has no hard disk, you must remove the DOS diskette from drive A: and then insert the diskette that contains the program you want to run in drive A:. Then select drive A from the Drives area of the Shell.

❏ If you have multiple hard disk drives, select the hard disk drive on which the program is stored from the Drives area.

❏ If the Directory Tree area shows several directories, select the directory on which the program is stored from the Directory Tree area of the Shell.

❏ In the Files Area, highlight the program's file name and press Enter (or double-click the file name with your mouse).

❏ If a dialog box opens, enter any necessary information and then press Enter.

The next section demonstrates how to use these steps to run the DOS CHKDSK program.

Running a DOS Program

The CHKDSK program is stored with the file name CHKDSK.EXE. On a hard disk, the program is usually stored in the DOS directory. For computers that do not have hard disks, the CHKDSK.EXE program is stored on the Shell or Shell\Help diskette that you created during the installation process.

Assuming that you are starting from the initial DOS Shell screen (which displays both the File List and Program List), use the following steps to run the CHKDSK program:

1. If your computer has no hard disk, be sure that the `Shell` or `Shell/Help` diskette is in drive A: and select `drive A` from the Drives area of the Shell.

NOTE: If you are using diskettes, and CHKDSK.EXE is not on the DOS Shell diskette, use the techniques discussed in Chapter 4 to locate the CHKDSK.EXE file on one of the other DOS diskettes.

---

2. Optionally, if you want to be able to view more file names, select `Single File List` from the View menu (though you can use any view you want).

3. If you have multiple hard disks, select the `disks` that DOS programs are stored on (typically drive C) from the Drives area.

4. If you have a hard disk, select the `DOS directory` from the Directory Tree area of the Shell.

5. Press `Tab` to move to the Files Area of the screen and then use the ↓ or ↑ key to move the highlighter to the CHKDSK.EXE file name.

6. When CHKDSK.EXE is highlighted (as shown in Figure 5.1), press `Enter`. (If you have a mouse, you can use the Scroll Bars to locate the CHKDSK.EXE file and double-click the file name).

The screen now displays information about your computer's memory (RAM) and the current hard disk or diskette. (If a question appears on the screen asking whether you want to convert lost clusters to chains, press the letter N and Enter.) Figure 5.2 shows an example of the information displayed by CHKDSK. Note that your screen probably shows completely different information.

Don't be concerned about the information that CHKDSK is now displaying; the important point here is that you were able to run this program. (When you do want to learn more about the information that CHKDSK displays, refer to Appendix B.)

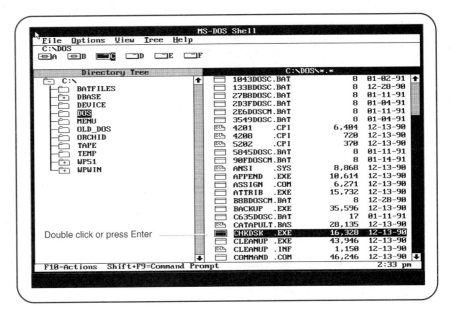

Figure 5.1. The CHKDSK.EXE file name is highlighted.

```
Volume Serial Number is 165C-4523

 33323008 bytes total disk space
   770048 bytes in 7 hidden files
    61440 bytes in 11 directories
 23158784 bytes in 771 user files
  9332736 bytes available on disk

     2048 bytes in each allocation unit
    16271 total allocation units on disk
     4557 available allocation units on disk

   655360 total bytes memory
   600384 bytes free


Press any key to return to MS-DOS Shell....
```

Figure 5.2. Sample output of the CHKDSK program.

NOTE: When a screen message tells you to press "any key", it means any "typewriter" key, such as a letter, the Spacebar, or Enter.

NOTE: Near the bottom of the screen, the prompt `Press any key to return to MS-DOS Shell...` appears. Go ahead and press a key now. The CHKDSK program ends, and you'll be returned to the DOS Shell File List.

Running an Application Program from the DOS Shell

The basic techniques for running application programs are essentially the same as those used to run DOS programs. The following exercise assumes that you (or someone else) has already purchased and installed the Lotus 1-2-3 program on your computer.

If your computer has a hard disk, the Lotus 1-2-3 manual recommends that you create a directory named 123 to store the 1-2-3 program on; it also tells you to start the program by entering the command `123` at the DOS prompt. Let's work through the exact steps required to run 1-2-3, both for computers with and without a hard disk. (Again, you cannot perform these exact steps unless you already have a copy of the 1-2-3 program installed on your hard disk or available on floppy diskettes.)

1. If your computer does not have a hard disk, remove the `DOS diskette` from drive A:, insert the Lotus 1-2-3 `System Disk` in drive A:, and then select `drive A` from the Drives area.

2. Optionally, select `Single File List` from the View menu if you'd like to switch to that view.

3. If you have multiple hard drives, select the `drive` that the 1-2-3 program is stored on.

4. If your computer has a hard disk, select the 123 `directory` from the Directory Tree area of the screen.

NOTE: Although several files are named 123 (see Figure 5.3), you know that 123.COM is the file that contains the program, because programs always have the file name extensions .COM, .EXE, or .BAT. (On a graphics screen, program files are also represented by a rectangular icon *without* the upper right corner folded down.)

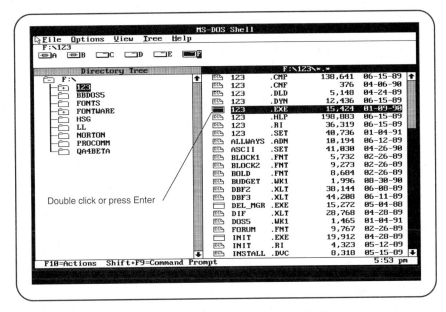

Figure 5.3. 123.EXE file name is highlighted.

5. Move to the Files area and use the S c r o l l   B a r, ↑ or ↓ keys to move the highlight to the 123.EXE file name. (If you are using a mouse, click once on the 123 . E X E file name.) Your screen now should resemble the one shown in Figure 5.3.

6. Press E n t e r or double-click the mouse.

After a brief pause, the Lotus 1-2-3 program spreadsheet appears on your screen, as shown in Figure 5.4. (Though its exact appearance depends on the version of 1-2-3 that you are using).

```
A1:                                                                    MENU
Worksheet  Range  Copy   Move  File  Print  Graph  Data  System  Add-In  Quit
Global   Insert  Delete  Column  Erase  Titles  Window  Status  Page  Learn
          A        B       C       D       E       F        G       H
 1
 2
 3
 4
 5
 6
 7
 8
 9
10
11
12
13
14
15
16
17
18
19
20
```

Figure 5.4. Lotus 1-2-3 spreadsheet program is "in control."

Exiting an Application Program

Unlike the CHKDSK program, which automatically returns control to DOS when it finishes its task, most application programs stay in control of your computer until you take specific steps to exit them. Because different programs require different steps for exiting, you must always find exact instructions in the program's documentation.

If you used the preceding steps to run the 1-2-3 program on your computer, it is probably still on your screen. To exit the 1-2-3 program and return to DOS, follow these steps:

1. Press the / key to display a menu of options at the top of the screen.

2. Press Q to select Quit from that menu.

3. When given the options No and Yes, press Y to select Yes.

4. When you see the message `Press any key to return to MS-DOS Shell...`, press a key to return to the DOS Shell.

Now you have used the DOS Shell to run both a DOS program and an optional application program. The basic steps described in these sections work for all programs that you might use on your computer. In addition, you can customize the DOS Shell to make it easier to run programs, as discussed in Chapter 11.

Running Programs from the File List

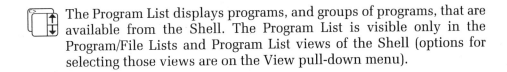 The Program List displays programs, and groups of programs, that are available from the Shell. The Program List is visible only in the Program/File Lists and Program List views of the Shell (options for selecting those views are on the View pull-down menu).

> NOTE: The icons for programs and group names look different in the Program List if you have a graphics monitor.

Initially, the Program List displays the Main program group (the title **Main** appears at the top of the window). As you'll learn in Chapter 11, you can add programs and groups to the Program List, so we cannot tell you exactly what options are available in the Program List on your particular computer (particularly if you share a computer with others).

It's likely, however, that your program list contains at least three programs (Command Prompt, Editor, and MS-DOS QBasic), and one group (Disk Utilities). The Command Prompt option performs a temporary (partial) exit from the Shell; the Editor option runs the DOS Editor (described in Chapter 10), and the MS-DOS QBasic option runs the BASIC language interpreter (a very large topic—see a book on Microsoft's Quick BASIC for details). The Disk Utilities group offers programs used for managing disks (described in Chapters 6 and 7).

To run a program listed in the Program List,

❑ If you are using the keyboard rather than a mouse, press Tab until the highlighter is in the Program List window.

> NOTE: A window is simply an area of the screen.

❏ If the program you want to run is in a group other than the one that's currently displayed, select the appropriate group name, either by double-clicking its name or by moving the highlighter to the name and pressing Enter.

❏ Select the name of the program you want to run, either by double-clicking its name or by moving the highlighter to the name and pressing Enter.

If you'd like to try this out in a hands-on manner, follow these steps:

1. If you are using the keyboard, press Tab until the highlighter gets to the Program List area of the screen.

2. Highlight Editor and press Enter (or double-click the Editor option) to run that program.

3. You'll see a dialog box asking for the name of the file to Edit. Skip this for the time being by pressing Enter or clicking the OK command button.

4. The opening screen for the Editor appears. (You'll learn how to use this program in Chapter 10.)

5. Press Escape to leave the opening screen. The Editor is now "in control". To get back to the Shell, you must exit (close) the Editor program.

6. Pull down the Editor's File menu by pressing Alt+F or by clicking File in its Menu Bar.

7. Select Exit by typing X, by clicking the Exit option, or by moving the highlighter to the Exit option and pressing Enter.

The Editor program is no longer running, and the Shell is back "in control." You have successfully run and exited a program from the Program List.

Note that the general technique of pulling down the File menu and selecting Exit is a common technique used to exit many programs. If you ever get into a program that you know little about and don't know how to exit, try selecting Exit from its File pull-down menu or the Exit or Quit option from its Menu Bar.

If you selected Command Prompt from the Program List, you can return to the Shell by typing EXIT at the command prompt and pressing Enter. (If you enter the DOSSHELL command, rather than EXIT, you'll start a second Shell, which is usually harmless but can make matters quite confusing.)

The same basic techniques can be used to run a program in a particular group. To try it,

1. Move the highlighter to the Disk Utilities group name and press Enter (or just double-click Disk Utilities if you are using a mouse. The names of program in the Disk Utilities group are displayed.

   You don't really want to use any of these programs until you learn more about them in upcoming chapters, but you could run any program now by highlighting its name and pressing Enter or by double-clicking its name (but don't do so now).

2. To get back to the Main group now, highlight Main and press Enter or double-click the Main option.

Again, you'll learn more about the Program List and how to customize it to best suit your needs in Chapter 11. For now, it's sufficient to know that this is an alternative means of running programs.

Running Programs by Dragging

 Yet another technique for running some programs is to drag a data file to its program. By a data file, I mean a file that contains data that a program created, such as a document created with your word processing program or a spreadsheet created with your spreadsheet program.

To use this technique, you must be able to recognize which data files belong to which programs. Furthermore, this procedure does not work with all programs, so you may have to experiment and do a little research in the documentation that accompanies your application program to determine whether you can use this technique. If you are not that experienced yet, you may want to keep this technique in the back of your mind.

The general procedure is fairly simple and convenient:

❑ In the Files List, use your mouse to move the highlighter to the data file that you want to work with.

❑ Hold down the left mouse button and drag to the program you want to use the icon that appears. (If the program is not currently visible, keep holding down the left mouse button and move to the arrows at the top or bottom of the Scroll Bar for the Files List to scroll.)

❏ When you see the program, move the highlighter to it and release the mouse button.

❏ You may see a dialog box asking for confirmation. If so, click Yes to proceed with the operation.

If the data file and program you have selected are compatible, and the program supports this capability, your program will run and load the data file you dragged to it.

If the data file and program are on separate drives and/or directories, you can use the Dual File Lists view to drag a data file to its program. If you have a hard disk, a mouse, and DOS 5, chances are you can use the following specific steps to try dragging a text (data) file— AUTOEXEC.BAT in this example—to the DOS Editor (EDIT.COM). (You will learn more about actually using the Editor and the role of the AUTOEXEC.BAT file in later chapters.)

1. Select drive C by clicking its name or icon in the Drives area of the Shell.

2. Switch to the Dual File Lists view by selecting Dual Files Lists from the View pull-down menu.

3. In the upper Directory Tree, click the C:\ (root directory) drive to select that directory. This is the directory where AUTOEXEC.BAT is located (if it exists).

4. In the lower Directory Tree, click the DOS directory (this is where the Editor program is located).

5. In the upper Files List window, use the Scroll Bars (if necessary) to scroll through file names until you can see the AUTOEXEC.BAT file.

6. Move the mouse pointer to the AUTOEXEC.BAT file name, and hold down the left mouse button (don't release the mouse button until I tell you to).

7. Drag to the Lower Files List area the icon that appears. Notice how the icon and the massage in the lower left corner of the screen change as you drag the icon through various file names in the Files List.

8. If EDIT.COM does not appear in the lower Files List, keep the left mouse button depressed and drag the icon to the up-arrow or down-arrow in the Files List's Scroll Bar until you see the EDIT.COM program's name in the Files List. Drag the icon away from the arrow to stop scrolling.

9. Move the icon to the `EDIT.COM` file name.

10. Now you can release the mouse button.

11. If you see a dialog box asking whether you are sure that you want to start EDIT.COM using AUTOEXEC.BAT as the initial file, click the `Yes` command button.

Your AUTOEXEC.BAT appears on the Editor's edit screen ready for editing. Of course, I have not described what the Editor program nor AUTOEXEC.BAT files are all about yet, but you have successfully "launched" (a flowery term for "run") the Editor with your AUTOEXEC.BAT file as the program to edit.

If you are a WordPerfect user, you could use this same general techniques to drag a WordPerfect document file to the WordPerfect program (WP.EXE). Should you be a spreadsheet user, you could probably apply this same general technique to drag a spreadsheet file to its spreadsheet program.

In this example, you've dragged your AUTOEXEC.BAT file to the DOS Editor program and could now use that program to change that file. If you are a beginner, however, you're probably wondering "now what do I do?". As we mentioned, you'll learn more about the Editor and AUTOEXEC.BAT file later in this book. For now, it's sufficient to know that you have successfully launched the Editor by dragging a file to it. As you gain experience you'll learn how to use this general technique with other programs.

Your best bet now (if you are not an experienced user) would probably be to leave the Editor program without making any changes to your AUTOEXEC.BAT file. Here's how:

1. Click the `File` option in the Menu Bar at the top of the screen.

2. Click the `Exit` option to leave the Editor.

You are back to the DOS Shell and have learned another alternative method of starting programs from the DOS 5 Shell. If you want to get back to your "normal" Program/File Lists view, click the View option in the Menu Bar and then select Program/File Lists by clicking that option.

Running Programs by Association

 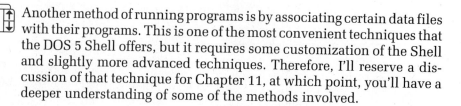 Another method of running programs is by associating certain data files with their programs. This is one of the most convenient techniques that the DOS 5 Shell offers, but it requires some customization of the Shell and slightly more advanced techniques. Therefore, I'll reserve a discussion of that technique for Chapter 11, at which point, you'll have a deeper understanding of some of the methods involved.

Running Programs from the DOS Command Prompt

 This section discusses techniques for running programs from the command prompt, without the aid of the DOS Shell. Remember, if you are using DOS 5, the command prompt is entirely optional.

Therefore, if you feel that learning an alternative technique might be confusing, you can skip to the chapter "Summary" to review important techniques and concepts.

Also remember that if you are using DOS 5, you must press the F3 (or Alt-F4) key to leave the DOS Shell and get to the command prompt.

The general steps for running a program from the command prompt are listed in the following:

❏ If your computer has no hard disk, you must remove the DOS diskette from drive A: and insert the diskette containing the program that you want to run into drive A:.

❏ If your computer has a hard disk, use the CHDIR (or CD) command to change to the directory that contains the program that you want to run.

❏ Type the file name that runs the program and press Enter.

The following section demonstrates how to use these steps to run the DOS CHKDSK program.

Running a DOS Program from the Command Prompt

NOTE: The DOS commands that you used in the previous chapter, such as DIR, PROMPT, CHDIR, and CD, are stored in RAM, so you don't need to change disk drives or directories to use those commands.

The DOS CHKDSK (short for Check Disk) program is stored in a file named CHKDSK.EXE. Exactly where the CHKDSK.EXE program is stored depends on your computer system and the version of DOS you are using. If you installed DOS on a hard disk, DOS automatically stored the CHKDSK.EXE on the root directory (for DOS 3) or the DOS directory (for DOS 4 and 5). If your computer has no hard disk, the CHKDSK.EXE program is stored on the DOS diskette (for DOS 3), on the Shell diskette (for DOS 4 or 5).

If you are at the Shell, press F3 or Alt-F4 to get to the command prompt. Then, to run the CHKDSK program:

1. If your computer has no hard disk, be sure the Shell or Shell/Help diskette is in drive A, and then be sure you're on that drive (type A: and press Enter).

2. If you have multiple hard drives, select the drive that DOS programs are stored on (for example, type C: and press Enter).

3. If your computer has a hard disk, type CD \DOS and then press Enter to go to the DOS directory.

4. To run a program, type its file name, without the extension. In this case, type CHKDSK and press Enter to run the CHKDSK program.

TIP: As you'll learn in Chapter 11, the DOS PATH command lets you run a program from any directory, avoiding the Bad Command or File Name error.

If the current diskette or hard disk directory does not contain the CHKDSK.EXE program, DOS displays the error message `Bad command or file name`. If that error occurs, you need to use the techniques discussed in Chapter 4 to search other DOS diskettes or other directories to find CHKDSK.EXE. Use the command `DIR C*.*` on each directory or each diskette (to view file names that begin with the letter C) until you find the directory or diskette that contains CHKDSK.EXE. When you find the correct diskette or directory, type the `CHKDSK` command and press Enter to run the program.

The CHKDSK program performs a somewhat simple task—it displays information about memory (RAM) and disk storage space. (If a question appears on the screen asking whether you want to convert lost clusters to files, press the letter `N` and Enter). Figure 5.2 shows an example of the information displayed by CHKDSK. Note that your screen probably shows completely different information.

Don't be concerned about the details that CHKDSK is now displaying; the important point here is that you were able to run this program. (When you do want to learn more about the information that CHKDSK displays, refer to Appendix B.)

Let's review the basic techniques you used. First, you located the file that contains the program you want to run (CHKDSK.EXE in this example). Then, you typed the program name, which is the same as the file name without the extension (CHKDSK in this example). After typing the file name, you pressed Enter, and DOS ran the program.

After the CHKDSK program ends, it automatically returns you to DOS. When you see the DOS command prompt, you know that CHKDSK is done and DOS is back in control. (You can now enter any DOS command that you wish.)

Running an Application Program from the Command Prompt

The basic techniques for running application programs are essentially the same as those used to run DOS programs. The following exercise assumes that you (or someone else) has already purchased and installed the Lotus 1-2-3 program on your computer.

If your computer has a hard disk, the Lotus 1-2-3 manual recommends that you create a directory named 123 to store the 1-2-3 program on; it also tells you to start the program by entering the command `123` at the DOS prompt when you're in the 123 directory. Let's work through the exact steps required to run 1-2-3, both for computers with and without a hard disk. (Again, you cannot perform these exact steps unless you already have a copy of the 1-2-3 program installed on your hard disk or available on floppy diskettes.)

1. If your computer does not have 1-2-3 installed on the hard disk, remove the DOS diskette from drive A: and insert the Lotus 1-2-3 System Disk into drive A:. Switch to that drive (type A: and press Enter).

2. If your computer has several hard disk drives, select the drive that the 123 program is stored on (for example, type C: and press Enter to get to drive C).

3. On a hard disk, change to the 123 directory by typing the command CD \123 and pressing Enter.

4. Type the program name 123 and then press Enter.

After a brief pause, the Lotus 1-2-3 program spreadsheet appears on your screen, as shown in Figure 5.4. (Depending on your version of 1-2-3, your screen may look different). You won't actually use the 1-2-3 program here. You need to study a book or the documentation that comes with the Lotus 1-2-3 software package to learn how to use 1-2-3. (Lotus 1-2-3 might not look impressive when it first appears on the screen, but it is actually a very powerful and useful program for managing and analyzing business and financial information!)

However, the important point here is that you have performed the necessary steps to run an application program. The general techniques you used to run Lotus 1-2-3 hold true for all other application programs. However, always remember to check the documentation that comes with an application program for detailed information about running that program, such as which diskette to insert, which directory to access, and the command required to run the name of the program.

Exiting an Application Program

Unlike the CHKDSK program, which automatically returns control to DOS when it finishes its task, most application programs stay in control of your computer until you take specific steps to exit them. Because different programs require different steps for exiting, you must find exact instructions in the program's documentation.

If you used the preceding steps to run the 1-2-3 program on your computer, it is probably still on your screen. To exit the 1-2-3 program and return to DOS, follow these steps:

1. Press the / key to display a menu of options at the top of the screen.

2. Press Q to select Quit from the menu.

3. When given the options No and Yes, press Y to select Yes. This returns you to the DOS command prompt, which indicates that DOS is back in control. You can now use DOS to run another program.

Although the preceding exercises did not help you to understand or to use the Lotus 1-2-3 program, the general techniques that you used to start and exit the program are important: You will use these same general techniques to start and use all programs on your computer. (Again, the specific techniques that you need to run, use, and exit an optional application program are included in the documentation that comes packaged with that program.)

To recap, the basic procedure you use to start a program at the command prompt is as follows: First, if the program is not installed on your hard disk (or your computer doesn't have a hard disk), you must insert the appropriate program diskette in drive A:. If your computer has a hard disk, you must go to the appropriate disk drive (for example, C:) and then go to the program's directory, using the CHDIR (or CD) command. Then type the file name (without the extension) that starts the program. The required diskettes, directories, and program names are discussed in the documentation that comes with any application program that you purchase.

About Bad Command or File Name

One of the most common error messages beginners face is Bad Command or File Name. Most often, this message is caused by forgetting to go to a program's drive and directory before entering the command to run the program. (Though misspelling a command or not using spaces correctly causes the same error). Chapters 7 and 11 offer techniques to simplify running programs.

Starting More Than One Program at a Time

The DOS 5 Shell lets you perform several operations that you can't perform from the command prompt. One of the most useful Shell-only operations is called *task swapping*.

In all versions of DOS before DOS 5, you could only start one program at a time; you started it, worked with it, and then exited it to return to DOS. If you wanted to see the data in another program, you had to exit the first program, start the second, exit the second, and then start the first again. This was a time-consuming and tedious task. with the DOS 5 Shell, however, you can start two or more programs and then swap between the programs or the Shell with a single key combination.

The practical uses for this feature are many. For example, if you're writing a weekly business report with a word processor but you often need to refer to figures in a database, perform recalculations in a spreadsheet, and create charts with a graphics program, you previously would have had to open and close these applications scores of times.

These time-consuming, repetitive tasks are just what you bought your computer to avoid. The DOS 5 task-swapping feature provides a welcome convenience to DOS users: You simply open all of these applications and then swap from program to program as you need them to create your report.

Enabling the Swapper

Before you can take advantage of task swapping, you must first *enable the Swapper*; that is, you must first use the Options menu to change one of the default settings of the Shell. After you make this change, DOS saves the new setting and automatically starts the Task Swapper whenever you use the Shell.

To activate the Task Swapper,

1. If you are at the command prompt, enter EXIT (or DOSSHELL, depending on how you last exited the Shell) and press Enter to get back to the Shell.

2. Press Alt-0 or click Options in the Menu Bar to pull down the Options menu.

3. Select Enable Task Swapper.

If you pull down the Options menu again, you'll notice that a diamond-like *bullet* appears to the left of the Enable Task Swapper option. That bullet symbol is used throughout the Shell to signify that an option is on, or active.

The Enable Swapper option is called a *toggle*; it has only two states— enabled or disabled, on or off. To *toggle* the option off (disable the Task Swapper), simply follow the previous steps exactly. Select the option once to turn it on; select it again to turn it off.

The Active Task List Display

After you enable the Swapper, the Program List section of the Shell divides into two areas: one titled Main (or the active "program group" name) and the other called the Active Task List. The Active Task List lets you know which programs you have already started and therefore, which programs are currently open.

If your Shell is currently displaying the Program List view, the Active Task List occupies the entire right side of the screen (see Figure 5.5); if you are using the Program/File Lists view, the Active Task List section is a small box in the lower right corner of the screen (see Figure 5.6).

You can select either view from the View pull-down menu.

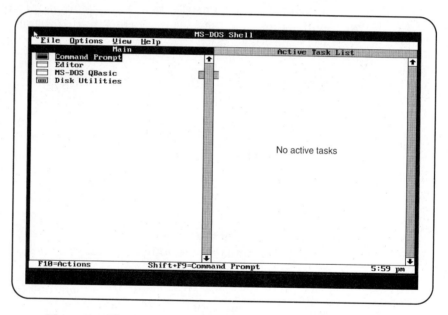

Figure 5.5. The Active Task List box in the Program List screen.

How the Task Swapper Operates

After you've enabled the Task Swapper, you can start a program and then press a key combination to return to the Shell from which you can start another program. You can repeat this process as many times as necessary.

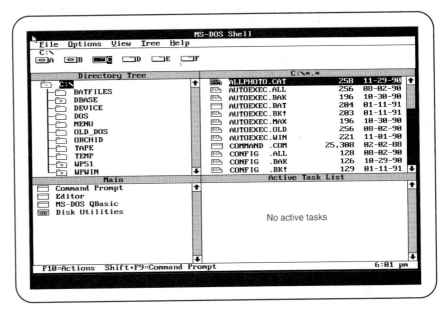

Figure 5.6. The Active Task List box in the Program/File Lists screen.

Although all of the programs that you have started are technically "open," they are not all "active." Only the currently selected program is actually running. What about the other unselected programs?

Assume that you've started a program from the Shell and then issued the command that returns you to the Shell. DOS immediately takes a "snapshot" of memory and saves that information to a disk file; then it starts the Shell program. When you return to the previously started program, DOS exits the Shell and reloads the saved disk file into memory; this restores your computer's memory to its previous state (which includes the program and data that was stored there before you switched to the Shell), and that program resumes running.

NOTE: Windows 3, which is basically an alternative DOS Shell, does allow multiple programs to run simultaneously on many computers.

Remember, you cannot start a spreadsheet recalculation or large printing task, for example, and assume that the operation will continue after you switch to another program. When you leave the current program, DOS suspends its activity and restores that activity only when you switch back to the program. Only one program can be "running" at a time.

Swapping Between Programs

To run multiple programs available from the Active Task List, first be sure the Enable Swapper option in the Options menu is turned on and then use the following general steps.

❑ If your monitor is not displaying the Active Task List, select `Program/File Lists` from the View menu.

❑ Start a program in the usual manner, using either the `Files List` or `Program List`, as described previously in this chapter.

❑ After your program has completed all of its startup operations and is active, press `Alt-Tab`, `Alt-Esc`, or `Ctrl-Esc`. This causes DOS to go back to the Shell.

The Active Task List on the screen now includes the name of the program that you just left. You can now use steps two and three to start another program. Each new program name will be listed in the Active Task List.

To switch to an already running (open) program, select its name from the Active Task List. With the mouse, double-click the program name; with the keyboard, Tab to the Task List, use the arrow keys to highlight the program name, and press Enter.

Closing Open Programs

If you are finished using a program and you no longer need to swap to it, you exit (close) that program as you normally would. After the program ends, DOS returns you to the Shell from which you can switch to another program. Note that the Active Task List no longer displays the name of the program that you just closed.

NOTE: Always close active programs and exit the Shell before you turn off your computer. Otherwise, you could lose data.

You cannot use the F3 or Alt-F4 keys to exit the Shell until you have closed all open programs. You must select the programs one by one from the Active Task List, exiting them in the usual fashion. When the Task List no longer displays any program names, you can exit the Shell.

You can, however, get to the command prompt by pressing Shift+F9 or by selecting Command Prompt from the Main program group, even while programs are listed in the Active Task list. Remember, however, that when you temporarily exit the Shell in the manner, you enter the EXIT command (not DOSSHELL) at the command prompt to get back to the Shell.

Never turn off the computer while programs are still open (while their names are displayed in the Active Task List box)! If you do, the data that you entered into those programs will probably be lost. Always close those programs and exit the Shell before turning off your computer.

> NOTE: Deleting a program from the Active Task List is a last resort! Use this method only if a program refuses to accept your usual exit commands.

If a program ever "locks up" or freezes so that you can't exit it as you normally would, use the following steps to recover.

1. Press `Alt-Esc` to return to the Shell.

2. Then highlight the `program's name` in the Active Task List. With the mouse, click the name once; with the keyboard, `Tab` to the Task List and use the arrow keys to position the highlight over the name.

3. Press the `Del` key.

This is a "last-resort" procedure! Figure 5.7 shows the warning message that DOS displays before you delete a program from the Task List. Although this procedure closes the program, it might cause you to lose some of the data that you've entered. It also destabilizes DOS and can disrupt future operations. After you have deleted the program name, immediately close any other programs that may be open, exit the Shell, and then reboot your computer. When the DOS Shell returns, everything will be fine again.

Back to the Defaults

Once you activate the Task Swapper, it remains enabled even in future DOS sessions until you turn it back off. If you want to disable the swapper now, you must first empty the Active Task list by ending any running programs. Then select Enable Task Swapper from the Options pull-down menu.

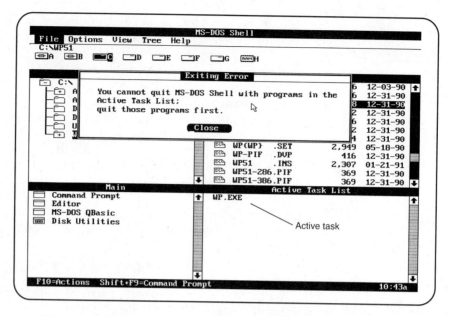

Figure 5.7. Warning message displayed for application still active

Summary

This chapter has covered several alternative techniques for running programs, including using the Files and the Program lists, dragging a data file to its program, and typing the program's name at the command prompt:

❏ To run a program from the Files List of the Shell, first select the program's drive and directory locations from the Drives and Directories areas of the Shell and then select the program's name from the Files List. (Programs always have the file name extension .COM, .EXE, or .BAT).

❏ You can start some programs by using your mouse to drag a data file to its program file.

❏ You can select groups and run programs in the Program List by selecting (highlighting and pressing Enter or double-clicking) group and program names.

❏ To start a program from the command prompt, you need to go to the program's drive, then to its directory (using the CD command), and then type the name of the program.

 ❏ The DOS 5 Shell Task Swapper lets you start several programs and easily switch from one to another without exiting and restarting each program from scratch. Select Enable Task Swapper from the Options pull-down menu to activate the swapper.

Managing Programs and Files

In Part 1 of this book, you learned how to perform essential DOS operations that you will probably use on a daily basis in your work with the computer. After reading those chapters, you should be able to find your way around any DOS computer, whether it be your personal computer or one you share with coworkers or fellow students.

Part 2 focuses on more specific techniques for actually putting the computer to work. The techniques discussed in this section are essential to using your computer effectively; you will use them regularly as you gain experience with your computer. For example, Part 2 covers the following topics:

- ❑ How to format new diskettes for use on your computer.

- ❑ How to make copies of diskettes.

- ❑ How to create directories and subdirectories on your hard disk and diskettes to better organize your files.

- ❑ How to perform basic file operations such as copying, erasing, moving, and protecting files.

- ❑ How to use advanced "power tips" to increase your efficiency and make your work easier.

The first three chapters in this part provide many hands-on exercises that you can try for yourself. The last chapter provides general examples for using advanced techniques to manage large numbers of files and directories.

Managing Your Diskettes

As you know from Chapter 1, diskettes store information and computer programs. If your computer does not have a hard disk, you must use diskettes to store all your computer files. Even if your computer has a hard disk, you still need to use diskettes to copy new programs onto your hard disk and to store backup copies of hard disk files.

This chapter focuses on techniques for preparing diskettes to store information, for making backup copies of files, and for comparing diskettes. The later sections of this chapter explain the important features of modern diskettes.

What You Need to Work Through This Chapter

To do the sample exercises in this chapter, you need at least two new, blank diskettes. If you do not have any blank diskettes available, you still might want to read through this chapter to get an overview of the formatting procedure; then, you can do the exercises later, when you have some blank diskettes.

Formatting Diskettes

When you purchase an application program for use on your computer, the package contains a diskette (or sometimes several diskettes) with the program's files stored on it. You can use these diskettes with your computer at any time, because they are already *formatted* (prepared) for use on your computer.

On the other hand, when you purchase a box of new, blank diskettes, they are not ready for use on your computer. They first must be formatted, using the techniques described in this chapter, before you can store files on them.

Formatting is required because different computers use different types of disk drives and operating systems. Although DOS is the most widely used operating system in the world, other microcomputer operating systems are available and each requires a different diskette format. The formatting procedure prepares a new, blank diskette for use with a particular type of computer and a particular operating system.

Format with Caution!

In all versions of DOS before DOS 5, formatting a diskette permanently erases all information that is stored on that diskette. If you use those versions of DOS to format a diskette that already contains information or programs, you cannot use DOS to access that information or run those programs. Therefore, you need to exercise a great deal of caution when formatting diskettes with DOS 3.x and 4.

NOTE: The DOS 5 FORMAT command performs a "safe" format on floppy disks. If you format a disk by mistake, you can use the UNFORMAT command to restore the files on the disk.

By default, the DOS 5 FORMAT command performs a "safe" format on floppy disks that already contain data. It deletes certain DOS "system" information from the disk and makes the disk appear to be empty; however, it doesn't actually erase the information during the formatting operation. If you accidentally reformat an already formatted disk using DOS 5, you can use the UNFORMAT command (described later in this chapter, as well as in Appendix B) to restore the files on the disk.

Although DOS 5 lets you recover from an accidental format, preventing such an occurrence is such a simple procedure that you probably never will need to use the "disaster-recovery" UNFORMAT command. Be sure you follow the instructions in the next section: They offer the "ounce of protection" that saves the aggravation, lost time, and potentially lost data of an accidental format.

Checking a Diskette Before You Format It

In some situations, you might not be sure whether a particular diskette has been formatted. However, a quick and easy way to tell the difference between formatted and unformatted diskettes is to ask DOS to show you the contents of the disk. If the diskette is not already formatted, DOS displays a message informing you that it cannot read the disk so that you know the disk has never been formatted.

As an example, assume that you have a diskette in hand and want to format it. Just to play it safe, you want to check to see whether the diskette already contains important files. Here's how to do so:

> NOTE: Chapter 1 discussed the proper method for inserting and removing diskettes from the floppy disk drives.

❏ If your computer has a hard disk, put the diskette that you want to format into disk drive A:.

❏ If your computer has two floppy disk drives and no hard disk, place the diskette that contains the DOS Shell in drive A: and insert the diskette you want to format into drive B:.

If you are using DOS 5, and the DOS Shell is currently displayed on your screen, use the following steps to check the diskette:

1. Go to the disk drive that contains the diskette to be formatted by selecting its name (either A: or B:) in the Drives section of the Shell.

> NOTE: To get more information about any error message, press F1 or select the Help command button while the message is displayed.

2. If your screen displays a `Warning!` window with the message `General failure` (as shown in Figure 6.1), you've attempted to access an unformatted diskette. It is now safe to proceed with the formatting procedure.

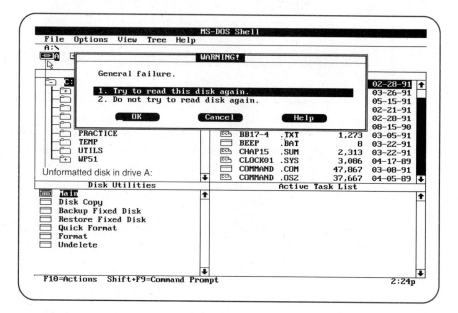

Figure 6.1. Warning message displayed when trying to access an unformatted diskette.

3. Remove the warning message from your screen by pressing the `Esc` key.

4. Skip the next three steps.

 If you are using DOS 3 (or the optional DOS 4 or DOS 5 command prompt), use the following steps to check the diskette:

1. Use the `DIR` command, followed by the name of the drive that contains the diskette that you want to format, to see whether the diskette contains any files. (For example, if the diskette to be formatted is in drive A:, type `DIR A:`. If the diskette to be formatted is in drive B:, type `DIR B:`.)

2. Press `Enter`.

3. If your screen displays an error message, such as `General failure reading drive`, followed by the drive name, the diskette is not yet formatted. Press the letter `A` to select Abort from the options that appear.

NOTE: DOS 3 and 4 permanently erase the files; DOS 5 erases the files' names, but leaves their data intact.

If you did not get an error (or warning) message when checking the diskette, the diskette is already formatted and does not need to be reformatted. However, if the DIR command listed file names, formatting that diskette will erase all he files on that diskette. Do not proceed with formatting that disk unless you are certain you want to erase all of its files.

NOTE: If DOS displays an error message during the formatting procedure, refer to the "Troubleshooting" section near the end of this chapter.

Proceeding with the Format

Once you've determined that you want to format a particular disk, here's how to do so using the DOS 5 Shell:

1. If your computer has a hard disk, select the hard disk (usually `C`) from the Drives area.

2. If your computer does not have a hard disk, place the `DOS Shell diskette` in drive A:. Access that drive by selecting drive `A` from the disk drives area of the File List.

3. Using the View menu, switch to the `Program/File Lists` view.

4. Select `Disk Utilities` from the Programs List (the bottom left section of the screen under the `Main` title bar) by highlighting and pressing `Enter` or by double-clicking.

> NOTE: You cannot reformat a write-protected diskette; see the section "Diskette Write Protection."

5. Select the `Quick Format` option, either by highlighting it and pressing `Enter` or by double-clicking it with your mouse.

6. When the `Format dialog box` appears (as shown in Figure 6.2), it initially suggests a disk drive for formatting (either a: or b:).

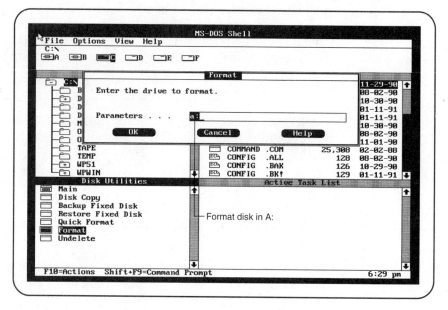

Figure 6.2. The Format dialog box.

7. If the suggested drive is not the one containing the diskette you want to format, type the name of the drive that contains the diskette (either `A:` or `B:`). Use the Backspace, arrow, and Delete (Del) keys to make changes or corrections as necessary. Do not reformat a hard disk drive (C:, D:, E: or any higher letter) unless you know exactly what you are doing and are willing to lose all the files on that disk.

8. Press `Enter` or use your mouse to click the `OK` box once.

9. Skip the next four steps.

If you are using DOS 3 or the optional DOS 5 command prompt, follow these steps to start the formatting process:

1. If your computer has a hard disk, access the hard disk, typically by typing C: and pressing Enter.

2. If your computer does not have a hard disk, insert your DOS (or DOS Shell) diskette in drive A:.

3. Type the FORMAT command followed by the name of the drive that contains the diskette that you want to format. For example, to format the diskette in drive A: type FORMAT A:. If the diskette to be formatted is in drive B:, type FORMAT B:.

4. Press Enter.

At this point, DOS displays a message similar to the following one. (Your message reflects the drive name you specified in the dialog box, in place of x.)

```
Insert new diskette for drive x:
and press ENTER when ready...
```

Assuming that the disk is already in its drive (because you just checked its contents), press Enter to proceed with the formatting.

NOTE: The drive light goes on when the disk drive is in use. Never remove a diskette when the drive light is on.

After the disk drive light goes on, you'll probably hear some whirring and buzzing as DOS formats the diskette. DOS keeps you informed of its progress as it does its work (different versions of DOS present different progress messages).

Regardless of the progress message that your screen displays, DOS lets you know when the formatting is complete by showing a message such as Format complete.

Electronic Labels

DOS Versions 3.3, 4, and 5 next display the following message:

```
Volume label (11 characters, ENTER for none)?
```

NOTE: The VOL and LABEL commands referenced in Appendix B let you view and optionally change a disk's electronic label.

A *volume label* (also called an *electronic label*) is a brief descriptive title (no more than 11 characters) that you can store on the diskette. This label appears on your screen during certain DOS operations and is useful for reminding you of the diskette's contents. However, the label is entirely optional and has no effect on your use of the diskette. For now, skip the volume label option by pressing Enter.

Available Diskette Space

Next, DOS displays the number of bytes of disk space available on the newly formatted diskette. If DOS encountered any flawed areas on the diskette while it was formatting, DOS disables those areas so that they cannot store files. This prevents the flawed areas from corrupting data or making certain files unreadable later.

Depending on the version of DOS you are using, your screen might also display information about *allocation units* and a *volume serial number*. You don't need to be concerned about these items now. (Chapter 15 discusses some of these "technical details.")

Finally, DOS displays the prompt

```
QuickFormat another (Y/N)?
```

This last prompt lets you know that you can format another diskette by pressing a Y. If you press N (for no), DOS ends the FORMAT program. For now, press N and then press Enter. (If prompted, press any key to return to the Shell).

The new diskette is now formatted and ready for use with your computer. However, unlike the DOS Startup diskette, this new diskette can only be used to store files; it cannot be used to start your computer. It is possible to format a new diskette so that it can be used to start a computer, but you don't need to be concerned about this yet. (When you do need further information on this topic, see the FORMAT and SYS command entries in Appendix B.)

At this point however, you've learned how to format a diskette for use with your computer. Remember, when you buy a box of new diskettes, they must be formatted before you can use them.

Format Versus Quick Format

You may have noticed that the Disk Utilities group contains two options for formatting: Quick Format and Format. The general steps for using these options are identical, but the way they perform the job differs somewhat: Quick Format checks to see whether the disk is already formatted and if so, saves information required to unformat the disk and then quickly reformats the disk by erasing all of its information. If the disk has never been formatted, this option asks for permission to perform an unconditional format.

Format, like Quick Format, checks to see whether the disk is already formatted and if so, saves information required to unformat the disk. Then it completely reformats the disk (which takes longer than deleting its information). If the disk has not already been formatted, this option proceeds with an unconditional format without asking for permission.

An "unconditional" format is basically a first-time format of a previously unformatted disk. No unformatting information is saved during an unconditional format (because there is none to save).

DOS 5 command prompt users can select the type of format to perform by using optional switches with the FORMAT command. See FORMAT in Appendix B for more information.

Unformatting a Disk

If you do accidentally reformat a previously formatted disk, chances are you can "unformat" it and get your original files back. You need to perform the unformat right away, however. Otherwise, any new files you save to the disk will start to overwrite the "invisible" ones that you can restore by unformatting.

Also, if you save any new files to the disk after reformatting it and then unformat that disk, the files saved after the reformatting will be replaced by the files that were on the disk before it was reformatted.

In this section, I'll assume that you are unformatting floppy disks. If you do accidentally reformat a hard disk, and want to unformat, be sure to read about the UNFORMAT command in Appendix B for additional information and warnings.

Unformatting a floppy disk is a pretty simple process:

1. Place the accidentally reformatted disk in drive A or B (if you don't have a hard disk, keep your disk in drive A and put the reformatted disk in drive B).

2. If you are at the DOS 5 Shell, select Exit from the File pull down menu (or press F3) to get to the command prompt (optionally, you can press Shift+F9 if you have programs running in the Active Task List).

3. Make sure that the disk drive containing the UNFORMAT program is the currently selected one (for example, type C: and press Enter if you have a hard disk; type A: and press Enter if you have floppies).

4. Type unformat followed by a blank space and the name of the drive containing the disk you want to unformat (for example, UNFORMAT A: to unformat the disk in drive A).

5. Press Enter.

6. As prompted, insert the disk to be unformatted into the appropriate drive (A: or B:) if you haven't already done so and press Enter.

7. You will see warnings reminding you that UNFORMAT should only be used to unformat a disk that has accidentally been reformatted and then additional instructions depending on the situation, as described in the sections that follow.

Unformatting with a Valid MIRROR File

Whenever you reformat a previously formatted disk, DOS places information required to unformat the disk in an "invisible" file called the MIRROR file. (Mirror is actually a program developed by Central Point Software and licensed to Microsoft to use as part of DOS 5).

When you attempt to unformat a disk, DOS first looks for this MIRROR file, and if it finds one, it tells you the date and time that the file was used and that the file has been validated.

Next, it asks whether you are sure you want to update the system area of the disk (which is just a roundabout way of asking whether you really want to unformat the disk). Press Y to proceed.

When the UNFORMAT is complete, you'll see a message indicating that the system area has been rebuilt and a message indicating that you may need to reboot the system (though you would probably only need to reboot if the system hangs—that is, becomes unresponsive). You can use the DIR command to check the current contents of the disk (for example, DIR A: or DIR B:).

Unformatting Without a Mirror File

If you accidentally reformatted a disk with a version of DOS prior to version 5 or you formatted to a different density (described later in this chapter), or unconditionally reformatted the disk using the /u switch with the FORMAT command (described in Appendix B), the disk will not have a Mirror file on it.

When you UNFORMAT such a disk, you'll see a message indicating that the MIRROR file cannot be found and an option to search the hard disk for it. Press Y to proceed.

You then see additional warnings and messages and a prompt asking for permission to perform the "search phase," where the UNFORMAT command analyses the disk to be unformatted. Press Y to proceed.

When the search phase is complete, you may see a message indicating that no files or subdirectories were found, so therefore the disk cannot be unformatted. The program then ends with the prompt `No action taken`. That particular disk cannot be unformatted.

On the other hand, if the search phase indicates that UNFORMAT can possibly unformat the disk (even without the aid of the invisible MIRROR file), you'll see information to this effect and an option to proceed with the format. Press Y to select Yes and follow the prompts that appear on the screen.

For additional information about the UNFORMAT command, refer to Appendix B.

Copying Diskettes

As mentioned earlier in this chapter, you can use formatted diskettes to make backups (copies) of the files on a hard disk or for storing data from computers without a hard disk. Occasionally, you might also want to make a copy of an entire diskette—either as an extra (archival) backup or as a means of sharing data with co-workers.

> NOTE: Some application programs are stored on *copy-protected* diskettes to prevent users from giving away free copies of the program. These diskettes cannot be copied.

DOS provides a utility that enables you to make an exact duplicate of any diskette that is not copy-protected. This same utility can also format a new diskette (if necessary) before it makes the copy.

When you copy a diskette, DOS needs to know which drive contains the *source* diskette and which contains the *destination* (or *target*) diskette. As the names suggest, the source of the copy is the diskette that contains the files you want to copy; the destination (or target) diskette is the blank diskette that you want to copy the files to. Figure 6.3 illustrates this concept.

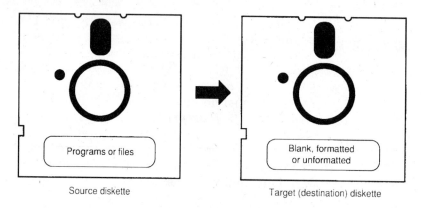

Source diskette   Target (destination) diskette

Figure 6.3. Files are copied from the source diskette
to the destination diskette.

Note that the Disk Copy utility can only copy an entire diskette to another diskette of the same *media*. That is, you cannot use the Disk Copy utility to copy from a hard disk to a diskette or from a 5.25-inch diskette to a 3.5-inch diskette. Nor can you use the Disk Copy utility to copy files between low- (double-) density and high-density disks (see the section called "Diskette Storage Capacities" later in this chapter for a definition of disk density). Chapter 8 discusses techniques for copying files among various types of disks.

NOTE: If you use a DOS diskette to start your computer, use the Disk Copy utility to make some extra backup copies of your startup diskette.

To practice using the Disk Copy utility, select a diskette (such as one of your DOS diskettes) to copy and get a new, unformatted diskette to store the copy on. Then, follow the next series of instructions, according to the version of DOS that you are using.

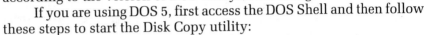 If you are using DOS 5, first access the DOS Shell and then follow these steps to start the Disk Copy utility:

1. If your computer doesn't have a hard disk, insert your D O S Shell diskette into diskette drive A:.

2. Using the View menu, switch to the Program/File Lists view.

3. Select Disk Utilities from the Programs List (the bottom left section of the screen under the Main title bar). Using the keyboard, press the Tab key to move to the Main section, press the ↓ key to highlight the option, and then press Enter; using a mouse, merely double-click the option.

4. From the Disk Utilities screen, which appears next, select Disk Copy.

    This displays a dialog box for the Disk Copy utility, as shown in Figure 6.4. The dialog box suggests possible source and destination drives, but you can change these suggestions by typing over them. Use the usual Backspace, Delete (or Del), ←, and → keys to make corrections, as described in the next steps:

NOTE: Be sure to separate the source and destination diskette drives with a blank space.

5. If your computer has only one floppy disk drive (or two or more nonmatching disk drives), change the suggested source and destination drives to a: a: or b: b: by typing over the suggested drive names.

6. If your computer has two matching floppy disk drives, leave the suggested source and destination as a: b:.

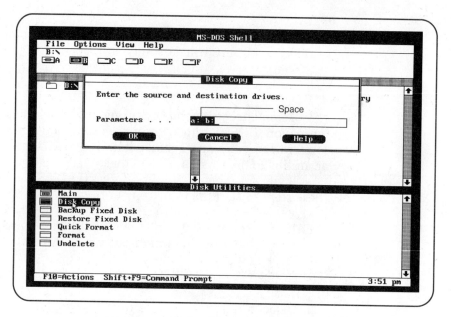

Figure 6.4. Dialog box for the Disk Copy utility.

7. Press Enter (or click the OK box with your mouse).

8. Proceed with the following section.

     If you are using DOS 3 or the optional DOS 5 command prompt, follow these steps to start the Disk Copy utility:

1. If your computer does not have a hard disk drive, insert your DOS diskette in drive A:. (Insert the Shell diskette if you are using DOS 4.)

2. If your computer has a hard disk, access the root directory of the disk drive with the DOS directory by typing CD \ and pressing Enter.

3. Type diskcopy followed by the name of the drive that contains the source diskette, in turn followed by the name of the drive that contains the destination diskette. Separate the two names with a blank space (by pressing the Spacebar). For example, if your computer has two matching floppy disk drives, type the command DISKCOPY A: B: or if your computer has only one floppy disk drive, type the command DISKCOPY A: A:.

4. Press Enter.

Additional messages that appear on the screen depend on what type of diskette you are copying and whether or not you are using one disk drive or two. After DOS tells you to insert the source and destination diskettes, follow the instructions as they appear on the screen.

NOTE: If you encounter a problem during the Disk Copy procedure, refer to the Troubleshooting section near the end of this chapter.

If you are copying using a single diskette drive, you might see the messages `Insert SOURCE diskette...` and `Insert TARGET diskette` several times. These messages are actually telling you to reinsert the same source and target disk, as I'll explain.

When you copy a diskette using a single drive, DOS reads as much information as will fit into memory (RAM) from the source drive, asks for the TARGET drive, and copies all the information from memory back onto that drive.

Now, if you have 640K of memory and are copying 720K diskettes, it stands to reason that DOS cannot read 720K of data into 640K of RAM. Hence, it asks for the source disk, copies data from it, asks for the target disk, and copies data to it.

Then it asks again for the source disk, copies the rest of the data from it, asks for the target disk and copies data to it once again. You may be requested to reinsert the same source and destination disks several times to complete the copy.

Remember that Disk Copy is not finished copying the current disk until you see the message `Copy another diskette (Y/N)` on your screen. Press the letter `N` if you do not want to copy any other diskettes. Then, as indicated on the screen, press any key. If you are using DOS 5, you can also select Main to leave the DOS Utilities screen and to display the Main Group of the Program List.

Comparing Diskettes

You can also compare the contents of two disks, or just certain files, but only at the command prompt, not in the Shell. Here are some additional commands you can learn about in Appendix B if you need to compare disks or files:

DISKCOMP compares the entire contents of two or more disks

COMP compares two or more files

FC compares two or more files

Also, for information on copying (instead of comparing) files from the command prompt, see

COPY copies individual files or groups of files

XCOPY is an extended version of COPY.

Features of Modern Diskettes

So far, this book has discussed several terms for using diskettes with DOS. Now, I discuss the features of diskettes in a little more detail.

Diskette Write Protection

Like cassette and VCR tapes, diskettes can be used in either of the following two modes:

Read/Write: You can format the diskette and freely store, retrieve, and erase information on it.

Write-Protected: You can only read files (information) from the diskette. You cannot reformat it, nor can you change, delete, or add new information to the diskette.

In most cases, you use diskettes in their read/write status. However, when you want to be sure that the information on a diskette is not inadvertently altered or destroyed, you can change its status to Write-Protected (also called *read-only* status).

You change the status of a 5.25-inch diskette to Write-Protected by covering the notch in the side of the disk with a small adhesive tab. (These tabs are usually included in a new box of diskettes.) Figure 6.5 illustrates the write-protect notch of a 5.25-inch diskette and shows how the adhesive tab fits over it.

The 3.5-inch diskettes usually include one or two write-protect notches that can be opened or closed by moving a sliding door. If the door is closed, the diskette has read/write status. Opening the door changes the status of the diskette to write-protected, as shown in Figure 6.6. (With diskettes that have two doors, you must open both doors to fully write-protect the disk, and you must close both doors to provide full read/write access.)

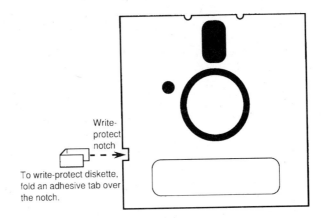

To write-protect diskette, fold an adhesive tab over the notch.

Write-protect notch

Figure 6.5. Write-protection on a 5.25-inch diskette.

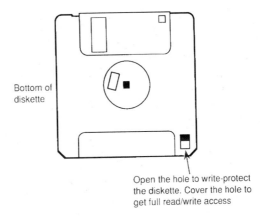

Bottom of diskette

Open the hole to write-protect the diskette. Cover the hole to get full read/write access

Figure 6.6. Write-protection on a 3.5-inch diskette.

Note that some diskettes, particularly those in application software packages, have no write-protect notch or door. These diskettes are "permanently" write-protected so that you can never inadvertently erase files stored on the diskette.

Diskette Storage Capacities

As discussed in Chapter 1, diskettes come in two basic sizes: 3.5-inch and 5.25-inch. In addition to the difference in physical sizes, diskettes also differ in the amount of information they can store. The storage capacity of modern diskettes is determined mostly by how densely (tightly) the diskette stores information.

Table 6.1 compares the storage capacities of diskettes—in terms of the number of files and the number of bytes (characters) diskettes can hold. Remember, K is the abbreviation for kilobyte (about 1,000 characters), and M is the abbreviation for megabyte (about 1 million characters).

Table 6.1. Comparison of various diskette sizes and storage capacities.

Diskette Size	Maximum Density	Maximum Files	Bytes
5.25-inch	Low (or Double)	112	360K
5.25-inch	High	224	1.2M
3.5-inch	Low	112	720K
3.5-inch	High	224	1.44M

Which type of diskette you can use is determined by the disk drives you have in your computer. The physical size difference (5.25-inch versus 3.5-inch) of diskettes is obvious from looking at the diskette (as shown in Chapter 1). You might not be sure of the capacities of your drives, however. If you are in doubt, check the documentation that came with the computer or ask your computer dealer.

When you purchase blank 3.5-inch diskettes for use in your computer, be forewarned that the box in which the diskettes are packaged might be a bit confusing because 3.5-inch diskettes are often sold in two sizes—1-megabyte and 2-megabyte. Note that this apparently conflicts with Table 6.1, which states 3.5-inch diskettes have either a capacity of 720K or 1.44M.

However, the 1-megabyte and 2-megabyte capacities printed on the package refer to *unformatted* diskettes. The required formatting procedure stores information on the diskette that occupies space, thus leaving the diskettes with reduced storage capacities.

> NOTE: The 5.25-inch diskettes also are sometimes rated as single- or double-sided. However, because all IBM microcomputers (and compatibles) use double-sided diskettes, single-sided 5.25-inch diskettes are rarely sold.

Diskette Compatibility

Some leeway is provided in using diskettes of different storage capacities within different disk drives. The basic rule of thumb is that a disk drive can use diskettes that are equal to or less than the drive's own total capacity. That is, a high-capacity drive can read both high-capacity and low-capacity diskettes. A low-capacity disk drive, however, can only use low-capacity diskettes.

If you use a high-capacity drive to copy files to a low-capacity diskette, you might not be able to use that diskette in a low-capacity drive. Several factors determine the compatibility between drive capacities and diskette capacities, including the version of DOS that you are using. For complete information on this topic, see the FORMAT command reference in Appendix B.

About Tracks and Sectors

When you use DOS to format and copy diskettes, you see messages on your screen that provide information about *tracks, sectors, sides, allocation units,* and other terms that refer to the structure of the diskette in use. Although DOS occasionally displays such information on your screen, you don't need to be concerned about any of these terms now. They all refer to "structures" that DOS handles automatically "behind the scenes."

Why then does DOS present information about tracks, sectors, and other technical issues, if that information is not important to users? Well, the truth is that the information is useful, but only to a handful of computer engineers and software developers. (These people probably comprise less than 1 percent of all computer users.)

Just as you can drive a car without knowing the technical inner workings of its transmission and voltage regulator, you can use your computer for years without knowing anything about tracks, sectors, and allocation units. However, the more you use your computer, the more interested you probably will become in some of these technical issues, including how your computer manages information at its most technical level. When your curiosity gets the better of you, feel free to read Chapter 15 to find out just how the computer "does it."

Troubleshooting

NOTE: DOS 5 users: Remember that you can press the Help key (F1) for "instant help" whenever the error message window is displayed on the screen.

Should you encounter a problem while doing any of the exercises in this chapter, DOS probably will display one of the following error messages. Locate the error message that is displayed on your screen and try the recommended solutions:

❏ **Attempted write-protect violation:** You tried to copy data onto (or to format) a write-protected diskette. If you are using 5.25-inch diskettes, remove the write-protect tab (if possible) or use a different diskette. If you are using 3.5-inch diskettes, close the write-protect slot(s) (if possible) or use another diskette. (See the section "Diskette Write Protection" in this chapter for more information.)

❏ **Bad command or file name:** You either misspelled the command name or the program you attempted to run is not available on the current drive or directory. If the problem is simply one of misspelling, retype the command (using proper spelling) and press Enter.

NOTE: The exercises presented in this book assume a standard organization of DOS files; however, your computer might be organized differently.

If you are sure you typed the command correctly, the program is not available on the current drive or directory. The Format and Disk Copy utilities described in this chapter require that DOS have access to the following programs (files):

Utility	File Required
Format	FORMAT.COM
Disk Copy	DISKCOPY.COM

Use the general techniques described in Chapter 5 to search other diskettes or hard disk directories for the appropriate files. When you locate the appropriate file, start the utility from that diskette or directory.

❏ `Drive letter must be specified`: You tried to use the FORMAT utility without specifying a disk drive. Try again, but specify either `A:` or `B:` as the drive to format.

❏ `Drive types or diskette types not compatible`: You tried to use incompatible disk drives or incompatible diskette types during a Disk Copy procedure. Try using one diskette drive (for example, `a: a:`) rather than two (for example, `a: b:`). If that does not work, the diskettes are incompatible and cannot be copied using that procedure. You'll need to use the Copy option from the File pull-down menu or the COPY command at the command prompt instead.

❏ `Invalid drive specification`: You specified a disk drive that does not exist on your computer. For example, you specified drive B: with a computer that has no drive named B:, or you omitted a drive name where one is required.

❏ `File not found`: You tried to view the names of files on a diskette that has no files stored on it, or you used an ambiguous file name that does not match any of the file names on the diskette. (Note that the diskette is already formatted for use, and you don't need to reformat it.)

❏ `Parameter format not correct`: Most likely, you omitted a parameter or left out a blank space. For example, when using the Disk Copy and Disk Comp utilities, entering `a:a:` or `b:b:` produces this error because the drive names are not separated by a space. Try the command again, this time inserting the required blank space between the drive names (for example, `a: a:`, or `b: b:`).

❏ `Required parameter missing -`: You did not completely specify optional parameters. For example, you must include a drive name with the Format utility, and you must provide two drive names (separated by a blank space) with the Disk Copy utility.

❏ `Write protect error`: Same as `Attempted write-protect violation`.

Summary

This chapter provided useful techniques to help you use diskettes with your computer. Following is a summary of these techniques:

❏ New diskettes must be formatted before you can use them on your computer. Be sure that you format only diskettes that do not already contain programs or other files.

❏ To write-protect 3.5-inch diskettes—thereby preventing files from being modified, changed, or erased—slide the write-protect door(s) to the "open" position.

❏ To write-protect 5.25-inch diskettes—thereby preventing files from being modified, changed, or erased—cover the write-protect notch with an adhesive tab.

❏ For detailed information about diskette and drive compatibilities, see the reference to the FORMAT command in Appendix B.

❏ To format a diskette from the DOS command prompt, enter the FORMAT command followed by the name of the drive that contains the diskette to be formatted.

❏ To copy a diskette from the DOS command prompt, enter the DISKCOPY command followed by the names of the source and destination disk drives.

❏ DOS 5 users can format diskettes by selecting Disk Utilities from the Program List's Main Group screen and then Format from the Disk Utilities screen.

❏ To use the DOS Shell to make an exact copy of a diskette, select Disk Utilities from the Program List's Main Group and then select Disk Copy from the Disk Utilities screen.

Managing Your Hard Disk

Chapter 4 discussed ways in which your computer's hard disk might already have files organized into directories and subdirectories, and it showed techniques for searching those directories and subdirectories. This chapter focuses on techniques for creating your own directories and offers tips on how to best organize a hard disk (or high-capacity diskettes) for quick and easy access to your files.

Even though directories and subdirectories are used primarily on hard disks, they can be used on floppies as well. Therefore, even if your computer doesn't have a hard disk, you may want to experiment with some of these techniques. To do so, put a formatted diskette in drive A: or B: of your computer. Then, anywhere that you see a reference to hard disk drive C:, substitute drive A: or B: (depending on which drive you want to use).

Naming Directories

As you might recall from Chapter 4, a directory on a disk is a place in which you can store files (like a drawer in a file cabinet). Each directory can have a name of as many as eight characters. No directory name can contain blank spaces or any of the following characters:

```
" / \ [ ] ; : * < > | + = , ?
```

Rather than remember all the symbols you cannot use in directory names, it's easier to limit yourself to using letters, numbers, underscores (_), and hyphens (-).

Also, do not use any of the following names as directory names—DOS uses these as the names of *devices* (as you'll learn later in this book):

```
CLOCK$    CON      AUX      COM1     COM2     COM3
CON       LPT1     LPT2     LPT3     NUL      PRN
```

Table 7.1 lists examples of valid and invalid directory names.

Table 7.1. Examples of valid and invalid directory names.

Directory Name	Status
MYBOOKS	valid
ACCT_REC	valid
ACCTSREC	valid
GL	valid
UTILS	valid
1989_TAX	valid
ACCT REC	invalid (contains a blank space)
ACCT:REC	invalid (contains colon)
GENERAL_LEDGER	invalid (too long)
PRN	invalid (same as device name)

You can use any combination of upper- and lowercase letters when naming a directory. However, when DOS displays the name, it automatically converts lowercase letters to uppercase.

A disk may also contain subdirectories, which are also places to store files. Whereas directories branch off the "root," subdirectories branch off other directories. Thus, subdirectories are "beneath" directories in the directory tree. Subdirectory names follow the same rules as directory names. However, a subdirectory name is preceded by the higher-level directory name and a backslash.

For example, ACCTSREC\QTR1 refers to a subdirectory named QTR1, which is beneath the directory named ACCTSREC. Note that the backslash separates the two names; it is not part of either name.

Simplifying the Terminology

Before you continue your exploration of directories and subdirectories, I'll simplify the terminology a bit. To begin with, the only difference between a directory and subdirectory is that a subdirectory name appears beneath a directory name on a directory tree. Other than that one small difference, directories and subdirectories are basically the same thing—a place on a disk in which you can store files.

> NOTE: As you gain experience with DOS, you'll see that many messages on your screen also use the terms *directory, subdirectory,* and *path* interchangeably.

However, referring to something like \ACCSREC\QTR1 as both directory and subdirectory can be confusing. To simplify matters, DOS uses the term *path.* This is actually a very descriptive name, because the series of directory and subdirectory names actually describe a path to follow to find a particular file. For example, the path \ACCSREC\QTR1 indicates that to get to the QTR1 directory, DOS must follow a path starting at the root directory (\), going down one level to the ACCSREC directory, and then down one more level to the QTR1 directory. Similarly, the path \SALES\BOB tells DOS that to find the BOB directory, DOS would start from the root directory (\), move down one level to the SALES directory, and then down one more level to the BOB directory.

Creating a Directory

It's very easy to create a directory on a disk, but there is one important point that you need to keep in mind when creating your own directories: When you create a new directory, DOS automatically creates it below the current directory.

> NOTE: If you get an error message while doing any of the exercises in this chapter, refer to the "Troubleshooting" section near the end of this chapter, or if you are using the DOS Shell, press F1 for help.

As you know, the root directory is the highest-level directory in any directory tree. All directories that you create are below the root directory in the tree. In the exercise that follows, you will create a new directory, named PRACTICE, on hard disk drive C:. This directory will be one level beneath the root directory. Follow the appropriate steps for your version of DOS.

Hands-On: Creating a Practice Directory

 If you are using DOS 5 and the DOS Shell is displayed on your screen, follow these steps to create the PRACTICE directory:

> NOTE: If you have a mouse, use the usual point-and-click method to perform steps 1-5.

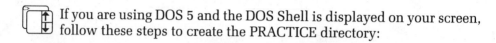

1. In the Drives area of the Shell, select the drive on which you want to create the directory (that is, C: or A:).

2. In the Directory Tree area of the shell, select the root directory by moving the highlight to the top of the tree.

3. Select Create Directory... from the File pull-down menu (shown highlighted in Figure 7.1).

4. When you see the Create Directory dialog box, type the new directory name PRACTICE (as shown in Figure 7.2).

5. Press Enter or click OK to create the directory. Note that the new directory name, PRACTICE, is in the directory tree, as in the example shown in Figure 7.3.

Creating a Practice Directory at the Command Prompt

 If you are using DOS 3 or the optional DOS 5 command prompt, you use the MKDIR (often abbreviated as MD) command (both are short for Make Directory) to create a new directory. To ensure that the new directory is created one level below the root directory, follow these steps exactly:

1. Go to the drive where you want to create the directory (that is, type C: to switch to drive C or type A: to switch to drive A) and press Enter.

2. To go to the root directory type the command CD \ and press Enter.

3. Next, type the command MD PRACTICE and press Enter.

4. To view the new directory tree, type TREE and press Enter.

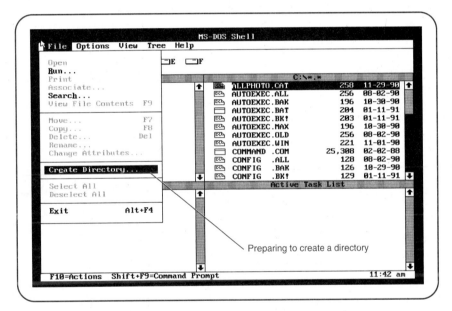

Figure 7.1. The File pull-down menu.

NOTE: Remember, you can enter the command TREE >PRN to print the directory tree.

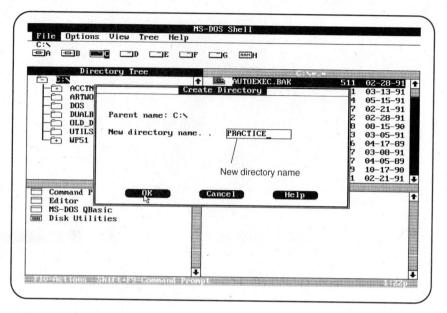

Figure 7.2. The Create Directory dialog box with a new directory name.

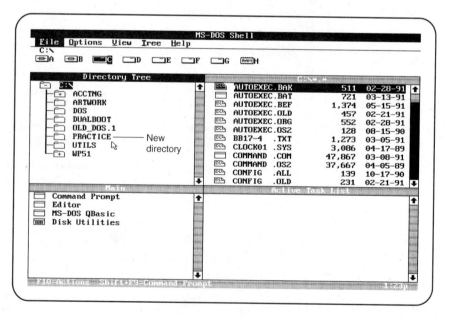

Figure 7.3. The PRACTICE directory is now in the directory tree.

The TREE display shows the names of all the directories and subdirectories on the disk. Depending on the version of DOS you are using, DOS displays the new directory name (with all other existing directory names) either in the format

```
DIRECTORY PATH LISTING...
Path: \PRACTICE
Sub-directories: None
```

or the format:

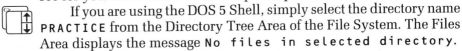

Because the PRACTICE directory that you just created is new, it does not yet contain any files. To verify this, change to the directory and see for yourself. Follow these simple steps:

If you are using the DOS 5 Shell, simply select the directory name `PRACTICE` from the Directory Tree Area of the File System. The Files Area displays the message `No files in selected directory`.

1. If you are using the DOS command prompt, type `CD PRACTICE` and press `Enter`.

2. Type `DIR` and press `Enter`.

DOS displays a screen similar to the following:

```
Directory of C:\PRACTICE

.            <DIR>     03-23-91    9:57a
..           <DIR>     03-23-91    9:57a
      2 File(s)               0 bytes
                     xxxxxxxx bytes  free
```

> NOTE: Remember, you can enter the command `PROMPT $P$G` to make DOS show the name of the current directory.

The bottom line of the DIR command says that there are `2 File(s)` on this newly created directory, and it appears as though these are named . and . . . However, . and . . are not truly files. Instead they are shortcut names for the current and parent (higher-level) directories. You will learn how to use these shortcut names in Chapter 9. For the time being, you need not be concerned about the . and . . symbols displayed by the DIR command.

Creating Subdirectories

As mentioned earlier, DOS automatically places any new directory that you create "beneath" the current directory in the tree. Therefore, to create a subdirectory, you merely change to the *parent* directory (the one that you want to be above the new subdirectory) and follow the same steps that you did to create the PRACTICE directory, but using the new subdirectory names.

As an example, create a subdirectory named TEST beneath the PRACTICE directory. Follow the appropriate procedure for your version of DOS.

Hands-On Example of Creating a Subdirectory in the Shell

If you are using the DOS Shell and the File List is displayed on your screen, follow these steps:

1. If you have not done so already, change to the PRACTICE directory by selecting its name from the Directory tree.

2. Press F10 or Alt to access the Menu Bar.

3. Select the File option by highlighting it and pressing Enter.

4. Select Create Directory....

5. Type the subdirectory name TEST and press Enter.

Note that the new directory name is indented beneath the PRACTICE directory name in the Directory Tree, as follows:

```
└─────PRACTICE
       └─────TEST
```

Hands-On Example of Creating a Subdirectory at the Command Prompt

 If you are using the command prompt, follow these steps:

1. If you have not already done so, change to the PRACTICE directory by typing `CD \PRACTICE` and pressing `Enter`.

2. Type the command `MD TEST` and press `Enter` to create the new directory.

3. To view the directory tree, type `TREE` and press `Enter`.

```
DIRECTORY PATH LISTING...
Path: \PRACTICE
Sub-directories: TEST
Path: \PRACTICE\TEST
Sub-directories: none
```

or in the format . . .

```
   └──────PRACTICE
            └──────TEST
```

You will use the new directories you created in this chapter to practice some file management techniques in the next chapter. However, now that you know how to create directories, there are some general tips and techniques that you should keep in mind before you start organizing your own hard disk into new directories. These general tips are discussed in the following sections.

Tips for Creating an Efficient Directory Tree

The whole purpose of dividing a hard disk into directories is to organize your files for easier access. If you create directories haphazardly, your files eventually become disorganized and difficult to keep track of. To avoid making a maze of your hard disk, keep in mind the following tips as you create your directory structure.

Tip #1: Don't Clutter the Root Directory

The initial DOS installation procedure automatically creates the root directory and stores a few files on it. Because the root directory is already there when you start using your computer, you might be tempted to use it as a sort of dumping ground for all your files or perhaps, for those "stray" files that do not seem to belong in any other directory.

However, the only files that really need to be in the root directory are AUTOEXEC.BAT, CONFIG.SYS, and a few others that DOS placed there when it was installed. (The purpose of these DOS files in the root directory is discussed in Chapters 10 and 11.)

Cluttering the root directory with extra files is like throwing manila file folders into a big, unmarked, cardboard box. After you install DOS on your computer and DOS stores its own files in the root directory, let DOS keep the root directory to itself. Before creating and storing your own files, make your own directories for related programs and files. In other words, start getting organized from the beginning. Instead of using a cardboard box, store all your information in clearly marked file drawers (that is, directories).

Tip #2: Keep All DOS Programs in a Single Directory

This tip is similar to tip #1: Once DOS stores its files in certain directories, just leave those files alone and do not use those directories to store other files. For example, installing DOS 5 on your computer automatically creates a directory named DOS. The installation process also stores most DOS files in this directory.

There is no major reason for you to move or copy DOS files from the DOS directory to other directories. Nor is there any reason for you to store other files in the DOS directory. Again, when you start creating and storing your own files, create and use your own directories.

Tip #3: Install Application Programs on the Recommended Drives

Whenever you buy an application program, the manual that comes with that program usually suggests that you create a unique disk or unique directory on your hard disk to store that program on. (In fact, the program might come with an automatic *installation program* that creates the appropriate directory for you on a hard disk.)

When you install an application program on a hard disk, use the directory name that the program's documentation recommends. Otherwise, you might find it difficult using that program's manuals, which probably assume that you followed their recommendations.

Tip #4: Make the Directory Tree Broad and Shallow

DOS allows you to be creative when constructing a directory tree. You can create subdirectories beneath directories, sub-subdirectories beneath subdirectories, and so on. However, the "deeper" you go in this scheme, the longer the path names become.

For example, you could create a series of subdirectories with a path name DBASE\BOB\PROJECTS\UPSALES; this involves four separate directories. However, when you want to change directories at the command prompt, or when you want to identify the location of a file in UPSALES, you will often have to type this entire path name. Trust me, it won't be long before you grow tired of typing `DBASE\BOB\PROJECTS\UPSALE`.

A second reason for keeping the directory tree broad and shallow is to provide easy access to all related files. For example, suppose that you have purchased two application programs for use with your computer: dBASE IV (a database management program) and Lotus 1-2-3 (a spreadsheet program). You store these programs in the directories that the manuals advise—DBASE and 123, respectively.

Now, assume that you need to create two new directories, one for storing your accounts-receivable data, and one for inventory data. You decide to name these directories ACCT_REC and INVENTRY. Further assume that you will use the dBASE IV program to handle some information in both accounts-receivable and inventory data and Lotus 1-2-3 to handle the rest of the data.

Given all this information, you have two options for creating the directory tree. A "deep" structure would look like the tree shown in Figure 7.4, with the directories containing accounts receivable and inventory files beneath the program directories. The problem with that directory tree is that it artificially divides the accounts receivable and inventory data into four separate directories: DBASE\ACCT_REC, DBASE\INVENTRY, 123\ACCT_REC, and \123\INVENTRY.

Figure 7.5 shows a better directory tree for organizing the various programs and your business data. Notice that each directory is on the same level (that is, the tree is shallower than the one in Figure 7.4).

The shallower directory tree has the distinct advantage of organizing both the accounts receivable files and the inventory files into their own clearly-named directories. The files are not artificially divided into subdirectories that are dependent on individual application programs. If you change inventory data, you need only do so on one directory.

Given this new tip, you might be wondering when you would ever want to create a subdirectory. Actually, using a subdirectory makes sense when all the files on it are relevant only to the parent directory. For example, when you install the dBASE IV program on your computer, the installation process automatically creates several directories, including DBASE, DBASE\SAMPLES, and DBASE\DBTUTOR.

This organization makes sense because the SAMPLES and DBTUTOR directories contain files that can be used only with dBASE IV. There is no artificial breakup of files, as there was in the example involving the ACCT_REC and INVENTRY directories, which were both used by the dBASE and 1-2-3 programs. Figure 7.6 illustrates this concept.

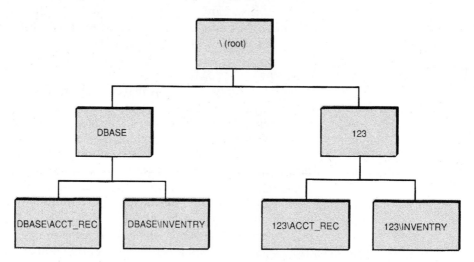

Figure 7.4. A deep directory tree.

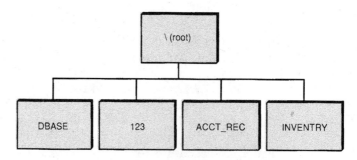

Figure 7.5. The preferred shallow directory tree.

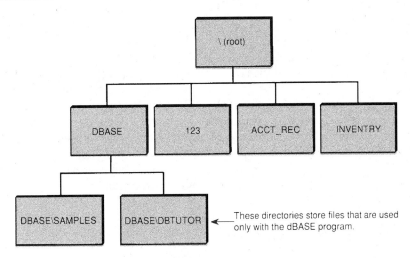

Figure 7.6. The SAMPLES and DBTUTOR directories contain files that are used only with dBASE IV.

Tip #5: Use the PATH Command to Simplify Access to Programs

As you already know, DOS normally requires that you access the directory that contains a program before you use that program. If you have not changed to the correct directory when you try to run a program, DOS displays the error message `Bad command or file name` because it cannot find the file that contains the program. This can be an inconvenience indeed.

Fortunately, DOS provides a simple and elegant way around this problem—the PATH command. In a nutshell, the PATH command tells DOS, "If you cannot find my program on this directory, check these other directories." For example, referring back to the shallow directory tree in Figure 7.5, suppose that you are currently accessing the INVENTRY directory, but you want to run the 1-2-3 program to manage your inventory data.

If you try to run 1-2-3 (or dBASE, for that matter) from the INVENTRY directory, DOS merely displays the `Bad command or file name` message because that program is not in the INVENTRY directory. However, if you first enter the command `PATH C:\123; C;\DBASE` at the command prompt, DOS "knows" that it also needs to check the directories named 123 and DBASE on drive C: before ending its search for the program. Hence, you'll be able to run your 1-2-3 and dBASE IV programs from any directory on the hard disk.

Once entered at the command prompt, the PATH command stays in effect for the entire current session (that is, until you turn off the computer). As an alternative to typing in the appropriate PATH command for your directory tree each time you turn on your computer, you can have DOS automatically enter the command for you as soon as you start the computer. This is by far the preferred method for using the PATH command.

Chapter 11 discusses specific steps for setting up a PATH command for your computer. For now, just keep in mind that this option is available to you. (Also, remember that Appendix B provides a complete reference for the PATH command.)

Troubleshooting

If you have a problem while creating or changing to a directory, you will probably see one of the following error messages. Try the suggested solution for each error message.

❏ `Access denied`: If you see this error message while trying to create a new directory from the DOS Shell, the directory name already exists. You cannot create two directories with the same name, so you cannot proceed with the command. (Press the Esc key to cancel the operation.)

❏ `Directory already exists`: You tried to create a directory that already exists. DOS returns you to the prompt and doesn't allow you to proceed with the command.

❏ `Invalid directory`: You tried to access a directory that does not exist or that does not exist beneath the current directory. Perhaps you merely misspelled the directory name in the command line. Try re-entering the command with the directory name spelled properly. If the problem persists, review Chapter 4 or study the CHDIR command reference in Appendix B.

❏ `Invalid switch`: Most likely, you used a forward slash (/) rather than a backslash (\) in the command. Try again, this time using the correct backslash (\) character.

❏ `Unable to create directory`: DOS displays this message when any one of the following errors occurs: 1) The directory that you tried to create already exists; 2) you tried to create a directory beneath a nonexistent directory; or 3) you specified a directory name that contains invalid characters or has the same name as a reserved device.

Check the existing directory tree structure, using either the DOS 5 File List or the DOS 3 TREE command, to determine which error occurred in your situation. (If necessary, you might also want to refer to the MKDIR and CHDIR commands in Appendix B for more details.)

Summary

This chapter taught you specific techniques for creating directories and presented some general tips on how to best organize your computer's directory tree.

❑ A directory name can consist of as many as eight characters, cannot contain blank spaces or reserved device names, and should contain only letters, number, hyphens (−), and underscores (_).

❑ The terms *directory* and *subdirectory* are often used interchangeably because each term refers to an area on the hard disk in which you store files. *Path* refers to the "route" (through various levels of directories) to files in subdirectories.

❑ When you create a new directory, DOS places that new directory beneath the current directory in the tree structure.

❑ To create a directory that is one level below the root directory, always begin by changing to the root directory.

C>

❑ To create a new directory from the command prompt, first change to the parent directory and then type MKDIR or MD followed by a blank space and the name of the new directory. Then, press Enter. (See the MKDIR reference in Appendix B for other optional methods.)

❑ To create a directory using the DOS Shell, first access the File List section of the screen and then change to the appropriate drive and parent directory. Then, press F10 or Alt to access the Menu Bar and select the Create Directory... option from the File pull-down menu. Type the name of the new directory and press Enter.

Managing Files

This chapter discusses how to manage your files by viewing, copying, erasing, moving, renaming, and protecting them. These general file management techniques will be useful in all your future work with your computer and DOS; in fact, you'll probably use some of these techniques every time you sit down at the keyboard.

If DOS 5 is installed on your computer, you can use the DOS Shell to perform file management operations. The basic procedure is as follows:

1. Be sure that you are using one of the File List only screens or that the cursor is in the File List section of the Program/File Lists screen.

2. Select a file (or files) for the operation.

3. Select the appropriate operation from the File pull-down menu.

Figure 8.1 illustrates the general procedure (discussed in more detail with each operation).

DOS 3 users (and of course, DOS 4 and 5 users who prefer the command prompt) can use several built-in DOS commands for these operations, including COPY, RENAME, ERASE, and TYPE. Remember, "built-in" commands are available in DOS at any time, so you can perform these operations on any disk drive and in any directory.

If you have any problems doing these exercises, refer to the Troubleshooting section near the end of the chapter. DOS 5 Shell users can also press the F1 key or select the Help menu to display help on the screen.

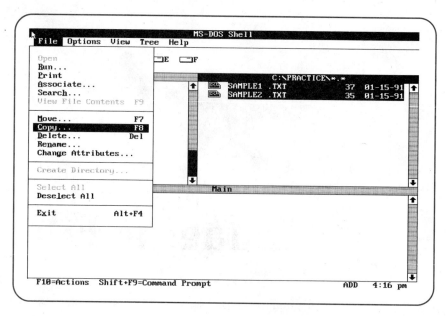

Figure 8.1. Performing file operations with the DOS 5 Shell.

Rules for Naming Files

When you start creating, copying, and renaming files, remember that DOS imposes certain restrictions on file names and that all file names must abide by these rules. This holds true even if you create files with an application program, such as a spreadsheet, a database management system, or a word processor.

The basic rules for creating file names (described briefly in Chapter 4) are as follows:

❏ The base name for the file can be no more than eight characters long and may not contain blank spaces.

❏ You can include an optional three-letter extension—preceded by a period—with any file name.

❏ You should restrict file names to only letters, numbers, hyphens (-), and underscores (_). (Use the period only to separate the base name from the extension.) The following characters can never be used in a file name: " . / \ [ ] : * < > | + : , ?

❏ Do not use any of these reserved device names as file names:
`CLOCK$ CON AUX COM1 COM2 COM3 CON LPT1 LPT2`
`LPT3 NUL PRN.`

❏ Try to use meaningful file names that describe the contents of the file. For example, instead of assigning the file name X.DAT to your first-quarter 1992 data file, use the more meaningful file name QTR1-92.DAT.

❏ As much as possible, try to use a similar pattern of file names for related files. (For example, you might use QTR1-92.DAT, QTR2-92.DAT, QTR3-92.DAT, and so on, for files that store quarterly data.) This helps make it easier to manage the files as groups when copying, moving, or erasing them.

❏ Avoid using the file name extensions `.BAT`, `.COM`, and `.EXE`, as these are reserved for programs. (You'll learn how to create your own .BAT program files in Chapter 13.)

Examples of valid and invalid file names are in Table 8.1.

Table 8.1. Examples of valid, and invalid, file names.

File Name	Status
ACCT_REC.DAT	Valid
X.ABC	Valid (but not very descriptive)
LEDGER.WKS	Valid
ABC-CO.LET	Valid
1990SUMM.TXT	Valid
READ.ME	Valid
PRNT.TXT	Valid
GENERAL-LEDGER.DAT	Invalid (base name is too long)
MY LETTER.DOC	Invalid (contains a blank space)
MY.LET.DOC	Invalid (contains two periods)
PRN.TXT	Invalid (PRN is a DOS device name)

File Name Extensions

You can assign any extension to a file name when you create a file. However, many application programs automatically assign their own extensions to file names. Some examples of commonly used file name extensions and the types of information that those files hold are listed in Table 8.2.

Table 8.2. Examples of commonly used file name extensions.

Extension	Contents
.BAT	A DOS "batch" program (discussed in Chapter 13)
.COM	A program that DOS can run
.EXE	A program that DOS can run
.TXT	Written text
.DOC	A document (written text)
.BAK	A backup (copy) of another file
.BAS	A BASIC program
.BMP	A Windows 3 bit-mapped (graphics) file
.WKS	A Lotus 1-2-3 (version 1) spreadsheet
.WK1	A Lotus 1-2-3 (version 2) spreadsheet
.XLS	A Microsoft Excel Spreadsheet
.MSP	A Microsoft Paint picture
.DBF	A dBASE database
.DB	A Paradox database
.OVL	An overlay file (discussed in Chapter 15)

Hands On: Creating Some Sample Files

To perform some of the file management techniques in this chapter, you need to create a few simple practice files, named SAMPLE1.TXT and SAMPLE2.TXT. There are many ways to create files on your computer.

I'll demonstrate a somewhat primitive technique in this chapter, only because the sample files are small and the technique is simple. As you gain experience with your computer, you'll probably want to use a word processor or EDIT, the new DOS 5 full-screen editor (discussed in Chapter 10), to create larger text files and programs.

If your computer has a hard disk, place these practice files in the PRACTICE directory. If your computer does not have a hard disk, place the sample files on a blank, formatted diskette. To create these files, follow the appropriate steps for your particular computer:

1. If you are using DOS 5, press the F3 key (or Alt-F4) to exit the Shell and display the command prompt.

2. If your computer has a hard disk, type C: and press Enter to access the hard disk. Then type CD \PRACTICE and press Enter to change to the PRACTICE directory.

3. If your computer does not have a hard disk, place a blank, formatted diskette in drive B:. Then, type B: and press Enter to access drive B:.

4. Type the command COPY CON SAMPLE1.TXT and press Enter.

5. Type the sentence This is the first sample text file. (Use the Backspace key to make corrections if necessary.)

6. Press Enter after typing the sentence.

7. Press Ctrl-Z (hold down the Ctrl key and press the letter Z) or press F6. This displays a ^Z on your screen.

8. Press Enter again.

After DOS displays the message 1 file(s) copied, the command prompt reappears. DOS has copied the sentence you typed on the screen into a file named SAMPLE1.TXT. To create the second sample file, follow these steps:

1. Type COPY CON SAMPLE2.TXT and press Enter.

2. Type the sentence I am the second sample text file. (Again, use the Backspace key to make corrections if necessary.)

3. Press Enter after typing the sentence.

4. Press Ctrl-Z (or F6) and then press Enter.

You have now created the two practice files you will use in later examples in this chapter. You did so by COPYing text from the CONsole (screen) to a file. Don't be concerned about memorizing this technique for creating files, however, because you'll learn a more practical method in Chapter 10.

If you are using DOS 5, type DOSSHELL and press Enter to return to the Shell. If you do not have a hard disk, be sure your Shell diskette is in drive A:. Then type A: and press Enter to access that drive. When the A> command prompt appears, type the command DOSSHELL and press Enter.

Selecting Files for Operations in DOS 5

You must display the File List section of the DOS Shell to perform the following file operations. To do so, choose any of the display options except Program List from the View menu.

If you are using DOS 5, you often need to select files from the Files Area before you perform an operation. Therefore, I'll review the general techniques for selecting file names. As with all DOS 5 operations, you can use either the keyboard or a mouse to select file names, as summarized in the following lists.

To select a single file using the keyboard:

1. Using the keyboard, press the Tab key until the highlight moves to the Files List of the screen.

2. Then use the ↓, ↑, PgUp, or PgDn keys to move the highlight bar to the file you want to select.

To select a single file with a mouse:

1. Move the mouse pointer to the name of the file you want to select in the Files List area.

2. Click once.

NOTE: To select all the file names in the Files List, select Select All from the Files pull-down menu.

To select two or more consecutive files using the keyboard:

1. Press the Tab key until the Highlight Bar gets to the File List area.

2. Use the ↓, ↑, PgUp, and PgDn keys to scroll the highlight to the first file you want to select.

3. Hold down the Shift key, then press ↓ or ↑ to highlight adjacent file names.

4. When the file names you want to select are highlighted, release the Shift key.

 To select two or more consecutive files using the mouse:

1. Move the mouse pointer to the name of the first file you want to select and click once.

2. Then hold down the Shift key, and click the last file in the group. (If you need to use the Scroll Bar to display more file names in a long list, continue holding down the Shift key as you scroll through the list.)

 To use the keyboard to select two or more nonconsecutive files on nonconsecutive groups of files:

> NOTE: When the Shell is in Add mode (Shift-F8), you can press the Spacebar to select a file and to deselect a selected file.

1. Press the Tab key until the highlight moves to the Files List.

2. Then use the ↓, ↑, PgUp, and PgDn keys to move the highlight bar to the first file you want to select.

3. Press Shift-F8 to initiate the Shell's Add mode, in which you can add file names to the current list of selections. (Note that the word ADD appears on the Reference Bar at the bottom of the screen.)

4. Use either keyboard technique described previously for selecting individual or groups of file names from the Files List.

To use the mouse to select two or more nonconsecutive files or nonconsecutive groups of files:

1. Select the first `file name` by single-clicking it.

2. Select additional file names by holding down the `Ctrl` key and single-clicking additional file names.

3. Select additional groups of adjacent file names by keeping the `Ctrl` key held down, holding down the `Shift` key, clicking the `last file name` in the group of adjacent file names, and then releasing the `Shift` (but not `Ctrl`) key.

On a graphics screen, a *selected* file is displayed with its icon in reverse video (that is, white on black rather than black on white). For example, in Figure 8.1, the files SAMPLE1.TXT and SAMPLE2.TXT are currently selected. On a text screen, selected files are represented by a right-pointing triangle to the left of the file name.

Deselecting Files

If you want to deselect one or more selected files

1. If you are in the Add mode and using the keyboard, move the `Highlight Bar` to the name of the file you want to deselect and press the `Spacebar`.

2. If you're using a mouse, hold down the `Ctrl` key and click the `name` of the file you want to deselect.

3. To deselect all of the currently selected file names, select `Deselect All` from the File pull-down menu.

Spacebar Versus Enter

Notice that when selecting files for an operation, as in this chapter, you always press the Spacebar. In earlier chapters, you saw how highlighting a program file name in the Files List and pressing Enter could be used to run a program.

If you accidentally press Enter rather than the Spacebar while trying to select a file name, or you double-click rather than single-click your mouse when selecting a file name, DOS "assumes" that you are attempting to *run* the file as though it were a program.

This minor (and common) mistake results in one of two actions. If the file you specify is not a program (or a file "associated" with a program), DOS beeps to inform you that it cannot "open" the file. However, if the file that you specify is an executable program (or a file "associated" with a program), DOS runs it.

To recover from this, exit the program (if necessary), and press a key when DOS displays the `Press any key to return to MS-DOS Shell` prompt at the lower right corner of your screen. When DOS redisplays the File List, use the ↑ and ↓ keys or click once with your mouse to properly select the appropriate file name.

Viewing the Contents of a File

DOS contains a built-in command you can use to look at the contents of any file. However, the contents of many files (particularly programs) might appear on the screen as strange characters or cause the computer to beep, because they contain instructions that only the computer can read.

The general steps for viewing the contents of a file are

1. Select the drive and directory that the file you want to view is stored on and `Directory Tree` areas of the Shell.

NOTE: The `View File Contents` option is available on the File pull-down menu only when a single file name is selected in the Files Area.

---

2. Highlight or single-click the name of the file you want to view in the `Files List` area of the Shell.

3. Select `View` from the pull-down menu.

4. When you finish viewing the contents of the file, press `Escape` or select `Restore View` from the View pull-down menu.

NOTE: Press F9 as a shortcut method of displaying the contents of a single file.

If you'd like to try this feature on your own, follow the steps to view the contents of the SAMPLE2.TXT file you created earlier. It appears on your screen as shown in Figure 8.2.

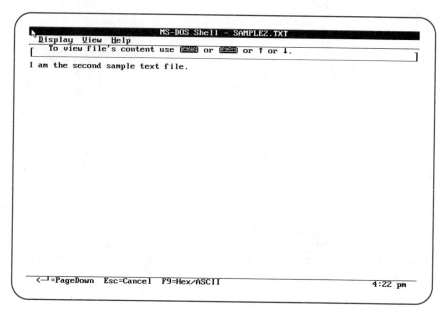

Figure 8.2. Contents of the SAMPLE2.TXT file displayed in ASCII format.

Because the SAMPLE2.TXT file is so small, you can see its entire contents. However, when viewing larger files, you might need to use the PgDn and PgUp keys or the ↑ or ↓ keys to scroll through the file, as the message at the top of the screen indicates. If you are using a mouse, you can click these icons to perform that action. For example, if you click once on the ↓ icon, the screen scrolls up one line.

Notice in the Title Bar at the top of the screen that DOS tells you that you are currently viewing the SAMPLE2.TXT file. Also notice that the Menu Bar now offers three choices: Display, View, and Help.

NOTE: To switch between the ASCII (text) and Hex displays, you can press the F9 key, as noted in the bottom line of the screen.

With the Display menu, you can choose to view a file in either ASCII format (as straight characters and symbols, as shown in Figure 8.2) or in Hexadecimal format, which lets you examine program files in great detail. If you now select the Hex option from the Display menu, you will see the screen shown in Figure 8.3. The left column of numbers represents the locations of the data in the file, the middle column shows the data in the file as two-digit hexadecimal (base 16) numbers, and the right column shows the numbers as ASCII characters. (The dots represent all hex values that are not standard ASCII characters.)

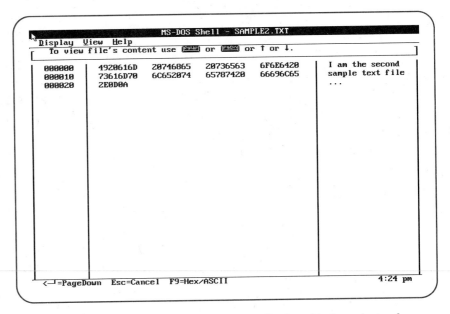

Figure 8.3. Contents of Sample2.TXT displayed in hexadecimal.

The View pull-down menu in the View File Contents screen provides options to Repaint the Screen (for example, to remove network messages) and an option to Restore the View (return to the Shell).

The Help menu is exactly the same as it is in the File and Program Lists. After viewing the contents of the file, press Esc or select the Restore View option from the View menu to return to the File List screen.

If you are using an earlier version of DOS or the optional DOS 5 command prompt, you can use the TYPE command to view the contents of a file. Use this method to look at the contents of the SAMPLE2.TXT file.

NOTE: Because DOS always requires that you press Enter after typing a command, from now on we'll use the term *enter* to mean *type the command and then press Enter.*

For example, when we say, "Enter the command TYPE SAMPLE1.TXT," that means you should type the command TYPE SAMPLE1.TXT and press the Enter key when you are at the command prompt. (If you are at the Shell, don't forget to first exit to the command prompt by pressing F3.)

1. If your computer doesn't have a hard disk, be sure to access drive B: by entering the command B:.

2. If your computer has a hard disk, be sure to change to the PRACTICE directory by entering C: to get to drive C: and then entering CD \PRACTICE to get to the PRACTICE directory.

3. Enter the command DIR to verify that the SAMPLE2.TXT file is on the current drive and directory.

4. Enter the command TYPE SAMPLE2.TXT.

After DOS shows the contents of the file, it redisplays the command prompt, as shown in Figure 8.4. (Your screen might also show preceding commands.)

Remember that if you attempt to view the contents of a program with the TYPE command, your screen will display strange symbols and might beep repeatedly. However, this does not harm the file; the information is stored as codes that only the computer can read.

Copying Files

Much of your work with DOS involves the copying of files. In fact, copying files is one of those truly basic procedures that every computer user seems to perform on nearly a daily basis. You make these copies for any or all of the following reasons:

❏ To backup important files.

❏ To transfer files between the hard disk and diskettes or between different sizes of disks (if your computer has both 5.25- and 3.5-inch disk drives.

❏ To use the same set of files on more than one computer.

The Shell offers two procedures for copying files: a general procedure through standard menu selections, and another using the mouse to "drag" a copy of the file to a new location—a very "Macintosh-like" action. Of course, you can always use the command prompt and the COPY command to make copies, too.

```
C:\>CD\PRACTICE

C:\PRACTICE>DIR

 Volume in drive C has no label
 Directory of C:\PRACTICE

 .            <DIR>        01-15-91    3:55p
 ..           <DIR>        01-15-91    3:55p
 SAMPLE1   TXT         37 01-15-91    3:56p
 SAMPLE2   TXT         35 01-15-91    3:57p
         4 file(s)            72 bytes
                        11511808 bytes free

C:\PRACTICE>TYPE SAMPLE2.TXT
I am the second sample text file.

C:\PRACTICE>
```

Figure 8.4. Contents of the SAMPLE2.TXT file are displayed.

The general procedure for copying files via the Shell is

1. In the Files List area of the Shell, select the file(s) you want to copy (as described under the previous heading "Selecting Files for Operations in DOS 5").

2. Select Copy from the File pull-down menu.

3. When the Copy File dialog box appears, type the destination of the copies (for example, type A:\ if you want to copy the selected files to the root directory of drive A).

4. Press Enter or select OK.

When making copies, you need to know two simple things; the *source* of the file that you want to copy (that is, the file's location) and the *destination* of the copy (that is, where you want to place the copy of the file). When you specify the source and location, DOS makes the following assumptions:

If you don't specify a drive, DOS assumes the current drive.

If you don't specify a directory, DOS assumes the current directory.

If you don't specify a file name in the destination, DOS assumes that it can give the copied file the same name as the original file.

You can place the wildcard characters ? and * in file names when you use the command prompt to copy groups of files, such as *.BAK to copy all files with the .BAK extension or *.* to specify all the files on a particular directory.

Because no two files in the same drive and directory can have the same name, attempting to copy a file to the same drive, directory, and file name results in DOS displaying a message to the effect that a file cannot be copied to itself.

This may make copying sound more complicated than it is, but copying files is pretty simple and straightforward as long as you just keep the source and destination clearly fixed in your mind. The sections that follow describe specific techniques for copying files. I describe the general menu operation first.

Making Backup Copies

Often it's a good idea to keep two copies of the same file on a directory. That way, if you accidentally delete a copy or make modifications to it that you later change your mind about, you have the other copy of the file to work with.

Use the following technique to copy SAMPLE1.TXT to a file named SAMPLE1.BAK on the PRACTICE directory. In this case, you will be placing the copy on the same drive and directory as the original file, so you must give the copy a unique name (SAMPLE1.BAK in this example). Here are the exact steps to follow:

1. At a DOS Shell File List screen, be sure that the SAMPLE1.TXT and SAMPLE2.TXT file names are displayed in the Files Area. (If they are not, use the usual techniques to access the appropriate drive and directory.)

2. Move the highlight to the SAMPLE1.TXT file name in the Files Area (or just click that file name with your mouse).

NOTE: Press F8 as a shortcut method of displaying the Copy dialog box.

3. Select Copy from the File pull-down menu.

4. When the dialog box appears, press the End or → key to move the cursor to the end of the suggested destination.

5. Type \SAMPLE1.BAK so that the dialog box looks like Figure 8.5. (You must use the backslash to separate the file name from the directory name.)

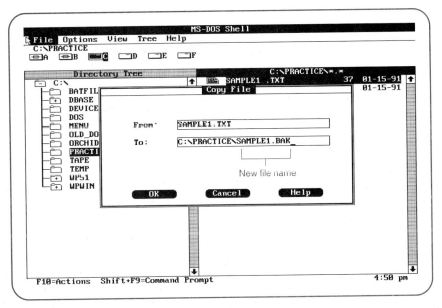

Figure 8.5. SAMPLE1.TXT copied to SAMPLE1.BAK.

6. Press Enter or click OK to perform the copy.

When DOS is finished copying, it lists the SAMPLE1.BAK file name in the Files Area. Now, on your own, try repeating the general procedure outlined in steps 1 through 6, but this time copy SAMPLE2.TXT to a file named SAMPLE2.BAK. When you finish making the second copy, your screen looks like Figure 8.6. (You can use the View File Contents option on the File pull-down menu to verify that the copied files match the originals.)

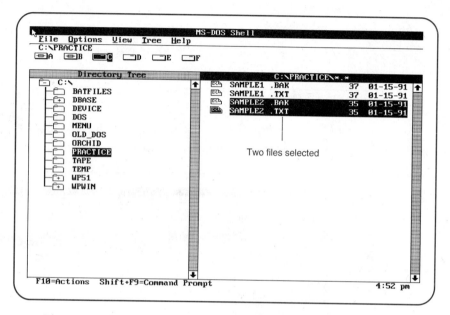

Figure 8.6. SAMPLE1.BAK and SAMPLE2.BAK in the Files Area.

 To make copies from the command prompt, use the COPY command followed by the source file name (the original) and the destination file name (the copy). To store copies of SAMPLE1.TXT and SAMPLE2.TXT in files names SAMPLE1.BAK and SAMPLE2.BAK, you could use the following two COPY commands (remember to press Enter after typing each command):

```
COPY SAMPLE1.TXT SAMPLE1.BAK
COPY SAMPLE2.TXT SAMPLE2.BAK
```

As a shortcut to using several commands to copy multiple files, you can use wildcards, provided that the names of the files being copied have a similar format. The file names SAMPLE1.TXT and SAMPLE2.TXT have a very similar format, with only one character differentiating the two names. Therefore, you can make copies of both files in a single operation by specifying SAMPLE?.TXT as the source name and

SAMPLE?.BAK as the destination name. (Recall from Chapter 4 that the ? character stands for any single character.) Here are the exact steps to follow:

1. If your computer has a hard disk, enter the command `CD \PRACTICE` to access the PRACTICE directory.

2. If your computer does not have a hard disk, insert the diskette that contains the sample files into drive B:; then enter the command `B:` to access the diskette in drive B:.

3. Be sure that the sample files are indeed on the current drive and directory by entering the command `DIR` to view all file names.

4. Enter the command `COPY SAMPLE?.TXT SAMPLE?.BAK`.

DOS displays the name of each original file as it makes the copies; then, it ends the process with the message `2 file(s) copied`. To verify that you now have two new files named SAMPLE1.BAK and SAMPLE2.BAK, enter the `DIR` command. (Also, verify that the copies contain exactly the same text as the originals by using the TYPE command to view the contents of each file.)

Copying to a Different Directory (same drive)

In some situations, you might want to store copies of files in multiple directories. To do so, you specify a file name as the source of the copy and a directory name as the destination. (The copied file will have the same name as the original file.)

You can copy several files to a new directory in a single operation. To demonstrate this procedure, store copies of SAMPLE1.TXT and SAMPLE2.TXT on the PRACTICE\TEST directory (which is currently empty). Use the following steps as appropriate for your version of DOS. (If your computer does not have a hard disk, you can create these files and directories on a diskette, or you can skip to the section "Copying to Different Disk Drives.")

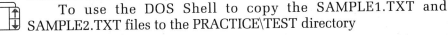

To use the DOS Shell to copy the SAMPLE1.TXT and SAMPLE2.TXT files to the PRACTICE\TEST directory

1. Select the `PRACTICE` directory from the Directory Tree area of the shell.

2. Select both the SAMPLE1.TXT and SAMPLE2.TXT file names by highlighting one, pressing Shift-F8 and using the arrow keys and Spacebar combination to highlight the other (or by clicking one with your mouse and then holding down the Ctrl key while clicking the other).

3. Select Copy from the File pull-down menu.

4. Press End and type \TEST to change the suggested destination to C:\PRACTICE\TEST as shown in Figure 8.7. (You must use the backslash to separate the directory names.)

5. Press Enter or select OK.

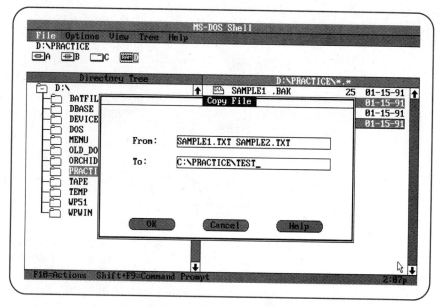

Figure 8.7. Dialog box to copy files to the PRACTICE\TEST directory.

When the operation is complete, the dialog box disappears. To verify that the PRACTICE\TEST directory now contains copies of SAMPLE1.TXT and SAMPLE2.TXT, move the highlight to the Directory Tree Area and select the TEST directory name. Note the names of the two copied files in the Files Area of the screen.

Copying to a Different Directory by Dragging

You can use the Shell also to copy files by dragging them to a new location.

The general procedure for copying files to a different directory is simple:

1. Hold down the `Ctrl` key.

2. Select all the `files` you want to copy by clicking them.

3. When you click the last file to be moved, do not release the `left button`.

4. With the left button still depressed, drag the file icon to the `Directory Tree Area`.

5. When the file icon is on the name of the directory to which you are copying the files, release the `left button` and then release the `Ctrl` key.

6. Select the `Yes` button in the Confirm Mouse Operation dialog box.

How does this procedure work? To find out, repeat the example in the previous section. To use the mouse to copy the SAMPLE1.TXT and SAMPLE2.TXT files into the TEST subdirectory, follow these steps:

1. Hold down the `Ctrl` key.

2. Click `SAMPLE1.TXT`.

3. Click `SAMPLE2.TXT`, but do not release the `left mouse button`!

4. Drag the mouse cursor into the `Directory Tree Area`. Notice that a three-line "file" icon appears in place of the mouse cursor.

5. Position the file icon on the TEST subdirectory name and release the `left mouse button` and then the `Ctrl` key. The Shell now displays the Confirm Mouse Operation dialog box, as shown in Figure 8.8.

6. Press `Enter` (or select Yes) to tell the Shell to copy the files to C:\PRACTICE\TEST.

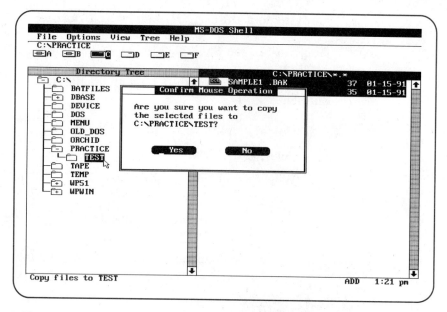

Figure 8.8. Confirm Mouse Operation dialog box to copy SAMPLE1.TXT and SAMPLE2.TXT to the TEST directory.

You can copy one file or an entire directory of files with the same easy procedure.

 To copy files to a new directory using the command prompt, specify the name of the file (or use wildcard characters to indicate a group of files) as the source, and specify the drive and directory name as the destination. For example, to copy SAMPLE1.TXT and SAMPLE2.TXT to the TEST directory (beneath the PRACTICE directory), follow these steps:

1. Enter the command `CD \PRACTICE` to access the PRACTICE directory.

2. Enter the command `COPY SAMPLE?.TXT C:\PRACTICE\TEST`.

DOS displays the names of the files as they are copied and then ends the operation with the message `2 file(s) copied`. To verify that the TEST directory indeed contains these new files, change to the directory by entering the command `CD TEST`, and then enter the `DIR` command to view the names of files stored there.

Note that both the PRACTICE and PRACTICE\TEST directories contain copies of the SAMPLE1.TXT and SAMPLE2.TXT files. Even though the files share the same name and content, they are completely independent of each other. Hence, changing or deleting these files on one directory has no effect on the copies on the other directory.

Copying to Different Disk Drives

NOTE: Some application programs are *copy-protected* with a structure that enables them to be used on only one computer. Although DOS can copy such programs, the copies will not work on different computers.

Copying files from one disk (or diskette) to another is one of the most common types of copying. If your computer has a hard disk, you use this basic procedure to copy application programs from their original diskettes onto your hard disk. You also use this technique to copy files from your hard disk to diskettes, an operation that lets you store extra backups or use files on other computers.

If your computer doesn't have a hard disk, use this procedure to copy files from one diskette to another so that you can store the copies in a safe place as backups, or you can copy files from one diskette to another so that you can use the same files on multiple computers.

Using Shell Menus to Copy Files to a Disk

To copy a file from one disk drive to another, specify the file(s) that you want to copy as the source, and specify the disk drive that you want to copy to as the destination. You can also specify a directory on the destination disk drive, but it must be a name of an existing directory. (DOS will not automatically create a new directory while copying files.) If you do not specify a directory on the destination drive, DOS places the copies in the current directory of that drive (usually the root directory).

To practice this procedure, copy the SAMPLE1.BAK and SAMPLE2.BAK files to a new diskette. To do so, you need a blank, formatted diskette (in addition to the one you might have used in earlier exercises). To prepare for the procedure, set up the diskettes as follows:

❏ If your computer does not have a hard disk, insert the source diskette (the one with SAMPLE1.BAK and SAMPLE2.BAK on it) in drive B: and insert the blank, formatted diskette in drive A:.

❏ If your computer has a hard disk, insert the blank, formatted diskette in drive A:.

Now, follow the appropriate steps for your computer:

1. At the File List screen, be sure to access the PRACTICE directory on your hard disk (or drive B: if you have no hard disk).

NOTE: When the Shell is in Add mode (Shift-F8), you can press Spacebar to select a file or press it again to deselect a highlighted file.

---

2. Select the SAMPLE1.BAK and SAMPLE2.BAK file names by highlighting one, pressing Shift-F8, and using the arrow keys and Spacebar combination to highlight the other (or by clicking one with your mouse and then holding down the Ctrl key while clicking the other).

3. Press F10 or Alt and then press Enter to access the File pull-down menu.

4. Select Copy....

NOTE: You must specify a directory for the operation, even if it is only the root directory.

---

5. Hold down the Del (or Delete) key until the suggested destination is completely erased; then type the new destination A:\, as shown in Figure 8.9.

6. Press Enter.

When copying is complete, the dialog box disappears from the screen.

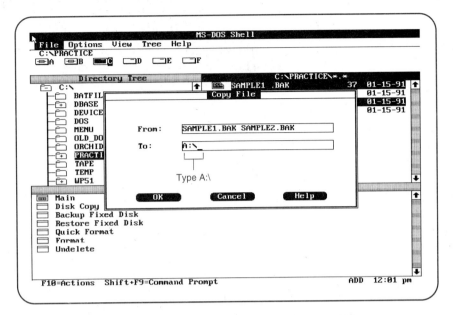

Figure 8.9. Dialog box to copy SAMPLE1.BAK
and SAMPLE2.BAK to drive A:.

Copying Files to a Disk by Dragging

Using the mouse procedure to copy files to a different disk drive is
similar to copying files to a different directory. However, you need to
use the Dual Files List if you want to be able to copy files from a directory
on one drive to a specific directory on the second drive. Here is the
general procedure:

1. Select Dual File Lists from the View pull-down menu.

2. Select the source drive and directory from the top
   Directory Tree and Files List.

3. Select the destination drive and directory from the
   Directory Tree and Files List near the bottom of the screen.

4. Select the files you want to copy from the top Files List.

5. Hold down the Ctrl key and drag the icon to whatever directory in the bottom Directory Tree you want to copy the files to.

6. Release the mouse button, then the Ctrl key, and respond
   to the confirmation box (if it appears).

If you simply want to copy files to the root directory of a different drive, as is common when you're copying from a hard disk to a floppy, you can simply drag the selected files to the drive's icon without using the Dual File Lists views. To try this particular technique, use the mouse to copy the SAMPLE1.BAK and SAMPLE2.BAK files to drive A: as listed in the following.

1. Hold down the `Ctrl` key.

2. Click `SAMPLE1.BAK`.

3. Click `SAMPLE2.BAK`, but do not release the left mouse button!

4. Drag the `mouse cursor` into the Drives Area. Notice that a three-line file icon appears in place of the mouse cursor. (You can release the Ctrl key now.)

5. Position the `file icon` on the drive A: icon and release the left mouse button. The Shell now displays the Confirm Mouse Operation dialog box.

6. Press `Enter` (or select `Yes`) to tell the Shell to copy the files to drive A:.

After the operation is complete, switch to drive A: to verify that the files were copied. If you look in the Files Area, you will see that both files have been copied in the root directory of the disk in drive A:. You can copy one file or an entire directory of files with the same easy procedure.

This is a convenient method for copying files from your hard disk to a floppy disk, thus creating backup copies of your important files. Although you can copy files to any disk drive listed in the Drives Area (whether it be a floppy drive, hard drive, or RAM drive), you can only copy to the root directory of the specified drive. This limits the value of this method for copying files to a hard drive, because most of the files on a hard disk drive should be stored in directories and subdirectories, not in the root directory.

1. If you have a hard disk, enter the command `CD \PRACTICE` to change to the PRACTICE directory, or if you do not have a hard disk, access drive B: by entering the command `B:`.

2. Enter the command `COPY SAMPLE?.BAK A:` to copy the sample backup files to the diskette in drive A:.

DOS displays the names of the files as they are copied and ends the operation with the message `2 file(s) copied`. To verify that the diskette in drive A: now contains the copied files, enter the command

DIR A: at the command prompt. (If you are using a system without a hard disk, remove the diskette from drive A:, and reinsert the DOS diskette after you verify the copy.)

General Precautions for Copying Files

Before you start copying files on your own, keep in mind this important point: If you copy a file to a disk drive or directory that already contains a file of the same name, the copied file replaces the original file. For example, suppose that a directory named ACCT_REC contains a file named CUSTLIST.DAT that lists 1,000 customer names and addresses. Now, suppose that you create another file named CUSTLIST.DAT in a directory named INVENTRY, but this file lists only two customer names and addresses.

Finally, suppose that you decide to copy the CUSTLIST.DAT file from the INVENTRY directory to the ACCT_REC directory. If you do so, the 1,000 names and addresses in CUSTLIST.DAT will be lost forever because DOS will *overwrite* (replace) the original CUSTLIST.DAT file on the ACCT_REC directory with the copy from the INVENTRY directory.

DOS 5 helps protect users from potential problems of this type. Whenever you copy a file using the DOS Shell File List, DOS first checks the destination drive or directory to see whether it already contains a file with the same name as the one it's about to copy. If DOS finds a file on the destination with the same name, it presents the warning shown in Figure 8.10.

As you can see, the Replace File Confirmation dialog box warns you when it is about to overwrite an existing file. The **Replace File:** message at the top of the box lets you know the path, name, creation date, and size of the file that the copy operation will overwrite. The **With File:** message displays the same information about the file that you are currently copying.

In the example in Figure 8.10, the dialog box warns you that the SAMPLE2.BAK file in the \PRACTICE\TEST directory will be overwritten by the SAMPLE2.BAK file from the \PRACTICE directory. If you select Yes, DOS replaces the file on the destination with the new copy and then proceeds to copy other files (if any). If you select No, the file is not copied, and DOS proceeds to copy other files (if any). If you select Cancel, DOS cancels the entire current copy operation.

This Replace File Confirmation dialog box can save you from inadvertently overwriting a new file with an old one. Whenever you see this box, check the dates and the sizes of the two files. The date specifies when the file was created or last modified; the size tells you how many characters the file contains. In general, you rarely want to copy an older file over a newer one or a smaller file over a larger one.

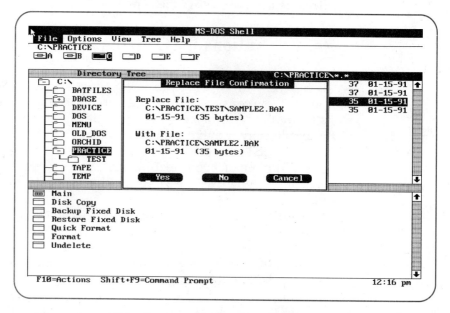

Figure 8.10. DOS 5 Replace File Confirmation dialog box warns you when it will overwrite an existing file.

When you work at the command prompt, DOS (any version) gives no warning when a copy procedure is about to replace an existing file—DOS simply replaces the file! Because of this, you should always check the destination directory (or drive) to see whether it contains a file that has the same name as the one you are about to copy. (Use the DIR command to do so.)

For example, say that you are planning to copy CUSTLIST.DAT from the INVENTRY directory to the ACCT_REC directory. (Because your computer probably does not have these directories, you cannot try this right now; this is just a hypothetical example.) Before you rush into the copy procedure, you decide to check the destination directory to see whether it already contains a file with this same name. You enter the command

```
DIR C:\ACCT_REC\CUSTLIST.DAT.
```

Now, suppose that DOS informs you there is already a file named CUSTLIST.DAT on the ACCT_REC directory, and DOS displays the file name and the following information:

```
Directory C:\ACCT_REC
CUSTLIST     DAT          35000      03-15-92      3:22p
```

The question you must now ask yourself: "Should I proceed with this copy, thus overwriting (replacing) the CUSTLIST.DAT file's contents with the INVENTRY directory's CUSTLIST.DAT file?"

To answer this question, you would first look at the basic file information for CUSTLIST.DAT on the INVENTRY directory. To do so, you would enter the command DIR CUSTLIST.DAT (you don't need to specify the drive and directory if you are already accessing the INVENTRY directory), and DOS might show you the following information about that file:

```
Directory C:\INVENTRY
CUSTLIST     DAT             50      06-20-92      8:00a
```

NOTE: The DOS 5 Replace File Confirmation dialog box automatically displays file dates and sizes when you are about to overwrite an existing file.

In this example, you would be very wise not to copy CUSTLIST.DAT from the INVENTRY directory to the ACCT_REC directory for one very important reason: As you can see in the two directory displays, the CUSTLIST.DAT file in the ACCT_REC directory contains 35,000 bytes (characters), whereas the CUSTLIST.DAT file in the INVENTRY directory contains only 50 bytes. If you were to proceed with the copy, you would lose at least 34,950 characters in the CUSTLIST.DAT file in the ACCT_REC directory. This could, indeed, be a rather unpleasant loss (particularly if you had no backups of the file being replaced).

Remember, even if you are planning to copy a group of files with a single COPY command, you can check the destination directory to see whether it already contains files with the same names as the files being copied. For example, suppose that you plan to copy *.TXT (all files with the extension .TXT) from the PRACTICE directory to the PRACTICE\TEST directory. To preview the current (PRACTICE) directory to see what files will be copied, enter the command DIR *.TXT. To check the destination directory for files with similar names, enter the command

```
DIR C:\PRACTICE\TEST\*.TXT
```

Renaming Files

As you gain experience using your computer and DOS wildcards, you'll notice what an advantage it is to name related files with file names that have a similar pattern. For example, suppose that you store quarterly data for your business in separate files. If you were to name these files in a haphazard manner, such as 1992QTR1.DAT, QTR2-92.INF, and 92-3-QTR.TXT, you could not use ambiguous file names to perform operations on these files as a group. However, if you renamed the files using a consistent format, such as QTR1-92.DAT, QTR2-92.DAT, and QTR3-92.DAT, you could more easily display or manage these related files using the ambiguous file names QTR?-92.DAT or QTR*.DAT.

It's easy to use DOS to rename a file, and you don't need to worry about accidentally replacing an existing file with a new one, because DOS will never allow you to do so. When you change the name of a file, the new name must be unique in the current directory (or diskette). If the new name is not unique, DOS displays a warning message and refuses to continue the operation.

You can use the usual DOS wildcard characters, ? and *, to simultaneously rename several files. To demonstrate, try renaming the SAMPLE1.BAK and SAMPLE2.BAK files on the PRACTICE directory to SAMPLE1.OLD and SAMPLE2.OLD. Use the following steps for your version of DOS:

1. If your computer has a hard disk, select the PRACTICE directory from the Directory Tree Area of the File List screen.

2. If your computer does not have a hard disk, be sure that disk drive B: contains the diskette that has the SAMPLE1.BAK and SAMPLE2.BAK files on it; then select B from the Drives Area.

3. Select the SAMPLE1.BAK and SAMPLE2.BAK file names by highlighting one, pressing Shift-F8, and using the arrow keys and Spacebar combination to highlight the other (or by clicking one with your mouse and then holding down the Ctrl key while clicking the other).

4. Press F10 or Alt and press Enter to pull down the File menu.

5. Select Rename....

The Rename File dialog box appears on your screen, as shown in Figure 8.11. Notice that the box displays the current name for the file, a blank box for entering a new name for the file, and a counter that keeps you informed of the number of operations you are performing. (In Figure 8.11, for example, SAMPLE1.BAK is 1 of 2, the first of two files that you are going to rename.)

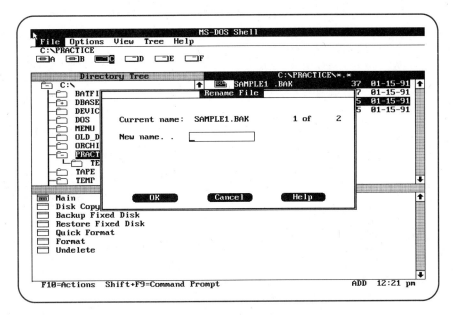

Figure 8.11. The Rename File Dialog box.

You must remember to enter a complete file name for each file. After you type the new file name and press Enter, DOS prompts you to rename the next file, until you've provided a new name for each selected file. (If you decide not to rename a particular file, press Enter without typing a new name.) As usual, you can also press F1 (or select the Help button) for help or press Esc to cancel the entire request.

To proceed with the renaming exercise, follow these steps:

6. Type SAMPLE1.OLD and press Enter.

7. Type SAMPLE2.OLD and press Enter.

The Files Area of your screen now displays the two files with the new names you provided.

NOTE: You can abbreviate the RENAME command as REN.

To rename files from the command prompt, use the RENAME command followed by the current name, a blank space, and the new name, as shown in this general format:

`RENAME currentname newname`

You can use wildcard characters to rename a group of files, but you need to exercise a little caution when doing so, as demonstrated later. For now, rename SAMPLE1.BAK and SAMPLE2.BAK to SAMPLE1.OLD and SAMPLE2.OLD by following these simple steps:

1. If your computer has a hard disk, enter the command `CD \PRACTICE` to change to the PRACTICE directory.

2. If your computer does not have a hard disk, be sure the diskette in drive B: has the `SAMPLE1.BAK` and `SAMPLE2.BAK` files on it and access drive B: by entering the `B:` command.

3. Type `RENAME SAMPLE?.BAK SAMPLE?.OLD`.

4. Press `Enter`.

To verify the results of the procedure, enter the `DIR` command to display the new files' names. As the directory display shows, DOS renamed the SAMPLE1.BAK and SAMPLE2.BAK files to SAMPLE1.OLD and SAMPLE2.OLD. Because you used the ? wildcard character, both files were included in the renaming operation.

In the future, when you use wildcard characters to rename groups of files, keep in mind one important rule: Don't shorten the names of two or more files using a single RENAME command. The reason for this rule is straightforward. Suppose that you attempt to rename SAMPLE1.OLD and SAMPLE2.OLD to SAMP1.OLD and SAMP2.OLD using the single command `RENAME SAMPLE?.OLD SAMP?.OLD`.

The problem here is that DOS does not "know" the last character in the file name (that is, 1 or 2) is the one that makes each file name unique. It therefore renames the first file to SAMPL.OLD. Then, it also attempts to name the second file SAMPL.OLD. When DOS sees that the file name SAMPL.OLD is already in use, it displays the error message `Duplicate file name or file not found` and cancels the renaming of the second file. (If you then entered the `DIR` command to see the names of files, you would see that only one of the files was renamed.)

If you want to shorten the names of several files, you must rename each file individually. Hence, in this example, rather than using the command `RENAME SAMPLE?.OLD SAMP?.OLD`, you would need to enter the following two commands:

```
RENAME SAMPLE1.OLD SAMP1.OLD
RENAME SAMPLE2.OLD SAMP2.OLD
```

Also keep in mind that you cannot provide a new drive or directory location for a file while renaming it. For example, the seemingly logical command `RENAME C:\PRACTICE\SAMPLE1.TXT A:SAMPLE1.BAK` displays the error message `Invalid parameter`, because the command attempts to rename a file in the PRACTICE directory while at the same time trying to move the file to the diskette in drive A:. Such operations are simply not allowed with the RENAME command. (However, the command `COPY C:\PRACTICE\SAMPLE1.TXT A:SAMPLE1.BAK` would work; it would leave SAMPLE1.TXT intact on the PRACTICE directory, while also putting a copy of that file—with the name SAMPLE1.BAK—on the diskette in drive A:.)

Deleting Files

From time to time, you probably will want to delete (or *erase*) files to make room for new ones or to unclutter your disks. However, if you are using any version of DOS before Version 5.0, you should be careful when deleting files because once you do, there is no turning back. That is, as soon as you erase a file, it is permanently gone! DOS erases a file very quickly; so, even if it took you days, weeks, or even 2MOVEmonths to create a file, DOS will "zap" it into oblivion before you can say "whoops."

If you are using DOS 5, you can use the UNDELETE command to recover accidentally deleted files. However, you must recover the deleted files immediately! If you perform other DOS operations, such as creating, copying, or combining files, you might overwrite the data in the deleted files, thus losing the information forever. (See the next section for a brief overview of how to "undelete" files in DOS 5.) If you ever accidentally delete a file or group of files, you can always consult the UNDELETE entry in Appendix B for details about file recovery procedures.

As with the other basic file operations discussed in this chapter, you can erase several files during a single operation. However, when doing so, you must exercise extreme caution to ensure that you do not inadvertently erase more files than you intended. Techniques that illustrate caution are built into the following exercises, which show you how to safely erase the SAMPLE1.OLD and SAMPLE2.OLD files.

The basic technique for using the DOS Shell to erase files is the same as it was for other operations, except that you must be absolutely sure that you've selected only the files that you want to erase. You do this by first "deselecting" all files, as discussed in the following steps:

1. Be sure that you are still accessing the PRACTICE directory if you are using a hard disk, or if your computer has no hard disk, that your current drive is drive B:.

2. With the File List screen displayed, press F10 or Alt and then press Enter to pull down the File menu.

3. If the last option Deselect All is available, select it. (If the option is shaded and unavailable, there are no selected files, so you can press the Esc key to close the menu.)

4. Now that you know that there are no selected files (which you might have otherwise overlooked), press Tab (or use your mouse) to move to the Files Area of the screen.

5. Select the SAMPLE1.OLD and SAMPLE2.OLD files using the usual technique.

> NOTE: Press the Del key as a shortcut method of displaying the Delete dialog box.

6. Press F10 or Alt and then press Enter to pull down the File menu.

7. Select Delete....

8. DOS displays the Delete File dialog box, which contains the names of the files to delete. Press Enter to proceed.

The Delete File Confirmation dialog box provides options that permit you to delete the current file (select Yes), skip (don't delete) the current file (select No), or cancel the entire operation (select Cancel), as shown in Figure 8.12. DOS displays a confirmation dialog box for each file that you previously selected for deletion. (This is an added precaution in case you forget to "deselect all" files before selecting new files for this operation.)

To delete the file whose name is shown next to the Delete prompt, select Yes by clicking the button with your mouse or by moving the underline cursor to that option and pressing Enter. To complete this exercise, proceed with the following steps:

9. Select Yes to delete SAMPLE1.OLD.

10. When the options appear for SAMPLE2.OLD, again select Yes to delete the file.

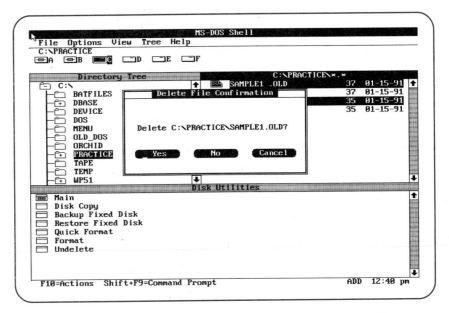

Figure 8.12. Options to delete a file or to cancel deleting a file.

After DOS erases both files, it redisplays the File List screen. Note that SAMPLE1.OLD and SAMPLE2.OLD are no longer listed in the Files Area, as Figure 8.13 shows.

 To erase files from the command prompt, use the ERASE (or DEL, for delete) command followed by the name of the file you want to erase.

 NOTE: DOS 5 users have some additional protection options when using the ERASE command at the command prompt. See the ERASE (also DEL) command reference in Appendix B for details.

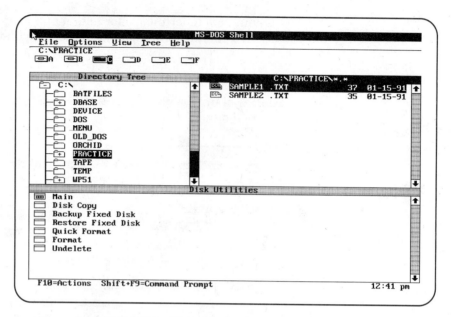

Figure 8.13. SAMPLE1.OLD and SAMPLE2.OLD have been deleted.

You can also use ambiguous file names to erase multiple files. For example, to erase SAMPLE1.OLD and SAMPLE2.OLD or the identical command DEL SAMPLE?.OLD, you could use the command `ERASE SAMPLE?.OLD`, but before you do so, look at some precautionary steps you can take so that you don't accidentally erase other files:

1. If your computer has a hard disk, be sure to change to the PRACTICE directory by entering `CD \PRACTICE`. If your computer does not have a hard disk, be sure that the diskette containing `SAMPLE1.OLD` and `SAMPLE2.OLD` is in drive B:, and access the drive by entering the `B:` command if necessary.

2. Before erasing SAMPLE?.OLD, first enter the command `DIR SAMPLE?.OLD` to see exactly which files fit this ambiguous file name pattern.

3. In this case, you should see only two file names, `SAMPLE1.OLD` and `SAMPLE2.OLD` (in addition to the usual information that the DIR command provides).

4. Because SAMPLE1.OLD and SAMPLE2.OLD are indeed the two files you want to erase, type the command `ERASE SAMPLE?.OLD` and press `Enter`.

5. Type DIR to see the names of remaining files, which will not include the deleted SAMPLE1.OLD and SAMPLE2.OLD files.

As mentioned at the beginning of this section, if you are using a version of DOS other than DOS 5, you need to exercise caution when erasing files, because once you do, the files are gone forever (which of course, is also a very good reason for always making backup copies of important files!). However, at a deeper, more technical level, the file is not really deleted. Instead, DOS changes the first character in the file name to make the file "invisible" and ready to be replaced by a new file. When you save a new file in the future, DOS then overwrites the "invisible" file with the new file's contents.

> NOTE: You can also protect files from being accidentally erased, as discussed in the section "Protecting Files" later in this chapter.

 DOS 5 is the first version of DOS to provide a built-in feature to locate and recover these invisible files. Therefore, it is possible to "undelete" an accidentally deleted file, as you will see in the next section. However, if you are using an earlier version of DOS, all hope is not lost; several third party vendors offer "undelete" utilities that work with files in DOS 3 and 4. If you don't own DOS 5, you should seriously consider purchasing one of these products for your computer. Do so now, before an accident actually occurs. (For a list of several of these utility packages, see Chapter 17.)

Remember, even if you use DOS 5 or own an unerase program, up-to-date backup copies of files are still the best way to protect yourself from accidentally losing files.

Undeleting Files with the DOS 5 UNDELETE Command

When DOS deletes a file, it doesn't really erase the data from the disk; it just changes the first character of the file name (to a σ—lowercase sigma) so that other DOS commands don't "see" the file. Although the information is still on the disk immediately after you erase the file, DOS commands no longer recognize that it is there, and they quickly overwrite the data with the new or modified files that you later save to disk.

NOTE: The DOS 5 Shell does not include an Undelete menu option. You must either type UNDELETE after selecting the Run command from the File menu, or you must type UNDELETE from the command prompt.

DOS 5 includes a utility that unerases files. The UNDELETE command searches for files that start with a σ so that you can restore the first character of the file name to a letter that DOS commands can recognize. Immediately thereafter, DOS can once again perform operations on that file.

The basic use of the command is quite simple, and if it is used immediately after a deletion, it is always effective. However, if you save, copy, or alter even one file after a deletion, your chances of recovering the deleted file decrease dramatically, because the new or revised file may overwrite part of the deleted file.

The UNDELETE entry in Appendix B gives an overview of the command usage. However, if you use the UNDELETE command immediately after accidentally erasing a file or files, the following brief procedure will always recover all of the deleted files in the current directory:

1. Be sure that the `current directory` is the directory that contains the deleted files.

2. Type `UNDELETE`. (If DOS responds with a `Bad command or file name` error message, type the full path name C:\DOS\UNDELETE.)

3. When UNDELETE asks whether you want to recover the specified file, press `Y` (for Yes).

4. When UNDELETE prompts you to enter the first character of the file, type the `original first letter`. (If you can't remember the original first letter, type any valid character that will create a unique name in the current directory.)

Repeat the previous steps until you have undeleted all of the files that you want to recover.

In the previous section, you deleted two files—SAMPLE1.OLD and SAMPLE2.OLD. Now assume that you haven't performed any other file operations and that PRACTICE is still the current directory. If you follow the steps in the preceding bulleted list (typing an `S` at both of the `Enter the first character of the filename` prompts), your screen will resemble Figure 8.14.

```
C:\PRACTICE>UNDELETE

Directory: C:\PRACTICE
File Specs: *.*

    Delete Tracking file not found.

    MS-DOS Directory contains    2 deleted files.
    Of those,    2 files may be recovered.

Using the MS-DOS Directory.

        ?AMPLE2  OLD        35  1-15-91  3:57p  ...A
Do you want to undelete this file? (Y/N)
Y _____  Type
Enter the first character of the filename.
S _____  Type
File successfully undeleted.

        ?AMPLE1  OLD        37  1-15-91  3:56p  ...A
Do you want to undelete this file? (Y/N)
Y
Enter the first character of the filename.
```

Figure 8.14. Using UNDELETE to recover two deleted files.

Type the DIR command to see that the two files have indeed been undeleted.

If you want to undelete a specific file (even if it is in another directory or on another drive), type the path and/or file name after the UNDELETE command. For example, if you are currently in the \DOS directory and want to undelete the SAMPLE1.OLD file in the PRACTICE directory, type

```
UNDELETE \PRACTICE\SAMPLE1.OLD
```

and answer the prompts accordingly.

Combining Files

You can copy and combine (merge) several individual text files into a single new file. This can be handy when, for example, you've created several files containing names and addresses and want to create a larger file combining all the names and addresses. The DOS 5 Shell does not provide any means of combining files, but all versions of the DOS command prompt do.

> NOTE: Don't forget to press Enter after typing each DOS command.

The basic technique for combining files is to use the COPY command. You must list as the source of the copy the names of files to be combined, separated by a plus (+) sign. You must provide as the destination a new, unique file name. Look at an example that combines the SAMPLE1.TXT and SAMPLE2.TXT files:

1. If you are using the DOS 5 Shell, press the `F3` key to exit the Shell and display the command prompt.

2. Be sure to access the correct drive or directory; enter the command `CD \PRACTICE` if you have a hard disk or enter `B:` if you don't have a hard disk.

3. Type the command `COPY SAMPLE1.TXT+SAMPLE2.TXT COMBO.TXT`. (Note the plus sign that joins the source files and also note the blank space in front of the new file name COMBO.TXT.)

4. To verify that the command worked, enter `DIR` to view the file names.

5. To view the contents of the new COMBO.TXT file, enter the command `TYPE COMBO.TXT`.

The TYPE command displays the contents of the COMBO.TXT files as follows:

```
This is the first sample text file.
I am the second sample text file.
```

Note that you should only combine *text* files. Never try to combine program files (that is, those with the file name extension .COM, .EXE, or .BAT.). If you combine program files, the resulting "program combination" file probably will not work at all, or if it does, it might do very strange things to your computer!

If you are a DOS 5 user, return to the DOS Shell now by typing the command `DOSSHELL` and pressing Enter. (If you do not have a hard disk, be sure to insert the Shell diskette in drive A:, access drive A: by typing `A:` and pressing Enter and then type `DOSSHELL` and press Enter).

Moving Files

As you gain experience in using your computer, you might occasionally decide to change the directory tree structure of the hard disk to better organize your files. When you do so, you probably will want to move, rather than copy, files from one directory to another.

The DOS 5 File List has a built-in menu option for moving files. However, earlier versions of DOS do not have a "move" command, so you must move files using a two-step operation:

1. Copy the file to the new directory.

2. Erase the file from the original directory.

Try a simple example: Move the new COMBO.TXT file from the PRACTICE directory to the PRACTICE\TEST directory. (These steps are described for a hard disk computer, but if you created these directories on a diskette, you can follow the instructions by substituting the correct drive name.) Follow the appropriate steps for your version of DOS:

1. Select PRACTICE from the Directory Tree to change to the PRACTICE directory.

2. Select COMBO.TXT from the Files Area of the screen.

> NOTE: Press F7 as a shortcut method of displaying the Move dialog box.

3. Press F10 or Alt and then press Enter to pull down the File menu.

4. Select Move....

5. Press the End key and type \TEST to change the destination to C:\PRACTICE\TEST, as shown in Figure 8.15.

6. Press Enter to start the operation.

When DOS finishes the operation, COMBO.TXT is no longer displayed in the Files Area. If you move the highlight to the Directory Tree Area of the screen and select TEST to change to that directory, you'll see that COMBO.TXT is now stored on that directory.

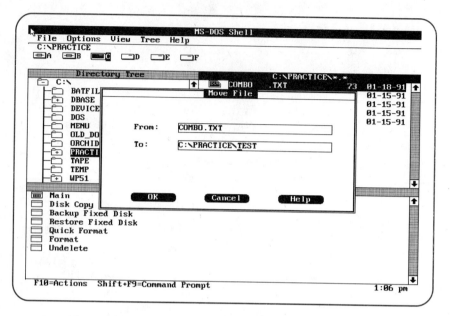

Figure 8.15. Dialog box to move COMBO.TXT from the
PRACTICE directory to the TEST directory.

NOTE: With the mouse-only procedure, use the Alt key to move
files; use the Ctrl key to copy files.

 DOS 5 users also have the ability to move files "graphically"; that
is, literally move a file's icon (and the file itself!) to a new location. This
is similar to the mouse-only copying procedure discussed earlier in this
chapter. However, instead of holding down the Ctrl key during the
operation, you hold down the Alt key.

To see how this procedure works, repeat the previous example.
Use the mouse to move the COMBO.TXT file into the TEST subdirectory
as described in the following steps:

1. Hold down the Alt key.

2. Click COMBO.TXT, but do not release the left mouse
   button!

3. Drag the mouse cursor into the Directory Tree Area. Notice
   that a three-line file icon appears in place of the mouse cursor.
   (You can release the Alt key now.)

4. Position the file icon on the TEST subdirectory name and release the left mouse button. The Shell now displays the Confirm Mouse Operation dialog box, as shown in Figure 8.16.

5. Press Enter (or select Yes) to tell the Shell to move the files to C:\PRACTICE\TEST.

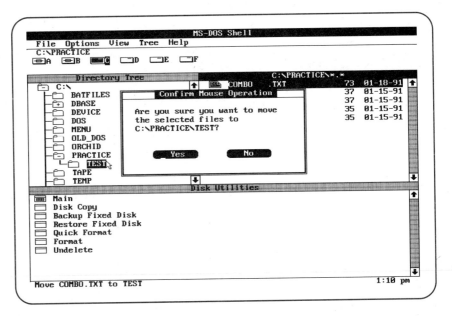

Figure 8.16. Confirm Mouse Operation dialog box to move COMBO.TXT to the TEST directory.

If you switch to the PRACTICE\TEST directory and look in the Files Area, you will see that both files have been moved into the TEST directory. Click the PRACTICE directory to verify that the file is no longer there.

To perform the same operation from the command prompt

1. Enter the command CD \PRACTICE to change to the PRACTICE directory.

2. Enter the command COPY COMBO.TXT C:\PRACTICE\TEST to copy the COMBO.TXT file to the TEST directory.

3. After DOS reports that it copied the file, verify the copy by entering the command DIR C:\PRACTICE\TEST\C*.* to view all file names on the TEST directory that begin with the letter C. Note that COMBO.TXT is listed there.

4. Because the copy was successful, you can now erase COMBO.TXT from the current directory (PRACTICE) by entering the command `ERASE COMBO.TXT`.

Notes on Move/Copy by Dragging

When using your mouse to move/copy files by dragging, there are a few points to keep in mind:

❏ If you hold down the Ctrl key while dragging files, the end result is always a copy (easy to remember because both Ctrl and Copy begin with the letter C).

❏ If you hold down the Alt key while dragging files, the end result is always a move.

❏ If you don't hold down either Ctrl or Alt while dragging a file, the end result depends on where you drag the files to:

If you drag the files to a different directory on the same drive, the result is a move.

If you drag the files to a different drive, the result is a copy.

This may seem confusing, but it's just DOS's way of trying to be "intuitive." The most common reason for "dragging" a file from one directory to another on the same drive is to move it; hence that's the default if you don't hold down Ctrl or Alt when dragging. The most common reason to drag a file to a different drive is to make a copy, and hence, that's the default if you don't hold down Ctrl or Alt in that situation.

Protecting Files

Each file on your diskette or hard disk is assigned several *attributes*. Whenever you store a new file or a copy of an existing file onto your disk, DOS automatically assigns that file the attribute *read-write*, which means that you can change or delete the file at any time. However, you can reset the attribute of any file to *read-only*, which means that you can view and use the contents of the file, but not change or delete the file.

Changing a file's attribute to read-only is a good way to ensure that the file is never accidentally erased. However, because setting the read-only attribute also prevents you from changing the file, it is inconvenient for data files that you need to update on a regular basis (such as mailing lists, bookkeeping data, and so on). Nonetheless, files that you never change (such as application programs and DOS programs) are good candidates for read-only protection.

To practice using this technique, change the attribute of the SAMPLE1.TXT and SAMPLE2.TXT files in the PRACTICE directory to read-only, and then you can see what happens when you try to erase those files. Follow the appropriate steps for your version of DOS:

1. Be sure that the `File List` is displayed on your screen and that you are accessing the `PRACTICE` directory (if you have a hard disk) or that you are accessing the drive containing the diskette with SAMPLE1.TXT on it (if you don't have a hard disk).

2. Move to the Files Area and select the `SAMPLE1.TXT` and `SAMPLE2.TXT` files in the usual manner.

3. Press `F10` or `Alt` and then press `Enter` to pull down the File menu.

4. Select `Change Attributes....`

5. At the Change Attribute dialog box, select `Change selected files one at a time` (see Figure 8.17).

   DOS displays the next Change Attribute dialog box on your screen, as shown in Figure 8.18. Note that each file has four attributes that you can change; however, for the time being, I'll confine the discussion to the Read only attribute. (The ATTRIB entry in Appendix B discusses the other options.) As you are instructed on the screen, to change an attribute, you must first move the highlight to it using ↑ or ↓ and then press the Spacebar.

6. Press ↓ to move the highlight to the `Read only` option.

7. Press the `Spacebar` (or click the option once with your mouse) to select the attribute. Note that a right-pointing triangle to the left of the option indicates that the read-only attribute is now turned on. (The Archive attribute may also be turned on; to turn it off, highlight `Archive` and press the `Spacebar`. Note that pressing the Spacebar "toggles" an option on or off.)

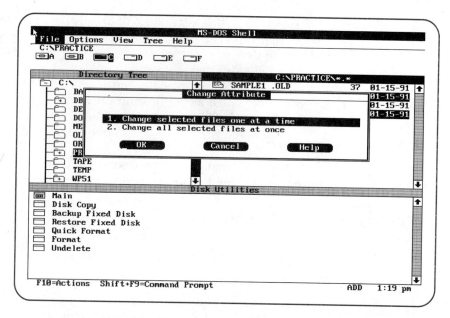

Figure 8.17. This Change Attribute dialog box appears when you select more than one file.

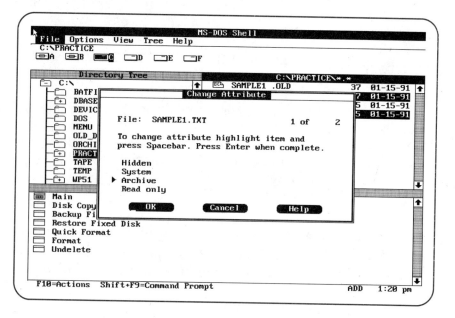

Figure 8.18. The Change Attributes dialog box.

8. Press Enter to set the attribute of that file to Read-only.

9. Repeat the procedure with the next file. When you press Enter, you will return to the File List.

Just to experiment, try to erase SAMPLE1.TXT now. Follow these steps:

1. Select the PRACTICE directory from the Directory Tree area of the Shell.

2. Select the SAMPLE1.TXT file name.

3. Select Delete... from the File pull-down menu.

   Notice the dialog box that appears (Figure 8.19).

4. Select No (or press Esc) to avoid deleting the file.

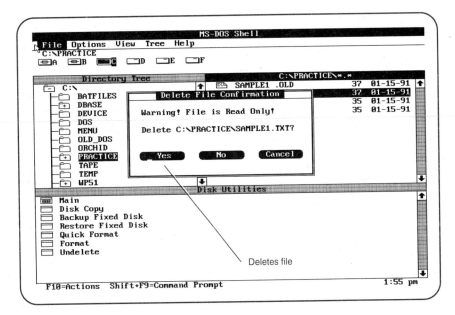

Figure 8.19. The Warning message displayed when you are about to delete a read-only file.

As you can see, changing a file to read-only gives you an extra level of protection against accidentally deleting an important file.

DOS 3 users (and DOS 5 users who prefer the command prompt) can use the ATTRIB (short for ATTRIBUTE) program to change a file's attribute. To the right of the ATTRIB command, you place the following symbols to assign or remove the read-only attribute:

+R   (to turn on the read-only attribute)

−R   (to turn off the read-only attribute)

To the right of the +R or –R symbol, specify the file (or an ambiguous file name) to which you want to assign the attribute. Here are the exact steps for changing the attribute of SAMPLE1.TXT to read-only (+R):

1. If your computer has a hard disk, enter the command CD \PRACTICE to access the PRACTICE directory (or enter B: to access the diskette that contains SAMPLE1.TXT).

2. Enter the command ATTRIB +R SAMPLE1.TXT.

Although nothing appears to happen because DOS just redisplays the command prompt, see what happens when you try to erase the file. Enter the command ERASE SAMPLE1.TXT. DOS displays the message Access denied because you cannot erase a file (via the command prompt) that has the read-only attribute assigned to it. (Enter the DIR command to prove to yourself that the file has not been erased.)

NOTE: ATTRIB is not a built-in command; DOS needs to have access to the ATTRIB.EXE file to run the program.

Resetting the Read-Write Attribute

At times you might need to change a file's attribute back to read-write so that you can modify or erase the file. Use the same basic procedure you used to turn on the read-only attribute. Because you really do not need to protect the SAMPLE1.TXT and SAMPLE2.TXT files, using the following steps changes them back to read-write files:

1. Select SAMPLE1.TXT and SAMPLE2.TXT from the Files Area of the File List screen.

2. Press F10 or Alt and then press Enter to pull down the File menu.

3. Select Change Attributes....

4. Select Change selected files one at a time.

5. Highlight Read only and press the Spacebar (so that the triangle marker disappears).

6. Press Enter.

Repeat the procedure with the next file.

To reinstate the Read-Write attribute by way of the command prompt, use the –R option with the ATTRIB command, as in the following step:

> C>

At the command prompt, enter the command ATTRIB –R SAMPLE1.TXT.

The SAMPLE1.TXT no longer has the read-only attribute turned on, so you can change it or erase it at the command line.

Renaming Directories

You can use DOS 5 to change easily the name of a directory. Rather than work through a sample exercise to demonstrate this technique (which you probably will not use often, other than to correct a misspelled directory name), I'll outline the general techniques for future reference. (You don't need to try the following steps if you don't want to change a directory name.)

NOTE: Techniques for renaming directories for DOS 3 users are discussed in Chapter 9.

To rename a directory using the DOS 5 Shell, you first need to ensure that none of the file names in the Files Area are selected (otherwise DOS renames the selected files rather than the directory). Here are the general steps you need to follow:

1. Access the File List screen.

2. Select the directory that you want to rename from the Directory Tree (by highlighting it or by clicking the directory name with your mouse).

3. Press F10 or Alt and then press Enter to pull down the File menu.

4. If the Deselect All option is available for selection, select it to ensure that no files are selected. (You would then need to redisplay the File pull-down menu.)

5. Select Rename....

6. When the Rename Directory dialog box appears (as shown in Figure 8.20), type the new name for the directory.

7. Press Enter.

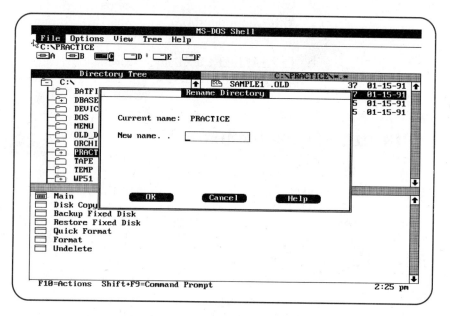

Figure 8.20. Dialog box to rename a directory.

After DOS completes the operation, the Directory Tree immediately displays the new directory name that you specified.

Deleting Directories

You can delete a directory at any time, provided you observe the following three rules:

❏ You cannot erase a directory that contains files. (You must first erase all the files.)

❏ You cannot delete a directory that is a parent to lower-level subdirectories (remember that you may need to expand the Directory Tree to see whether a directory has subdirectories.)

❏ You cannot delete the root directory.

All of the above rules are designed to protect the integrity of your files—by making it impossible for you to inadvertently erase all the files in a directory. (Also, because the root directory contains important DOS files, you are not permitted to delete it.)

> NOTE: Be sure that all the files in a directory are really expendable before you start deleting them.

To demonstrate the full series of steps you must execute to delete a directory, delete the TEST directory that you created earlier. First, you need to erase all the files in the directory before you can delete it, as outlined in the following steps. (If your computer does not have a hard disk, but you have created these directories on a diskette, you can follow the instructions by substituting the correct drive name for your computer.)

 If you are using DOS 5, you can delete a directory (if it contains no files) by using the Delete option from the File pull-down menu. Here are the exact steps:

1. Go to the TEST directory (if necessary, first expand the PRACTICE directory in the Shell and then select the TEST subdirectory).

2. Press Tab to move the highlight to the Files List area of the Shell.

3. Press F10 or Alt and then press Enter to pull down the File menu.

4. Select Select All. (This shortcut technique is much faster than selecting each file individually. After you select this option, note that all the files in the Files Area are indeed selected.)

5. Redisplay the File menu and then select Delete....

6. Press `Enter` to confirm the command.

7. When DOS presents the Delete File Confirmation dialog box, select `Yes` to delete the named file.

8. Continue until the `Files Area` displays `No files in selected directory`, indicating that the directory is now empty.

9. Redisplay the `File` menu.

10. Select `Delete....`

11. When the Delete Directory dialog box appears (as shown in Figure 8.21), select `Yes`.

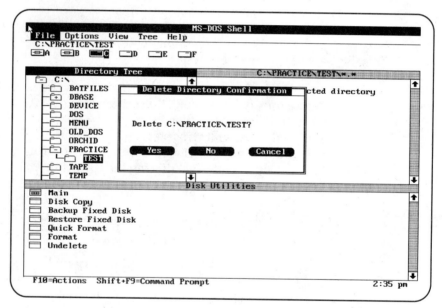

Figure 8.21. The Delete Directory dialog box.

When you return to the File List screen, notice that the TEST directory no longer exists beneath the PRACTICE directory.

 From the command prompt, you need to erase all the files on the directory that you want to delete. Then you need to access the parent directory and use the RMDIR or RD command (both are abbreviations for Remove Directory) to delete the directory. Here are the steps that enable you to remove the TEST directory:

NOTE: Remember, if your command prompt does not show the name of the current directory, enter the command PROMPT PG to make it display the current directory's name.

1. First enter the command CD \PRACTICE\TEST to access the TEST directory (beneath the PRACTICE directory).

2. Enter the command DIR and be sure that only the sample files used in this chapter are stored on the directory. (You can ignore the . and .. symbols.)

3. To erase all the files on the PRACTICE\TEST directory, enter the command ERASE *.*.

NOTE: DOS displays the Are you sure? (Y/N) warning message only when you try to delete all the files in a directory by using the ambiguous file name *.* (which matches all file names).

4. When you see the message Are you sure? (Y/N), type Y (for Yes) to erase all the files.

5. Enter the DIR command to verify that all files have been erased. (Again, you can ignore the . and .. symbols; DOS retains responsibility for creating and deleting these special directories.)

6. Change to the parent directory by entering the command CD... (This shortcut method is discussed in Chapter 9.)

7. Enter the command RD TEST.

To verify that the directory was deleted, change to the root directory (by entering the command CD \) and then enter the TREE command to view the directory tree. Notice that the PRACTICE directory no longer has the TEST subdirectory.

Please remember to be careful when deleting your own directories. Remember, if you are not using DOS 5, when you erase all the files in a directory, they are permanently lost.

Troubleshooting

If you make an error while managing files, DOS most likely will display one of the following error messages. Try using the suggested solutions to correct the error.

❏ `Access denied`: DOS displays this error message when one of the following problems arises:

> You tried to delete a directory that is not empty. (Erase all files in the directory first. Read-only files can be erased from the command prompt only after you change their attribute to read-write.)

or . . .

> You tried to create or rename a directory or file using a name that is already in use. (Use the TREE or DIR command to see whether the directory or file name already exists.)

or . . .

> You tried to create a file or directory using an invalid name. (Use a different name, avoiding the reserved device names and illegal characters.)

or . . .

> You tried to change or delete a read-only file. (Turn off the read-only attribute, using techniques described in the section "Resetting the Read-Write Attribute" in this chapter.)

❏ `All files in directory will be deleted!--Are you sure (Y/N)?`

> You entered a command that will erase all the files in a directory. Proceed with this command by typing Y (for Yes) or cancel the command by typing N (for No).

❏ `Attempt to remove current directory`

> You tried to delete the current directory. Enter the command `CD..` to move to the parent directory; then, try again.

❏ `Bad command or file name`

> Usually, you've tried to run a program that is not in the current directory or diskette, or you misspelled a command. This error message appears when you try to run the ATTRIB

command when the ATTRIB.EXE file is not in the current directory or diskette. (ATTRIB is a program, not a built-in DOS command.) Use the DIR command to search for the diskette or directory that contains the ATTRIB.EXE file and then try again, being sure to include the complete location and name of the file that you want to assign an attribute to. For example, the command `ATTRIB +R C:\PRACTICE \TEST\SAMPLE1.TXT` assigns the read-only attribute to the SAMPLE1.TXT file in the TEST subdirectory, regardless of your current directory.

❏ `Duplicate file name or file not found`

During a renaming operation, DOS was unable to find the file that you want to rename or was unable to rename the file because the file name already existed in the current directory. Use the DIR command to check current file names to determine which error is creating the problem; then, retry the command using an acceptable file name.

❏ `File cannot be copied onto itself`

The source and destination in a copy operation are identical, thus asking DOS to store two files with the same name in the same directory. Try again, being sure to specify a valid source and destination for the copy operation.

❏ `File creation error`

Either there is not enough room left on a diskette to store the new file, or you exceeded the maximum number of directory entries for the disk. (See Table 6.1 for directory limitations.)

❏ `File not found`

The file name specified in a command does not exist in the current directory or diskette. You are accessing the wrong directory or diskette, or you misspelled the file name. Check the Files Area in the DOS 5 File List or use the DIR command to see whether the file exists in the current directory or diskette.

❏ `Insufficient disk space`

(See `File creation error`)

❏ `Invalid drive specification`

You specified a disk drive (such as B:, C:, or D:), but there is no such drive on your computer. Try again, using a valid disk drive name.

❏ **Invalid filename or file not found**

> You tried to create or rename a file using an illegal file name. DOS also displays this error when you try to use the wildcard characters ? or * in a TYPE command, which can only accept a single, unambiguous file name.

❏ **Invalid parameter**

> Most likely, you used a forward slash (/) rather than a backslash (\) in a path name.

❏ **Invalid path, not directory, or directory not empty**

> While attempting to remove a directory, you either misspelled the directory name, specified a directory that has subdirectories, or specified a directory that still contains files. See the section "Deleting Directories" in this chapter for more information.

❏ **Invalid path or file not found**

> You tried to copy a file or change a file's attributes, but you used the name of a nonexistent directory or file. Use the DIR or TREE commands to determine the error and then try again with the proper directory and/or file names.

❏ **Invalid switch**

> A switch specified in your command is not available with the current command. Also caused by using a forward slash (/) rather than a backslash (\) in directory names.

❏ **No subdirectories exist**

> You ran the TREE command from a directory that has no subdirectories. Enter the command CD \ to access the root directory and then retry the TREE command.

❏ **Path not found**

> Your command specified the name of a directory that does not exist. Check your spelling or use the TREE command to check the directory tree for the correct path name.

❏ **Syntax error**

> You used the wrong format when you typed a command. Try again, being sure to use blank spaces, backslashes, and punctuation marks carefully. Also, be sure to put file names for the command in their proper order.

❏ `Write-protect error--Abort, Retry, Ignore` (or `Abort, Retry, Fail`)

You tried to store a new file on a diskette that is write-protected. Type A to abort the command and then remove the write-protect tab from the diskette (as discussed in Chapter 6).

Summary

This chapter discussed the basic file-management techniques needed for viewing, copying, renaming, deleting, moving, and protecting files. The next chapter expands on these techniques to help you manage even bigger jobs. For now, I'll review the basic techniques presented in this chapter:

❏ Regardless of which application programs you use on your computer, your file names need to conform to the rules imposed by DOS: an eight-character maximum length with no blank spaces or illegal characters, followed by an optional period and extension.

❏ To delete a directory, you must first erase all the files on it.

❏ From the command prompt, use the general format `TYPE` `filename` to view the contents of a file.

❏ From the command prompt, you can use the wildcard characters ? and * to perform operations on groups of files.

❏ At the command prompt, use the general format `COPY` `from-source-to-destination` to copy files.

❏ To rename a file from the command prompt, use the general format `RENAME` `old-filename new-filename`.

❏ To erase files at the command prompt, use the general format `ERASE` `filename`.

❏ To combine files into a single new file, use the general format `COPY` `file1+file2+file3 newfilename` where files to be combined are joined by plus signs and `newfilename` is the name of the resulting combined file.

❏ To move files from the command prompt, first use the COPY command to copy the file to the new directory and then use the ERASE command to delete the original file from the current directory.

❏ To protect files from accidental change or erasure at the command prompt, use the general format ATTRIB +R *filename* to turn on the read-only attribute.

❏ To delete a directory at the command prompt, first erase all the files on the directory by using the ERASE *.* command. Then access the parent directory and use the RMDIR or RD command to remove the directory.

To select a single file:

❏ Using the keyboard, move the Highlight Bar to the file you want to select.

❏ If you have a mouse, move the mouse pointer to the name of the file and click once.

To select two or more consecutive files:

❏ Using the keyboard, move the Highlight Bar to the first file of the group you want to select. Hold down the Shift key and press the ↑ or ↓ key until you have highlighted the entire group of files.

❏ If you have a mouse, click once on the name of the first file in the group you want to select. Then hold down the Shift key and click the last file in the group.

To select two or more nonconsecutive files:

❏ Using the keyboard, move the Highlight Bar to the first file you want to select. Press Shift-F8 to initiate the Shell's Add mode. Highlight the next file you want to select and then press Spacebar to select it. Continue with this procedure until you have selected all the appropriate files.

❏ If you have a mouse, click the name of the first file you want to select. Then hold down the Ctrl key and click the next file. Continue with this procedure until you have selected all the appropriate files.

❏ After selecting the files for an operation, pull down the File menu, either by pressing F10 or Alt and then Enter or by clicking the File option in the Menu Bar with your mouse.

❏ To view the contents of a file, select a single file name from the Files Area and then select the View File Contents option from the File pull-down menu. (Press F6 as a shortcut method of viewing a file.)

❏ Use the Copy... option in the File pull-down menu to copy a selected file (or files) to a new name on the current directory or to the same name in a different directory or disk drive. (Press F8 as a shortcut method of copying a file.)

❏ To copy files to a new directory or disk by dragging a file icon to a new location, hold down the Ctrl key, select the file or files, drag the file icon to the new directory or drive, and then release the left mouse button.

❏ To rename a file in the File List, select the file(s) you want to rename, and then select Rename... from the File pull-down menu.

❏ To delete files using the File List, select the files to delete and then select the Delete... option from the File pull-down menu. (Press Del as a shortcut method of deleting a file.)

❏ To move files using the File List, select the files to move and then select Move... from the File pull-down menu. (Press F7 as a shortcut method of moving a file.)

❏ To move files to a new directory or disk by dragging a file icon to a new location, hold down the Alt key, select the file or files, drag the file icon to the new directory or drive, and then release the left mouse button.

❏ To help protect a file from accidental change or erasure, turn on the read-only attribute by selecting Change Attributes... from the File pull-down menu.

❏ To rename a directory from the File List, select the directory name from the Directory Tree Area and then select Rename... from the File pull-down menu.

❏ To delete an empty directory from the Directory Tree Area in the File List, first erase (or move) all of its files, access the empty directory, and select Delete... from the File pull-down menu.

Power Tips for Everyone

So far, you've learned basic elements of DOS that you can use to run your computer effectively. Hopefully, the hands-on exercises have helped you see how DOS operates. However, when you begin working with your own programs and data, you will be managing many more directories and files than you worked with in the previous examples.

This chapter shows techniques that experienced DOS "power users" use every day to manage their files. In making the transition from "beginner" to "power-user" status, you need to keep in mind that your computer and DOS are designed to be *general purpose tools*. That is, using DOS effectively is not merely a matter of pushing the right button at the right time. Instead, using DOS effectively is a matter of knowing what tools are available and how and when to use those tools to solve a particular problem.

Therefore, beginning with this chapter, you will see fewer "hands-on" exercises, because there is no way of knowing exactly what files, programs, and directories are on your computer. Instead, I'll provide general examples of how and when to use a particular tool. As you read the chapter and gain experience using your computer, you'll see that these power tips will help you to work "smarter" rather than harder at your keyboard. The power tips are divided into two major categories, those for the DOS Shell and those for the command prompt. The usual icons mark the beginning of each section.

Power Tips for the DOS 5 Shell

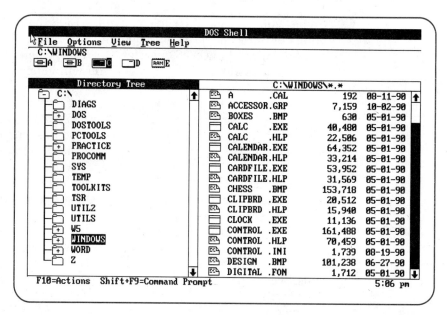 The DOS 5 Shell offers many advanced features to simplify managing directories and files on your computer. The first sections of this chapter will help you take advantage of these features and will become even more valuable as you gain experience and your file management problems become more complex.

Arranging File Names

As you know from previous experience, the File List area of the DOS 5 Shell displays the names of files in the current directory. If a directory contains more file names than can fit in the Files List, you can scroll through the file names using the ↑, ↓, PgUp, and PgDn keys, or you can click the Scroll Bar with a mouse (as discussed in Chapter 3). Figure 9.1 shows an example in which there are many more files in the current directory than can fit in the initial File List.

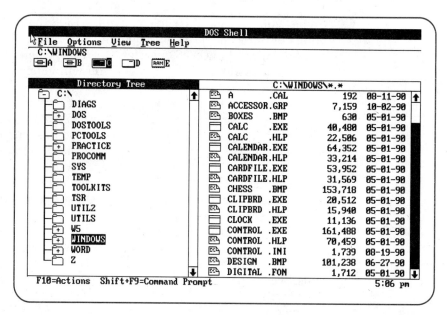

Figure 9.1. A sample File List with many files.

> NOTE: Refer to the inside front cover of this book if you need help making selections in the **File List**.

By default, DOS displays the names of all files in alphabetical order. You can rearrange the order of the display by pulling down the Options menu from the Menu Bar and selecting `File Display Options....` Doing so displays the Display Options dialog box, as shown in Figure 9.2.

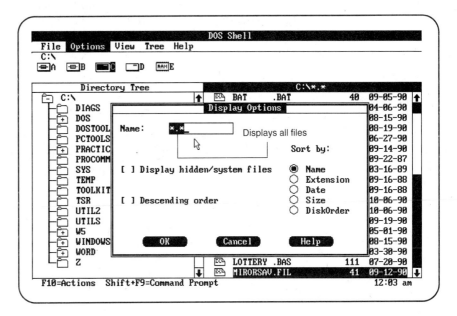

Figure 9.2. The Display Options dialog box.

Notice that there are four "fields," or areas that you can change. Initially, the cursor is in the `Name:` box, which lets you specify which files to display. The default specification (`*.*`) displays all files.

The next field, `Display hidden/system files`, enables the Shell to list files that have their hidden or system attributes set. Many utility programs create hidden files that contain valuable information about your directories and internal DOS files. DOS uses two "system" files (which are also hidden) and requires that they be stored in your root directory. Because most DOS commands do not work on hidden or system files, checking this box is of questionable value. To have the

Shell display these special files, press Tab to move the cursor to the brackets next to the `Display hidden/system files` prompt and press the Spacebar (or simply click between the brackets with the mouse). To toggle the option off, press the Spacebar (or click) again.

The next field, `Descending order`, reverses the normal order of a listing. For example, if you check this box (using the same procedure as with the previous box), the File List first displays files that begin with Z and ends with files starting with A.

Press Tab again (or use your mouse) to access the `Sort By:` field, which consists of five option buttons. When the cursor is in the `Sort By:` portion of the dialog box, you can use the ↑ and ↓ keys to access another sorting option and then press Enter to select that option. (Mouse users click once on an option button and then click once on the `Yes` button.) The effects of the various options are described in Table 9.1.

Table 9.1. Options for displaying file names.

Sort by Option	Effects
Name	File names are displayed in alphabetical order (the default selection).
Extension	File names are displayed in alphabetical order by extension.
Date	File names are displayed in descending date order (that is, the most recently created or modified files are displayed first).
Size	File names are displayed in descending (largest to smallest) order by size.
DiskOrder	File names are displayed in the order in which they were stored in the directory.

These options are useful for managing files several ways. For example, if you want to see groups of files with the same extension, select the `Extension` option. Because the file names are displayed in alphabetical order by extension, you can easily see all the directory's file names that have the same extension (such as the .BMP, or bit-mapped picture, files for Windows 3.0 in Figure 9.3).

Suppose that you want to see which files have been created or changed today (or recently). Select the `Date` option in the `Sort By:` section, and DOS displays all the files with the most recently created or modified files first.

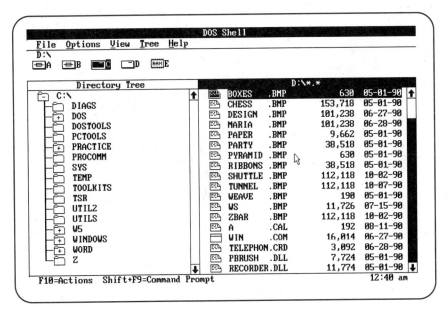

Figure 9.3. Sample file names arranged by extension.

The `DiskOrder` option displays file names in the order in which DOS stored them on the disk. Although this order might not be particularly useful in helping you find a file, it can help DOS perform operations a little more quickly, especially those that involve many files. When you initially select files for an operation, you should use one of the other `Sort By:` options to simplify the selection process; however, before you actually begin the operation, select the `DiskOrder` option to help make DOS more efficient.

Quickly Selecting Groups of File Names

Rearranging file names is only one way of managing large groups of files. By changing the `Name:` section in the Display Options dialog box from `*.*` to a more descriptive ambiguous files name, you can quickly isolate groups of file names for an operation.

For example, suppose that you want to copy some of the files with the extensions .TXT and .BMP from the current directory to a diskette. Instead of painstakingly selecting each file individually, you could use the Display Options dialog box to make the procedure a quick and easy one, as outlined below:

1. Select the Deselect All option from the File pull-down menu (if it is available) to cancel any currently selected files.

2. Pull down the Options menu from the Menu Bar, select File Display Options..., and change the file specifier to display only specific files (for example, from *.* to *.TXT to display only those files with the .TXT extension).

3. To select all these file names for an operation, select the Select All option from the File pull-down menu.

4. To isolate the next group of file names, select File Display Options... again from the Options pull-down menu and then change the file specifier (for example, from *.TXT to *.BMP).

5. Again, select all these files for the operation by selecting Select All from the File pull-down menu.

To verify that the appropriate files have been selected, select File Display Options... from the Options pull-down menu, and change the *.BMP file specifier to *.* (all files). You can also select another sort order for the file names by changing the Sort By: options. In Figure 9.4, the file names are listed in alphabetical order. As you can see, all files that have the .TXT and .BMP file extensions are selected. Now you can select any operation from the File pull-down menu to manage this group of files, or you could individually "deselect" files to exclude them from the operation. (In this example, you would select Copy....)

Selecting Files from Different Directories

In some operations, you might need to select files that are stored on separate directories (or disk drives). To do so, you must execute two basic steps:

1. Pull down the Options menu and enable the Select Across Directories option.

2. Simultaneously view the file names of two drives or directories by selecting Dual File Lists from the View pull-down menu.

To demonstrate the technique and capabilities of selecting files across directories, assume that you want to copy to drive A: all the files that have the extension .BAK from two directories, named PROCOMM and WINDOWS.

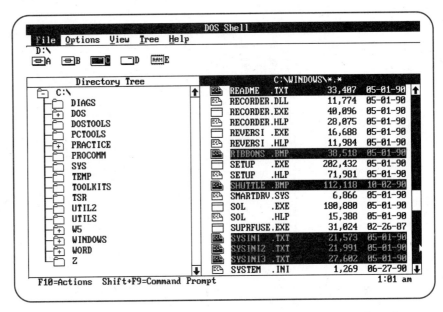

Figure 9.4. Files with the extension .TXT and .BMP are selected.

Your first step is to pull down the Options menu, use the ↓ key to highlight the `Select Across Directories` option and then press Enter (or you can simply click the option with the mouse). Notice that the menu immediately disappears without anything apparently happening. However, the next time you pull down the Options menu, you will notice a "bullet" next to the `Select Across Directories` option. This option is a "toggle" and works like the Enable Switcher toggle you learned about in Chapter 5: Select it once to turn it on; select it again to turn it off.

The preceding step is important when you want to use files from multiple directories in a single operation. If you forget to select the Select Across Directories option (see Figure 9.5), DOS automatically "deselects" files from the current directory as soon as you access another directory.

Next, to simplify your work, you can use the Dual File Lists view. To do so, pull down the View menu on the Menu Bar and then select `Dual File Lists`.

NOTE: Using the Dual File Lists screen and a mouse, you can "drag" an icon to copy or move a file from one directory to another directory on another drive (see Chapter 8 for a general description of this icon-dragging procedure).

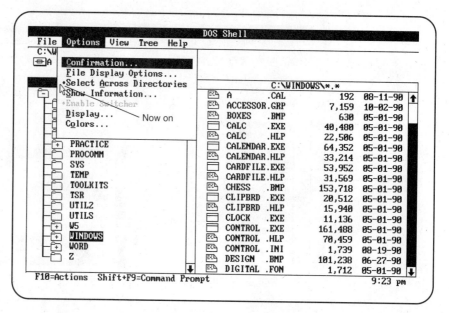

Figure 9.5. The Select Across Directories option is enabled.

The screen splits into two separate file areas. You can use the Tab key or your mouse in the usual manner to move the highlight around the screen. Notice that each window has its own Drives Area, Directory Tree, and Files List. Use the usual techniques to select drives, directories, and file names from each window. Figure 9.6 shows an example in which the top window is accessing the PROCOMM directory on drive C:, and the bottom window is accessing the WINDOWS directory on drive C:.

Because the Select Across Directories option is on, you can use the usual techniques to select files from the File List of both windows. For example, to select the .BAK files from both the PROCOMM and WINDOWS directories, first press F10 or Alt and then select `File Display Options...` from the Options pull-down menu. Change the file specifier in the `Name:` box to `*.BAK`. The `*.BAK` specifier appears at the top of the File List for both windows, and both windows display only those file names that have the .BAK extension, as shown in Figure 9.7.

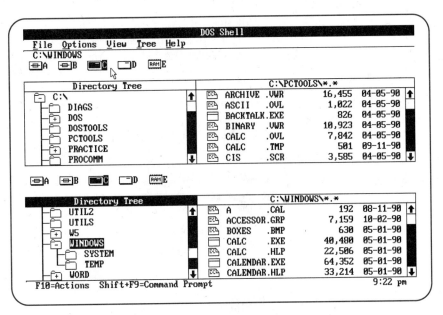

Figure 9.6. The File area split into two windows.

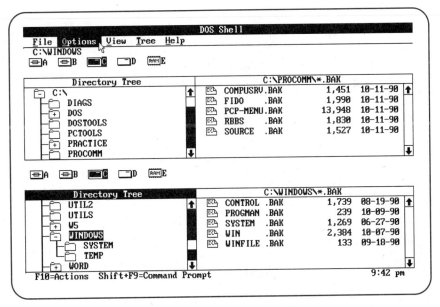

Figure 9.7. Both windows display only .BAK file names.

You still need to select all the files from both windows before performing your operation. You must do this individually for each window. That is, press the Tab key until the highlight is in the File List of the top window; press F10 or Alt and then press Enter to pull down the File menu; finally, select the Select All option. Press the Tab key a few times to move the highlight to the Files List of the bottom window. Again, press F10 or Alt, press Enter to pull down the File menu, and then select the Select All option. Notice that all the files with the .BAK extension are highlighted, as shown in Figure 9.8.

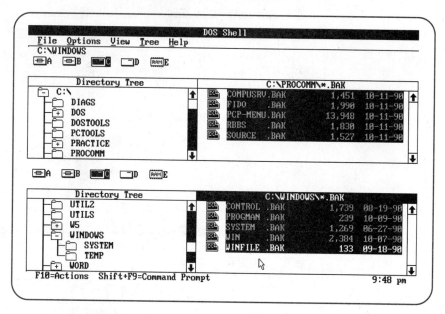

Figure 9.8. All .BAK files are selected on two directories.

> NOTE: You can also use the multiple file list to display the source and destination directories for Copy and Move operations.

Now that you've selected all the appropriate files for your operation, you can pull down the File menu and select an operation (such as Copy..., in this example). The operation automatically includes all the selected files from both directories.

You can also use the mouse to drag all selected files from both directories to a drive icon or to another directory in either of the displayed Directory Trees. See Chapter 8 for details about dragging file icons to a new location.

Selecting Files from Three or More Directories

NOTE: The Select Across Directories option is enabled when you see a "bullet" to the left of that selection in the Options menu.

Even though you cannot split the File List screen into more than two windows, you can still select files from more than two directories, as long as the Select Across Directories option is enabled. Using two windows isn't valuable when working with more than two directories, so switch back to the single File List screen by pressing F10 or Alt to access the Menu Bar and then selecting the Single File List option from the View pull-down menu.

Next, select Display File Options... from the Options pull-down menu and enter a file specifier in the Name: box that identifies the types of files you want to select. (Press Backspace or enter *.* to view all file names.) Now you can use the usual techniques to access various directories and to select files from each directory. Because the Select Across Directories option is enabled, DOS "remembers" all of the files that you select from each directory. This lets you move freely from directory to directory, so that you can select whatever files you need.

When you finish selecting files, merely pull down the File menu, and select the operation that you want to perform. (Remember, however, that the View File Contents option is available only when a single file name is selected.)

The next section discusses techniques that will help you to manage all your files and directories on a hard disk.

Searching All Directories for a File

As you add more directories and files to your hard disk, you might find it increasingly difficult to remember where every individual file is stored. You can use the DOS 5 File List to locate the directory quickly and easily that any file is stored in, even if you do not know the exact file name that you are looking for.

For example, suppose that you wrote a letter to a person named Smith, but you do not remember in which directory you stored the letter. Although you remember that you named the file SMITH, you aren't sure of the extension that you used after the base name. Fortunately, there's a quick way to search all the directories on your hard disk for a file beginning with the letters SMITH.

First, you must display the All Files screen, which displays all file names on all directories. To do so, press F10 or Alt to access the Menu Bar, pull down the View menu, and then select the `All Files` option. Your screen changes slightly, but don't be concerned about that.

Next, you must change the file specifier to SMITH.* (all files starting with the letters SMITH followed by any extension). To do so, select `Display File Options...` from the Options pull-down menu, and change the file specified in the `Name:` box to `SMITH.*`. Press Enter after you type the new file specifier.

As Figure 9.9 shows, the File List shows the names of all files that match the SMITH.* ambiguous file name. However, notice that the area that used to show the Directory Tree now displays specific file information instead.

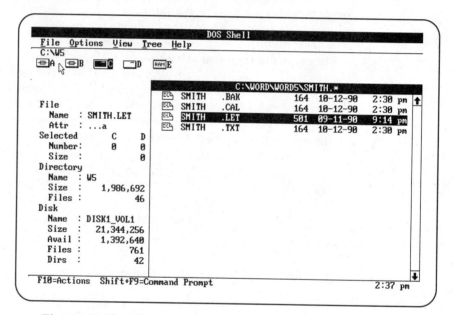

Figure 9.9. The File List's All Files screen showing SMITH.* files.

As you move the highlight through the file names in the File List, the left side of the screen displays the drive and directory on which the file is stored (as well as additional information). For example, notice in Figure 9.9 that SMITH.LET is stored on C:\W5 (the W5 directory on drive C:). Having located the file, you can select `Single File List` from the View pull-down menu and then use the Directory Tree to access both the W5 directory and the file.

Other Features of the All Files Screen

You can use the File List's `All Files` screen to manage your files much like you use the "normal" single-directory file display. This can be a great tool when you want to perform an operation on all directories, such as copying or deleting a group of files.

For example, suppose that you don't have much space left on your hard disk, so you decide to copy all the .BAK (backup) files to diskettes and then erase those files from your hard disk. To perform this operation quickly, first select the `All Files` option from the View pull-down menu to ensure that all directories are accessible. Then, select `Display File Options...` from the Options pull-down menu and change the file specifier in the `Name:` box to `*.BAK`. (Then press Enter as usual.)

The File List area displays all the .BAK files on the entire hard disk. Next, select `Select All` from the File pull-down menu to select all of these files. As Figure 9.10 shows, these few simple steps selected every single .BAK file on the entire hard disk.

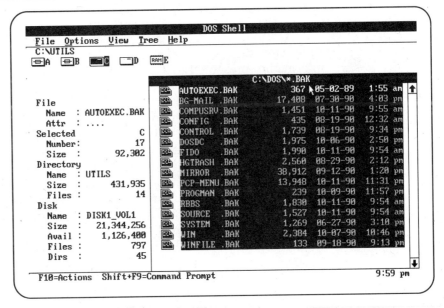

Figure 9.10. All .BAK files on the hard disk are selected.

> NOTE: See the next section, "Speeding Large Operations," for tips on speeding up copying and deleting operations.

Next, you can select any operation from the File pull-down menu as you normally would. In the current example, you would select `Move...` and then specify a destination for all the selected files to be moved to. When the move is complete, DOS displays the message `No files match file specifier` in the File List. Because you've just moved all the selected files to a floppy disk drive, your hard disk no longer contains any files with the .BAK extension.

> NOTE: To redisplay all the files on your hard disk, select `File Display Options` from the Options menu and change the Name: field to `*.*`.

Furthermore, if your computer has multiple disk drives, you can select new drives from the Drives Area at the top of the screen, and then you can select files from the multiple drives. DOS keeps track of all the files selected on all drives and directories. After you finish selecting files, DOS lets you perform file operations that might involve several disk drives and dozens of directories.

As a bonus, the All Files screen also displays important information about your disk, as summarized in Table 9.2. You can also view the information presented in Table 9.2 without displaying the File List's `All Files` screen. To do so, move the highlight to any file name in the Files List and then pull down the Options menu and select `Show information....` A window appears, as shown in Figure 9.11. Press Esc or select OK to leave the window; press F1 or Select Help to display a help window.

Remember, if you want to switch between the All Files screen and the "standard" screens so that you can select files from both, you should first pull down the Options menu and be sure that the `Select Across Directories` option is enabled (marked with a bullet, as described earlier in this chapter). Otherwise, DOS automatically deselects all files when you switch from the All Files display to other displays.

Table 9.2. Information displayed by the system `ALLFiles` view.

Heading	Displays
File Name	Name of the currently highlighted file
Attr	Attributes assigned to the file: a—placeholder for any unassigned attribute r—read-only attribute h—hidden attribute is on a—archive attribute is on (See ATTRIB in Appendix B for further details)
Selected	Drives that have been accessed
Number	Number of selected files on each drive
Size	Combined sizes of selected files
Directory Name	Directory that the highlighted file is stored on
Size	Amount of disk space used by the files in the directory
Files	Number of files stored on the directory
Disk Name	Electronic label assigned to disk (if any)
Size	Total storage capacity of disk
Avail	Total available disk space remaining on disk
Files	Total number of files stored on disk
Dirs	Total number of directories on disk

Speeding Large Operations

When you select a large group of files and then copy or erase them, DOS stops and asks for permission to erase or overwrite existing files. DOS also asks for permission to copy or move a file when you use a mouse to drag that file to a new location. These safety features are designed to help prevent accidentally erasing an important file or moving a file to an incorrect location. However, if you always take precautions before these operations and you are certain that you want to copy, delete, or move the selected files, the constant "checking for permission" can become tiresome.

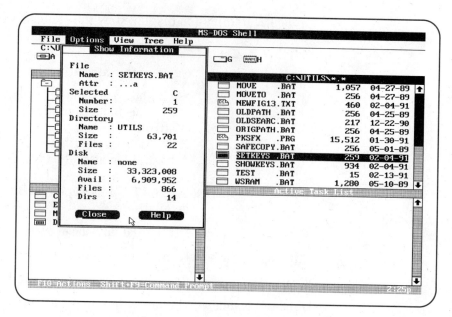

Figure 9.11. The Show Information window.

To prevent DOS from asking for permission before deleting or erasing a group of files, first select all the files for the operation. Then, press F10 or Alt and pull down the Options menu. Select `Confirma-tion...` to display the dialog box shown in Figure 9.12. Note that the `Confirm on Delete`, `Confirm on Replace`, and `Confirm on Mouse Operation` options are marked with an X.

You can turn off any (or all) options by moving the highlight to the option and pressing the Spacebar once (or by clicking the box with your mouse). Press Enter or select OK after you remove the Xs; then select the operation you wish to perform from the File pull-down menu.

> NOTE: Each time you start your computer, the Confirm on Delete, Confirm on Replace, Confirm on Mouse Operation options are automatically turned on.

Note that once you turn off these options (by removing the Xs), DOS leaves them off for future operations unless you turn them on again (by putting the Xs back into the boxes). In addition, after you leave the DOS Shell by pressing the F3 (or Alt-F4) key and then restart the Shell, DOS always turns on these options. However, if you leave the Shell by pressing Shift-F9 (as discussed in the next section), these options are not reset to on when you return to the Shell.

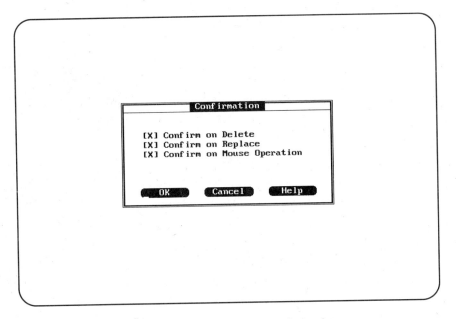

Figure 9.12. The Confirmation dialog box.

An Alternative Method of Leaving the Shell

In preceding examples in this book, you pressed the F3 key or the Alt-F4 key-combination to leave the DOS Shell and access the command prompt. To return to the DOS Shell, you typed the command DOS SHELL and pressed Enter. When you use this technique to exit and return to the Shell, DOS always resets the File List to its original settings and automatically deselects any selected files.

NOTE: The Shift+F9=Command message prompt always appears on the screen when this exiting technique is available.

If you want to switch back and forth between the command prompt and the Shell without losing any of your current settings or file selections, press Shift-F9 (hold down the Shift key and press F9).

When the command prompt appears, the top line on the screen displays information about the current DOS version, followed by the command prompt.

You can now enter any DOS commands and even change directories. When you are ready to return to the Shell, type EXIT and press Enter.

NOTE: You can also select the Command Prompt option from the Program List Main Group screen as an alternative to pressing Shift-F9.

This alternative technique for exiting the Shell has the advantage of retaining selected files and other settings when you return. However, keep in mind that DOS accomplishes this by keeping the Shell in memory (RAM), occupying about 7KB of space. If you inadvertently enter the DOSSHELL command—rather than EXIT—to return to the shell, a new copy of the Shell is stored in RAM. If you make this mistake many times, you probably will have so many DOS Shells in RAM that you cannot run other programs or memory conflicts "lock up" the computer, requiring that you reboot by simultaneously pressing the Ctrl, Alt, and Del keys, as discussed later in this chapter.

If you are at the command prompt, but you cannot remember whether you exited using F3 (or Alt-F4) or the Shift-F9 option, type EXIT and press Enter. If the Shell does not reappear, you must have used F3; type DOSSHELL and press Enter. No harm done!

Power Tips for Command Prompt Users

 DOS 3 users (and DOS 5 users who use the command prompt) have many powerful shortcut techniques at their disposal. These are discussed in the sections that follow. Note that several examples involve *external* DOS commands that are stored on disk rather than in RAM. If you have a problem using any of these commands, see the Troubleshooting section near the end of this chapter.

Please keep in mind that you can also refer to the inside back cover of this book for a quick summary of DOS commands and the operations they perform. All of the commands listed on those pages are described in more detail in Appendix B.

Shortcuts to Using Directories

NOTE: If your DOS prompt does not show the name of the current directory or path, enter the command `PROMPT $P$G` to change the prompt.

In previous chapters, you learned the basics of using the MKDIR (or MD) command to create new directories and the CHDIR (or CD) command to change directories. As discussed previously, entering the command `MD TEST` creates a new directory named TEST beneath the current directory. Entering the command `CD TEST` takes you to the TEST directory only if you are currently accessing the parent directory.

You can get a little more control over these commands by specifying the root directory name (\) as the starting point for the operation. For example, suppose that you are accessing a directory with the path name PRACTICE\TEST. If you enter the command `MD FINANCES`, DOS automatically creates the new directory beneath the current directory so that the full directory path actually becomes PRACTICE\TEXT\FINANCES.

However, if you enter the command `MD \FINANCES`, DOS uses the root directory as the starting point, thus placing the FINANCES directory one level below the root. In other words, entering the command `MD \FINANCES` is a shortcut for entering the following two commands:

```
CD \
MD PRACTICE
```

You can also use the root directory as the starting point for a CHDIR, or CD, command. The following examples show how different uses of the root directory (named \) affect the CD command:

`CD FINANCES`	Changes to the FINANCES directory only if that directory is exactly one level below the curent directory.
`CD \FINANCES`	Changes to the FINANCES directory from any level, provided that the FINANCES directory is exactly one level below the root directory.

```
CD \SALES\FINANCES
```
Changes to the FINANCES directory (beneath the SALES directory) from any directory on the disk (that is, regardless of the current directory).

Keep in mind that there is no quick-and-easy way to simultaneously access both a different drive and directory in a single command. For example, if you are currently accessing floppy disk drive A:, you cannot enter the command `C:\SALES\FINANCES` to change to the SALES\FINANCES directory on drive C:. Instead, you must first change drives and then change directories, by entering the following two commands:

```
C:
CD \FINANCES\SALES
```

The . and .. Shortcuts

As you might recall from previous chapters, the DIR command always displays two "file" names (. and ..) even though there are really no such files on the directory. The . and .. are symbols: . is an abbreviation for the current directory, and .. is an abbreviation for the parent directory. You can use these symbols as shortcuts in your commands.

For example, suppose that your current directory path is \SALES\FINANCES. To move up to the \SALES directory from FINANCES, you need enter only the `CD..` command. Entering the command `CD..` again takes you up another level to the root directory. (Entering `CD..` from the root directory does nothing, because there are no higher-level directories.)

The .. symbol can also be used to quickly switch between lower-level subdirectories. For example, suppose that your current directory path is FINANCES\SALES\1991 and you want to change to the lowest subdirectory on the following path FINANCES\SALES\1992. Instead of typing the lengthy command `CD \FINANCES\SALES\1992`, you need to enter only the command `CD ..\1992`.

You can use the .. symbol in any command. For example, suppose that you want to copy all the files from the \FINANCES\SALES\1991 path to the lowest directory on the \FINANCES\SALES\1992 path. If \FINANCES\SALES\1991 is the current directory, you can enter either the command `COPY *.* \FINANCES\SALES\1992` or the much shorter command `COPY *.* ..\1992` (because .. "fills in" the parent directory named \FINANCES\SALES).

> NOTE: In case you are wondering, experienced DOS users pronounce *.* as *star dot star*, .. as *dot dot*, and . as *dot*.

The . command can be used to specify the current directory's name. For example, suppose that your current directory path is \FINANCES\SALES and you want to copy all of SALES files to the next lower directory (on the \FINANCE\SALES\1992 path). Instead of typing the lengthy command `COPY *.* C:\FINANCES\SALES\1992`, use . to stand for the current directory by entering the command `COPY *.* .\1992`.

The . symbol can also be used to specify all the files on a directory, as a shorthand way of saying `*.*`. For example, if you really wanted to take a shortcut, you could enter the command `COPY . .\1992` rather than `COPY *.* .\1992`.

Furthermore, if the destination for the copy is the name of a directory that is exactly one level below the current directory, you really need not specify the parent directory or even the .. symbol. Hence, if the current path is \FINANCES\SALES and you want to copy all its files to the \FINANCE\SALES\1992 subdirectory, the ultimate shortcut command would be

```
COPY . 1992
```

In English, the command above says, "Copy everything from the current directory (.) to the subdirectory named 1992, which is one level below the current directory."

For beginners, the shorthand method of entering commands can be a bit abstract. If in doubt, use the longhand method. For example, even though the command `COPY C:\FINANCES\SALES\*.* C:\FINANCES\SALES\1992` takes a bit more typing than `COPY . 1992`, it still gets the job done and is much more explicit and easier to understand.

Incidentally, the fact that DOS allows you to use . in place of `*.*` is the reason that DOS always displays a warning message when you try to erase all the files on a directory. Some users, on seeing the . and .. symbols in the DIR display, might attempt to erase the "mysterious files" by entering the command `ERASE .`, which is identical to entering `ERASE *.*`.

> NOTE: The ERASE and DEL commands are identical.

Early versions of DOS displayed the message `Are you sure (Y/N)` before erasing the files, but many users simply pressed `Y`, for Yes, thinking they were erasing only one file—named `.`! This warning has been improved in DOS 5, which adds the message `All files in directory will be deleted!` when you enter the ERASE `.`, ERASE `..`, or ERASE `*.*` commands.

Shortcuts to Specifying Files

All DOS commands make "assumptions" about the locations of files based on the information you provide . . . and omit. You can omit any information from a command, as long as you want DOS to assume that the omitted information refers to the current drive, directory, and file name. Note in the following examples how DOS makes assumptions based on omitted information:

`C:\SALES\MYDATA.DAT`	Assumes that MYDATA.DAT is in the \SALES directory of disk drive C:.
`\SALES\MYDATA.DAT`	Assumes that MYDATA.DAT is in the \SALES directory of the current drive.
`MYDATA.DAT`	Assumes that MYDATA.DAT is in the current drive and directory.

You can use any *file specification* (that is, drive name, path, and file name) in any DOS command, both to save time in moving from one directory to the next and also to shorten commands. For example, if you are currently accessing disk drive D:, and you want to see the contents of C:\SALES\MYDATA.DAT, you don't actually need to change drives or directories. Instead, merely specify the drive, the full path, and the file name in the TYPE command, as follows:

```
TYPE C:\SALES\MYDATA.DAT
```

If you completely omit the destination in a COPY command, DOS assumes the destination is the current location. For example, suppose that you are currently accessing the \SALES directory of disk drive C: and you want to copy all the files from disk drive A: to this directory. You can completely omit the destination from the COPY command (because the destination is the current drive and directory) and specify only the source (diskette drive A:), as follows:

```
COPY A:*.*
```

In English, the previous command says, "Copy all files (*.*) from drive A: to here." To copy all the .BAK files from the \MARKTNG directory to the current directory, you could enter either

```
COPY \MARKTNG\*.*
```

or . . .

```
COPY C:\MARKTNG\*.*
```

In all these examples, the names of the copied files have been omitted, which ensures that the copies have the same names as the originals. Suppose, however, that you want to copy all the .WKQ files from a directory named \QUATTRO to floppy disk drive A:. In addition, you want to change the extensions on the copied files from .WKQ to .BAK. Assuming that your current directory is \QUATTRO, you could enter this command to perform both operations:

```
COPY *.WKQ A:*.BAK
```

Note that *.WKQ specifies the source of the copy (all .WKQ files on the current directory), whereas *.BAK specifies the names of the destination files (same first name, but .BAK extension).

All these shortcuts might be a little confusing at first, but remember shortcuts are optional, not required. If you want to copy all the files from the \SALES directory to the \MARKTNG directory, the command `COPY C:\SALES\*.* C:\MARKTNG` always works, regardless of what your current drive and directory are.

Sorting the DIR Display

The DIR command always displays file names in the order they were created, the oldest files first and the newest files later. If you prefer a more organized sort order, you can choose from two options: Use the SORT command in combination with the DIR command, or use one of the new switches added to the DIR command in DOS 5.

Programs such as the SORT command that rearrange output are called "filters." (Remember, as an external DOS command, the SORT.EXE file must be accessible from the current drive and directory.)

NOTE: The ¦ character, called *pipe*, is Shift-\ on most keyboards (hold down the Shift key and press \).

For example, to list file names in alphabetical order in the DIR display, enter the command

```
DIR | SORT
```

To print this alphabetical list of file names, enter the command

```
DIR | SORT >PRN
```

You can also sort file names in the DIR display by extension, size, or date. For details, see the SORT command reference in Appendix B.

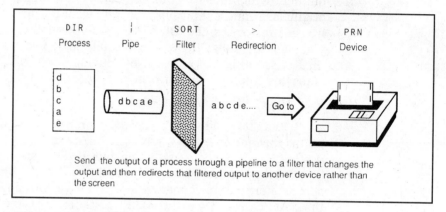

Send the output of a process through a pipeline to a filter that changes the output and then redirects that filtered output to another device rather than the screen

Figure 9.13. An illustration of how a pipe and filter work with a command.

With the DIR command in DOS 5, you can use an internal switch to duplicate the previous operations. For example, to list a directory's file names in alphabetical order, enter the DIR command with the /O: switch:

```
DIR /O:N
```

The /O: (or "option") switch lets you display files by name (N), extension (E), date and time (D), size (S), and with directories listed before files (G). If you add a minus sign (–) to any of the these letters, you reverse the order of the display. For example, the command

```
DIR /O:-N
```

displays files in reverse alphabetical order (with *Z* names first and *A* names last). For details about this handy new method of displaying directory listings, see the DIR command reference in Appendix B.

Displaying Files from a Certain Date

 You can have the DIR command display all the files on a directory that were created or last modified on a certain date. This is handy when you are looking for a file that you created earlier today or yesterday, but you cannot remember the full name of the file.

> NOTE: To use FIND with DIR or any other command, the DOS FIND.EXE file must be accessible from the current directory.

The first step is to use the CD command to change to the directory on which the file is stored. You then might want to enter the `DATE` command to check the current system date. Note that the format of the date used in the command must match the format displayed by the DIR command. Most versions of DOS use the `mm-dd-yy` format (see the previous sample command). However, some foreign versions of DOS might require the `dd-mm-yy` format (that is, 30-04-91) or the `yy-mm-dd` format (91-04-30). To determine the appropriate date format for your version of DOS, enter the `DIR` command and look at the date assigned to each file. (Press Enter at the prompt instead of entering a new date.)

Next, use the DIR command followed by the pipe (¦), the FIND command, and the date you're interested in enclosed in quotation marks. For example, to display the names of files that were created on April 30, 1991, you would enter the command:

```
DIR ¦ FIND "04-30-91"
```

Searching All Directories for a File

It is possible to use a single command to search all the directories on your hard disk from the command prompt. However, I must warn you that if you have an older, slower computer, the search can be quite time-consuming. Nonetheless, the technique is a valuable one, and it can come in handy in certain situations.

For example, suppose that you use the Microsoft Excel spreadsheet program to prepare a budget. After spending many hours, you save the spreadsheet file with the file name BUDGET. Because Excel automatically adds the extension .XLS to any spreadsheet that you save, the file actually is stored under the file name BUDGET.XLS.

Now, suppose that the next day, when you try to bring your BUDGET spreadsheet back into Excel, Excel tells you that it cannot find a file named BUDGET.XLS. Undoubtedly, your first reaction is a sinking feeling: Either you forgot to save the file or the computer somehow failed to save the file as you'd requested. (The latter reason is less likely to explain the missing file.)

What probably happened is that you indeed saved the file, but you were not paying attention to which directory you saved it in. Before you panic, search for the file in all the directories on your hard disk. You could use the `CD` and `DIR BUDGET.*` commands to access and search each directory, but there is an easier way.

The CHKDSK command provides an optional `/V` switch that displays the names of every file on the hard disk. You can see this for yourself by first changing to the directory that holds the CHKDSK.COM file and then entering the command `CHKDSK /V`.

You can also use the CHKDSK /V command in conjunction with the FIND command to restrict the search to a particular file name or a string of characters. Remember, however, that both the CHKDSK.COM and FIND.EXE files must be on the current directory; otherwise, DOS merely displays the infamous `Bad command or file name` error message.

Look at exactly how you can quickly search all the directories on your hard disk for a file named BUDGET. First, change to the directory in which CHKDSK.COM and FIND.COM are located. Then enter the command

```
CHKDSK /V ¦ FIND "BUDGET"
```

Notice that you must separate the two commands with the pipe character (¦), you must enclose in double quotation marks the file name you are searching for, and you must enter the file name in uppercase letters. This is the basic syntax of all searches.

After a pause (which might be either a few seconds or a few minutes), your screen displays the location and name of all files that contain the name BUDGET, as in the example shown in Figure 9.14.

If your missing file appears on the list, you know exactly where to find it. For example, if you were looking for BUDGET.XLS (the spreadsheet created with the Microsoft Excel program), you know that it is stored in a directory named WINDOWS. You can COPY it from that directory to whatever directory you intended to store it on in the first place.

Of course, another common error is misspelling a file name while saving it, but not realizing you've made such an error. For example, you might have typed BUDHET, rather than BUDGET, when you saved the spreadsheet.

```
C:\>chkdsk /v | find "BUDGET"
        C:\ACCTNG\Q1BUDGET.DAT
        C:\WP\WPFILES\BUDGET.TXT
        C:\WINDOWS\BUDGET.XLS
        C:\DBASE\BUDGET89.DBF
        C:\DBASE\BUDGET89.MDX

C:\>
```

Figure 9.14. Results of searching all directories for the BUDGET file.

You cannot use the * and ? wildcard characters with the FIND command, but you can narrow or broaden the search by searching for more or fewer characters. For example, entering the command

    CHKDSK /V | FIND "BUD"

displays all file (and directory) names that contain the letters BUD.

The CHKDSK and FIND commands are also handy for finding program files that have a particular extension, such as .COM or .EXE. For example

    CHKDSK /V | FIND ".COM"

displays the names of all files on all directories that have the .COM extension. The command

    CHKDSK /V | FIND ".EXE"

displays the names of all files on all directories that have the .EXE extension.

If your search presents more files than can fit on the screen, you can channel the output to the printer instead. Merely redirect the output to the printer by using the >PRN symbol, as in the following example:

    CHKDSK /V | FIND ".EXE" >PRN

If, however, the CHKDSK.COM, FIND.EXE, and MORE.COM files are all available from the current disk and directory, enter the following command to pause for a keypress after each screenful of information:

```
CHKDSK /V ¦ FIND ".EXE" ¦ MORE
```

FIND is also handy for searching for specific words or phrases within files. You can even use it to search for text or files that do not match some value (that is, display all files that do not have the .EXE extension). See the reference to the FIND command in Appendix B for additional applications.

Refining Your Copies

> NOTE: To use XCOPY, the XCOPY.EXE file must be accessible from the current drive and directory.

DOS Version 3.2 and all later versions include a program named XCOPY.EXE (for eXtended COPY) that can help you more specifically select files for copying. Two of this command's eight optional switches are particularly handy:

/D:date	Copies files that were created or changed on (or after) a specified date.
/S	Copies all files from the current directory and all subdirectories beneath it.

To demonstrate the power of XCOPY, suppose that at the end of the day, you want to copy new and modified files from your hard disk onto a floppy diskette in drive A:. Furthermore, you are certain that you've been working with files only in the \FINANCES and \FINANCES\SALES directories. Assuming that today's date is April 30, 1991, and that you are currently accessing the \FINANCES directory, you could enter the following command to copy only the files that were created or modified on (or after) the current date:

```
XCOPY *.* A: /D:04-30-91 /S
```

Note that the current date is specified in the mm-dd-yy format. However, if you are using a foreign version of DOS, you must use the appropriate format for your dates, as displayed by the DATE and DIR commands. Note also that the /S switch copies files from all subdirectories beneath the \FINANCES directory, but because the /D switch is also set, only those files that were created or modified on or before April 30, 1991 are copied. If you start the XCOPY command from the root directory and use the /S switch, DOS copies all files from all directories on the disk.

XCOPY offers several other features that can help you speed and refine file copying. See the XCOPY command reference in Appendix B for more details.

Renaming Directories

Unlike DOS 5, earlier versions of DOS do not provide an easy way of renaming a directory. Instead, you need to create a new directory with the name you want to use, copy all the files from the old directory to the new directory, erase the files from the old directory, and then delete the old directory. Look at an example in which you change the name of a directory named BOOKS to BOOKS_92. (Both the new and old directories are one level below the root.)

First, you would enter the command CD \BOOKS to change to the existing directory. You might want to enter the DIR command and make a note of how many files are in the directory.

Next, enter the command MD \BOOKS_92 to create the new directory. Note the use of the backslash to ensure that the new directory is one level below the root directory. If you had entered MD BOOKS_92 DOS would have created the new directory below the current directory.

Your next step is to enter the command COPY *.* \BOOKS_92 to copy all the files from the current directory to the new directory. To verify that all the files have been copied, enter the command DIR \BOOKS_92 and be sure it contains the same number of files as the BOOKS directory.

When you are certain that all the files have been copied, enter the ERASE *.* command to delete the files from the current directory. When DOS asks whether you are sure, press Y and Enter. Enter the DIR command to be sure all the files have been erased. (You might need to change the attributes on read-only files to erase them.)

Now you can delete the BOOKS directory. First, move up to the root directory by entering the CD \ command. Then, enter the RD \BOOKS command to remove the empty directory. Now all the files that used to be in the BOOKS directory are in a directory named BOOKS_92, and the BOOKS directory no longer exists. Use the usual CD \BOOKS_92 command to change to the new directory.

A Simple Way to Correct Errors

Aren't you annoyed when you type a long command like `COPY C\MARKTNG\BUDGET*.* C:\SALES\BUDGET` and DOS responds with an error message like `Path not found`? You look at the command and realize that because you left out the colon after the C in the source, you have to type the whole line again. Well, guess what? You do not have to retype the entire command: DOS always remembers the last command you entered, and it provides several keys to help you change that command. The most commonly used of these special editing keys are

F1 (or →)	Recalls one character from the previous command.
F2	Pressing F2, then any character, recalls all characters up to, but excluding, the typed character.
F3	Recalls all remaining characters from the previous command.
F4	Pressing F4, then any character, deletes all characters up to, but excluding, the typed character.
FS	Re-edit current command before pressing the Enter key.
Ins (or Insert)	Lets you insert new characters into the command.
Del (or Delete)	Deletes one character from the previous command.
Backspace	Erases the character to the left of the cursor.
Esc	Cancels all current changes. Press Enter after Esc to redisplay the command prompt.

To fix the example command above, you would first press → six times to recall the first six characters, as follows:

```
C> COPY C
```

NOTE: After you press the Ins (or Insert) key, you can insert as many characters as you need.

Next, press the Ins (or Insert) key so that you can insert a character; then press the colon so that the command now looks as follows:

```
C> COPY C:
```

Finally, press the F3 key to recall all the remaining characters from the previous command. The screen displays the following:

```
COPY C:\MARKTNG\BUDGET\*.* C:\SALES\BUDGET
```

and you can press the Enter key to enter the newly corrected command.

Look at a different example. Suppose that you type the command `DOR C:\SALES` to view the names of files on the SALES directory. Of course, DOS returns the error message `Bad command or file name` because there is no command called `DOR`. To correct the error, press → (or F1) to recall the D, press the letter `I` (this replaces the letter O), and then press F3 to retrieve the rest of the command.

The screen now shows `DIR C:\SALES`, so you can press Enter to enter the command. (Note that in this example, the letter *I* replaced the letter *O*; it was not inserted before the letter *O* because you did not press the Ins key before typing the letter I.)

Another common error occurs when you type a path containing a directory name that does not belong. For example, suppose that you enter the command `COPY C:\SALES\MARKTNG\*.* A:` and DOS returns `Path not found`. You look at the command and remember that \MARKTNG is at the same level as \SALES, not below it. Therefore, you need to remove \SALES from the command.

To do so, press the F2 key, then the letter S to bring back all characters up to the S,

```
COPY C:\
```

Next you want to delete all characters up to, but excluding, the first letter *M*. Press the F4 key and then press the letter M. (The deletion has no immediate effect on the screen.) Next, press the F3 key. Now the screen shows

```
COPY C:\MARKTNG\*.* A:
```

Because the command is now correct, you can press Enter to execute the operation.

Besides being handy for correcting errors, the ability to retrieve the preceding command is valuable for entering several similar commands. For example, suppose that you want to copy a file named TEMPLATE.WK1 to four different directories, named SALES\QTR1, SALES\QTR2, SALES\QTR3, and SALES\QTR. To do so, first enter the initial command, which might look as follows:

```
COPY C:\123\TEMPLATE.WK1 C:\SALES\QTR1
```

Press Enter, and when the copy is finished, press F3 to recall the command. Press Backspace once to change the command to

```
COPY C:\123\TEMPLATE.WK1 C:\SALES\QTR
```

Then, press 2 to change the command to

```
COPY C:\123\TEMPLATE.WK1 C:\SALES\QTR2
```

and again press Enter. You can repeat the general procedure to copy the file to the SALES\QTR3 and SALES\QTR4 directories.

Canceling a Command

Suppose that you start a process, such as copying a large group of files, but then you change your mind after DOS begins carrying out its orders. You can interrupt the command (any command) by pressing either Ctrl-C or the Break key. (The Break key on most keyboards is Ctrl-Pause— hold down the Ctrl key and press the Pause key. On other keyboards, you press Ctrl-Scroll Lock or Ctrl-Break.)

WARNING: Rebooting deletes all data stored in RAM and makes no attempt to save any data to the disk. Avoid pressing Ctrl-Alt-Del when a program other than DOS is in control of your computer.

Although it's unlikely, there may be times when your computer gets "hung up," and nothing you do at the keyboard can get it working correctly again. In such cases, you can *reboot* the system (also called a *warm boot*) by simultaneously holding down the Ctrl, Alt, and Del keys. (If your computer has no hard disk, put your DOS Startup diskette in drive A: before you press Ctrl-Alt-Del.)

Your screen will go blank for a while. Then DOS goes through a start-up process similar to when you first turn on the computer. Everything then should be back to normal.

Troubleshooting

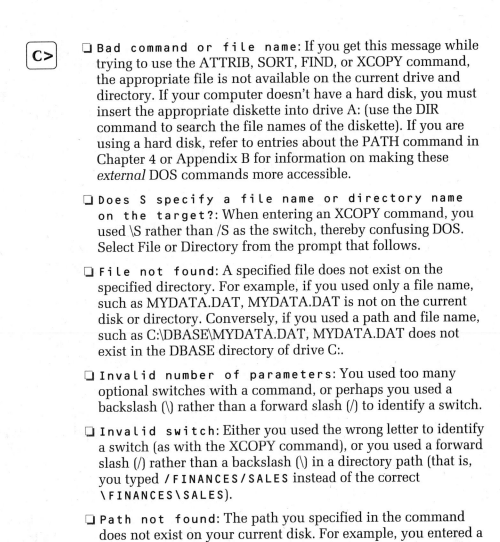

❏ `Bad command or file name:` If you get this message while trying to use the ATTRIB, SORT, FIND, or XCOPY command, the appropriate file is not available on the current drive and directory. If your computer doesn't have a hard disk, you must insert the appropriate diskette into drive A: (use the DIR command to search the file names of the diskette). If you are using a hard disk, refer to entries about the PATH command in Chapter 4 or Appendix B for information on making these *external* DOS commands more accessible.

❏ `Does S specify a file name or directory name on the target?:` When entering an XCOPY command, you used \S rather than /S as the switch, thereby confusing DOS. Select File or Directory from the prompt that follows.

❏ `File not found:` A specified file does not exist on the specified directory. For example, if you used only a file name, such as MYDATA.DAT, MYDATA.DAT is not on the current disk or directory. Conversely, if you used a path and file name, such as C:\DBASE\MYDATA.DAT, MYDATA.DAT does not exist in the DBASE directory of drive C:.

❏ `Invalid number of parameters:` You used too many optional switches with a command, or perhaps you used a backslash (\) rather than a forward slash (/) to identify a switch.

❏ `Invalid switch:` Either you used the wrong letter to identify a switch (as with the XCOPY command), or you used a forward slash (/) rather than a backslash (\) in a directory path (that is, you typed `/FINANCES/SALES` instead of the correct `\FINANCES\SALES`).

❏ `Path not found:` The path you specified in the command does not exist on your current disk. For example, you entered a command like `COPY C:\SALES\*.* A:`, but your hard disk does not have a directory named SALES.

Summary

The power tips presented in this chapter will help you use your computer more effectively and with much less effort. Following is a summary of the power techniques you've learned:

❏ To cancel an operation before DOS finishes it, press the Break key (Ctrl-Pause or Ctrl-Scroll Lock on most computers).

❏ At the command prompt, you can use the . symbol to refer to the current directory, and the .. symbol to refer to the parent directory.

❏ Enter the command `DIR ¦ SORT` to view file names in alphabetical order. Alternatively, you can use the DIR /O:N switch to list file names alphabetically.

❏ Enter the command `DIR ¦ FIND` followed by a date in `mm-dd-yy` format to locate files that were created or modified on or after a particular date.

❏ DOS versions 3.2 and higher offer the XCOPY command to help you gain more control over copy operations (discussed in detail under XCOPY in Appendix B).

❏ The →, F1, F3, F4, Ins, Del, and Backspace keys can be used as shortcuts for correcting errors in commands and for repeating a series of similar commands.

❏ To rearrange the order of file names in the File List in the `File List` section of the Shell, pull down the Options menu and select `File Display Options...`; then press Tab and select a sort order from the `Sort by:` options.

❏ To quickly select all files with a similar extension from the File List, first pull down the Options menu and select `File Display Options....` Then enter an ambiguous file name in the `Name:` box and press Enter. Finally, pull down the File menu and select the `Select All` option.

❏ If you want to perform an operation with files that are stored on separate directories, pull down the Options menu and enable the Select Across Directories option, either by highlighting it and pressing Enter or by clicking the option once with your mouse.

❏ To gain access to all files on a disk—regardless of the directories they are stored on—pull down the View menu, and select All Files.

❏ To prevent DOS 5 from asking for permission before erasing or overwriting files or before performing a mouse operation, pull down the Options menu, select Confirmation..., and remove the Xs from the Confirm on Delete, Confirm on Replace, and/or Confirm on Mouse Operation options.

❏ To leave the DOS Shell without disrupting current settings or selected file names, press Shift-F9.

❏ To return to the DOS Shell after pressing Shift-F9, enter the command EXIT rather than the usual DOSSHELL command.

Customizing Your System

The next three chapters discuss techniques that let you customize many of the elements of your computer system, including the keyboard, screen displays, the printer, and the hard disk. In addition, DOS 4 and 5 users learn techniques for customizing the DOS Shell. The techniques presented in these chapters make your computer easier and simpler to use.

Topics in the following chapters include

❏ Creating and editing DOS text files with the DOS 5 Editor.

❏ Simplifying hard disk usage by making important programs accessible from all directories.

❏ Customizing the DOS Shell so that you can run programs merely by selecting Shell options.

❏ Important techniques for backing up your hard disk and recovering from a hard disk crash.

❏ Taking advantage of special screen features, such as color, blinking, and reverse video.

❏ Using your printer effectively.

❏ Customizing the actions of function keys so that they perform special operations.

Creating and Editing Files

While reading subsequent chapters, you might want to use two special DOS files to configure your computer. One file, named CONFIG.SYS, tells DOS how to *configure* (set up) your hardware (described in more detail later). You use a second file, named AUTOEXEC.BAT, to customize and simplify the use of your computer.

> NOTE: Don't worry if you cannot find your own AUTOEXEC.BAT or CONFIG.SYS file right now; your computer might not even have them yet.

To *edit* (change) these files, you use a program called an *editor*. There are hundreds of editors available for DOS microcomputers: These include word processing programs, such as WordPerfect, and small "desktop" text editors that come with programs such as Sidekick and PC Tools Deluxe. In addition, DOS comes with two somewhat simplified text editors—EDLIN (which is in all versions of DOS) and EDIT (which is in only DOS 5).

EDLIN is a decade-old "line editor" that is both clumsy and difficult to use. Avoid using it. If you have DOS 5, use the EDIT editor instead. Optionally, you can use your favorite word processor, as long as you remember a few basic rules of thumb.

Using a Word Processor to Edit DOS Text Files

Word processors are by far the easiest and most powerful tools for editing DOS text files. However, there is one catch to using a word processor: Most word processors assume you are creating documents that people will be reading, rather than files that DOS will be reading. Because of this, most word processors insert special formatting characters into files.

The word processor uses these formatting characters to display the document on the screen or to compose a page for the printer, but it never actually shows them on the screen, so you normally don't see them.

> NOTE: The `Bad command or file name` error message is sometimes caused by hidden formatting characters, but other problems, such as misspelling a command, also cause this error message to appear.

However, DOS sees the formatting characters, and it becomes quite confused by them. As soon as DOS encounters one of these formatting characters in either the AUTOEXEC.BAT or CONFIG.SYS file, it stops trying to read the file and returns an error message, such as `Bad command or file name`. This has been known to drive many computerists half crazy, because they cannot see the formatting characters that DOS sees, and therefore they cannot figure out what is wrong.

To show you the "invisibility" of these formatting characters, look at an example using WordPerfect as the word processing program. Figure 10.1 shows the contents of a sample AUTOEXEC.BAT file displayed on the screen by WordPerfect.

The WordPerfect screen does not appear to contain any strange-looking formatting characters in the text, just the normal letters, numbers, and punctuation symbols from the keyboard. (The last line is displayed by WordPerfect and is not part of the file.)

Now, suppose that after you change the file on the WordPerfect screen, you save it. Later, when you restart the computer and DOS attempts to read the file, it displays an error message (such as `Bad command or file name`). When you use your word processing program to view the file, everything appears to be in order.

Before you waste a lot of time trying to figure out what's wrong, check a file to see whether it contains special characters by using DOS, not the word processing program, to display the contents of the file. DOS displays all characters—including any special formatting characters that the word processor is hiding.

```
rem *********************************AUTOEXEC.BAT
c:\dos\mode com1:9600,n,8,1,r
c:\dos\mode lpt1:,,b
prompt $p$g
path c:\dos;d:\pdox35
loadhigh f:\mouse1\mouse
loadhigh c:\dos\print.exe /d:lpt1
loadhigh c:\dos\doskey.com
c:\dos\mirror c: /tc /td /te /tf
md h:\temps
set temp=h:\temps
path h:\temps;c:\dos;c:\wp51;d:\utils;d:\dbase;f:\fontware
rem set dtl_lblopt=on
call macros
dosshell




C:\AUTOEXEC.BAT                              Doc 1 Pg 1 Ln 3.5" Pos 1"
```

Figure 10.1. Sample AUTOEXEC.BAT file on WordPerfect's screen.

5 ⎹ DOS 5 users can look at the contents of any file by selecting its name from the Files List and then selecting `View File Contents` from the File pull-down menu. As you can see in Figure 10.2, WordPerfect was indeed hiding some strange-looking formatting characters, particularly at the top of the file. This is definitely not a plain ASCII text file and therefore, is not a file that DOS can read.

> NOTE: ASCII is pronounced *AS-key.*

Incidentally, a "plain text" file (one that contains only letters and numbers and no strange formatting codes) is also called an ASCII file (or ASCII text file). ASCII is an acronym for American Standard Code for Information Interchange and as the name implies, is a standardized means of representing letters and numbers in computers.

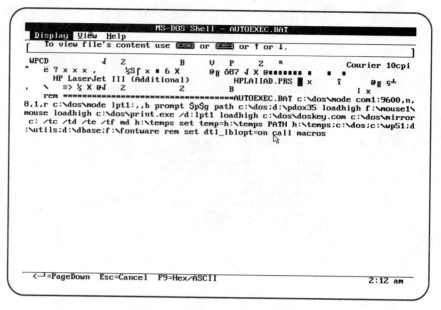

Figure 10.2. DOS's view of the WordPerfect file.

 Command prompt users can use the TYPE command to view the contents of a file. In this example, entering the command `TYPE C:\AUTOEXEC.BAT` shows that the file is not an ASCII text file, as Figure 10.3 illustrates.

Therefore, if you use a word processor to edit DOS text files, there are two very important points to keep in mind:

❏ You must take special steps to ensure that all DOS text files are saved in ASCII text format.

❏ The only way you can see whether a text file contains formatting codes is by using the `View File Contents` option in the DOS Shell File List or by using the TYPE command at the DOS command prompt.

We'll discuss both points in more detail later.

WARNING: Never use a word processing program to edit a program file with the .COM or .EXE extension. These are not DOS text files.

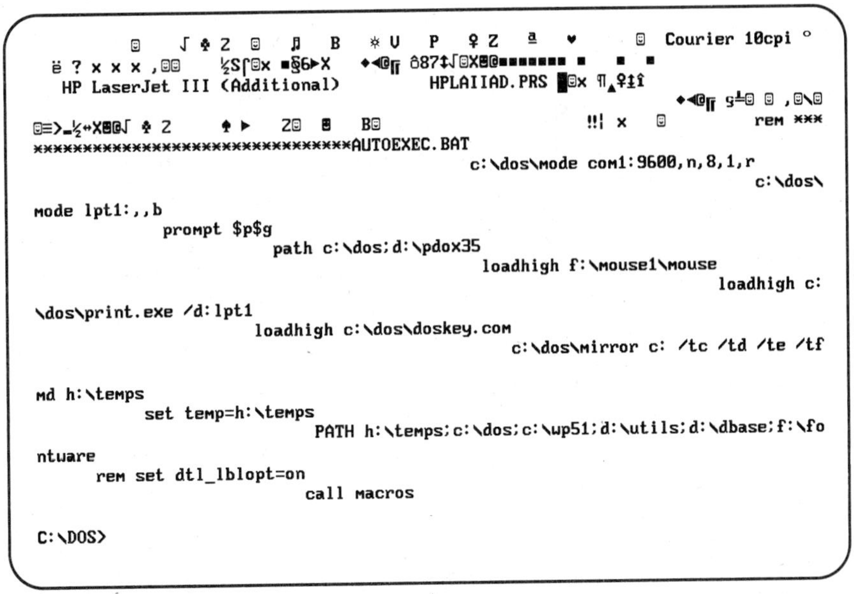

```
 ⊟    ♫ ♦ Z  ⊟   ♫  B   ☀ U   P   ♀ Z   ª   ♥       ⊟  Courier 10cpi  °
ë ? x x x ,⊟⊟    ½S⌐⊟x ∎§6►X   ◆◄⊞⎕ ∂87‡⌡⊟X⊟⊞∎∎∎∎∎∎∎ ∎   ∎ ∎
HP LaserJet III (Additional)        HPLAIIAD.PRS ▌⊟x ¶▲♀‡î
                                                         ◆◄⊞⎕ g⊥⊟ ⊟ ,⊟\⊟
⊟≡>_½�++X⊟⊟⌡ ♦ Z      ♦ ►    Z⊟  ⊟  B⊟            !! x    ⊟         rem ✻✻✻
✻✻✻✻✻✻✻✻✻✻✻✻✻✻✻✻✻✻✻✻✻✻✻✻✻✻✻✻✻✻✻AUTOEXEC.BAT
                                            c:\dos\mode com1:9600,n,8,1,r
                                                                  c:\dos\
mode lpt1:,,b
             prompt $p$g
                      path c:\dos;d:\pdox35
                                        loadhigh f:\mouse1\mouse
                                                           loadhigh c:
\dos\print.exe /d:lpt1
                  loadhigh c:\dos\doskey.com
                                         c:\dos\mirror c: /tc /td /te /tf

md h:\temps
        set temp=h:\temps
                         PATH h:\temps;c:\dos;c:\wp51;d:\utils;d:\dbase;f:\fo
ntuare
      rem set dtl_lblopt=on
                           call macros

C:\DOS>
```

Figure 10.3. The TYPE command's view of a non-ASCII file.

This chapter discusses general techniques for creating and editing DOS text files using the popular WordPerfect word processing program. However, we cannot do much more than explain how to display the file on the screen and how to save it properly. To learn the editing features of your word processor, you need to refer to that program's documentation or to a book that explains that program.

NOTE: Before using your own word processing program, be sure to read the section "Where to Store AUTOEXEC.BAT and CONFIG.SYS" later in this chapter.

If you have a word processing program other than WordPerfect, you need to learn how to use it to create, edit, and save ASCII text files. In particular, if you are using one of the following word processing programs, look for information describing the options listed next to each program's name:

Program	Topic for ASCII Files
DisplayWrite	ASCII COPY TO FILE
Microsoft Word	Save UNFORMATTED

Program	Topic for ASCII Files
MultiMate	CONVERT program, or ASCII format
Sprint	File Translate, Export ASCII file
WordStar	Nondocument mode

Editing DOS Text Files with WordPerfect

If you currently own a copy of WordPerfect and have installed it on your computer, you can use it to edit DOS text files. Assuming you have a hard disk (which is practically a necessity with WordPerfect), here are the basics of using WordPerfect to edit DOS Text files, starting at the DOS 5 Shell:

1. In the Drives area of the Shell, select the drive that WordPerfect is stored on.

2. Select the name of the WordPerfect directory (usually WP51 for WordPerfect 5.1) from the Directory Tree Area.

3. Move the highlight to the file name WP.EXE in the Files List.

4. Run the program by pressing Enter or by double-clicking the highlighted name.

5. At the WordPerfect Edit screen, press Text In/Text Out (Ctrl-F5), select DOS Text, select Retrieve (option 2).

6. Type the location and name of the file you want to edit (for example. C:\AUTOEXEC.BAT) and press Enter.

The file (if it exists at the location you specified) appears on the WordPerfect Edit screen, like the example shown in Figure 10.1 (Don't worry if your AUTOEXEC.BAT file looks different or if you don't understand what the commands in the file mean right now; you'll learn about them soon.)

NOTE: Don't worry if the symbol ^Z appears at the bottom of the file. You can leave it there, or you can type over it, but do not type a ^Z into the file if you erased the existing one.

Now you can use any of WordPerfect's capabilities to change the file (but, again, I cannot explain how to use the program here). When you finish making changes, you need to save the file in ASCII format.

Saving an ASCII File with WordPerfect

When you save an ASCII text file that's been created or changed by WordPerfect, be sure to follow these steps:

1. Press Text In/Text Out, `Ctrl-F5`.

2. Select `DOS Text`, then `Save`.

3. Press `Enter` to accept the suggested location and file name when the screen displays the `Document to be saved` prompt.

4. Press `Y` when the screen asks whether to `Replace` the original file with the new file.

5. To exit WordPerfect, press Exit (`F7`).

6. When the message `Save document? (Y/N)` appears, press `N` (otherwise, you'll replace the ASCII Text file version that you just saved with a formatted version that DOS can't read).

7. When the `Exit WP? (Y/N)` message appears, press `Y`.

Now you're back to DOS.

Using EDIT to Edit DOS Text Files

NOTE: EDIT is a DOS 5 program; if you have an earlier version of DOS and must use EDLIN, see the EDLIN entry in Appendix B.

The DOS Editor (which I'll refer to as EDIT) can also be used to edit DOS text files. This full-screen text editor is easy to learn, comes with extensive on-line help, and performs several sophisticated operations, such as *global search-and-replace* and *block moves*.

Another advantage to using EDIT is that it always stores its files in ASCII text format, so you never have to worry about formatting codes being embedded in your files.

Running EDIT

The Editor is stored in a file named EDIT.COM. If you are using diskettes, EDIT.COM is stored on the Edit disk of your installed DOS disks. You need to put that disk in drive A to use the Editor. If you are using a hard disk, EDIT.COM is stored in your DOS directory.

1. Select Editor in the Program List near the bottom of the screen by double-clicking or highlighting and pressing Enter.

2. When the File to Edit dialog box appears, type the complete location and name of the file you want to edit (for example C:\AUTOEXEC.BAT) and press Enter (or select OK).

If you prefer to use the DOS 5 command prompt, enter the EDIT command followed by the name of the file you want to edit. For example, EDIT C:\AUTOEXEC.BAT.

The file you specified (if it exists) appears on the screen, ready for editing, as in the example shown in Figure 10.4.

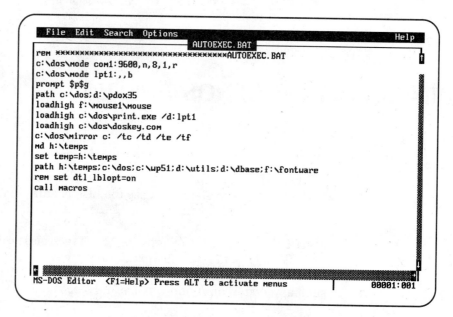

Figure 10.4. EDIT's editing screen.

Using EDIT's Help Screens

5 Like the Shell, EDIT offers context-sensitive help. You can get to the help screen by pressing F1 at any time or by selecting Help from the · upper right corner of the screen (by clicking or pressing Alt+H).

EDIT also offers a Survival Guide, which you can view by pressing F1 when no particular menu or option is selected. You can also get to the Survival Guide by running EDIT without providing the name of the file to edit (either by entering the command EDIT alone at the command prompt or by leaving the Open File dialog box empty when starting EDIT from the Shell. When you do so, you'll see the opening screen shown in Figure 10.5, and you can then press Enter to go to the Survival Guide.

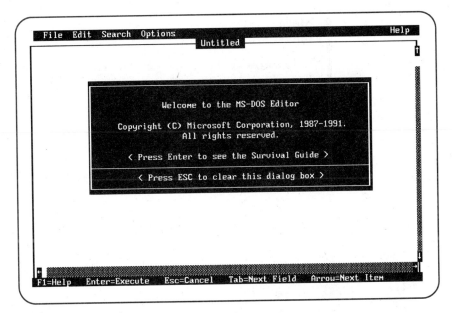

Figure 10.5. The EDIT "Welcome" screen.

In the Survival Guide, you'll see certain topics enclosed in triangular brackets. For more information on one of those topics, move the cursor to it and press Enter, or double click the topic with the mouse. Table 10.1 lists other keys and mouse operations that you use with Edit's help system.

Table 10.1. EDIT help keys.

Actions	Keystrokes
Display EDIT Help	F1 (or click the right mouse button)
Exit Help	Esc
Display "Getting Started"	Shift-F1
Pull down the Help menu	Alt-H
Move to next topic	Tab
Move to previous topic	Shift-Tab
Move to next topic starting with char	char
Move to previous topic starting with char	Shift-char
Display previous topic (20 accesses are stored)	Alt-F1 (or double-click the Back button)
Display the next Help topic	Ctrl-F1
Display the previous Help topic	Shift-Ctrl-F1
Switch between help window and edit screen	F6

To leave the help screens, press Escape.

Basic Menu Operations

 Using EDIT's menus is identical to using the menus in the DOS Shell. From the keyboard

1. Press the Alt key to activate the Menu Bar

2. Press the first letter of a menu you want to view.

3. Use the arrow keys to position the highlighter to the option you want, then press Enter.

Of course you can select menu items in EDIT using your mouse:

1. Point to and then click in the Menu Bar the name of the `menu` that you want to view.

2. To select an option from a menu, point to and then click the `option`.

Like the Shell's pull-down menus, menu options that are followed by an ellipsis (`...`) lead to a dialog box when selected. If there's a shortcut key available for the option, the shortcut key is shown to the right of the option (there are four examples on the Edit pull-down menu).

Typing in EDIT

The main role of EDIT, of course, is to let you create and edit text. If you want to try some of the techniques I'll be talking about, start with a "practice" file. Here's how:

1. If you are already in the Editor, exit (select `Exit` from the File pull-down menu).

2. If you are at the command prompt, run the Shell (type `DOSSHELL` and press `Enter`).

3. If the Main group is not displayed in the Program List near the bottom of the screen, select `Main`.

4. Select `Editor` from the Program List (by highlighting and pressing `Enter` or by double-clicking).

5. Type `PRACTICE` and press `Enter` or click `OK`.
   Notice that the name of your file is PRACTICE.TXT (displayed in reverse video below the center of the Menu Bar). EDIT automatically adds the file extension `TXT` to any file name for which you do not specify an extension.

Before you begin typing text in your practice file, you should realize that EDIT is not a word processor—you will not want to use it to create lengthy or complex documents. The most noticeable of EDIT's limitations are

no word wrap	When you type more than 80 characters on one line, the words don't automatically wrap to the next line; instead, your characters are entered on the same line and your screen display shifts to the right.
no undo feature	If you accidentally delete a block of text, you cannot recover it; you have to retype the entire block.
no automatic backup	When you change an existing file and then quit the editor, EDIT does not create a backup of the original file.

NOTE: ASCII files created by Microsoft Word and WordPerfect may contain extremely long lines that make the files unsuitable for viewing in EDIT.

The word-wrap limitation requires an additional comment. If you load ASCII files created by word processors that do not insert carriage returns at the end of their screen lines (that is, that use automatic word wrap), EDIT will extend those lines off the right side of the screen until it reads a carriage return. Thus, your document might have a width of several thousand characters—not an ideal size for viewing on an 80-column display! When you use your word processor, remember to press ↵ at the end of each line (instead of relying on automatic word wrap), so your document won't have such wide lines.

To create a practice file, type the following text. (Remember, you must press Enter at the end of each line of text to move to the next line. Press Enter twice if you want an extra blank line.)

```
Knowledge is of two kinds.
We know a subject ourselves,
or we know where we can find
information about it.

Boswell, Life of Johnson,
1775
```

When you finish, your screen should look like Figure 10.6.

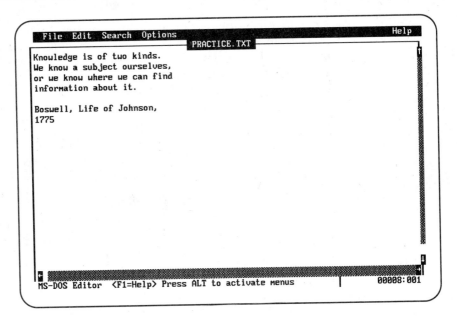

Figure 10.6. Some sample text typed on the Edit screen.

Cursor Movement in EDIT

To edit a document, you must first be able to move the *cursor* to specific locations in your text. The cursor shows your current location—that is, the location at which a character will appear when you next press a key. EDIT's *editing cursor* is a small underline character.

> NOTE: The editing cursor is a small underline character; the *mouse cursor* is a small dark block.

 Note, however, if you are using a mouse, your screen also displays a block-like mouse cursor. The mouse cursor lets you quickly change locations in your text without having to use the keyboard. Position the mouse cursor at a new location and click the left mouse button; the editing cursor immediately moves to the new location. For example, to use the mouse to move the editing cursor from anywhere in your practice text to the first character, position the mouse cursor on the K in `Knowledge` and click the left mouse button.

If you are using the keyboard, you have many cursor movement keys from which to choose. However, in small documents, you probably will only need to use the arrow keys to move throughout your text. The ← and → keys move the cursor one character to the left or right, and the ↑ and ↓ keys move the cursor one line up or down.

In EDIT, you use two sets of keyboard commands for most actions—a Microsoft set and a WordStar-compatible set. If you already know the WordStar editing commands, you will be able to use most of the functions of EDIT immediately. Table 10.2 includes the complete list of keyboard commands for moving the editing cursor throughout your text.

Table 10.2. EDIT cursor-movement keys.

Actions	Microsoft Keystrokes	WordStar-Compatible Keystrokes
Left one character	←	Ctrl-S
Right one character	→	Ctrl-D
Left one word	Ctrl-←	Ctrl-A
Right one word	Ctrl-→	Ctrl-F
Up one line	↑	Ctrl-E
Down one line	↓	Ctrl-X
First indention of current line	Home	
Beginning of current line	Ctrl-Q,S	
Beginning of next line	Ctrl-Enter	Ctrl-J
End of line	End	Ctrl-Q,D
Top of screen	Ctrl-Q,E	
Bottom of screen	Ctrl-Q,X	
Sets bookmarks (maximum of 4)	Ctrl-K,0-3	
Accesses set bookmarks	Ctrl-Q,0-3	

The last two commands require a little explanation. Because EGA and VGA displays can show many more words on a single screen than can a CGA display, EDIT has a built-in feature—*bookmarks*—that you can use to move the cursor quickly around the screen. Bookmarks are preset locations in your document that can be accessed by a simple combination of keys.

For example, to set a bookmark, move the cursor to a location in the first line on your screen and press

`Ctrl-K`

Then, press a number from 0 through 3. If you place the 0 bookmark in line 1 and the 1 bookmark in line 6, you can instantly move the editing cursor to bookmark 0 by pressing

`Ctrl-Q 0`

and then quickly move to bookmark 1 by pressing

`Ctrl-Q 1`

You can insert as many as four bookmarks on a screen at any one time. Although you probably don't need this feature on a standard 25-line display or if you use a mouse, it can be helpful for keyboard users with high-resolution VGA monitors.

Text-Scrolling in Edit

With EDIT, you can not only move the cursor around the screen, you can also move the text itself. For example, if you want to display the next *page* (screenful) of text, it would be tedious to move the cursor to the last line of the screen and then press the ↓ key 25, 43, or 60 times (depending on your video display adapter). Instead, you can press the PgDn key. Likewise, to display the previous screenful of text, you need only press the PgUp key. EDIT contains a full array of such text-scrolling keys, as shown in Table 10.3.

Table 10.3. Text-scrolling keys.

Actions	Microsoft Keystrokes	WordStar-Compatible Keystrokes
Up one line	Ctrl-↑	Ctrl-W
Down one line	Ctrl-↓	Ctrl-Z
Up one page	PgUp	Ctrl-R
Down one page	PgDn	Ctrl-C
Left one window	Ctrl-PgUp	
Right one window	Ctrl-PgDn	

NOTE: Chapter 3 includes a complete discussion of mouse operations.

 If you are using a mouse, click the vertical Scroll Bar (or drag the Slider Box) to move toward the beginning or end of your file, and you only click the horizontal Scroll Bar (or drag the Slider Box) to move the display right or left on a long line. For a complete discussion of these mouse operations, see the "Using Scroll Bars" section of Chapter 3.

Because EDIT doesn't have word wrap but can load documents with lines longer than 80 columns, you may need to use the Ctrl-PgDn key combination (or click the horizontal Scroll Bar with the mouse) to view the text at the end of a long line.

Practice using all of the cursor-movement and text-scrolling commands. When you feel comfortable with them, you are ready to begin editing.

Editing a Document

5 EDIT includes a full array of editing commands. However, for editing simple files, such as AUTOEXEC.BAT and CONFIG.SYS, or for jotting down quick notes, you can get by with a few basic editing keys. Type your text and erase any mistakes with the commands listed in Table 10.4.

Table 10.4. Basic Editing Keys in EDIT.

Key	Purpose
Backspace or Ctrl-H	Delete character to left of cursor
Del or Ctrl-G	Delete character at the cursor
Ctrl-T	Delete from the cursor to the end of the word
Ctrl-Y	Delete entire line
Ctrl-QY	Delete from the cursor to the end of the line
Ins or Ctrl-V	Switch between Insert and Overwrite modes

Most of the commands in Table 10.4 are straightforward and easy to understand. However, the last item is best illustrated by an example.

Assume that you have your PRACTICE file on the screen and that you want to change the word `kinds` in the first line to `types`. Using the commands in the previous table, you could perform this operation in several different ways. After you move the editing cursor to the `k` in `kinds` you could

Type `type` and press Del four times

or

press Del four times and type `type`

or

press Ctrl-T and type `types`

and so on. However, there is a simpler method.

By default, EDIT is in *insert* mode. When you type a character, it is inserted at the cursor location; all characters to the right move farther to the right. If you type `type` here, the word `kinds` will move to the right, and you'll have to perform another operation to delete it.

The EDIT program includes another editing mode called *overstrike*. If this mode is active, a typed character replaces the character at the cursor location. To activate overstrike mode, press the Ins key or type Ctrl-V. Notice how the cursor changes from a flashing underline to a large flashing rectangle. These two cursors provide an instant visual method for letting you know which mode you are currently using. After you press the Ins key, type

`type`

Note that these characters replace the previously displayed characters.

You usually use overstrike mode when you want to replace large blocks of text instead of inserting text; that saves you the extra operation of deleting the text. When you finish changing the example text, press Ins again to return EDIT to insert mode.

Selecting (Highlighting) Text

You can more efficiently perform most editing operations that involve more than a few characters if you *select*, or highlight, the text first. For example, although you can delete three lines of text by holding down the Del key, you can perform the same operation more quickly by selecting the three lines and then pressing the Del key once.

If you know how to move the cursor, you know how to select text—hold down the Shift key while pressing the cursor-movement keys. To select text

Position the cursor on the first (or last) character you want to select.

Hold down the Shift key,

Move the cursor in the appropriate direction.

For example, if you are using the keyboard, follow these steps to select the word Information in your PRACTICE file:

1. Move the cursor to the I in the fourth line on the screen.

2. Hold down the Shift key.

3. Press Ctrl-→.

Note that you can use any appropriate cursor-movement command for step 3 (that is, you could also press → eleven times). However, you will be more productive if you always select the most efficient command.

Notice that all of the characters in the word are highlighted (displayed in reverse video), as shown in Figure 10.7. Any editing operation you now perform affects the entire word. That is, if you press the Del key, Information is erased.

If you are using the mouse, follow these steps to select the word Information in your PRACTICE file:

1. Click the left mouse button on the I in the fourth line on the screen.

2. Hold down the Shift key.

3. Drag the mouse cursor to the space following the word (be sure that the entire word is highlighted in reverse video).

4. Release the left mouse button.

Remember, selected text—be it two characters, one line, or a hundred lines—is manipulated as a single block, so be careful which key you press after you've selected text. EDIT lacks an undo feature, so if you select several lines and then accidentally press the Del key, you will have to retype every word!

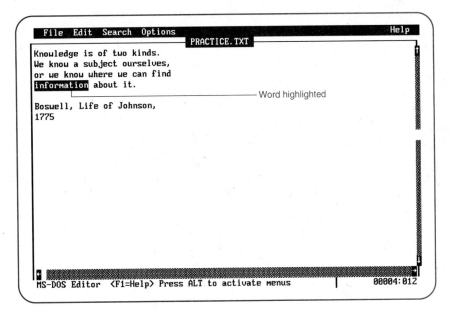

Figure 10.7. Selecting text in EDIT.

Table 10.5 lists all of EDIT's text-selection keys.

Table 10.5. Text-selection keys.

Actions	Microsoft Keystrokes	WordStar-Compatible Keystrokes
Left one character	Shift-←	
Right one character	Shift-→	
Left one word	Shift-Ctrl-←	
Right one word	Shift-Ctrl-→	
Current line	Shift-↓	
Line above	Shift-↑	
Screen up	Shift-PgUp	
Screen down	Shift-PgDn	
To beginning of file	Shift-Ctrl-Home	
To end of file	Shift-Ctrl-End	

To cancel a selection ("unselect" selected text), press any cursor movement key, or if you are using a mouse, click anywhere in the EDIT window.

Moving Selected Text

You've already selected a word; now select a larger block of text and then move it to another location. Although you can select individual words or characters on a line, when you try to include text from more than one line, EDIT forces you to select entire lines instead.

For example, assume that you want to move

```
Boswell, Life of Johnson,
1775
```

to the beginning of your document. Here's how:

1. Move the cursor to the `first line` you want to move (the line beginning with `Boswell`).

2. Drag the mouse down or hold down the `Shift` key and press ↓, so your screen looks like Figure 10.8.

3. Next, select `Cut` from the Edit pull-down menu. The bottom two highlighted lines in the work area immediately disappear from the PRACTICE file.

   Although the text seems to be deleted, EDIT has actually placed it in a *buffer*—an area in memory—called the *Clipboard*. The text in the Clipboard is still available for you to use. To redisplay the two lines of text that you have cut to the Clipboard, you must first move the cursor to the line of the document where you want to insert the text. (Remember, EDIT is line oriented: Multiple-line text is inserted at the line indicated by the cursor. Your cursor can be anywhere within that line.)

   To proceed with our example:

4. Move the cursor to the first line of the document.

5. Select `Paste` from the Edit menu.

The deleted two lines immediately reappear at the top of your document, as in Figure 10.9. That's all there is to moving blocks of text: Cut them to the Clipboard and then paste them back in at another location.

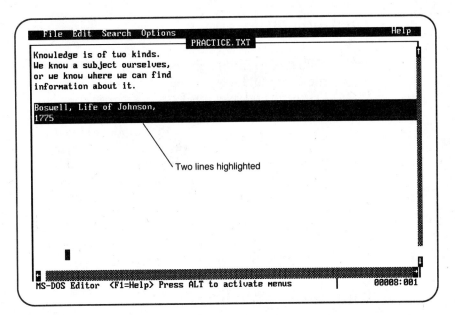

Figure 10.8. Selecting two lines of text.

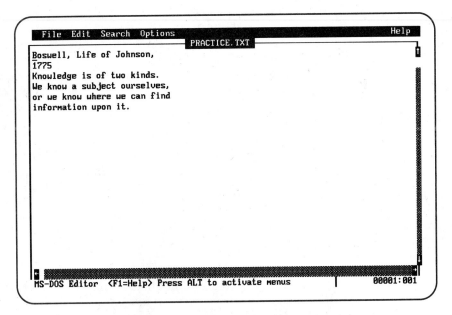

Figure 10.9. Text moved to the top of the document.

The Clipboard

Note that even though you've pasted your selected text back into the file, those cut lines still remain in the Clipboard. Therefore, positioning the cursor and selecting Paste again would paste another copy of the text into the Clipboard.

Your text remains in the Clipboard until you cut or copy another piece of text into it. However, the Clipboard can hold only one piece of text at a time. Therefore, if you perform another cut or copy operation, the first block of text is lost and only the second selection is retained.

For example, highlight the date in the second line of the file. Then, cut it from the text using the Cut command from the Edit menu or by pressing `Shift-Del`. Move the cursor to the end of the first line and paste the contents of the Clipboard back into the document. Notice that only the last cut operation is inserted.

Copying Selected Text

Another important editing operation involves selecting a block of text and copying it to another location. The procedure is similar to the operation for moving text. For example, copy the title, author, and date (now on the first line of your document) to the end of the PRACTICE file.

To try this procedure, select (highlight) the first line of text. Then select Copy from the Edit pull-down menu. (You can also use the shortcut Ctrl-Ins key combination.) Although nothing seems to happen on the screen, you've actually copied the selected text to the Clipboard. Now you can create a duplicate of the selected text anywhere in the document.

For example, position the cursor in the blank line below your current text and select the Paste option from the Edit menu or press the shortcut Shift-Ins key combination. Your screen resembles Figure 10.10. You can make as many copies of this line as you want because the Clipboard retains this text until your next cut or copy operation.

Deleting Selected Text

Your example text now contains identical first and last lines. Delete the first lines:

1. Move the cursor to the first letter in the first line (the `B` in `Boswell`) by using the arrow keys or clicking that letter.

2. Highlight the first two lines by holding down the Shift key and pressing ↓, or by dragging the mouse down.

3. Press the Del key or choose the Clear option from the Edit menu.

   This deletes the lines, but does not save the text to the Clipboard. The selected text is irretrievably lost, and the Clipboard retains the text it was assigned in its last cut or copy operation. In this example, the Clipboard still contains the line Boswell, Life of Johnson, 1775 from your previous copy.

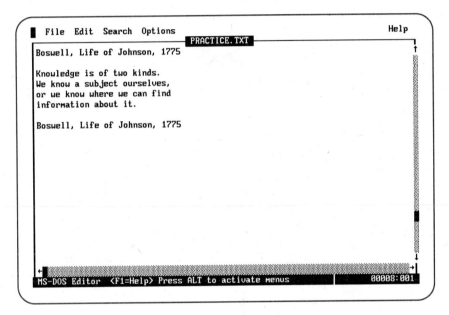

```
  File  Edit  Search  Options                                    Help
                           PRACTICE.TXT
 Boswell, Life of Johnson, 1775                                         ↑

 Knowledge is of two kinds.
 We know a subject ourselves,
 or we know where we can find
 information about it.

 Boswell, Life of Johnson, 1775




                                                                       ↓
                                                                       →
 MS-DOS Editor  <F1=Help> Press ALT to activate menus       00008:001
```

Figure 10.10. Copying and pasting a line into a document.

EDIT includes three basic editing procedures. Be sure that you know and understand these operations (all of which are included in the Edit menu):

Cut (Shift-Del)	Deletes selected text from the file and stores that text in the Clipboard.
Copy (Ctrl-Ins)	Copies selected text into the Clipboard, but does not delete that text from the file.
Clear (Del)	Deletes selected text from the file and discards that text.

Table 10.6 lists all of the pertinent commands for these basic EDIT editing procedures and other related operations.

Table 10.6. Insert and copy keys.

Actions	Microsoft Keystrokes	WordStar-Compatible Keystrokes
Toggles insert and overstrike modes	Ins	Ctrl-V
Copies selected text to the Clipboard	Ctrl-Ins	
Moves selected text to the Clipboard	Shift-Del	
Moves current line to the Clipboard	Ctrl-Y	
Moves text from cursor to the end of line to the Clipboard	Ctrl-Q,Y	
Pastes the contents of the Clipboard to current cursor position	Shift-Ins	
Inserts a blank line below the cursor position	End-Enter	
Inserts a blank line above the cursor position	Home,Ctrl-N	

Finding Text

EDIT also contains easy-to-use Find (search) and Change (global search-and-replace) commands. For example, If you want to see whether your text uses the word we, first pull down the Search menu and then select the Find option. Notice that the word at the current cursor location (in your text) is automatically inserted into the Find What field.

In this case, type we in the Find What field. You can specify a string of as many as 127 characters. Although the dialog box is too small to display all this text at one time, characters will scroll to the left so that you can enter the complete string.

Next, tab to the Match Upper/Lowercase check box. You use this check box to specify whether the search will be case-sensitive (that is, if upper- and lowercase letters match exactly). If you select this check box (by clicking it with the mouse or by tabbing to it and pressing the Spacebar), EDIT will find only two matches for we (in the third line). If you don't check this box, EDIT will find three matches—because it also finds the We in the second line.

Finally, tab to the next check box, Whole word. If this box is checked, the search finds strings only if entire words match other entire words; that is, a search for we will find only that word. However, if the box is not checked, a search for we will not only find We and we, but also the we in Boswell (in the last line).

After you enter your settings, select OK. A highlight in the work area immediately selects the first occurrence of your text (if any exists). To see whether the document contains other occurrences of your text, select the Repeat Last Find option from the Select menu or press the F3 function key.

Notice that the cursor highlights each instance of your string and cycles through the document again if you continue to press F3.

Replacing Text

5 If you need to change all occurrences of a string, you could use the Find option, delete the string, and then add the new string; however, that procedure would be incredibly time-consuming. To perform this operation quickly and efficiently, EDIT offers a much simpler global search-and-replace" feature called Change.

For example, if you decide to change the word or to and throughout the document, highlight an instance of or in text and then select Change from the Search menu. Notice that EDIT has already inserted the word into the Find What field. (You also could have typed the word into the field instead of highlighting it in text.)

Next, tab to the Change To field and type the word and. The string in this field replaces all occurrences in the document of the string in the Find What field (or). Once again, be careful with the settings that you choose for the Match Upper/Lowercase and Whole word check boxes. If you don't select Whole word, some global replaces can produce unpredictable results; for example, this exercise would result in the following "word":

Infandmation

That's probably not what you had in mind.

After you've filled in all the fields and set the check boxes, begin the search-and-replace operation by selecting either the Find and Verify or the Change All button at the bottom of the dialog box. If you are sure that you want every instance of a string to be replaced, select Change All. EDIT changes all occurrences of the string in your document and then displays a dialog box that lets you know the operation is complete. Select OK to return to the work area.

If you are not sure whether every occurrence of a string should be changed, select the Find and Verify button. Try the following exercise with the PRACTICE file:

1. Position the cursor at the beginning of the file

2. Open the Search menu.

3. Select the Change option.

4. Enter the word or in the Find What field.

5. Enter the word and in the Change To field.

6. Turn off both check boxes (toggle the option buttons so that no X appears between the brackets).

7. Now, select the Find and Verify button.

Notice that a Change dialog box opens at the bottom of your screen and prompts you to choose one of four actions:

Change	Change the specified string to the new string
Skip	Leave the current highlighted text as it is but continue searching for other text to replace
Cancel	Abandon the search and replace operation
Help	Display information that will help you execute this procedure correctly

In this example, select Change. Notice that the word or (in line three) has now been changed to and. The highlight next jumps to the next instance of or, which, because you did not specify Whole word, falls in the middle of the word `Information`. Obviously, you don't want to make this change, so select Skip. Although this change was not made, the search for additional changes continues until the last instance of the string has been found. Then, a dialog box signals that the change operation is complete. Select OK to return to the work area.

Table 10.7 summarizes EDIT's Find and Change commands.

Table 10.7. Find and change keys.

Actions	Microsoft Keystrokes	WordStar-Compatible Keystrokes
Repeat; finds the same text	F3	Ctrl-L
Searches for text	Ctrl-Q,F Changes text	Ctrl-Q,A

Printing a Document

5 When you finish typing and editing your text, you might want to print a hard copy of your efforts. To do so, select the Print option from the File menu. This opens the Print dialog box, which displays the following two option buttons:

```
( ) Selected Text Only
(.) Complete Document
```

If you have not selected (highlighted) any text in the document, EDIT makes the Complete Document button the default option. (The bullet within the parentheses indicates which button is currently active.) However, if you previously had highlighted text within the document, EDIT would have displayed the Selected Text Only option as the default.

In this case, you want to print the entire document, so be sure that the Complete Document radio button is activated and then select `Yes`. If your printer is connected correctly, the entire PRACTICE file prints.

If your printer is not turned on or is not on-line, EDIT displays a Device Fault dialog box warning you that an error has occurred. Whenever you see an error message such as this, refer to the context-sensitive help system to help you rectify the problem.

In this case, press F1 or select the Help button. This displays a dialog box listing four common mistakes that can generate that particular error message. After you read the information thoroughly, press OK to clear the help message; then, press OK again to clear the Device Fault dialog box. After you correct the printer problem, you can try to print the document again.

Saving a File

5 Anything you do on the Edit screen, whether you are creating a new file or changing an old one, takes place only on the screen and in the computer's memory. Your work is not saved until you explicitly save it. To do so, select Save from the File pull-down menu.

Because you specified the name of the file (PRACTICE.TXT) before you began this example session, EDIT automatically saves your text (including any changes) to that file. After EDIT saves your work to disk, it redisplays the main work area.

Saving a Previously Unnamed File

5 If you start EDIT without specifying a file name, type some text, and then try to save the file using the Save option, EDIT displays a Save dialog box.

The Save dialog box contains several fields. If you want to save your file in the current directory (which is listed below the words File Name), type a valid DOS name into the File Name field and then press Enter or select OK. If you want to specify another directory and/or drive, move the cursor to the Dir/Drives field, and use the up and down arrow keys to select the appropriate path name for the file. If you are currently in a subdirectory, select the .. symbol to move to the parent, or next higher, directory. (Of course, you can always type the complete path name into the File Name box without accessing the Dir/Drives field.)

After you enter the correct name and location, select OK.

Creating a New Text File

 Assume that you return to your document, add some more text, and then decide to begin a new file. Select the File menu and then choose the New command.

Notice that EDIT does not immediately create a new file. Because you have made changes to your work but have not yet saved them to disk, EDIT opens a dialog box that permits you to do so. You can select Yes to save your document and the latest changes, No to discard all of your changes, or Cancel to abandon the operation and return to the document.

The more you use EDIT, the more you will appreciate this safety feature; it helps prevent your accidentally losing a great deal of hard work. In this example, save your changes to PRACTICE.TXT by selecting Yes.

EDIT immediately saves the changes, closes PRACTICE.TXT, and opens a new file. Because you haven't yet named this new document the title area near the top of the screen reads Untitled.

Type the following text:

```
No need for alarm.
This is just a test.
```

Naming an Untitled Text File

 Remember, you created this second document with the New command, and it doesn't yet have a name. To name the file, select the Save As option from the File menu.

If you are using the keyboard, type Alt-F and then press the hot key A or move the highlight to the Save As option with the up and down arrow keys and press Enter. Of course, if you are using a mouse, click Save As.

This is the same dialog box that EDIT displayed when you selected the Save command (except that this box is entitled `Save As`). Use it the same way. In this example, type

```
TEST.TXT
```

to save the file in the current directory. Note that EDIT automatically adds the .TXT file name extension if you don't specify an extension.

Exiting the Editor

 To exit the EDIT editor after you've created and saved your file, select the File menu (Alt-F) and then press X or select the Exit option. This returns you to the command line because in this example you started EDIT from the DOS prompt. However, when you start EDIT from the DOS Shell, the Exit command returns control to the Shell.

Notice that the EDIT program ended immediately because you had just saved your work. However, assume that you made additional changes to the file but forgot to save them. Now, when you exit the EDIT program by selecting the Exit option from the File menu, the program does not immediately end.

Because you have not yet saved your changes to disk, EDIT opens the Save dialog box to permit you to do so. You can select Yes to save your document and the latest changes, No to discard all of your changes, or Cancel to abandon the exit operation and return to the document.

This important safety feature will not let you exit the editor unless you either save changes to your file or explicitly cancel those changes. However, the editor lacks an important feature that most other text processors offer: EDIT doesn't make backup copies of the original file.

Although EDIT prevents you from accidentally closing an unsaved file, when you select the Yes option from the Save dialog box, the contents of your original file are discarded and only the edited version of the file exists. That is, if you edit your AUTOEXEC.BAT file and then save it, your original AUTOEXEC.BAT file is lost forever; it is not saved in AUTOEXEC.BAK (as it would be in EDLIN or most word processors).

Therefore, if you are using EDIT to change important files such as AUTOEXEC.BAT or CONFIG.SYS, you would be prudent to make a backup of your original file before you begin editing, by entering these commands:

```
COPY AUTOEXEC.BAT AUTOEXEC.BAK
EDIT AUTOEXEC.BAT
```

Now, if you make a mistake in your file and you want to reedit the original file, you can use the .BAK file.

Customizing the Editor

 The Options selection in the Menu Bar pulls down a menu that lets you change some EDIT display settings. If you have a color monitor, you can select the Display option to change the current EDIT screen colors. You can also use this option to change two other display settings.

Note that both the EDIT.COM and QBASIC.EXE programs use the same initialization file—QBASIC.INI. Therefore, any display changes that you make to EDIT (such as changing colors) automatically affect the default QBASIC screen, and vice versa.

Changing Colors

When you select Display from the Options menu, the dialog box that appears is divided into two main sections—the Colors field and the Display Options field. The highlighted colors in the Foreground and Background boxes of the Colors field are your current color selections, as shown in Figure 10.11.

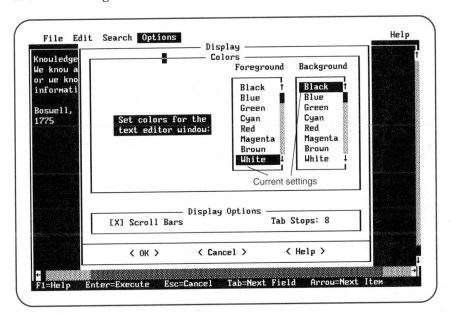

Figure 10.11. The Display option dialog box.

To change these colors, move the flashing underline cursor to the Background box and use the arrow keys (or the Scroll Bars) to move the highlight, thus changing the EDIT background color. Notice that the left side of the Colors field actually shows the new color (and the current foreground color) as it will look on your screen.

If you have an EGA or VGA adapter, you can create many exotic combinations. Color selection is a remarkably individual matter. Popular color schemes include White on Blue, Black on Cyan, and Blue on White. Choose whatever combination of colors suits your personality.

Note that whatever changes you make in this dialog box are saved in the QBASIC.INI initialization file and will also affect the QBASIC environment.

Other Display Options

If you use a mouse, be sure that the Scroll Bars check box has an X in it; that selection displays Scroll Bars, which let you use the mouse to move through your documents. If you use the keyboard, you can turn off the Scroll Bars by toggling off the X. This gives you an extra column and row in which you can type text. However, you probably should continue to display the Scroll Bars—even if you only use the keyboard—as explained in the following paragraph.

Inside the horizontal and vertical Scroll Bars is a small box that moves as you move the cursor through your document. This Slider Box is a helpful indicator as to your current location in a lengthy document. Therefore, the Scroll Bars offer a convenient feature that is not offset by the addition of one mere extra column and row.

The Tab Stops field determines how many spaces a Tab keypress will advance the cursor. The default setting is eight spaces, an indention used by many programmers. If you use EDIT strictly for writing DOS files, notes, and letters, you might want to reset this field to five spaces, a standard paragraph indention.

When you finish changing the settings in the Display dialog box, select OK to initiate your changes. Select Cancel to return to the original settings.

Specifying a Help Path

The Help Path option lets you set the path to the EDIT.HLP file in case you are using the EDIT program in a directory other than the directory that contains the help file. You probably won't need to set this field because the default installation places both EDIT.COM and EDIT.HLP in the \DOS directory and specifies this directory in the system PATH command set in your AUTOEXEC.BAT file. However, if you decide to relocate the help file to another directory, you can specify that directory name in this dialog box.

Command Line Switches

  You can control some of EDIT's display features when you start the program from the command line. The following switches to the EDIT command modify the setup of the editor's display:

/B   You can use a monochrome monitor with a color graphics card or see EDIT in monochrome on a color monitor.

/G   Executes a fast update of a CGA monitor. If your monitor displays flickering dots, your hardware doesn't support this option. You will have to restart EDIT without the /G option.

/H   Displays the maximum number of lines your hardware permits.

/NOHI   To use a monitor that does not support high intensity. Do not use this switch with Compaq laptop computers.

If you have an EGA or VGA monitor, you probably will use the /H switch often. This switch lets EDIT display 43 (EGA) to 60 lines (VGA) of text at a time, which is most helpful when you are creating or editing long documents and want to see as much text on the screen as possible. To use this switch (or any of the others), type a command line similar to the following:

```
EDIT filename /H
```

More About EDIT

The basic EDIT editing skills you learned in this chapter are enough to enable you to create or modify any of the files discussed later in this book. However, as mentioned earlier, if you are going to be creating and editing large text files, you'd be wise to invest in a good word processing program.

Be sure to read—and remember—the information in the next section about storing your AUTOEXEC.BAT and CONFIG.SYS files. You'll need to keep in mind these important points in all your future work with these two special files.

Where to Store AUTOEXEC.BAT and CONFIG.SYS

Regardless of which editor you use to create or modify your AUTOEXEC.BAT and CONFIG.SYS files, it is extremely important to remember that both these files must be stored so that DOS can automatically read them when you first start the computer. Recall from Chapter 2 that when you turn your computer on, it automatically reads the root directory of the hard disk (or the diskette in drive A:) for instructions on how to boot up.

After the computer gets going, DOS searches the same diskette or directory for two files—CONFIG.SYS and AUTOEXEC.BAT—to see whether they contain any additional start-up instructions. If DOS does not find these files on the current diskette or directory, it assumes that they do not exist and completes its start-up operations. DOS neither searches other disk drives or directories nor displays any error messages to warn you of a problem.

In other words, if you create or modify either the AUTOEXEC.BAT or CONFIG.SYS using the wrong diskette or directory, your efforts will be fruitless. DOS will never see your changes, and you will probably find yourself at wit's end trying to figure out why DOS is ignoring your customization commands. Read on and remember the important points discussed in the sections that follow.

Storing AUTOEXEC.BAT and CONFIG.SYS on a Hard Disk

If your computer has a hard disk, and you always start your computer with the floppy disk drives empty, the AUTOEXEC.BAT and CONFIG.SYS must be stored on the root directory of the hard disk drive that your computer boots from. On virtually all computers, this is disk drive C:.

Figure 10.12 illustrates the proper location of the AUTOEXEC.BAT and CONFIG.SYS files, using the DOS 5 **File List** screen's Directory Tree as a guide. (If you are using DOS 5, your computer probably already has these two files stored in the root directory of drive C:.)

Using a hypothetical directory tree hierarchy as a guide, Figure 10.13 shows the proper location of the AUTOEXEC.BAT and CONFIG.SYS files. (If you are using DOS 3, your computer might not have these files, but if it does have them, they are stored in the root directory of drive C:.

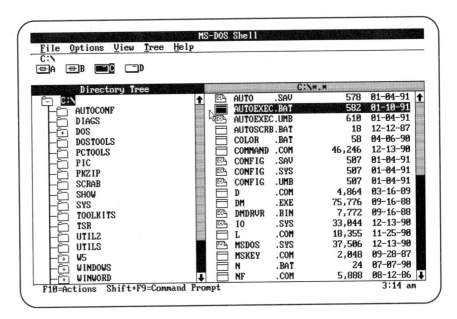

Figure 10.12. The DOS 5 File List view of the proper location of the AUTOEXEC.BAT and CONFIG.SYS files.

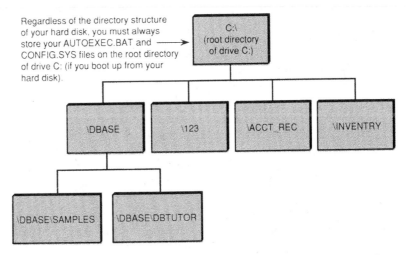

Figure 10.13. The proper location of the AUTOEXEC.BAT and CONFIG.SYS files on a sample directory tree.

Regardless of the version of DOS that you use, or whether you use EDIT or another text editor to edit the AUTOEXEC.BAT and CONFIG.SYS files, you must remember to specify the complete location and file name of the file you want to edit. To be safe, never assume that the root directory is the current directory. Instead, when you edit the AUTOEXEC.BAT file, be sure to specify `C:\AUTOEXEC.BAT` as the file name. When you edit CONFIG.SYS, be sure to specify `C:\CONFIG.SYS` as the file to edit. By preceding the file name with C:\, you are certain to store your changes in the root directory of drive C:.

Any changes you make to either CONFIG.SYS or AUTOEXEC.BAT take effect when you restart your computer, as discussed later in this chapter.

Storing AUTOEXEC.BAT and CONFIG.SYS on a Diskette

NOTE: Often, the root directory is the only directory on a diskette.

If you usually start your computer with a diskette in drive A:, you must be certain to save your AUTOEXEC.BAT and CONFIG.SYS files on the root directory of that diskette. Storing these files (or changes to these files) on any other diskette will be fruitless, because DOS doesn't look elsewhere for these files.

To clarify, I'll first define the diskette that you put into drive A: before turning on your computer as your *Startup* diskette, regardless of the label you personally placed on that diskette. Figure 10.14 illustrates the importance of storing the AUTOEXEC.BAT and CONFIG.SYS files on the Startup diskette.

If your text editor (be it a word processing program or DOS's EDIT) is stored on a diskette other than the Startup diskette (the DOS 5 floppy diskette installation stores EDIT on the Edit disk), you should start your computer as usual by placing your Startup diskette in drive A:. Then, when you create or edit the AUTOEXEC.BAT or CONFIG.SYS file, you need to be certain that you do so on the Startup diskette. If your text editor is not stored on the Startup diskette, you should use the following procedure:

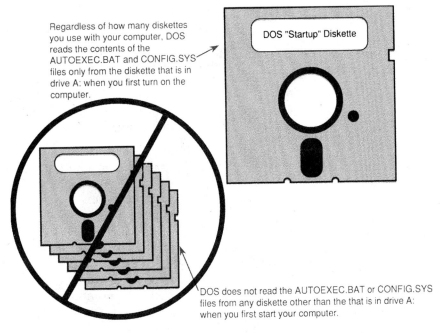

Regardless of how many diskettes you use with your computer, DOS reads the contents of the AUTOEXEC.BAT and CONFIG.SYS files only from the diskette that is in drive A: when you first turn on the computer.

DOS "Startup" Diskette

DOS does not read the AUTOEXEC.BAT or CONFIG.SYS files from any diskette other than the that is in drive A: when you first start your computer.

Figure 10.14. If you start your computer from a diskette, be sure to store your AUTOEXEC.BAT and CONFIG.SYS files on the root directory of your Startup diskette.

NOTE: Unfortunately, different diskette sizes might store EDIT.COM on different diskettes, so only you can determine which diskette that EDIT.COM is stored on.

1. Remove the Startup diskette from drive A: and put it in drive B:.

2. Put the diskette that contains your editing program in drive A: (so that you can run the editing program).

3. Stay on drive A: and use the proper command to run your editing program.

4. When specifying the name of the file to be edited, be sure to specify the root directory of drive `B:` (to edit a file on your Startup diskette). For example, if you want to edit the AUTOEXEC.BAT file on your Startup diskette, specify `B:\AUTOEXEC.BAT` as the file to be edited. If you want to modify the CONFIG.SYS file on your Startup diskette, specify `B:\CONFIG.SYS`. After making your changes, save the file using the appropriate method for your editor.

5. Then remove both diskettes from their drives and put the `modified Startup` diskette back in drive `A:`.

Your changes will take effect when you restart your computer, as discussed later in this chapter.

If your diskette size permits EDIT.COM to be stored on the Startup diskette, you don't need to be concerned about using disk drive B:. Leave your Startup diskette in drive A: and after the EDIT command, specify the name of the file that you want to edit. For example, to edit the AUTOEXEC.BAT file, enter the command `EDIT AUTOEXEC.BAT`. To edit the CONFIG.SYS file, enter the command `EDIT CONFIG.SYS`. After making your changes, save the file using the usual Save command, as described earlier.

Your changes will take effect when you restart your computer, as discussed later in this chapter.

Special Warning for DOS 5 Users

  Regardless of the editor that you use to modify your AUTOEXEC.BAT file, DOS 5 users must be aware that your AUTOEXEC.BAT file might contain the DOSSHELL command. This command automatically starts the Shell when you turn on the computer.

As soon as DOS encounters the DOSSHELL command in the AUTOEXEC.BAT file, it stops reading the AUTOEXEC.BAT file and starts the Shell. Therefore, if your AUTOEXEC.BAT file contains the DOSSHELL command, be sure after you make changes that DOSSHELL is the last command in your AUTOEXEC.BAT file.

When Your Changes Take Effect

After you first modify or create either the CONFIG.SYS or AUTOEXEC.BAT file on your computer, nothing new will happen. That's because DOS reads these files and executes their commands at boot-up time (that is, when you first start your computer). If you want to activate any changes you made to CONFIG.SYS, or AUTOEXEC.BAT, you must reboot.

Rebooting is a simple procedure. If you start your computer from a diskette rather than the hard disk, be sure to put the Startup diskette in drive A:. If you start your computer from a hard disk, make sure the floppy disk drives are empty. To reboot, press Ctrl-Alt-Del (hold down the Ctrl key, hold down the Alt key, and then press the Del key). Then release all three keys. DOS reads your modified CONFIG.SYS or AUTOEXEC.BAT files (assuming that you stored them correctly, as discussed previously in this chapter) as it restarts the system.

Note that it is not absolutely necessary to reboot to activate commands in the AUTOEXEC.BAT file. Instead, you can activate the AUTOEXEC.BAT batch file by entering the command AUTOEXEC at the command prompt. You'll learn more about batch files, like AUTOEXEC.BAT, in Chapters 13 and 14.

Troubleshooting

If you make an error while typing some of the exercises in this chapter, you will probably see one of the following error messages. Locate the appropriate error message and try the suggested solution.

❑ `Bad command or file name`: You tried to run a program (perhaps EDIT) that is not available on the current drive or directory. Try a different diskette, disk drive, or directory.

❑ **If DOS ignores changes in your AUTOEXEC.BAT or CONFIG.SYS file**: (This is not a DOS error message, instead it's a common problem.) If DOS seems to be ignoring changes you made to either your AUTOEXEC.BAT or CONFIG.SYS file, be sure to read the section titled "Where to Store AUTOEXEC.BAT and CONFIG.SYS."

Summary

As you read future chapters, you might want to create or edit DOS text files, particularly the files named CONFIG.SYS and AUTOEXEC.BAT. To do so, use any text editor, word processor, or the DOS EDIT editor. In summary

❏ If you use a word processor, you must save your file as an ASCII text file.

❏ The easiest way to see whether a file contains word processing codes is to use the DOS Shell's View File Contents option or the command prompt TYPE command.

❏ If a text file contains formatting characters, you must remove them or DOS will not be able to read the file.

❏ The DOS 5 full-screen EDIT editor never stores formatting characters in a file.

❏ When creating or editing a file with any text editor (or EDIT) remember to accurately specify the complete location and name of the file you want to create or edit.

❏ After editing either the CONFIG.SYS or AUTOEXEC.BAT file, be sure to store these files in the root directory of the appropriate hard disk drive or diskette; otherwise, DOS will ignore any changes you've made.

❏ Changes that you make to the CONFIG.SYS or AUTOEXEC.BAT file do not take effect until you restart your computer.

❏ If you are editing the AUTOEXEC.BAT file for DOS 5 and want the Shell to appear automatically when you start the computer, be sure that the DOSSHELL is the last command in the AUTOEXEC.BAT file.

Simplifying Working with Your Hard Disk

This chapter presents techniques to simplify using your hard disk. In particular, it focuses on techniques for making your favorite programs readily accessible from any directory on your hard disk. Of course, you can use similar techniques to manage programs on diskettes. However, because many application programs use at least one diskette, this chapter is really geared toward hard disks, which can store dozens of large application programs.

A Sample Directory Tree

To understand ways of customizing your hard disk, you need a sample directory tree. Needless to say, it is unlikely that your computer has exactly the same directory structure as the example. Nonetheless, you can apply the general techniques that you learn in this chapter to customize any hard disk, regardless of the specific programs or directories stored on it.

To start, assume that you have a complete set of software, including a database management system, spreadsheet, and word processor. In addition, you have numerous smaller utility programs, such as a calculator program, an appointment scheduler, a mouse driver (for your mouse), and others. Also assume that you stored all your DOS programs, such as FORMAT.COM and TREE.COM, in a directory named DOS.

To be as realistic as possible, this example uses specific brand names for the major application programs and the mouse, as listed in Table 11.1. The names of the directories that contain these programs are also included in the table.

Table 11.1. Sample software collection and directories.

Program	Product Name	Directory
Database manager	dBASE IV	DBASE
Spreadsheet	Excel	WINDOWS
Word processor	WordPerfect	WP
Utilities	(several)	UTILS
Operating System	DOS	DOS
Mouse driver	Microsoft Mouse	MOUSE1

In addition to all your programs, suppose that you store data for your business on two directories, named ACCTNG and SALES. Finally, assume that your hard disk contains numerous subdirectories of files that are used only with specific programs. Given this collection of programs and data, your directory structure might look like Figure 11.1.

As you can see, the sample directory tree adheres to the advice presented in Chapter 7; the tree is broad and shallow, each major application program is stored on its own directory, and each application uses the manufacturer's recommended directory name. Also, the ACCTNG and SALES directories are stored at the same levels as the major programs. Finally, subdirectories, such as PIF and DBTUTOR, contain files that pertain only to their parent directories (WINDOWS and DBASE, respectively).

Now that the directory tree is established, you need to make it easy to gain access to any and all programs. For example, while accessing the ACCTNG directory, you want to be able to run at any time your spreadsheet, word processing, database management, utility, and DOS programs.

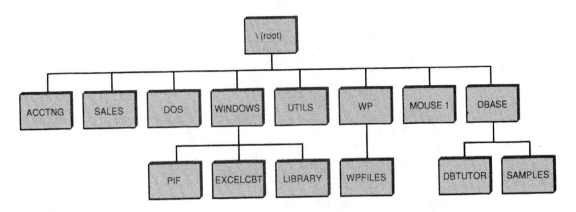

Figure 11.1. A sample directory tree.

Setting Up a Search Path

As you know from preceding chapters, if you attempt to run a program that is not in the current directory (or drive), DOS displays the error message `Bad command or file name`. This can be inconvenient, if not maddening.

The solution to this problem is the all-important PATH command. This command tells DOS to look in other directories if it cannot find the requested program in the current directory. The general syntax of the PATH command is

`PATH d:pathname;d:pathname;d:pathname ...`

in which

`d:` is the name of a drive

`directory` is the name of a directory on the drive

`;` separates each drive and directory name

You can list to the right of the PATH command as many drive and directory names or pathnames as you wish, as long as you remember to separate each sequence with a semicolon and restrict the total number of characters on the line to 128 or fewer.

You can include the root directory in the search path by including its name (\) in the PATH command. For example, the following PATH command tells DOS to search both the root and DOS directories of drive C:

```
PATH C:\;C:\DOS
```

The order of directory names in the PATH command affects the time that DOS requires to find a particular program. A little planning can ensure that DOS locates and runs your programs as quickly as possible; that is the topic of the next section.

Planning the Perfect Path

First, remember that the PATH command searches only for *executable* files, which always have the file name extension .BAT, .COM, or .EXE. Therefore, it serves no purpose to include in the PATH command directories that contain only data files (such as ACCTNG and SALES in the sample directory tree.

Second, keep in mind that DOS searches all the directories—from left to right—in the PATH command, until it finds the program you requested. For example, suppose that you set up your PATH command as follows:

```
PATH C:\DOS;C:\WP;C:\WINDOWS;C:\DBASE
```

When you run the DBASE program from the ACCTNG or SALES directory, DOS first searches the current directory for the dBASE program; then it looks in the DOS directory, the WP directory, the WINDOWS directory, and finally, the DBASE directory.

> NOTE: The DIR command shows how many files are stored on a directory; however, it counts ., .., and any subdirectories as "files," even though they are not truly files.

Therefore, you should consider two factors when determining the order of the directories in your PATH command:

1. How many files are in each directory

2. Which programs do you use most often

If a particular directory contains an exceptionally large number of files, you might want to list it as the last directory in the PATH command so that it is searched as a "last resort," when DOS determines that no other directory contains the requested program.

If you use a particular program far more frequently than other programs, you probably should list its directory (or pathname) first in the PATH command; that way, its directory is the first one searched. For example, as a writer and programmer, I use my word processing program more than any other, and therefore, I always list its directory first in my PATH command.

Also, remember that you don't need to include every directory that contains a program in the PATH command. For example, the MOUSE1 directory in the example directory tree includes a program that allows you to use a mouse with some applications. However, that program needs to be run only once (at the beginning of each DOS session) to install the mouse. Therefore, you don't need to include the MOUSE1 directory in the PATH command, because it doesn't contain any programs that you need, and DOS never needs to search it.

To be more specific about the sample directory tree in Figure 11.1, assume that you use your DOS commands and word processing program frequently and that you use your database manager, spreadsheet, and utility programs less frequently. Furthermore, assume that the WINDOWS directory has, by far, the most files in it.

WARNING: Do not put any blank spaces—other than the one immediately to the right of the PATH command—in your list of directories. DOS stops reading directory names from the PATH command as soon as it encounters a blank space.

The ideal PATH command takes into consideration individual program usage. In the example situation, you could obtain maximum speed of access to all programs with this command:

```
PATH C:\DOS;C:\WP;C:\DBASE;C:\UTILS;C:\WINDOWS
```

or perhaps this one:

```
PATH C:\WP;C:\DOS;C:\UTILS;C:\DBASE;C:\WINDOWS
```

Both PATH commands tell DOS to first search the most frequently used directories, DOS and WP, and then to search the less frequently used directories. The crowded WINDOWS directory is always the last directory searched.

How to Enter a PATH Command

You can enter the PATH command at the command prompt at any time. (DOS 4 and 5 users need to exit the Shell first.) Before you type a new path, enter the command

```
PATH
```

to have DOS display the current PATH. DOS displays either the message No Path, if no path has been defined, or the currently defined path. (Your AUTOEXEC.BAT file might have predefined a PATH when you first started the computer.)

WARNING: If your computer has a hard disk, it's best not to include floppy drives A: or B: in your PATH command, because if either floppy drive is empty while DOS is searching for a file, you'll get the General Error Reading Drive error message. You always need to put diskettes in drives A: and B: to avoid the error message.

You define a new path by typing the PATH command with the proper *syntax* (separating each drive and directory or pathname specification with a semicolon). After you enter the PATH command, the defined path stays in effect until you turn off the computer, reboot, or define a different path. For example, when you enter the following command at the command prompt

```
PATH C:\DOS;C:\WP;C:\DBASE;C:\UTILS;C:\WINDOWS
```

the programs on the DOS, WP, DBASE, UTILS, and WINDOWS directories are accessible from all directories for the remainder of the current session.

Rather than enter the PATH command each time you start the computer, include the PATH command in your AUTOEXEC.BAT file. That way, DOS automatically defines the path for you as soon as it boots the computer. (This is particularly helpful for other people who might use your computer but are less knowledgeable about DOS.)

Before you actually modify your AUTOEXEC.BAT file, look at its current contents. To do so (assuming that the DOS command prompt is on your screen), enter the following command:

```
TYPE C:\AUTOEXEC.BAT
```

Entering this command produces one of the following three results:

> NOTE: Your AUTOEXEC.BAT file might display `SET PATH=` rather than `PATH`, but you can consider these the same thing.

❑ DOS displays an AUTOEXEC.BAT file that contains a defined PATH (or SET PATH=) command. In this case, you can always change the existing path.

❑ DOS displays the AUTOEXEC.BAT file, but the file does not contain a PATH (or SET PATH=) command. In this case, you can add a PATH command to the file.

❑ DOS displays a message, such as `File not found - AUTOEXEC.BAT`. In this case, you can create your own AUTOEXEC.BAT file and then put a PATH command in it.

Regardless of the result you get when you view the contents of your AUTOEXEC.BAT file, the general editing techniques you learned in Chapter 10 help you define the PATH command in your own AUTOEXEC.BAT file. Because this might be your first editing experience, use the DOS EDIT program to work through an example. However, before you begin editing, you need to know exactly where to place the PATH command in the AUTOEXEC.BAT file.

Positioning the PATH Command in AUTOEXEC.BAT

> NOTE: If your AUTOEXEC.BAT file already contains commands, do not remove any of the existing commands unless you know exactly what you are doing. Remember, Appendix B provides a reference to all DOS commands.

Basically, you can place the PATH command anywhere in the AUTOEXEC.BAT file, as long as the entire command is no longer than 128 characters and no other commands are on the same line. Always remember however, if you are using DOS 4 or 5 and your AUTOEXEC.BAT file already contains the DOSSHELL command, DOSSHELL must be the last command in the AUTOEXEC.BAT file.

Figure 11.2 shows a sample AUTOEXEC.BAT file that includes the command

```
PATH C:\WP;C:\DOS;C:\UTILS;C:\DBASE;C:\WINDOWS
```

```
@ECHO OFF
SET COMSPEC=C:\DOS\COMMAND.COM
PATH C:\WP;C:\DOS;C:\UTILS;C:\DBASE;C;\WINDOWS
VERIFY OFF
PROMPT $P$G
C:\MOUSE1\MOUSE
APPEND /E
APPEND C:\DOS
PRINT \D:LPT1
DOSSHELL
```

Figure 11.2. A sample AUTOEXEC.BAT file with a PATH command.

Notice that the PATH command includes all the directories that contain frequently used programs from the example directory tree depicted in Figure 11.1.

Notice also that the sample AUTOEXEC.BAT file includes the command `C:\MOUSE1\MOUSE`. This line runs the mouse driver program (named MOUSE.COM in this example), which installs the mouse when the computer first boots up. Because the MOUSE1 directory is not included in the preceding PATH command, DOS must be told the exact location of the MOUSE.COM program (C:\MOUSE1 in this example) so that it can find and execute the MOUSE.COM program.

Modifying the AUTOEXEC.BAT File

As described in Chapter 10, you can use any word processor that can retrieve and save DOS text files, as well as the DOS Editor (or earlier EDLIN) program to edit AUTOEXEC.BAT. Use whichever technique you prefer now to open your AUTOEXEC.BAT file on the editing screen. (Remember, it's C:\AUTOEXEC.BAT on a hard disk).

Modifying an Existing PATH   If your AUTOEXEC.BAT file already contains a PATH or SET PATH= command, move the cursor to the PATH command's line. Then use the cursor-movement and editing keys (as discussed in Chapter 10) to make changes or delete the current line and type an entirely new PATH command.

When you finish and are satisfied with the new PATH command, press the Alt-F key combination, X, and Enter to save your changes and exit. To verify your changes from the DOS command prompt, enter the command TYPE C:\AUTOEXEC.BAT and press Enter. Remember, the new PATH command does not take effect until you either run the AUTOEXEC.BAT program or reboot (press Ctrl-Alt-Del) the computer.

Adding a PATH Command to an Existing AUTOEXEC.BAT file   If your computer already has an AUTOEXEC.BAT file, but it does not contain a PATH (or SET PATH=) command, you can add the PATH command. It's best to put this near the top of the AUTOEXEC.BAT file so that any other commands in the file can search the directories specified in the PATH.

For example, suppose that you decide to insert your new PATH command as the third line in an existing AUTOEXEC.BAT file. To do so, first move the cursor to the second line in the file and press the End-Enter key-combination to insert a new blank line. Then type the complete PATH command and check to see whether the command is correct. To save your changes and exit EDIT, press the Alt-F key combination, X, and Enter.

If you want to verify your change from the DOS command prompt, type the command TYPE C:\AUTOEXEC.BAT and press Enter. Remember, the new PATH command does not take effect until you either run the AUTOEXEC.BAT program or reboot (press Ctrl-Alt-Del).

Understanding the Effects of a PATH Command

Remember, DOS refers to the PATH command only when you attempt to run a program that is not in the current directory. PATH has no effect on displays, such as the DOS 5 Files List, or on the output of the DIR command.

Furthermore, DOS uses the PATH command only when searching for a program to run; it does not search for a file specified in conjunction with a command. For example, if you enter the command TYPE MYFILE.TXT at the command prompt to view the contents of a file named MYFILE.TXT, DOS searches PATH for the TYPE command, but it searches only the current directory for the MYFILE.TXT file, regardless of the PATH search path. DOS "knows" that the TYPE command is trying to view the contents of the MYFILE.TXT file, and that you are not trying to run a program that has the .BAT, .EXE, or .COM extension.

On the other hand, when you enter a command at the command prompt that DOS does not recognize as one of its own built-in (internal) commands, such as DBASE, DOS "knows" that you are trying to run a program. In this case, DOS indeed searches all the directories (and pathnames) specified in the PATH command for file names DBASE.BAT, DBASE.COM, or DBASE.EXE.

Overlays Can Disrupt a Path

I should mention one technical detail that might cause problems in some circumstances. That is, most large application programs are actually divided into several separate files—the main program, with its .COM or .EXE file, and additional *overlay* files, which often have extensions such as .OVL, .OV1, .OV2, and so on.

The main (.EXE or .COM) program for the application needs to be able to find its overlay files to run properly. If it cannot find the overlays in the current directory or disk, it usually displays an error message, such as `Cannot find overlay...`, and then it returns control to DOS.

If you are using major application programs and you installed the programs in the directories that the manufacturers recommended, you probably will never encounter this problem. However, if you run into an overlay file problem, there is a solution: You need to use the APPEND command, in addition to (or rather than) the PATH command, to gain proper access to the program. For details, see the reference to the APPEND command in Appendix B.

A Note on DOS External Commands

 You know the difference between DOS internal commands, which are accessible at any time, and external commands, which are actually stored on disk as programs. External commands are accessible only when DOS can find the appropriate file on the current directory (or in the defined PATH).

If you want to be sure that all internal and external DOS commands are available at all times, you need to take only two actions: First, be sure that all the DOS external command programs are stored in one directory and second, include that directory in your PATH command. Table B.1 at the beginning of Appendix B provides a quick summary of internal and external DOS commands.

Adding Your Own Commands to the DOS Shell

5 DOS 5 users can further simplify the use of their hard disk by adding commands and groups to the DOS Shell. For example, notice in Figure 11.3 that the `Program List` Main Group in the Program List near the bottom of the screen now includes a new group named `Application Programs`.

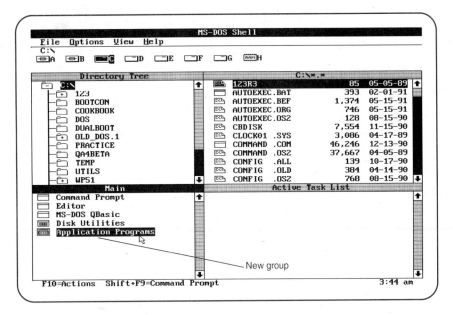

Figure 11.3. A new group added to the Program List screen.

Selecting the new `Application Programs` option displays a new group of options, as Figure 11.4 shows. Selecting an option from this group runs a specific program (from the example programs in Table 11.1).

You can add your own groups and options to the DOS Shell at any time. To demonstrate the basic steps involved, the following sections will create a group from which you can run several application programs. This example also uses the hypothetical directory tree shown in Figure 11.1.

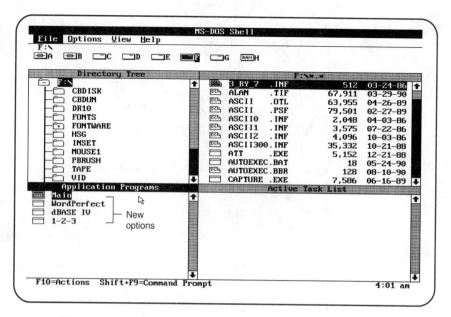

Figure 11.4. A new group of options for running programs.

Adding a New Group

Currently, your DOS Shell probably consists of two groups, the Main Group, which is displayed on your screen when you first start the Shell, and the Disk Utilities group, which is displayed when you select Disk Utilities from the Main Group screen. To add a new group, start by displaying the "higher level" group screen. For example, if you want the new Application Programs group to be accessible from the Main Group screen, be sure that the Main Group screen is displayed and that the highlight is in the Program List Area.

Next, use the usual menu selection techniques to activate the Menu Bar (the Alt or F10 key) and pull down the File menu, as shown in Figure 11.5.

From the pull-down menu, select the New... option. In the New Program Object dialog box, select the Program Group button (by clicking it with the mouse or by using the up or down arrow keys) and press Enter to add the new group. This displays the Add Group dialog box, which asks for some required and some optional information, as shown in Figure 11.6.

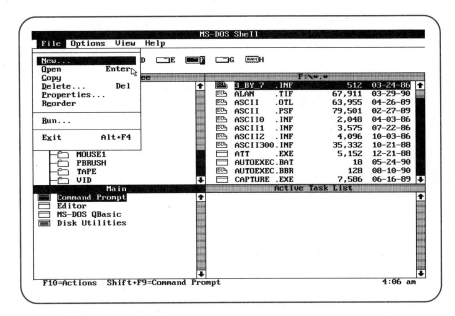

Figure 11.5. The File menu displayed for the Program List.

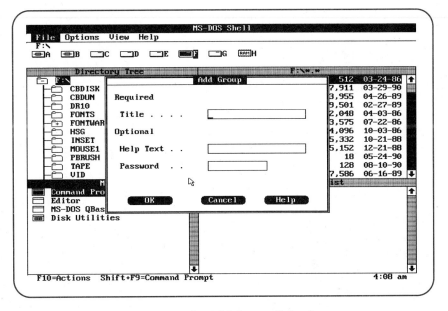

Figure 11.6. The Add Group dialog box.

As usual, use the Tab and Shift-Tab keys to move from box to box and the Backspace, Ins, Del, and arrow keys to make corrections, as necessary. Each of the options in the dialog box is discussed in the sections that follow.

The Group Title

NOTE: Remember that you can always press the F1 key (or click an option in the Help menu with the mouse) for additional help whenever you are using the DOS Shell.

The group Title should briefly describe the contents of a "group" of programs. It can be as many as 23 characters long and may contain blank spaces and punctuation marks. The group title will appear as an option on the higher-level group screen. (For example, the Application Programs option in Figure 11.4 is a group title on the Main Group screen. The group title also appears at the top of the group's screen. (In Figure 11.4, `Main Group` is the title of the currently displayed group.)

After you type the group title in the appropriate box, press Tab to move to the next box—the Group Help Text.

The Group Help Text

You can add your own help message to a group. After you add the message, your help text appears in the Help window whenever you highlight the group title and press the F1 key. You can enter as many as 255 characters, including spaces and punctuation, to the Help box. Later, when DOS displays your help text, it automatically formats the text to fit inside the Help window.

If you want a sentence or paragraph in your help text to begin on a new line, end the preceding line with a ^m (pronounced `caret m`.) To type the ^m, first type an uppercase 6 (hold down the Shift key and type the number *6* above the letters *T* and *Y* on the keyboard). Then release the Shift key and type the letter `m`, so that it looks just like ^m on the screen. If you want to place a blank line between two lines, use two ^m's (^m^m). Each additional ^m after the first one inserts another blank line in the final help text.

The Group Password

If you want to limit access to the new group, you can assign a password to it. The password can be as many as 20 characters long and may contain blank spaces. Keep in mind that once you enter a password, only people who know the password will be able to gain access to the group.

NOTE: If you forget the password for a group, you can edit the groups's `password=` line in the DOSSHELL.INI file to change or delete the password.

Be sure you write the password on a piece of paper (checking your spelling both on the screen and on the paper very carefully), and then put that piece of paper in a safe place. If you forget the password later, even you will not be able to access the new group (unless you are an advanced user and can change or delete the group's `password=` line in the DOSSHELL.INI file.)

If you do not want to assign a password to the group, leave this option blank.

A Sample Group

Figure 11.7 shows a completed sample Add Group dialog box. The group title is Application Programs; however, only a small portion of the help text is visible. The entire help text is as follows (note the use of ampersands to start sentences on new lines):

This group lets you run the Word Processing, Spreadsheet, and Database Management programs. Each program is automatically started in its own directory.

In this example, the Password option in the Add Group dialog box is blank, which indicates that no password is required to access the new group.

After defining your new group, select the OK button to save it. The group title, `Application Programs`, then appears on the current group screen, as shown previously in Figure 11.3.

If you add help text to your group, you can view it by moving the highlight to the group name (Application Programs in this example) and pressing F1. The first lines of your custom help text appear in the help window, and you can use the usual scrolling techniques to view remaining text. Press Esc to leave the help window. Figure 11.8 shows the custom help text for the Application Programs group.

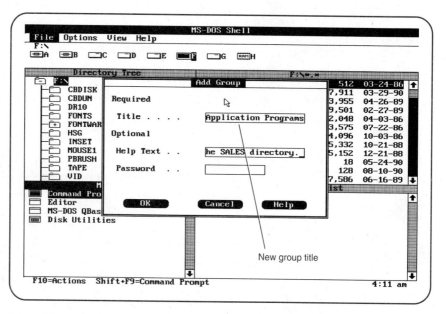

Figure 11.7. A new group defined on the Add Group dialog box.

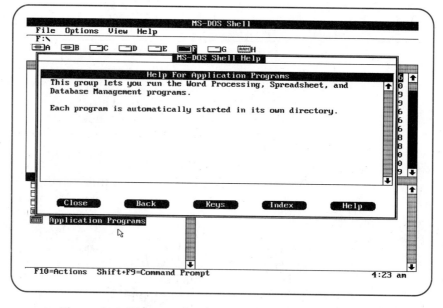

Figure 11.8. Help text for the Application Programs group.

Adding Programs to the Group

When you first create a new group, it doesn't contain any programs other than the option to return to the Main group. Therefore, if you select the group name from the Main Group screen (either by highlighting it and pressing Enter or by double-clicking the group name with your mouse), DOS initially shows only the `Main` option on the screen (clicking that option returns you to the Main group). Note, however, that the group title appears at the top of the screen, as you can see in Figure 11.9.

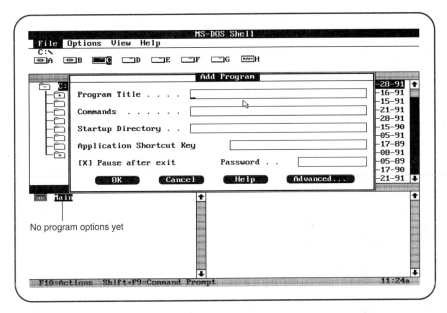

Figure 11.9. A new group before adding program options to it.

To add a new program item to the group, first pull down the File menu from the Menu Bar and then select the `New` option. At the New Program Object dialog box, press Enter or select OK to select Program Item (note that this option is the default selection). This displays the Add Program dialog box, as shown in Figure 11.10.

Note that the Add Program box contains two required items—Program Title and Commands—and several optional items. All items are described in the following sections.

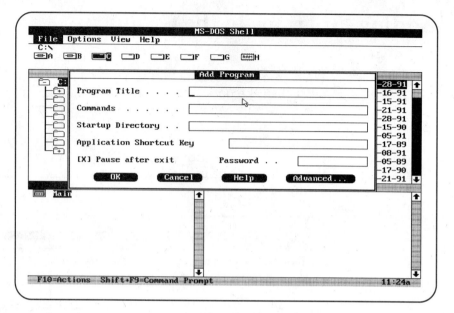

Figure 11.10. The Add Program dialog box.

The Program Title

The program title can be as many as 23 characters long and may include blank spaces and punctuation marks. This is the title that appears on the group screen and the one that you select to run the program. Typically, you should use either the program's commercial name (such as dBASE IV) or a description of the program (such as Database Manager). After you type the program title, press Enter or Tab to move to the next item.

The Program Commands

NOTE: See Chapter 13 if the program that you want to run from the Shell is a batch (.BAT) file.

In the Commands box, you need to type the commands that DOS uses to start the program. If several commands are required, separate each command with a space, a semicolon (;), and another space (for example,

EDIT C:\AUTOEXEC.BAT ; COPY C:\AUTOEXEC.BAT D:\BACKUPS ; EDIT C:\CONFIG.SYS ; COPY C:\CONFIG.SYS D:\BACKUPS). Each command is executed in sequence, from left to right. You can enter as many valid DOS commands as necessary, but the text in the `Commands` box cannot exceed 500 characters.

The Startup Directory

NOTE: The purpose of overlay files, which usually have file name extensions like .OVR or .OVL, are discussed in detail in Chapter 16.

The `Startup Directory` option lets you define a directory to switch to before running the program. If the program's home directory (that is, its location) is not included in the PATH statement, enter the program's home directory as the Startup Directory (so DOS can find the program).

If the program's home directory is in the PATH, you can leave the Startup Directory option empty to start the program from whatever happens to be the current directory, or you can specify any other directory.

For example, suppose that your spreadsheet program is stored on C:\MYSHEET, and C:\MYSHEET is in the PATH. You store your spreadsheets on C:\MYSHEET\MYFILES. In that case, you could make C:\MYSHEET\MYFILES the Startup Directory for that spreadsheet. That way, the spreadsheet program will (probably) automatically use \MYSHEET\MYFILES to store and retrieve files. (I say "probably" because it depends on the particular spreadsheet program that you use).

The Application Shortcut Key

When you enable the Task Swapper (via the Options menu), you can have several applications open at one time. If you want to jump from the current application to another open application, you usually have to press Alt-Tab to cycle through open applications until you reach the one you want.

Use the `Application Shortcut Key` option box to specify a key-combination (Alt plus a key, Ctrl plus a key, or Shift plus a key) that automatically starts this program if 1) the Task Swapper is active and 2) the application is currently in the Active Task List.

When you define a shortcut key, keep two things in mind: 1) try to select "mnemonic" combinations (for example, Alt-W for WordPerfect, Alt-D for DBASE IV, and so on) and 2) do not choose a key-combination that might have another meaning in your applications (for example, do not choose Alt-F to start FOXPRO if Alt-F pulls down a `File` menu).

Pause After Exit

When you run a program from the Shell, a brief, almost imperceptible transition is made to the command prompt, and then control shifts to the program you are running. When you finish with that program and exit to DOS, there is an equally brief transition from the command prompt to the Shell. You hardly notice any of this—if everything goes right.

However, if DOS encounters a problem while trying to access a program, it displays an error message on the command prompt screen, not on the Shell screen. This is inconvenient because the command prompt screen is displayed so briefly that it is impossible for you to read the error message.

You can force DOS to pause and display the command prompt screen before returning to the Shell. This gives you a chance to read any error messages that might have appeared if something went wrong. To make DOS pause at the command prompt screen, select the Pause After Exit check box. You must then press a key to return to the DOS Shell.

NOTE: When you first add a program to a group, always be sure this box is checked. That way, if you make a mistake in the dialog box, you'll be able to see the error message, which in turn, might help you solve the problem.

Now, if there is a problem that prevents DOS from running the program, DOS displays an error message that briefly describes the problem. The Pause After Exit option lets you read that message before control returns to the Shell.

For example, the error messages `Bad command or file name` indicates that the DBASE program is not available from the current directory or that you made a mistake in the dialog box. (Perhaps you misspelled the directory name or startup command.)

After you read the error message, press a key to return to the Shell. Then check for possible errors in the startup sequence by using the techniques described in the later section entitled "Changing a Program or Group."

With the `Pause After Exit` check box, you can control whether or not the DOS Shell is displayed immediately after this program ends. The box has an `X` in it by default. Leave the check when you don't want the Shell to be automatically displayed after the current program ends. You should also leave the box checked when you want to read the output of a program before returning to the Shell. For example, if you add the DOS MEM program to one of your groups, be sure this box is checked so that you can read the information on the screen.

To cancel this option, click the check box or use the Tab or arrow keys to move the highlight to the box and then press the Spacebar. The `X` immediately disappears; now, after the program you're using ends, the Shell will be displayed immediately.

The Program Password

The Password option on the Add Program dialog box is identical to that used with the Add Group dialog box (and the same warning still applies). However, entering a password here restricts access only to this specific program rather than to the group as a whole. (Leave this item blank if you do not want to require a password.)

The Advanced Dialog Box

The Advanced dialog box lets you specify additional details about the current program item. You can enter help text, reserve the minimum conventional and extended memory this program needs, limit the extended memory that the program can use, set video modes, disable task swapping, and disable the DOS Shell's reserved shortcut keys. To display the Advanced dialog box, select the Advanced button at the bottom right of the Add Program dialog box.

The Help Text

The Help Text option for adding programs is identical to that for adding help text to a group. However, the help message that you enter here should refer only to the specific program being added, not to the group as a whole. This text will be displayed whenever you select this program item and press the F1 key. (Leave this item blank if you do not want to add help text.)

Conventional Memory KB Required

Use this option box to specify the minimum amount of conventional memory (in kilobytes) that the program needs in order to run. For example, if your program requires a computer that has at least 256 KB, you could enter 256 in this box. If less than 256 KB is available on your system when you select this program, DOS will display an `Insuffi-cient Memory` prompt and then return control to the Shell. If you do not enter a number in this box, DOS uses a default value of 128.

XMS Memory KB Required

This option box lets you specify the minimum amount of extended memory (in kilobytes) that the program needs in order to run. The default value is zero. For example, if your program requires 512 KB of extended memory for large data files, you should enter 512 in this box. If less than 512 KB of extended memory is available on your system when you select this program, DOS will display an `Insufficient Memory` prompt and then return control to the Shell.

XMS Memory KB Limit

This option box lets you specify the maximum amount of extended memory (in kilobytes) that the program can use. It sets this limit by controlling the amount of extended memory that can be swapped by the program. For example, when you select this program, if you enter 256 in this box, your program can access only 256 KB of extended memory. If you do not enter a number in this box, DOS uses a default value of 384. Of course, if your system has less than 384 KB of extended memory, the default value will be the total amount of available extended memory.

The Video Mode Options

This option lets you specify the video mode—Text or Graphics—that will be used when you run this program.

The Text option displays only ASCII characters when running the program. If your program doesn't include graphics characters in its output, you should select this option to speed disk swapping operations. The Graphics option lets the program display bit-mapped graphics (if your hardware supports this type of graphics display). For example, you would select Text for a simple text editor and select Graphics for a full-blown, WYSIWYG ("what you see is what you get") word processor.

Prevent Program Switch Box

If you select this option (by placing an X in this check box), you disable task swapping when this application is running. For example, if you check this box for your word processor, when you run that program from the Shell, you will not be able to return to the Shell with Ctrl-Esc or switch to another open application with the Alt-Tab key combination. You will have to end your word processing program if you want to return to the Shell.

Reserve Shortcut Keys Boxes

If your program uses one of the DOS Shell's reserved key combinations (Alt-Esc, Alt-Tab, or Ctrl-Esc) to perform an essential operation, check the appropriate box to disable the Shell's use of that key combination. For example, if Alt-Tab performs a recalculation in your spreadsheet program, the only way you can use this command is to check the Alt-Tab box to disable the Shell's use of this key combination.

A Sample Program Definition

Figure 11.11 shows a completed sample Add Program dialog box, created to provide access to the dBASE IV program. The program title is dBASE IV. The program command is DBASE, the Startup Directory is \DBASE on hard disk drive C: (where the program is stored), and the Application Shortcut Key is Alt-D. The Password option was left blank so that everyone has unrestricted access to the dBASE program. Also, as soon as the application ends, control immediately returns to the DOS Shell.

In the Advanced box, I entered the following help text, which is displayed whenever you select this program and press F1:

```
Select this option to run the dBASE IV program.^m
^m
You will automatically be changed to the DBASE directory.^m
^m
When the dBASE Control Center appears on the screen, you can
change to another directory by selecting "Disk Utilities..."
from the Tools pull-down menu. Then select "Set default
drive:directory" from the DOS pull-down menu.
```

NOTE: You can also run a program by highlighting its option on the screen and selecting Open from the File pull-down menu.

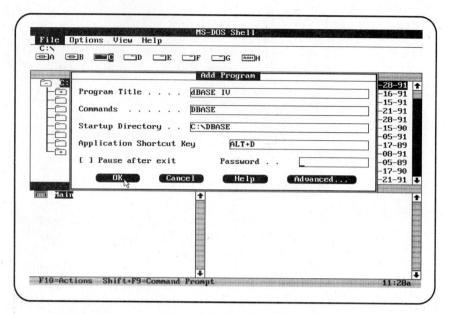

Figure 11.11. Add Program dialog box designed to start dBASE IV.

Figure 11.12 shows the Applications Programs screen with the new program title **dBASE IV** added. Pressing F1 while this option is highlighted displays the custom help text for this option. Selecting this option, by highlighting and pressing Enter or by double-clicking with a mouse, immediately starts the dBASE IV program.

When you finish using dBASE IV and exit to DOS, you are automatically returned to the Application Programs group screen.

Startup Box for a Word Processor

It is not absolutely necessary to use a program's "home" directory as the starting point for a program that you access from a group screen. If the program's directory is specified in the PATH command of your AUTOEXEC.BAT file, you can start the program from any directory.

> NOTE: The "real" name of your WordPerfect directory may vary; for example, WordPerfect 5.1 is generally stored in a directory named \WP51.

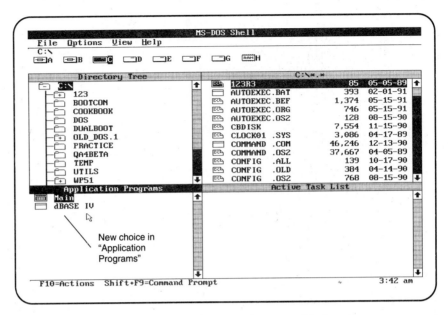

Figure 11.12. The dBASE IV option added to the
Application Programs group.

A good example is the WordPerfect program, which is stored in the WP directory. As you can see in our hypothetical directory structure (Figure 11.1), the directory tree shows a subdirectory named WPFILES beneath the WP directory. This subdirectory stores files that are used only with WordPerfect.

The reason for creating the WPFILES subdirectory is that most people (myself included) tend to save a lot of "junk" files with word processing programs, such as old letters, memos, and notes. If you do not erase these from time to time, they eventually accumulate into a huge collection of file names.

In this example, we're assuming the WP directory is in the search PATH. However, DOS shouldn't be forced to search through a lot of junk file names each time you try to run a program. Hence, the \WP\WPFILES path name leads to a directory used as a storage area for general word processing files (such as memos, letters, and notes).

To ensure that anyone who uses the computer also stores their general word processing files in this directory, you can make this the default directory from which WordPerfect is started. To do so, you must first be certain that the WP is included in the PATH command (preferably in the AUTOEXEC.BAT file, so there is no chance of your forgetting to enter the PATH command at the command prompt).

Then, when you add the WordPerfect program to a group, add \WP\WPFILES to the Startup Directory box. Figure 11.13 shows the appropriate Add Program dialog box for adding WordPerfect to the Application Programs group. (Remember, if you want to add custom help text, you must enter the help message in the Advanced dialog box.)

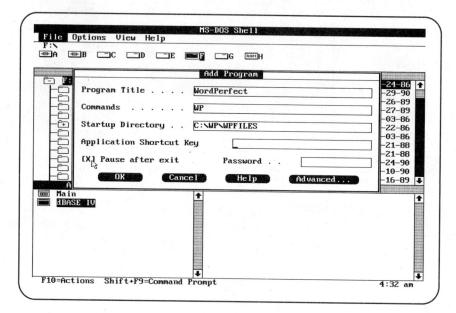

Figure 11.13. Add Program dialog box for WordPerfect.

NOTE: Depending on your version of WordPerfect, you might also need to change the Location of Files for Documents using Shift-F1,L,D within the WordPerfect program. See your WordPerfect documentation.

This startup sequence ensures that when you "casually" save a WordPerfect file without specifying a different directory, the file will be stored on the \WP\WPFILES directory. (However, WordPerfect still allows you to save and edit files on other directories if you so desire.)

As usual, after completing the Add Program dialog box, select the OK button to save your changes and return to the current group screen.

Leaving a Group Screen

To leave a group screen (other than the Main Group) and return to the Main Group, press the Escape (Esc) key. You can also select the `Main` option at the top of your group option list. If you are in a subgroup, select the top item until you return to the Main group.

Changing a Program or Group

You can always change the contents ("properties") of a group or program dialog box. To do so, use the following steps:

1. Highlight the `group` or `program` name on the screen.

2. Press `F10` or `Alt` to access the Menu Bar.

3. Select the `Properties...` option from the File menu.

NOTE: If you cannot see the cursor in the dialog box, try pressing the Ins (or Insert) key to make it larger.

This displays the contents of the group or program in the Group Properties or Program Item Properties dialog box. Table 11.2 lists the editing keys that you can use to make changes. After completing your changes, select the OK button to save the revisions. To abandon your changes, press Esc or select the Cancel button.

Table 11.2. Keys used to enter and edit dialog box entries.

Key	Effects
Tab	Moves cursor to the next option
Shift-Tab	Moves cursor to the previous option
→	Moves cursor right one character
←	Moves cursor left one character
Home	Moves cursor to the start of text in the box
End	Moves cursor to the end of text in the box

Continues

Table 11.2. *(continued)*

Key	Effects
Del (or Delete)	Deletes the character at the cursor
Backspace	Moves the cursor left and erases the character
F1	Displays help
Esc	Abandons the current changes

Deleting a Program or Group

To delete a group or program item, use the following steps:

1. Highlight the `group` or `program` name on the screen.
2. Press `F10` or `Alt` to access the Menu Bar.
3. Pull down the File menu and select the `Delete...` option or press `Del`.

In either case, when you select `Delete...`, the DOS Shell presents two options:

1. Delete this item
2. Do not delete this item

Select the first option to perform the deletion; select the second option to cancel the operation.

Copying Programs to Other Groups

If you want the same program to be accessible from different groups, highlight the program's name, press F10 or Alt, and pull down the File menu. Select `Copy....` Notice the instructions in the Reference Bar at the bottom of the screen:

```
Display Group to Copy To, then press F2. ESC to cancel
```

Move the highlight to the group to which you want to copy the program item. When the destination group screen appears, press F2 to complete the copy. (You also have the option of pressing Esc to abandon the copy.)

Rearranging Options in a Group

To rearrange the program items in a group, first move the highlight to the program item that you want to move. Then press F10 or Alt, pull down the File menu, and select `Reorder....` The Reference Bar at the bottom of the screen displays the following instructions:

`Select location to move to, then press Enter. ESC to cancel`

As instructed, move the highlight to the new position for the current option and press Enter. If you are using a mouse, you can double click the new location. If you change your mind, press Esc to cancel the operation.

Creating Custom Dialog Boxes for Program Items

If you've used any programs from the Disk Utilities... screen, you probably noticed that DOS displays a dialog box in which you can enter additional information before DOS runs the program. For example, when you select `Quick Format` from the Disk Utilities... screen, DOS presents the dialog box shown in Figure 11.14.

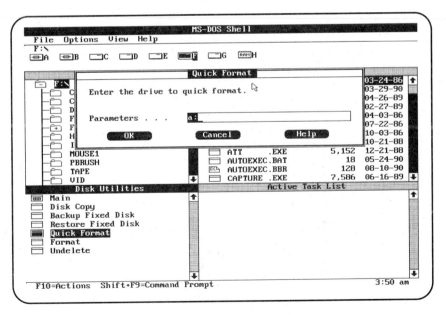

Figure 11.14. The Startup Dialog Box for the FORMAT program.

When you add your own programs to a group, you can also design a dialog box to be displayed before DOS runs the program. To create a customized dialog box that appears whenever you select your program, you must first add a space and then `%1` after your command in the Commands box of the Add Program dialog box.

For example, assume that you want a dialog box to open every time you start your WordPerfect program. If you've already created this program item in your Applications Programs group, you must first add the `%1` variable to the program's command line. To do so, use the following steps:

1. Highlight the `WordPerfect option`.

2. Press `F10` or `Alt` to activate the Menu Bar.

3. Pull down the File menu and select the `Properties...` option to display the WordPerfect Program Item Properties dialog box.

4. Change the command in the Commands box to read `WP %1`.

5. Select the `OK` button.

This causes the Shell to display another dialog box—Program Item Properties. Use the four fields here to create the new dialog box that will appear whenever you select the WordPerfect program.

Window Title

In this field you can enter a title that will be displayed at the top of your customized WordPerfect dialog box. In the WordPerfect example I've been using, you might enter `Run WordPerfect` in the Window Title field.

Program Information

In this optional field you can enter text that will appear under the title of the customized dialog box. You might include a brief description of the current program to let the user know exactly what this program will do. In the current example, you might enter

```
WordPerfect is a word processor you can use to create and edit files.
```

Prompt Message

In this field you can specify a *prompt* that helps the user enter the correct information in the dialog box. In the WordPerfect example, you might use the prompt

```
Enter name of file to edit...
```

so that the user knows to enter a file name. With other programs, you might list a series of valid parameters that the user could enter.

Default Parameters

In this field you can specify a default parameter for the program—that is, a parameter that is always listed in your customized dialog box when the program is selected. The user can automatically accept that default value by pressing Enter.

For example, look at the startup dialog box for the FORMAT program in Figure 11.14. The dialog box offers the a : parameter as the default. If you want to format the diskette in drive A:, press Enter; if you want to format a diskette in another drive, type the new drive letter (the new parameter automatically replaces the default value).

Enter a default parameter when you are reasonably sure that the user actually will use that parameter. Because most people format diskettes in drive A:, this is an excellent choice for the FORMAT command. However, this type of default value appears to be useless for our WordPerfect example. After all, you can't specify a file name; you don't know which file the user will need to edit.

Multiple Custom Dialog Boxes

You can create multiple customized dialog boxes for a single program by inserting additional % parameters (%1, %2, and so on) after your command in the Commands box of the Add Program dialog box.

For example, assume that you want two dialog boxes to open every time you start a particular program—one in which you specify a directory for a file and the other in which you specify the actual filename. To do so, include two or more replaceable parameters after the startup command.

For example, referring back to the dialog box in Figure 11.13, if you were to change the Command box from

```
WP
```

to

```
WP %1 %2
```

two dialog boxes would appear before the WordPerfect program was actually run. You could use these to specify two separate startup options for WordPerfect; perhaps the name of the document to edit and also the name of a macro to execute immediately at startup.

Using Prompt Box Entries from Multiple Commands

If you want more than one startup sequence command to use the entry in your customized dialog box, use the "% variables" to save and repeat entries. You can define as many as 10 such variables.

For example, examine the following program startup command sequence (in the Commands box of the Add Program dialog box). Notice that the directory name entered in response to the instruction `Enter directory to store files on` is stored as %1. The `Enter name of file to edit` dialog box is stored as %2.

```
CD \%1 ; WP %2 ; DIR C:\%1\%2
```

The DIR C:\%1\%2 command in the startup sequence retrieves the values entered into the two prompt boxes and inserts them into the DIR command. For example, if you entered \WP\WPFILES as the directory to store the file on and BOB.LET as the file name, DOS actually executes the command `DIR C:\WP\WPFILES\BOB.LET`, thereby displaying the directory entry for the file returning to the Shell.

More Dialog Box Examples

To see other examples of program startup sequences, go to the Disk Utilities group and move the highlight to any option on that screen. Press F10 or Alt, pull down the File menu, and select the Properties option. Press Tab to move the cursor to the Commands box. To see the startup sequence for the command, scroll through the Commands box using the usual ← and → keys.

Associating Data Files with Programs

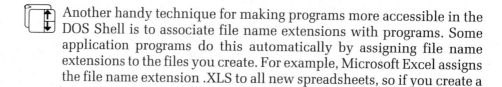 Another handy technique for making programs more accessible in the DOS Shell is to associate file name extensions with programs. Some application programs do this automatically by assigning file name extensions to the files you create. For example, Microsoft Excel assigns the file name extension .XLS to all new spreadsheets, so if you create a

spreadsheet named INCOME, Excel automatically stores that spreadsheet in a file named INCOME.XLS.

On the other hand, some application programs do not automatically assign extensions to file names. In these cases, you can devise your own naming scheme to identify a program's data files. For example, when you use a word processor, always use the extensions .TXT (for text) and .DOC (for document) for the files that you create.

When you set up an association between an application and a filename extension, DOS automatically loads the appropriate program when you select the file name from the Files List. The program doesn't even need to be in the same directory as the file you select.

To associate a file name extension with a program, you must first know the program name, which is the command you use to start the program followed by the extension .COM, .EXE, or .BAT. Then highlight that program in the Files List and select `Associate...` from the File pull-down menu. DOS then asks you for the extension (or extensions) to associate with that program. Look at an example.

Suppose that you use the WordPerfect word processing program on your computer, and you typically use it to create files with the extensions .DOC and .TXT. To associate these extensions with the WordPerfect program, first use the Directory Tree Area of the File List to change to the directory that contains the WordPerfect program (usually named WP).

NOTE: To ensure that only one file name is selected when associating extensions to a program, select `Deselect All` from the File pull-down menu before you select a file to associate.

Next, highlight the name of the file that contains the WordPerfect program (WP.EXE) (or click your mouse once) to select that file name. Press F10 or Alt and then press Enter to pull down the File menu. Finally, select `Associate...`.

This displays the Associate File dialog box in which you type in the extension(s) to associate with that program. Do not include the leading period in your extensions (for example, type DOC not .DOC). If you are assigning multiple extensions, separate each with a blank space. Press Enter after you finish typing the extensions. Figure 11.15 shows an example that associates the extensions .TXT and .DOC with the WordPerfect program. (Note also that WP.EXE is selected in the Files List.)

After you make the association between the WordPerfect program and the .TXT and .DOC file name extensions, you'll always have quick and easy access to WordPerfect for editing files. In the future, whenever you select a file with one of those extensions from the Files List (by highlighting its name and pressing Enter, or double clicking it with your mouse), DOS automatically runs the WordPerfect program and displays the selected file for editing.

Note that you don't need to change to the WordPerfect program's directory; DOS finds the program for you and runs it, while you remain in the current directory. However, be aware that the Associate capability works only with application programs that permit *command line options*. Consult the documentation that came with your application program to determine whether 1) it provides this capability and 2) it supports only specific extensions.

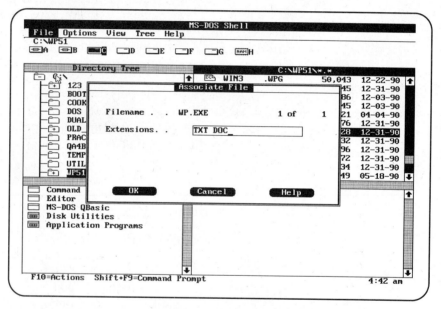

Figure 11.15. Associating the .TXT and .DOC extension with WordPerfect (WP.EXE).

For example, the documentation for the dBASE IV program explains that you can run dBASE IV and have it automatically load a dBASE command file, but only if the command file has the extension .PRG. For example, if a file named INVENTRY.PRG exists in the current directory, you can enter the command DBASE INVENTRY to start DBASE and the INVENTRY.PRG program simultaneously. Therefore, you can associate the .PRG extension to the dBASE IV program in the DOS Shell.

Refer to the documentation that comes with an application program to determine which file name extensions can be associated with it. To give you some general examples, Table 11.4 lists nine common application programs, the directories in which they are typically stored, the name of the program file, and acceptable extensions that you can associate with the program.

> WARNING: Never enter the extensions .COM, .EXE, or .BAT in the Associate file dialog box. Files with these extensions are programs themselves, not data files that can be associated with programs.

Table 11.4. Sample application programs and associated extensions.

Application Program	Hard Disk Directory	Program's File	Associated Extensions
dBASE III PLUS	DBASE	DBASE.EXE	.PRG
dBASE IV	DBASE	DBASE.EXE	.PRG
Paradox (Version 3)	PARADOX3	PARADOX3.EXE	.SC
R:BASE	RBFILES	RBASE.EXE	.CMD
Excel	WINDOWS	EXCEL.EXE	.XLC, .XLM, .XLS
Lotus 1-2-3	123	123.COM	.SET
Quattro	QUATTRO	Q.EXE	.WKQ
WordPerfect	WP	W.EXE	<any>
WordStar (Version 4)	WS4	WS.EXE	<any>

Note that the WordPerfect and WordStar word processing programs do not automatically assign extensions to file names; therefore, you can associate any extension you wish to these programs. However, limit yourself to only those extensions that you use when working with these programs, such as .TXT, .DOC, and .LET.

Refer to the sample directory tree presented in Figure 11.1. A quick examination shows that you should probably associate extensions with your dBASE and EXCEL programs, in addition to the extensions you've already associated with WordPerfect. Using the information from Table 11.3, you know that you should associate the .PRG extension with the

DBASE.EXE program in the DBASE directory and the .XLC, .XLM, and .XLS extensions with the EXCEL.EXE program in the WINDOWS directory. Doing so provides quick and easy access to all three programs from the data files on any directory.

Simplifying Hard Disk Backup Procedures

I've discussed the importance of making copies (backups) of files to protect yourself from accidental erasures, disk problems, and so on. Backing up the files on your hard disk is especially important, because if your hard disk *crashes*, you probably won't be able to recover any of the files stored on it. A hard disk crash can be caused by any number of problems, the most common being that some moving part wears out or breaks.

NOTE: Chapter 16 shows how a hard disk operates and the moving parts involved.

Undoubtedly the thought of your hard disk crashing—and destroying all of your files—is unnerving. Rest assured, this is not something that happens all the time. I've personally had three hard disks crash in 12 years. Ironically, two of these crashes were within several days of each other. (Apparently, the new hard disk that I installed to replace the old one was defective, because a few days later, it also crashed.) However, hard disk crashes are not the only events that can deprive you of your files. Natural disasters, such as fires and lightning-induced power surges, as well as not-so-natural disasters, such as burglars and malicious computer programs called *viruses*, can also destroy your files. If you store your backup files in the same building as your computer, some of these disasters can also ruin your backup diskettes. (You can protect valuable data by storing backups in a diskette-sized safe deposit box at the bank or in a fireproof safe.)

Speaking of disasters, even if your computer is insured, the work you put into creating your files is not. In fact, chances are that none of your software is covered by insurance. Even if an insurance company offers you a refund for the loss of your computer hardware, you will have recouped only a small portion of your actual investment of time and money.

> NOTE: When you upgrade to DOS 5, the SETUP program auto-matically lets you back up your entire system before it installs the new DOS programs.

This section examines techniques for backing up your entire hard disk and for recovering data from the backups. Of course, backing up an entire hard disk can take quite a bit of time, so it is not the kind of task you want to do every day. However, during the course of any single day, you will probably create or change only a few files. Because backing up these few files can be done quickly and is easily performed at the end of each day, I'll also discuss techniques for making more frequent backups.

Backing Up the Entire Hard Disk

DOS provides a command, named BACKUP, that can back up files from your hard disk onto a series of diskettes. Unlike the COPY and XCOPY commands, BACKUP stores files in a special condensed *image* format. This allows BACKUP to store copies of files that are larger than the capacity of a diskette. It is important to remember, however, that backup copies created with the BACKUP command can only be restored onto your hard disk using the DOS RESTORE command (discussed later in this chapter).

Calculating the Number of Diskettes Required

Backing up your hard disk is an operation that requires several diskettes. You can calculate how many diskettes you'll need by dividing the total number of bytes of data stored on your hard disk by the capacity of one diskette. To find out how many bytes of storage space are currently being used on the hard disk, use the CHKDSK command. (Remember, CHKDSK is an external command, and DOS must be able to find CHKDSK.COM when you enter the command.)

For example, suppose that you enter the command CHKDSK at the command prompt and that DOS displays the following information about your hard disk (other information that CHKDSK displays is not relevant at the moment):

```
33323008 bytes total disk space
 .
 .
 .
18071552 bytes available on disk
```

Given that your disk has a total of 33,323,008 bytes of storage space and that 18,071,552 bytes are still available, then your disk must contain 15,160,456 bytes of data (33,232,008 minus 18,071,552). To calculate the number of 360KB diskettes required to back up that much data, use the formula *data/diskette storage capacity* or in this case:

```
15,160,456/360,000
```

which results in 42 diskettes. If you are using 1.2MB diskettes, you would calculate the number of diskettes required by using the following figures:

```
15,160,456/1,200,000
```

which results in 13 diskettes.

Sometimes the BACKUP procedure requires fewer diskettes than the calculation determines because it stores files in a somewhat compacted format. However, the data stored on your hard disk will probably grow in the future, so there is no harm in labeling a few extra diskettes for future backups.

After you determine the number of diskettes required to back up your hard disk, place labels on each diskette and number them. Be sure to number them consecutively, starting at 1. For example, you would label the first three diskettes:

HARD DISK BACKUP #1

HARD DISK BACKUP #2

HARD DISK BACKUP #3

and so on . . ..

If you have more than one hard disk drive, you must back up each separately, and therefore you need to calculate the number of diskettes required for additional hard disks as well. Create one set of backup diskettes for each hard disk. Number each set starting with 1 and label them accordingly, as in these examples:

HARD DISK BACKUP C: #1

HARD DISK BACKUP C: #2

HARD DISK BACKUP C: #3

and so on . . .

HARD DISK BACKUP D: #1

HARD DISK BACKUP D: #2

HARD DISK BACKUP D: #3

and so on . . ..

DOS Versions 3.3 through 5 can automatically format the diskettes when you initiate the BACKUP procedure. If you are using an earlier version of DOS, you need to format each of these diskettes before you start the backup procedure.

WARNING: See the following commands in Appendix B for warnings about using them with BACKUP: APPEND, ASSIGN, SUBST, and JOIN.

After you label all the diskettes (and format them, if necessary), you can begin the backup procedure. BACKUP requires the following basic syntax:

`BACKUP drive...:file(s)... destination switches`

Drive:file(s) specifies the hard disk to back up.

file(s) represents a single file name or an ambiguous file name of files to back up. (For example, *.* backs up all files on the hard disk.)

destination is the floppy disk drive in which the backup diskettes are placed.

switches represents various options that control how files are backed up.

The most commonly used optional switches are listed in Table 11.5. (See Appendix B for additional, less frequently used switches.) Note that the optional switches are always preceded by a forward slash (/).

Table 11.5. Switches commonly used
with the BACKUP command.

Switch	Description
/A	Adds new and modified files to existing backup diskettes
/L	Creates a log on the current directory of the hard disk that lists all backed up files
/M	Backs up new and modified files only
/S	Backs up files from all subdirectories beneath the current directory

Keep in mind that BACKUP is an external DOS command, and it requires access to a file named BACKUP.EXE. Automatic formatting also requires that the FORMAT.COM file be available from the current directory. Before starting the backup procedure, either access the directory that contains these files or be sure that the appropriate directory is included in the current PATH specification.

To start the backup procedure, follow the appropriate steps for your version of DOS:

NOTE: DOS 4 and 5 users, note that the Backup option "suggests" a source, destination, and switch for backing up the hard disk. Look at the startup sequence for this option; it displays the suggestion by using the /D and /R options discussed earlier in this chapter.

---

1. Insert backup diskette number 1 in drive A:.

2. From the Main Group screen, select Disk Utilities.

3. Select Backup Fixed Disk.

4. Press the End key, the Spacebar, and then add the switch /L to the suggested prompt, as shown in Figure 11.16.

5. Press Enter (or click OK once).

If you are backing up from the command prompt, follow these steps:

1. Insert backup diskette number 1 in drive A:.

2. Type the command BACKUP C:*.* A: /S /L and press Enter.

Regardless of whether you used the DOS Shell or the command prompt to start the backup procedure, the steps shown had you enter C:*.* A: /S /L as the source, destination, and switches. The C:*.* entry starts the backup at the root directory (that is, C:\ represents the root directory of drive C: and *.* specifies all files). The A: entry specifies drive A: as the destination. The /S switch tells DOS to include all directories beneath the starting directory (the root directory in this example) and /L creates a log file (BACKUP.LOG) on the current directory of the hard disk.

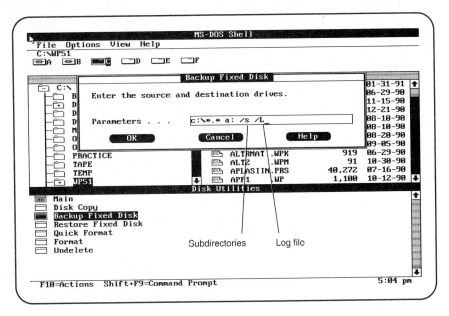

Figure 11.16. Dialog box for the Backup Fixed Disk option.

After you enter BACKUP, DOS provides instructions on how to proceed. (These instructions vary slightly in different versions of DOS.) The first message is

```
Insert backup diskette 01 in drive A:
WARNING! Files in the target drive A:\ root directory will be erased
Press any key to continue...
```

Double-check to be sure that you placed backup diskette number 1 in drive A:. Then press a key to continue.

If the BACKUP command automatically formatted the diskette in drive A:, DOS displays information about the diskette, followed by the prompt `Format another (Y/N)?`. Press N and Enter to proceed.

Your screen now shows the directory and path of each file as it is backed up. After filling one diskette, DOS prompts you to insert the diskette you labeled number 2 and repeat the formatting and backing up process. This procedure is repeated until all the files on the hard disk are backed up. Follow the instructions as they appear on the screen; always answer N whenever DOS asks whether you want to format another diskette; and be sure to place the correctly numbered diskette into drive A: when prompted.

When DOS finishes the backup, the command prompt or Shell reappears on the screen. Remove the diskette in drive A: and write the word *Last* on the label, because DOS might require you to insert this last diskette in drive A: at some time in the future. (A later example will demonstrate this requirement.)

Printing the Log File

NOTE: Refer to the section "Controlling the Printer" in Chapter 12 if you have problems printing the BACKUP.LOG file.

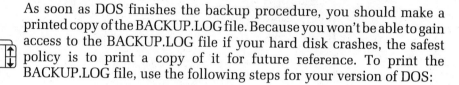

As soon as DOS finishes the backup procedure, you should make a printed copy of the BACKUP.LOG file. Because you won't be able to gain access to the BACKUP.LOG file if your hard disk crashes, the safest policy is to print a copy of it for future reference. To print the BACKUP.LOG file, use the following steps for your version of DOS:

1. If you are using the DOS Shell, display the `File List`.

2. Change to the `DOS directory` by highlighting its name in the Directory Tree (or by clicking it once with the mouse).

3. Press the `Tab` key to move to the Files List.

4. Move the highlight to the `BACKUP.LOG` file and press the `Spacebar` (or click your mouse once) to select that file name.

5. Press `F10` or `Alt` and then press `Enter` to pull down the File menu.

6. Select `Print....` (Note that this option is available only if you have loaded the resident portion of the PRINT program—by typing `PRINT /D:PRN` at the command line—before you started the Shell.)

1. If you are working from the command prompt, type `TYPE C:\BACKUP.LOG > PRN`.

2. Press `Enter`.

The printout of the BACKUP.LOG file displays the date and time of the backup, as well as the diskette number, directory, and file name of each backed-up file, as in the example shown in Figure 11.17. (Note that your printout will reflect the date, time, directories, and file names of your hard disk.)

```
24-17-90  16:30:00

001   \CONFIG.SYS
001   \012345.678
001   \AUTOEXEC.BAT
001   \DOS\COUNTRY.SYS
001   \DOS\COMMAND.COM
001   \DOS\DISKCOPY.COM
001   \DOS\DISPLAY.SYS
001   \DOS\FDISK.COM
001   \DOS\FORMAT.COM
001   \DOS\KEYB.COM
001   \DOS\KEYBOARD.SYS
001   \DOS\REPLACE.EXE
001   \DOS\SYS.COM
001   \DOS\ASSIGN.COM
001   \DOS\ATTRIB.EXE
001   \DOS\BASIC.COM
001   \DOS\BASICA.COM
001   \DOS\COMP.COM
001   \DOS\DEBUG.COM
001   \DOS\DISKCOMP.COM
001   \DOS\EDLIN.COM
```

Figure 11.17. A partial sample BACKUP.LOG file printout.

The information in the BACKUP.LOG file might come in handy in the future if you ever need to restore a few files from your backup diskettes. Later sections will demonstrate this procedure.

Files Stored on Backup Diskettes

As mentioned earlier in this chapter, the BACKUP command stores an image of your hard disk on one or more diskettes; it does not store individual files. Therefore, you might be surprised if you look at the directory of one of your backup diskettes.

For example, if you put one of the backup diskettes into drive A: and then enter the command DIR A: from the DOS command prompt, you will see only two file names listed, as follows:

```
BACKUP      001      1,210,709      04-17-91   04:30p
CONTROL     001          3,001      04-17-91   04:30p
```

001 is the number of the backup diskette label

The next column represents the size of the combined files on the diskette.

04-17-91 and 04:30P represent the date and time of your last backup. (The DOS 5 File List screen shows the date but not the time.)

Neither the COPY nor XCOPY commands can retrieve files from these BACKUP or CONTROL files. Only the RESTORE command, discussed later, can perform this operation.

Updating the Backup Diskettes

After you initially create your backup of the entire hard disk, you can use a few shortcut techniques to quickly update the backups. In particular, you might want to use the /M (for *modified*) and /A (for *add*) switches to back up only modified files.

The /M switch causes BACKUP to copy only those files that have their *archive bit* turned on. The archive bit is stored with the file name and other attributes (such as read-only) in every file, and DOS automatically turns it on when you create or edit a file. When you back up a file using the BACKUP command, DOS turns off the Archive bit, and the bit remains off until you modify the file again.

The /A switch adds new and modified files to the existing backup diskettes instead of replacing the existing backups. If you do not use the /A switch, DOS automatically reformats the backup diskette, thereby erasing all the backup files that are already on that diskette. Basically, you want to use the /A switch whenever you want to back up only new and modified files, instead of going through the time-consuming process of backing up the entire hard disk.

> NOTE: DOS 5 users can select Backup from the Disk Utilities screen to update the backup diskettes, but they must be sure to change the suggested entry in the dialog box to include the /M and /A switches.

To back up modified files and add new files to the existing backups, first be sure that all your numbered backup diskettes are available. Then, while still accessing the hard disk, enter a BACKUP command with the general format `BACKUP C:\*.* /M /A /S / L:filename` where `filename` assigns a name other than BACKUP.LOG to the new backup log file. You might make the file name represent the current date, but be sure not to use any invalid characters. For example, if you are updating your backup diskettes on April 15, 1992, you might want to enter the command.

```
BACKUP C:\*.* A: /M /A /S /L:Apr15_92.LOG
```

When you press Enter, DOS prompts you to insert your last (highest-numbered) backup diskette in drive A:. (This is the diskette you labeled "Last" after the original backup.) Depending on the number of new and modified files that need to be backed up, DOS might prompt you to insert additional diskettes.

If backing up new or modified files requires you to use additional diskettes, write *Last* on the new highest-numbered diskette and erase it from the label of the diskette that was previously labeled Last.

You also might want to print a copy of the new log file. Keep it handy in case you need to restore only certain files from your backup diskettes.

NOTE: The XCOPY command, discussed in Appendix B, is also a useful tool for making daily backups of new and modified files.

Remember, it's a good idea to store backup diskettes off-site—away from the computer—in case of fire or theft. If you use the /A option to update your backup diskettes, you need to keep only the diskette labeled *Last* (or better yet, a copy of that diskette) near the computer for daily updates. As you fill more backup diskettes, store them off-site with the other, lower-numbered diskettes.

Recovering From a Hard Disk Crash

If your hard disk crashes and you need to install a new hard disk, you must first format (and partition, if necessary) the hard disk and then install DOS as though you had bought a brand new computer. (See Appendix A for a detailed discussion of these topics.) Then, when the hard disk is physically ready to accept data, you can use your backup diskettes to recreate your original directory tree and copy all of your files to the new hard disk.

NOTE: Appendix B discusses all the switches available for both the BACKUP and RESTORE commands.

You must use the RESTORE command to copy backup files from your diskettes to the hard disk. To ensure that all directories are recreated and that files are placed in their original directories, you must use the /S switch. In addition, you probably should use the /P switch as well. This switch causes RESTORE to pause and ask for permission before updating a file that already exists on the hard disk with an "older" copy of the file. For example, if you've upgraded to a newer version of DOS since the hard disk crashed, you do not want to replace your new DOS files with the old DOS files on the backup diskettes—the /P switch helps prevent you from doing so.

The general syntax for restoring all the files from the backup diskettes is as follows:

```
RESTORE drive destination /S /P
```

drive is the name of the drive that will hold the backup diskette(s).

destination is the name and the root directory of the hard disk being restored and is followed by the *.* file specifier.

NOTE: There is no need to "practice" restoring a hard disk; the entire operation is "automatic." Use the RESTORE command only when necessary.

For example, to restore the entire hard disk from backup diskettes in drive A:, you would type the command

```
RESTORE A: C:\*.* /S /P
```

After you press Enter to enter the command, DOS prompts you to insert the backup diskettes in sequentially numbered order. Because you specified the /P switch, DOS might stop and ask for permission before replacing an existing file with an older one. In most cases, you should answer No to keep the newer version of the file on the hard disk.

When RESTORE completes it operation, it redisplays the DOS command prompt. Use the appropriate commands to examine the files on your hard disk and notice that all your original files and directories are back in place.

Restoring Only Specific Files

In some cases, you might need to restore only a few files. For example, suppose that you tried to erase all the .BAK files on your DOS directory, but you inadvertently entered the command ERASE *.BAT, which erases all your *batch files* instead. (Batch files are discussed in Chapter 13.) You need to restore these files from your backup diskettes, but you certainly do not need to restore all of the files on your hard disk.

In this situation, you need to restore only those files that have the extension .BAT into the current directory (DOS in this example). To do so, enter the command

```
RESTORE A: C:  \DOS\*.BAT /P
```

Note that the /P switch is optional; it helps prevent overwriting newer files with older files. DOS prompts you to insert your backup diskettes, in numbered order, until it has restored all the specified files.

You can speed the process of restoring only certain files by checking your printed copies of the backup .LOG files. When you locate the diskette number that contains the files you want to back up, insert that diskette into drive A: rather than the one that DOS suggests. DOS will display the message `WARNING! Diskette is out of se-quence. Replace diskette or continue if OK.` Leave the diskette in drive A: and press any key to start the restoration process from that diskette.

Troubleshooting

If you make an error while trying the techniques in this chapter, one of the following messages will probably appear on your screen. Locate the appropriate error message and try the recommended solution.

- ❏ `Bad command or file name:` You either misspelled a command or the program is not available on the current diskette, directory, or in the currently defined PATH of directories.

- ❏ `General failure reading drive A:` The diskette in drive A: is probably not formatted. Press `A` to abandon the operation; then format the diskette.

- ❏ `Invalid drive in search path:` Your command includes a drive name that does not exist on your computer.

- ❏ `Last backup diskette not inserted:` DOS requested that you put the last backup diskette in the destination drive, but you put in a different diskette. Try your highest-numbered diskette.

❑ **System files restored. Target disk may not be bootable**: Versions of DOS prior to 3.3 copy the system files during backup and restore operations. You probably need to use the SYS command (see Appendix B) to recopy system files from your newer version of DOS back to the root directory. (This makes your hard disk bootable again.)

❑ **Target is full. The last file was not restored**: The hard disk on which you are restoring files has no more storage space, and the last-listed file name was not restored. This occurs when your backup diskettes contain more data than the hard disk can store. You probably need to manually create all new directories on your hard disk and then use the RESTORE command independently for each directory to restore only specific files.

❑ **Warning! Diskette is out of sequence. Replace diskette or continue if OK**: The backup diskette in drive A: is not the one that DOS requested. Replace it with the properly numbered diskette. However, if you are certain that you want DOS to search only the current diskette because you know it contains the files you want to recover, leave the out-of-sequence diskette in the drive. Then press any key to continue. DOS asks to search only higher-numbered disks in future prompts.

❑ **Warning! Files in the target drive A:\ root directory will be erased**: DOS is telling you that the current backup will replace previously backed up files. This message does not appear when you use the /M and /A switches to update a previous backup.

Summary

This chapter focused on techniques that help make your use of a hard disk more efficient, easier, and safer. The following is a summary of the most important points:

❑ Use the PATH command to permit DOS to search specific directories for program files with the .COM, .EXE, and .BAT extensions. This lets you run programs from any directory on your hard disk and avoids the Bad command or file name error.

❑ Hard disk crashes, as well as other disasters, can destroy all the files on a hard disk. Keep backup copies of files off-site so that you can recover from any type of loss.

❑ The BACKUP command can back up either an entire hard disk or new and modified files.

❑ You cannot use COPY or XCOPY to recover files that were saved with the BACKUP command; you must use the RESTORE command.

❑ DOS 5 users can provide easier access to programs by creating, modifying, and deleting groups and program items in the DOS Shell. To access the options that perform these operations, pull down the File menu when the Program List section of the Shell is active.

❑ By associating selected file name extensions with programs, DOS 4 and 5 users can run programs by selecting file names with the associated extension from the Files List of the DOS Shell.

Managing the Standard Devices

This chapter discusses techniques for managing the standard devices attached to virtually all computers—the screen, the printer, and the keyboard. Because you've gotten this far in the book, the devices connected to your computer are probably functioning quite well. However, as you'll see in this chapter, there are some fancy techniques that you can use to customize the features of these devices.

Note that nearly all of the examples in this chapter use the command prompt. That's because the DOS Shell, while easy to use, does not offer as much flexibility as the command prompt in many situations.

 Remember, if you are using DOS 5 and want to try the command prompt examples in this chapter, you must press the F3 key or the Alt-F4 key-combination to exit the DOS Shell and display the command prompt.

Directing Actions to Devices

DOS offers many commands and techniques for controlling devices. Several techniques use the redirection symbols (listed in Table 12.1) in conjunction with DOS device names (listed in Table 12.2) to manage the flow of information to and from various devices.

Table 12.1. DOS redirection symbols.

Redirection Symbol	Meaning
<	Read input from *device*
>	Send output to *device*
>>	Send output to *file* without overwriting existing text

Table 12.2. DOS device names.

Device Name	Description
CON	The keyboard (for input) and screen (for output) (CONsole)
COM1	First serial (COMmunications) port
COM2	Second serial port
COM3	Third serial port
COM4	Fourth serial port
AUX	Another name for COM1 (AUXiliary serial port)
LPT1	First parallel printer (Line PrinTer) port
LPT2	Second parallel printer port
LPT3	Third parallel printer port
PRN	Same as LPT1 (PRiNter)
filename.ext	(Although not actually a device, a file can sometimes be used as though it were device)

If you've followed the command prompt examples in this book, you've already seen redirection symbols and device names. For example, the command DIR > PRN sends output from the DIR command to the printer. The command TREE > PRN sends output from the TREE command to the printer.

Note that Table 12.2 shows that some names define a *port*. You can think of a port as a plug on the back of your computer to which a device, like the printer, is attached. For example, if you have two printers attached to your computer on ports LPT1 and LPT2, entering a command such as `DIR > LPT2` sends output to your second printer rather than the first.

If you use the `> PRN` symbol and device name, but it does not send output to the printer, perhaps you have a *serial* printer attached to the COM1 port. In that case, try entering command `DIR > COM1`. In fact, if you are not sure which port your printer is hooked to, you can experiment with different device names and the `DIR >` command until you find the device name that accesses the printer.

As you will see, DOS offers you great flexibility in using device names and redirection symbols, but the command that uses them must be logical. For example, the command

```
DIR < PRN
```

makes no sense because the printer cannot "send" anything to the DIR command. (In fact, the printer cannot send anything to any device; it can only accept output from the computer.) However, the command `DIR > PRN` command makes sense because the DIR command can certainly send its output (text) to the printer.

Managing the Screen

DOS 5 users have already seen how to change the colors of the DOS Shell and how to use the Scroll Bar and PgUp and PgDn keys to scroll through long lists of directory and file names (Chapter 3). This section focuses on techniques for managing the screen at the command prompt. These techniques work for all versions of DOS.

Clearing the Screen

 NOTE: You cannot clear the screen while using EDIT or while EDLIN is displaying the * prompt.

Many times when you use the DOS command prompt, the screen becomes cluttered with old command lines and the output of those commands. You can eliminate that clutter by clearing the screen. Enter the command `CLS` (short for CLear Screen), and press Enter. Everything but the command prompt (which now appears at the top left corner of the screen) is cleared from your screen.

Controlling Scrolling

Some DOS commands show far more lines of information than the screen can display at one time, and text scrolls off the screen too quickly for you to read. You've already seen how to use the /P switch with the DIR command so that DOS pauses after each screenful of information is presented. Several more techniques for controlling scrolling are discussed in the next few sections.

Starting and Stopping Scrolling

Whenever large amounts of text are scrolling off the screen, you can always freeze the display by pressing Ctrl-S (hold down the Ctrl Key and press the letter S). Scrolling stops immediately. To resume scrolling, press any character key, the Spacebar, or Ctrl-S.

If your keyboard has a key labeled Pause, you can press that key instead of Ctrl-S to stop scrolling. To resume scrolling after pressing Pause, press any other key.

Using the MORE Command

In some cases, you need to be pretty quick on the keyboard to use the Ctrl-S or Pause key effectively, especially with today's high-speed computers. As an alternative, you can use the MORE command to have DOS automatically pause as each screenful of information is presented.

MORE is an *external* command. That is, it's actually a program stored in a file named MORE.COM. To use MORE, the MORE.COM file must be accessible from the current drive and directory. (If you get the `Bad command or file name` error when you first try to use the command, keep reading and try the alternative techniques discussed later in this section.)

There are two different syntaxes for using MORE. When you need to display the contents of lengthy text files, enter the MORE command, followed by the < redirection symbol, followed by the name of the file whose contents you wish to view. The general syntax for this usage is

```
MORE < filename.ext
```

(*filename.ext* is the name of the file you wish to view).

When you want to use MORE in conjunction with another DOS command, use the second general syntax as shown in the following sentence. In this case, type the complete command, followed by the pipe character ¦ and the MORE command. This general syntax is as follows:

```
DOS command ¦ MORE
```

For example, assume that after you buy a new application program, you notice that a file named READ.ME is included on the program diskette. You want the computer to pause each time the screen is filled with text so that you have time to read all the information. To do this, enter either this command:

```
MORE  < A:READ.ME
```

or this command:

```
TYPE A:READ.ME ¦ MORE
```

> NOTE: Notice how the MORE < READ.ME command uses the *input* redirection symbol to send the contents of the READ.ME file into the MORE program.

Although both commands use the MORE command in different ways, the result is the same. DOS displays one screenful of text and the prompt `-- More --`. When you see this prompt, press any key to see the next screen. Optionally, you can press Ctrl-C or Break to stop viewing the file. (To press Break, press Ctrl-Pause or Ctrl-Scroll Lock, depending on which key is marked Break on your keyboard.)

If the MORE command is not available on the current drive, directory, or PATH, change to the diskette or directory that contains the MORE.COM file (usually the DOS directory in Versions 4 and 5 or the root directory in earlier versions) and specify both the location and name of the file you want to view. For example, if you want to view the contents of a file named README.DOC in a directory named QUATTRO, first change to the drive and directory that contains the MORE.COM file. Then enter the command

```
MORE < C:\QUATTRO\README.DOC
```

or

```
TYPE C:\QUATTRO\README.DOC ¦ MORE
```

If your computer doesn't have a hard disk, put the DOS diskette that contains the MORE.COM program into drive A: and insert the diskette that contains the file whose contents you want to view in drive B:. Assuming that the file you want to view is named README.TXT and that the current drive is drive A:, enter the command

```
MORE < B:README.TXT
```

or

```
TYPE B:README.TXT ¦ MORE
```

Remember, if you have a hard disk, you can make external commands, such as MORE, more accessible by setting up an appropriate PATH command, as discussed in Chapter 11.

NOTE: As mentioned in Chapter 4, TREE is also an external command, and it requires access to the program TREE.COM.

You can use MORE with any command that displays data. For example, the TREE /F command can display the names of all files in all directories of your hard disk. To see its output one screen at a time, enter the command

```
TREE C:\ /F ¦ MORE
```

Customizing the Command Prompt

In Chapter 4, you learned that you can enter the command PROMPT PG to change the DOS command prompt so that it displays the current drive and directory. You can actually do quite a bit more to alter the command prompt. Table 12.3 lists all the codes that you can use with the PROMPT command to customize your command prompt.

Table 12.3. Symbols used with the PROMPT command.

Code	Effect
$$	Displays the $ character
$_	Breaks prompt onto a second line
$B	Displays the ¦ character
$D	Displays the current date

Code	Effect
$E	Generates an escape character
$G	Displays the > character
$H	Backspaces one character
$L	Displays the < character
$N	Displays the current drive
$P	Displays the current drive and directory
$Q	Displays the = character
$T	Displays the current time
$V	Displays the current version of DOS
<other characters>	other characters are displayed literally

You can use these codes to change the prompt at any time. For example, the last entry in the table means that any characters other than the listed codes are displayed *literally*, or exactly as you type them in the prompt command. If at the command prompt you type

`PROMPT At your service -- Please enter a command:`

and press Enter, every command prompt that DOS displays thereafter will read `At your service -- Please enter a command:`.

Next, enter this command:

`PROMPT $D $B $T$G`

When you press Enter, the command prompt displays the current date ($D) followed by a blank space, the ¦ symbol ($B), another blank space, the current time ($T), and the > symbol ($G). (Note that the blank spaces in the prompt correspond to the blank spaces you typed in the PROMPT command.)

`Thu  04-19-1992 ¦ 10:31:42.70>`

NOTE: The $_ symbol uses the underscore character, not the hyphen. That is, it's $_ rather than $-.

To break a lengthy prompt into two lines, use the $_ character where you want to split the prompt. For example, if you enter the command

```
PROMPT $D$_$T$G
```

DOS displays a command prompt with the current date on one line and the current time and a > symbol on the second line, as follows:

```
Thu  04-19-1992
10:32:42:68>
```

The $V (version number) symbol does not break the command prompt into two lines, so you need to use the $_ symbol. For example, if you enter the command

```
PROMPT $V$_$D$G
```

the command prompt displays the current version of DOS on one line and the current date and the > symbol on the next, as follows:

```
IBM DOS Version 5.00
Thu 04-19-1992
```

You can use the Backspace code ($H) to erase parts of a prompt. For example, suppose that you want your command prompt to display the current date minus the year, followed by the ¦ character, the current drive and directory, and the > symbol. To do so, you must type this command:

```
PROMPT $D$H$H$H$H$H $B $P$G
```

When you press Enter, DOS displays a new prompt that resembles the following (of course, it will display today's date and your current directory):

```
Thu 04-19 ¦ C:\DOS>
```

Note that the command uses five Backspace ($H) symbols to erase the last five characters of the current date (/1992).

You can also combine text and codes in the PROMPT command. For example, type this command:

```
PROMPT Today is $D$_Current drive and directory is $P$G
```

When you press Enter, the prompt appears as follows (with today's date displayed in place of Mon 01-01-92 and your current drive and directory in place of C:\DOS):

```
Today is Mon 01-01-92
Current drive and directory is C:\DOS>
```

If you want to return to your more familiar command prompt, enter the command PROMPT PG.

Using ANSI Codes to Control the Screen and Keyboard

 Many years ago when computers were all room-size giants, the American National Standards Institute (ANSI) developed a standardized coding system for managing the interface between keyboards, computers, and monitors. They did so to make software more *portable*, that is, so that programs could be used without modification on many different types of computers and monitors.

DOS comes with a *device driver*, stored in a file named ANSI.SYS, that uses the ANSI coding system to send characters and images to your screen. The file is called a "device driver" because it literally drives a device; that is, it tells a device (in this case, your monitor) what to do.

To see whether your computer is currently set up to accept ANSI codes, you have to use the TYPE command to view the contents of your CONFIG.SYS file. Because CONFIG.SYS is always stored on the startup drive or directory, the file is easy to find—if it in fact exists.

On a hard disk, enter the following command at the DOS command prompt:

    TYPE C:\CONFIG.SYS

On a computer that boots from a diskette, insert your Startup diskette in drive A:, be sure that drive A: is your current drive, and enter the command

    TYPE CONFIG.SYS

If your computer can accept ANSI codes, the CONFIG.SYS file contains the command DEVICE = followed by the location and name of the ANSI.SYS file. For example, on a computer that boots from the hard disk, you should see either the command

    DEVICE = C:\ANSI.SYS

or perhaps the command

    DEVICE = C:\DOS\ANSI.SYS

On a computer that starts from a diskette, you should see the command

    DEVICE = A:\ANSI.SYS

NOTE: Some programs require that your CONFIG.SYS file load the ANSI.SYS file. These programs' documentation will inform you of this requirement.

If your CONFIG.SYS file does not set up the ANSI.SYS device driver, you can modify the file using the general techniques described in Chapter 10. However, it is not absolutely necessary to do so, unless you want to customize screen colors at the command prompt or redefine keys on your keyboard (as discussed later in this chapter).

To modify your CONFIG.SYS file to include the ANSI.SYS device driver, you first must be sure that DOS can find the ANSI.SYS file as soon as you turn on the computer. That is, if you boot your computer from a diskette, the ANSI.SYS file must be stored on that diskette. The CONFIG.SYS file must also contain the command

```
DEVICE = ANSI.SYS
```

If your computer boots from a hard disk, locate the directory that contains ANSI.SYS FILE (probably the root directory or the DOS directory). When you modify the CONFIG.SYS file, be sure to specify the complete path and file name in the DEVICE command, as in the following examples:

```
DEVICE = C:\ANSI.SYS
```

or

```
DEVICE = C:\DOS\ANSI.SYS
```

After you change the CONFIG.SYS file, remember that modifications do not take effect until you reboot the computer. However, from then on, DOS automatically issues these commands every time you start your computer.

Modifying Screen Colors and Attributes

5 DOS 5 users already know how to change the color scheme of the DOS Shell. If you are using another version of DOS (or you prefer the DOS 5 command prompt), you can use ANSI codes to customize the screen colors displayed at the command prompt, provided that your computer is set up to accept ANSI codes (as discussed in the preceding section).

To color the screen, you use the PROMPT command in conjunction with special codes called *escape sequences*. An escape sequence is a series of characters that begin with the Escape (or Esc) key character. Recall from Table 12.3 that you can use the $e symbol in the PROMPT command to specify the Escape key character.

The general syntax for using an Escape sequence in the PROMPT command is as follows:

```
PROMPT $e[xxm
```

in which x x is a one-digit *attribute* number or a two-digit color number. Table 12.4 lists the complete escape sequences for controlling screen colors on monitors that are capable of displaying color.

Table 12.4. Escape sequences for changing screen colors.

Color	Foreground	Background
Black	$e[30m	$e[40m
Red	$e[31m	$e[41m
Green	$e[32m	$e[42m
Yellow	$e[33m	$e[43m
Blue	$e[34m	$e[44m
Magenta	$e[35m	$e[45m
Cyan	$e[36m	$e[46m
White	$e[37m	$e[47m

Table 12.5 lists the escape sequences for controlling special attributes on both color and monochrome screens. You can use these special attributes in conjunction with colors (on color monitors). Note that these one-digit escape sequences are similar to the two-digit codes used for coloring the screen.

Table 12.5. Escape sequences for changing screen attributes.

Attribute	Escape Sequence
None	$e[0m
High intensity	$e[1m
Underline (monochrome only)	$e[4m
Blinking	$e[5m
Reverse video	$e[7m
Invisible	$e[8m

> NOTE: Be sure to use the lowercase letters *e* and *m* in the escape sequences. If you make a mistake, the DOS prompt displays all characters literally from the point of the error to the right. Retype the command to correct it.

The following gives you practice using some of these escape sequences at the DOS command prompt. However, keep in mind that you might not see any changes until you either clear the screen or start typing again.

To switch the screen display to reverse video, enter the following command:

```
PROMPT $e[7m
```

> NOTE: Reverse video reverses the foreground and background colors or shades used on your screen. For example, if your screen normally displays dark letters on a light background, reverse video displays light letters against a dark background.

Not much seems to happen at first (other than the fact that the command prompt disappears). However, watch what happens when you enter any command that displays text, such as DIR. The displayed text appears in reverse video, as shown in Figure 12.1.

After changing screen colors or attributes, you can enter a new PROMPT command to redefine the command prompt, without losing the current attributes or colors. For example, to redisplay the familiar command prompt, enter the command `PROMPT $P$G`.

Now try the blinking attribute; enter the command

```
PROMPT $e[5m
```

To see the results, enter a command (such as `DIR`) that displays text on the screen. Notice that the reverse video attribute remains in effect, and now blinking has been added to that attribute.

To return to the normal screen display, remove all attributes by entering the command

```
PROMPT $e[0m
```

Then enter the `CLS` command to clear the screen and the `PROMPT $P$G` command to redisplay your command prompt.

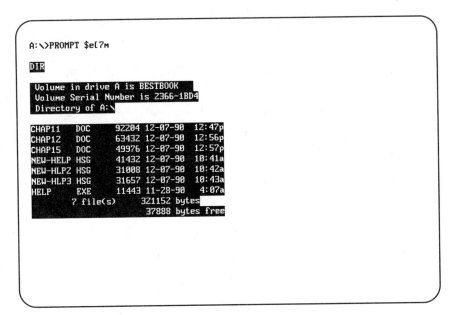

Figure 12.1. Sample display in reverse video.

WARNING: If you set the screen foreground and background to the same color, you won't be able to see what you are typing on the screen. If you cannot see what you are typing, carefully enter the command PROMPT $e[0m$P$G or press Ctrl-Alt-Del to reboot.

If you have a color monitor, try some different color schemes. Use any combination of the foreground and background color escape sequences shown in Table 12.4. For example, to display yellow text on a blue background, enter the command

```
PROMPT $e[33m $e[44m
```

Then enter a command that displays text (such as DIR). If yellow looks more like brown, switch to high intensity by entering the command

```
PROMPT $e[1m
```

Again, enter a command to display text (such as DIR) and see the effects of these PROMPT commands.

You can use any combination of screen attributes, colors, and the command prompt style codes in a single PROMPT command if you wish. For example, to simultaneously set the screen colors to high-intensity red letters on a black background and also define the command prompt, enter the command

```
PROMPT $e[40m$e[1m$e[31m$P$G
```

Keep in mind that DOS reads the "code strings" defined in the PROMPT command every time it displays the command prompt. Therefore, you can turn on an attribute at the beginning of the prompt and then turn it off at the end of the prompt, so that only the command prompt itself uses the defined attribute.

For example, suppose that you want to display your screen in normal colors, but you want to display the command prompt in reverse video. To do so, first return to the normal screen colors and attributes by entering the commands

```
PROMPT $e[0m$P$G
```

and

```
CLS
```

Next, enter a PROMPT command that turns on reverse video, displays the command prompt, and then turns off reverse video, as follows:

```
PROMPT $e[7m$P$G$e[0m
```

As Figure 12.2 shows, only the command prompt is displayed in reverse video.

Saving PROMPT Settings

The one problem with designing a custom command prompt that uses fancy display attributes and colors is that DOS "forgets" it as soon as you turn off the computer. However, you can have DOS immediately activate your custom prompt at startup by including the PROMPT command in your AUTOEXEC.BAT file.

> NOTE: Remember, you can only use screen attributes and colors if your CONFIG.SYS file loads the ANSI device driver.

```
C:\DOS>PROMPT $e[7m$P$G$e[0m

C:\DOS>DATE
Current date is Mon 02-04-1991
Enter new date (mm-dd-yy):

C:\DOS>TIME
Current time is 12:10:42.24p
Enter new time:

C:\DOS>
```

Figure 12.2. The command prompt is displayed in reverse video.

You can place the PROMPT command on any line in the AUTOEXEC.BAT file. (However, DOS 4 and 5 users must remember to leave the DOSSHELL command as the last command in AUTOEXEC.BAT.) Figure 12.3 shows a sample AUTOEXEC.BAT file that contains the command `PROMPT $e[7m$P$G$e[0m`. Remember, you must edit the AUTOEXEC.BAT as a DOS text file, and you must store it in the root directory on the proper drive for your computer. Refer to Chapter 10 for details, if necessary.

Controlling the Screen's Character Size

NOTE: You can also use the MODE command to configure other devices. See Appendix B for details.

Normally, DOS displays 80 columns of text across the screen. However, you can double the size of the letters on the screen by telling DOS to display only 40 columns of text across the screen. To do so you must use the DOS MODE command. Table 12.6 lists the codes that you can use with the MODE command to control the display on your monitor.

```
@ECHO OFF
SET COMSPEC=C:\DOS\COMMAND.COM
PATH C:\WP;C:\DOS;C:\UTILS;C:\DBASE;C:\WINDOWS
VERIFY OFF
PROMPT $e[7m$P$G$e[0m
C:\DOS|MOUSE.COM
APPEND /E
APPEND C:\DOS
PRINT /D:LPT1
DOSSHELL
```

Figure 12.3. Sample AUTOEXEC.BAT file with a customized PROMPT command.

NOTE: Changing the character size affects command prompt screens only, not the DOS Shell or EDIT.

MODE is an external DOS program. To use MODE, the MODE.COM file must be accessible from the current diskette or directory (otherwise, DOS displays the `Bad command or file name` error message). If you are using the DOS 5 Shell, you should exit the Shell using the F3 key (not the Shift-F9 key) so that the copy of the Shell remaining in RAM does not conflict with the MODE program that will be loaded into memory.

If you have a color monitor, and you are currently looking at the command prompt, try the MODE command by entering the following:

```
MODE 40
```

Next, enter any command that displays text (such as DIR). As Figure 12.4 shows, the display uses much larger characters.

To switch back to the 80-column display, enter the command

MODE 80

Table 12.6. Options for controlling the screen display with MODE.

Code	Effect
40	Sets the display width to 40 characters on a color graphics screen. (Does not affect colors.)
80	Sets the display width to 80 characters on a color graphics screen. (Does not affect colors.)
BW40	Sets the display width to 40 characters and colors to black and white on a color graphics screen.
BW80	Sets the display width to 80 characters and colors to black and white on a color graphics screen.
CO40	Sets the display width to 40 characters and allows color on a color graphics creen.
CO80	Sets the display width to 80 characters and allows color on a color graphics screen.
MONO	Sets the display width to 80 characters and allows only a monochrome display. The only setting available with monochrome display adapters.)

Controlling the Printer

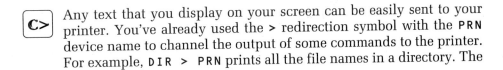

Any text that you display on your screen can be easily sent to your printer. You've already used the > redirection symbol with the PRN device name to channel the output of some commands to the printer. For example, DIR > PRN prints all the file names in a directory. The command TYPE *filename.ext* > PRN prints the contents of a file. There are other ways to send information to the printer as well, as the sections that follow describe.

```
C:\>DIR

   Volume in drive C has no label
   Volume Serial Number is 201A-2C4C
   Directory of   C:\

   SALES           <DIR>       01-02-90    1:05p
   012345    678          109 06-17-88   12:00p
   COMMAND   COM        37637 06-17-88   12:00p
   DOS             <DIR>       03-13-89    4:13p
   ACCTNG          <DIR>       01-02-90    1:06p
   BACKUP    LOG        40076 04-18-89    5:50p
   AUTOEXEC  BAT          256 04-20-90   11:50a
   AUTOEXEC  BAK          256 04-19-90    2:23p
   CONFIG    SYS          256 04-19-90    2:23p
   MOUSE1          <DIR>       05-05-88    6:05p
   WP              <DIR>       05-06-88    9:13a
   WINDOWS         <DIR>       05-09-88    3:14p
   DBASE           <DIR>       06-09-88    8:17a
   UTILS           <DIR>       11-07-88    9:05a
        14 File(s)      17192960 bytes free

C:\>
```

Figure 12.4. Screen displaying 40 characters per line.

Copying Screen Text

NOTE: To print screen displays using the Shift-PrintScreen key combination, see the section titled "Printing Graphics" later in this chapter.

When the command prompt is displayed, you can send an exact copy of whatever is on your screen (called a *screen dump*) to the printer by pressing the Shift-PrintScreen key (on some keyboards, PrintScreen is abbreviated Print Scrn or Prt Sc).

To try this procedure, be sure that the DOS command prompt is displayed on your screen and then enter the command DIR /W. Then press Shift-PrintScreen (hold down the Shift key and press the PrintScreen key).

There are two points to keep in mind about using the PrintScreen key to "dump" text from the screen to the printer. First of all, those of you who have laser printers may not see the printed results immediately. Instead, you may need to eject the current page from the printer to see the printed screen dump (as discussed in the next section).

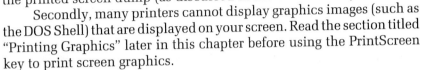

Secondly, many printers cannot display graphics images (such as the DOS Shell) that are displayed on your screen. Read the section titled "Printing Graphics" later in this chapter before using the PrintScreen key to print screen graphics.

Ejecting a Page

Most printers allow you to eject a page from the printer by pressing buttons on the front of the printer. However, it is often easier to let DOS do it; use the DOS ECHO command with the form-feed character (Ctrl-L) and the printer redirection symbol (> PRN). To use this technique, follow these steps:

1. Type **ECHO** and press the **Spacebar**.

2. Press **Ctrl-L** (hold down the Ctrl key and press the letter L; the screen displays **^L**).

3. Press the **Spacebar** and type **>PRN**.

   At this point, your command should look as follows:

   ECHO ^L PRN

If it does, press **Enter**, and your printer will eject the current page.

Keeping Track of the Top of the Page

One of the most common complaints one hears about computers and printers is that the computer does not properly print text on pages. For example, your computer might start printing a new page in the middle of one piece of paper, keep printing that same page onto the second piece of paper, and then start printing the next page on the third piece of paper. This can be very irritating!

If your printer uses tractor-feed (continuous-form) paper, you can follow two simple rules to avoid this problem:

❏ Be sure that the page perforation is directly above the printer's printing head before you turn on the printer and computer.

❏ After you turn on the printer and computer, never manually "crank" the paper through the printer to get to the next page.

The reasoning behind these two rules is quite simple. First, whenever you start your computer, DOS "assumes" that top of a page is aligned just above the printer head. Second, DOS keeps track of the top of each page by counting the number of lines it sends to the printer. If the paper is not properly aligned when you start the computer, DOS is "off the mark" at the outset. Even if the paper is aligned properly when you turn on the computer, DOS cannot detect you manually cranking paper through the printer. When you do that, its count of how many lines of the page have been moved through the printer becomes incorrect, and it no longer can properly align text on the page.

> NOTE: Ctrl-J (^ J) is called the *line feed* character because it "feeds" one blank line to the printer.

Now, you might be wondering how you can eject a partially printed page or insert extra blank lines without manually cranking the printer platen. Well, use the `ECHO ^L > PRN` command discussed previously to eject the entire page. If you only want to move the paper a few lines on the current page, use the command `ECHO ^J >PRN` (press Ctrl-J to type the ^J symbol). After you type the command and press Enter, you can print additional blank lines by pressing F3 and Enter. (Recall that F3 repeats the previous DOS command.)

Note that some printers also provide buttons, such as "Set TOF" (Top Of Form), to help you keep track of alignment. See your printer manual for additional information about page alignment and the use of printer control buttons.

Slaving the Printer

Another way to send text to the printer is to *slave* the printer so that it prints all text as it appears on the screen. Use the Ctrl-PrintScreen keys as a toggle to slave and *unslave* the printer.

For example, at the command prompt, hold down the Ctrl key and press the PrintScreen (or Print Scrn or Prt Sc) key; then, release both keys. Now enter any command that displays text, such as DIR. When you press Enter, the printer prints everything that appears on your screen (including the DIR command itself).

To unslave the printer, press Ctrl-PrintScreen again. Now the printer is no longer a slave to the screen. (If you've been trying the examples, type the `ECHO ^L >PRN` command to eject the printed page from the printer.)

Another way to slave the printer is to make it copy exactly what you type at the keyboard. Although doing so turns your computer into an overpriced typewriter, the technique is handy for quick and easy jobs like addressing envelopes. The basic procedure is to use the COPY command with CON (the DOS device name for the console) as the source and PRN as the destination.

For example, to address an envelope, put the envelope into the printer. Then enter the command `COPY CON PRN` at the command prompt, as shown at the top of Figure 12.5. After you enter this command, the command prompt disappears, and you can type any text you wish. (Use the Backspace key to make corrections.) In the figure, I inserted several blank lines by pressing Enter a few times; then I typed name and address, which I indented using the Spacebar.

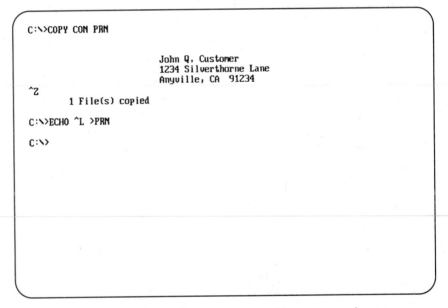

```
C:\>COPY CON PRN

                        John Q. Customer
                        1234 Silverthorne Lane
                        Anyville, CA  91234
^Z
        1 File(s) copied

C:\>ECHO ^L >PRN

C:\>
```

Figure 12.5. Using the computer to address an envelope.

After you type the name and address, type Ctrl-Z (which appears as ^Z) and press Enter. At this point, DOS prints the text on the printer and displays the message `1 File(s) copied` on the screen. To eject the envelope from the printer, enter the `ECHO ^L PRN` command.

Copying Files to the Printer

You've already seen how to use the TYPE command and the > PRN redirection symbol to print the contents of a file. You can also use the COPY command to copy the contents of text files to the printer. In addition, because COPY (unlike TYPE) permits ambiguous file names, you can print several files with one command.

To copy a file to the printer, use the standard COPY command syntax, specifying the name of the file you want to print as the source and the device name PRN (for printer) as the destination. For example, if you wanted to print all the files that have the extension .BAT from the root directory of drive C:, enter the command

```
COPY C:\*.BAT PRN
```

Keep in mind that you can only print text files, not programs or files that use special formatting codes. When in doubt, first view the contents of the file using the TYPE command. If the file's contents look okay on the screen, they will look fine on the printer as well.

Printing Graphics

NOTE: All programs that are capable of displaying graphs are also capable of printing them on any dot matrix or laser printer, so you might never need to use the GRAPHICS program and Shift-PrintScreen keys to print a graph.

If you have an IBM, Epson, or compatible printer that is capable of displaying graphics, you can use Shift-PrintScreen to copy a graphics image from the screen to the printer only after you've loaded into memory the DOS GRAPHICS program. To load the GRAPHICS program, change to the directory that contains the file named GRAPHICS.COM and then enter the command GRAPHICS at the command prompt.

After you run the GRAPHICS program, it stays in memory (RAM) until you turn off the computer. (It uses about 5KB of memory while *resident* in RAM.) For the remainder of your session with the computer (that is, until you turn off your computer or reboot), you can use the Shift-PrintScreen key to "dump" both text and graphics to your printer.

If your screen displays low-resolution graphics, graphics images are printed in the normal vertical format. If you use a high-resolution graphics screen, your graphics images will be printed sideways (horizontally) across the page. (If in doubt about low- and high-resolution graphics, try the procedure and see what happens; you can't do any harm).

If you always want to have the option to print graphs using Shift-PrintScreen, include the GRAPHICS command in your AUTOEXEC.BAT file. In fact, if you are using DOS 5, the installation process might already have performed this step for you. Use the View option or TYPE command to view the contents of your AUTOEXEC.BAT.

If you see the command A:\GRAPHICS or C:\DOS\GRAPHICS, the graphics program is automatically loaded as soon as you start your computer. You can print graphics at any time by pressing Ctrl-PrintScreen (provided that your printer is capable of printing graphics).

Entering the GRAPHICS command by itself is generally sufficient for printing graphs with Ctrl-PrintScreen. However, you can use several options with the GRAPHICS command to control color printers and to reverse the colors on the printed copy. For more details, see the discussion of the GRAPHICS command in Appendix B.

Controlling Dot Matrix Print Size

If you have an IBM or Epson dot matrix printer (or any compatible printer), it is probably printing at the default setting of 80 characters per line and six lines to the inch. You can use the MODE command to change the number of characters per line to 132 and/or the number of lines printed per inch to 8.

If you have the right printer, and the MODE.COM file is available in the current drive or directory, you can try some of the various combinations by entering the following commands (be sure to press Enter after typing each command):

```
MODE LPT1:COLS=132 LINES=6
DIR >P
MODE LPT1:COLS=132 LINES=8
DIR >P
MODE LPT1:COLS=80 LINES=8
DIR >P
MODE LPT1:COLS=80 LINES=6
DIR >P
```

Controlling Laser Printer Print Size

If you have a Hewlett-Packard LaserJet printer, you can use a few tricks to take advantage of its special features, such as compressed print and landscape mode. However, the required codes are awkward to type at the command prompt. Therefore, in Chapter 14, you will create your own program, named JETSET.BAT, to facilitate using your laser printer's special features.

Background Printing

The main problem with using commands such as TYPE CONFIG.SYS > PRN and COPY C:*.BAT PRN to print text files is that you have to wait until the printing is done before you can use your computer again. As an alternative, you can tell DOS to print *in the background*, therefore allowing you to continue using the computer while the printer is printing.

DOS accomplishes this background printing by using small *slices* of time when the computer is doing nothing else to send some text to the printer. For example, while you are reading something on the screen or thinking about what you want to do next, DOS can send quite a bit of text to the printer. Most printers, in turn, can store some text in a *buffer* (memory inside the printer) and therefore can accept data from the computer faster than the printer can print it. For example, in 2 seconds DOS might be able to send enough text to keep your printer busy for a minute or two.

Although background printing is quite easy, each version of DOS uses a slightly different technique, so I'll discuss each version separately. Note that the PRINT command offers several options in addition to those described in this chapter. See Appendix B for details.

Using Print from the DOS Shell

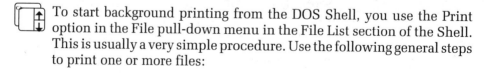 To start background printing from the DOS Shell, you use the Print option in the File pull-down menu in the File List section of the Shell. This is usually a very simple procedure. Use the following general steps to print one or more files:

1. First, be sure the Shell is displaying the File List. If both the File List and the Program List are displayed, be sure that the highlight is currently in one of the File List areas.

2. Use the Drives Area and the Directory Tree Area of the Shell to select the drive and directory that contains the file you want to print.

NOTE: The Print option (like the TYPE command) can only reliably print ASCII text files. If in doubt about the contents of a file, use the View File Contents option to preview the file. If the file's contents look okay on the screen, the printed copy will probably be fine as well.

---

3. Move the highlight to the Files List and select as many as 10 files to print by highlighting the appropriate file names.

4. After selecting files to print, press F10 (or Alt) and Enter to pull down the File menu (as shown in Figure 12.6).

NOTE: If the Print option is shaded and unavailable on the File pull-down menu, press Esc to leave the menu and continue reading the following instructions.

---

5. Select the Print option.

DOS immediately begins printing each file. If you selected multiple files, each file begins on a new page. Notice that you can continue to use your computer as DOS prints the files; you can even select additional files to print.

If you were unable to complete the steps above because the Print option on the menu was shaded and unavailable, but you are sure that you selected at least one file name to print, the PRINT command is not initialized. To initialize PRINT, press the F3 key to display the command prompt, type PRINT /D:LPT1, and press Enter. Then enter the command DOSSHELL to return to the Shell. Select the file(s) to print from the Files List again; then select Print from the File pull-down menu.

You can add the PRINT /D:LPT1 command to your AUTOEXEC.BAT file, provided that the PRINT.COM file is available from the startup directory or diskette when you first turn on the computer. For example, if you boot from a hard disk and PRINT.COM is stored on the DOS directory, add the command C:\DOS\PRINT /D:LPT1 to your AUTOEXEC.BAT file.

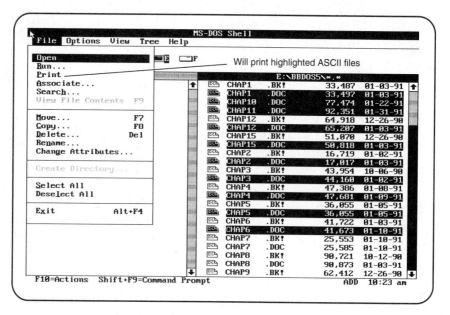

Figure 12.6. The File pull-down menu.

If you start your computer from a diskette and PRINT.COM is on the Startup diskette, add the command `PRINT /D:LPT1` to your AUTOEXEC.BAT file. Be sure to place this command before the DOSSHELL command in AUTOEXEC.BAT.

Using PRINT from the Command Prompt

To use the PRINT command from the command prompt, first be sure that the PRINT.COM file is available on the current diskette or directory (or is in a directory defined in your path command). Then enter the command PRINT followed by the location and name of the file you want to print. For example, to print a copy of the AUTOEXEC.BAT file on a hard disk, enter the command

    PRINT C:\AUTOEXEC.BAT

If this is the first time you've used PRINT in the current session, DOS displays the message

    Name of list device [PRN]:

PRN is the device name of your main printer. To use this suggested device name, press Enter. DOS then displays the message

    C:\AUTOEXEC.BAT is currently being printed

and begins printing. In addition, the command prompt immediately appears on your screen, ready to accept new commands while DOS is printing your file.

You can even enter additional PRINT commands while DOS is printing a file. DOS puts other files that need to be printed in the *queue*, and it prints them when the printer becomes available. You can put a maximum of 10 files into the queue for printing (unless you use the /Q switch, described in Appendix B, to expand the size of the queue).

Checking the Queue

If you want to see the names of the files that are currently lined up in the queue for printing, enter the command PRINT with no additional file names or switches.

Canceling a Print Job

PRINT provides two switches for canceling a print job: /T terminates all printing, and /C cancels the printing of a specific file or group of files. For example, suppose that you enter the command

```
PRINT C:\DOSBOOK\CHAP?.TXT
```

to print a group of files (for example, CHAP1.TXT, CHAP2.TXT, and so on). After DOS displays a message such as

```
C:\DOSBOOK\CHAP1.DOC is currently being printed
C:\DOSBOOK\CHAP2.DOC is in queue
C:\DOSBOOK\CHAP3.DOC is in queue
```

the DOS prompt reappears, and you can type new commands. The printer then prints each file in the queue.

NOTE: Users of DOS 4 and 5 must exit the Shell and use the PRINT /C or PRINT /T command at the command prompt to terminate a printing job.

To remove a file from the queue so that it is not printed, use the PRINT command followed by the file name and the /C switch. For example, to remove CHAP2.DOC from the queue, enter the command:

```
PRINT C:\DOSBOOK\CHAP2.DOC /C
```

To cancel the printing of the current file and all remaining files in the queue, use the /T switch with the PRINT command, as follows:

```
PRINT /T
```

DOS then displays a message such as `All files canceled by operator. Print queue is empty` to inform you that all printing has stopped. (If your printer contains a buffer, it might continue to print for a short time.)

Using PRINT with Application Programs

> NOTE: PRINT might not be able to use the formatting codes, such as boldface and underlining, that your word processor offers.

Most application programs, such as spreadsheets and word processors, store special codes in the files you create. If you try to print such a file directly, using the PRINT command, the output will probably be a mess. However, virtually all application programs provide the capability to *print to a file*, or to store a copy of the file in ASCII text format. (Refer to the application program's manual for specific instructions.) You can use the DOS PRINT command to print any file that has been stored in ASCII text format.

For example, suppose that you use the Lotus 1-2-3 program as your spreadsheet. Each month, you prepare a budgeted income statement, a portion of which appears on the 1-2-3 worksheet screen shown in Figure 12.7. Furthermore, assume that at the end of the year, you want to print all 12 budget sheets, but you want to use the DOS PRINT command to print in the background so that you can continue to use your computer.

Now, suppose that the spreadsheet files are stored in files named BIS_JAN.WK1, BIS_FEB.WK1, and so on to BIS_DEC.WK1. To see what format these files are in, change to the directory that contains the files and enter the command

```
TYPE BIS_JAN.WK1
```

If your screen shows a lot of "happy faces" and other strange characters, you cannot use the PRINT command to print the file. You need to copy the file so that the copy contains only ASCII text characters.

```
A1:                                                             MENU
Printer  File
Send print output directly to a printer
          A       B       C        D       E      F      G      H
      1                            ABC Company
      2                       Budgeted  Income  Statement
      3
      4
      5   SALES                               $450,000
      6
      7   Cost of Goods Sold:
      8       Finished goods, beginning inventory   $68,500
      9       Cost of goods, manufactured          $313,500
      10        Cost of goods available for sale    $110,000
      11      Less finished goods, ending inventory $203,500
      12      Total cost of goods sold            $246,500
      13  Gross profit on sales
      14
      15  EXPENSES
      16
      17      Administrative expenses              $85,000
      18      Selling expenses                     $35,000
      19      Interest expenses                    $75,000
      20      Total expenses                      $195,000
```

Figure 12.7. A sample Lotus 1-2-3 spreadsheet.

Like most application programs, you can use Lotus 1-2-3 to store a copy of a file in ASCII text format. 1-2-3 provides this capability by letting you "print" the spreadsheet to a file rather than directly to the printer. (If you actually own Lotus 1-2-3, the command is /PF, which selects Print and File from the menus.) In this example, you need to print all 12 Budgeted Income Statement spreadsheets to files, for example, BIS_123.WKI for the spreadsheet and BIS_123.PRN for the ASCII file.

When you finish that job, you could exit 1-2-3 and return to DOS. To be sure the new .PRN files contain only ASCII characters, you could enter the command TYPE BIS_123.PRN at the command prompt. Next, you would enter the command

```
PRINT BIS_???.PRN
```

to print all 12 files. (This assumes that you used the /Q switch, discussed in the PRINT command entry in Appendix B, to initialize the PRINT command to handle more than 10 files.) Now DOS can print all 12 files in the background, and you are free to use your computer for other jobs.

Treating Files as Devices

You've already seen how to use a file as input to the MORE command (when you used the command `MORE < READ.ME`). You can also use file names as output devices. For example, instead of entering a command such as `DIR > PRN` to channel the output from the DIR command to the printer, you could enter a command such as `DIR > MYFILES.TXT`. This command stores the output from the DIR command in a file named MYFILES.TXT.

Storing the output from commands in files can be very handy. For example, when you use the > PRN directive to send output to the printer, you need to wait for printing to finish before you can use your computer. However, if you channel output to a file (which is much quicker than sending output to the printer), you can use the PRINT command to print the output file in the background.

Also, if you have a word processing program, you can use it to edit the output file in any way you wish. That is, you can add special printer features (such as boldface or underline), reorganize the pagination, add margins, and so on. You can even merge the output file into an existing document. In fact, virtually all application programs, including spreadsheets and database managers, let you import these DOS output files for further use.

The following example demonstrates the power of using a file as a device that accepts output from a command. Assume that you want to print a listing of all the files in three directories on your hard disk— the root directory, the DOS directory, and the WP directory (the last two of which your computer might not actually have).

Instead of printing the file names immediately, you decide to store them in a file so that you can print them later using the PRINT command. Suppose that you want to store the output from the three DIR commands in a file named MYFILES.TXT in the WP directory.

Starting at the DOS command prompt, enter the following commands to change to the WP directory and send a list of all the file names in the root directory to the file named MYFILES.TXT:

```
CD \WP
DIR C:\ > MYFILES.TXT
```

The DIR command displays nothing on the screen, because its output was sent to the MYFILES.TXT file. Now, to add the file names from the DOS directory to the MYFILES.TXT file, you need to enter the command

```
DIR C:\DOS >> MYFILES.TXT
```

Notice that this command uses the >> redirection symbol. This symbol *adds* (or *appends*) the new output to the MYFILES.TXT file, instead of *replacing* its contents. Again, the DIR command displays nothing on the screen, but when the DOS prompt reappears, you know that the output is stored in the file.

Finally, to add the list of file names from the WP directory to the MYFILES.TXT file, enter this command:

```
DIR >> MYFILES.TXT
```

Before printing the MYFILES.TXT file, take a quick look at it to be sure it actually contains the file names from all three directories. To do so, enter the command

```
TYPE C:\WP\MYFILES.TXT
```

or the command

```
MORE < C:\WP\MYFILES.TXT
```

Now that you are convinced that the MYFILES.TXT actually contains the text you want, you can enter the final command:

```
PRINT C:\WP\MYFILES.TXT
```

You are now free to use your computer while the PRINT command prints the contents of the MYFILES.TXT file in the background.

You could also preview, edit, and print the MYFILES.TXT file with your word processing program. To do so, run your word processing program in the usual manner and specify C:\WP\MYFILES.TXT as the file to edit.

Customizing the Keyboard

If your CONFIG.SYS file includes the DEVICE=ANSI.SYS command (as discussed earlier in this chapter), you can customize your keyboard to perform special tasks. It's extremely unlikely that you would want to redefine one of the standard keys, such as making the A key generate the letter Z (although you could do so if you had the desire). A more practical application uses the procedure to assign functions to special key combinations that are not already defined by DOS, such as Ctrl-F3 or Alt-F7.

The general procedure for redefining function keys is very similar to the one used for defining screen attributes and colors. You use the PROMPT command followed by an escape sequence. However, you must also include a code that indicates the key you want to redefine, the character or characters you want the key to display (enclosed in quotation marks), the number 13 (which is the code for the Enter key), and finally, a lowercase *p* (rather than an *m*), which signals the end of the sequence. This general syntax is as follows:

```
PROMPT $e[0;key number;"characters to type";13p
```

The numbers used to specify keys that you might want to redefine are listed in Table 12.7. Those marked with an asterisk already serve useful functions in DOS (and particularly the DOS Shell), so you should avoid redefining those keys.

Table 12.7. Numbers assigned to function keys.

Key	Number	Key	Number	Key	Number	Key	Number
F1*	59	Shift-F1	84	Ctrl-F1	94	Alt-F1*	104
F2*	60	Shift-F2	85	Ctrl-F2	95	Alt-F2	105
F3*	61	Shift-F3	86	Ctrl-F3	96	Alt-F3	106
F4*	62	Shift-F4	87	Ctrl-F4	97	Alt-F4	107
F5*	63	Shift-F5	88	Ctrl-F5	98	Alt-F5	108
F6*	64	Shift-F6	89	Ctrl-F6	99	Alt-F6	109
F7	65	Shift-F7	90	Ctrl-F7	100	Alt-F7	110
F8	66	Shift-F8	92	Ctrl-F8	101	Alt-F8	111
F9*	67	Shift-F9*	92	Ctrl-F9	102	Alt-F9	112
F10*	68	Shift-F10	93	Ctrl-F10	103	Alt-F10	113

* Already assigned a function by DOS.

Suppose that you want to redefine the Shift-F10 key (number 93) so that it displays the names of files when you press it. First, enter the following command at the command prompt:

```
PROMPT $e[0;93;"DIR";13p
```

After you press Enter, the command prompt is no longer visible, so enter the command PROMPT PG to redisplay it.

To test your new function key assignment, press Shift-F10 (hold down the Shift key and press the F10 key). Your screen displays the names of files on the current drive or directory.

Awkward commands that are difficult to remember are especially good candidates for redefinition as function keys. For example, in order to use the GRAPHICS command to prepare a wide-carriage IBM Personal Graphics Printer to print graphics screens, you might need to enter the command `GRAPHICS GRAPHICSWIDE /R /PRINTBOX:LCD` (see the GRAPHICS command in Appendix B for details). The following command assigns the appropriate command to the Shift-F8 key:

```
PROMPT $e[0;92;"GRAPHICS GRAPHICSWIDE /R /PRINTBOX:LCD";13p
```

After you initially enter the command, your prompt will disappear. You can enter another PROMPT command, such as `PROMPT $p$g` to bring back your original command prompt.

To set up your printer to print graphics displays, you need only press Shift-F8. Note, however, that the function key will work only during the current session (before you turn off the computer) and only if the GRAPHICS.COM program is available from the current drive and directory.

Assigning Multiple Commands to a Function Key

You can assign two or more commands to a function key, as long as you use the 13 (Enter) code to separate them. For example, the following command sets up the Shift-F7 key so that it first clears the screen (CLS) and then displays a wide directory listing (DIR /W):

```
PROMPT $e[0;90;"CLS";13;"DIR /W";13p
```

Using Function Keys to Type Text

Redefining function keys can be handy for more than entering commands. For example, assume that you regularly need to type your return address on envelopes. The following command sets up the Shift-F6 key to do this job for you, assuming of course, that you substitute your own name and address for John Q. Melon's. Note that you must type the command as one long line, even if it wraps to the next screen line. (Also, the entire escape sequence cannot exceed 128 characters.) Be sure to include blank spaces only where indicated.

```
PROMPT $e[0;89;"COPY CON PRN";13;"John Q. Melon";13;"123 Oak Tree
Lane";13;"Glendora, CA 91749";13;26;13;"ECHO";12;">PRN";13p
```

After you define the key, pressing Shift-F6 displays the output shown in Figure 12.8 on your screen (which, as you may notice, looks somewhat similar to that in Figure 12.5). Of course, the name and address are also sent to the printer.

```
C:\DOS>PROMPT $e[0;89;"COPY CON PRN";13;"John Q. Melon";13;"123 Oak Tree Lane";1
3;"Glendora, CA 91740";13;26;13;"ECHO ";12;" >PRN";13p

PROMPT $P$G

C:\DOS>COPY CON PRN
John Q. Melon
123 Oak Tree Lane
Glendora, CA 91740
^Z
          1 File(s) copied       Pressing Shift-F6
                                  produced all of this.
C:\DOS>ECHO ^L >PRN

C:\DOS>
```

Figure 12.8. Result of pressing Shift-F6 after redefining the key.

I'll review this key definition so that you can see how it works. First, COPY CON PRN;13 types the COPY CON PRN command and presses Enter so that the following text is sent to the printer. Then, the name, address, and city, state, zip lines are typed, each followed by the Enter key code so that they are placed on separate lines.

The 26 code that you see in the command causes DOS to press Ctrl-Z, the code necessary to end the COPY CON PRN command (it appears as ^Z in Figure 12.8). Then the sequence "ECHO ;12;" >PRN";13p types the ECHO ^L PRN command and presses Enter to eject the page from the printer.

How did I know that the 26 code would type Ctrl-Z and that the 12 code would type Ctrl-L? Easy—the Ctrl key combinations are numbered from 1 to 26, starting at A. That is Ctrl-A is number 1, Ctrl-B is 2, and so on. Because L is the 12th letter of the alphabet, its numeric code is 12, and because Z is the 26th letter of the alphabet, its numeric code is 26.

The main problem with redefining function key definitions is that they are lost the moment you turn off your computer. Nor are key definition commands particularly good candidates for the AUTOEXEC.BAT file, because other commands may reset them during the startup procedure. However, as you'll learn in Chapter 13, you can store many key definitions in a *batch file*; then you need to type only one command to reinstate all your custom key definitions.

However, keep in mind that many application programs, including word processors and spreadsheets, assign their own commands to the function keys. Therefore, your custom key definition might work only when the DOS command prompt is displayed.

Resetting the Function Keys

To reset a function key to its original definition, follow the 0;*key number* portion of the command with a semicolon and a repeat of the 0;*key number*. For example, to reset the Shift-F10 key (number 93) to its original definition, enter the command:

```
PROMPT $e[0;93;0;93p
```

DOSKEY and Commercial Keyboard Customizing Packages

In Chapter 15, you will learn how to use the new DOS 5 DOSKEY command to create *macros*, which also let you quickly execute long, complicated commands. Because you can give these macros descriptive names, they are sometimes easier to remember and use than redefining the function keys.

You can also use commercial *keyboard macro* programs to customize your keyboard. Most of these programs let you redefine a key by recording a series of keystrokes; therefore, you don't have to deal with long strings of strange symbols. Many can also be used in conjunction with other programs on your computer, so your custom key definitions are not lost when you switch from one program to the next. Following are the names and manufacturers of some keyboard macro programs:

Keyworks
Alpha Software Corp.
1 North Ave.
Burlington, MA 01803
(617) 229-2924

ProKey
Rosesoft, Inc.
P.O. Box 45880
Seattle, WA 98145-0880
(206) 282-0454

SuperKey
Borland International, Inc.
4585 Scotts Valley Dr.
Scotts Valley, CA 95066
(408) 438-8400

Troubleshooting

This section lists common error messages that DOS might display while trying some of the examples in this chapter. If you use one of these messages, try the recommended solution.

❏ `Errors on list device indicate that it may be off-line. Please check it:` The printer is either disconnected, turned off, or is currently off-line. Check your printer to be sure it is on-line (see your printer manual if necessary).

❏ `Invalid parameter:` A switch or option used in a command is misspelled or the forward slash (/), backslash (\), or pipe (¦) characters are used incorrectly.

Summary

This chapter presented commands and techniques for managing and configuring standard devices—the screen, printer, and keyboard.

❏ In general, you can use the <, >, and >> redirection symbols and the DOS device names to channel output that normally appears on the screen to a different device. (File names can often be used as though they are device names.)

❏ The CLS command clears the screen.

❏ The Ctrl-S and Pause keys, as well as the MORE command, allow you to control the scrolling of text on the screen.

❏ You can use the PROMPT command to customize the command prompt.

❏ If your CONFIG.SYS file loads the ANSI.SYS file during startup, you can use the PROMPT command to control screen attributes and colors and to assign text and commands to function keys.

❏ The Shift-PrintScreen key combination copies to your printer whatever is on the screen.

❏ The Ctrl-PrintScreen key combination slaves the printer so that all future screen displays are sent to the printer. (You must press Ctrl-PrintScreen again to unslave the printer.)

❏ To print ASCII text files in the background so that you can continue to use your computer during printing, use the PRINT command (or select the Print option on the DOS 5 File List's File pull-down menu).

Programming DOS

The next three chapters discuss DOS *batch files* and DOS 5 *macros*. Batch files are basically DOS text files that contain a group, or batch, of commands that DOS executes in sequence; macros are user-created commands (often consisting of several DOS commands) that execute as though they are actually internal DOS commands. In essence, batch files and macros are your own DOS commands and programs. The general techniques you learned for modifying DOS text files also allow you to create and edit batch files.

The skills you will learn in these chapters include

❏ How to create and run batch files and macros.

❏ How to make your batch files and macros create useful commands that simplify your work.

❏ How to make batch files easy to use—for yourself and for others.

❏ How to create batch files and macros that accept options from the command line.

❏ How to use advanced programming techniques, such as looping, decision-making, branching, and calling, to add more power and flexibility to your batch files.

Many of the powerful and practical sample batch files and macros presented in these chapters will come in handy in your own work with your computer. In a sense, they offer new, easy-to-use commands that DOS "forgot."

Creating and Using Batch Files

So far, your experience with DOS commands has consisted of typing a single command and then pressing Enter to execute that command. As an alternative to this one-command-at-a-time approach, you can store a series of commands in a single file and then have DOS automatically execute every command in the file. Files that contain multiple DOS commands are called *batch files* (because they process a "batch" of commands at one time).

All DOS batch files have the file name extension .BAT. The AUTOEXEC.BAT file discussed in previous chapters is such a batch file. However, AUTOEXEC.BAT is different from other batch files because DOS automatically executes all the commands in AUTOEXEC.BAT as soon as you start your computer.

> NOTE: AUTOEXEC is an abbreviation for AUTOmatically EXECuted.

You run all other batch files as though they were programs. That is, at the command prompt, you type the name of the batch file and press Enter. From the DOS 5 File List, you highlight the name of the batch file in the Files List and then press Enter or double-click the mouse.

When DOS executes the commands in a batch file, it does so in first-to-last order. That is, it executes the first (top) command, then the second command, then the third command, and so on, until there are no more commands to be executed. In a sense, DOS "sees" the commands in a batch file as though each were being typed at the command prompt independently.

Creating and Storing Batch Files

Batch files must be stored as ASCII text files. Therefore, you can use any of the techniques described in Chapter 10 to create and edit your own batch files. The name you assign to a batch file must follow the basic rules of all DOS file names—no more than eight characters in length, no blank spaces, and no punctuation other than the underscore and hyphen. The file name extension must be .BAT.

When naming a batch file, be sure not to give it the same name as a .COM or .EXE file. For example, if you have the dBASE program on your computer, do not create a batch file named DBASE.BAT. Otherwise, when you enter the command DBASE, DOS will run only DBASE.BAT or DBASE.EXE, but not both. Whether it runs DBASE.BAT or DBASE.EXE depends on the current directory and PATH statement: On any single directory, a file with the .COM extension is given priority, followed by a file with the .EXE extension, followed by a file with the .BAT extension. For example, if the current directory contains both a file named DBASE.EXE and a file named DBASE.BAT, the DBASE.EXE file will be executed when you type DBASE and press ↵.

On the other hand, if you have three files named DBASE.COM, DBASE.EXE, and DBASE.BAT on three different directories, DOS will run whichever one it encounters on the current directory. If none of those files is in the current directory, DOS will run whichever one it encounters first in the current PATH statement, regardless of whether it has the .COM, .EXE, or .BAT extension.

Because batch files provide useful tools to make your work easier, they should be stored where they are easily accessible when you need them. Keep in mind, however, that if a batch file includes any DOS external commands, such as CHKDSK, TREE, SORT, FIND, or MORE, the associated DOS program files (CHKDSK.COM, TREE.COM, SORT.EXE, FIND.EXE, and MORE.COM) must also be accessible from the current diskette, directory, or PATH.

Remember that DOS executes commands in a batch file exactly as though they were typed at the command prompt. Therefore, if your batch file contains a misspelled command or an external program or command that is not available from the current diskette, directory, or defined PATH, DOS will display the usual `Bad command or file name` error message when it attempts to execute that command.

Creating Your Own Batch Files

You'll be creating many useful batch files in these chapters, and you will probably want to use them from time to time in your own work. To ensure that these batch files are easily accessible and that they can find the DOS external programs that they require, you must know how to prepare a diskette or directory for storing batch files. Please read whichever of the two following sections is appropriate.

Preparing Batch Files for a Computer Without a Hard Disk

If your computer doesn't have a hard disk, you should store your batch files on a single diskette. Create this diskette by following these steps:

1. Start your computer in the usual manner, with the `Startup diskette` in drive A:.

2. If the DOS Shell appears, press `F3` to display the command prompt.

3. Insert a new, blank diskette in drive B:, type the command `FORMAT B: /S`, and press Enter. (If DOS displays the `Bad Command or File Name` error message, you need to insert the diskette that contains the FORMAT.COM file into drive A: and try again.)

> NOTE: DOS needs to find COMMAND.COM in order to run a batch file. When you used the /S switch in the FORMAT command, DOS automatically copied COMMAND.COM to your diskette.

4. If DOS asks for a volume label after it finishes formatting, type UTILITIES and then press Enter. Answer N when asked about formatting another diskette.

5. Using the COPY command (or the Copy option in the DOS Shell), copy all the files listed in Table 13.1 to the diskette in drive B:.

6. After you copy all the required files to the new diskette, use the DIR B: command (or the DOS Shell File List) to be sure that the diskette in drive B: contains all the files listed in Table 13.1 plus the COMMAND.COM file.

7. Remove the diskette from drive B: and label it *Custom Utilities*.

Table 13.1. External DOS commands used
by the sample batch files.

Command Used	File Required
CHKDSK	CHKDSK.COM
EDLIN	EDIT.COM*
FIND	FIND.EXE
MORE	MORE.COM
SORT	SORT.EXE
TREE	TREE.COM
XCOPY	XCOPY.EXE

* Required only if you use EDIT to create and edit batch files.

Whenever you create, edit, or use a batch file, do so on the new disk that you've labeled *Custom Utilities*. (In later sections we will refer to this diskette as the Custom Utilities diskette.) You can use the Utilities diskette in either drive A: or B: of your computer. However, be sure that after inserting the diskette into its drive, you remember to access the appropriate drive.

If you aren't going to use the EDIT editor to create and edit your batch files, you should put your word processing diskette in drive A: and access drive A:. Then insert your Custom Utilities diskette into drive B:. Whenever you create or edit a batch file, be sure to specify B: before the file name (for example, B:D.BAT to create or edit the D.BAT batch file).

Preparing Batch Files for a Computer with a Hard Disk

If your computer has a hard disk, you should store all your custom batch files in a single directory. In this example, you'll store them in a directory named UTILS. Remember, however, that your batch files require that DOS have access to the external programs listed in Table 13.1.

To give yourself maximum access to your batch files, and to give the batch files access to the external DOS commands that they need, include in your PATH command both the UTILS directory and the directory that contains the external DOS files. Follow these steps:

1. If you are using the DOS 5 Shell, press F3 or Alt-F4 to display the command prompt.

2. To create the UTILS directory, type the command MD \UTILS and press Enter.

3. Using the CD and DIR commands, determine which directory on your hard disk contains the external commands listed in Table 13.1. (In Versions 4 and 5, check the DOS directory; in earlier versions of DOS, check the root directory.)

4. Modify your AUTOEXEC.BAT file so that the PATH command includes both the new UTILS directory and the directory that contains the external DOS command.

> NOTE: If you are using DOS 4 or 5, remember that if your AUTOEXEC.BAT file includes the DOSSHELL command, it must be the last command in the AUTOEXEC.BAT file.

To complete step 4, you must use techniques that were described in Chapters 10 and 11. Don't forget, if you start your computer from the hard disk, AUTOEXEC.BAT must be stored on the root directory of drive C:.

> NOTE: Remember that the only blank space in a PATH command should be the one immediately after the word PATH.

If your external DOS commands are stored in the directory named DOS, be sure that the PATH command in your AUTOEXEC.BAT file includes the DOS and UTILS directories (in addition to your other frequently used directory names) as follows:

```
PATH C:\DOS;C:\UTILS
```

If your external DOS commands are stored in the root directory, be sure that your AUTOEXEC.BAT file PATH command includes both the root and the UTILS directories (in addition to your other frequently used directory names) as follows:

```
PATH C:\;C:\UTILS
```

After modifying your AUTOEXEC.BAT file, be sure to save it. Doing so will bring you back to the command prompt. You can then execute the modified AUTOEXEC.BAT file using either of two methods. You can reboot the computer (by pressing Ctrl-Alt-Del), or you can enter the AUTOEXEC command directly at the command prompt.

If you decide to use the latter method, first enter the command CD \ to make sure the root directory is current. Then type AUTOEXEC and press Enter. DOS executes each command in the AUTOEXEC.BAT file. This latter technique works because AUTOEXEC.BAT is a batch file, and any batch file can be executed by entering its name as a command. The only thing that makes AUTOEXEC.BAT unique among batch files is that it is the only batch file that DOS looks for and executes automatically when you first start your computer.

If your computer starts with the DOS Shell displayed, press F3 or Alt-F4 to display the command prompt. To verify that AUTOEXEC.BAT has set up the proper path, type the command PATH and press Enter. DOS shows the currently defined path.

In the future, whenever you want to create or change a batch file, either change to the UTILS directory or if you prefer to work from a different directory, specify C:\UTILS as the location for the batch file. For example, to create or edit the D.BAT batch file from any directory, specify C:\UTILS\D.BAT as the name of the file.

A Simple Practice Batch File

A good practice batch file is one that is simple to create and use. I'll start with a batch file that contains only two simple commands—DIR/W and VER. You can name this simple batch file D.BAT. (Admittedly, D.BAT won't dazzle you with its power; still, it demonstrates many of the fundamental principles of batch files.)

To use the DOS EDIT editor to create this batch file, see the following steps. (If instead, you use another editor or word processor, remember to save the file in ASCII text format.)

1. Type `EDIT \UTILS\D.BAT` and press `Enter`.

2. Type `DIR /W` in the first line and press `Enter`.

3. Type `VER`.

4. To pull down the File menu, press `Alt-F`.

5. To exit EDIT, press `X`.

6. Press `Y` to save your changes and end the EDIT program.

7. To verify that the file was saved, type `TYPE \UTILS\D.BAT` and press `Enter`.

The batch file that appears on the screen consists of the following two lines:

```
DIR /W
VER
```

Running Your First Batch File

To *run* (execute the commands in) a batch file, use the same basic technique that you use to run any program—type the file name without the extension and press Enter. In this example, press the letter `D` and then press Enter.

As mentioned earlier, you can also use the DOS Shell to run the D.BAT batch file. First, use the File List to access the drive or directory that contains the file. Then highlight `D.BAT` in the Files List and press Enter (or double-click the mouse).

This batch file displays a wide listing of the file names on the current diskette or directory (the DIR /W command) and then the current version of DOS (the VER command), as shown in Figure 13.1. (Your screen, of course, shows different file names.) Note that the figure shows the exact series of events that took place.

Although this is not a terribly exciting batch file, it does provide one convenience: Whenever you want to see a wide directory listing, you enter the letter D at the command prompt, rather than DIR /W. You save a few keystrokes, which is very handy if you don't like to (or can't) type.

```
C:\UTILS>D

C:\UTILS>DIR /W

 Volume in drive C has no label
 Volume Serial Number is 159A-619B
 Directory of C:\UTILS

[.]             [..]            ADDPATH.BAT     COPYTO.BAT      PKSFX.PRG
COMMAND.COM     D.BAT           COUNTIN.BAT     FF.BAT          JETSET.BAT
LOOKFOR.BAT     LOOKIN.BAT      LOOKIN2.BAT     MOVE.BAT        MOVETO.BAT
OLDPATH.BAT     OLDSEARC.BAT    ORIGPATH.BAT    SAFECOPY.BAT    SETKEYS.BAT
SHOWKEYS.BAT    WSRAM.BAT
          22 file(s)        64082 bytes
                          3334144 bytes free

C:\UTILS>VER

MS-DOS Version 5.00



C:\UTILS>
```

Figure 13.1. Results of running the D.BAT batch file.

If you made a mistake and your batch file does not work properly, use EDIT (or another text editor) to make corrections. Again, refer to Chapter 10 if you need reminders about how to edit a file.

Using Echo to Display Text

You've already used the DOS ECHO command (with the > PRN directive) to send a special code to the printer. You can also include the ECHO command to send a message from a batch file to the screen. For practice, modify the simple D.BAT batch file so that it sends the rather frivolous message That's all folks! to the screen after it executes the DIR /W and VER commands. Here are the steps to follow if you are using the EDIT editor:

1. At the DOS command prompt, type the command EDIT \UTILS\D.BAT and press Enter.

2. To move the editing cursor to the end of the file, press Ctrl-End or click on the third line with the mouse.

3. Type `ECHO That's all folks!`.

4. To pull down the File menu, press `Alt-F`.

5. To exit EDIT, press `X`.

6. Press `Y` to save your changes and end the EDIT program.

7. To verify that the file was saved, type `TYPE \UTILS\D.BAT` and press `Enter`.

Your batch file now contains the following three lines:

```
DIR /W
VER
ECHO That's all folks!
```

To run your modified D.BAT batch file, type the letter `D` at the command prompt and press Enter. Your new batch file still displays a wide directory of file names and shows the current DOS version number. In addition, these lines appear beneath the file names:

```
C\UTIL>ECHO That's all folks!
That's all folks!
```

The ECHO command displayed the `That's all folks!` message, but it did so twice, as Figure 13.2 shows. That happened because DOS automatically displays commands stored in batch files before it executes them. That is, DOS displayed the entire command `ECHO That's all folks!`, then executed that command, and then displayed the results of the command—the sentence `That's all folks!`.

Preventing Double Echoes

If you are using Version 3.3 or later of DOS, you can prevent DOS from displaying a command before executing it by preceding the command with an ā symbol. (If you are using an earlier version of DOS, you can do so by putting the command `ECHO OFF` at the top of the batch file, as discussed in the section "Hiding All Commands" later in this chapter.)

If you are using Version 3.3 (or later) of DOS, use following the steps to change the ECHO command in the D.BAT batch file to @ECHO:

1. Type `EDIT \UTILS\D.BAT` and then press `Enter`.

2. To move the editing cursor to the third line of the file, press ↓ twice or click on the `first character` of the `third line` with the mouse.

3. Type the @ symbol.

4. To pull down the File menu, press `Alt-F`.

5. To exit EDIT, press `X`.

6. Press `Y` to save your changes and end the EDIT program.

7. To verify that the file was saved, type `TYPE \UTILS\D.BAT` and press `Enter`.

```
C:\UTILS>DIR /W

 Volume in drive C has no label
 Volume Serial Number is 159A-619B
 Directory of C:\UTILS

[.]               [..]             ADDPATH.BAT      COPYTO.BAT       PKSFX.PRG
COMMAND.COM       D.BAT            COUNTIN.BAT      FF.BAT           JETSET.BAT
LOOKFOR.BAT       LOOKIN.BAT       LOOKIN2.BAT      MOVE.BAT         MOVETO.BAT
OLDPATH.BAT       OLDSEARC.BAT     ORIGPATH.BAT     SAFECOPY.BAT     SETKEYS.BAT
SHOWKEYS.BAT      WSRAM.BAT
         22 file(s)         64082 bytes
                          3334144 bytes free

C:\UTILS>VER

MS-DOS Version 5.00

C:\UTILS>ECHO That's all folks!
That's all folks!


C:\UTILS>
```

Figure 13.2. Results of using an ECHO command in D.BAT.

After you complete Step 7, your screen shows the following modified D.BAT file:

```
DIR /W
VER
@ECHO That's all folks!
```

To run the new batch file, press the letter `D` and Enter. This time notice that the `That's all folks!` message appears only once at the bottom of the list of file names, as in Figure 13.3.

```
C:\UTILS>D

C:\UTILS>DIR /W

 Volume in drive C has no label
 Volume Serial Number is 159A-619B
 Directory of C:\UTILS

[.]            [..]           ADDPATH.BAT     COPYTO.BAT     PKSFX.PRG
COMMAND.COM    D.BAT          COUNTIN.BAT     FF.BAT         JETSET.BAT
LOOKFOR.BAT    LOOKIN.BAT     LOOKIN2.BAT     MOVE.BAT       MOVETO.BAT
OLDPATH.BAT    OLDSEARC.BAT   ORIGPATH.BAT    SAFECOPY.BAT   SETKEYS.BAT
SHOWKEYS.BAT   WSRAM.BAT
        22 file(s)        64082 bytes
                        3334144 bytes free

C:\UTILS>VER

MS-DOS Version 5.00

That's all folks!


C:\UTILS>
```

Figure 13.3. The @ECHO message appears only once in D.BAT.

Using Remarks to Comment Batch Files

Although the D.BAT file is relatively simple, batch files can be quite large and complicated (as you will see in later examples). To make it easier for you—and for others who use your batch file—to understand the purpose of commands in the batch file, add *comments* (also called *remarks*) to the file. A comment is like a note to yourself. DOS realizes that the comment is only for humans to read and therefore completely ignores the line.

To add a comment to a batch file, start the line with the command REM (short for *remark*).

If you are using Version 3.3 or later of DOS, you can use the command @REM to put a comment in a batch file, which prevents DOS from displaying the remark when it executes the batch file. You can test this now by adding a comment to the D.BAT batch file by using the following steps:

1. Type EDIT D.BAT and press Enter.

2. To move the editing cursor to the third line of the file, press ↓ twice, or click on the first character of the third line with the mouse.

3. To insert a comment above the third line (if you are using DOS Version 3.3 or later), type the command @REM Show closing message.... (If you are using an earlier version, leave out the leading @ sign.) Press Enter.

4. To pull down the File menu, press Alt-F.

5. To exit EDIT, press X.

6. Press Y to save your changes and end the EDIT program.

7. To verify that the file was saved, type TYPE \UTILS\D.BAT and press Enter.

The batch file now contains the following commands (without the @ symbols if you are using DOS 3.2 or earlier):

```
DIR /W
VER
@REM Show closing message...
@ECHO That's all folks!
```

You can test the D.BAT batch file by entering the command D at the command prompt. If you are using DOS 3.3 or later and added the @REM command, you will see that the D.BAT file does its job without displaying the comment to the right of the REM command. (Again, comments preceded by REM are for "human consumption only.")

If you are using an earlier version of DOS, the REM command line will be displayed on your screen but will have no effect on DOS. Again, if you are using a version of DOS prior to 3.3, you cannot precede a command with @ to hide it during execution, but you will learn an alternative technique shortly.

Later examples use REM comments to label each batch file with a name and a general purpose. These comments at the top of the file will make it easier for you to determine which batch file you are viewing in the figures in this book.

Passing Parameters to a Batch File

So far, the D.BAT file is little more than a shortcut for typing the longer command `DIR /W` and displaying the current DOS version number. However, it lacks one feature that the DIR command offers—the capability of specifying types of files. For example, with DIR, you can enter a command such as `DIR *.EXE /W` to limit the listing to files that have the .EXE extension. However, if you enter the command `D *.EXE`, DOS still lists the names of all the files on the current diskette or directory because it ignores the `*.EXE`.

Change the D.BAT file so that it accepts and uses a *parameter* (additional text entered at the command prompt), such as the *.EXE specifier in the previous example. The basic technique is to use *percent variables* as placeholders for additional command line entries. The first extra entry is always named %1, the second is named %2, the third is named %3, and so on. When you type a batch file name and additional parameters on the command line, each parameter passed to the % variables must be separated by a blank space.

To permit a single parameter to be passed to the DIR command in the D.BAT file, edit the first line of the file to read

```
DIR %1 /W
```

Type `TYPE \UTILS\D.BAT` and press Enter to check the contents of the batch file.

If you are using DOS 3.3 or later, your batch file should contain the following commands (with all the blank spaces in the right places):

```
DIR %1 /W
VER
@REM Show closing message...
@ECHO That's all folks!
```

If you are using Version 3.2 or earlier of DOS, your D.BAT batch file should look the same, but without the @ symbol in front of the REM and ECHO commands.

Now, try using a file specifier with the D command. For example, when you enter the command `D *.COM`, DOS displays only the names of files (if any) on the current directory that have the extension .COM. If D.BAT is the only file on your current directory, try viewing the contents of a different directory. For example, enter the command `D C:\*.COM` to view the .COM files on the root directory of your hard disk or enter the command `D C:\DOS\*.COM` to view the names of the .COM files on your hard disk's DOS directory.

D.BAT now has the flexibility of the DIR command. That's because the parameter you type next to the D command gets passed to the DIR command in your batch file. For example, look closely at Figure 13.4; notice at the top of the screen that I entered the command `D C:\DOS\*.COM` to view .COM files in the DOS directory. Also notice that the batch file *substituted* the C:\DOS*.COM parameter into its own DIR command (in place of the %1 variable).

```
C:\UTILS>D C:\DOS\*.COM

C:\UTILS>DIR C:\DOS\*.COM /W

 Volume in drive C has no label
 Volume Serial Number is 159A-619B
 Directory of C:\DOS

FORMAT.COM      KEYB.COM        MODE.COM        SYS.COM         UNFORMAT.COM
DOSKEY.COM      MIRROR.COM      MORE.COM        REBUILD.COM     DOSSHELL.COM
TREE.COM        EDIT.COM        MSHERC.COM      DISKCOMP.COM    DISKCOPY.COM
ASSIGN.COM      GRAFTABL.COM    GRAPHICS.COM    COMMAND.COM
        19 file(s)        266508 bytes
                         3328000 bytes free

C:\UTILS>VER

MS-DOS Version 5.00

That's all folks!


C:\UTILS>
C:\UTILS>
```

Figure 13.4. Results of entering D C:\DOS*.COM.

What happens now if you enter the old D command without specifying a drive, directory, or file name? Well, the batch file acts exactly as it did before. DOS substitutes nothing for %1, so the command that DOS executes is once again DIR /W. (If you enter the command D and examine the DIR command displayed on the screen by the batch file, you will see that this is indeed the case.)

Try passing two parameters to the D batch file. Notice that when you type the following command:

```
D  *.*  /S
```

the /S has no effect, because it is a second optional parameter on the command line (that is, a blank space separates it from the first parameter, *.*). B.DAT completely ignores this second parameter because the batch file contains no %2 variable to handle it.

The Importance of Proper Spacing

The most common errors that people make when using % variables in batch files involve blank spaces: Sometimes, people forget to include necessary blank spaces; other times, they add spaces when they are not needed. For example, if the first line in D.BAT looked as follows:

```
DIR%1/W
```

your batch file would not work. That's because when you enter a command, such as D C:*.*, to execute the batch file, DOS substitutes the parameters into the command exactly as it is told to. That is, the batch file actually tries to execute the following command:

```
DIRC:\*.*/W
```

Because DOS has no idea what DIRC means, it displays the familiar Bad command or file name message.

Surrounding the %1 variable with blank spaces, as follows:

```
DIR %1 /W
```

ensures that blank spaces are also included during the substitution. Therefore, when you enter the command D C:*.* to execute the batch file, the parameter is substituted into the %1 variable in exactly the same way:

```
DIR C:\*.* /W
```

and DOS has no problem interpreting that command.

Hiding All Commands

Regardless of which version of DOS you are using, you can prevent batch file commands from being displayed before execution by adding ECHO OFF command to the top of your batch file. ECHO OFF tells DOS not to echo the commands to the command prompt, but instead to display the results of the commands.

If you are using DOS 3.3 or later, you can make the first command in your batch file @ECHO OFF, which even prevents the ECHO OFF command itself from being echoed. To test the ECHO OFF command for yourself, add the command to D.BAT. Your batch file should now contain the following commands (but without the @ signs if you are using DOS 3.2 or earlier):

```
@ECHO OFF
DIR %1 /W
VER
@REM Show closing message...
@ECHO That's all folks!
```

When you enter D to run the batch file, notice that none of the commands from the batch file are displayed; only the results of each command appear on the screen, as Figure 13.5 shows.

```
C:\UTILS>D

Volume in drive C has no label
Volume Serial Number is 159A-619B
Directory of C:\UTILS

[.]             [..]            ADDPATH.BAT     COPYTO.BAT      PKSFX.PRG
COMMAND.COM     D.BAT           COUNTIN.BAT     FF.BAT          JETSET.BAT
LOOKFOR.BAT     LOOKIN.BAT      LOOKIN2.BAT     MOVE.BAT        MOVETO.BAT
OLDPATH.BAT     OLDSEARC.BAT    ORIGPATH.BAT    SAFECOPY.BAT    SETKEYS.BAT
SHOWKEYS.BAT    WSRAM.BAT
         22 file(s)        64082 bytes
                         3334144 bytes free

MS-DOS Version 5.00

That's all folks!

C:\UTILS>
C:\UTILS>
```

Figure 13.5. Only the results of commands from D.BAT are displayed.

As a general rule, don't include the ECHO OFF or @ECHO OFF command when you first build a batch file. You are better off seeing the commands as they are executed so that if the batch file fails to run properly, you can see which command caused the error. This is especially important when you use percent variables, because if you cannot see how the command is executed after the substitution takes place, you might have trouble figuring out what went wrong. Only after you have created, tested, and perfected your batch file should you insert the ECHO OFF or @ECHO OFF command at the top of the file.

For the remaining batch file examples in this book, I assume that you are using one of the later versions of DOS, Version 3.3, 4, or 5. That is, I include @ signs in front of certain commands to prevent them from being echoed on the screen.

If you are using Version 3.2 or earlier, you must remember to omit these @ signs from your batch file. Initially, your batch file will echo commands to the screen. After testing and perfecting a batch file, however, you can add the ECHO OFF command to the top of the batch file to hide the echoes.

Now that you have some basic tools to help you create and develop batch files, you can move ahead and start creating more practical and more powerful batch files.

A Batch File to Search for Files

As you might recall from Chapter 9, you can search every directory on a hard disk by using the CHKDSK and FIND commands. For example, entering the command `CHKDSK /V | FIND /I "budget"` displays all the files that contain the name `budget`. However, wouldn't it be easier if you could perform this operation by entering a simple command such as `LOOKFOR  BUDGET`? Of course, so create a batch file named LOOKFOR.BAT to handle the job.

> NOTE: Actually, I wanted to name this batch file FIND.BAT so that I could enter the command `FIND  BUDGET`, but because DOS already includes a program named FIND.EXE, this would have created a conflict.

The LOOKFOR.BAT batch file uses three external commands `CHKDSK`, `FIND`, and `MORE`. Remember, these are external commands and require access to the CHKDSK.COM, FIND.EXE. and MORE.COM files. As discussed earlier in this chapter, these files must be on the same diskette as the LOOKFOR.BAT file or if you have a hard disk, in the same directory or in a directory specified in the PATH command.

1. Type `EDIT  LOOKFOR.BAT` and press `Enter`.

2. Type `@REM **************** LOOKFOR.BAT` (type any number of asterisks) and press `Enter`.

3. Type `@REM Searches all directories for a file.` and press `Enter`.

4. Type `@ECHO Did you remember to use UPPERCASE?`

5. Type @ECHO (press Ctrl-C to cancel) and press Enter.

6. Type @ECHO Searching... and press Enter.

7. Type CHKDSK /V | FIND "%1" | MORE and press Enter.

8. To pull down the File menu, press Alt-F.

9. To exit EDIT, type X.

10. Press Y to save your changes and end the EDIT program.

11. Type TYPE LOOKFOR.BAT and press Enter to view the file.

Figure 13.6 shows the completed LOOKFOR.BAT batch file. The asterisks in the first line of the batch file are decorative: They make the name of the batch file stand out. The second line is an explanation of what the batch files does. The three @ECHO commands display messages on the screen as the batch file is executing (as you will soon see).

```
@REM ************************* LOOKFOR.BAT
@REM Searches all directories for a file.
@ECHO Did you remember to use UPPERCASE?
@ECHO (Press Ctrl-C to cancel)
@ECHO Searching...
CHKDSK /V | FIND "%1" | MORE
```

Figure 13.6. The LOOKFOR.BAT batch file.

 NOTE: DOS 5 also offers the /S switch, which you can use in lieu of CHKDSK /V. See DIR in Appendix B.

Notice that in the last command, the %1 variable is not surrounded by blank spaces within the quotation marks of the FIND command. The reason for this is that when you enter a command such as LOOKFOR BUDGET, you want the word BUDGET to be inserted into the FIND command without any blank spaces, as follows:

```
CHKDSK /V | FIND "BUDGET"
```

If you had inserted blank spaces in this example

```
CHKDSK /V | FIND " %1 "
```

during execution, the substitution would result in the following:

```
CHKDSK /V | FIND " BUDGET "
```

The FIND command would then look for the word BUDGET surrounded by blank spaces. Of course, because file names cannot contain blank spaces, the command would never find a matching name.

Notice that the CHKDSK command line includes the MORE command. This ensures that DOS pauses if LOOKFOR displays more file names than can fit on one screen. A single keypress then displays the next screenful of names. (MORE does not affect the display if all the file names fit on one screen.)

Test this batch file by using LOOKFOR to display the names of all files that have the .BAT extension. Enter the command

```
LOOKFOR .BAT
```

(Be sure to use uppercase letters for .BAT.) After you press Enter (and perhaps wait a while), your screen displays all file names that have the .BAT extension. Figure 13.7 shows the results on my computer.

```
C:\UTILS>LOOKFOR .BAT
Did you remember to use UPPERCASE?
(press Ctrl-C to cancel)
Searching...

C:\UTILS>CHKDSK /V | FIND ".BAT" | MORE

C:\AUTOEXEC.BAT
C:\UTILS\ADDPATH.BAT
C:\UTILS\COPYTO.BAT
C:\UTILS\D.BAT
C:\UTILS\COUNTIN.BAT
C:\UTILS\JETSET.BAT
C:\UTILS\LOOKFOR.BAT
C:\UTILS\LOOKIN.BAT
C:\UTILS\LOOKIN2.BAT
C:\UTILS\MOVE.BAT
C:\UTILS\OLDPATH.BAT
C:\UTILS\ORIGPATH.BAT
C:\UTILS\SAFECOPY.BAT
C:\UTILS\SETKEYS.BAT
C:\UTILS\SHOWKEYS.BAT

C:\UTILS>
```

Figure 13.7. Results of the LOOKFOR.BAT command.

Notice at the top of the figure that you can see where I entered the command `LOOKFOR .BAT`. The next three lines display messages from the ECHO commands in the batch file. The command `CHKDSK /V |  FIND ".BAT" | MORE` is the final command that the batch file executes. Note that the .BAT parameter was substituted into the command in %1 position. The remainder of the screen shows the locations and names of all the files on my hard disk with the .BAT extension.

If your LOOKFOR.BAT batch file is working properly, you might want to insert the @ECHO OFF commands as the first line. This prevents the CHKDSK command line from being displayed on the screen when you use LOOKFOR.BAT in the future.

Because the FIND command does not support the wildcard characters ? and *, you cannot use these with your new LOOKFOR command. However, you can enter any partial file name to achieve the same basic result. For example, LOOKFOR MYTEXT displays all file names that contain the characters MYTEXT. The command `LOOKFOR .C` displays all file names that contain .C, (such as .COM, .CHK, .COS, and so on).

CHKDSK /V displays both directory names and file names, so if your search parameter includes a directory name, all the files in that directory are displayed. For example, LOOKFOR DBASE displays the names of all files in the dBASE directory. To prevent that from occurring, include the period in the file name. For example, the command `LOOKFOR DBASE.` displays only file names that have DBASE. in them (for example, DBASE.EXE, SQLDBASE.STR, DBASE.PIF, and others).

NOTE: If you have DOS 5, you can create a SEARCH macro that replaces CHKDSK with the enhanced DIR command (see Chapter 15).

If you are using Version 5 of DOS, you can make this command even more convenient. When you use DOS 5, you can add the /I switch to the FIND command to make its operation *case-insensitive*; that is, it will search for files that have the .BAT extension if you type `LOOKFOR .BAT` or `LOOKFOR .bat`. Just change the last line in LOOKFOR.BAT to the following:

```
CHKDSK /V | FIND /I "%1"
```

Interrupting a Batch File

You can stop any executing batch file by pressing Ctrl-Break or Ctrl-C. DOS then displays the message `Terminate batch job? (Y/N)?`. Press `Y` to stop the batch file execution and return to the command prompt or press `N` to resume the batch file execution. (Note that the LOOKFOR.BAT batch file displays a reminder that the batch file can be canceled by pressing Ctrl-C. This reminder is presented because the batch file can take a long time to complete on some computers, and you might get tired of waiting.)

A Batch File that Ejects a Printed Page

If you have a laser printer, you probably need to eject pages from it often. If you are tired of typing the entire command `EJECT ^L > PRN` to perform this simple task, you can create a batch file to do the job for you. Give this new batch file the name FF.BAT (for Form Feed).

> NOTE: If you have DOS 5, you can create an FF macro that is faster and more versatile than this batch file (see Chapter 15).

Note that this batch file requires you to enter a *control character* (Ctrl-L) in the file. With most text editors, you can either type the control character itself (for example, press Ctrl-L) or type the ASCII code for the control character. For example, to type a Ctrl-A character, you might hold the Alt key, type 001 on the numeric keypad, then release the Alt key. Ctrl-B is Alt 002, Ctrl-C is Alt 003, and so forth. However, EDIT doesn't allow you to perform the first operation, and you can only perform the second operation by using a little trickery.

Recall that pressing the Alt key tells EDIT to highlight the options in the Menu Bar; this usurpation of the Alt key prevents you from entering the ASCII code of control characters. However, you can disable EDIT's default operation of the Alt key—so that you can use Alt as part of a command—by pressing the Ctrl-P combination first. Then you can use the Alt key to enter the ASCII code.

For example, use the following procedure to create the FF.BAT file, which includes the Ctrl-L control character:

1. Type EDIT FF.BAT and press Enter.

2. Type @REM **************** FF.BAT (use any number of asterisks; they are merely decorative) and press Enter.

3. Type @REM Send a form—feed to the printer. and press Enter.

4. Type @ECHO and then press the Spacebar (not Enter).

5. Type Ctrl-P (to disable EDIT's use of the Alt key).

6. Hold down the Alt key and type 012 *on the numeric keypad*; then release the Alt key. Ctrl-L (ASCII character 12) appears on your screen as the "female" symbol (♀).

7. Press the Spacebar again.

8. Type > PRN and so the complete line shows ECHO (female) > PRN (see Figure 13.8).

9. To pull down the File menu, press Alt-F.

10. To exit EDIT, press X.

11. Press Y to save your changes and end the EDIT program.

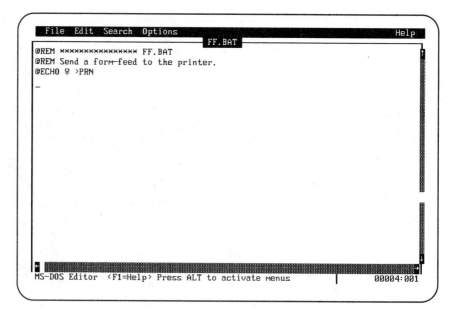

Figure 13.8. The contents of the FF.BAT batch file.

Be aware that if you use the TYPE command to view the contents of the file, your screen might display the ♀ symbol as ^L (the caret is the standard notation for the Ctrl key). Some programs display Ctrl-key combinations as graphics characters (EDIT); others display them in Ctrl-key notation (EDLIN, DOS). Don't worry about this; different software and hardware use different methods to refer to the same character. For example, ASCII 12, Ctrl-L, Alt-0-1-2, and ♀ all represent the same character under different circumstances. A rose is a rose is a rose . . ..

Now try using the FF.BAT batch file. If your printer is hooked up and ready to go, you can eject a page by typing `FF` and pressing Enter. Isn't that better than typing the long, cryptic command `ECHO ^L > PRN`?

Extending the Path

Suppose that you use many different programs on your computer, and you often need to change your PATH setting. For example, suppose your AUTOEXEC.BAT file assigns the path

```
PATH C:\DOS;C:\WP;C:\UTILS
```

and this path is adequate for your usual needs. Occasionally, however, you use programs that require an expanded path. Rather than force DOS to always search these seldom-used directories, you just type the new PATH command as you require it.

Well, if you regularly need to do this, you will find it very tiring to have to retype the entire PATH command repeatedly. Wouldn't it be better if you could just enter a command like `ADDPATH C:\DBASE` to add C:\DBASE to your current PATH setting? You can easily create a batch file to provide this feature. However, before you begin, you need to learn a few new things.

Accessing the DOS Environment

DOS stores the current settings for various commands in an area of memory called the *DOS environment* (or *environment* for short). You can examine the contents of the environment at any time: Enter the command `SET` at the command prompt. DOS then displays your system's environment, as in the following example (yours will be different):

```
COMSPEC=C:\DOS\COMMAND.COM
APPEND=C:\DOS
PROMPT=$P$G

PATH=C:\DOS;C:\WP;C:\UTILS
```

A batch file can copy any information from the environment by specifying the environment *variable name* within percent signs. For example, if you insert %PATH% in a batch file and then later executed the file, the current path would be substituted for %PATH%. (You'll soon see an example of this.)

A batch file can also use the SET command to store information in the environment. In fact, you can even store information in the environment from the command prompt. To illustrate this, follow these steps:

1. At the command prompt, type SET VAR1=TEST and then press Enter.

2. Type SET and press Enter.

The first step creates an environmental variable called VAR1, which contains the word TEST. The second command displays the current contents of the environment, which now includes

```
VAR1=TEST
```

To remove the new variable from the environment, enter the command

```
SET VAR1=
```

and press Enter. (Enter the SET command again to verify that the variable has been removed.)

What are the practical implications of this? As you'll see, both the %PROMPT% variable and the SET command play an integral part in the new ADDPATH.BAT batch file. Use the following steps to create ADDPATH.BAT:

1. Type EDIT ADDPATH.BAT and press Enter.

2. Type @REM *************** ADDPATH.BAT (use any number of asterisks) and press Enter.

3. Type @REM Extends the current path, and press Enter.

4. Type @REM and remembers the previous path. and press Enter.

5. Type `SET EXPATH=%PATH%` and press `Enter`.

6. Type `PATH %PATH%;C:\%1` and press `Enter` (if you do not have a hard disk named C:, substitute a different drive name).

7. Type `@ECHO Path is now %PATH%` and press `Enter`.

8. To pull down the File menu, press `Alt-F`.

9. To exit EDIT, press `X`.

10. Press `Y` to save your changes and end the EDIT program.

The complete ADDPATH.BAT file should match Figure 13.9. To understand how it works, assume that the current path is `H:\TEMPS;C:\DOS;C:\WP51;C:\UTILS` and that you run the batch file by entering the command `ADDPATH DBASE`. The first command following the comments substitutes the current path for %PATH% so that the command actually becomes `SET EXPATH=H:\TEMPS;C:\DOS;C:\WP51;C:\UTILS`. Then when it executes, it stores the current path setting in the environment using the variable name EXPATH. (This variable is important in the next batch file that you will create, which allows you to "undo" a change made by ADDPATH.)

```
@REM *********************** ADDPATH.BAT
@REM Extends the current path,
@REM and remembers the previous path.
SET EXPATH=%PATH%
PATH %PATH%;C:\%1
@ECHO Path is now %PATH%
```

Figure 13.9. The ADDPATH.BAT batch file.

Then the current path is again substituted for %PATH% in the next command so that that line becomes

```
PATH H:\TEMPS;C:\DOS;C:\WP51;C:\UTILS;C:\%1
```

Next, the parameter from the command line, DBASE in this example, is substituted into the position held by %1 so that the command is finally expanded to

```
PATH H:\TEMPS;C:\DOS;C:\WP51;C:\UTILS;C:\DBASE
```

After both substitutions are made, DOS executes the complete command, which defines the new path as

`H:\TEMPS;C:\DOS;C:\WP51;C:\UTILS;C:\DBASE`

The last command, `@ECHO Path is now %PATH%`, displays the new PATH setting on the screen informing you that you have selected a new path. How did %PATH% end up in containing the new path information? Because when you execute a command such as `PATH H:\TEMPS;C:\DOS;C:\WP51;C:\UTILS;C:\DBASE`, as this batch file does, DOS automatically adjusts the environment accordingly, so %PATH% now shows the current (altered) path.

Try using this batch file. First, enter the command `PATH` and press Enter to view your current PATH setting on the screen. Then enter the ADDPATH command with the name of any other directory on your hard disk. For example, using the hypothetical directory tree from Chapter 11, you might enter the command

`ADDPATH WINDOWS`

Your screen displays quite a bit of activity, as Figure 13.10 shows. To see whether ADDPATH did its job, enter the command `SET` when the command prompt reappears. Notice that the environment now contains both the new path (next to PATH=) and the previous path (next to EXPATH=), as shown at the bottom of the figure.

```
C:\UTILS>ADDPATH WINDOWS

C:\UTILS>SET EXPATH=C:\DOS;C:\WP;C:\UTILS

C:\UTILS>PATH C:\DOS;C:\WP;C:\UTILS;C:\WINDOWS
Path is now C:\DOS;C:\WP;C:\UTILS;C:\WINDOWS

C:\UTILS>
C:\UTILS>

C:\UTILS>SET
COMSPEC=C:\DOS\COMMAND.COM
PROMPT=$p$g
TEMP=h:\temps
EXPATH=C:\DOS;C:\WP;C:\UTILS
PATH=C:\DOS;C:\WP;C:\UTILS;C:\WINDOWS

C:\UTILS>
```

Figure 13.10. Results of the command ADDPATH WINDOWS.

If your ADDPATH command is working properly, you can clean up its display by adding the @ECHO OFF command to the top of the batch file.

Restoring the Original Path

The OLDPATH.BAT batch file is the opposite of ADDPATH: It removes the last-added directory name from the path list. It's particularly handy for correcting a mistake. For example, while using ADDPATH, suppose that you add the drive name out of habit to the directory name. Because ADDPATH automatically adds the drive name, entering a command like ADDPATH C:\WINDOWS produces this faulty new path:

C:\DOS;C:\WP;C:\UTILS;C:\C:\WINDOWS

Notice that there is an extra C:\ before the WINDOWS directory name. DOS can't handle this, so you need to correct the path definition. The OLDPATH.BAT batch file lets you make this correction just by typing the command OLDPATH (rather than by retyping the entire PATH command). To provide feedback, OLDPATH also shows you that it has reinstated the current path to

C:\DOS;C:\WP;C:\UTILS

After running OLDPATH.BAT, you need only enter the correct command, ADDPATH WINDOWS, for DOS to set up the new, correct PATH command.

To create the OLDPATH.BAT batch file, follow these steps:

1. Type EDIT OLDPATH.BAT and press Enter.

2. Type @REM *************** OLDPATH.BAT and press Enter.

3. Type @REM Removes the latest addition to the PATH. and press Enter.

4. Type PATH %EXPATH% and press Enter.

5. Type @ECHO Path is back to %PATH% and press Enter.

6. To pull down the File menu, press Alt-F.

7. To exit EDIT, press X.

8. Press Y to save your changes and end the EDIT program.

Your OLDPATH.BAT batch file should match the file in Figure 13.11. The first two lines are comments. In the next command, the previously defined path (which, you recall, was stored in the EXPATH environmental variable) is substituted for %EXPATH%. Therefore, the command expands to `PATH C:\DOS;C:\WP;C:\UTILS` (using the previous example path) when DOS executes it. This resets the PATH definition to the previous definition. The last command displays the new current path definition.

```
@REM ************************ OLDPATH.BAT
@REM Removes the latest addition to the PATH.
PATH %EXPATH%
@ECHO Path is back to %PATH%
```

Figure 13.11. The OLDPATH.BAT batch file.

You can run the OLDPATH batch file only after you've used the ADDPATH batch file to add a new path (because ADDPATH creates the EXPATH variable). To test this batch file, enter the command `OLDPATH` at the command prompt. (This batch file accepts no parameters.) Notice that the path that you added with the previous ADDPATH command is now removed from the PATH definition. (To further verify this, enter either the command `PATH` or the command `SET`.)

ADDPATH for Multiple Disk Drives

As it is currently designed, ADDPATH.BAT can only be run on a computer that has a hard disk drive named C:. If you want your ADDPATH.BAT batch file to allow you to include other hard disk drives, change the following line:

```
PATH %PATH%;C:\%1
```

to

```
PATH %PATH%;%1
```

When using this new ADDPATH batch file, you must include the drive name with the ADDPATH command. For example, to add the PARADOX3 directory from drive F: to the current PATH setting, you must enter the command

```
ADDPATH F:\PARADOX3
```

Reinstating the Original Path

Let's develop a third related batch file, named ORIGPATH, that always resets your PATH command to its original setting in the AUTOEXEC.BAT file. First, you need to change your AUTOEXEC.BAT file to include the command `SET ORIGPATH=%PATH%`. Be sure to place this command beneath the PATH command in your AUTOEXEC.BAT file, because the PATH must be defined before the SET ORIGPATH command stores it in the ORIGPATH variable. Figure 13.12 shows a sample DOS 5 AUTOEXEC.BAT file with the appropriate SET ORIGPATH command in it. (This figure includes comments that describe the purpose its commands.)

```
@ECHO OFF
REM *********************** AUTOEXEC.BAT
REM --- Put COMSPEC in the environment.
SET COMSPEC=C:\DOS\COMMAND.COM
REM --- Set up the PATH
PATH C:\WP;C:\DOS;C:\UTILS
REM --- Store an extra copy of current PATH in the environment.
SET ORIGPATH=%PATH%
REM --- Turn off verification to speed processing.
VERIFY OFF
REM --- Install the mouse driver.
C:\MOUSE1\MOUSE
REM --- Make all DOS 4 files accessible.
APPEND /E
APPEND C:\DOS
REM --- Initialize PRINT.COM and design the command prompt.
PRINT /D:LPT1
PROMPT $P$G
REM --- Go straight to the DOS Shell.
DOSSHELL
```

Figure 13.12. Sample DOS 5 AUTOEXEC.BAT file.

Now you can create a simple batch file, named ORIGPATH.BAT, that looks like the one in Figure 13.13. Any time you want to reinstate the original PATH definition, enter the command `ORIGPATH`. The command `PATH %ORIGPATH%` in that batch file resets the path to the setting defined by the original PATH command in AUTOEXEC.BAT. (Remember, however, that the SET ORIGPATH command in AUTOEXEC.BAT is not executed until you either run AUTOEXEC.BAT or you reboot your computer.)

```
@REM ********************** ORIGPATH.BAT
@REM Restores original path from AUTOEXEC.BAT.
@ECHO OFF
PATH %ORIGPATH% ECHO Path is now %PATH%
```

Figure 13.13. The ORIGPATH.BAT batch file.

Using Batch Files to Assign Tasks to Keys

Chapter 12 showed you how to assign your own commands or keystrokes to any function key (after you installed the ANSI.SYS system via the CONFIG.SYS file). That is, you use the command PROMPT $e[0; followed by 1) a special code for the key (see Table 12.7), 2) the keystrokes you want to display enclosed in quotation marks, and 3) the letter p, which signals the end of the sequence. A couple of drawbacks to using this approach are

❑ As soon as you turn off the computer, your custom key definitions are lost.

❑ The codes are abstract and difficult to remember and therefore are not easy to type from memory each time you start your computer.

A simple batch file can solve these problems. To demonstrate, you'll create a batch file named SETKEYS.BAT that assigns the tasks listed in Table 13.2 to the keys listed in that table. The third column of the table indicates the code number used in the PROMPT command to signify the key.

Figure 13.14 shows the complete SETKEYS.BAT batch file. Using Figure 13.14 as your source, start EDIT and follow the same procedures that you used in previous examples to create batch file.

NOTE: The commands typed by these custom function keys will be easier to understand later when you actually use them and see them typed out.

Table 13.2. Examples of tasks assigned to function keys.

Key	Job Performed	PROMPT Key Code
Alt-F2	Send linefeed to the printer	105
Alt-F3	Eject page from printer	106
Alt-F4	Copy new and modified files to drive A:	107
Alt-F5	Start the DOS Shell	108

```
@REM *********************** SETKEYS.BAT
@REM Assign tasks to Alt-function keys.
PROMPT $e[0;105;"ECHO ";10;" >PRN";13p
PROMPT $e[0;106;"ECHO ";12;" >PRN";13p
PROMPT $e[0;107;"XCOPY C:\*.* A: /S /M /W";13p
PROMPT $e[0;108;"DOSSHELL";13p
PROMPT $P$G
```

Figure 13.14. The SETKEYS.BAT batch file.

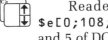   Readers should note that the command `PROMPT $e[0;108;"DOSSHELL";13p` is available only to users of Versions 4 and 5 of DOS. This command enables you to press Alt-F5 to start the DOS Shell. (The DOSSHELL.BAT and other SHELL programs stored in the DOS directory or on the Shell diskette must be available from the current diskette or directory for this command to work properly.)

    After you have entered the entire SETKEYS.BAT file and exited EDIT, type `TYPE SETKEYS.BAT` to view your file. Be sure it looks exactly like the screen in Figure 13.14. (If it does not, use EDIT to make corrections.)

Testing SETKEYS.BAT

If you need additional information about the commands assigned to these functions keys, refer to Appendix B.

To test your SETKEYS batch file, type the command `SETKEYS` at the command prompt and press Enter. This causes a list of PROMPT commands to quickly scroll past your screen. To ensure that each key works, try it (referring back to Table 13.2 for a reminder of what each key is supposed to do). Note that the Alt-F2 and Alt-F3 keys require that the printer be on-line and ready to accept data.

Because Alt-F4 copies new and modified files from the hard disk to a diskette in drive A:, you should also test this only on a hard disk system and only with a blank, formatted diskette already inserted in drive A:.

Note also that the Alt-F4 key combination is designed for you to use on a day-to-day basis for copying recently modified files. If you have not performed a BACKUP command recently (see Chapter 11), this function key probably will try to copy too many files to the diskette. If it runs out of diskette space while copying, DOS will display the message `Insufficient disk space` and then redisplay the command prompt. (No harm done, though.)

Summary

This chapter has discussed the basics of creating your own commands via batch files. The basic techniques you've learned here will allow you to create nearly any batch file that you might require. Remember, any command that you can type at the command prompt can be placed in a batch file. This includes commands that run other programs, such as DBASE, WP, or EXCEL.

In the next chapter, you'll expand your knowledge of batch files by learning about commands that are allowed only in batch files. But first, review the important points discussed in this chapter.

❑ Any commands that you normally enter at the command prompt can be stored as a group in a batch file.

❑ Batch files must have the extension .BAT and should not have the same name as any file with a .COM or .EXE extension.

❑ You execute all the commands in a batch file by running the file exactly as you would run any other program on your computer.

❑ To prevent a command from appearing on the screen before it is executed, precede the command with an @ character (versions 3.3 and later).

❑ You can pass parameters from the DOS command line to your batch file by using the names %1, %2, %3, and so on, as placeholders.

❑ To stop the execution of a batch file, press Ctrl-C or Ctrl-Break.

❏ You can have a batch file read information from the environment by surrounding variable names with % signs. (For example, %PATH% reads the current PATH setting.)

❏ You can use the SET command to store data in the environment. (When you use the SET command alone, it displays the contents of the environment.)

❏ If ANSI.SYS is installed on your computer, you can use the PROMPT $e[0; commands in a batch file to customize the function keys.

Extending the Power of Your Batch Files

This chapter presents some advanced techniques that you can use to create bigger and better batch files. The sample batch files that you will develop are practical programs you will find useful in your own work.

This chapter assumes that you already know how to use the EDIT text editor described in previous chapters. Therefore, we will no longer present the step-by-step instructions required to create each batch file. Remember, Chapter 10 provides general information about creating and editing any DOS text file.

Decision Making in Batch Files

A batch file can use two commands—IF and IF NOT—to make a decision about whether to perform some operation. The basic syntax for the IF command is as follows:

```
IF condition command
```

in which `condition` is some situation that DOS can evaluate as being either true or false. If the condition proves true, the command next to it is executed. If the condition proves false, the command next to it is ignored.

You can reverse the effects of the condition by using the IF NOT command, as shown in the following syntax:

```
IF NOT condition command
```

In this command, if the condition is not true, the command is executed. If the condition is true, the command is ignored.

The three basic techniques for using the IF command are discussed in the sections that follow.

Using IF to Check for Files

The `IF EXIST filename` version of IF checks to see whether the file specified in `filename` exists. For example, the following command looks for a file named MYDIARY.TXT in the current directory. If the file exists, the command `TYPE MYDIARY.TXT` is executed; otherwise, the `TYPE MYDIARY.TXT` command is ignored.

```
IF EXIST MYDIARY.TXT TYPE MYDIARY.TXT
```

The next command checks to see whether a file named CHAP1.TXT already exists in a directory named \BAKFILES. If the file does not yet exist, the COPY command copies CHAP1.TXT from the current directory to the \BAKFILES directory; if the CHAP1.TXT files does exist on the \BAKFILES directory, the COPY command is not executed.

```
IF NOT EXIST \BAKFILES\CHAP1.TXT COPY
CHAP1.TXT \BAKFILES
```

This general syntax is useful in batch files when you want to be sure that a COPY operation does not overwrite an existing file. (You'll soon see an example of this usage.)

You also can use wildcard characters in the `filename` portion of the command. For example, the following command displays the message `No batch files here` if the current directory does not contain any files with the .BAT extension.

```
IF NOT EXIST *.BAT ECHO No batch files here
```

Using IF to Compare Strings

As you probably recall, a *string* is any character or group of characters. You can also use the IF command to compare two strings by using the general syntax

```
IF string1 == string2 command
```

which (in English) says, "If the first string matches the second string, do `command`." You can also use the syntax

```
IF NOT string1 == string2 command
```

which says, "If the first string does not match the second string, do `command`."

The IF command recognizes two strings as identical if they are exactly the same, including uppercase and lowercase letters. For example SMITH matches SMITH, but SMITH does not match Smith.

Typically, you use IF to see whether a passed parameter or an environmental variable equals a set value. For example, the command

```
IF %1 == Martha ECHO Hello Martha!
```

displays the message `Hello Martha` if the %1 variable contains the name `Martha`.

If either string is left blank, DOS returns the error message `Syntax error`. If there is a possibility that one of the strings might be left blank, follow both strings in the IF command with an extra character, such as a period. For example, suppose you create a batch file that requires you to enter a parameter at the command prompt. The following command checks to see whether the parameter is blank and if so, displays the message `A parameter is required` if the parameter.

```
IF %1. == . ECHO A parameter is required
```

Remember that %1 is merely a placeholder for the first option entered at the command prompt. Therefore, if %1 contains `Joe`, the previous command becomes `IF Joe. == . ECHO A parameter is required` before it is executed. Because `Joe.` is not the same as `.`, the ECHO command is ignored.

However, if you don't include a parameter at the command prompt, the command becomes `IF . == . ECHO A parameter is required` before execution. In this case, the two strings (`.` and `.`) are identical, so the ECHO command is executed. You'll see a practical example of this technique in MOVE.BAT and in other batch files presented in this chapter.

Testing for Command Errors

NOTE: See the IF command in Appendix B for a reference to all ERRORLEVEL values.

A third variation of the IF command is used in conjunction with commands such as `BACKUP`, `FORMAT`, and `RESTORE`. These commands all return an ERRORLEVEL value after they are executed. If the operation is completed successfully, ERRORLEVEL is zero. If the operation could not be completed, ERRORLEVEL is some number greater than zero.

The general syntax for using ERRORLEVEL in an IF command is as follows:

```
IF ERRORLEVEL number command
```

The command is executed only if the ERRORLEVEL value is greater than or equal to the `number`. For example, the BACKUP command returns an errorlevel value in the range of 1 to 4 when the backup operation cannot be completed. In the following sample batch file, the IF command signals DOS to display the message `Backup not fully completed!` if an error occurs during the BACKUP command:

```
REM ********************** QUICKBAK.BAT
REM Backs up new and modified files only.
BACKUP C:\*.* A:\ /S /M
IF NOT ERRORLEVEL 0 ECHO Backup not fully completed!
```

Many of the batch files presented later in this chapter contain practical examples of the IF command. First however, you need to learn about the GOTO command, which helps add even more decision-making power to your batch files.

Skipping a Group of Commands in a Batch File

> NOTE: You can use GOTO only in batch files; it is not a valid command at the command prompt nor in a DOSKEY macro.

As you know from the previous chapter, DOS usually executes commands in a batch file from the top down. However, you can force DOS to skip commands or repeat commands by using the GOTO command to perform a technique called *branching*.

The GOTO command tells DOS to skip a group of commands until it finds a *label*. When it finds the label, it resumes execution at the first command after the label. The label itself must be preceded by a colon in the batch file (but you do not include the colon in the GOTO command).

For example, the following sample batch file contains the command `GOTO NearBottom` and the label `:NearBottom`:

```
@ECHO OFF
ECHO I'm line 1
ECHO I'm line 2
GOTO NearBottom
ECHO I'm line 3
ECHO I'm line 4
:NearBottom
ECHO I'm line 5
ECHO I'm line 6
```

If you ran this batch file, your screen would display

```
I'm line 1
I'm line 2
I'm line 5
I'm line 6
```

Notice that the two ECHO commands between the GOTO NearBottom command and the :NearBottom label were completely ignored. That's because the GOTO command branched execution to the first command after the NearBottom label, and therefore DOS never "saw" the ECHO commands for lines 3 and 4.

Copying Files Without Overwriting

To demonstrate a practical application of the IF and GOTO commands, Figure 14.1 shows a batch file named SAFECOPY.BAT that copies files from one drive or directory to another only if no files at the destination will be overwritten. (This is different from the DOS COPY command, which will overwrite files at the destination.)

```
@ECHO OFF
REM ************************* SAFECOPY.BAT
REM Checks for overwriting before copying files.
IF EXIST %2\%1 GOTO ErrMsg
COPY %1 %2\%1
GOTO Done
:ErrMsg
ECHO Files on %2 will be overwritten!
ECHO Copy aborted
:Done
```

Figure 14.1. The SAFECOPY.BAT batch file.

Look at how SAFECOPY.BAT works: Assuming that you create this batch file on your own computer, you would enter the command `SAFECOPY *.BAT \DOS` to use SAFECOPY.BAT to copy all the .BAT files from your current directory to a directory named \DOS.

First, in the command `IF EXIST %2\%1 GOTO ErrMsg`, the %1 and %2 variables are replaced with the source and destination for the copy. Hence, the command becomes `IF EXIST \DOS\*.BAT GOTO ErrMsg` before execution. This checks to see whether any files on the \DOS directory have the extension .BAT. If any do, control branches to the label `:ErrMsg`, thereby skipping the COPY command.

If the GOTO command did not branch control to the :ErrMsg label, the command `COPY %1 %2\%1` becomes `COPY *.BAT \DOS\*.BAT` after substitution. When this command executes, it copies all .BAT files to the \DOS directory.

After a successful copy, the `GOTO Done` command passes control to the label named `:Done` so that the ECHO commands that display the error message are ignored. (These must be skipped because the batch file shouldn't display the error messages after a successful copy operation.)

The :ErrMsg label (short for *error message*) marks the location to which the GOTO ErrMsg command passes control when the IF EXIST %2\%1 command proves true. Because this label is beneath the COPY command, the COPY command is not executed when control is passed to this label.

The commands ECHO Files on %2 will be overwritten! and ECHO Copy aborted display the error message on the screen. Note that if the COPY command is executed, the GOTO Done command skips over these commands, so the error message is not displayed. The :Done label marks the end of the batch file, where execution ends and control returns to the command prompt.

As you will soon see, "asking questions" with IF and branching with GOTO can help you to build more "intelligent" batch files. But first, look at a few more optional techniques that can make your batch files even smarter.

Pausing for a Keystroke

Another useful command that you can use in batch files is PAUSE. This command temporarily stops execution of the batch file and displays the message Press any key to continue.... This pause is usually used to give a person a chance to insert a diskette in a drive. However, it can also be used to give you the option of pressing Ctrl-C to terminate the batch file in the event of an unexpected situation.

> NOTE: NUL is sometimes called the "garbage can" device, because anything sent to it just disappears.

You can redirect the message displayed by PAUSE to a device called NUL (for null) if you want to hide the stock message and create your own. For example, look at the following series of commands:

```
@ECHO OFF
ECHO File(s) will be overwritten!
ECHO Press Ctrl-C, then Y, to abandon the operation
ECHO or any other key to proceed and overwrite... PAUSE > NUL
COPY %1 %2
```

When executed, these commands display the following on the screen:

```
File(s) will be overwritten!
Press Ctrl-C, then Y, to abandon the operation
or any other key to proceed and overwrite...
```

Pressing any key other than Ctrl-C (or Ctrl-Break) resumes processing normally so that the COPY command below the PAUSE command is executed normally. However, pressing Ctrl-C (or Ctrl-Break) during this pause cancels execution of the batch file and displays the confirmation message:

```
Terminate batch file (Y/N)?
```

Pressing Y at this point finally terminates the batch file and returns to the command prompt. The COPY command is not executed. In essence the PAUSE command lets the user (the person who happens to be using the batch file at the moment) make a decision based on information provided by the messages on the screen.

Figure 14.2 shows a modified version of SAFECOPY.BAT that uses this alternate technique. Rather than absolutely refusing to overwrite files during a copy procedure, the batch file explains that files will be overwritten and asks for permission to proceed with the operation.

```
@ECHO OFF
REM *********************** SAFECOPY.BAT
REM Modified version that gives the user the
REM choice about whether to proceed.

REM --- If no files will be overwritten, proceed to GoAhead.
IF NOT EXIST $2\%1 GOTO GoAhead

REM --- Present message and opportunity to cancel...
ECHO File(s) will be overwritten!
ECHO Press Ctrl-C, then Y, to abort operation
ECHO or any other key to proceed and overwrite...
PAUSE > NUL

REM --- IF Ctrl-C was not pressed during pause,
REM --- execution proceeds with rest of commands.
:GoAhead
COPY %1 %2\%1
```

Figure 14.2. The modified SAFECOPY.BAT batch file.

This version of SAFECOPY.BAT begins with the command IF NOT EXIST %2\%1 GOTO GoAhead, which sends control directly to the label :GoAhead and bypasses the messages that directly follow.

The ECHO commands present the messages warning that a file (or files) will be overwritten. Then a PAUSE waits for a keypress. Pressing Ctrl-C during the pause and then pressing Y terminates execution of the batch file so that the COPY command is never reached.

Use the EDIT editor to create both versions of SAFECOPY.BAT. Test each one by trying to copy the same file to the same directory twice. On the second attempt, one batch file will not allow you to recopy the file, and the other will warn you about the operation.

Soon you will develop a similar batch file, named MOVE.BAT, that safely moves files from one drive or directory to another. First however, the next section will teach you a few tricks that you can use to make your batch files display more readable messages.

Improving Batch File Messages

If you develop batch files that display many messages and warnings on the screen, you should use some of the techniques discussed in the sections that follow.

Making Your Batch File Beep

You can easily make your batch file sound a beep when it presents an important message. If you are using the EDIT editor to create your batch files, type the ECHO command, followed by a blank space and the message. However, before you press Enter to move to the next line, you have to insert a Ctrl-G control character. You do this by using the following steps (while in EDIT):

1. Type **Ctrl-P** (which enables you to use the Alt key to enter an ASCII control character).

2. Hold down the **Alt** key.

3. Type **007** (the ASCII code for Ctrl-G) on the numeric keypad.

4. Release the **Alt** key.

Your screen now displays a bullet character (•), as in the following example:

```
ECHO Files will be overwritten!•
```

Later, when you run the batch file, DOS will sound the beep whenever the message is displayed on the screen. (This technique is often used by programs to get your attention and warn you of a potential problem.)

Displaying Blank Lines from a Batch File

If you want a batch file to display a blank line on the screen, follow the ECHO command with a period (no blank spaces). You can try this directly at the command prompt. That is, if you enter the command

```
ECHO
```

DOS displays the message ECHO is on (or ECHO is off). However, if you enter the command

```
ECHO.
```

DOS displays only a blank line.

A Batch File to Move Files to a New Directory

Now, I will combine most of the techniques discussed in preceding sections to develop a powerful batch file named MOVE.BAT that can move files from one directory to another. On the surface, you might think that such a batch file need only contain two commands

```
REM *********************** MOVE.BAT
COPY %1 %2
ERASE %1
```

If this MOVE.BAT file were stored on your computer, and you wanted to move the files named CHAP1.TXT, CHAP2.TXT, and so on up to CHAP19.TXT to a directory named \DONE, you would enter the command MOVE CHAP*.TXT C:\DONE. The first command would become COPY CHAP*.TXT C:\DONE, which would copy all the files from the current directory to the directory named \DONE. Then the second command would become ERASE CHAP*.TXT, which would erase those copied files from the current directory.

NOTE: DOS 5 users already have a safe technique for moving files from one directory to another—the Move option in the File pull-down menu of the File List.

However, what if you entered the command MOVE CHAP*.TXT C:\DONE without realizing that you had not yet created a directory named \DONE? Because DOS would not find a directory named \DONE, it would assume you meant a file named DONE on the root directory! First DOS would copy CHAP1.TXT to the file named DONE. Then it would copy CHAP2.TXT to the file named DONE, overwriting the current contents of the DONE file, and so on. When the COPY command was completed, the file named DONE on the root directory would contain only a copy of CHAP17.TXT.

This is a disaster when the second command in the batch file, ERASE CHAP*.TXT, is executed. Now you've got a problem. Not only has MOVE.BAT sent copies of the first 16 chapters to nowhere, but it has erased the originals as well!

Figure 14.3 shows a better version of the MOVE.BAT batch file, which is loaded with safety features to prevent problems. It even warns you if the MOVE operation is going to overwrite files on the destination directory so that you can bail out before any overwriting takes place. (Blank lines are included in the batch file to help you isolate individual groups of commands, or *routines*).

Look at how the improved version of MOVE.BAT works. As an example, suppose that you run MOVE.BAT with the command

```
MOVE CHAP*.TXT C:\DOSBOOK
```

The first line turns off ECHO, and the next three lines are the usual comments. The first command, IF %2. == . GOTO ErrMsg1, checks for an initial error. This command verifies that two parameters were entered next to the MOVE command. If %2 (the second parameter) were left blank, this command passes control to the :ErrMsg1 label. In this example, the executed command would be IF C:\DOSBOOK. == . GOTO ErrMsg1, and because C:\DOSBOOK. is not the same as ., execution resumes with the next command.

The next command, IF NOT EXIST %1 GOTO ErrMsg2, checks to see whether the files being copied exist in the current directory. In this example, after substitution takes place, the command becomes IF NOT EXIST CHAP*.TXT GOTO ErrMsg. If no files in the current directory match the ambiguous file name CHAP*.TXT, this command passes control to the :ErrMsg2 label. Again, this is just a safety precaution that ensures that the command has been entered correctly at the command prompt.

```
@ECHO OFF
REM ********************** MOVE.BAT
REM Move file(s) to a new destination.
REM %1 is source, %2 is destination.

REM Make sure two parameters were passed.
IF %2. == . GOTO ErrMsg1

REM Make sure source exists
IF NOT EXIST %1 GOTO ErrMsg2

REM Check to see whether overwriting will occur.
IT NOT EXIST %2\%1 GOTO MoveIt

REM Provide warning before overwriting;● is Ctrl-G.
ECHO WARNING! %1 file(s) already exist on %2●
ECHO Press Ctrl-C now to cancel operation or
ECHO any other key to overwrite files on %2
PAUSE > NUL

:MoveIt
COPY %1 %2\%1 > NUL
REM Double-check before erasing.
IF NOT EXIST %2\%1 GOTO ErrMsg3
ERASE %1 GOTO Done

:ErrMsg1
ECHO You must provide a source and destination, for example.
ECHO MOVE *.BAK \BAKFILES
ECHO moves all .BAK files to the \BAKFILES directory.
GOTO Done

:ErrMsg2
ECHO %1 does not exist on current directory!
GOTO Done

:ErrMsg3
ECHO Destination directory does not exist or source invalid
ECHO (Source may not contain a drive or directory name)
ECHO -- Operation canceled --

:Done
```

Figure 14.3. A better MOVE.BAT batch file.

The next command, `IF NOT EXIST %2\%1 GOTO MoveIt`, checks to see whether any files in the destination directory have the same names as the files in the source directory. In this example, the command becomes `IF NOT EXIST C:\DOSBOOK\CHAP*.TXT GOTO MoveIt`. If none of the files on the C:\DOSBOOK directory match CHAP*.TXT, the GOTO command branches control directly to the :MoveIt label. However, if file names on the destination directory match files to be moved, the next commands are executed:

NOTE: Remember, the • symbol (which represents the control character Ctrl-G) causes the computer to beep.

```
ECHO WARNING! %1 file(s) already exist on %2•
ECHO Press Ctrl-C now to cancel operation or
ECHO any other key to overwrite files on %2
PAUSE > NUL
```

These commands display the message warning that files will be overwritten. After substitution, the actual message displayed is as follows:

```
WARNING! CHAP8.TXT file(s) already exist on C:\DOSBOOK
ECHO Press Ctrl-C now to cancel operation or
ECHO any other key to overwrite files on C:\DOSBOOK
```

the PAUSE > NUL command waits for a keystroke but does not display its own message. At this point, pressing Ctrl-C cancels the batch file, so no files are moved. Pressing any other key passes control to the next commands.

:MoveIt is the label for the block of commands that perform the actual copying and erasing. First the command COPY %1 %2\%1> NUL is converted to COPY CHAP*.TXT C:\DOSBOOK\CHAP*.TXT. (Ignore the > NUL for now; it just hides the messages that COPY normally displays and can be omitted from the batch file if you prefer.)

Notice that the COPY command repeats the file name in the destination. This ensures that entering an invalid directory names does not lead to problems. For example, if this batch file had used the command COPY %1 %2, the command to be executed in this example would be COPY CHAP*.TXT C:\DOSBOOK. If the directory named C:\DOSBOOK does not exist, this command would copy the CHAP*.TXT files to a file named DOSBOOK on the root directory (as discussed earlier).

However, the command COPY %1 %2\%1 becomes COPY CHAP*.TXT C:\DOSBOOK\CHAP*.TXT. In this case, DOS must assume that \DOSBOOK is a directory name. Therefore, if the \DOSBOOK directory cannot be found, DOS cancels the operation and displays the error message Path not found. This safety procedure prevents you from inadvertently copying files to the root directory.

Before erasing any files in the current directory, the command IF NOT EXIST %2\%GOTO ErrMsg3 becomes IF NOT EXIST C:\DOSBOOK\CHAP*.TXT GOTO ErrMsg3. This command checks the destination directory to verify that it contains the files that were (presumably) copied by the preceding COPY command. If anything went wrong during the COPY operation, the destination directory will not contain the copied files. In that case, this command passes control to the :ErrMsg3 label so that the ERASE command does not erase any files.

If (and only if) all went well up to this point, the `ERASE %1` command expands to `ERASE CHAP*.TXT`. This erases all copied files from the source directory. Because every possible error has been checked, it is now safe to proceed with this ERASE command.

The next command, `GOTO Done`, branches control to the :Done label to bypass the error messages. Following this command are the various labels and error messages to which the preceding IF commands would have passed control in the event of an error. These are simple ECHO commands that provide information about the specific error that was encountered. As you can see in the following code lines, each routine branches control to the :Done label after displaying its error message so that the following ECHO commands are not displayed:

```
:ErrMsg1
ECHO You must provide a source and destination, for example,
ECHO MOVE *.BAK \BAKFILES
ECHO moves all .BAK files to the \BAKFILES directory.
GOTO Done

:ErrMsg2
ECHO %1 does not exist on current directory!
GOTO Done

:ErrMsg3
ECHO Destination directory does not exist or source invalid
ECHO (Source may not contain a drive or directory name)
ECHO -- Operation canceled --

:Done
```

In some ways, MOVE.BAT might seem almost paranoid in its concern with safety. However, considering that this batch file erases files, safety is certainly something that cannot be stressed too strongly.

Tips for Using MOVE.BAT

Keep in mind that MOVE.BAT is designed to move files only from the current directory to a different directory. You cannot specify a drive or another directory in the source.

For example, you cannot enter a command such as `MOVE C:\WP\WPFILES\SALEMEMO.DOC   \SALES` to move the SALEMEMO.DOC file from the \WP\WPFILES directory to the \SALES directory. Instead, you must first change to the \WP\WPFILES directory by entering the command `CD \WP\WPFILES` at the command prompt. Then you can move the SALEMEMO.DOC file from that directory to the \SALES directory by entering the command `MOVE  SALEMEMO.DOC \SALES`. Of course, if you make a mistake, MOVE.BAT certainly will let you know before any damage is done!

Repeating Commands in a Batch File

Another high-powered technique that you can use in batch file is *looping*. Looping allows you to repeat a command several times. The command you use for looping is FOR, which uses the following general syntax:

```
FOR %%letter IN (items) DO command
```

where `letter` is a single letter (*a* through *z* or *A* through *Z*), `items` is either a list of items separated by blank spaces or an ambiguous file name (which represents several files), and `command` is the command that is executed during each pass through the loop.

Each time the loop is executed, the `%%letter` variable assumes either the next value in the list of items or the next file name in the list produced by the ambiguous file name.

Even though you normally use the FOR command in a batch file, you can actually try an example at the command prompt. However, when using FOR at the command prompt, you use `%letter` rather than `%%letter`.

Now test the command: Assuming that the command prompt is displayed on your screen, enter this command:

```
FOR %c IN (Item1 Item2 Item3) DO ECHO %c
```

When you press Enter, your screen shows the following:

```
C:\UTILS>ECHO Item1
Item1

C:\UTILS>ECHO Item2
Item2
```

```
C:\UTILS>ECHO Item3
Item3

C:\UTILS>
```

(Where C:\UTILS> is simply the DOS command prompt.)

Notice what happened. In the first pass through the loop, %c was replaced by the first item in the list, so the first command executed was `ECHO  Item1`. During the second pass through the loop, %c was replaced by the second item in the list, so the command executed was `ECHO Item2`. In the third pass through the loop, Item3 was substituted for %c, so the command executed was `ECHO Item3`. The next section examines a more practical application of looping.

LOOKIN.BAT: A Batch File to Search for a Word

LOOKIN.BAT is a batch file that can search through the contents of text files for a specific word. The more files and information you store on your computer, the more useful this batch file becomes. For example, suppose that you use EDIT to create a file, named PHONE.TXT, that contains people's phone numbers, as shown in Figure 14.4. (Your file would probably contain many more names and numbers.) If you created LOOKIN.BAT, you could quickly retrieve Bonnie Baker's number by entering the command

```
LOOKIN PHONES.TXT Baker
```

```
Arthur Adams              (213)555-0146
Bonnie Baker              (619)555-9302
Charlie Charisma          (415)555-0954
Donna Daring              (213)555-8765
Edie Estoval              (415)555-7676
Frankly Fastidious        (619)555-9443
Gina Garrog               (714)555-3232
Harry Hampton             (212)555-6543

(many more names could follow...)
```

Figure 14.4. A file containing names and phone numbers.

Your screen would display the following:

```
--------------- PHONES.TXT
Bonnie Baker                          (619)555-9302

Press any key to print this list
or Ctrl-C to abort.
```

Another situation in which LOOKIN.BAT is useful is when you forget the name of a file you've created. If you know the directory in which the file is stored and can think of a distinctive word that is stored in the file, you can use LOOKIN to quickly search a large group of files for that word.

For example, if you wrote a letter to Albert Smith but cannot remember the name of that particular file (other than the fact that it probably had the extension .LET), you would enter the following command to search all .LET files on the current directory for the word *Albert*:

```
LOOKIN *.LET Albert
```

Figure 14.5 shows sample results of running LOOKIN.BAT for the theoretical example above. Note that the name *Albert* appears in only the QUIKNOTE.LET file.

```
c:\WP\WFPILES:LOOKIN *.LET Albert
Searching for Albert in *.LET...
Results of scanning *.LET files for Albert


---------- ACCTNG.LET

---------- COVER.LET

---------- GRANDMA.LET

---------- QUIKNOTE.LET
Albert J. Smith
Dear Albert:

---------- ZOO.LET

Press any key to print this list
or press Ctrl-C to abort.
```

Figure 14.5. Sample results of a search with LOOKIN.BAT.

Figure 14.6 shows the entire LOOKIN.BAT batch file. Use the usual EDIT techniques to create LOOKIN.BAT on your own system.

```
@ ECHO OFF
REM *********************** LOOKIN.BAT
REM Searches multiple text files for a word.
REM ----- %1 is file(s) to be searched,
REM ----- %2 is word to search for.

REM ----- Erase TEMPFILE.TXT if it exists.
IF EXIST TEMPFILE.TXT ERASE TEMPFILE.TXT

REM ----- Search files with FIND,
REM ----- redirect output to TEMPFILE.TXT.
ECHO Searching for %2 in %1...
FOR %%c IN (%1) DO FIND "%2" %%c >> TEMPFILE.TXT

REM ----- Display the results.
ECHO Results of scanning %1 files for %2
TYPE TEMPFILE.TXT ¦ MORE

REM ----- Present option to print the results.
ECHO.
ECHO Press any key to print this list
ECHO or press Ctrl-C to abort.
PAUSE > NUL
ECHO Results of scanning %1 files for %2 > PRN
TYPE TEMPFILE.TXT > PRN
ECHO ♀ > PRN
```

Figure 14.6. The LOOKIN.BAT batch file.

NOTE: The DOS 5 FIND command includes the /I switch, which tells FIND to ignore case. If you are using DOS 5, use the command `FOR %%c IN (%1) DO FIND /I "%2" %%c >> TEMPFILE.TXT` in the previous batch file.

LOOKIN.BAT also offers some unique features that you have not seen in previous batch files. Therefore, I'll discuss the purpose of each command in LOOKIN.BAT (excluding the REM comment lines). For the purposes of example, assume that you executed LOOKIN.BAT with the command `LOOKIN *.LET Albert`.

First, the command `IF EXIST TEMPFILE.TXT ERASE TEMPFILE.TXT` erases the file named TEMPFILE.TXT from the current directory (if it exists). As you will see, LOOKIN.BAT channels its output to this file so that you later have the option of printing the results of LOOKIN.BAT after viewing them on the screen.

Next, the command ECHO Searching for %2 in %1 displays a message that tells you what operation is taking place. In this example, the message on the screen would be Searching for Albert in *.LET.

The next command, FOR %%c IN (%1) DO FIND "%2" %%c >> TEMPFILE.TXT, executes the command FIND "%2" every time a new file name matches the *.LET ambiguous file name. For example, if the first file to be searched is APRIL90.LET, this command becomes FIND "Albert" APRIL90.LET. The >> TEMPFILE.TXT portion of the command channels the output to the TEMPFILE.TXT file without erasing existing text in TEMPFILE.TXT. This loop is repeated until all *.LET files have been searched.

The next command, ECHO Results of scanning %1 files for %2, displays a message on the screen: in this example, it is Results of scanning *.LET files for Albert. Then the command TYPE TEMPFILE.TXT ¦ MORE displays the results of the search, which are stored in the file TEMPFILE.TXT. The ¦ MORE option pauses the display after each screenful of information and waits for a keypress.

The ECHO. command prints a blank line on the screen. The next two ECHO commands display the message

```
Press any key to print this list
or press Ctrl-C to abort.
```

The PAUSE > NUL command pauses without displaying a message. Pressing Ctrl-C during this pause terminates batch file execution; pressing another key resumes execution at the next command.

Your screen now displays a bullet character (•), as in the following example:

```
ECHO Files will be overwritten!•
```

Later, when you run the batch file, DOS will sound the beep whenever the message is displayed on the screen. (This technique is often used by programs to get your attention and warn you of a potential problem.)

If you do not press Ctrl-C to cancel the operation, the next three commands send the message Results of scanning *.LET files for Albert and the contents of the TEMPFILE.TXT to the printer. The last command, ECHO ♀ > PRN, then ejects the page from the printer. (Remember, ^L is entered by pressing Ctrl-L). You can omit this last command if you are not using a laser printer.

Tips for Using LOOKIN.BAT

> NOTE: The DOS 5 FIND command can ignore the case of text. If you are using DOS 5 and include /I in the FIND command, your search text doesn't need to match text exactly.

LOOKIN.BAT can search any file or group of files in any directory for any single word. Remember, however, that because it uses the DOS FIND command to perform this search, the command is *case-sensitive* in versions of DOS preceding DOS 5. That is, the command `LOOKIN PHONES.TXT BAKER` would not find Baker. (An improved version of LOOKIN.BAT, named LOOKIN2.BAT and presented later in this chapter, offers a way around this limitation for users of earlier versions of DOS.)

Also, if you use LOOKIN.BAT to search files that you created with a word processor, the results might not be accurate. The reason for this is that the word processor may use formatting codes that change the word that FIND is looking for. If in doubt, use the TYPE command to view the contents of your word processing file to see how it is stored.

If your word processor changes the last character of every word, you should use LOOKIN.BAT to search for all the characters in a word except for the last. For example, suppose that you want to search through a group of files with the extension .DOC for the word "banana". However, you created these .DOC files with WordStar, which alters the last character of many words in a document. Entering the command `LOOKIN *.DOC banan` would yield more accurate results than the command `LOOKIN *.DOC banana`.

LOOKIN.BAT displays only the `Searching...` message while the search is taking place. Depending on the speed of your computer and the amount of text being searched, the delay might be anywhere from a few seconds to several minutes. In most cases, however, the search probably will be surprisingly fast.

COUNTIN.BAT: A Variation of LOOKIN.BAT

LOOKIN.BAT displays the name of every file searched and the lines of text in each file that contain the word you are looking for. As an alternative, you can create COUNTIN.BAT, which displays the names of files that contain the word you are looking for and the number of times the word appears in that file.

This can be a useful command in many situations. For example, assume that you've stored each chapter for a book in files named CHAP1.TXT, CHAP2.TXT, CHAP3.TXT, and so on. If you wanted to see which chapter first introduced the term *reboot,* you could enter the command `COUNTIN CHAP*.TXT reboot`. The results of this search, shown in Figure 14.7, reveal that the word *reboot* is first mentioned in Chapter 3 (CHAP3.TXT) and is also included in several other chapters.

```
C:\WPJWPFILES>COUNTIN *TXT reboot
Counting for "reboot" in *.TXT files
"reboot" appears in the following *.TXT files

---------- CHAP3.TXT: 2
---------- CHAP5.TXT: 10
---------- CHAP10.TXT: 1

Press any key to print this list
or press Ctrl-C to abort.
```

Figure 14.7. Results of the command COUNTIN *.TXT reboot.

If you already created LOOKIN.BAT, use it as a starting point for developing COUNTIN.BAT, because the two batch files are very similar. To do so, at the command prompt, enter the command `COPY LOOKIN.BAT COUNTIN.BAT`. Then enter the command `EDIT COUNTIN.BAT`. Now, you need to change only a few lines, rather than create an entirely new file. Figure 14.8 shows the complete COUNTIN.BAT file.

Note that the FIND command in the line that begins `FOR %%C...` now includes the /C switch. This switch tells the FIND command to count rather than display the words being searched for.

The two lines that begin with TYPE commands have been changed to `TYPE TEMPFILE.TXT ¦ FIND "-" ¦ FIND /V " 0" ¦ MORE`. The TYPE command sends the results of the search (stored in TEMPFILE.TXT) to the filters that follow the command. The first filter, `FIND "-"`, limits the output to those lines that begin with a hyphen, because these are the only lines that contain file names (as you can see in Figure 14.7).

That output is then passed through the second filter, `FIND /V " 0"`, which filters out all lines that contain a zero preceded by a blank space. (The leading blank space is included so that only lines with an exact count of zero are excluded, but not lines that contain a zero, such as those with a count of 10 or 20 or lines with a file name like SPRING90.TXT). The final output is passed through the MORE filter, which pauses the screen display every 24 lines.

```
@ECHO OFF
REM ********************** COUNTIN.BAT
REM Searches multiple text files for a word.
REM ----- %1 is file(s) to be searched,
REM ----- %2 is word to search for.

REM ----- Erase TEMPFILE.TXT if it exists.
IF EXIST TEMPFILE.TXT ERASE TEMPFILE.TXT

REM ----- Search files with FIND /C
REM ----- redirect output to TEMPFILE.TXT.
ECHO Counting for "%2" in %1 files.
FOR %%c IN (%1) DO FINE /C "%2" %%c >> TEMPFILE.TXT

REM ----- Display the results.
ECHO "%2" appears in the following %1 files.
TYPE TEMPFILE.TXT ¦ FIND "-" ¦ FIND /V " 0" ¦ MORE

REM ----- Present option to print the results.
ECHO.
ECHO Press any key to print this list, ECHO or press Ctrl-C to abort.
PAUSE > NUL
ECHO "%2" appears in the following %1 files > PRN
TYPE TEMPFILE.TXT ¦ FIND "-" ¦ FIND /V "0" > PRN
ECHO ♀ > PRN
```

Figure 14.8. The COUNTIN.BAT batch file.

A few messages and comments have also been altered slightly. After making your changes, save your work and exit EDIT in the usual manner. The basic technique for using COUNTIN.BAT is identical to that for using LOOKIN.BAT. The only difference is the format of the displayed results.

Passing Multiple Parameters to DOS Commands

Looping is also valuable for passing multiple parameters to DOS commands that usually accept only a single parameter. For example, if you want to erase the files APPLE.TXT, BANANA.DOC, and CHERRY.LET using the DOS ERASE command, you must enter three separate commands:

```
ERASE APPLE.TXT
ERASE BANANA.DOC
ERASE CHERRY.LET
```

However, with the next batch file, MERASE.BAT (Multiple ERASE), you can specify as many as nine files to erase and any of those file names can contain wildcard characters. To erase the three files listed previously using MERASE, you need only enter the command

```
MERASE APPLE.TXT BANANA.DOC CHERRY.LET
```

Figure 14.9 shows the complete MERASE.BAT file. To demonstrate how the batch file works, assume that you created it and then entered the command `MERASE APPLE.TXT BANANA.DOC CHERRY.LET` to erase three files. This command stores the following values in the % variables:

```
%1= APPLE.TXT
%2= BANANA.DOC
%3= CHERRY.LET
```

%4 through %9 are empty (blank).

WARNING: In Figures 14.9 through 14.12, the last line, starting with FOR %%c, is broken only to fit within the margins of this book. If you type one of these batch files, don't break that last line.

```
@ECHO OFF
REM *********************** MERASE.BAT
REM Accepts as many as nine file names to erase.
FOR %%c IN (%1 %2 %3 %4 %5 %6 %7 %8 %9) DO IF NOT %%c. == .
    ERASE %%c
```

Figure 14.9. The MERASE.BAT batch file.

In the first pass through the loop, %%c assumes the value of %1, or APPLE.TXT in this example. Therefore, the command `IF NOT %%c. == . ERASE %%c` expands to `IF NOT APPLE.TXT == . THEN ERASE APPLE.TXT`. Because `APPLE.TXT` and `.` are not the same, the command `ERASE APPLE.TXT` is executed, and the file is erased.

During the next pass through the loop, %%c takes the value of %2, or BANANA.DOC. Once again, the IF test proves true, so the ERASE BANANA.DOC command is executed, and the BANANA.DOC file is erased. In the third pass through the loop, %%c assumes the value of %3, or CHERRY.LET. Again, the IF test proves true, and CHERRY.LET is erased.

During the fourth pass through the loop, %%c takes the value of %4, which is empty. In this case, the command `IF NOT %%c. == .` proves false (because %%c. does equal .), so the ERASE command is ignored. In fact, in all remaining passes through the loop, the IF NOT command proves false; therefore, no more files are erased and the batch file ends, returning control to the command prompt.

There are no built-in safety features in this batch file: It is as immediate in its erasing as the regular DOS ERASE command. However, DOS 4 and 5 users can add the /P switch to the right of the ERASE %%c command. This forces the ERASE command to pause and ask for permission before deleting each file. Figure 14.10 shows this safer version of MERASE.BAT.

```
@ECHO OFF
REM ************************* MERASE.BAT
REM Accepts as many as nine file names to erase.
FOR %%c IN (%1 %2 %3 %4 %5 %6 %7 %8 %9) DO IF NOT %%c. == .
     ERASE %%c /P
```

Figure 14.10. Safer version of MERASE.BAT
(works only with DOS 4 and 5).

You can use this general looping technique to pass as many as nine parameters to any DOS command. However, it's a little trickier passing multiple parameters to a command that requires two or more parameters, such as COPY. For example, if you try to create a batch file named MCOPY that can accept multiple file names, as in the command

```
MCOPY LETTER.TXT MYFILE.DOC A:
```

and also the command

```
MCOPY APPLE.TXT BANANA.DOC Qtrl_90.WKS ABC.LET A:
```

you might think you will have a difficult time—the reason being that in the first command, the destination (A:) is the third parameter (%3), but in the second command, the destination is the fifth parameter (%5). However, there is a simple solution to this problem. If you use a syntax that places the destination first, your batch file can always "assume" that the destination is %1.

For example, you can create a batch file named COPYTO.BAT that accepts as many as eight file names to copy, using the general syntax

```
COPYTO destination file1 file...file8
```

where any of the eight file names can contain wildcards. That is, you could enter the command

```
COPYTO A: APPLE.TXT BANANA.DOC CHERRY.LET
```

where A: is the destination and the rest are file names to be copied to drive A:, or you could enter the command

```
COPYTO A: *.TXT *.LET *.LET *.DOC *.BAK LETTER?.TXT
```

to copy all the specified files to drive A:.

Figure 14.11 shows the COPYTO.BAT batch file. It works on the same basic principle that MERASE.BAT does; however, the %1 variable is not included in the list of items for the loop command. The FOR loop processes only the file names (%2 through %9), whereas the destination (%1) is repeatedly used as the destination in the COPY command.

```
@ECHO OFF
REM ************************* COPYTO.BAT
REM Accepts as many as eight file names to copy.
REM %1 is destination, %2 through %9 are file names.
FOR %%c IN (%2 %3 %4 %5 %6 %7 %8 %9) DO IF NOT %%c. == .
    COPY %%c %1
```

Figure 14.11. The COPYTO.BAT batch file.

You can use this looping technique to pass multiple parameters to a batch file as well. However, this technique is a little different, and it also varies with different versions of DOS, as the next section explains.

Passing Control from One Batch File to Another

Because batch files are essentially customized DOS commands, they can be used like any other DOS command, either at the command prompt or in a batch file. In all versions of DOS, one batch file can pass control to another batch file, but in doing so, the first batch file relinquishes all control to the second batch file, and any additional commands in the first batch file are not executed. Look at a simple example.

The following BAT1.BAT file contains two ECHO commands. However, note that a command between them executes a batch file named BAT2.BAT:

```
@ECHO OFF
REM ****** Bat1.BAT
ECHO I am the first line in BAT1.BAT.
```

```
BAT2
ECHO I am the last line in BAT.BAT.
```

BAT2.BAT, shown below, contains one ECHO command:

```
@ECHO OFF
REM ******* Bat2.BAT
ECHO       I am the only line in BAT2.BAT.
```

If you were to create both of these batch files and then enter the command BAT1, your screen would display the following:

```
I am the first line in BAT1.BAT.
    I am the only line in BAT2.BAT.
```

As you can see, the second ECHO command in BAT1.BAT was never executed. That's because after the BAT2 command was executed, all control passed to BAT2.BAT. When BAT2.BAT finished its job, all execution stopped.

NOTE: If you are using a version of DOS prior to 3.3, replace the CALL command with COMMAND /C in the sample batch files that follow. Be sure to follow the /C with a blank space.

With DOS versions 3.3 and later, you can have one batch file *call* another so that when the second batch file finishes, it returns control to the first. That way, execution resumes normally, and the first batch file can finish executing its remaining commands. To use this technique, use the CALL command.

For example, look at the following BAT1.BAT file. Notice that the only difference between this version and the previous version is that BAT1.BAT uses the command CALL BAT2, rather than just BAT2, to pass control to the BAT2.BAT batch file:

```
@ECHO OFF
REM ******* Bat1.BAT
ECHO I am the first line in BAT1.BAT.
CALL BAT2
ECHO I am the last line in BAT.BAT.
```

With this version of BAT1.BAT, entering the command BAT1 produces these messages on the screen:

```
I am the first line in BAT1.BAT.
    I am the only line in BAT2.BAT.
I am the last line in BAT.BAT.
```

Notice in this example that when BAT2.BAT finished its job, it returned control to BAT1.BAT, and execution resumed normally at the first command beneath the `CALL BAT2` command. (Versions of DOS prior to 3.3 need to use the command `COMMAND /C BAT2` in place of `CALL BAT2` to achieve the same result.)

With this latter technique you easily can create batch files that use other batch files. When used in conjunction with the FOR command, CALL can pass multiple parameters to batch files that normally accept only a fixed number of parameters.

For example, the previously described MOVE.BAT batch file accepts only two parameters—the source of the move and the destination of the move. Now, couple this batch file with a similar batch file named MOVETO.BAT, which uses this different syntax:

> `MOVETO destination file1 file2...file8`

where `destination` is the drive or directory to which files are being moved and `file1 file2...file8` represents as many as eight file names to be moved. Therefore, this single command

> `MOVETO C:\WP\WPFILES *.TXT *.DOC *.LET`

moves all .TXT, .DOC, and .LET files from the current directory to the WP\WPFILES directory.

The command

> `MOVETO A: *.BAK LETTER.TXT NOTE.TXT JUNE90.WKS`

moves all .BAK files, plus the files LETTER.TXT, NOTE.TXT, and JUNE90.TXT, to drive A:. Again, you can list as many as eight file names, and any or all of those names can contain wildcard characters.

The real beauty of this technique is that you don't even need to modify the existing MOVE.BAT batch file to use it. Instead, you can call it from the MOVETO.BAT batch file and still get all the benefits of the safety features it offers. Figure 14.12 shows the MOVETO.BAT batch file.

```
@ECHO OFF
REM ************************* MOVETO.BAT
REM Moves multiple files
REM %1 is destination, %2 through %9 are file names.

FOR %%c IN (%2 %3 %4 %5 %6 %7 %8) DO IF NOT %%c. == . MOVE
    %%c %1
```

Figure 14.12. The MOVETO.BAT batch file.

> NOTE: Basically, MOVETO.BAT uses the same technique to pass multiple parameters that COPYTO.BAT uses. The only real difference is the use of the CALL command in the FOR loop.

Now, look at how MOVETO.BAT does its job. The following discussion assumes that you enter the command `MOVETO \WP\WPFILES APPLE.TXT BANANA.TXT CHERRY.TXT`.

First, the %variables immediately receive these values:

```
%1= \WP\WPFILES
%2= APPLE.TXT
%3= BANANA.TXT
```

%4= CHERRY.TXT %5 through %9 are blank

On the first pass through the loop, %%c is replaced with %2, which is APPLE.TXT. The command `IF NOT %%c. == .` proves true, so the command `CALL MOVE %%c %1` becomes `CALL MOVE APPLE.TXT \WP\WPFILES`. This executes the MOVE command with these parameters, and MOVE.BAT moves the file.

When control returns to MOVETO.BAT, the next pass through the loop is executed, and %%c takes the value of %3, which is BANANA.TXT. The `IF NOT %%c. == .` test proves true, so the command expands to `CALL MOVE BANANA.TXT \WP\WPFILES`. Once again, MOVE.BAT moves the file and returns control to MOVETO.BAT.

On the next pass through the loop, %%c takes on the value of %4, which is CHERRY.TXT. Once again, the IF test proves true, the command `CALL MOVE CHERRY.TXT \WP\WPFILES` is executed, and MOVE.BAT moves the file. Again, it returns control to MOVETO.BAT.

During the next pass through the loop, %%c assumes the value of %5, which is empty. The test `IF NOT %%c. == .` proves false in this case, so the CALL MOVE command is not executed. In fact, because all remaining %variables are empty, the CALL MOVE command is never again executed. After the last pass through the loop, execution ends and control returns to the command prompt.

Passing More Than Nine Parameters

As mentioned earlier, you can use up to nine %variables (%1 through %9) in a batch file. However, you can pass more than nine parameters to a batch file and gain access to those above %9 by *shifting* all other parameters to the left (that is, to a smaller %variable number). The command to shift parameters is (not surprisingly) SHIFT.

The SHIFT command is much different than the FOR...IN...DO looping method you used in previous examples to pass multiple parameters to a command, so I'll stop here and discuss SHIFT in its own light.

Suppose that you created a batch file named SAMPLE.BAT and entered the following command to execute the batch file:

```
SAMPLE A B C D E F G H I J K
```

The first nine %variables would receive the following values:

```
%1 = A
%2 = B
%3 = C
%4 = D
%5 = E
%6 = F
%7 = G
%8 = H
%9 = I
```

The SHIFT command shifts all the parameters from their current positions to the next lower-numbered %variable. For example, if SAMPLE.BAT contained a SHIFT command, after that command was executed, the %variables would contain

```
%1 = B
$2 = C
%3 = D
%4 = E
%5 = F
%6 = G
%7 = H
%8 = I
%9 = J
```

Executing the SHIFT command again would have this effect:

```
%1 = C
%2 = D
%3 = E
%4 = F
%5 = G
%6 = H
%7 = I
%8 = J
%9 = K
```

The next SHIFT command would result in the following:

```
%1 = D
%2 = E
%3 = F
%4 = G
%5 = H
%6 = I
%7 = J
%8 = K
%9 =
```

Notice that because there were no additional parameters on the command line, %9 is now blank. Each time a SHIFT command is executed in the future, the variables continue to be shifted, and the "blanks" follow accordingly. If you executed SHIFT enough times, all the % variables would eventually be empty.

NOTE: The maximum number of parameters that you can pass to a batch file is limited by the maximum allowable length of any DOS command, which is 127 characters.

To use the SHIFT command effectively, you usually couple it with the decision-making power of the IF command and the branching ability of the GOTO command. Look at an example of this by creating a modified version of the LOOKIN.BAT batch file, named LOOKIN2.BAT, that can accept any number of parameters.

In its current state, LOOKIN.BAT can search for only one word. If you are using a version of DOS other than DOS 5, LOOKIN.BAT is case-sensitive; therefore, a truly thorough search for all occurrences of a word such as "tomato" would require at least three commands, as follows:

```
LOOKIN *.TXT tomato
LOOKIN *.TXT Tomato
LOOKIN *.TXT TOMATO
```

With LOOKIN2.BAT, you could accomplish this same goal by entering the single command

```
LOOKIN2 *.TXT tomato Tomato TOMATO
```

In fact, you could search for any number of words using this same basic syntax.

Figure 14.13 shows the LOOKIN2.BAT batch file. Many of the commands in LOOKIN2.BAT are identical to the commands in

LOOKIN.BAT. This section will focus on those commands that are unique to LOOKIN2.BAT.

```
@ECHO OFF
REM *********************** LOOKIN2.BAT
REM Searches multiple text files for multiple words.
REM ----- %1 is file(s) to be searched,
REM ----- %2 is word to search for.

REM ----- Erase TEMPFILE.TXT if it exists.
IF EXIST TEMPFILE.TXT ERASE TEMPFILE.TXT

REM Put %1 in the environment for future use.
SET FileName=%1

REM ----- Search files with FIND,
REM ----- redirect output to TEMPFILE.TXT.
:NextWord
ECHO Searching for %2 in %FileName%...
ECHO Search for %2 in %FileName% >> TEMPFILE.TXT
FOR %%c IN (%FileName%) DO FIND "%2" %%c >> TEMPFILE.TXT

REM Store a form-feed in TEMPFILE.TXT.
ECHO ♀ >> TEMPFILE.TXT

REM Shift and repeat search if more words to search for.
SHIFT
IF NOT %2. == . GOTO NextWord

REM ----- Clean up the environment.
REM ----- Display the results.
SET FileName=
TYPE TEMPFILE.TXT | MORE

REM ----- Present option to print the results.
ECHO
ECHO Press any key to print this list
ECHO or press Ctrl-C, then Y, to abort.
PAUSE > NUL
TYPE TEMPFILE.TXT > PRN
```

Figure 14.13. The LOOKIN2.BAT batch file.

To describe the basic technique that LOOKIN2.BAT uses to search for multiple words, assume that you execute the batch file with the command LOOKIN2 *.TXT Apple Banana Cherry. This sets up the %variables as follows:

```
%1= *.TXT
%2= Apple
%3= Banana
%4= Cherry
```

%5 through %9 are blank.

First, the command `SET FileName=%1` stores the first parameter (for example, *.TXT) in the environment, using the variable name `FileName`. This ensures that if a later SHIFT command erases the *.TXT stored in %1 from the list of parameters, the batch file can still gain access to *.TXT.

:NextWord is a label that marks the beginning of the commands used for printing messages and performing the search. The next two ECHO commands display messages: The first displays its message on the screen; the second sends its message to the TEMPFILE.TXT file, where it later will be displayed as a heading for TEMPFILE.TXT. Note that both commands use %FileName% to display *.TXT, rather than %1. On the first search, therefore, the message displayed on the screen is

```
Searching for Apple in *.TXT
```

The command `FOR %%c IN (%FileName%) DO FIND "%2" %%c >> TEMPFILE.TXT` searches all files that match the file name *.TXT for the word currently stored in %2. This is similar to the same command in LOOKIN.BAT, but %FileName% is used in place of %1 so that *.TXT is taken from the environment. This loop searches all .TXT files for the word `Apple` and then stores the results in TEMPFILE.TXT.

The next command, `ECHO ♀ >> TEMPFILE.TXT`, sends a form-feed to TEMPFILE.TXT. (Remember, ♀ represents Ctrl-L and is generated in EDIT by typing Ctrl-P and then Alt-0-0-7 when you create the batch file.) This form-feed ejects the paper from the printer after the batch file prints the contents of TEMPFILE.TXT. Ejecting the page after printing ensures that the results of each word-search start printing on a new page.

Next, the command SHIFT shifts all parameters to the left (or to the next lower number). Therefore, the %variables now contain the following values:

```
%1= Apple
%2= Banana
%3= Cherry
%4=
```

The next command, `IF NOT %2. == . GOTO NextWord`, checks to see whether %2 is blank. In this example, %2 currently contains the word `Banana`, so the command `GOTO NextWord` is executed, and control branches to the :NextWord label.

The commands below :NextWord are executed, but because %2 now contains `Banana` (not `Apple`), the message, heading, and FIND search are adjusted accordingly. For example, the command `ECHO Searching for %2 in %FileName%` now displays the message

`Searching for Banana in *.TXT`

After the FOR loop searches the *.TXT files for the word `Banana` and stores the results in the TEMPFILE.TXT file, the SHIFT command is executed again. Now the %variables contain

```
%1= Banana
%2= Cherry
%3=
%4=
```

The command `IF NOT %2 == . GOTO NewWord` once again passes control up to the :NewWord label, and once again the message, heading, and search are updated. However, %2 now equals `Cherry`, and that is the word that is searched for. The command `ECHO Searching for %2 in %FileName%` now displays the following message on the screen:

`Searching for Cherry in *.TXT`

Once again, after completing the search for the word `Cherry`, the SWITCH command is executed. Now the %variables contain

```
%1= Cherry
%2=
%3=
%4=
```

This time, the command `IF NOT %2. == . GOTO NewWord` does not pass control to the :NewWord label, because %2 is empty. Therefore, processing resumes with the next command in the batch file.

The command `SET FileName=` sets the FileName variable to "nothing" and thus removes it from the environment. Then the command `TYPE TEMPFILE.TXT | MORE` displays the results of the searches, all of which have been stored in the TEMPFILE.TXT. The remaining commands print the TEMPFILE.TXT file, exactly as they did in the original LOOKIN.BAT batch file.

Including Escape Sequences in Batch Files

Many printers require that you send Escape key sequences to activate special features. For example, the Hewlett-Packard LaserJet printers use the Escape key sequences shown in Table 14.1 to activate various printing modes. The table signifies the Escape key character as {ESC}, as your printer manual might.

Table 14.1. Escape-key codes that control the HP LaserJet printer.

Print Mode	Escape Sequence
Portrait (normal)	{ESC}E{ESC}&l0O
Landscape	{ESC}E{ESC}&l1O
Compressed Portrait	{ESC}E{ESC}&l0O{ESC}&k2s
Compressed Landscape	{ESC}E{ESC}&l1O{ESC}&k2s
Reset to default mode	{ESC}E

> NOTE: Different printers require different codes to activate their features; check your printer manual for a complete list of these codes.

Note that the characters used for portrait modes (l0O) are a lowercase l, the number zero (0), and an uppercase letter o. The characters used for the landscape modes (l0O) are a lowercase letter l, the number 1, and an uppercase letter o.

If you want your batch file to send Escape character sequences to the printer, you might have trouble typing them into your batch file. For example, if you use the EDIT editor, the moment you press the Esc key, EDIT assumes that you want to cancel a command.

> NOTE: If you use an editor other than EDIT, refer to that program's documentation for instructions on how to enter the Escape character into a file.

 If you are using EDIT, you must use the following procedure to enter an Escape character:

1. Press Ctrl-P (to disable any special meaning for the next command).

2. Press Ctrl-V. This displays a small underline character (_).

3. Then type a left square bracket ([).

The characters initially appear on your screen as _[. Note that even though _[appears to be two characters, DOS interprets it as a single Escape key character. Therefore, if you want to send to your printer an Escape key character followed by a [character, first press Ctrl-P, Ctrl-V, and then [to signify the Escape key, and then type [for the bracket. These appear on your screen as _[[.

The _ symbol appears on the screen only when you are in EDIT. When you use the DOS TYPE command to list the file, the letter character is no longer displayed, so what originally appeared as _[appears as a space and a [.

Creating JETSET.BAT

5 This section shows you how to create a batch file named JETSET.BAT that you can use to set the print mode for a LaserJet printer. Figure 14.14 shows the entire JETSET.BAT file as it appears when displayed in EDIT. This is a tricky batch file to type; remember, when you see the _ character in the following figure, you must type Ctrl-P and then Ctrl-V to generate it.

Remember, you can use EDIT's Copy and Paste commands to copy similar lines. Then you can make only a few changes to those lines instead of typing the lines from scratch. Be sure to pay close attention to the differences between the lowercase l letter and number 1 and to the uppercase O letter and the number 0.

Line 41 must be entered by typing ECHO, followed by a blank space, a press of the Ctrl-P key, a press of the Ctrl-L key, another blank space, and then > PRN. After you have typed the entire batch file, press Alt-F; then type X and press Y to save your work and return to the command prompt.

Using JETSET.BAT

After you create JETSET.BAT, you can select a print mode for an HP LaserJet by entering the command JETSET followed by a one- or two-letter code (in upper- or lowercase letters) as follows:

JETSET P	Switches to Portrait (normal) mode
JETSET L	Switches to Landscape (horizontal) mode
JETSET CP	Switches to Compressed Portrait mode
JETSET CL	Switches to Compressed Landscape mode

```
@ECHO OFF
REM *********************** JETSET.BAT
REM -------------------- Sends printer control codes to a LaserJet.

REM ----- Make sure parameter passed is valid.
FOR %%c IN (P p L l CP cp CL cl) DO IF %1. == %%c. GOTO Ok

REM -- If parameter matches none of items checked in loop
REM -- above, there must be an error. Display help below.

ECHO JETSET requires one of the following codes:
ECHO
ECHO      P  Portrait (normal)
ECHO      L Landscape
ECHO      CP Compressed Portrait
ECHO      CL Compressed Landscape
ECHO
ECHO Example: To switch to Compressed Landscape mode, enter JETSET CL.
ECHO
GOTO End

REM Valid parameter was entered; send appropriate code to the printer.

:Ok
IF %1. == P. ECHO _[E_[&l0O > PRN
IF %1. == p. ECHO _[E_[&l0O > PRN
IF %1. == CP. ECHO _[E_[&l0O_[&k2S > PRN
IF %1. == cp. ECHO _[E_[&l0O_[&k2S > PRN
IF %1. == L. ECHO _[E_[&l1O > PRN
IF %1. == l. ECHO _[E_[&l1O > PRN
IF %1. == CL. ECHO _[E_[&l1O_[&k2S > PRN
IF %1. == cl. ECHO _[E_[&l1O_[&k2S > PRN

REM ----- Ask about performing a test to verify success.
ECHO
ECHO Printer set -- press any key to verify
ECHO or Ctrl-C, then Y, to exit...
PAUSE > NUL

REM -- Proceed with test (print directory) if Ctrl-C not pressed.
ECHO This is a test. > PRN
ECHO ♀ > PRN

ECHO Remember that other programs might set the
ECHO printer back to Portrait (normal) mode!
:End
```

Figure 14.14. The JETSET.BAT batch file.

If you enter the command JETSET without a code (or with an invalid code), the screen displays the following help message:

```
JETSET requires one of the following codes:

P   Portrait (normal)
```

```
L    Landscape
CP   Compressed Portrait
CL   Compressed Landscape
```

Example: To switch to Compressed Landscape mode, enter JETSET CL

When you enter a valid code, JETSET displays the following message:

```
Printer set -- press any key to verify
or Ctrl-C, then Y, to exit...
```

If you press any key other than Ctrl-C (or Ctrl-Break), JETSET sends the line This is a test to the printer and then ejects the page so that you can verify that the proper mode has been set. If you press Ctrl-C, the newly selected print mode stays in effect, but the test sentence is not printed.

If you proceed with the test, the screen also displays the reminder message:

```
Remember that other programs might set the
printer back to Portrait (normal) mode!
```

You should test each of the possible codes that JETSET offers. If a particular command, such as JETSET CL, does not set the correct mode for your printer, you might have an error in the escape sequence in JETSET.BAT. Use EDIT to make corrections, always referring to Figure 14.14 as a guide.

How JETSET.BAT Works

When you first run JETSET.BAT, the %1 variable takes the value of the parameter entered next to the JETSET command. The command FOR %%c IN (P p L l CP cp CL cl) DO IF %1. == %%c. GOTO Ok compares %1 to each acceptable option (both uppercase and lowercase). If the %1 parameter matches one of the acceptable options, the GOTO command passes control to the label :Ok.

If the %1 variable does not match one of the acceptable options, the help messages beneath the FOR loop (lines 11 through 19 in Figure 14.14) are displayed instead. After the help messages are displayed, the GOTO End command skips the IF commands that send escape sequences to the printer, and therefore the print mode is not altered.

Lines 24 through 31 compare %1 to each acceptable option. When an IF command finds a match between %1 and an acceptable option, the ECHO command sends the appropriate escape sequence to the printer (that is, > PRN). Lines 34 through 37 present the message that explains the optional test, and then execution waits for a keypress. If you do not press Ctrl-C, line 40 sends a simple sentence to the printer, and line 41 ejects the page from the printer. Lines 43 and 44 display the reminder message on the screen.

Accessing Batch Files from the Shell

You learned in Chapter 11 how to create new groups in the DOS Shell and how to access programs from a group. You can use those same basic techniques to create a group screen for your batch files.

Figure 14.15 shows the Main Group screen with the addition of a new group called Custom Utilities. Figure 14.16 shows an example of how you could design the Custom Utilities group screen. Note that the options on this screen refer to the batch files created in this and the previous chapter.

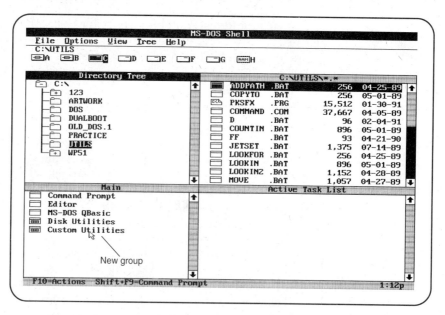

Figure 14.15. DOS Shell Main Group with a new group added.

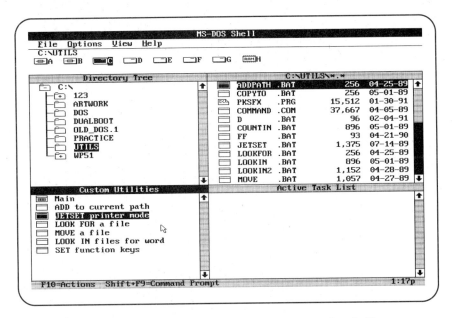

Figure 14.16. A new group screen for accessing batch files.

Figure 14.17 shows the Program Item Properties dialog box for the JETSET printer mode option. Enter `JETSET` as the Program Title, enter `JETSET %1` as the startup Command, and toggle off the Pause After Exit check box. When you select OK, you must fill in the Program Item Properties dialog box for the `%1` parameter, as shown in Figure 14.18.

This set of fields creates the dialog box that appears when you select the JETSET program. Type `JetSet` as the Window Title, type `Enter mode (P, L, CP, or CL)` as the Program Information, and type `Mode...` as the Prompt Message. If you want the batch file to display a default value (perhaps L), enter that value in the Default Parameters field.

The startup sequence assumes that the directory that contains JETSET.BAT is listed in the current PATH setting. Therefore, the startup sequence does not change directories before running JETSET.

Once you've created the dialog boxes for running JETSET.BAT, you can run it from the Custom Utilities program group by highlighting its name and pressing Enter or by double-clicking its name. You'll see the dialog box in Figure 14.19. See Chapter 11 if you need additional help with creating program groups and items in the DOS 5 Shell.

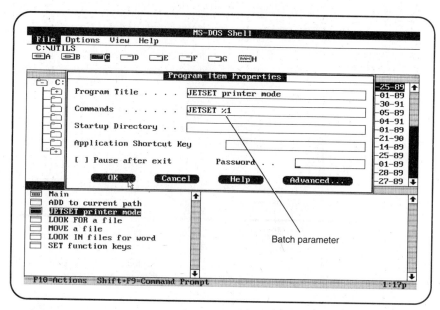

Figure 14.17. The Program Item Properties screen for JETSET.BAT.

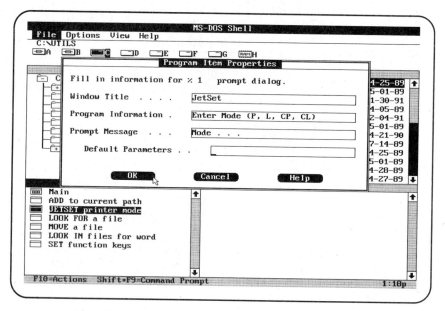

Figure 14.18. The Program Item Properties screen for
JETSET's %1 parameter.

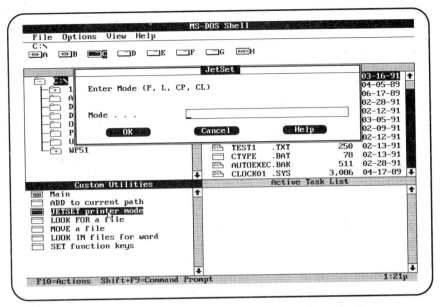

Figure 14.19. The dialog box that appears after selecting JETSET Printer mode.

Creating Your Own Shell

If you are the principal user of a computer that other users share, you might want to create your own DOS Shell. This shell won't be as fancy as the DOS 5 Shell, but it can give less knowledgeable users much easier access to programs. In addition, you can also restrict beginners to certain directories (at least, until they learn how to use DOS on their own).

The basic idea is straightforward. Create a batch file (perhaps named MENU.BAT) that displays a menu of all the programs that you want to make available to other users. Label the options by assigning a number or a letter to each option, as in the example shown in Figure 14.20.

Next, create a batch file that uses the option number or letter as its name, that contains the necessary commands to run the requested program, and (optionally) re-executes the MENU.BAT batch file when the user exits the requested program.

```
@ECHO OFF
REM ************************ MENU.BAT
REM Provide a "shell" for running programs.
CLS
ECHO ===========================================
ECHO
ECHO              What do you want to do?
ECHO
ECHO              1. Use WordPerfect
ECHO              2. Use Microsoft Excel
ECHO              3. Use dBASE IV
ECHO              4. Show what the function keys do
ECHO              5. Go to DOS Command Prompt
ECHO
ECHO ===========================================
ECHO
ECHO Enter a number (1-5); then press Enter...
ECHO
ECHO ===========================================
PROMPT $e
```

Figure 14.20. The MENU.BAT batch file.

For example, the user uses Option 1 on the Menu screen to run the WordPerfect program. Therefore, you need to create a batch file named 1.BAT that will go through the steps required to run the WordPerfect program (because when the user types 1 and presses Enter, DOS will naturally look for a program named 1.EXE, 1.COM, or 1.BAT). Figure 14.21 shows a sample 1.BAT batch file.

```
@ECHO OFF
REM ************************ 1.BAT
REM Run WordPerfect from the \WP\WPFILES directory.
CD \WP\WPFILES
WP
CD \UTILS
MENU
```

Figure 14.21. The 1.BAT batch file.

When the user types 1 and presses Enter, DOS assumes that 1 is a "normal" command, and it looks for a file named 1.BAT (or 1.COM or 1.EXE). This executes 1.BAT, which first changes to the C:\WP\WPFILES directory and then runs the WordPerfect program. When the user exits WordPerfect, the CD \UTILS directory changes back to the \UTILS directory and then the MENU command again executes the MENU.BAT batch file.

You could create similar batch files, named 2.BAT and 3.BAT, to run Microsoft Excel, dBASE IV, or any other program that is available on your system.

Option 5 uses the batch file 5.BAT, shown in Figure 14.22, to remove the MENU display from the screen and redisplay the command prompt.

```
REM *********************** 5.BAT
REM Return to command prompt from MENU.BAT.
PROMPT $P$G
CLS
```

Figure 14.22. The 5.BAT batch file redisplays the command prompt.

As an alternative to making users enter the command MENU, you could make the following two lines the last two commands in your AUTOEXEC.BAT file:

```
CD \UTILS
MENU
```

This automatically displays the help screen as soon as you start the computer. (DOS 5 users would have to delete the DOSSHELL command to do this.)

When you consider that you can customize the function keys to have them automatically enter DOS commands and you can also create batch files such as MENU.BAT to create a type of DOS Shell, you can see that DOS is indeed a very flexible and powerful tool. With these techniques you can customize your system in just about any way you can imagine, and they make your "personal computer" very personal indeed.

Summary

This chapter presented advanced commands and techniques for creating batch files and developed several useful batch files to demonstrate their use. As you gain experience with DOS, you certainly will be able to create some interesting "customized commands" of your own.

❏ The IF command allows a batch file to test for a condition and then react accordingly.

❏ The GOTO command reroutes the normal sequence of execution in a batch file.

❏ The PAUSE command temporarily stops batch file execution and waits until you press a key.

❏ Redirecting output of a command to the NUL device hides any messages that the command normally displays.

❏ To make a batch file display a blank line, type ECHO.

❏ To make a message in a batch file sound a beep, use the Ctrl-G character (by pressing Ctrl-P and then Alt-0-2-2 in EDIT).

❏ The FOR command sets up a loop to repeatedly execute a command in a batch file.

❏ The CALL command passes execution to another batch file, but it permits execution to resume at the next command in the calling batch file.

5 ❏ To use EDIT to enter Escape-key sequences in a batch file, press Ctrl-P, then Ctrl-V, and then type [.

The Power of DOSKEY

NOTE: If you are using a version of DOS prior to version 5, nothing in this chapter will work for you—better skip it.

5 DOSKEY (or DOSKey), introduced in version 5 of DOS, is a powerful new tool for DOS command line users. DOSKEY enhances command-line capabilities in four ways.

- ❏ Uses **command line "history"** to display, edit, and run previously executed commands
- ❏ Uses **enhanced command-line editing** to modify earlier commands rather than retype them
- ❏ Uses the **command separator** to place several commands on a single line
- ❏ Uses the **macro generator** to create, run, and save *macros*, which are like your own custom DOS internal commands

This chapter covers all these DOSKEY features.

Activating DOSKEY

 To activate DOSKEY from the command prompt, type

DOSKEY

and press Enter. Optionally, add the command DOSKEY to your AUTOEXEC.BAT file if you want DOSKEY's features to be available every time you start your computer.

> NOTE: Chapter 17 explains how to use LOADHIGH to load DOSKEY into reserved memory, thus saving space in conventional memory for other programs.

When you run DOSKEY, the program installs itself in memory and creates a *buffer* (a portion of memory) that will hold the commands and macros. The program and buffer occupy 4KB of memory. Indeed, if you are using a computer with an 80286 or 80386 processor, you may even be able to load DOSKEY into reserved memory so that it doesn't use any conventional memory at all.

Selecting a Buffer Size

> NOTE: For a complete explanation of DOSKEY macros, see the section "Creating and Executing Macros" later in this chapter.

By default, DOSKEY creates a 512-byte (1/2KB) memory buffer in which it stores your previous commands and any macros that you create. If the length of your average DOS command is between 10 and 16 characters, the default DOSKEY buffer can store approximately 32 to 50 commands. If you enter more commands than the buffer can hold, DOSKEY stores the most recent and deletes the oldest.

Remember, too, that the buffer must also store macros. If you use many macros (each of which may be as long as 127 characters), DOSKEY might not have much memory left to store the DOS commands that you type on the command line.

If you want to set aside more memory for the buffer, you can include the /BUFSIZE= switch when you start DOSKEY. For example, the following command sets aside 1KB of buffer space for DOSKEY:

```
DOSKEY /BUFSIZE=1024
```

If your computer has limited memory and you use few macros, you might want to reduce the DOSKEY buffer to conserve memory for your programs. For example, this command reduces the buffer size to 256 bytes (1/4KB):

```
DOSKEY /BUFSIZE=256
```

Changing the Buffer Size

> NOTE: You cannot change the buffer size, but you can run another copy of DOSKEY with a new buffer size. See "Running Multiple DOSKEY Sessions" near the end of this chapter.

Be aware that once DOSKEY is installed, you cannot change its buffer size, so again, it's probably to your benefit to determine a buffer size and place the appropriate command in your AUTOEXEC.BAT file. For example, if you put the following command in AUTOEXEC.BAT

```
DOSKEY /BUFSIZE=1024
```

you'll have a DOSKEY with a 1KB buffer available each time you start your computer.

Reusing Recorded Commands

One of the easiest, and most useful, features of DOSKEY is its *command-line history*, so called because it records a "history" of commands entered at the command prompt. You can repeat any previous command in this history without retyping, which can be a real timesaver in situations where you need to use the same command or commands repeatedly.

For example, say that during your current session, you checked your directory listing, changed directories, formatted a disk, ran a program, and then copied some files to a floppy diskette. With DOSKEY, you can display, edit, or reuse all of these recorded commands.

NOTE: See Table 15.1 for a complete list of keys for accessing your command-line history.

Press the F7 function key to display your command-line history. The previously described example session might resemble Figure 15.1 (but depends entirely on whatever commands you've entered since initially entering the DOSKEY command).

```
1:    DIR /A
2:    CD /WP
3:    FORMAT A: /F:360 /U /V:MEMOS
4:    WP
5:    COPY *.DOC A:
```

Figure 15.1. A sample command-line history.

To reuse a recorded command, you must first redisplay it (and optionally, change it); then press Enter. Table 15.1 lists the keys that you can use to redisplay recorded commands.

Table 15.1. Recalling command lines.

Key	Function
↑	Scrolls backward through recorded commands
↓	Scrolls forward through recorded commands
Page Up	Displays the first command in the buffer
Page Down	Displays the last command in the buffer
F7	Displays all commands in the buffer
F8	Searches for commands that start with the text you specify
F9	Recalls a command by its number
Alt+F7	Deletes all commands from the buffer

As you can see from Table 15.1, DOSKEY offers many options for redisplaying commands. For example, you can press ↑ to move through your previous commands one command at a time. If you want to redisplay your first command, you need only press the Page Up key.

> NOTE: For a quick reminder of DOSKEY options and keys, you can enter `DOSKEY /?` at the command prompt. You can also refer to DOSKEY in Appendix B.

If you want to redisplay a command after you've entered many, you could press ↑ until you find the correct command. However, DOSKEY offers two faster methods. You can press F7 to redisplay a numbered list of all your commands, press F9, and then enter the number of the line you want to recall, or you can type the first few characters of the command and press F8.

For example, suppose that the seventh command of your current session was `REPLACE C:\*.TXT A: /R`, and you want to redisplay the commands. One way to do so would be to

1. Press `F7`, which displays a numbered list of stored commands.

2. Press `F9`, which displays the `Line number:` prompt.

3. Press `7`, which selects the command `REPLACE C:\*.TXT A: /R` (numbered as 7:).

4. Press `Enter`, which displays the seventh command on the current command line.

As an alternative, you could use these steps:

1. Type `R`.

2. Press `F8` to display the first command in the buffer that starts with an `R`.

3. Continue pressing `F8` until you display the command `REPLACE C:\*.TXT A: /R`.

(Note that for step 1, you could enter more characters—such as `RE` or `REP`—to limit the search to a more specific command name.)

At this point, you can either press Enter to execute that command, or you can edit the command line with DOSKEY's expanded command-line editing features. (See the next section.)

The last command in Table 15.1, Alt-F7, erases all the commands stored in the DOSKEY memory buffer. You don't really need to use this command; DOSKEY automatically deletes the oldest stored commands when the buffer fills so that your most recent commands are always available.

Editing Recorded Commands

With DOS, you can perform rudimentary editing of the current command line and recall the previous command, as explained in the section "A Simple Way to Correct Errors" in Chapter 9. However, DOSKEY expands your command-line editing options (see Table 15.2) and facilitates your editing of any command line currently stored in the DOSKEY memory buffer.

Table 15.2. Keys used to edit commands.

Key	Function
← →	Positions the cursor to any character in the command
Home	Moves to the start of the command
End	Moves to the end of the command
Ctrl-←	Moves back one word
Ctrl-→	Moves forward one word
Backspace	Deletes the character to the left of the cursor
Delete (Del)	Deletes the character at the cursor
Ctrl-End	Deletes all characters from the cursor to the end of the line
Ctrl-Home	Deletes all characters from the cursor to the beginning of the line
Ins	Inserts newly typed characters at the cursor position
Esc	Erases the currently displayed command

DOSKEY's features can make your command-line work more productive and less repetitious. For example, suppose that you used the command `REPLACE C:\*.TXT A: /R` earlier in your session to update files with the .TXT extension. Now you want to use the same command to update files with the .DOC extensions.

If DOSKEY were active, you could recall and change the command by doing the following:

1. Type `RE` and press `F8` to recall the command.

2. Press the ← key nine times (or press `Ctrl-←` twice and then ← four times) to move the cursor to the first `T` in the command line.

3. Type `DOC`; notice that these characters overtype the original characters (`TXT`).

4. Press `Enter` to run the modified command (`REPLACE C:\*.DOC A: /R`).

Notice that pressing the ← key does not erase characters; it just moves the underline cursor to the left. Also notice that, by default, DOSKEY is in *overstrike* editing mode; that is, any text you type replaces existing text (as shown in the previous example). However, DOSKEY also has an insert mode in which the characters you type are inserted into text without overwriting the original text. Pressing the Ins key switches between Insert and Overwrite modes.

NOTE: To put DOSKEY into *insert* mode for the current command, press the Ins key.

The overstrike mode cursor is an underline; the insert mode cursor is a block.

For example, if you want to modify the previous command to include spreadsheet files in your C:\123 directory, you could use the following steps:

1. Press ↑ to recall the previous command—`REPLACE C:\*.DOC A: /R`.

2. Use the cursor-movement commands listed in Table 15.2 to move the cursor to the `*` character.

3. Press the `Ins` key to initiate insert mode. (Notice that the underline cursor changes to a flashing block character.)

4. Type `\123` to add the new directory name to the command.

5. Press → twice to move the cursor to the first `T` in the extension.

NOTE: The Ins key is a toggle: press it once to start insert mode; press it again to return to overstrike mode.

---

6. Press `Ins` again. (This restarts overstrike mode.)

7. Type the new extension `WK3`.

8. Press `Enter` to run the modified command (`REPLACE C:\123\*.WK3 A: /R`).

   Note that you could have remained in insert mode for the entire operation by replacing step 6 in the previous list with the following procedure:

   Press the `Del` key three times.

   Pressing Del erases the character at the cursor. Because you are still in insert mode, the new characters you type are inserted into the current line.
   You can always tell your current mode by looking at the shape of the cursor:

   A block cursor indicates insert mode

   An underline cursor indicates overstrike mode

NOTE: To start DOSKEY in insert mode, use the command `DOSKEY /INSERT`. Then, whenever you edit a command line, your characters will be inserted into the current line. If you press Ins, you will temporarily start overstrike mode; however, when you edit a new command, DOSKEY will default to insert mode.

Entering Several Commands on One Command Line

With DOSKEY installed, you can also type multiple commands on a single line, up to a maximum of 127 characters. To do so, you must press Ctrl-T between each command. A paragraph symbol (¶) appears where you press Ctrl-T.

For example, to clear the screen and change the system date and time, you can enter the command

```
CLS ¶ DATE ¶ TIME
```

in which ¶ is generated by pressing Ctrl-T (you don't need to insert spaces before and after the character). When you press Enter, each command plays its normal row in left-to-right order (that is, CLS is executed, then DATE, then after completing the prompt presented by the DATE command, the TIME command is executed).

This feature can be quite handy, especially when you combine it with the procedures you learned for recalling and editing stored commands. For example, assume that you created several memos in the current directory of your hard disk and then saved them on a blank disk with the command

```
FORMAT B: /F:720  XCOPY *.TXT B: /V /M
```

which formats a 720KB 3 1/2-inch floppy diskette in drive B: and then copies all new or changed files (with the /M switch) to that diskette.

One advantage of executing both commands on a single line is that the lengthy process of formatting and copying becomes one operation; you don't have to wait for formatting to be completed before copying. If you have Windows 3 or a similar multitasking DOS Shell, you could go off to another program and be doing some other work while these commands are doing their job).

The second advantage, of course, is that you could redisplay and modify this lengthy command to format another disk and copy other files, as described earlier in the "Reusing Recorded Commands" section.

Although all the DOSKEY features I've discussed so far are easy and convenient, the most powerful feature of all is macros.

DOSKEY Macros

The term *macro* means large (the opposite of micro). A macro is a "large command" executed as a single command, but in doing its job, executes several other commands. In this sense, macros are much like batch files. However, there are also many differences between macros and batch files:

❏ Macros are stored in memory rather than on disk, which means they run a little faster but also disappear the moment you turn off the computer.

❏ Whereas a batch file consists of many commands on separate lines, macros have all their commands on one line (each command separated by $T).

❏ There's no limit to the length of a batch file, but a macro cannot exceed 127 characters in length.

❏ You can terminate a batch file by pressing Ctrl-C or Ctrl-Break once, but these keys terminate only the current command in a macro.

❏ The replaceable parameters in batch files are expressed as %0 through %9. In macros, you use $* through $9. Macros also use unique characters for piping and redirection (see Table 15.3).

❏ You cannot use the common GOTO and ECHO OFF batch file commands in macros.

❏ Neither a batch file nor another macro can start a macro. A macro may, however, start a batch file and a batch file may create macros.

You'll learn more about these differences in the sections that follow, and you'll also see several example macros.

Creating and Executing Macros

To create a macro, use the following general format:

```
DOSKEY name=command $T command $T ...
```

where *name* is the name of the macro, *command* is the command that the macro is to execute, and $T (typed by pressing Ctrl-T) separates multiple commands, if any. A blank space must separate the DOSKEY command and the macro name that follows it; all other blank spaces are optional.

Macro Piping and Redirection

You've learned how to use the >, <, ¦ , and other characters for piping and redirection in preceding chapters. You cannot use these same characters directly in macros. Instead, you must use special symbols that stand for these characters, as shown in Table 15.3.

Table 15.3. Macro creation codes.
Redirection and Piping Characters Used in Macros

Character	Macro Equivalent	Purpose
<	$L or $l	Redirects input
>	$G or $g	Redirects output
>>	$GG or $gg	Appends output to a file
|	$B or $b	Redirects output from one command to another
Other Special Characters		
¶	$T or $t	Separates commands
$	$$	The $ (dollar sign) symbol
%1 through %9	$1 through $9	Replaceable variables
%0	$*	Special replaceable variable that accepts all text on the command line after the macro name

The macro codes are easy to remember because they are all mnemonics. For example, $L is the Less than symbol, $G is the Greater than symbol, $B is the vertical Bar symbol, $T separates Two commands, and $* uses the DOS "all" character (*) to mean "all text on the command line." Upper- and lowercase differences don't matter.

Use these codes in macros exactly as you would use the literal characters in a batch file or the command line. That is, if the command you want to execute needs the >> redirection character, use the code GG in place of >> in your macro. The GG will be converted to >> automatically when you execute the macro. You'll see examples in the sections that follow.

Some Sample Macros

Here are a few sample macros to give you an overview of the kinds of things you can do with macros, as well as some specific examples to work with.

Macros to Shorten Commands

 The simplest macros are those that execute a longer command using a shorter one. For example, if you are tired of typing DOSSHELL every time you want to switch from the command prompt to the Shell, you could create a macro named DS (or just D for that matter) that executes the DOSSHELL. To create the DS macro (assuming DOSKEY has been loaded by now), type

```
DOSKEY DS = DOSSHELL
```

and press ↵.

To test the macro, type DS and press Enter. (Press F3 to return to the command prompt after you get to the Shell.)

Don't forget that the DS macro you just created is available for the current session only; it will be erased as soon as you reboot or turn off the computer. I'll describe how to make macros more permanent in a moment.

Macros to Customize Commands

Another handy feature of macros is the capability of customizing an existing command to your liking. For example, when you enter the MEM command, you see a brief report of the status of memory. To get a more complete report, without it whizzing by too quickly to read, you need to enter MEM /C ¦ MORE.

Optionally, you could change the MEM command so that it always performs what the lengthier MEM/C ¦ MORE command does. To do so, you create a macro named MEM by typing this command at the command prompt:

```
DOSKEY MEM = MEM /C $B MORE
```

Now when you enter the command MEM, the MEM macro will be executed, which in turn executes the command MEM/C ¦ MORE. (The $B in the macro is converted automatically to the split vertical bar at execution time.) Hence, you've changed the MEM command to better suit your needs.

A Note on Macro Names

Even though MEM is a "normal" DOS command, the MEM macro is executed automatically when you enter MEM as a command. That's because whenever you enter a command at the command prompt, DOS always first checks to see whether a macro has the same name as the command you entered, and if so, DOS executes the macro.

There's one potential little problem here though. Suppose that you really do want to run the original MEM command to get a brief report on the status of memory. How do you tell DOS to "skip the macro and execute the original command?" Easy. Press the Spacebar before typing the command so that there is a blank space between the command prompt and the command.

For example, to run the original MEM command rather than the MEM macro you just created, put a blank space in front of the command, like this:

```
C:\DOS> MEM
```

instead of typing the command right at the prompt like this:

```
C:\DOS>MEM
```

The blank space between the command prompt and the MEM command tells DOS to "ignore the macro named MEM (if any) and execute the original DOS MEM command."

Macros to Create New or Multiple Commands

Multiple commands within a macro must be separated by the characters $T, which are automatically changed to the paragraph symbol (¶) when you execute the macro.

As an example, suppose that you want to create a macro named PTREE that prints the complete directory tree of the current drive and then ejects the printed page from the printer. To do so, you would enter this command at the command prompt:

```
DOSKEY PTREE = TREE \ /A $G PRN $T ECHO ^L $G PRN
```

where TREE \ /A $G PRN is translated to TREE \ /A > PRN during execution; the \ means "start from the root directory," the /A means "use ASCII codes" (you can omit /A if your printer prints graphics), and > PRN, of course, means "send output to the printer." The $T marks the end of one command and the beginning of the next.

When typing the second command, ECHO ^L $G PRN, be sure to press Ctrl-L to type the ^L symbol. When executed, this command becomes ECHO ^L >PRN which, as you know from previous chapters, ejects the current page from the printer.

Once you create this macro, all you need to do is type PTREE and press ↵ anytime you want a printed copy of the current directory.

Macros That Accept Variables

Like batch files, a macro can contain replaceable parameters that take on a value from the command line, like most "normal" DOS commands. For example, the normal DOS COPY command can take any source or destination, which gives you unlimited abilities for copying files.

To mimic this capability of accepting data from the command line in macros, use $1, $2, and so on through $9, as placeholders (technically called *replaceable parameters*) for text that comes from the command line.

To demonstrate, create a macro that, like the TYPE command, can type the contents of any file. Rather than displaying the contents at breakneck speed on the screen, this TYPE macro pauses after each screenful of text. Name this macro STYPE (for Slow Type).

To create the macro, type this command at the command prompt:

```
DOSKEY STYPE = TYPE $1 $B MORE
```

and press Enter.

NOTE: Replaceable variables in batch files are preceded by the % symbol; replaceable variables in macros are preceded by the $ symbol.

This macro tells DOSKEY to create a macro called `STYPE` that executes the command `TYPE filename ¦ MORE`, where `filename` can be entered when entering the command at the command prompt (like the normal TYPE command) and will be inserted where the $1 placeholder appears. The `$B MORE` becomes `¦ MORE` when the macro is executed so that the display pauses after each screenful of text.

To use this macro, type STYPE and a file name. For example, suppose that you enter this command at the command prompt (after creating the macro):

```
STYPE A:\README.DOC
```

to type a file named README.DOC on the disk in drive A. Before executing the STYPE macro, DOS replaces the $1 with the file name you've provided and converts the $B symbol to a pipe (¦). Hence, before the STYPE macro is executed as a DOS command, it is converted to this:

```
TYPE A:\README.DOC ¦ MORE
```

Hence, your new STYPE command acts like the old TYPE command but pauses for a keypress after each screenful is displayed (assuming the document being typed is more than a screenful in length).

Macro to Search Multiple Directories

You can pass up to nine parameters to a macro using the placeholders $1, $2, $3, and so forth. In the command line, each parameter to be passed must be separated by a single blank space.

For example, suppose that you want to create a macro named `SEARCH` that searches all the directories on a drive using a simple syntax like

```
SEARCH C: *.BAK
```

where `SEARCH` is the command, `C:` is the drive to search, and `*.BAK` is the file name pattern to look for. Notice that a blank space separates the command (SEARCH) from the first parameter (C:), and another blank space separates the first parameter (C:) from the second parameter (*.BAK). You'll need two placeholders in the macro, $1 and $2, to accept these two parameters.

To create the SEARCH macro, enter this command at the command prompt:

```
DOSKEY SEARCH = DIR $1\$2 /S
```

If after creating the macro you enter the command

```
SEARCH C: *.BAK
```

you'll see a listing of all the .BAK files (if any) on drive C, or you could enter the command

```
SEARCH D: QTR*.*
```

(if you have a drive D) to search all the directories on drive D for file names that begin with the letters QTR.

NOTE: See "Macro to Search Multiple Drives and Directories" later in this chapter for a more powerful version of this macro.

How does the macro work? Well, when you enter the command SEARCH D: QTR*.*, the $1 and $2 are replaced by the parameters from the command line like this:

```
DIR D:\QTR*.* /S
```

NOTE: For more information on the DIR command, see DIR in Appendix B.

The D:\ tells the search to start at the root (highest level) directory, the QTR*.* defines the file name pattern to search for, and /S means "including all subdirectories." (Because the search begins at the root directory, "all subdirectories" includes every directory on the drive.)

The $* DOSKEY Parameter

If you don't know exactly how many parameters you want to pass to a macro, you can use $* to mean "all parameters to the right of the command in the command line."

For a practical application, consider the ATTRIB command, which can accept six possible parameters (H, S, A, R, /S, and a file name or patter) to assign attributes to a file or file. Now, suppose that you create the following macro named A that executes the ATTRIB command followed by two parameters:

```
DOSKEY A = ATTRIB $1 $2
```

The macro would use two parameters separated by a space, as follows:

```
A -R *.BAK
```

would run correctly. But the command

```
A -H -H *.BAK /S
```

would cause problems because you've elected to use six valid ATTRIB options, but the A macro can only accept the first two. One solution would be to define the A macro as

```
DOSKEY A = ATTRIB $1 $2 $3 $4 $5 $6
```

NOTE: For a quick review of ATTRIB or any other DOS command use the /? switch at the command prompt (for example, ATTRIB / ?) or refer to Appendix B.

The $* replaceable variable offers a much simpler solution. The following macro:

```
DOSKEY A = ATTRIB $*
```

uses $* as the placeholder, which accepts any number of parameters (as one long string of text) to the right of the command line. That is, entering

```
A -R +A -S -H C:\*.* /S
```

is perfectly okay and is simply converted to the following valid DOS command before being executed:

```
ATTRIB -R +A -S -H C:\*.* /S
```

Displaying Available Macros

If you forget which macros are available at the moment or forget the name of a particular macro, enter this command at the command prompt:

```
DOSKEY /MACROS
```

or optionally, enter the abbreviated version DOSKEY /M. A list of all current macros will be displayed, as in the following example:

```
DS=DOSSHELL
MEM=MEM /C $b MORE
PTREE=TREE \ /A $g PRN $t ECHO ^L $g PRN
STYPE=TYPE $1 $b MORE
SEARCH=DIR $1\$2 /S
A=ATTRIB $*
```

As usual, you can use ¦ MORE to pause after each screenful or >PRN to print all available macros, like this:

```
DOSKEY /M >PRN
```

Don't forget to eject the page after printing the macros.

NOTE: The /I switch is used with FIND to ignore upper- and lowercase.

You can also use the /HISTORY switch (or abbreviated /H switch) with DOSKEY to review all the recorded commands in the current session. For example, the command

```
DOSKEY /H
```

displays the entire DOSKEY history (excluding any commands that have been "bumped" because the buffer was filled). The command

```
DOSKEY /H | FIND "DOSKEY" /I > PRN
```

displays only commands that begin with the word `DOSKEY`, which narrows down the display a bit, but again excludes any early commands that have been "bumped."

Editing Macros

The command you enter to create a macro is recorded just like any other command you enter at the command prompt. Therefore, you can change any existing macro by using the keys presented in Table 15.1 to locate the command used to create the macro, then use any of the keys listed in Table 15.2 to make your changes.

Optionally, retype the macro definition from scratch. The new macro will replace the old one instantly.

Deleting Macros

To delete a macro, use the following general format:

```
DOSKEY macroname =
```

where *macroname* is the name of the macro you want to delete. Entering this sets the macro equal to "nothing," which essentially erases the macro.

For example, if you wanted to delete the PTREE macro, type

```
DOSKEY PTREE =
```

and press Enter. This deletes the macro and frees all the space it used in the DOSKEY buffer.

If you want to delete all your current macros, DOSKEY provides an easy shorthand method—press Alt-F10.

Batch File Commands in Macros

Macros are very similar to batch files; you can also use most of the batch file commands that you used in the last two chapters in your macros. The only two batch commands that don't work in macros are GOTO and ECHO OFF.

Obviously GOTO won't work because it looks for a "label" on another line, and after all, a macro is by definition a one-line entity. This is unfortunate because the lack of a "branching" command denies your macros of much of their "decision-making" capabilities.

However, a macro can call a batch file using the CALL command. I'll examine this strategy a little later.

Because the ECHO OFF command doesn't work within a macro, you will always see your macro commands typed before they are executed. (In case you are wondering, preceding the macro commands with the @ symbol won't suppress the displays either.)

All other batch file commands, including PAUSE, ECHO, IF, and FOR work within a macro. The next section contains an example that uses the FOR command.

Macro to Search Multiple Drives and Directories

Chapter 14 described the FOR loop, which can be used to repeat a command or another batch file repeatedly. You can also use FOR loops in macros, provided you remember to use a single % where you would normally use double percent signs (%%) in a batch file.

A very handy example is a macro that can search all the directories on all the hard disk drives of your computer. This is particularly handy if you have several hard drives (for example, C:, D:, E:, and F:) and lots of directories and need to perform a general search for a file you've "lost."

I'll name this macro ADSEARCH (for All Drive Search) and give it a simple syntax. For example, to search all drives and directories for a "lost" file name MYFAVE.TXT, you would enter the command

```
ADSEARCH MYFAVE.TXT
```

What could be simpler?

Here's the command you need to enter at the command prompt to create this macro:

```
DOSKEY ADSEARCH = FOR %C IN (C: D: E: F:) DO DIR %C\$1 /S/B
```

Be sure to include only valid hard drives for your system within the parentheses. For example, if you have hard disk drives C and D only, you'd enter this command instead:

```
DOSKEY ADSEARCH = FOR %c IN (C: D:) DO DIR %c\$1 /S/B
```

To try it, pick the name of a file that you know is on your disk and see whether the macro can find it. For example, if you have the WordPerfect program, enter the command

```
ADSEARCH WP.EXE
```

You'll see the DIR command executed for each hard drive on your system, but you will see the WP.EXE file listed only next to its home drive and directory.

Making Macros Permanent

As I've mentioned, all macros are erased from memory the moment you turn off or reboot your computer. Obviously, this is a major inconvenience if you create a handy supply of macros, because it necessitates creating all your macros every time you restart your computer.

As stated before, however, a batch file can create macros. The solution to the inconvenience of losing macros when you turn off your computer is to create a batch file, named MACROS.BAT perhaps, that can create all your favorite macros at once, even automatically each time you start your computer. Here's the general procedure:

1. Use the DOSKEY /MACROS command to display all current macros but reroute the output to a batch file, C:\DOS\MACROS.BAT, for example.

2. Edit `C:\DOS\MACROS.BAT` to ensure all syntax is correct and to convert command-prompt control characters to edit control characters.

3. In the future, enter the command `MACROS` to recreate all your macros or include the command `CALL MACROS` in your AUTOEXEC.BAT file to recreate all macros automatically at the beginning of each new session.

The following sections look at each step in more detail.

Rerouting Macros to a Batch File

To create the C:\DOS\MACROS.BAT batch file so that you can easily recreate your favorite macros in the future, enter the following command at the command prompt:

```
DOSKEY /MACROS >> C:\DOS\MACROS.BAT
```

Nothing will appear on the screen, but when the command prompt reappears, the DOS directory on drive C will hold a file named MACROS.BAT that you can edit into a viable batch file, as described in the next section.

Editing Your MACROS.BAT Command File

To edit the "rerouted" DOSKEY output in MACROS.BAT into a viable batch file, you need to load that batch file into a text editor. To do so, enter this command at the command prompt:

```
EDIT C:\DOS\MACROS.BAT
```

Your EDIT screen will look something like Figure 15.2 (but the appearance of your screen depends entirely on the macros you've created on your own computer).

The first problem with this current version of MACROS.BAT is that the syntax of every command is incorrect. For example, DOS cannot execute the command

```
DS=DOSSHELL
```

The proper syntax to create the DS macro is

```
DOSKEY DS=DOSSHELL
```

You need to edit this file (using the basic EDIT techniques described in Chapter 10) to make the batch file look like Figure 15.3.

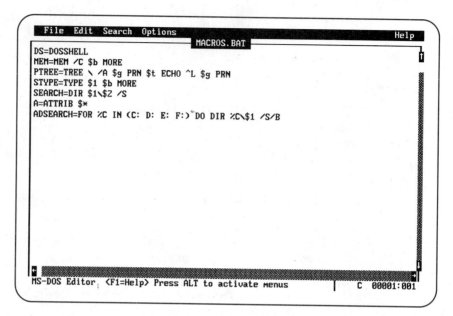

Figure 15.2. A MACROS.BAT file created using /MACROS.

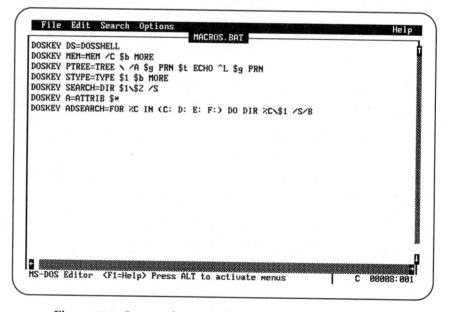

Figure 15.3. Corrected syntax after using /MACROS to create
MACROS.BAT.

In many cases, you could save this edited file and be done. In this case however, you're not quite ready to save the file, because you still need to change the ^L in the PTREE macro to EDIT's version of a control character.

NOTE: The need to change control characters to some other format depends on your particular editor. If you are not using EDIT to edit MACROS.BAT, you may not need to make the conversion.

Converting Control Characters

Before you save your edited MACROS.BAT file, you must search for any control characters that were sent to that file using the > or >> redirection symbol and change them to EDIT's version of that character.

As described in Chapter 10, the way to place a control character in a file created by EDIT is to press Ctrl-P, hold down the Alt key, and type on the numeric keypad the ASCII number for that control character.

Furthermore, you can see that the PTREE macro in Figure 15.3 contains the control character Ctrl-L (it appears as ^L in that macro). If you want the macro to work correctly, you need to delete ^L and replace it in EDIT with ASCII character 12.

You know you need ASCII character 12 in this case, because L is the 12th letter of the alphabet. A ^A character would need to be replaced with ASCII character 1, a ^B with ASCII character 2, and so forth up to a ^Z, which would need to be replaced with an ASCII 26, because Z is the 26th letter of the alphabet.

To change ^L to ASCII character 12 in this example, you need to follow these steps:

1. Move the cursor to the ^ (caret) at the start of ^L.

2. Press Del twice to delete ^L.

3. Press Ctrl-P. (Hold down the Ctrl key, press P, then release both keys; nothing seems to happen, but EDIT is now ready to accept a control character.)

4. Hold down the Alt key and using the numeric keypad rather than the number at the top of the keyboard, type the number 012.

5. Release the Alt key.

6. If the blinking cursor is on the $ rather than on a blank space, you should insert a blank space. To do so, press the Ins key and then press the Spacebar.

Figure 15.4 shows the MACROS.BAT file after this change is made. Notice that the ⌃L character in the PTREE command now looks like the Greek female symbol, which is how Ctrl-L (⌃L) is supposed to look on the EDIT screen.

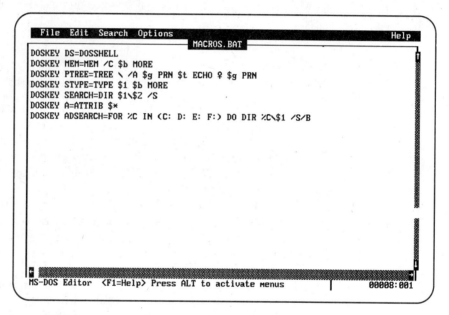

Figure 15.4. MACROS.BAT after changing ⌃L to ASCII 12.

Saving the Finished MACROS.BAT File

When you've finished making your changes to MACROS.BAT, save it as you would any other file in EDIT. That is,

1. Press Alt to access the Menu Bar.

2. Pres F to pull down the File menu.

3. Type X to select Exit.

4. Type Y to select Yes, save the file, and exit EDIT.

Now you are back to the command prompt. In future sessions with your computer, you can simply enter the command `MACROS` at the command prompt to reactivate all your macros, but you'll probably find it more convenient to change your AUTOEXEC.BAT file so that DOSKEY is executed and your macros are installed automatically each time you start your computer, as described in the next section.

Automatically Installing Macros at Startup

If you want DOSKEY and your macros to be readily available each time you start your computer, you'll need to add the appropriate commands to your AUTOEXEC.BAT file. As described earlier, you can alter your AUTOEXEC.BAT file at any time. Bring it into EDIT or enter this command at the command prompt:

```
EDIT C:\AUTOEXEC.BAT
```

Your current AUTOEXEC.BAT file will appear on the EDIT screen.

Next, using the EDIT techniques described in Chapter 10, add the commands

```
DOSKEY
CALL C:\DOS\MACROS
```

to your AUTOEXEC.BAT file to initiate DOSKEY and install your macros. Be aware, however, that if your AUTOEXEC.BAT file contains the command DOSSHELL to run the Shell, that command should be the last command in your AUTOEXEC.BAT file, because you don't want the Shell to "take control" of your system until every command in AUTOEXEC.BAT has been executed.

For example, Figure 15.5 shows a sample AUTOEXEC.BAT file with the appropriate commands for this example placed near the end of the AUTOEXEC.BAT file, just above the DOSSHELL command.

If you're a DOS 5 whiz and want to load DOSKEY and other programs into reserved memory (as described in Chapters 16 and 17), you could modify your AUTOEXEC.BAT file as shown in Figure 15.6 to load DOSKEY, and your macros, without wasting much conventional memory.

Either way, both DOSKEY and your macros will be readily available each time you start your computer.

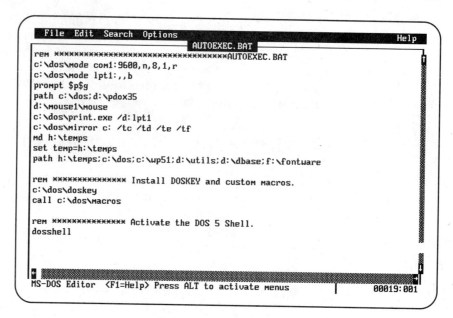

Figure 15.5. A sample AUTOEXEC.BAT file to install DOSKEY and macros via MACROS.BAT.

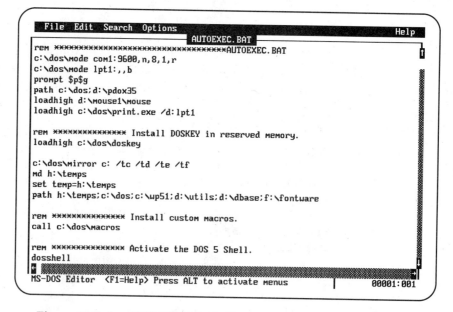

Figure 15.6. An AUTOEXEC.BAT file to install DOSKEY in reserved memory and activate your macros.

Adding New Macros to MACROS.BAT

If you create a new macro at the command prompt and decide to add that macro to your MACROS.BAT file to make it a permanent macro, use the same basic techniques you used to create the original MACROS.BAT file. For example, suppose that you enter the following command to create a macro that ejects the current page from the printer when you enter FF (for form feed) at the command prompt:

```
DOSKEY FF = ECHO ^L $G PRN
```

To add that macro to your MACROS.BAT file, reroute output from DOSKEY /MACROS or DOSKEY /HISTORY to your C:\DOS\MACROS.BAT file, making sure to use the append (>>) redirection character. For example, you could enter this command, which isolates only the command used to create the FF macro:

```
DOSKEY /H ¦ FIND "DOSKEY FF" /I >> C:\DOS\MACROS.BAT
```

Next, you could enter the command

```
EDIT C:\DOS\MACROS.BAT
```

to check your MACROS.BAT file.

Then you'll need to edit to make sure each command is valid and to delete any extraneous lines that do not specifically create macros. Remember, too, that if any new macros contain control characters, you need to replace them with EDIT's control characters.

In this example, you'd need to replace the ^L character with the ASCII 12 symbol (as described earlier) to complete the job so that the completed MACROS.BAT file looks like Figure 15.7.

Converting Batch Files to Macros

Like the FF macro created in the preceding example, many other batch files that you constructed in Chapters 13 and 14 will also run as macros. This brings up an interesting question: Which of your batch files should you convert to macros and which should you leave as batch files? Use the following guidelines to determine whether you should create a macro or a batch file:

Use a Macro

If you want immediate access to the "custom" command from any drive or directory.

If you want to "customize" an existing DOS command (as in our MEM macro described earlier).

If you have adequate free memory to store it.

If the command is less than 127 characters.

Use a Batch File

If you use the command rarely.

If your command must make a "decision" and branch to an alternate location (that is, if it uses GOTO).

If your computer is short on memory and you don't want to increase the size of the DOSKEY buffer to handle the new command.

If the command requires more than 127 characters.

If the batch file is better, safer, or more "bullet-proof" than the shorter macro version.

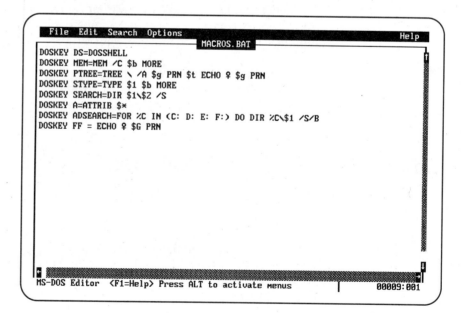

Figure 15.7. MACROS.BAT file with the new FF macro definition added.

I'll review some of the batch files created in preceding chapters and discuss why, or why not, each would be a good candidate for a macro.

FF, the form-feed batch file, is a perfect example of a batch file that can (and should be) converted to a macro: It's short, you will probably use it often, and it doesn't occupy a lot of memory. In the preceding chapter, you saw how to convert that batch file to a macro and add that macro to the MACROS.BAT file.

The three PATH-changing batch files, ADDPATH, OLDPATH, and ORIGPATH, are not good candidates for macros. One reason is that the capability of accessing environmental variables with %variable% is unique to batch files. You also probably would not use those batch files often enough to justify loading them into memory.

The SETKEYS batch file is much too long to be trimmed down to the 127-character maximum length of a macro.

The QUICKBAK batch file isn't a particularly good candidate for a macro because the minuscule time savings gained by converting it hardly justifies loading it into memory. On the other hand, it is brief and could easily be converted to a macro using this command:

```
DOSKEY BACKUP=BACKUP C:\*.* /S /M $T IF NOT ERRORLEVEL 0 ECHO
Backup not complete!
```

> NOTE: The preceding and two other commands in this chapter are shown on two lines because of space constraints in this book. When you type these commands, do so on one line.

Notice that the batch file's two commands are separated by the $T code and that the warning message is shortened to save memory.

The SAFECOPY batch file meets many of the criteria for a macro, but it can't be converted because it requires a GOTO command. However, if you modify the concept behind it, you can use the following workaround conversion:

```
DOSKEY SAFECOPY=IF NOT EXIST $2\$1 COPY $1 $2\$1
```

This macro isn't as sophisticated as the batch file version and doesn't display any information to the user, but it does everything the SAFECOPY batch file does. For example, if you type SAFECOPY DATA.DTA \DB and the DATA.DTA file does not exist in the DB directory, the macro will copy the file. However, if DATA.DTA does exist, the macro will end without copying the file because the IF NOT condition was not met.

The MOVE batch file is too long and complex to be converted to a macro. The GOTO command (which isn't allowed in macros) is required to exercise the numerous safety features in that program.

At first glance, the LOOKIN batch file appears to be too long and complicated for a macro; however, with some judicious pruning and limiting of features, this batch file turns into an excellent macro. Consider the following conversion:

```
DOSKEY LOOKIN=IF EXIST TEMP.TXT DEL TEMP.TXT $T FOR %C IN ($1) DO FIND
/I "$2" %C $G$G TEMP.TXT $T TYPE TEMP.TXT $B MORE
```

Notice that we had to eliminate the printing capability and that we used shorter file names. Notice also that the %%C notation used in the FOR command in batch files must be converted to the command line notation %C when used in a macro. The three main commands are separated by $T codes, and the ¦ symbol is represented by the $B code.

LOOKIN2.BAT must use a GOTO command and therefore cannot be converted to a macro. The JETSET batch file is obviously too long and complicated to be a macro, but it brings up an interesting point: If you have installed ANSI.SYS in your CONFIG.SYS file, you can use a macro to send "escape sequences" to your system's hardware devices.

For example, if you have a color monitor and have included the DEVICE = C:\DOS\ANSI.SYS command in your CONFIG.SYS file, you can change screen colors to jazz up your commands a bit. For example, here's a modified version of the STYPE macro that displays its output in a unique color. (You would type it as one long line.)

```
DOSKEY STYPE=PROMPT $$e[33;44m $$e[1m $T TYPE $1 $B MORE $T PROMPT
$$e[0m$$P$$G
```

The PROMPT $$e[33;44m $$e[1m command sends an escape sequence ($$e[) that changes your system's foreground color to yellow (33) and background color to blue (44). The DOSKEY code for the $ symbol, $$, is used throughout the macro. After the TYPE $1 $B MORE command, the PROMPT $$e[0m$$P$$G section resets your system's colors to the default ($$e[0m) and then restores your system prompt to display the current drive and directory ($$P).

Running Multiple DOSKEY Sessions

With DOS 5, you can keep multiple versions of DOSKEY in memory at the same time; each memory-resident DOSKEY program maintains its own buffer of commands and macros. Though the practical implications of multiple DOSKEYs may be few, it's worth knowing how this works if you are a power user who runs multiple instances of the command prompt.

To start a new DOSKEY buffer with its own commands and macros, without replacing the original DOSKEY, you first need to get to a secondary DOS command prompt. There are several ways to do so:

1. Start the Shell and then temporarily exit the Shell by pressing `Shift-F9` or by selecting `Command Prompt` from the Program List.

2. Run a `program` and then temporarily exit that program to the DOS command prompt.

3. At the command prompt, type `COMMAND` and press `Enter`.

No matter which technique you use to get to the secondary command prompt, you can use the following command to install a new DOSKEY buffer:

`DOSKEY /REINSTALL`

or if you're using reserved memory (Chapter 17), you can enter this command:

`LOADHIGH DOSKEY /REINSTALL`

With the following message, DOS reports that it has created a new copy of DOSKEY:

`DOSKey installed.`

The new DOSKEY buffer in the secondary shell contains none of the previous commands typed at the command line; it is a totally new copy of DOSKEY and its buffer is initially empty. You can now load a new set of macros, which are completely independent of the macros in your original version of DOSKEY. If you run the MEM command as follows:

`MEM /C ¦ MORE`

and scroll through the list of programs in memory, you will notice two copies of DOSKEY.

To get back to your original DOSKEY buffer and macros, you first need to enter the command `EXIT` at the secondary command prompt to leave that prompt. Then exit the current program or Shell as you normally would so that you're back to the original DOSKEY and command prompt. To verify your return, press F7 to list commands or enter DOSKEY /MACROS to list current macros.

Summary

This chapter has taught you all about DOSKEY, a new feature introduced in DOS 5 that offers

❏ Command line history to display, edit, and run previous commands.

❏ Enhanced editing of commands.

❏ A command separator so that you can place several commands on a single line.

❏ A macro generator to create, run, and save macros.

❏ Activation by typing DOSKEY at the command prompt and pressing Enter.

❏ ↑, ↓, Page Up, Page Down, F7, F8, and F9 to recall commands.

❏ ←, →, Ctrl-←, Ctrl-→, Home, End, Delete, and other editing keys to alter recalled command lines.

❏ Ctrl-T to separate commands on a single line.

❏ The syntax DOSKEY *macroname* = *commands* to create macros.

❏ $G (>), $L (<), GG (>>), $B (¦) for piping and redirection in macros.

❏ $T to separate commands, $1 through $9 in place of %1 through %9 as replaceable parameters, and $* to accept multiple parameters.

❏ DOSKEY /MACROS (or DOSKEY /HISTORY) command to review current macros.

❏ Sending macro definitions to a batch file by using the general syntax DOSKEY /MACROS >> *filename*. Then use EDIT to work on the resulting batch file.

❏ Macros available at the start of every session by adding to your AUTOEXEC.BAT file 1) commands to load DOSKEY and 2) a command to execute the batch file that creates macros.

❏ The DOSKEY /? (at the command prompt) for quick on-line help. (Also refer to DOSKEY in Appendix B as needed.)

Advanced DOS Techniques

As you become more experienced in using your computer, you probably will need to start using more advanced options and capabilities, such as extended memory, expanded memory, RAM disks, and other features. Using these capabilities effectively requires a more detailed knowledge of the way things work "inside" the computer.

If you have a computer that contains an 80286, 80386, or 80486 microprocessor and more than 640KB of memory, DOS 5 automatically creates *extended memory* when you install the operating system. Although DOS 5 takes care of this automatically—without you even having to know what extended memory is—the new operating system also includes several other memory management options that will help you increase the power of your computer. To be able to use these new DOS 5 features, you first need to understand how your computer's memory is organized and accessed.

The next three chapters provide the technical information that you will need to understand and use the more advanced options and features of your computer. In summary, you will learn:

❑ How a computer stores information.

❑ How your computer's memory is organized.

❑ Reasons for the 640KB RAM limit and methods for overcoming that limitation.

❏ How disks store and organize information.

❏ How the computer communicates with devices and other computers through serial and parallel communications.

❏ How to get the most from your computer by using advanced features such as RAM disks, extended memory, expanded memory, and disk caching.

❏ How to resolve common problems, such as diskette, data, and program incompatibilities.

❏ Options for networking computers and for allowing several computers to share devices such as printers and modems.

To get started, let's take a look inside the computer and see exactly what makes it tick.

What Makes It Tick?

You can drive a car without knowing anything about the internal workings of the transmission or the voltage regulator. Similarly, you can use a computer effectively without knowing a great deal about its technical internal workings. However, if you want to use advanced options, such as extended and expanded memory, or write complex programs of your own, you must have a basic understanding about the way things work in a computer.

This chapter explains at a more technical level the way your computer operates. The information presented here will help you better understand the techniques presented in Chapter 17, which describes how to use DOS 5's advanced memory management features, or if you are using an earlier version of DOS, install optional devices on your computer.

How Computers Store Information

Although you interact with your computer with the same alphabet (A to Z) and numbers (0 to 9) that you use in your daily communications, the computer actually works on a completely different principle known as the *binary* numbering system. The binary system uses only two digits—0 and 1. Why only two digits? Because all the internal workings of the computer use electronic (or in the case of disks, magnetic) switches that can be in either of one or two states—off (0) or on (1).

Each of these on/off switches is called a *bit* (short for Binary digIt). Although on and off offer only two possible states, combining two binary digits offers four unique combinations, as follows:

00
01
10
11

A group of three bits offers eight possible unique combinations:

000
001
010
011
100
101
110
111

Notice the progression. One bit offers two combinations. Two bits offer four (2^2) unique combinations. Three bits offer eight (2^3) unique combinations.

Modern microcomputers use a group of eight bits to store an individual character. Using eight bits permits a total of 256 (2^8) unique combinations of bits. A group of eight bits is called a *byte*. As you might recall from Chapter 1, I pointed out that one byte equals one character; so the word *cat* uses three bytes of storage space.

The complete ASCII character set consists of 256 unique characters. If you look at the ASCII character set (shown in Appendix C), you will see that there are exactly 256 unique characters, numbered 0 to 255. Each of these characters is represented by a unique set of eight bits. For example, the letter *A* is represented by the byte *10000001*, the letter *B* is represented by the byte *10000010*, the letter *C* is represented by the byte *10000011*, and so on.

Hexadecimal Numbering System

If you look at Appendix C, you will notice that two numbering systems are displayed: The decimal numbers are listed in the normal sequence of 0 to 255; the hex (short for *hexadecimal*) numbers are listed from 00 to FF. The hexadecimal numbering system is often used as a shorthand method of expressing binary numbers.

The decimal numbering system is based on 10 unique digits, 0 through 9. After you count to 9, you start using the two-digit numbers 10, 11, 12, 13, and so on to 99. Although the decimal numbering system is convenient for humans, who have 10 fingers to count on, it does not accurately reflect the computer's way of storing information, which is based on eight-bit bytes.

The hexadecimal numbering system uses 16 unique digits, 0 through 9 and A through F. In hex, you don't start using two digit numbers until you get to F:

```
0
1
2
3
4
5
6
7
8
9
A
B
C
D
E
F
10
```

Because F is the largest single digit in hex, FF is the largest two-digit pair, just like 9 is the largest single-digit in decimal, and 99 is the largest two-digit number. Notice that the ASCII table in Appendix C conveniently ends at hexadecimal FF—the largest possible two-digit number in hex. This convenience, of course, is no accident.

Simply stated, any character in the ASCII alphabet can be represented by a two-digit hexadecimal number. In fact, the first 16 hexadecimal numbers (0, 1, 2, 3 through F) are often expressed as 00, 01, 02, 03, through 0F, to maintain the two-digit consistency.

Why Is a Kilobyte 1,024 Bytes?

The hexadecimal numbering system provides some insight into why you often encounter certain numbers, such as 64, 512, and 1,024, when working with computers. If computers were based on the decimal system, you would see the more familiar multiples of 10. For example, if you start with 1 and continue multiplying by 10, you generate the following familiar sequence of numbers:

$$1 \times 10 = 10$$
$$10 \times 10 = 100$$
$$100 \times 10 = 1,000$$
$$1000 \times 10 = 10,000$$

and so forth.

But computers are based on the number 2, so the significant numbers of this base are all multiples of 2. Therefore, if you repeatedly multiply by 2, you come up with these numbers:

$$2 \times 2 = 4$$
$$4 \times 2 = 8$$
$$8 \times 2 = 16$$
$$16 \times 2 = 32$$
$$32 \times 2 = 64$$
$$64 \times 2 = 128$$
$$128 \times 2 = 256$$
$$256 \times 2 = 512$$
$$512 \times 2 = 1,024 \text{ (1 Kilobyte)}$$

and so on, to

$$2^{16} = 65,536 \ (64\text{KB})$$
$$2^{20} = 1,048,576 \ (1 \text{ Megabyte})$$

You might occasionally encounter numbers that are one or two less than a number listed above. For example, DOS allows a command entered at the command prompt to have a maximum length of only 127 characters. However, after you type a DOS command, you have to press Enter—and Enter is another character. That makes the actual length of the complete command 128 characters.

Converting Hex to Decimal

If you do not get involved in the technical aspects of DOS and your computer, you will probably never need to use hexadecimal numbers. In case you do, several tools are available to provide help.

To determine the hexadecimal number of an ASCII character, refer to Appendix C of this book. If you frequently make conversions between hexadecimal and decimals number, you should purchase a calculator designed for programmers. You could also buy a program that offers a "pop-up" calculator, such as Borland's SideKick.

However, if you rarely make hexadecimal and decimal conversions and you don't want to spend money on such a specialized tool, you can use Table 16.1 to convert hexadecimal numbers as high as FFFF to their decimal equivalents.

Table 16.1. Converting hexadecimal numbers to decimal.

Thousands digit		Hundreds digit		Tens digit		Ones digit	
Hex	Decimal	Hex	Decimal	Hex	Decimal	Hex	Decimal
0	0	0	0	0	0	0	0
1	4,096	1	256	1	16	1	1
2	8,192	2	512	2	32	2	2
3	12,288	3	768	3	48	3	3
4	16,384	4	1,024	4	64	4	4
5	20,480	5	1,280	5	80	5	5
6	24,576	6	1,536	6	96	6	6
7	28,672	7	1,792	7	112	7	7
8	32,768	8	2,048	8	128	8	8
9	36,864	9	2,304	9	144	9	9
A	40,960	A	2,560	A	160	A	10
B	45,056	B	2,816	B	176	B	11
C	49,152	C	3,072	C	192	C	12
D	53,248	D	3,328	D	208	D	13
E	57,344	E	3,584	E	224	E	14
F	61,440	F	3,840	F	240	F	15

To use Table 16.1, total the decimal values for each digit in the hex number. For example, the one-digit hex number F converts to 15 in decimal. The two-digit hex number 9F is 144 + 15, or 159 decimal. The hex number 100 is 256 + 0 + 0, or 256 decimal. The hex number CD1 is 3,072 + 208 + 1, or 3,281 decimal. The number 1010 hex is 4,096 + 0 + 16 + 0 or 4,112 decimal. The hex number FFFF is 61,440 + 3,840 + 240 + 15 or 65,535 decimal.

Converting Decimal to Hex

Converting decimal numbers to hex involves repeatedly dividing the number (and then subsequent quotients) by 16 while converting the remainder of each division to its hexadecimal equivalent until the quotient is zero. The result of the first division produces the ones-digit in the hex number. The result of the second division produces the tens-digit in the hex number, and so on. Figure 16.1 depicts how to convert the number 751 to hexadecimal.

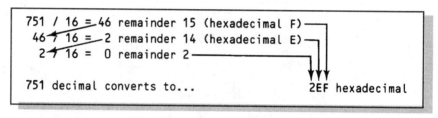

```
751 / 16 = 46 remainder 15 (hexadecimal F)
 46 / 16 =  2 remainder 14 (hexadecimal E)
  2 / 16 =  0 remainder 2

751 decimal converts to...              2EF hexadecimal
```

Figure 16.1. Converting 751 decimal to its hexadecimal equivalent.

How Memory Is Organized

Your computer's main memory (RAM) consists of *RAM chips*. If you were to remove the cover from your computer and look inside, you would see these RAM chips as small, black, rectangular wafers plugged into a larger board. Actually, the black wafer is the *chip carrier*, and it is much larger than the actual chip to make handling easier. If you could see through the chip carrier, you would see the actual RAM chip, which is actually small enough to fit on your thumbnail (see Figure 16.2).

A RAM chip consists of thousands of tiny *transistors*, or switches, each of which can be either turned on (1) or off (0). A typical RAM chip contains 262,144 of these tiny switches (which gives you an idea of how small each switch is). Each switch represents one bit. As you know, it takes eight bits (a byte) to store one character, so a RAM chip that has

262,144 switches can store 32,768 bytes (or 32 Kilobytes) of information. (From a purely technical standpoint, the bits on a single chip are not actually organized into bytes. Instead, a byte is "spread across" multiple chips.)

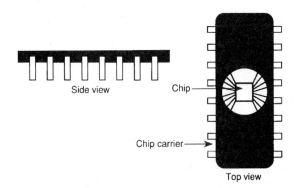

Side view   Chip

Chip carrier ➞

Top view

Figure 16.2. A RAM chip, inside the chip carrier.

The switches in RAM operate very quickly, which permits the computer to run at amazing speeds. However, these switches work only when they receive electrical power. As soon as you turn off the computer, all the switches go off. This is why (as Chapter 1 discussed) RAM is volatile and why you need to use disks to store information permanently.

Read-Only Memory (ROM)

There is more to memory than RAM. Your computer also contains Read-Only Memory (ROM) in addition to RAM. A ROM chip is similar to a RAM chip, except that it is preprogrammed to perform certain tasks; it cannot be used for storing data or programs. ROM occupies certain areas of your computer's total memory, as you will see in a moment.

Memory Maps

The total memory (RAM and ROM combined) in a computer is often displayed in a *memory map*. A memory map displays how memory is divided into areas that perform specific jobs. Figure 16.3 shows a sample memory map for a computer with 640KB RAM.

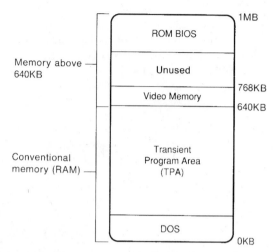

Figure 16.3. How memory is allocated in modern microcomputers.

Memory above 640KB is used for specific jobs that the computer needs to perform regularly. The first 128KB above the 640KB *address* (position in memory)—that is, from the 640KB address to the 768KB address—is usually used for managing the video display.

The remaining 256KB at the high end of memory is partially unused and partially used by the ROM BIOS (the Basic Input/Output System), which controls the "traffic" of data being received from, and sent to, various devices such as the keyboard, screen, and printer.

> NOTE: DOS 5 offers the new commands DOS, DEVICEHIGH, EMM386, and LOADHIGH to let you access reserved memory (see Chapter 17).

5 Prior to DOS 5, the 384KB area above the 640KB address (called *reserved* memory) was nearly "off-limits" to the average user, because the computer reserves this area for its own "managerial" tasks. However, as discussed in Chapter 17, DOS 5 offers the LOADHIGH and DEVICEHIGH commands, that let you load device drivers and TSR programs into that area of memory. In this chapter, you'll also see how that area of memory is used to manage expanded memory.

How DOS and Programs Use RAM

As you know, DOS is a program. When you first start your computer, a part of DOS is stored in RAM automatically (which incidentally, explains why some DOS commands are *internal* commands, whereas others are *external* commands; the internal commands are already in RAM, and therefore DOS does not need to read instructions from a file stored on disk to perform an operation).

The exact amount of RAM that DOS uses is dependent on the specific version of DOS that you are using, but all versions of DOS use some RAM. When you enter the CHKDSK or MEM command at the DOS command prompt, DOS displays both the total memory available (for example, 655360 bytes, which is 640KB) and the total number of bytes free (for example 565552). If you subtract the free (available) bytes from the total number of bytes, the difference is the number of bytes occupied by DOS (and perhaps other programs, as discussed later).

When you run a program, a copy of that program is loaded into RAM, which ensures maximum processing speed. The largest program that you can run is determined by how much memory is available after DOS has already been loaded into RAM. This remaining area is sometimes called the Transient Program Area (or TPA), because it is used for programs that "come and go."

For example, when you use your spreadsheet program, a copy of that program is stored in RAM. When you exit your spreadsheet program and load your word processing program, the copy of the spreadsheet program in RAM is erased, and a copy of your word processing program is stored in RAM. This is the reason that you usually use only one program at a time. However, as discussed in the next section, not all programs are transient.

Memory-Resident Programs

Some programs remain in memory after you start them so that you can have quicker access to the features they offer. These are often called TSR programs (for Terminate-and-Stay-Resident). Some of the DOS external commands, such as PRINT.COM, GRAPHICS.COM, and MODE.COM, stay resident in RAM if you initialize them. When you activate additional devices, such as a mouse, the mouse-driver software also occupies some RAM.

In addition to the DOS TSR programs, many application programs stay resident in memory after loading. These programs remain in memory so that you can access them at any time just by pressing a key (sometimes called a *hot key*). You don't even need to be at the command prompt to run a loaded TSR program.

For example, SideKick Plus, a TSR program from Borland International, provides handy tools such as a phone list, an appointment calendar, a calculator, and other useful tools. After you load SideKick into RAM, you can access it by pressing a special key, even while you are running another program such as your spreadsheet or word processor.

Typically, TSR programs are loaded into RAM from the top down. When you load multiple TSR programs, DOS automatically keeps track of where the current TSR program ends in memory and stores the next TSR immediately beneath the existing TSRs.

NOTE: Though Figure 16.4 doesn't show it, some of DOS is actually stored near the top of the 640KB mark. Nonetheless, it occupies a specific amount of memory.

All of these TSRs use additional memory, thus reducing the size of the remaining TPA. For example, Figure 16.4 shows how much RAM remains after loading DOS's PRINT.COM, MODE.COM, the DOS 4 Shell, a mouse driver, and some hypothetical TSR program (which I'll just refer to as Favorite TSR).

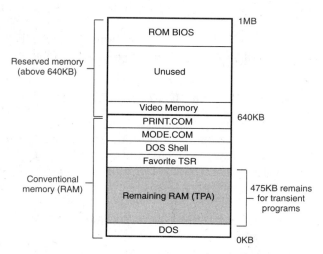

Figure 16.4. Memory after loading some TSR programs.

As you can see in the figure, of the original 640KB, only 457KB of memory remains after loading several TSR programs. Any program that requires more than 457KB of RAM will not be able to run (DOS would display the message Insufficient Memory).

DOS 5 Memory Allocation

NOTE: Chapter 17 discusses DOS 5 memory management in more detail.

As you'll learn in Chapter 17, one of the advantages DOS 5 has over its predecessors is that you can load TSRs (and device drivers) into the unused reserved memory above 640KB, thereby saving conventional memory. Comparing Figure 16.4 to Figure 16.5 shows how much conventional memory is saved by using the otherwise unused blocks of reserved memory.

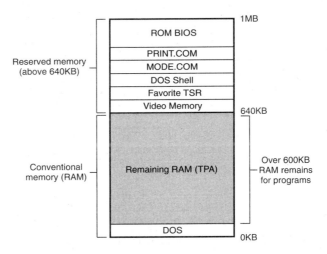

Figure 16.5. DOS 5 can load TSRs into otherwise unused reserved memory.

Granted, DOS 5 conserves precious conventional memory, but what if you really need a lot of memory, for example, to store a huge spreadsheet requiring several megabytes? As you might recall, spreadsheet programs store all the current spreadsheet's data in RAM. Even if you didn't load the additional TSRs, you might not have enough RAM to create the spreadsheet model you want.

You may think you can solve this problem by buying more RAM chips. However, this is not the case. As the next section shows, for original IBM PCs, XTs, and compatibles, the 640KB RAM limitation is not so easily expanded.

Why the 1MB Memory Limit?

The reason for the 1MB (RAM plus ROM) memory limit can be traced to the microprocessor that manipulates the data and instructions stored in RAM. As you might remember, RAM stores data for the microprocessor, but the microprocessor actually does all the work. For the microprocessor (the central processing unit, or CPU) to locate and manipulate the data stored in RAM, it needs to assign each byte an *address*.

The address of a particular byte in RAM is similar to the addresses of the houses in your community. Each house has a unique address so that the Post Office can deliver the mail. Each byte in memory also has a unique address so that the CPU can transfer information to and from RAM as needed.

The CPU of computers that use the 8086 and 8088 microprocessors, such as the IBM PC, XT, and compatibles, use 20 bits for storing memory addresses. This provides for 2^{20}, or 1,048,576, directly *addressable* locations in memory. The number 1,048,576 is referred to as 1 megabyte. Because there is no way to express a number larger than 1,048,576 using 20 bits, 1MB is the highest numbered memory location that the 8086 and 8088 microprocessors can address.

Overcoming the 640KB RAM Limit

Throughout the years, many innovations have been developed to break the 640KB RAM limit so that more space would be available for larger programs and bigger spreadsheets. The sections that follow discuss the three main approaches to overcoming this limitation.

Program Overlays

The oldest approach to running large programs in a smaller area of RAM has been to divide the program into a main file, which usually has the .COM or .EXE extension, and into separate *overlay* files, which often have extensions such as .OVL, .OVR, or .OV1, .OV2, .OV3 and so on. For example, the dBASE IV database management system program, when stripped of its optional elements, consists of the following essential files:

```
DBASE.EXE
DBASE1.OVL
DBASE2.OVL
DBASE3.OVL
DBASE4.OVL
DBASE5.OVL
DBASE6.OVL
```

There are also other files, such as those containing help screens and other messages, that must be considered part of the entire program. The size of all these combined files is a massive 2,239,747 bytes— clearly larger than the 640KB (that is, 655,360 bytes) limit that DOS allows on an IBM PC or XT.

In programs that use overlays, only the .COM or .EXE file is copied into RAM when you run the program. This file typically contains the most often-used capabilities of the program so that these features are readily available when you want them. The .COM or .EXE file also reserves space in RAM, called the *overlay area*, that is meant to hold additional specialized instructions.

When you request a feature not currently available in RAM, the program quickly copies the overlay file that contains that feature into the overlay area, where it replaces the current overlay. That is, only one overlay file can be stored in RAM at a time. Figure 16.6 illustrates this concept, using the dBASE IV program as an example.

Because only one overlay can be in use at a time in RAM, a program might need to swap overlays quite often, which involves copying the overlay from the disk into the overlay section of RAM. This can be a somewhat slow process (in the computer world, a two- or three-second delay is "interminable"), so it wasn't long before computer designers started seeking more efficient ways to extend the capabilities of RAM.

Extended Memory

The 80286 microprocessor, developed by Intel Corporation, offered a different solution to the 640KB memory limit—*extended memory*. This microprocessor uses a 24-bit addressing scheme that can access as much as 16MB of RAM. The IBM AT and compatible computers use the 80286 microprocessor.

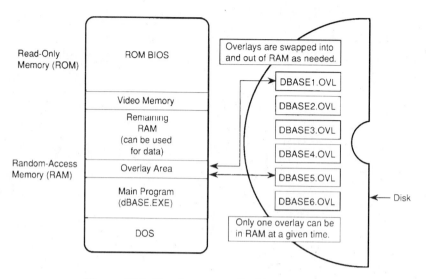

Figure 16.6. Overlays are called into RAM as needed.

The 80386 and 80486 microprocessors, which use a 32-bit addressing scheme, followed the 80286. The IBM PS/2 Model 80, the COMPAQ 386, and similar computers use the 80386 microprocessor. These computers also offer extended memory above the 640K limit.

Until Version 5, DOS was never designed to take advantage of the additional memory made available by the 80286 and 80386 microprocessors. DOS was designed for the earlier 8086 and 8088 microprocessors, which use the 20-bit addressing scheme. Because most application programs were designed for use with DOS, these microprocessors also were incapable of using extended memory effectively.

DOS 5, however, includes a new extended-memory manager program—HIMEM.SYS—which lets you access the enormous potential extended memory of the 80286 (16 megabytes) and 80386/80486 (4 gigabytes—4,000MB) microprocessors. If your computer has one of these processors and more than 640KB of RAM memory, and you are using DOS 5, Chapter 17 will show you how to use HIMEM.SYS and extended memory most effectively.

One tool that allows DOS to partially take advantage of the extended memory of the 80286 and 80386 microprocessors first appeared in Version 3 of DOS. It offers a means of treating extended memory as though it were a disk drive. This disk drive in extended memory is often called a *RAM disk*, or a *virtual disk*, because DOS interacts with it exactly as it does with all other disk drives in the computer.

NOTE: DOS 3, 4, and 5 can also use a part of "conventional" RAM memory as a virtual disk.

Fooling DOS into thinking that extended memory is a disk drive circumvents the problem of being able to address only 1MB of memory. All versions of DOS can access as much as 32MB from a disk drive, so by telling DOS that extended memory is another disk drive, you can easily access the 80286's maximum 16MB of extended memory.

NOTE: Chapter 17 discusses specific instructions for using DOS 3, 4, or 5 to create a RAM disk in your computer.

This virtual drive is actually composed of RAM chips and therefore does not use a spinning disk or moving drive heads. This makes it operate at speeds that are 10 to 20 times faster than a disk.

To take advantage of the extended memory as a virtual disk, you typically copy all the overlay files for a program or the data that you want to work with (or both, if they will fit) from a real disk to the virtual disk. Then you run the program as usual. DOS still runs the program in *conventional memory* (RAM) and still swaps overlays into and out of RAM from the virtual disk. However, the swapping is much quicker because there is no slow mechanical disk drive involved.

Similarly, if the program needs to read and write data to a disk, these operations are also much quicker if the information is stored on the virtual disk. Figure 16.7 illustrates this concept.

Treating extended memory as though it were a disk does not really give you more RAM for running programs. It makes the movement of data into and out of RAM quicker, because there is no real disk drive involved. As you'll see in the next section, a different technique, called *expanded memory* was also devised to allow "extra" RAM to be treated as conventional RAM.

Expanded Memory

Most software developers were more interested in expanding RAM than in speeding the flow of information between RAM and a disk. This is particularly true of spreadsheet developers, because spreadsheet programs must store in RAM all the data for the current worksheet. The size of a spreadsheet was therefore limited to the amount of RAM available after DOS, any TSR programs, and the spreadsheet program itself were loaded into RAM.

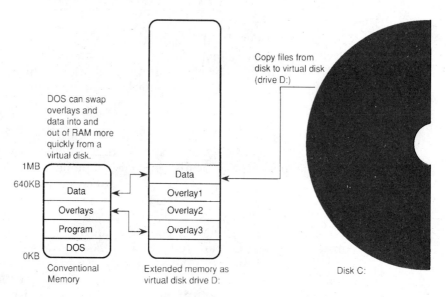

Figure 16.7. How DOS uses a virtual disk in extended memory.

Many spreadsheet users complained that 640KB was not enough room for their spreadsheet applications. The only solution to this problem, when using DOS as the operating system, was to find a means for allowing data beyond the 640KB limit to "spill over" into additional RAM chips. Of course, data that was stored in these chips had to be as accessible as it was in conventional RAM and this presented a tricky problem, because DOS had no way of directly addressing the data beyond the 640KB in RAM.

Three companies—Lotus Development Corporation, the maker of the 1-2-3 spreadsheet program, Intel, the maker of microprocessors, and Microsoft, the maker of DOS—joined forces to develop what is now known as the Lotus-Intel-Microsoft (LIM) standard for *expanded* memory. The word *expanded* is important here, because the LIM standard did, indeed, expand RAM beyond the 640KB limit.

From a technical standpoint, this swapping of memory (also called *paging*) is trickier than you might think, because as mentioned earlier, the area of addressable memory between 640KB and 1MB is typically reserved for video memory, hard disk management, and other BIOS (Basic Input/Output System) operations.

In most systems however, a good-sized chunk of memory in this area is unused. LIM takes control of 64KB of this unused memory, and uses it as a "switching area" for swapping data into, and out of, expanded memory on an "as needed" basis, as Figure 16.8 illustrates.

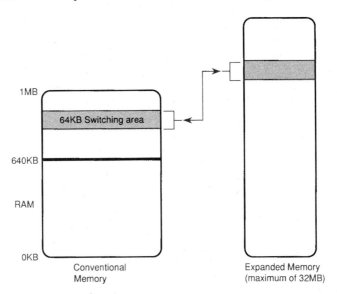

Figure 16.8. Expanded memory (EMS) uses 64KB of addressable memory as a switching area for DOS.

Even though the LIM technique involves some swapping of data into and out of the 1MB of memory that DOS can address, it is very different from the technique of using extended memory as a virtual disk. In the virtual-disk approach, DOS "sees" whatever is in extended memory as being stored on a disk. If you try to copy a file from a virtual disk into RAM, and there is not enough room in RAM to accommodate the data, DOS will deny the request with the `Insufficient Memory` error message.

> NOTE: Specifically, the LIM approach sends data into memory in 16KB chunks called *pages*. Thus, the 64KB area in ROM can handle four pages at a time.

However, with the expanded-memory approach, the swapping is limited to the switching area memory, so DOS never issues the

Insufficient Memory message. That's because the EMS approach, in a sense, "tricks" DOS into thinking that it's working with data that is stored within the 1MB limit. In other words, the LIM approach lets DOS work with more RAM than it can actually handle by feeding it small chunks of data on an as-needed basis.

Spreadsheet programs that take advantage of expanded memory could now let users create much larger worksheets. As a worksheet grows in size beyond the 640KB limit, the LIM approach swaps the overflow quickly and automatically into and out of expanded memory so that conventional RAM is no longer a constraint.

The example in Figure 16.9 shows the Microsoft Excel spreadsheet program stored in RAM and accessing a huge spreadsheet that extends beyond the 640KB limit.

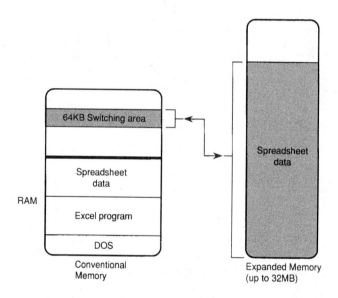

Figure 16.9. A huge Excel spreadsheet "spills over" into expanded memory.

The Current Standards

The basic LIM standard for expanded memory has evolved and improved since Version 3.2. The two main standards used today are the EEMS (Enhanced Expanded Memory Specification) and the LIM 4.0 standard. Whereas the original LIM 3.2 specification allowed a maximum of 8MB of expanded memory, the current specification allows as much as 32MB of expanded memory.

Many alternatives are available for installing expanded memory on a computer. Before DOS 5, the most common technique was to purchase a separate EMS board (hardware) and install it inside the computer. The board includes a *device driver* (a program) that manages the switching of data between expanded memory and addressable memory.

There are also EMS *emulators*, which mimic expanded memory using extended memory or even the hard disk. These are "software-only" products that do not require additional hardware, and DOS 5 includes one (EMM386.EXE) for use on 80386 and 80486 systems. If you own a computer that uses one of these microprocessors, see Chapter 17 for a detailed discussion of techniques for using HIMEM.SYS and EMM386.EXE to install and emulate expanded memory.

The Future of DOS?

One solution to breaking the 640KB limit was the development of an entirely new operating system, called *OS/2* (for Operating System 2). A second solution has been the development of DOS "extenders" and new shells, like Windows 3.0. Both products are developed by Microsoft, (the same people who brought you DOS). Both OS/2 and Windows are specifically designed to work with new 80286, 80386, and 80486-based computers that offer two operating modes: *Protected mode*, which takes full advantage of memory above 640KB, and *real mode*, which runs most standard DOS programs in conventional RAM.

Protected mode allows multiple programs to run simultaneously in protected memory above the 1MB limit of conventional memory. For example, with OS/2 or Windows, your computer can simultaneously print invoices, age your accounts receivable, and recalculate a large spreadsheet, all while you work with your word processing program. Figure 16.10 shows how memory is used in this example.

Both OS/2 and Windows 3 offer more graphical user interfaces (GUI), which are icon-based rather than text-based. The GUI interface is also more mouse-oriented than DOS (much like the Macintosh, in case you are familiar with that machine.)

How Disks Are Organized

A diskette or a hard disk stores information on a surface that is coated with hundreds of thousands—or millions—of tiny magnetic particles.

As you might know, magnets have a positive pole and a negative pole. If you've ever played with two magnets, you know that when you push two positive (or two negative) poles toward each other, the magnets repel one another. When you push a negative pole toward a positive pole, the magnets attract each other.

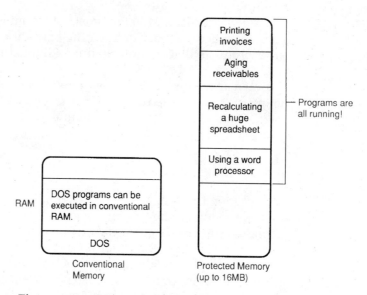

Figure 16.10. OS/2 and Windows 3 can run several programs simultaneously in protected memory.

Each magnetic particle on a computer disk can have one of two states—positive (represented as + or 1) or negative (represented as – or 0). Not surprisingly, each of these magnetic particles can represent one bit of data, and as you know, eight bits form a byte (a character).

If you could see the positive and negative magnetic poles on the tiny magnetic particles on a diskette, the word *cat* would look something like the following:

    –+––––++ –+––––––+ –+–+–+––

Using binary numbers, you would express the + signs as 1s, and the minus signs as 0s, as follows:

    01000011 01000001 01010100

If you check an ASCII chart that shows the eight-bit byte for each character in the ASCII character set, you'll see that these are indeed the bytes used to represent the letters *c*, *a*, and *t*. Of course, the computer must convert these bytes to ASCII characters when it displays them on the screen or sends them to the printer, because the word *cat* more meaningfully expresses to humans this feline animal than does 01000011 01000001 01010100.

How a Disk Drive Reads and Writes Data

Floppy disk drives and hard disk drives use the same basic principle for reading information from and writing information to the magnetic medium of a disk. As the disk spins, the *read/write head* moves across the surface (although never actually touching the disk) in much the same way that a needle on a stereo turntable moves across a spinning album. As the recording head moves above the disk, it either reads the magnetic bits or it changes their arrangement to store information.

Some older disk drives can read only one side of a diskette, because they only have one recording head. These drives use single-sided diskettes that can store only 160KB or 180KB of information. Figure 16.11 depicts the action of a disk drive with only one recording head.

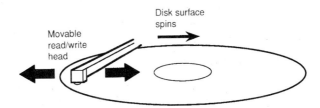

Figure 16.11. A disk drive that reads only single-sided diskettes.

Most modern disk drives have two recording heads, one for the top of the diskette and one for the bottom. These drives use double sided diskettes, with the most popular storage capacities being 360KB, 720KB, 1.2MB, and 1.44MB. Figure 16.12 depicts the action of a disk drive that has two recording heads.

A hard disk usually contains several spinning disks, referred to as *platters*. Each platter typically has two heads so that data can be read from or written to both sides. Figure 16.13 shows this arrangement of platters and heads.

Although the hard disk in Figure 16.13 *physically* consists of multiple platters, DOS can *logically* access the multiple platters as though they were one huge disk, named C:. How DOS logically accesses a hard disk is determined by how you *partition* the hard disk using the FDISK program (discussed in Appendix A).

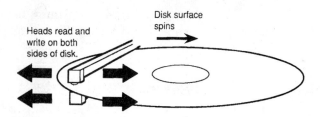

Figure 16.12. A disk drive with two recording heads.

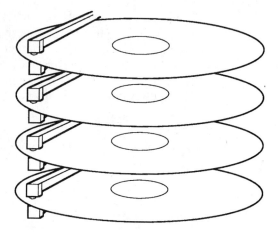

Figure 16.13. A hard disk with multiple platters.

Versions of DOS prior to 4.0 could only access a maximum of 32 megabytes of information on any logical hard disk. Therefore, if the combined hard disk platters offered 40 megabytes of disk storage, DOS had to do something like accessing the first 32 megabytes as drive C: and then accessing the remaining 8 megabytes as drive D:. The physical number of platters in the hard disk is not important—only the storage capacity matters.

Low-Level Formatting

When DOS first formats a disk, it performs a *low-level format*, which divides the surface of the diskette into *tracks* (rings) and *sectors* (slices), as Figure 16.14 shows. Each sector represents one *allocation unit* of data and stores a specific number of bytes, usually either 512KB or 1,024KB.

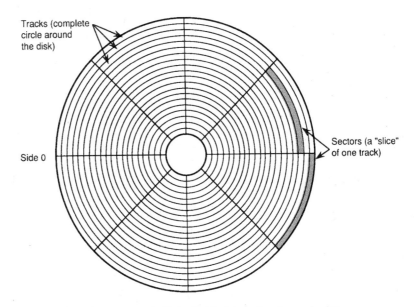

Figure 16.14. A disk divided into tracks and sectors.

Double-sided diskettes and hard disks are further divided into *cylinders*. A cylinder is the combination of all the corresponding tracks on each side of each platter, as Figure 16.15 illustrates. For example, a hard disk that has four double-sided platters contains eight tracks numbered "1." The combination of these eight tracks would be referred to as cylinder number 1.

When DOS writes a large file to a disk, it attempts to store data in a single cylinder of multiple sides (or platters) rather than in multiple tracks of a single platter. For example, when storing a file on the 10th track of a disk, DOS first fills track 10 on side 0, then track 10 of side 1, then track 10 of side 2, then track 10 of side 3, and so on. This makes reading and writing data quicker, because the heads are simultaneously positioned to the appropriate track (the heads always move in tandem, never independently).

High-Level Formatting

After the basic tracks, sectors, and cylinders are laid out on the surface of the disk, DOS performs a high-level format. During this phase, groups of sectors are set aside for storing information that DOS will later use to keep track of files. Each of these DOS information areas is discussed in the sections that follow.

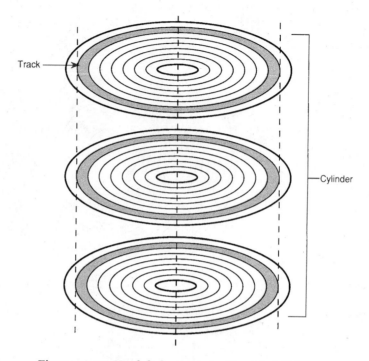

Figure 16.15. Hard disks (and double-sided diskettes)
are also divided into cylinders.

The Boot Record

The first sector on a disk stores the *boot record*. This is where the computer looks for startup information when you first turn it on. The boot record contains information about the format of the disk, such as the number of bytes per sector, the number of sectors per track and cylinder, and so on. The boot record also lists the names of the *system files* that contain the instructions that start the computer.

The system files needed to start DOS on an IBM computer are IBMIO.COM and IBMDOS.COM. On other microcomputers, these files are usually called IO.SYS and MSDOS.SYS. In most versions of DOS, the first two files are hidden; that is, their names do not appear when you list file names.

NOTE: A third file, named COMMAND.COM, is also copied to a disk that has been formatted with the /S switch. COMMAND.COM interprets DOS commands and batch files, issues prompts, and loads and executes other programs.

When you format a disk with the FORMAT /S command, DOS copies the two system files and COMMAND.COM to the disk so that you can use the disk to boot the computer. If you do not use the /S switch, the system files are not copied, and the disk cannot boot the computer. Furthermore, the space that would have been occupied by the startup files is eventually allocated to other files, so you cannot copy the system files later. (Actually, you can use the /B switch to reserve space for the system files, as discussed under the FORMAT command in Appendix B.)

The Directory Sectors

Another group of sectors on the disk is dedicated to storing the directory. In the directory sectors, the following information about each files is stored in a 32-byte area:

❏ The name and extension of the file.

❏ The status of file attributes, such as Read-Only and Archive.

❏ The time that the file was created or last changed.

❏ The date that the file was created or last changed.

❏ The size of the file.

❏ The starting cluster number.

All this information is stored in hexadecimal notation. However, when you use the DIR command to view the directory sectors of a disk, DOS converts the hex numbers to decimal before displaying them on the screen.

DOS never displays the starting cluster number on your screen. Instead, DOS uses this information to find the file. It would be a waste of time for DOS to have to search the entire disk each time you requested a file. Instead, it looks up the file name in the directory sectors and finds the corresponding *starting cluster number*, which pinpoints the exact track on the disk that contains the beginning of the file.

The File Allocation Table

Every disk also reserves a group of sectors that store the File Allocation Table (FAT). This table is a map that tells DOS where to find fragments of files that have been stored in *noncontiguous sectors*. Files are often fragmented into noncontiguous sectors when they are altered or expanded after new files have been stored next to them.

For example, suppose that you create a file named CUSTLIST.DAT that contains 50 names and addresses. Now, suppose that when you save this file, DOS stores it in sectors 5 through 10. Later, you create another file which DOS stores in sectors 11 through 15. If you then add some names to CUSTLIST.DAT, the entire file will not fit into sectors 5 through 10 anymore, and because sectors 11 through 15 are already taken, DOS must store the rest of CUSTLIST.DAT elsewhere (perhaps starting at sector 16).

The FAT keeps track of the various sectors in which a fragmented file is stored. Actually, the FAT keeps track of the *clusters* (or groups of sectors) in which files are stored. When you tell DOS to retrieve a file, it finds the starting cluster number stored with the file's name in the directory sectors. Then it starts reading the file at that location.

After reading all the data in the starting cluster, DOS looks up the file's starting cluster number in the FAT. The FAT, in turn, tells DOS the next cluster number (if any) in which more of the file is stored. DOS then accesses this cluster and reads more of the file. This process is repeated until DOS encounters a special code in the file that says "no more clusters; the entire file has been read."

The FAT is a crucial element of a disk. If the FAT is erased or destroyed, DOS can no longer access the files, because it doesn't know where they are stored. For this reason, DOS actually keeps two copies of the FAT on the disk. If the first table is ruined, DOS uses the other copy.

The Data Sectors

The Data Sectors are the sections of the disk in which the actual files and subdirectories beneath the root directory are stored. These remaining sectors are by far the largest area on the disk.

Table 16.2 shows the total number of sectors allocated to various data areas on different types of diskettes. Figure 16.16 shows how you can envision a disk after DOS has formatted it and allocated space to specific areas.

Table 16.2. Sector allotment for various diskette sizes.

	5.25-inch		3.5-inch	
Storage capacity	360KB	1.2MB	720KB	1.44MB
Boot record (sectors)	1	1	1	1
FAT sectors	4	14	10	18
Directory sectors	7	14	7	14
Data sectors	354	2,371	713	2,847
Bytes per sector	1,024	512	1,024	512
Sectors per cluster	2	1	2	1

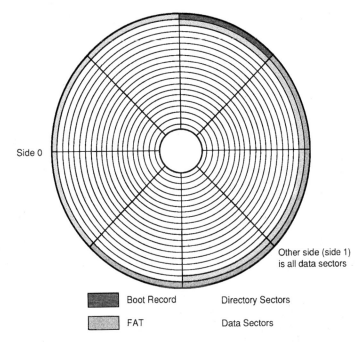

Side 0

Other side (side 1) is all data sectors

■ Boot Record   Directory Sectors

▨ FAT   Data Sectors

Figure 16.16. Space allocation on a formatted disk.

The allocation schemes for the various sections of hard disks vary greatly from one disk to another. These are determined during formatting by taking into account the amount of available storage space, the partitioning, the number of cylinders and heads, and other factors.

Serial and Parallel Communications

Computers use two basic techniques for sending data through wires to peripheral devices: 1) serial communication, in which bits are sent in a single-file stream, and 2) parallel communication, in which eight bits are sent in parallel through eight wires. Figure 16.17 shows the difference between these two methods, where the word *cat* (binary 01000011 01000001 01010100) is being sent to a peripheral device.

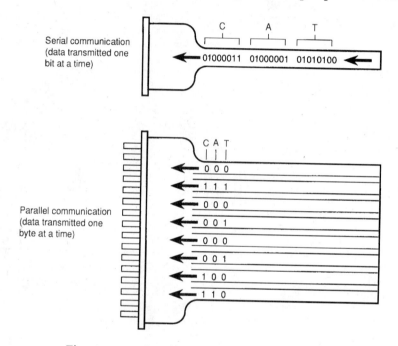

Figure 16.17. Serial and parallel communications.

Although the figure shows the parallel cable as a flat group of wires, the separate wires are usually wrapped around a core so that the cable is actually cylindrical.

NOTE: Serial communication is sometimes called *asynchronous communication*, because the devices involved must take turns sending and receiving; they cannot do so in a simultaneous (that is, synchronized) manner.

The serial communication technique is used when multiple wires are not available. For example, when sending data through phone lines via a modem, serial communication is used because the phone lines do not have the eight wires necessary for parallel communications. Serial communications are generally slower because the receiving device receives only one bit at a time.

Parallel communication is faster than serial communication because the receiving device receives one byte (that is, eight bits at a time). Most modern high-speed printers use parallel communications.

If you were to look at the back of your computer with all the plugs removed, you would see that some of the ports are male (that is, the pins protrude from the port). These are usually serial ports. The parallel ports on the back of the computer are usually female; the pins protrude from the plug at the end of the cable.

In most situations, you do not need to do anything special with DOS to use the serial and parallel ports. Other software automatically manages the ports. However, you can configure both the parallel and serial ports, if necessary, using the DOS MODE command. (See Appendix B for details.)

Summary

When you start using the more advanced features of your computer and DOS, you need a deeper understanding of the way things work. This chapter presented a brief overview of the technical inner workings of your computer. In summary

❑ The basic unit of storage in a computer is a binary digit (*bit*), which can be either on (1) or off (0).

❑ A single character is stored as a group of eight bits, called a *byte*.

❑ Internally, computers use a binary (base 2) rather than a decimal (base 10) counting system. Programmers use the more convenient hexadecimal (base 16) numbering system.

❑ A computer's conventional memory consists of up to 640KB of RAM and 384KB of ROM, for a total of 1MB of memory.

❑ Extended memory can be used as an effective extension of RAM by DOS 5's HIMEM.SYS memory manager. It can also be used as a virtual disk, which "appears" to DOS as any other disk, but is much faster because there are no moving parts.

❏ Expanded memory (which can be created on a 386 or 486 computer with the DOS 5 EMM386.EXE program) can be used by DOS as though it were additional conventional RAM.

❏ During formatting, a disk is divided into tracks, sectors, and clusters, which organize data for rapid storage and retrieval.

❏ In serial (or asynchronous) communications, data is sent one bit at a time.

❏ In parallel communications, data is sent one byte at a time.

Getting the Most from Your Computer

Chapter 16 described the basics of memory, disk storage and retrieval, and so forth. If I could summarize everything expressed in that chapter into two statements, those statements would be

❏ Memory (which includes RAM, extended, and so on) is fast, but there is a limited amount of it, and it "forgets" everything as soon as the power is shut off.

❏ Disk storage and retrieval is relatively slow, but there is generally lots of it, and it never "forgets" anything, regardless of whether the power is turned on or off.

In this chapter, the focus is on getting the most out of your computer—that is, getting maximum speed and performance (which all types of memory offer) while avoiding the slower bottlenecks that overdependence on disk storage provide. In particular, I'll look at

❏ Activating extended and/or expanded memory (if your system has such memory).

❏ Conserving precious conventional memory (RAM) by using upper memory blocks (if you have DOS 5 and a 386 or 486 computer).

❏ Using a RAM disk to speed some disk operations by as much as twentyfold.

❏ Using a disk cache to speed disk storage and retrieval in general.

DOS 5 offers by far the most options for configuring and optimizing the performance of your system. Even if you're using an earlier version of DOS, however, you'll probably be able to use many of the options presented in this chapter.

Activating Extended Memory

The first step in optimizing your system is ensuring that, if your computer has extended memory, it's being used. If you are using DOS 4 or 5, you can do so by entering the command

```
MEM
```

at the command prompt. If your computer has extended memory, you should see some information about it, as in the following example (though the numbers are likely to vary even if you have extended memory).

```
4194304 bytes total contiguous extended memory
      0 bytes available contiguous extended memory
4194304 bytes available XMS memory
```

NOTE: XMS is simply a type of "available" extended memory.

In this particular example, the first line informs you that this computer has about 4MB of installed extended memory. The second line tells you that none (0 bytes) of the extended memory is unused. The last line tells you that there is about 4MB of XMS memory, which says that all of the extended memory in this computer is currently available for use.

The device driver that converts "wasted" extended memory to usable XMS memory is named HIMEM.SYS. Chances are, if you have Windows 3 and/or DOS 5, the command to activate extended memory is already in your CONFIG.SYS file and looks something like this:

```
DEVICE = C:\DOS\HIMEM.SYS
```

The reason this command is already in your CONFIG.SYS file is because either Windows 3 or DOS 5 (or both) detected the available extended memory while you were installing the program(s), and hence the installation procedure automatically modified your CONFIG.SYS file to include this command.

If on the other hand, you enter the DOS 4 or 5 MEM command and saw a description of extended memory like this:

```
4194304 bytes total contiguous extended memory
4194304 bytes available contiguous extended memory
```

you can assume that while the current computer has about 4MB of installed extended memory, all of it is unusable and wasted. That's because "available" extended memory is not usable until it's under the control of a extended memory manager (or device driver).

> NOTE: Chapter 10 discusses techniques for creating and modifying DOS ASCII files, such as CONFIG.SYS and AUTOEXEC.BAT.

If this were the case, you would most likely want to locate the HIMEM.SYS file (most likely on the C:\DOS or C:\ directory of a hard disk) and modify the CONFIG.SYS file so that it activates HIMEM.SYS. For example, if the HIMEM.SYS file is on the C:\DOS directory, you need to add this command to your CONFIG.SYS file (preferably above other DEVICE= commands):

```
DEVICE=C:\DOS\HIMEM.SYS
```

After you save the modified CONFIG.SYS file, reboot the system and check the output of the MEM command, you should find that all of your extended memory has been converted to XMS memory, which means programs designed to use XMS memory can now do so.

As you'll see, there's quite a bit more you can do with extended memory.

Activating Expanded Memory

> NOTE: DOS 4 and 5 commands can *simulate* expanded memory in the extended memory on any 386 or 486 computer. For details see "Emulating Expanded Memory on 80386/80486 Computers" later in this chapter.

Expanded memory, in many ways, is sort of an "old-fashioned" version of extended memory, but is nonetheless a means of letting programs access RAM above the 640KB limit. Exactly how you install expanded memory on your system is determined by many factors, including your computer's microprocessor, the type of expanded memory board you have, and your version of DOS. However, the deeper your understanding of the principles of expanded memory, the easier it will be for you to install it.

As mentioned in Chapter 16, DOS uses a "switching area" in conventional memory above the 640KB RAM limit to manage data stored in expanded memory. This area is divided into four contiguous 16KB blocks of memory called *pages*. Typically, these pages are named P0, P1, P2, and P3. Combined, these four pages create the 64KB switching area, which is called the *page frame*.

Some device drivers for expanded memory require that you specify the *segment* address in memory at which the page frame begins (called the page frame's *base* address). Furthermore, some of these device drivers require that you specify this segment address in hexa-decimal (which can make matters even more confusing).

Figure 17.1 shows an example memory map of addresses in the range of 0KB to 1MB (all memory below extended and/or expanded memory) with segment addresses expressed in hexadecimal. The base address for the 64KB page frame is usually a segment at or above C400.

A starting address of C400 is usually considered the lowest "safe" starting point for the 64KB page frame that the expanded memory manager can use, because this is the first segment above RAM and video memory that is almost certainly unused.

Figure 17.2 shows a more detailed view of the 16KB segment addresses from C000 to EC00. In this example, segments D000 to DC00 are used for the 64KB page frame. Segment D000 starts the first 16KB page (P0), segment D400 starts the second page (P1), D800 starts the third page (P2), and DC00 starts the fourth page (P3).

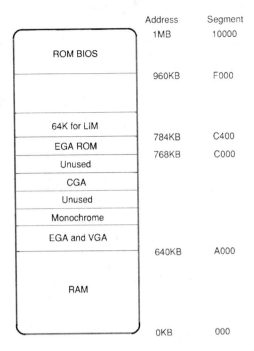

Figure 17.1. A detailed memory map with segment addresses.

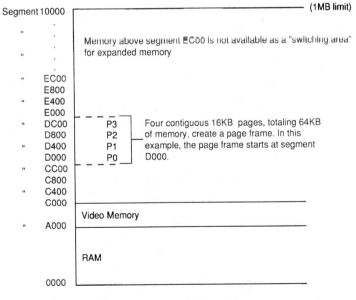

Figure 17.2. Four 16KB pages form a 64KB page frame
that begins at segment D000 in memory.

Notice in Figure 17.2 that the segments increase in increments of 400 hex. You can use any of the segments shown in the range of C400 to EC00 as the base address for the expanded memory manager's page frame.

As mentioned earlier, your expanded memory manager may be able to find a suitable base address on its own, and therefore, you may not even need to bother with these details. The sections that follow present a few general examples of installing expanded memory. Because different computers and different expanded memory adapters use different techniques. however, you should refer to the manual that came with your computer or expanded memory adapter for details.

Example of Installing Expanded Memory

PC DOS 4, the version of DOS 4 that is delivered with IBM computers, contains a device driver named XMA2EMS.SYS that supports the LIM (EMS) standard for expanded memory. To use XMA2EMS.SYS on an IBM 80286 computer, your computer must be using one of the following optional expanded memory adapters (or a compatible adapter that conforms to the LIM 4.0 standard):

> NOTE: Computers that use the 80386 processor can emulate expanded memory without an expanded memory adapter, as discussed later in this chapter.

❏ IBM 2MB Expanded Memory Adapter

❏ IBM PS/2 80286 Expanded Memory Adapter /A

❏ IBM PS/2 80286 Memory Expansion Option

Use the XMA2EMS.SYS device driver as you would any other device driver: Add the name to a DEVICE command in your CONFIG.SYS file. Specify a base segment address for the page frame in the range of C000 to E000, the most commonly used page frame address being D000.

> NOTE: The strange name XMA2EMS is an abbreviation for *eXpanded Memory Adapter to EMS* (the LIM specification).

For example, to use all of the memory in your expanded memory adapter, your CONFIG.SYS file must contain the command

```
DEVICE=C:\DOS\XMA2EMS.SYS FRAME=D000
```

The expanded memory becomes active the next time you start your computer (or when you reboot). To verify that the memory is available, enter the **MEM** command at the DOS command prompt. Your screen then displays a message similar to the following (your numbers, of course, will depend on memory availability in your computer):

```
655360 bytes total memory
655360 bytes available
539664 largest executable program size

1441792 bytes total EMS memory
1048576 bytes free EMS memory
```

If you want to use only a portion of expanded memory (perhaps assigning the other portion to a RAM disk), use the /X: switch at the end of the command and follow it by the number of 16KB pages of EMS. For example, suppose that your computer has 4MB of expanded memory, but you want to use only 2MB of it. Recall that 1 megabyte is 1,024KB, so 2MB is 2,048KB. Dividing 2,048 by 16 gives you 128 (the number of 16KB pages). Therefore, the command to put in your CONFIG.SYS file is

```
DEVICE=C:\DOS\XMA2EMS.SYS FRAME=D000 /X:128
```

If your expanded memory board offers 1MB (1024KB) of expanded memory, and you want to use half of that (512KB), you need to specify 32 (that is, 512/16=32) pages in your CONFIG.SYS file, as follows:

```
DEVICE=C:\DOS\XMA2EMS.SYS FRAME=D000 /X:32
```

Again, after you place the appropriate command in the CONFIG.SYS file and reboot, use the **MEM** command to verify that the expanded memory is available. From now on, any program that supports expanded memory, such as Microsoft Excel or Lotus 1-2-3 Version 3, will automatically use the expanded memory to store data beyond the 640KB limit.

Installing Expanded Memory with MS-DOS

If you are using MS-DOS Versions 3, 4, or 5 on a non-IBM microcomputer, the exact techniques that you use to install expanded memory depend primarily on your expanded memory adapter. In most cases, you still need to modify your CONFIG.SYS file to include the DEVICE=*driver name* command.

The *driver name* you use is determined by the expanded memory board in your computer. For example, the AST Rampage board uses a driver named REMM.SYS. The Intel Above Board uses a driver named EMM.SYS. COMPAQ computers that use the 80286 processor and an expanded memory adapter require a driver named CEMMP.SYS.

Refer to the documentation that came with your expanded memory adapter (or your computer) for specific instructions about modifying your CONFIG.SYS file. The documentation for a program that can use expanded memory may provide additional useful information. For example, the Microsoft Excel package contains a disk (the Utilities Disk) that includes device drivers for many different expanded memory adapters, as well as documentation for using the drivers.

Emulating Expanded Memory on 80386/80486 Computers

The 80386 and 80486 microprocessors can *emulate* expanded memory using extended memory or even a disk file; you do not need to have an expanded memory adapter installed in your computer. Both PC DOS 4 and MS-DOS 5 contain drivers that enable you to create and manage this "simulated" expanded memory.

About the only reason you would even want to emulate expanded memory on a 386 or 486 computer would be to run a program that absolutely requires expanded memory and cannot use extended memory. These days, such programs are few and far between. Then again, just in case you do run into this problem, you will need to solve it, so I'll talk about solutions.

The exact techniques you use to emulate expanded memory on a 386 or 486 will vary from computer to computer, and you will need to refer to the documentation that came with your 80386 computer for details. However, the following examples might help you better understand the procedures outlined in your documentation.

Emulating Expanded Memory with PC DOS 4

If you have an IBM 80386 computer, such as the PS/2 Model 80, and you are using IBM PC DOS 4, you can emulate expanded memory by using the XMAEM.SYS device driver. This device driver emulates the IBM PS/2 80286 Expanded Memory Adapter/A, which conforms to the LIM 4.0 EMS standard.

Your CONFIG.SYS file must contain two DEVICE commands, each specifying a different device driver. To use all the extended memory on an 80386 computer as expanded memory, you must add these two commands (in the order shown) to your CONFIG.SYS file:

```
DEVICE=C:\DOS\XMAEM.SYS
DEVICE=C:\DOS\XMA2EMS.SYS FRAME=D000
```

The first command, in essence, tells DOS that expanded memory must be emulated because no expanded memory adapter is installed. The second command then installs the expanded memory as though an adapter existed.

You can also set aside a specific amount of extended memory to be used for expanded memory, by specifying the number of 16KB pages. For example, you need 64 pages to specify 1MB of expanded memory (that is, 1MB is 1,024KB bytes, and 1024 divided by 16 is 64). Place this value to the right of the XMAEM.SYS driver name in your CONFIG.SYS file, as follows:

```
DEVICE=C:\DOS\XMAEM.SYS 64
DEVICE=C:\DOS\XMA2EMS.SYS FRAME=D000
```

Remember that the expanded memory is not installed until the next time you start the computer (or until you reboot). You can then verify that the expanded memory is installed by entering the MEM command at the command prompt.

Emulating Expanded Memory with MS-DOS Version 5

NOTE: In addition to simulating expanded memory, DOS 5's EMM386.EXE can also let you access reserved memory, as described a little later in this chapter.

If you are using DOS 5 on a 386 or 486 computer with extended memory, and you need to run a program that requires expanded memory, you can use the DOS 5 EMM386.EXE (Expanded Memory Manager for 386) program emulate expanded memory.

WARNING: If you also use Microsoft Windows 3.0, use the versions of HIMEM.SYS and EMM386.EXE that come with DOS 5, not the versions that came with your Windows package.

Because the 386 and 486 computers use extended memory to emulate expanded memory, extended memory must be activated before expanded memory is emulated. This is accomplished simply by ensuring that the DEVICE= command that activates HIMEM.SYS comes before the DEVICE= command that activates EMM386.EXE in the CONFIG.SYS file.

Secondly, you should specify how much extended memory you want to use to emulate expanded memory, and finally you must end the command with the word RAM. For example, here are a pair of commands in a sample CONFIG.SYS file that activate extended memory and then set aside 1MB (1024K) of the extended memory for use as expanded memory (note that HIMEM.SYS comes before EMM386.EXE):

```
DEVICE=C:\DOS\HIMEM.SYS
DEVICE=C:\DOS\EMM386.EXE 1024 RAM
```

Note that the amount of memory to allocate to emulate expanded memory (the 1024 in the preceding example) must be less than (or equal to) the total amount of extended memory available to you. However, because more programs use extended memory than expanded memory, you'll probably want to use only 1/4 to 1/2 of your extended memory to emulate expanded memory in most situations.

If your CONFIG.SYS file included those commands when you started your computer, you checked available memory using the MEM command, the resulting report might show the following (assuming the current computer has 4MB of extended memory installed):

```
 655360 bytes total conventional memory
 655360 bytes available to MS-DOS
 578912 largest executable program size

1441792 bytes total EMS memory
1048576 bytes free EMS memory

4194304 bytes total contiguous extended memory
      0 bytes available contiguous extended memory
3145728 bytes available XMS memory
```

In this case, there are now 3,145,728 bytes (about 3MB) of extended (XMS) memory available, because about 1MB (1,048,576 bytes) are being used to emulate expanded (EMS) memory.

As you'll see in the sections that follow, the EMM386.EXE driver plays a dual role in DOS 5. Even if you don't use it to emulate expanded memory, you can use it to access upper (reserved) memory, which conserves precious conventional RAM memory.

Conserving Conventional Memory (RAM)

One of the biggest advantages that DOS 5 offers over all its predecessors is the ability to conserve precious conventional memory. The advantages of conserving conventional memory are twofold:

❑ Programs that store all their data in RAM (such as some spreadsheet programs) can store more data, thereby allowing for larger spreadsheets.

❑ Programs that swap data into and out of RAM on an as-needed basis (such as word processors and database managers) run faster because they need to do less swapping.

Some people find it hard to envision how conserving space in conventional memory can result in increased speed for getting a job done. A practical analogy can help. Suppose that you have to move one ton of dirt. You have one truck that can hold 1/2 ton of dirt and another that can hold one ton of dirt. If both trucks go exactly the same speed, which one gets the job done faster? Obviously, the bigger truck gets the job done faster because it can do the job in one trip rather than two.

In a computer sense, the more conventional memory (RAM) that's available to hold data, the fewer time-consuming trips to the disk that are required to swap data into and out of RAM.

Figure 17.3 shows a "typical" memory configuration right after a computer is first booted. As you can see, DOS, as well as device drivers and memory resident programs, are in conventional memory (RAM) below the 640K mark. In this hypothetical example, 506KB of conventional memory remains for running programs and storing data.

In DOS 5, there are two main ways to recapture some of the conventional memory that's currently lost to DOS, the drivers, and the TSR's:

❑ Store DOS itself in the High Memory Area; which is the first 64K of extended memory above the 1MB mark.

❑ Store Device Drivers and memory resident (TSR) programs in previously "reserved" memory between the 640K and 1MB marks.

I'll look at each method in the next two sections.

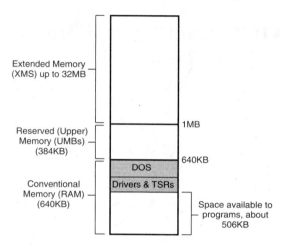

Figure 17.3. DOS, drivers, and TSR programs in conventional memory.

Storing DOS in High Memory

If you have DOS 5 and a computer with extended memory, a quick and easy way to conserve about 40K of conventional memory is to store DOS itself in the High Memory Area, which is the first 64K of extended memory. This is an ideal place to store DOS, because very few programs that access extended memory operate in this area, so there is no conflict between DOS and other programs.

Chances are, if you have extended memory, the DOS 5 installation procedure is already loading DOS in high memory. To find out, you can enter the MEM command at the command prompt. If you see

```
MS-DOS resident in High Memory Area
```

as the last line to that entry, there's nothing more you can do in this section. Skip to the next section.

On the other hand, if the MEM command informs you that extended memory is available on this computer and also shows

```
64KB High Memory Area available
```

you'll probably want to put DOS in high memory by adding the command DOS = HIGH to your CONFIG.SYS file. The command that activates HIMEM.SYS must precede the DOS=HIGH command:

```
DEVICE = C:\DOS\HIMEM.SYS
DOS = HIGH
```

After making this change and restarting your computer, entering the MEM command will not only show that DOS is now in the High Memory Area, but the "largest executable program size" will be about 40K larger than it was before.

Looking at it as shown in Figure 17.4, you can see that DOS is now up above the 1MB mark, leaving 542K of conventional memory for programs; a savings of nearly 40K of memory.

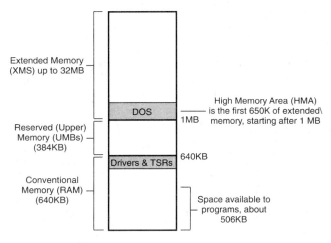

Figure 17.4. Memory with DOS loaded in the high memory Area.

Using Upper Memory Blocks (Reserved Memory)

As you learned in Chapter 16, *reserved* memory, or what Microsoft refers to as the *upper memory area*, is the 384KB of system memory that DOS reserves for its own use, for device drivers, and for various video and BIOS routines. As it turns out, the 384KB of memory that Microsoft originally set aside for itself is much more than was ever needed, so Microsoft (and others) began using chunks of that reserved memory— at first to create expanded memory so that all computers could break the (now extinct) 640KB limit.

> NOTE: If you use Windows 3 on a 386 or 486 computer with
> DOS 5, see "Windows 3 and UMBs" later in this chapter.

5   With DOS 5, however, Microsoft has introduced tools that can free
large blocks of upper memory to anyone with a 386 or 486 computer.
These tools—the programs HIMEM.SYS, EMM386.EXE, DOS,
DEVICEHIGH, and LOADHIGH—let you use all the memory in your
computer . . . even the memory DOS has kept to itself for the past decade.

I've already briefly discussed the EMM386.EXE, which can be
used to emulate expanded memory within extended memory. Because
EMM386.EXE already manages the use of reserved (upper) memory to
create the frames through which expanded memory is accessed, Microsoft decided to also give it other reserved-memory management
powers; that is, you can use EMM386.EXE to load your own drivers and
programs into reserved memory.

If you have a 386 or 486 computer, this can buy you over 100KB
of "free" memory, which in the past has been largely inaccessible and
wasted, unless you used products from third-party vendors (such as
Quarterdeck and Digital Research) to gain access to that memory.

> WARNING: If you use upper memory blocks, you will not be able
> to run Windows 3.0 in "standard" (/S) mode. (See "Troubleshoot-
> ing" later in this chapter for alternatives.)

Accessing the upper memory area is primarily a matter of adding
a few simple commands to your CONFIG.SYS and AUTOEXEC.BAT
files, as I will soon show. However, your system might include device
drivers and video systems that must use specific areas of upper
memory. These programs might cause memory conflicts that lock up
your system when you start installing programs in upper memory. Read
the "Troubleshooting" section later in this chapter before you begin
using upper memory.

If you have persistent problems, you may need to manually lock
out programs from sections of upper memory. Refer to the HIMEM.SYS
and EMM386.EXE entries in Appendix B for more details; then consult
Microsoft's DOS 5 documentation for additional information. Finally,
if you are having a problem with a specific program or device driver, the
technical support department of the company that manufactures that
program or driver may be able to solve the problem for you quite easily.

Accessing the Upper Memory Area

Most of the commands you use to access upper memory blocks must be placed in your system's CONFIG.SYS file. The general procedure for using upper memory blocks is as follows:

In CONFIG.SYS

❏ Activate extended memory with HIMEM.SYS.

❏ With the DOS=UMB command, tell DOS you plan use upper memory blocks.

❏ Install the EMM386.EXE expanded-memory emulator to manage the upper memory area.

❏ Load device drivers or programs into upper memory with the DEVICEHIGH command.

In AUTOEXEC.BAT

❏ Load memory-resident programs into upper memory with the LOADHIGH (LH) command.

Note that these commands must appear in your CONFIG.SYS file in the preceding order.

Every system will use different device drivers and TSRs, and some systems will require that you use one or more of the many switches that manually control the HIMEM.SYS and EMM386.EXE drivers.

Two examples that set up upper memory follow. This first sample CONFIG.SYS file is for a simple 386 system in which no hardware conflicts have occurred and all commands use their default settings.

```
DEVICE=C:\DOS\HIMEM.SYS
DOS=HIGH,UMB
DEVICE=C:\DOS\EMM386.EXE NOEMS
DEVICEHIGH C:\DOS\ANSI.SYS
DEVICEHIGH C:\WINDOWS\MOUSE.EXE /Y
```

Note that this CONFIG.SYS file follows the general outline that I described earlier.

❏ `DEVICE=C:\DOS\HIMEM.SYS` activates extended memory, as required, before any commands beneath are executed.

❏ `DOS=HIGH,UMB` kills two birds with one stone: It places DOS itself in the High Memory Area (as described earlier) and then "prepares" DOS to start using upper memory blocks (UMBs).

❑ `DEVICE=C:\DOS\EMM386.EXE NOEMS` activates the 386 (and 486) expanded memory emulator, but the NOEMS switch tells it that you're not really interested in emulating expanded memory (EMS). Hence, the command "assumes" you want to use upper memory blocks for drivers and TSR programs.

❑ The remaining `DEVICEHIGH=` commands replace what might otherwise have been plain DEVICE= commands, so the device drivers will be loaded into upper memory blocks rather than conventional memory.

The AUTOEXEC.BAT file for this same computer might include the following commands:

```
LOADHIGH C:\DOS\MODE\COM1:9600,N,8,1,R
LOADHIGH C:\DOS\MODE LPT1:,,B
LOADHIGH C:\DOS\PRINT.EXE /D:LPT1
LOADHIGH C:\DOS\DOSKEY
D:
CD\UTILS
LOADHIGH SYSCTRL.COM
C:
C:\DOS\MIRROR C:
PATH C:\DOS, D:\TEMPS
```

In this case, the command LOADHIGH (followed by a blank space) precedes every command that might otherwise not be preceded by any command. LOADHIGH forces the program to be loaded into upper memory rather than conventional memory. For example, the AUTOEXEC.BAT command

```
C:\DOS\PRINT.EXE /D:LPT1
```

correctly loads the resident portion of the DOS 5 Print program, but into conventional memory. However, the command

```
LOADHIGH C:\DOS\PRINT.EXE /D:LPT1
```

loads it into upper memory, preserving about 5.6K of RAM (conventional memory).

NOTE: HIMEM.SYS, EMM386.EXE, DOS=, DEVICEHIGH, and LOADHIGH are also referenced in Appendix B.

If you can get most of your drivers and TSR programs into upper memory, only a small amount of DOS and perhaps other programs needs to remain in conventional memory. Figure 17.5 shows an example with DOS in the High Memory Area, most drivers and TSR programs in upper memory, and only a small residual portion of DOS left in conventional memory, leaving 627 of conventional memory available.

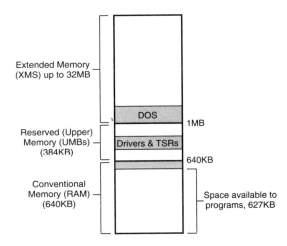

Figure 17.5. Drivers and TSR programs moved to upper memory.

Exploring Conventional and Upper Memory

As you probably know by now, with the MEM command you can examine your current memory situation in detail. Once you activate upper memory blocks by adjusting your CONFIG.SYS and AUTOEXEC.BAT file (and reboot, of course), you can get information about upper memory as well. You can use the /C switch with MEM for the clearest report and use piping and redirection as usual.

For example, entering the command

```
MEM /C ¦ MORE
```

pauses the display after each screenful of text. Entering

```
MEM /C >PRN
```

prints the report (though as usual, you'll probably need to eject the printed page from the printer). Figure 17.6 shows a hypothetical MEM /C report.

As you can see, the report shows the contents of both Conventional and Upper Memory, the size in decimal and in hex of every driver and program in memory, and the remaining amount of free memory.

```
Conventional Memory :

    Name                 Size in Decimal         Size in Hex
-------------         ----------------------      -------------
    MSDOS               15568     ( 15.2K)           3CD0
    SETVER                384     (  0.4K)            180
    HIMEM                1168     (  1.1K)            490
    EMM386               8208     (  8.0K)           2010
    COMMAND              2624     (  2.6K)            A40
    FREE                   64     (  0.1K)             40
    FREE               627120     (612.4K)           991B0

Total   FREE :         627184     (612.5K)

Upper Memory :

    Name                 Size in Decimal         Size in Hex
-------------         ----------------------      -------------
    SYSTEM             163840     (160.0K)          28000
    RAMDRIVE             1184     (  1.2K)            4A0
    ANSI                 4208     (  4.1K)           1070
    MODE                  464     (  0.5K)            1D0
    MOUSE               12784     ( 12.5K)           31F0
    PRINT                5760     (  5.6K)           1680
    DOSKEY               4144     (  4.0K)           1030
    SYSCTRL             14848     ( 14.5K)           3A00
    MIRROR               6528     (  6.4K)           1980
    FREE                   64     (  0.1K)             40
    FREE                  144     (  0.1K)             90
    FREE                 4400     (  4.3K)           1130
    FREE                  144     (  0.1K)             90
    FREE                 5008     (  4.9K)           1390
    FREE                 4512     (  4.4K)           11A0
    FREE                   80     (  0.1K)             50
    FREE                 4800     (  4.7K)           12C0
    FREE                 1040     (  1.0K)            410
    FREE                 1904     (  1.9K)            770
    FREE                 6016     (  5.9K)           1780
    FREE                 6016     (  5.9K)           1780
    FREE                 4800     (  4.7K)           12C0
    FREE                10848     ( 10.6K)           2A60
    FREE                 5408     (  5.3K)           1520
    FREE                20496     ( 20.0K)           5010
    FREE                37808     ( 36.9K)           93B0

Total   FREE :         113488     (110.8K)

Total bytes available to programs
(Conventional+Upper) :                  740672   (723.3K)
Largest executable program size :       626960   (612.3K)
Largest available upper memory block :   37808   ( 36.9K)

    4194304 bytes total contiguous extended memory
          0 bytes available contiguous extended memory
    3372032 bytes available XMS memory
            MS-DOS resident in High Memory Area
```

Figure 17.6. An example MEM/C report.

Figure 17.7 shows the CONFIG.SYS and AUTOEXEC.BAT files that were in effect on the 386 computer that printed the report shown in Figure 17.6. Take a look at the relationship between the MEM /C report and the contents of CONFIG.SYS and AUTOEXEC.BAT.

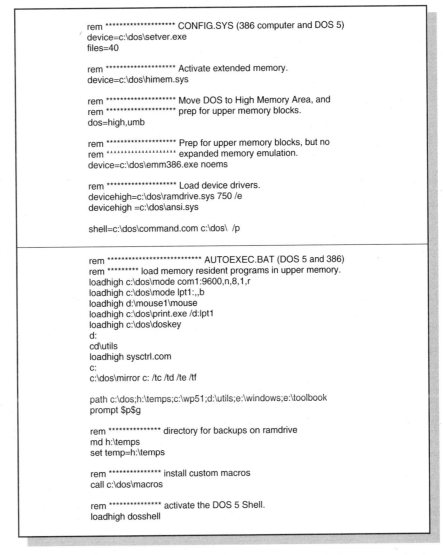

```
rem ******************** CONFIG.SYS (386 computer and DOS 5)
device=c:\dos\setver.exe
files=40

rem ******************** Activate extended memory.
device=c:\dos\himem.sys

rem ******************** Move DOS to High Memory Area, and
rem ******************** prep for upper memory blocks.
dos=high,umb

rem ******************** Prep for upper memory blocks, but no
rem ^^^^^^^^^^^^^^^^^^^^ expanded memory emulation.
device=c:\dos\emm386.exe noems

rem ******************** Load device drivers.
devicehigh=c:\dos\ramdrive.sys 750 /e
devicehigh =c:\dos\ansi.sys

shell=c:\dos\command.com c:\dos\  /p
```

```
rem *************************** AUTOEXEC.BAT (DOS 5 and 386)
rem ********* load memory resident programs in upper memory.
loadhigh c:\dos\mode com1:9600,n,8,1,r
loadhigh c:\dos\mode lpt1:,,b
loadhigh d:\mouse1\mouse
loadhigh c:\dos\print.exe /d:lpt1
loadhigh c:\dos\doskey
d:
cd\utils
loadhigh sysctrl.com
c:
c:\dos\mirror c: /tc /td /te /tf

path c:\dos;h:\temps;c:\wp51;d:\utils;e:\windows;e:\toolbook
prompt $p$g

rem ************** directory for backups on ramdrive
md h:\temps
set temp=h:\temps

rem ************** install custom macros
call c:\dos\macros

rem ************** activate the DOS 5 Shell.
loadhigh dosshell
```

Figure 17.7. A sample CONFIG.SYS and AUTOEXEC.BAT file.

Even though the DOS=HIGH command is used in the CONFIG.SYS file, the uppermost 15.2K of conventional memory are used by MS-DOS. As mentioned earlier, this is because not all of DOS can be loaded in the HMA and 15.2K remains in Conventional memory (partially to manage the fact that the rest of DOS is in the High Memory Area).

SETVER, HIMEM, EMM386, and COMMAND.COM occupy the memory below MS-DOS. None of these drivers can operate correctly in upper memory, so you simply cannot use DEVICEHIGH commands to install these drivers. No way around that.

In upper memory, the first 160K is already in use by the computer (SYSTEM), so is off limits. The driver for a RAM disk (RAMDRIVE, described a little later in this chapter), occupies the next 1.2K of memory. The various memory resident programs loaded via the LOADHIGH commands in AUTOEXEC.BAT occupy about the next 47.6 bytes. Here are a few additional comments:

> SYSCTRL is a general purpose "desktop" program (a freebie from the PC Source magazine) that I use for notes and reminders. It fits easily into upper memory.

> Even though the LOADHIGH command is not used in AUTOEXEC.BAT to load the MIRROR program, it loads there automatically if upper memory is available.

> You don't see DOSSHELL in upper memory, even though there's a LOADHIGH DOSSHELL command in the AUTOEXEC.BAT file. The reason is that I used F3 to exit to the command prompt before entering the MEM /C command to print the report. Hence, DOSSHELL was removed from upper memory before printing the report.

> One way around this would have been to use Shift+F9 to temporarily exit the Shell, which would leave it in upper memory. Entering EXIT to return to the Shell would, in turn, keep the Shell in upper memory.

NOTE: The DEVICEHIGH command can be used only in the CONFIG.SYS file, but the LOADHIGH command can be used both in AUTOEXEC.BAT and directly at the command prompt.

Note that because I exited the Shell using F3, entering the command DOSSHELL now would reload the Shell into conventional, not upper memory. However, I could enter the command

```
LOADHIGH DOSSHELL
```

to reload the Shell into upper memory and start using the Shell.

Notice in the output of the MEM /C report, even with so many DEVICEHIGH and LOADHIGH commands in use to store things in upper memory, that there's still 110.8K of unused upper memory available for yet more drivers and memory resident programs.

Loading Drivers that Allocate Memory

If a particular device driver allocates memory after it's loaded and loads it into upper memory, chances are that DOS will not provide enough memory for that driver to do its job properly, possibly locking up your entire system.

If you know how much memory that driver needs, however, and can determine that there is sufficient upper memory available based on the output from the MEM /C command, you can use the size= option in the DEVICEHIGH command to allocate sufficient memory to the driver. You must, however, express in hexadecimal the amount of memory needed.

For example, say that a given device driver needs to allocate up to 30KB of memory. From your MEM /C report, you've already determined that there is a FREE memory block available in upper memory that's at least 30K in size.

First, you need to convert 30KB to bytes; (30*1024) gives 30,720. Then convert that value to hexadecimal to (7800). Then add the appropriate command to your CONFIG.SYS file to allocate memory and load the device driver. For example, the following command allocates 30K (7800 H) bytes of upper memory to a driver called MYDEVICE.SYS:

```
DEVICEHIGH SIZE = 7800 C:\DOS\MYDEVICE.SYS
```

Maximizing Disk Performance

So far I've talked about ways to activate and conserve various types of memory. As mentioned however, disk drives are very often the real culprit behind slow computer performance. In the next sections, I'll discuss techniques for improving and maximizing disk drive speed and performance.

Using a RAM Disk

As discussed in Chapter 16, a RAM disk (or virtual disk) is a portion of memory set up to simulate a disk drive. The advantage of a RAM disk is that it is 10 to 20 times faster than a *physical* (that is, "real") disk drive. The disadvantages are

❏ Everything is erased from the RAM disk as soon as you turn off the computer.

❏ Some programs might not have enough memory space after you assign part of memory to the RAM disk (depending on how you set up the RAM disk).

The disadvantages of RAM disks, however, can by bypassed if you 1) only use the RAM disk to store temporary files and 2) use extended or expanded memory, rather than conventional RAM, for the RAM disk, as I'll discuss in the sections that follow.

Creating a RAM Disk in Conventional Memory

You can use conventional memory for your RAM disk. However, you first need to realistically determine how much memory is available. Before you make this appraisal, be sure to load all of your usual memory-resident programs, such as SideKick, as well as any DOS memory resident programs that you use regularly, (such as PRINT.COM, MODE.COM, GRAPHICS.COM, and so on).

Next, at the command prompt, you can enter the CHKDSK or the DOS 5 MEM command. Using CHKDSK, the last two lines displayed show the current available amount of conventional memory, as in the following example:

```
655360 total bytes memory
542832 bytes free
```

The DOS 5 MEM command displays three lines of information about conventional memory, as in the following example:

```
655360 bytes total conventional memory
655360 bytes available to MS-DOS
542832 largest executable program size
```

NOTE: To determine how much RAM an application program requires, check that program's documentation.

In the previous examples, the computer has 655,360 total bytes of memory, of which 542,832 bytes are free. (Dividing 542,832 by 1024 translates to about 530KB.) To determine a realistic size for your RAM disk, subtract the amount of RAM that your largest program requires from the amount of available memory.

Remember, too, that spreadsheet programs, such as Lotus 1-2-3, store data in RAM, and therefore you must also leave enough room to include your largest spreadsheet.

For example, assuming that Lotus 1-2-3 (Version 2) requires about 179KB of RAM and that your largest spreadsheet requires 50KB of RAM, the maximum amount of RAM available for a RAM disk would be about 301KB (530KB of available memory minus 179KB for 1-2-3 and 50KB for the largest spreadsheet). Because you wouldn't want to run out of memory during a crucial operation and because spreadsheets have a tendency to grow, play it safe and round that number down considerably, perhaps to 256KB.

To create a RAM disk, you need to modify your CONFIG.SYS file to include the command `DEVICE=device-driver`. If you are using MS-DOS, the *device-driver* for creating a RAM disk is named RAMDRIVE.SYS. Therefore, the general technique for installing a RAM disk using MS-DOS is to add a command to your CONFIG.SYS file that uses the following syntax:

```
DEVICE=d:\path\RAMDRIVE.SYS size sectors entries
```

PC DOS users with IBM machines must use the VDISK.SYS device driver rather than RAMDRIVE.SYS. Check your startup diskette or the root (C:) or C:\DOS directory of your hard disk to see whether it contains RAMDRIVE.SYS or VDISK.SYS. Use whichever device driver is available for your computer. (You might also need to check the documentation that came with your computer for additional details.)

VDISK.SYS uses the same basic syntax as RAMDRIVE.SYS, as follows:

```
DEVICE=d:\path\VDISK.SYS size sectors entries
```

NOTE: See the reference to RAMDRIVE.SYS in Appendix B for additional details concerning restrictions and defaults on RAM disks.

Whether you use VDISK.SYS or RAMDRIVE.SYS, you need to replace the italicized parameters with the following information:

d:path is the name of the drive and directory where the RAMDRIVE.SYS or VDISK.SYS file is located.

size is the size (in kilobytes) of the RAM disk (if omitted, DOS creates a 64KB RAM disk).

sectors is the size of each sector on the RAM disk—128, 256, or 512 bytes.

entries is the maximum number of file names in the root directory of the RAM disk, within the range of 2 to 512 (if this parameter is omitted, DOS permits 64).

You can omit parameters only if you've specified parameters to the left. For example, if you want to allow 128 directory entries, you cannot use the command `DEVICE=RAMDRIVE.SYS 128` or `DEVICE=VDISK.SYS 128` because DOS will think that the 128 refers to the size of the disk in kilobytes. Instead, you must specify both the size of the disk and the size of each sector (even if they are equal to the defaults), as in the following example:

```
DEVICE=RAMDRIVE.SYS 64 256 128
```

When DOS creates a RAM disk, it automatically assigns the next available drive name to it. For example, if your computer has one hard disk named C:, the RAM disk is automatically named D:. If your computer has hard drives C:, D:, E:, F:, and G:, the RAM disk is automatically named H:.

Now, suppose that you want to create a 256KB RAM disk in conventional RAM. If you are using MS-DOS and RAMDRIVE.SYS is stored on the \DOS directory of drive C:, you must add the following command to your CONFIG.SYS file:

```
DEVICE=C:\DOS\RAMDRIVE.SYS 256
```

If you are using MS-DOS and VDISK.SYS is stored on the root directory, you must add this command to the CONFIG.SYS file:

```
DEVICE=C:\VDISK.SYS 256
```

NOTE: The exact information that appears on your screen depends on your version of DOS and other factors.

After you modify the CONFIG.SYS file, DOS automatically creates the RAM disk each time you start your computer in the future or after you reboot. Information about the RAM disk appears on your screen during the bootup procedure, as follows:

```
Microsoft RAMDrive version 3.05 virtual disk H:
        Disk size Sector size adjusted
        Directory entries adjusted
        Buffer size: 256k
        Sector size: 512 bytes
        Allocation unit: 1 sectors
        Directory entries: 64
```

In this case, DOS named the RAM disk D: and gave it a 256KB storage capacity. DOS used its internal default values for the sector size and directory entries, because you omitted values for these parameters in the DEVICE command in the CONFIG.SYS file. Each sector is 512 bytes, and you can store a maximum of 64 files on the RAM disk.

From now on, you can use the RAM disk exactly as you would any other disk drive. (However, don't forget that everything is erased from the RAM disk as soon as you turn off the computer.) If you are using the DOS Shell, you'll notice that the drive name is included in the Drives Area of the File System, with a special RAM icon in the drives area.

Assume that your computer has one physical hard disk named C: and one RAM disk named D:. You can switch to the RAM disk from either the DOS Shell File System or from the command prompt by entering D: (as in this example). If you were to enter the command CHKDSK D: to check the RAM disk, your screen would show something like the following:

```
Volume MS-RAMDRIVE created 6-06-91 12:00a

    258560 bytes total disk space
       512 bytes in 1 directories
    258048 bytes available on disk

       512 bytes in each allocation unit
       505 total allocation units on disk
       504 available allocation units on disk

    655360 total bytes memory
    279424 bytes free
```

As you can see, the RAM disk has about 256KB of storage space available. Actually, it has a little less—256KB is actually 262,144 (256 * 1024) bytes. However, some of the RAM disk sectors are formatted as the boot record, FAT, and directory area, and these occupy some of the disk space. DOS automatically adds the disk volume label, MS-RAMDRIVE in this example, when the RAM disk is created.

Notice that the CHKDSK display shows only 279,424 bytes of memory (RAM) available. That's because DOS and your TSR programs occupy memory and also because a large part of RAM is now dedicated to the RAM disk, as shown in Figure 17.8.

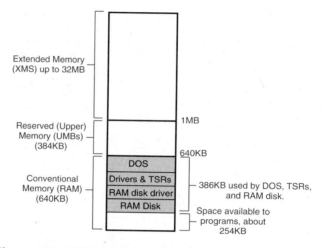

Figure 17.8. A RAM disk installed in conventional memory.

Installing a RAM Disk in Extended Memory

If your computer has extended memory, you should use that rather than conventional RAM for your RAM disk. Doing so saves precious conventional memory for running programs and generally lets you create much larger RAM disks (since you're likely to have more than 640K of extended memory). As mentioned earlier, you can easily determine how much extended memory is available by entering the MEM command.

> NOTE: To convert megabytes to kilobytes, multiply by 1024. For example, the maximum size of a RAM disk when 4MB of extended memory is available is 4,096K (4 * 1024).

Before you can use extended memory for a RAM disk, the extended memory must be placed under the control of an extended memory driver. In DOS 5 (and machines that run Windows 3), this is easily accomplished using the HIMEM.SYS driver. The command that loads HIMEM.SYS (e.g. DEVICE=C:\DOS\HIMEM.SYS in your CONFIG.SYS file) must come before the command that loads the RAM disk device driver.

To use extended memory for your RAM disk, activate the previously described VDISK.SYS or RAMDRIVE.SYS device driver in your CONFIG.SYS file, but follow the command with the /E (for Extended memory) switch. For example, to use MS-DOS to create a 1MB RAM disk with 512 byte sectors in extended memory, add the following command to your CONFIG.SYS file:

```
DEVICE=C:\DOS\RAMDRIVE.SYS 1024 512 /E
```

Note that the command assumes that the device driver is stored on the C:\DOS drive and directory. If your device driver is stored elsewhere, change C:\DOS\ to reflect the actual location of RAMDRIVE.SYS (or VDISK.SYS).

After you add the appropriate command to your CONFIG.SYS file, the RAM disk is automatically installed in extended memory every time you start your computer. For example, suppose that your computer has one hard disk named C:. After you add the appropriate DEVICE= command to your CONFIG.SYS file and boot up, your RAM disk is set up as drive D:. When you enter the following command at the command prompt:

```
CHKDSK D:
```

your screen displays information using the following general format:

```
volume MS-RAMDRIVE created 6-06-91 12:00a

1042944 bytes total disk space
    512 bytes in 1 directories
1042432 bytes available on disk

    512 bytes in each allocation unit
   2037 total allocation units on disk
   2036 available allocation units on disk

 655360 total bytes memory
 603728 bytes free
```

In this example, the RAM disk has 1,042,944 bytes of storage space available. The boot record, FAT, and directory sectors of the RAM disk occupy 512 bytes in one directory, leaving 1,042,432 bytes for storage. Each sector (allocation unit) holds 512 bytes. Conventional RAM memory still has 603,728 bytes free, because the RAM disk is in extended memory.

If you are using DOS 4 or 5, you could enter the MEM command to check available memory after installing this RAM disk in extended memory. You would notice that the "bytes available XMS memory" measurement is now smaller, because the RAM disk now uses some of that previously available extended memory.

Installing a RAM Disk in Expanded Memory

> NOTE: DOS 5 includes the EMM386.EXE program, which lets 386 and 486 computers *emulate* expanded memory within the extended memory created by HIMEM.SYS.

If your computer has expanded rather than extended memory, you can use all or a portion of the expanded memory for a RAM disk. Keep in mind, however, that programs that use (or require) expanded memory will not be able to access that portion of expanded memory that you've designated for a RAM disk.

To convert expanded memory to a RAM disk, your CONFIG.SYS file must first install and activate the expanded memory, as discussed earlier in this chapter. If the commands in the CONFIG.SYS file for installing expanded memory are not executed before the DEVICE=RAMDRIVE.SYS command used to install RAM disk, an error will occur, and the RAM disk will not be installed.

The exact command syntax required for installing a RAM disk in expanded memory depends on your version of DOS and whether or not you are using the DOS device driver, or a particular computer manufacturer's device driver, to install the RAM disk.

If you are using DOS 4 or 5, and its VDISK.SYS device driver, you use the /X switch in the DEVICE=VDISK.SYS command to install the RAM disk in expanded memory. If you are using MS-DOS 3.2 or later, and the RAMDRIVE.SYS device driver, you use the /A switch in the DEVICE=RAMDRIVE.SYS command.

Because different expanded memory boards use difference drivers, it's impossible to give a universally applicable example of using expanded memory for a RAM disk. Suppose, however, that you have a 2MB expanded memory adapter in your computer, and the command DEVICE=C:\DOS\MYEMS.EXE in your CONFIG.SYS file activates that expanded memory. To use 1MB of that expanded memory as a RAM drive, you could need to add this command to your CONFIG.SYS file (below the command that activates expanded memory):

```
DEVICE = C:\DOS\RAMDRIVE.SYS 1024 /A
```

where 1024 is the size of the RAM drive (1MB) and /A specifies expanded rather than conventional memory.

Using Upper Memory with RAMDrive

Even if you use extended or expanded memory for your RAM disk, the RAM disk device driver (which occupies about 1.2K of memory) remain in conventional memory (RAM). If you're using DOS 5, a 386 or 486 computer, and upper memory blocks (discussed earlier in this chapter), you can move this driver into upper memory, using the DEVICEHIGH command.

Just use the DEVICEHIGH command rather than the DEVICE command to load the RAM drive and be sure all the commands for activating extended and upper memory precede the command for installing the RAM disk, as in the following example, which installs a 1MB (1024K) RAM disk in extended memory (due to /E), and puts the 1.2K driver for the RAM disk in upper rather than conventional memory:

```
****************************** CONFIG.SYS
DEVICE=C:\DOS\HIMEM.SYS
DOS=HIGH,UMB
DEVICE=C:\DOS\EMM386.EXE NOEMS
DEVICEHIGH = C:\DOS\RAMDRIVE.SYS 1024 /E
```

If you were to enter a MEM /C command and reboot after making this change to your CONFIG.SYS file, you would see that neither the RAM disk nor the device driver for the RAM disk occupies any conventional memory.

Figure 17.9 shows this "ideal" placement of DOS, the HMA (High Memory Area), drivers, TSRs, and the RAM disk driver in UMBs (upper memory blocks) and the RAM disk itself in extended memory. Only some "residual" DOS files remain near the top of conventional memory (indicated by shading near the 640K mark). If you compare this figure to Figure 17.8, you can see the substantial savings in conventional memory.

Installing Multiple RAM Disks

If you want to create multiple RAM disks—for example drives D:, E:, and F:—include multiple DEVICE=RAMDRIVE.SYS (or VDISK.SYS) commands in your CONFIG.SYS file. DOS automatically assigns the next available drive name to each RAM disk.

However, you should also include a LASTDRIVE command in your CONFIG.SYS file to prepare DOS for the multiple virtual drives. Insert the LASTDRIVE command in your CONFIG.SYS file using the general syntax

```
LASTDRIVE=drive letter
```

in which *drive letter* is the name (without the colon) of the last
virtual drive. For example, if your computer has a hard disk named C:,
and you want to add three 512KB RAM disks in 1.5MB of extended
memory, include the following commands in your CONFIG.SYS file:

```
LASTDRIVE=F
DEVICE=C:\DOS\RAMDRIVE.SYS 512 /E
DEVICE=C:\DOS\RAMDRIVE.SYS 512 /E
DEVICE=C:\DOS\RAMDRIVE.SYS 512 /E
```

DOS automatically assigns these drives the names D:, E:, and F:.

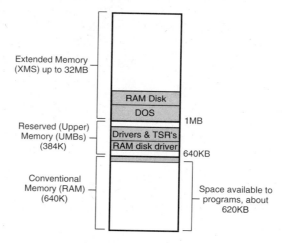

Figure 17.9. A RAM drive using no conventional memory.

The first command prepares DOS to support drives named A:, B:,
C:, D:, E:, and F:. The first DEVICE command sets up a 512KB hard disk,
named D: (because the name C: is already assigned to the physical hard
disk). The second DEVICE command automatically assigns the name E:
to the 512KB RAM disk. The third DEVICE command assigns the name
F: to the last 512KB RAM disk.

Using a RAM Disk Safely

As mentioned earlier, a major disadvantage of using a RAM disk is that
as soon as you turn off the computer, all data stored on the RAM disk
is immediately erased. A virtual disk acts so much like a physical disk
drive that you can very easily forget this important fact and lose all your
data.

One of the best applications for a RAM disk is to use it only for
temporary files that many programs create and erase automatically.
You don't care about losing these files when you turn off the computer

because they are only useful in the current session anyway. In fact, you may not even be aware of their existence, because programs that use temporary files typically create and erase them "behind the scenes."

Many modern programs check the DOS environment for a variable named TEMP, which tells them what drive and directory to use to store temporary files. Once your CONFIG.SYS file contains the command(s) required to activate a RAM disk, you can alter your AUTOEXEC.BAT file to 1) create a directory on the RAM disk and 2) set the TEMP variable to that drive and directory.

For example, suppose that you've used whatever technique works for you to create a RAM disk, and that the RAM disk is drive D:. To use D: for temporary files, you would add these commands to your AUTOEXEC.BAT (not CONFIG.SYS) file:

```
MD D:\TEMPFILS
SET TEMP=D:\TEMPFILS
```

The first command creates a directory named TEMPFILS on drive D: (the RAM disk in this example). The advantage to creating a directory on the RAM drive is that the root directory of a RAM disk can only hold a limited number of files (usually 64), whereas a subdirectory below the root can hold any number of files.

The command SET TEMP=D:\TEMPFILS tells any program that searches the environment for the TEMP variable name to use the RAM disk for temporary files. Hence, that program will be able to create and manage temporary files 10 to 20 times faster than it could when using the physical drive.

Using a Disk Cache to Speed Performance

While a RAM disk is great for temporary files and some disk-intensive operations, most of your work will still involve interacting directly with your actual disk drives. Hence, you want to be sure your disks are always running at top speed to ensure maximum overall performance.

One way to maximize the speed of a disk drive is through a disk *cache* (pronounced *cash*) to speed up processes that involve disk Input/Output (I/O). These processes include all operations that read data from the disk into RAM (Input) and write data from RAM to the disk (Output). The cache operates as an intermediary between the disk and RAM.

When a program requests data from the disk, DOS stores the data in the cache and then sends copies to the program (in RAM). When the program changes the data and returns it to the disk, DOS stores only the modified data in the cache. Although the program might change several items of data and send them to the disk for safe keeping, DOS actually stores these changes in the cache.

When the program finishes making changes to the data or the cache becomes filled, DOS copies all the modified data in the cache to the disk for safe storage. This single transfer is much more efficient than writing small chunks of modified data to the disk on a piecemeal basis (see Figure 17.10).

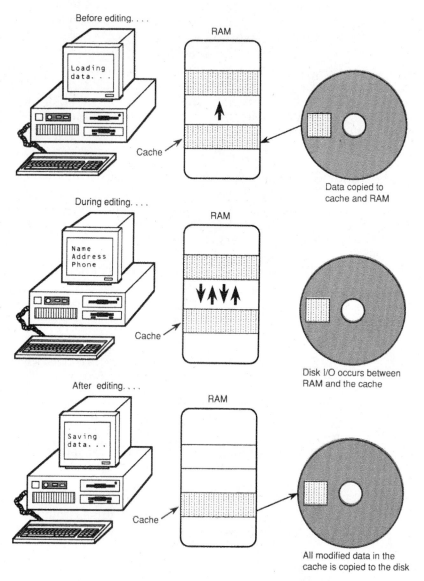

Before editing. . . .

RAM

Loading data. . .

Cache

Data copied to cache and RAM

During editing. . . .

RAM

Name
Address
Phone

Cache

Disk I/O occurs between RAM and the cache

After editing. . . .

RAM

Saving data. . .

Cache

All modified data in the cache is copied to the disk

Figure 17.10. A disk cache acts as an intermediary between RAM and a disk.

Sophisticated caching programs also keep track of how often data in the cache is being used. When more space is needed in the cache to store new data, the least used data is saved to disk and discarded from the cache to make room. This method makes the cache more efficient, because the cache tends to maintain data that is being modified frequently rather than only occasionally.

Some caching programs can also "look ahead" when a program requests data from the disk, reading a little more data than the program requests in anticipation that the program will soon request the additional data. Later, if the program requests the additional data, it's already in the cache and DOS doesn't need to access the disk.

The only disadvantage to a disk cache is that it is usually stored in RAM, thereby consuming some of your valuable memory. You might be able to use extended or expanded memory for your disk cache, but this is dependent on your version of DOS and your specific disk cache program.

Some computers provide their own disk cache programs, which are separate from DOS. For example, the IBM PS/2 Models 50 through 80 provide a disk cache program named IBMCACHE. Many COMPAQ computers provide a program named CACHE to manage disk caching. Refer to the owner's manual, or to the DOS manual, that came with your computer for information about using its unique disk-caching system.

DOS 5 (and Windows 3) provide the versatile SMARTDrive disk cache in extended, expanded, or reserved memory without wasting conventional memory.

Using the SMARTDrive Disk Cache

NOTE: If you are using both Windows and DOS 5, be sure you install the DOS 5 version of SMARTDRV.SYS ... not the Windows version.

The SMARTDrive disk cache was originally developed for use with Microsoft Windows. Now, Microsoft has included it in the DOS 5 package. To use SMARTDrive, your computer must have extended or expanded memory and, of course, a hard disk. Consider using SMARTDrive if your system has 512KB or more of free extended memory or 256KB or more of free expanded memory. Whether you should install this cache on your system also depends on the type of computing you do.

Remember, a disk-caching program speeds the reading of data from your hard disk. If you use programs that perform many disk operations (databases, for example, which are notorious for their frequent disk reads), SMARTDrive will significantly increase the performance of your system. If, however, you use your computer primarily as a word processor or for running entertainment programs, a disk cache will be of little or no value.

SMARTDrive works equally well in either extended or expanded memory. If your system includes both types of memory, use whichever has the most available memory. However, do not use SMARTDrive if you are already using another disk cache; this wastes memory and also produces a cache-within-a-cache situation, which may actually slow down disk operations! Disable your original cache before you install SMARTDrive.

NOTE: See the SMARTDRV.SYS entry in Appendix B for a complete discussion of the switches and usage of this command.

Activating SMARTDrive

To install the basic SMARTDrive disk cache in extended memory, add the following command in your CONFIG.SYS file:

```
DEVICE=C:\DOS\SMARTDRV.SYS
```

By default, SMARTDrive is installed in extended memory. To install the cache in expanded memory, add the /A switch to the previous command, as follows:

```
DEVICE=C:\DOS\SMARTDRV.SYS /A
```

In either case, be sure that the command that activates extended or expanded memory precedes the command that loads SMARTDRV.SYS in the CONFIG.SYS file.

If you do not specify a size for the cache in your DEVICE= command, SMARTDrive uses a default cache size of 256KB. Of course if your system doesn't have that much extended or expanded memory, SMARTDrive simply uses whatever you have.

The size of the cache (which holds your data in RAM) directly affects the efficiency of the program. The more information that SMARTDrive can access from RAM (rather than from the slow mechanical disk drive), the more efficient it will be. Although, you can actually specify a cache-size of 128KB, the minimum *effective* cache size is probably about 512KB. Microsoft recommends that the *optimum* SMARTDrive cache is 2MB. Note that unless you are working with huge data files, very large caches (from 2MB to 8MB) can actually degrade your system's performance!

If you have 2 megabytes of expanded memory, you can establish a large SMARTDrive disk cache with the following command in your CONFIG.SYS file:

```
DEVICE=C:\DOS\SMARTDRV.SYS 2048 /A
```

Note that the size follows the file name and must be expressed in kilobytes. To install this 2MB cache in extended memory, simply omit the /A switch; SMARTDrive installs itself in extended memory by default.

Putting SMARTDRV.SYS in Upper Memory

Even though the SMARTDrive cache is placed in extended (or expanded) memory, the driver for the cache is still placed in conventional memory, occupying about 21K.

If you are using a 386 or 486 computer, DOS 5, and upper memory blocks, you can put that driver into upper memory by using DEVICEHIGH rather than the DEVICE command to install SMARTDrive, as in the sample CONFIG.SYS commands shown below:

```
REM*************************** Sample
CONFIG.SYS

DEVICE = C:\HIMEM.SYS
DOS = HIGH,UMB
DEVICE = C:\DOS\EMM386.EXE NOEMS
DEVICEHIGH=C:\DOS\SMARTDRV.SYS 1024
```

In the last line, a 1MB (1024K) disk cache is placed in extended memory (automatically, since HIMEM.SYS has already activated extended memory), and the 21K driver is placed in upper memory.

Warnings About SMARTDrive

If you have partitioned your hard disk with some third-party disk management programs (most notably ONTRACK's Disk Manager and the SPEEDSTOR disk manager), the SMARTDrive program will refuse to load. Instead, as your system boots, the following message will appear on your screen:

```
Microsoft SMARTDrive Disk Cache version 3.11
SMARTDrive: Incompatible disk partition detected.
```

If you later type MEM /P or MEM /C, you will see that the SMARTDrive cache was not installed in memory.

The previously mentioned third-party disk management programs include routines that let hard disks work with computers that have outdated BIOs and that let users create larger partitions than earlier versions of DOS permitted. SMARTDrive is incompatible with these routines and can corrupt data if used in conjunction with them. As a safety feature, Microsoft by default won't permit SMARTDrive to work with these disk managers.

However, if you are using a newer computer with a recent BIOS and you have not created any partitions larger than 32MB, SMARTDrive will probably work correctly on your system. You may need to add the /P (which stands for "partition") switch to the end of the DEVICE = command for installing SMARTDrive. This switch forces SMARTDrive to run with all disk management programs.

Because you risk losing data by forcing SMARTDrive to operate with potentially incompatible programs, be sure you contact the technical support personnel at Microsoft and/or at the makers of your disk management software before you actually use this switch.

Other Ways to Improve Hard Disk Performance

There are a few additional techniques that you can use to get maximum speed and performance from your hard disk. These are described in the sections that follow.

Check Your PATH

One of the most common causes of slow disk response times, particularly when you're trying to run a program, is a PATH statement that forces DOS to look through hundreds or thousands of file name before finding the program you want. For example, suppose that whenever you try to run WordPerfect 5.1 (which is stored on the C:\WP51 directory), there seems to be an extremely long delay before the program starts.

> NOTE: Chapter 11 and Appendix B also discuss the PATH command.

Suppose that you then check the PATH statement in your AUTOEXEC.BAT file and find something like

```
PATH = C:\DOS;D:\UTILS;E:\WINDOWS;E:\TOOLBOOK;C:\WP51
```

Part of the delay in running in WordPerfect, in this case, may be the time required to search the current directory and every directory that precedes C:\WP51 in the PATH statement. If you changed that PATH statement to

```
PATH = C:\DOS;C:\WP51;D:\UTILS;E:\WINDOWS;E:\TOOLBOOK
```

DOS would be able to find the WordPerfect much more quickly.

The sheer number of files on a directory can also affect performance. For example, referring to the PATH statement above, if both the C:\DOS and C:\WP51 directories contain 1,000 files each, that's up to 2,000 file names that need to be searched when DOS is looking for the WordPerfect program.

Deleting any unnecessary files, or moving some files to other subdirectories to minimize the number of files in the directories that are listed in the PATH command can also greatly improve performance.

For example, if you moved all the documents, graphics, macros, and other files from your C:\WP51 directory onto subdirectories (for example, C:\WP51\DOCS, C:\WP51\GRAPHICS, C:\WP51\MACROS, and so forth) DOS would no longer need to search through the names of all those files when looking for the WordPerfect program.

Incidentally, WordPerfect and many other programs make it especially easy to store files in this manner, via a "Location of Files" feature that you can use to specify subdirectories for storing various types of files. Check the documentation that came with your particular program to see what it has to offer along these lines.

Setting Up Buffers

NOTE: The BUFFERS command in DOS 4 and 5 provides the look-ahead capabilities but not the frequency-checking of a disk cache.

The BUFFERS command acts a sort of "primitive" disk cache system and is available in most versions of DOS. To use the buffers command, simply add

```
BUFFERS = buffers
```

where *buffers* is a number in the range of 20 to 50 to your CONFIG.SYS file. The best values for *buffers* varies with the size of your hard disk:

Hard Disk Capacity	Value for *buffers*
Less than 40MB	20
40 - 79MB	30
80 - 119MB	40
120MB or more	50

See the BUFFERS entry in Appendix B for information about this command, including the *look-ahead* feature (also called *secondary cache*) available in DOS version 4 and 5.

Using FASTOPEN

The FASTOPEN program, which comes with DOS 5, acts like a cache but is specifically designed for use with programs that regularly open and close large numbers of files, such as database management systems and language compilers.

> NOTE: FASTOPEN can not use extended memory; only conventional or expanded memory.

FASTOPEN uses the basic syntax

```
FASTOPEN drive:[=n] [...] [/X]
```

where *drive:* is the name of the drive to track files on, *n* is the number of files to track, ... represents additional drives and numbers, and /X tells FASTOPEN to use expanded (not extended) memory.

You can use FASTOPEN right at the command prompt. For example, this command tells FASTOPEN to track the names of 40 files on drive C: as they're being open and closed:

```
FASTOPEN c:=40
```

Of course, you can also start FASTOPEN automatically at the beginning of each session by placing the FASTOPEN command in your AUTOEXEC.BAT file. For example, the AUTOEXEC.BAT command below tracks 10 files (each) on drives C:, D:, and E:, using expanded rather than conventional memory:

```
C:\DOS\FASTOPEN.EXE C:=10 D:=10 E:=10 /X
```

Note that in order for the preceding command to work correctly, the CONFIG.SYS file must have already activated expanded (EMS not XMS) memory.

> NOTE: Both FASTOPEN and INSTALL are referenced in Appendix B.

If you have DOS 4 or 5, you can use the INSTALL=command to load FASTOPEN from your CONFIG.SYS file, as in the example

```
INSTALL=C:\DOS\FASTOPEN.EXE C:\20
```

Finally, if you're using DOS 5 with upper memory blocks, you can use LOADHIGH either from the command prompt or in your AUTOEXEC.BAT file to install FASTOPEN in upper memory as in this example:

```
LOADHIGH=C:\DOS\FASTOPEN.EXE C:=10 D:=10 E:=10 F:=10
```

Defragmenting Your Hard Disk

As you erase old files and create new ones, DOS frees and reuses space as it becomes available. As a disk becomes older and fuller, many files may become fragmented, meaning that bits and pieces of a single file are spread throughout the disk rather than in consecutive factors. When this occurs, the drive head must move excessively (as you may actually be able to hear) when you read and write files. The end result is slow disk speed.

To regain speed, you need to defragment the files. DOS does not have much to offer in terms of defragmenting other than the CHKDSK command with the /F switch (see CHKDSK in Appendix F). There are some third-party programs available that offer much better defragmenting capabilities, as discussed under "Increasing Hard Disk Efficiency" in Chapter 18.

Adjusting Your Hard Disk Interleave

Another means of increasing hard disk performance is by adjusting the drive's interleave, which is in essence the ratio of disk revolutions to read/write attempts. You'll need a third-party program to adjust your disk interleave and I can recommend

SpinRite
Gibson Research Corporation
22991 La Cadena
Laguna Hills, CA 92653
(714) 830-2200

Troubleshooting

Using upper memory is a boon to most 386 and 486 computer users but can be tricky. However, some device drivers and memory-resident programs will not run correctly (or at all!) in the upper memory area. This portion of memory has always been off-limits to programs; therefore, some programs might not expect to be running within these addresses.

If a program won't load into upper memory, don't immediately write it off as being incompatible with DOS 5; you might have made a basic installation error instead. If you can't get drivers or programs to load into upper memory, check the following items first:

❏ Be sure your CONFIG.SYS file includes lines similar to the following (in this order):

```
DEVICE=C:\DOS\HIMEM.SYS
DEVICE=C:\DOS\EMM386.EXE NOEMS
DOS=UMB
```

or

```
DEVICE=C:\DOS\HIMEM.SYS
DEVICE=C:\DOS\EMM386.EXE RAM
DOS=HIGH,UMB
```

The HIMEM.SYS line must appear first; DOS= must include the UMB switch; and EMM386.EXE must include either the NOEMS or RAM switch.

❏ Be sure that you use the DEVICEHIGH command in your CONFIG.SYS file to load device drivers into upper memory. Note that HIMEM.SYS and EMM386.EXE cannot be loaded into upper memory; they must already be in effect before you can access the upper memory region.

❏ Be sure that you use the LOADHIGH (or LH) command in your AUTOEXEC.BAT file to load memory-resident programs into upper memory.

If the program you are trying to load into upper memory blocks returns an error message when you reboot your computer, but the computer finishes its startup sequence, you will have to load the driver or TSR in conventional memory. Simply change the appropriate CONFIG.SYS DEVICEHIGH command to DEVICE or delete the LOADHIGH command from your AUTOEXEC.BAT file.

NOTE: A "system disk" is a bootable diskette: the UNINSTALL diskette, the Startup diskette from a floppy installation, or a diskette created by the SYS command.

If your computer locks up when you first reboot after loading a program into upper memory, note the error message that DOS displays on your screen—that will tell you which program or driver is causing the problem. If you want to use that program, you will have to load it into conventional memory. However, now you will not be able to start your computer in the normal way: The balky program in upper memory is preventing your computer from finishing its boot sequence. To correct this, you must boot your system with a "system" disk, edit either CONFIG.SYS or AUTOEXEC.BAT to disable the incompatible program and then reboot your computer.

Because some programs may fail to run in upper memory, the following procedure is the safest way to load your upper memory area:

❏ Before you start, be sure you have already created a bootable system diskette.

❏ Use the MEM /C command to determine how much memory you have available in the upper memory area. Note this figure so that you have a rough idea of how many of your programs you will be able to load into upper memory.

❏ Edit the CONFIG.SYS file and use the DEVICEHIGH command to load your largest device driver into upper memory.

❏ Reboot your system.

❏ If your system successfully loads the driver into upper memory, try to load the next largest driver into upper memory from CONFIG.SYS and reboot. If the driver refuses to load, change the DEVICEHIGH command to DEVICE and then add the next driver. If the driver locks up your system, reboot with a system diskette in drive A, change the offending DEVICEHIGH command to DEVICE, and then try to load another driver into upper memory.

❏ Continue with the preceding procedure until you have installed all the appropriate drivers from CONFIG.SYS.

❏ Edit your AUTOEXEC.BAT file and use the LOADHIGH (LH) command to load your largest TSR into upper memory.

❏ Reboot your system.

❏ Follow the preceding guidelines, testing one program at a time, loading larger programs before smaller programs.

❏ As you load more and more drivers and programs into upper memory, occasionally use the MEM /C command to be sure that you still have free memory available in the upper memory area.

This type of "incremental" loading of the upper memory area—loading and testing one driver or TSR at a time—lets you know immediately which programs will or will not work. You could try to load all your drivers and programs into upper memory in one operation; if they all load and work correctly, you will have saved yourself some time. However, if one or more fail, you should use the previously described procedure to systematically load the upper memory area.

Sometimes a memory-resident program will successfully load into upper memory, but later it will not function correctly. This program might not be able to recognize upper memory addresses or might expect to "see" free memory regions around it. If any of your drivers or TSRs become "flaky" (that is, work for a while, but fail intermittently), remove the appropriate DEVICEHIGH or LOADHIGH commands and then load the program into conventional memory.

Older device drivers might expect to have much of the upper memory area to themselves. (After all, the entire area has been off-limits to general-purpose programs for more than a decade.) If this is the case, you might have to manually lock out part of the upper memory region.

You can restrict certain blocks of upper memory by using one or more switches when you install the EMM386.EXE expanded-memory emulator. For details about using the /X switch to prevent programs from using specific locations in upper memory, see the EMM386.EXE entry in Appendix B.

Windows 3 and UMBs

As of the writing of this book, a couple of potential problems still exist between Windows 3 and DOS 5, as described next.

Windows and Expanded Memory

Windows 3 has its own capability for emulating expanded memory and can do so automatically when a program needs expanded memory. However, if your CONFIG.SYS file contains a NOEMS switch with EMM386

```
DEVICE = C:\DOS\EMM386.EXE NOEMS
```

programs requiring expanded memory in Windows may fail to run.

To fix this, change the line in your CONFIG.SYS file to

```
DEVICE = C:\DOS\EMM386.EXE RAM
```

You'll still be able to use all your DEVICEHIGH and LOADHIGH commands; DOS will set aside 16KB of upper memory for page frame switching with expanded memory.

Windows in Standard Mode

You cannot use Windows 3 in Standard (/S) mode if you use upper memory blocks. For the EMM386.EXE program to remap upper memory so that you can load programs there, it must run in "protected mode." Because Windows Standard Mode must also run in protected mode, a conflict results, and Windows 3.0 will not run. You can, however, run Windows 3.0 in either Real mode or 386 Enhanced mode.

If you have a Windows 3.0 program that must run in Standard mode, you can create an alternate CONFIG.SYS file that does not access upper memory or try to load drivers and program there. This is most easily done by copying and modifying files.

For example, say that your current CONFIG.SYS file does use upper memory, as in the following example:

```
REM ********************* CONFIG.SYS
REM **************** Boot with UMBs.
DEVICE = C:\DOS\HIMEM.SYS
DOS = HIGH,UMB
DEVICE = C:\DOS\EMM386.EXE NOEMS
DEVICEHIGH = (etc.. etc..)
```

Furthermore, suppose that your AUTOEXEC.BAT file also includes some LOADHIGH commands.

First, you could enter these commands to make copies of the files:

```
COPY C:\CONFIG.SYS CONFIG.UMB
COPY C:\CONFIG.SYS CONFIG.WIN
COPY C:\AUTOEXEC.BAT AUTOEXEC.UMB
COPY C:\AUTOEXEC.BAT AUTOEXEC.WIN
```

Next, use EDIT (or whatever) to modify CONFIG.WIN so that it does not turn on upper memory blocks nor contain any DEVICEHIGH commands:

```
REM ********************* CONFIG.WIN
REM **** Boot for WINDOWS /S (n UMBs)
DEVICE = C:\DOS\HIMEM.SYS
DOS = HIGH
DEVICE = (etc.. etc..)
```

Also, use EDIT (or whatever) to remove the LOADHIGH commands from the AUTOEXEC.WIN file. (You need only remove the command LOADHIGH or LH and the blank space to the right, not the entire line that starts with LOADHIGH.)

Next, you could create a batch file named BOOTWIN.BAT, preferably on C:\DOS or some other directory in the PATH, that contains these commands:

```
COPY C:\CONFIG\WIN C:\CONFIG.SYS
COPY C:\AUTOEXEC.WIN C:\AUTOEXEC.BAT
```

> NOTE: If you have a "warm boot" utility that reboots on command, make it the last command in your BOOTWIN.BAT and BOOTUMB.BAT to avoid having to press Ctrl-Alt-Del to reboot.

Create a second batch file named BOOTUMB.BAT, again storing it on some directory in the path, that contains the commands

```
COPY C:\CONFIG.UMB C:\CONFIG.SYS
COPY C:\AUTOEXEC.UMB C:\AUTOEXEC.BAT
```

In the future, if you need to run Windows in Standard mode, first enter the command

```
BOOTWIN
```

at the command prompt. Then when the command prompt reappears, reboot (press Ctrl+Alt+Del). When you want to run DOS or use upper memory blocks, enter this command at the command prompt:

```
BOOTUMB
```

then reboot after the command prompt appears.

Multiple Boot Configurations

The preceding recommendation is a somewhat primitive technique for creating multiple CONFIG.SYS and AUTOEXEC.BAT files on a single computer for differing situations. A more elegant (and perhaps easier) approach to dealing with multiple boot configurations is through a utility that serves that purpose.

For example, you can use BootCon to define any number of CONFIG.SYS and AUTOEXEC.BAT files that you want. Then when you're first booting up your computer, a menu appears listing all the available boot configurations. You just "point-and-shoot" at your choice to load your preferred configuration. Following is information about BootCon:

BootCon
Modular Software Systems
115 W. California Blvd., Suite 113
Pasadena, CA 91105
(818)440-9104

Summary

Extended, expanded, and upper memory blocks offer alternatives to conventional memory with its 640K limitations. You can use RAM disks, caching, and other features to speed up your system by minimizing disk access time. Many of these options are specific to a particular computer, and their features are made available to DOS through the use of device drivers. You might need to refer to the manuals that came with your computer or option board for information about using these features. In summary

- ❏ Extended memory is available on many 80286, 80386, and 80486-based computer systems and is generally activated by the command DEVICE=C:\DOS\HIMEM.SYS in the CONFIG.SYS file.

- ❏ Expanded memory allows DOS to access memory beyond the 640KB RAM limit via a 64KB page frame in the hexadecimal range of C000 to E000.

- ❏ The specific device driver that you use for expanded memory depends on the expanded memory adapter installed in your computer and perhaps on the version of DOS that you are using.

- ❏ The 80386 and 80486 microprocessors can emulate expanded memory using either extended memory or a disk file.

- ❏ Computers that use 80386 and 80486 microprocessors can take advantage of the HIMEM.SYS, DOS=, and EMM386.EXE commands to gain access to "upper memory blocks," an area of memory that was off-limits to DOS users before version 5 (except as a means of accessing expanded memory).

- ❏ The DEVICEHIGH command loads device drivers specified in your CONFIG.SYS file into upper memory, and the LOADHIGH (or LH) command loads memory-resident programs specified in your AUTOEXEC.BAT file into upper memory.

❏ A RAM disk simulates a disk drive in conventional RAM, extended memory, or expanded memory and permits quicker disk operations.

❏ On most computers, the device driver for installing a RAM disk is named RAMDRIVE.SYS or VDISK.SYS.

❏ To use extended memory rather than conventional RAM for a RAM disk, use the /E switch with the VDISK.SYS or RAMDRIVE.SYS device driver. To use expanded memory for a RAM disk, use the /X switch for VDISK.SYS and the /A switch for RAMDRIVE.SYS.

❏ Because files stored on a RAM disk are erased as soon as you turn off the computer, use the safety procedure of creating batch files that automatically copy data from a RAM disk to a physical disk when you exit a program.

❏ Disk caching is a technique that speeds disk I/O by acting as an intermediary between RAM and the disk.

| 5 |

❏ DOS 5 provides a full-featured disk-caching program named SMARTDRV.SYS. Individual computer manufacturers often provide their own disk-caching programs as well.

Solutions to Common Problems

This chapter, the final tutorial section of the book, discusses tips and techniques for using DOS to solve common computer problems. The seemingly unrelated topics in this chapter represent the most commonly asked questions (in my experience) about how to use DOS to effectively handle "real-world" problems. I hope the following sections will save you hours of frustration by helping you solve pesky problems that sometimes arise as you work with your computer.

Remember that Appendix B provides additional technical details about all DOS commands and options.

I hope that these topics cover any questions that you might now have. However, even if you do not have a specific question or unresolved problem at the moment, reading about the solutions to these common problems will better prepare you to resolve them when they arise.

Solving Disk Format Incompatibility Problems

From the gradual extinction of the 8-inch floppy disk in the early 1980s, until 1986 when the IBM PS/2 line of computers emerged, the 5.25-inch diskette was the standard among microcomputers. Since then, many computers, particularly laptops, come equipped with the new 720KB and 1.44MB 3.5-inch drives, thus causing compatibility problems for anyone who must use both types of machines.

Unless you already have a computer that has both 5.25-inch and 3.5-inch drives installed or are willing to pay an outside service to make the transfers, you have only two alternatives to solving the 5.25 versus 3.5-inch incompatibility problem:

❏ If you have you two computers, one with a 5.25-inch drive and one with a 3.5-inch drive, you can solve the problem inexpensively with software.

❏ If you have only one computer and one drive size, you'll need to resort to the most expensive hardware solution of adding another drive.

Each option is discussed in more detail in the following text.

Software Solutions

Suppose that you have a laptop computer that has one or two 3.5-inch disk drives and a desktop computer that uses 5.25-inch diskettes. How do you get data from one machine to the other? Well, because you can easily transport the laptop, merely connect it to the desktop computer with a cable and use software to transfer data from a program on one machine to a similar program on the other machine.

Several software companies offer programs that make the laptop-to-desktop (and vice versa) transfers quick, easy, and uncomplicated. Some (although not all) of the programs also include the necessary cable. The following list includes the names of some of these programs and the companies that offer them. Your computer or software dealer can offer more alternatives.

The Brooklyn Bridge
White Crane Systems
6889 Peachtree Industrial Blvd., #151
Norcross, GA 30092
(404) 394-3119

Fastwire II
Rupp Brothers
P.O. Drawer J
Lenox Hill Station
New York, NY 10021

Lap-Link Plus
Traveling Software, Inc.
18702 North Creek Pkwy.
Bothell, WA 98011
(206) 483-8088

Paranet Turbo
Nicat Marketing Corp.
207-788 Beatty St.
Vancouver, B.C.
Canada V68 2M1
(604) 681-3421

5.25-Inch High-Density/Low-Density Conversions

All disk drives can read diskettes that are the appropriate size and the same or lower density. For example, a 1.2MB high-density disk drive can read both 1.2MB 5.25-inch diskettes and 360KB 5.25-inch diskettes. A 360KB 5.25-inch drive can read 360KB diskettes but not the higher density 1.2MB diskettes.

Similarly, a 1.44MB 3.5-inch diskette can read both 720KB 3.5-inch diskettes and 1.44MB 3.5-inch diskettes. However, a 720KB 3.5-inch diskette drive cannot read a higher-density 1.44MB 3.5-inch diskette.

DOS also allows you to format diskettes that can be used in the same types of drives or in those of lower density. For example, suppose that your desktop computer uses 1.44MB 3.5-inch drives, but your laptop uses 720KB 3.5-inch diskettes drives. How would you format a diskette and copy files to it so that you could use it with your laptop?

One solution is to use the laptop to format a 720KB diskette and then to copy files from the desktop computer hard disk to that diskette.

An alternative solution, if your laptop is not available, is merely to tell DOS to format the blank 3.5-inch diskette in the 1.44MB drive for use in a 720KB drive. Using DOS 4 or 5, the command would be `FORMAT B: /F:720`. (See the FORMAT entry in Appendix B for other solutions.) Then COPY the files that you need from your hard disk to the 720KB diskette in drive A:. Your laptop will have no problem using this diskette and the copied files.

The same basic solution can be used with most 5.25-inch diskettes. To format a disk for use in a 360KB drive, using a high-capacity 1.2MB drive, you can use the /F:360 switch with the FORMAT command (in DOS 4 or 5) or the /4 switch with the FORMAT command (in DOS 3). Again, refer to the FORMAT command in Appendix B if necessary.

The one exception to the use of the /F:360 and /4 switches is the IBM PC AT computer. With the AT, you can still use the `FORMAT A:` `/F:360` or `FORMAT A:` `/4` command to format the disk in drive A: as a 360KB diskette, but as soon as you copy a file onto that diskette, it is no longer readable in a 360KB drive!

This problem has caused much frenzied hair-pulling among IBM AT users who need to share data on computers with 360KB drives. Fortunately, there is a fairly inexpensive software solution to this problem. A program named COPY AT2PC converts files saved in the IBM AT's high-density format to low-density format so that they can be read in low-density drives. For more information, contact the following company, or ask your computer or software dealer for other alternatives:

COPY AT2PC
Microbridge Computers International
655 Sky Way #125
San Carlos, CA 94070
(800) 523-8777

Hardware Solutions

You cannot reconcile the incompatibility of 5.25-inch and 3.5-inch diskettes if you have access to only one computer with only one type of drive. In this case, you must install a drive for each diskette size that you want to use. This solution is considerably more expensive than the software solutions mentioned previously, but it might be the only alternative in some situations.

If there is room in your computer's main unit for an additional floppy disk drive, either above, below, or beside existing drives, you may be able to add another *internal* drive. If there is not room for another floppy drive in the main system unit, you may still be able to add an *external* floppy disk drive. Which solution is best for your computer depends on your computer's current configuration and power supply. For advice, you'll need to consult a qualified computer technician who is familiar with your computer.

Regardless of how you configure the multiple floppy drives on your computer, always remember the following two tips:

❏ A computer that contains a hard disk, one 1.44MB 3.5-inch drive, and one 1.2MB 5.25-inch drive (and the previously mentioned COPY AT2PC program if you have an IBM AT) provides total accessibility to all diskette sizes and densities.

❏ If you decide to install your own extra disk drive, follow the manufacturer's instructions carefully. If the manufacturer does not supply a specific device driver for activating the new drive, see the DRIVER.SYS entry (the DOS device driver for external drives) in Appendix B.

Computer dealers, manufacturers, and service technicians are good sources for helping you determine which solution is best for you. If you specifically want to add a 3.5-inch disk drive to your existing 5.25-inch drive system, you might want to examine the following products:

Manzana Third Internal Plus
Manzana Host Powered Plus
Manzana Microsystems Inc.
7334 Hollister Ave. Suite I
P.O. Box 2117
Goleta, CA 93118
(805) 968-1387

PC Connection 3.5-inch Internal Drive
PC Connection
6 Mill St.
Marlow, NH 03456
(603) 446-3383

Sysgen Bridge-File 3.5-inch Systems
Sysgen, Inc.
556 Gilbralter Dr.
Milpitas, CA 95035
(800) 821-2151

Solving Data Incompatibility Problems

Different software products use incompatible formats for storing their data; the reason this occurs is that each product uses the most efficient storage technique for its own internal program structure. However, there are many situations in which you might want to use data from one application program with a different program. For example, you might want to use Lotus 1-2-3 to print a graph from information stored in a dBASE IV database.

Basically, whenever you want to import or export data from spreadsheet or database management programs, you can usually find a way to do so either directly or by using ASCII text files as an intermediary format. For example, dBASE III PLUS can import data from and export data to Lotus 1-2-3. Similarly, Lotus 1-2-3 can import and export dBASE III PLUS data. For information regarding data transfers between applications, you should refer to the documentation that came with the application programs (not a DOS book or manual).

In a few cases, you might not be able to directly import or export data. However, virtually all software products are capable of importing and exporting DOS text files (or ASCII text files). Some products also let you decide whether you want to use *delimited* format or *fixed-length* format for the text file. In virtually all cases, the *delimited* format is much easier to work with. (But check your program's user manual for specific advice.)

For example, suppose that you want to export data from your old "GoodBase" program to dBASE IV, but GoodBase has no capability to export to dBASE IV. If GoodBase can export ASCII text files (and nearly every product can), use that capability to create an ASCII file that contains your data. Then run dBASE IV and import the data from the ASCII text file. (To continue this example, you need to refer to the dBASE IV documentation for additional information.)

Unfortunately, importing and exporting data among word processing programs is a bit more complicated, because each uses a very different method for storing formatting codes for printer features such as underlining, boldface, and so on.

Some word processors offer programs that allow you to import documents from and export documents to other word processing programs. For example, the WordPerfect word processor comes with a program named CONVERT that translates the codes in documents created on several other word processors into WordPerfect format. Similarly, the WordPerfect CONVERT program can also translate WordPerfect documents into other formats (including ASCII text).

However, if you don't own WordPerfect or you need to perform other types of transfers with word processing programs, you need additional help. For example, suppose that you use only the WordStar program, but you need to send your document to a company that requires WordPerfect (or DisplayWrite or Microsoft Word or other) format.

Several independent software companies offer solutions to this problem. Following is a list of some of these products and the companies that manufacture them. Be sure to determine whether or not a specific program supports the word processing formats you require. Your computer or software dealer might be able to provide additional alternatives.

R-Doc/X
Advanced Computer Innovations
30 Burncoat Way
Pittsford, NY 14534-2216
(716) 383-1939

Software Bridge
Systems Compatibility Corp.
401 North Wabash #600
Chicago, IL 60611
(800) 333-1359

Word for Word
Design Software Inc.
1275 West Roosevelt Rd.
West Chicago, IL 60185
(312) 231-4540

Using Older Programs with Newer Computers

> NOTE: In some cases, you can also use the simpler APPEND command (discussed in a later section) to solve problems in running programs.

Some very old ("ancient" in terms of computer age) DOS programs will not run under later versions of DOS. This is particularly true of programs that were designed to run under Version 1 of DOS, which was created for the first IBM PC.

You might be able to run these older programs under current versions of DOS by experimenting with several DOS commands designed to handle this situation. In particular, review the entries in Appendix B for the following commands:

ASSIGN   Reroutes program requests to a different disk drive. For example, use ASSIGN to use a program that "insists" on reading and writing data on drive B: (even if you have no drive B:).

FCBS	Tells DOS to use the Version 1 File Control Block system of managing files rather than the "file handles" approach used by later versions of DOS. Use this command when DOS displays the error message `FCB unavailable`.
JOIN	Tells DOS to treat a disk drive as though it were a directory for a program on another drive.
STACKS	Tells DOS to allocate more *stacks* than normal (the default is 9). Use this when DOS displays the error message `Fatal: Internal Stack Failure, System Halted.`
SUBST	Forces DOS to access a subdirectory as though it were a separate disk drive. Use this command when running DOS Version 1 programs on a hard disk subdirectory rather than on a floppy disk.

Using the DOS commands in this list can be risky because these commands "trick" DOS into actions it would not normally perform; therefore, treat them with the utmost caution. Use these commands only when you have no alternative (and heed the warnings listed in Appendix B). You should also consult the DOS manual that came with your computer for additional information about these easily misused commands.

Using Programs from Other Computers

If you import programs (not data) to your DOS computer from an incompatible computer, such as a Macintosh or a UNIX-based micro-computer, do not expect to use these programs with DOS. All application programs are designed for use with a specific operating system and microprocessor. No amount of tinkering or translation will make your Macintosh or UNIX program run under DOS.

If you want to use a specific program, such as Microsoft Excel, on both your PC and your Macintosh, you must purchase two separate copies of that program: Microsoft Excel and Microsoft Excel for the Mac. You can then exchange Excel-created *data* between your PC and Macintosh, using special hardware and transfer programs. However, the programs themselves can run only under the operating system they were designed for.

Running Older Programs with DOS 5

Some programs designed to run with earlier versions of DOS may not be able to run properly when DOS 5 is installed. For this reason, the SETVER command is included with DOS 5, which "fools" such programs into thinking that an earlier version of DOS is running. For more information, see SETVER in Appendix B.

Similarly, some older programs cannot run in the extra memory space that DOS 5 offers. Such programs often return the message `Packed File Corrupt` when you try to run them in DOS 5. Refer to the LOADFIX command in Appendix B if you have this problem when using DOS 5.

What to Do When Programs Cannot Find Their Overlays

Most (although not all) application programs are designed to be easily accessed from a hard disk; these programs can be activated from any drive or directory as long as the application's home directory is included in the current PATH setting. However, there is no guarantee that this procedure will work as expected, especially if you use a directory name other than that recommended by the manufacturer of the program.

For example, suppose that you use an early version of WordStar (Version 4) as your word processing program, and you install it on a directory named \EDITOR rather than the manufacturer's recommended directory \WS4. If you include the \EDITOR directory in your PATH command, DOS can always find the main WordStar program, WS.EXE, in the \EDITOR directory.

However, WordStar will search only the current directory and the (nonexistent) \WS4 directory for its overlay files (such as WSMSGS.OVR). If your current directory is not \EDITOR, when you enter the WS command, WordStar appears to get started, but then the following error messages appear on the screen:

```
Cannot find overlay C:WSSPELL.OVR
Cannot find messages C:WSSPELL.OVR
```

Because WordStar can't find its overlay (.OVR) files in either the current (nonexistent) \WS4 directory, it "bails out" and returns control to DOS.

The PATH command tells DOS to search the \EDITOR directory, so why can't WordStar find these overlay files? The answer to this question is that PATH searches only for files with the .BAT, .COM, and .EXE extensions. The overlay files for which WordStar is searching have the extension .OVR and therefore cannot be detected by the DOS PATH command. This is not a "bug" of any kind; it's simply the way DOS and WordStar (Version 4) operate.

Versions 3.3 and later of DOS offer a solution to this problem—the APPEND command. APPEND searches directories for all files except those with the .BAT, .COM, or .EXE extension. Therefore, the solution to the previous problem is a simple one. First, keep the \EDITOR directory in the current PATH setting so that DOS searches the \EDITOR directory for WordStar's main program WS.EXE. However, also list the \EDITOR directory in an APPEND command so that DOS searches the \EDITOR directory for the required overlay (.OVR) files.

> NOTE: See Chapter 10 if you need help editing your AUTOEXEC.BAT file.

All of the problems in this WordStar example can be resolved by adding these two commands to your AUTOEXEC.BAT file (assuming that all of the WordStar files are stored on a directory named \EDITOR on hard disk drive C:):

```
PATH C:\EDITOR
APPEND C:\EDITOR
```

After DOS receives these commands, you can access the WordStar program from any directory. The PATH command tells DOS to search the \EDITOR directory for the main program (WS.EXE, in this example). The APPEND command tells DOS to search the \EDITOR directory for any other files (for example, WSSPELL.OVR and WSMSGS.OVR) that WordStar requires.

For more details about using the APPEND command effectively, see the APPEND reference in Appendix B. If you are not already familiar with the PATH command, see Chapter 11 first; then study the PATH entry in Appendix B to gain a thorough understanding of this important DOS command.

Increasing Hard Disk Efficiency

As a hard disk becomes older and more packed with programs and data, you might notice a decrease in the speed at which it accesses files. A large part of this loss of efficiency is caused by *file fragmentation*, in which portions of files are scattered throughout the disk by the repeated saving, modifying, and erasing of files (as discussed in Chapter 17).

> NOTE: Another benefit of defragmenting files is that it reduces wear and tear on the mechanism that moves the drive head.

When a file is severely fragmented, the drive head must move around the disk a great deal to read the many scattered sectors that constitute the complete file. When this happens, you will notice that the hard disk drive in-use light remains on for a long time when reading the file. (You might also hear the drive head mechanism grinding away within the unit as it searches the disk for stray sectors.)

There are several optional file *defragmenting* programs available that can help you to rearrange your hard disk so that files are stored in contiguous sectors rather than in fragments. These programs rearrange the files so that each is stored in a contiguous series of sectors and the drive head doesn't need to search throughout the disk to read a file.

Following is a list of popular defragmenting programs, including names and addresses of their manufacturers. Your computer salesman or software dealer can also provide you with alternative programs.

Disk Optimizer
SoftLogic Solutions, Inc.
1 Perimiter Rd.
Manchester, NH 03103
(800) 272-9900

FastTrax
Bridgeway Publishing Co.
2165 East Francisco Blvd., Suite A1
San Rafael, CA 94912
(415) 485-0948

Mace Utilities
Paul Mace Software
123 N. First St.
Ashland, OR 97520
(800) 523-0258

Norton Utilities 5.0
Peter Norton Computing
10201 Torre Ave.
Cupertino, CA 95014
(213) 453-2361

PC Tools Deluxe
Central Point Software
15220 N. W. Greenbrier Pwky. #200
Beaverton, OR 97006
(503) 690-8090

Warnings About Using Disk Defragmenting Programs

Before you use a defragmenting program on your hard disk, pay heed
to the following advice:

❏ Backup your entire hard disk—using the DOS COPY, XCOPY,
or BACKUP commands—just in case something goes wrong.

❏ If your hard disk contains any copy-protected programs, such
as earlier versions of Lotus 1-2-3, Symphony, or dBASE III,
"uninstall" them before you use the defragmenting program.

If you don't follow the second item of advice before defragmenting
your hard disk, you probably will no longer be able to use the copy-
protected program on your hard disk without inserting the "key"
diskette in drive A:.

Alternatives to Defragmenting

Remember that file fragmentation is not the only cause of inefficient
hard disk accessing, nor is it the only solution. If your PATH command
forces DOS to search directories that contain many files, extensive file
searches will slow access times. As discussed in Chapter 11, putting the
most crowded directories near the end of your PATH command forces
DOS to search these directories only as a last resort.

Disk caching (discussed in Chapter 17) also speeds disk accessing
considerably.

Defragmenting Floppy Disks

Virtually all defragmenting programs are designed for hard disks. If you need to defragment a floppy disk, the process is simple, provided that you have two compatible floppy disk drives. First, format a new, blank diskette. Then use the DOS COPY (not DISKCOPY) command to copy all the files from one floppy to the other.

The COPY command individually copies each file into contiguous sectors on the destination diskettes. In the future, merely use the newly created disk rather than the original. You should immediately notice an increase in access speed (and hear much less drive-head noise) when using the new copy.

Prolonging the Life of Hard Disk Data

There are a few products designed to extend the life of data on the disk, as well as the life of the disk itself, which also can help protect the data and the disk and also can increase performance. However, I know of only one such product that does not require erasing and reformatting your entire hard disk (a process that could take hours if not days). That product is

> SpinRite
> Gibson Research Corporation
> 22991 La Cadena
> Laguna Hills, CA 92653
> (714) 830-2200

Vaccines for Computer Viruses

Computers don't catch diseases, but they can catch a *virus*—a program intentionally designed by "high-tech vandals" to wreak havoc on your computer. Fortunately, "virused" programs are extremely rare. No reputable software manufacturers would even consider selling virused programs because doing so would immediately put them out of business. However, a few virused programs do find their way into the world of *public-domain software* (software whose authors freely distribute their work to computer users through bulletin boards and communication networks).

Some viruses have become so widespread and have infected so many computers that they've earned their own titles. Some well-known virus programs include the Pakistani-Brain Teaser, the Trojan Horse, the Time Bomb, and the Nuke.

Some viruses are relatively harmless and simply display a comical message on a given date and time. Others may interfere with the computer's basic input/output operations, causing a severe performance slow-down or a scrambling of data on the screen. One particularly nasty virus just occasionally reverses two numbers on the screen (not at all funny to companies who rely on their computers for accounting and inventory management).

Some viruses are very dangerous. It's been said that a virus program actually burned out the monitors on quite a few computers. Others can damage all the files on a disk beyond any hope of recovery. One particularly famous virus, known as the Internet virus, actually crippled an entire nationwide network of computers.

Virused programs are particularly dangerous because they usually do their damage long after you use them, sometimes even after you've erased them from your disk! Most do so by modifying an important DOS file named COMMAND.COM, which is called into action whenever you run a program. A virused COMMAND.COM file can randomly erase a tiny part of your hard disk each time that you run any program. Eventually, these tiny erasures will cripple specific programs and perhaps even make the entire disk unusable.

One step you can take to help prevent many virused programs from damaging your own programs and data is to turn on the read-only attribute for the COMMAND.COM file so that no program can change it. Because no legitimate program would ever have reason to change the COMMAND.COM file, the only effect this change has is to disable virused programs.

To protect your COMMAND.COM file, first determine where it is located. A shortcut method for doing so is to enter the command SET at the command prompt. The SET command might display several lines of information, but you need only be concerned with the line that starts with COMSPEC=, because this specifies where COMMAND.COM is located.

Next, enter the ATTRIB +R command followed by the full path and name of the COMMAND.COM file. For example, if the SET command displays COMSPEC=C:\COMMAND.COM, enter the command ATTRIB +R C:\COMMAND.COM. If the SET command displays COMSPEC=C:\DOS\COMMAND.COM, enter the command ATTRIB +R C:\DOS\COMMAND.COM.

Although DOS redisplays the command prompt after you press Enter, you can be assured that COMMAND.COM is now protected from change, which protects your data from many (although unfortunately not all) virus programs. Other executable files are also targets for viruses. (To be safe, you can apply the read-only attribute to all files that have the .COM or .EXE extension.)

If you plan to use a lot of public-domain software, you might want to take the extra precaution of investing in antivirus software. There are several programs available on the market, including

Flu-Shot +
Software Concepts Design
594 Third Ave.
New York, NY 10016
(212) 889-6431

Certus
Foundation Ware
2135 Renrock
Cleveland, OH 44118
(216) 932-7717

Mace Vaccine
Paul Mace Software
400 Williamson Way
Ashland, OR 97520
(503) 488-2322

Your computer salesman or software dealer might be able to provide additional virus protection packages.

Communicating with Remote Computers

If you need to communicate with remote computers via the telephone lines, you have two alternatives:

- ❑ Install a modem (short for MOdulator/DEModulator), which allows two computers to send and receive data and programs.

- ❑ Buy a FAX board, which allows a computer to send and receive text and graphics (but not programs) to and from any FAX machine or any other computer with a FAX board.

The sections that follow discuss the strengths and weaknesses of each type of communication capability. Of course, you are not limited to selecting only one. However, a FAX board does require that your computer have a slot available to hold the board, as does an internal modem. The only way to know for sure how many slots are available in your computer is to remove the cover on your system unit. These hardware matters are beyond the scope of this book, so if you are in doubt, consult a computer service technician.

Modems

A modem is the most flexible means of sending data and programs from one computer to another. You also need a modem to communicate with large external database services such as The Source, Compuserve, Knowledge Index, Dow Jones, Prodigy, and the Official Airline Guides.

Perhaps the single most important feature to consider when purchasing a modem is the *baud rate*. The baud rate is the speed at which data is sent and received (measured in bits per second). The most common baud rates used in serial communications (that is, transmissions through phone lines) are 300, 1200, 2400, and 9600 baud. A modem's listed baud rate is its maximum rate of data transfer. Hence, buying a modem that can transmit and receive at 9600 baud provides the most flexibility for communicating with all other modems, both fast and slow.

A modem also requires *communications software* that manages the streams of data being sent and received by the connected computers. There are two major types of communications software available for modems. With the standard communications packages you can perform basic communications operations, such as sending and receiving files.

Most modems are packaged with their own communications software. However, that software might offer only limited operations, especially compared to some of the more widely used communications packages available from independent software dealers. You may want to examine the following full-featured packages:

Crosstalk Mark IV
Crosstalk XVI
Crosstalk Communications
1000 Holcomb Woods Pkwy.
Roswell, GA 30076-2575
(404) 998-3998

ProComm Plus
Data Storm Technologies, Inc.
1621 Towne Drive, Suite G
Columbia, MI 65205
(314) 474-8461

If your job entails writing programs for others to use or training people to use computers, you might need to use remote access software with your modem rather than the standard communications packages. These programs not only let you send and receive files, you can also use them to control a remote computer from your own computer or watch the activity of a user on a remote computer. A few vendors of remote access software are

Carbon Copy
Carbon Copy Plus
Meridian Technology, Inc.
7 Corporate Park, Suite 100
Irvine, CA 92714
(714) 261-1199

PC Anywhere
Dynamic Microprocessor Associates, Inc.
60 East 42nd St., Suite 1100
New York, NY 10165
(212) 687-7115

The real trick to using a modem effectively is ensuring that the two communicating computers use the same settings for sending and receiving files. You can use your communications software to adjust numerous settings for communicating with other computers, as follows:

Baud Rate	Usually 300, 1200, 2400, 4800, or 9600
Parity	None, Odd, Even, Mark, or Space
Data Bits	5, 6, 7, or 8
Stop Bits	1 or 2

The *parity* setting represents the characters that are used to detect errors during communications. The *data bits* setting establishes the number of bits that will be used to represent each character of transmitted data. The *stop bits* setting represents the number of bits used to separate groups of data bits.

Perhaps the most common setting used for sending and receiving files is `1200 N-8-1`, which is an abbreviated way of expressing: 1200 baud, None (parity), 8 data bits, and 1 stop bit. A common setting for communicating with remote database services is `1200 E-7-1` (1200 baud, Even parity, 7 data bits, and 1 stop bit). If you're not sure of the proper settings when you first access a remote computer, either one of these settings is a good "first guess" to try.

Again, adjusting the settings for communications via modem is a matter of using your communications software correctly. For more information, consult your computer dealer or a book that specializes in communications.

FAX Boards

A second way of communicating via telephone lines is through *facsimile transmission* (FAX). The beauty of FAX is that it allows you to communicate with a worldwide network of FAX machines and other computers with FAX boards without having to worry about settings such as baud rate, parity, and stop bits.

The FAX standard for facsimile transmission has changed a few times throughout the years. Currently, the most widely used standard is named Group 3, although a new standard (Group 4) is emerging. When you select a FAX board for your computer, try to select one that supports at least the Group 2 and Group 3 standards.

Using a FAX board in your computer is not exactly like owning a complete FAX machine. The main reason is that a FAX board can only send and receive files, not text or graphics that are already printed on paper. If you want to be able to send printed text, as well as files, you need to invest in an additional *scanner*. You can also buy a FAX machine that supports both paper and computer file transmissions.

Computer FAX is still in its infancy in many ways. Your computer dealer can offer up-to-date alternatives for installing a FAX board on your computer. If you want to survey the market on your own, contact the following FAX board manufacturers for additional information:

Connection CoProcessor
Intel PCEO
Mainstop CO3-07
5200 NE Elam Young Pkwy.
Hillsboro, OR 97124-6497
(800) 538-3373

JT-FAX 9600
Quadram Limited Partnership
1 Quad Way
Norcross, GA 30093
(800) 548-3420

FaxMail 96
Brook Trout Technology, Inc.
110 Cedar St.
Wellesley Hills, MA 02181
(617) 235-3026

Be aware that, unlike modems, when you receive a file via FAX, it is not a simple text file that can be edited with your word processor. Instead, it's a graphic file that can only be viewed and printed with certain programs. Therefore, if you need to transmit "editable" text from one location to another, a modem is almost certainly preferable to a FAX board.

The same is true of scanners. They are a great way to "capture" printed graphics, diagrams, logos, signatures, and such, and to use them in your printed documents. However, the text they capture will probably be inaccessible to your word processor or other text editor.

There are programs that can translate scanned text to editable ASCII files, but they tend to be expensive, slow, and only partially accurate.

Incidentally (speaking of scanners), I once saw a demonstration that used a scanner connected to a computer as an input device and also had a voice synthesizer as an output device. As the operator fed printed text into the scanner, the voice synthesizer read each word out loud, in perfect English. As the demonstrators pointed out, the implications of this demonstration are enormous for visually handicapped persons.

Sharing Data, Printers, and Other Devices

As a company expands its use of microcomputers, sharing resources among computers often becomes an important issue. For example, if one office uses four computers, it is more cost-effective to connect all four computers to one expensive laser printer than to purchase a separate printer for each computer. If several computers need up-to-the-minute access to important data, such as a customer list or inventory, you need to link the computers so that all users can have access to the same data.

The solutions to the resource-sharing problems are many and varied, as are the costs involved. The sections that follow briefly describe some alternatives that you may want to look into to solve these problems.

Peripheral Sharing Devices

The most inexpensive (and most limited) device for connecting several computers and peripherals is called the *peripheral sharing device*. This device allows multiple computers to share devices and send files to one another. Peripheral sharing devices, however, do not allow multiple users to access the same data at the same time.

For example, suppose that you have several computers in one office, but you do not want to spend the money to equip each computer with a printer, plotter, and modem. A peripheral sharing device is an inexpensive means of providing all connected computers access to a single printer, plotter, and modem.

The names of several peripheral sharing devices, and the companies that manufacture them, are included in the following list. Your computer dealer may be able to offer other alternatives.

The Logical Connection
Fifth Generation Systems, Inc.
11200 Industriplex Blvd.
Baton Rouge, LA 70809
(800) 873-4384

EasyLAN
Server Technology, Inc.
140 Kifer Ct.
Sunnyvale, CA 94086
(800) 835-1515

ManyLink
ManyLink for Work Groups
NetLine
2155 North 200 West, Suite 90
Provo, UT 84604
(801) 373-6000

If you need true multiuser capability, in which several users on separate computers not only share devices but also have simultaneous access to the same data, you need either a Local Area Network (LAN) or a multiuser operating system. These vary considerably in price and performance.

Selecting which alternative is best for your situation is a matter of accessing the potential complexity of the LAN and your requirements for operational speed and data-handling capabilities. A thorough investigation into these matters is beyond the scope of this book. Talk with a LAN consultant or study a book that specializes in local area networks. The sections that follow, however, provide an overview of the features and capabilities of these systems and can help you determine which alternatives merit further investigation.

Multiuser Operating Systems

Multiuser operating systems permit as many as 64 people to simultaneously share data stored in a single file. Typically, one 80386-based microcomputer acts as the *file server*, which stores all programs and data; multiple users then directly access this information through *dumb terminals*, which usually consist only of a keyboard and a monitor.

Although switching to a multiuser operating system means leaving DOS behind, these systems are all designed to "mimic" DOS and run your DOS application programs. Therefore, your knowledge of DOS (and existing DOS programs) remains useful.

The main disadvantage to some multiuser operating systems is that they do not provide adequate security for data and programs. That is, any user at any terminal can access all files on the 80386. That means, for example, that anybody can look into a payroll database to see another person's salary or peek into files that contain employment reviews (if they have the nerve).

If security is not a major issue, however, a multiuser operating system can be an inexpensive solution to your networking needs, provided that you have (or are prepared to buy) an expensive 80386-based computer. Some products that you might consider are

PC-MOS/386
The Software Link
3577 Parkway Lane
Norcross, GA 30092
(800) 451-LINK

Concurrent DOS/386
Digital Research, Inc.
60 Garden Ct.
Monterey, CA 93940
(408) 649-3896

Other alternatives that you might want to consider are the UNIX and AIX operating systems. Although not specifically designed to mimic DOS, newer versions of these operating systems provide multiple users with the ability to run DOS-based application programs. Your best bet in researching these alternatives is to contact your computer dealer or a knowledgeable consultant.

DOS-Based LANs

DOS-based LANs are more expensive than multiuser operating systems, but they tend to outperform the operating systems both in terms of the number of users supported and the speed at which operations are performed. DOS-based LANs are generally less expensive than LANs that use dedicated, non-DOS operating systems (discussed in the next section). However, they provide many of the same features, including multiuser access to data, sharing of devices, and security structures that prevent access to sensitive data.

Installing a DOS-based LAN requires both hardware (a networking board in each computer and a system of cabling) and software, which manages the connections and data transfer. The expense can be considerable—as much as $600 or more per computer—and unless you feel confident about connecting a great deal of sophisticated computer hardware, you should plan on paying a consultant for the time required to install the entire network.

Some DOS-based LANs that you might want to consider are

DNA Networks
DNA Networks, Inc.
351 Phoenixville Pike
Malvern, PA 19355
(800) 999-3622

ELS Netware II
Novell, Inc.
P.O. Box 9500
Provo, UT 84601
(801) 379-5900

LAN Smart
Localnet Communications, Inc.
3303 Harbor Blvd., Suite E-8
Costa Mesa, CA 92626-9979
(714) 549-7942

LANtastic
Artisoft Inc.
3550 N. 1st Ave. #330
Tucson, AZ 85719
(602) 293-6363

Non-DOS Based LANs

The high-end, non-DOS based LANs provide the best performance and the greatest flexibility of all the LAN alternatives. As you might expect, they are also much more expensive. Most also require that a single computer be used as the file server, which is dedicated to managing data, programs, and network connections. Typically, the cost of the file server alone is $3,000 to $6,000, an investment that often turns away potential office network users.

Non-DOS based LANs use their own operating systems; however, most are capable of running DOS application programs without a hitch. If you are thinking about investing in a high-powered non-DOS LAN, you should first check with a LAN consultant or your computer dealer.

Solving the "Too Many Files Are Open" Problem

Some application programs—particularly database management programs such as dBASE and Paradox—allow you to simultaneously work on several open data files. Many sophisticated "3-D" spreadsheet programs, such as Lotus 1-2-3 (Version 3), can also simultaneously manage multiple open files. In most cases, these programs can handle more open files that DOS initially allows.

When one of these application programs attempts to manage more open files than DOS allows, DOS displays an error message, such as `Too many files are open`. This error message can be confusing: Although your current application program displays the error message on the screen, the message is actually coming from DOS, not your application program.

If you search through the manuals that came with your application program, you will eventually discover that DOS, not the application program, is to blame. A true DOS whiz knows the source of the message and also knows that the only solution to this problem, regardless of the application program that presents the message, is to change the number of *file handles* allotted by the FILES command in the DOS CONFIG.SYS file.

When you first install DOS 5 on your computer, it determines a "reasonable" number of files that can be open simultaneously and sets the FILES command in the CONFIG.SYS file to that number (usually about 10 to 15). To verify this for yourself, view the contents of your

CONFIG.SYS file. If your computer has a hard disk, enter the following command at the DOS command prompt:

```
TYPE C:\CONFIG.SYS
```

If you start your computer from a floppy disk, put the Startup disk in drive A: and enter the following command at the DOS command prompt:

```
TYPE A:\CONFIG.SYS
```

Your CONFIG.SYS file probably will display a line that begins with `FILES=` and ends with a number in the range of 8 to 255. For example, your CONFIG.SYS file might include the command

```
FILES=15
```

which tells DOS to permit no more than 15 simultaneously open files.

Some application programs automatically adjust the FILES setting (and in some cases, the BUFFER setting) in your CONFIG.SYS when you install them. If you bypass the installation process or upgrade to a higher version of DOS after installing such a program, the FILES and BUFFERS settings might not match the number required by the application program. When this happens, the `Too many files are open` error message begins to appear.

The solution requires that you refer to the documentation that came with the application program (usually the section that discusses how to install the program). Then use EDIT or another editor (discussed in Chapter 10) to modify the CONFIG.SYS file on your hard disk drive C: root directory or on the floppy disk that you use to start DOS. For example, if the manual states that 44 files and 22 buffers should be available to DOS, modify your CONFIG.SYS file to contain the following instructions:

```
FILES=44
BUFFERS=22
```

Place these commands anywhere in the CONFIG.SYS file, as long as each is on a separate line. Save the edited file and then reboot by pressing Ctrl-Alt-Del. DOS reads the new CONFIG.SYS file each time you start your computer in the future, and DOS should no longer display the `Too many files are open` error message. (See the FILES and BUFFERS entries in Appendix B for more details about these commands.)

Using Foreign Language Alphabets

If your work requires you to use non-English languages, and your current version of DOS uses the English alphabet, DOS contains several features that allow you to switch to a non-English alphabet and non-English formats for dates, currency, and decimal placement. The exact techniques you use depend on your version of DOS.

Rather than describe the entirely different techniques here, this section refers to the appropriate entries in Appendix B. If you are using DOS 3.0 through 3.2, refer to the following entries in Appendix B:

```
COUNTRY
KEYB
SELECT (for IBM PC DOS only, prior to version 3.3)
```

If you are using DOS Version 3.3 through 5, see the following entries in Appendix B:

```
NLSFUNC
CHCP
SELECT
KEYBOARD
DISPLAY
MODE
GRAFTABL
COUNTRY
KEYB
DEVICE
```

Summary

This marks the end of the tutorial chapters in this book. By now you should be able to use the more technical Appendix B without any problems. The first few pages of Appendix B discuss the best ways to use that reference section.

I hope that this book has served you well and that you are now using your computer, DOS, and your favorite programs like a true computer whiz. Thanks for reading!

Installing DOS

Even if you are a beginner, chances are that you won't have to install DOS on your computer. If you use a computer at work or school, someone else already installed DOS. Even if your computer is fresh out of the box, and you've never even turned it on before, your computer dealer might have already installed DOS for you. (Nearly all computer dealers install DOS so that they can test the computer before they ship it to you.)

If you are not sure whether DOS is already installed, read Chapter 1; then try starting your computer, using the appropriate startup steps described in Chapter 2. If your computer refuses to start, it might be because DOS is not already installed. On the other hand, you might simply be using the wrong disk to start your computer.

DOS needs to be installed only once, and reinstalling DOS after it has already been installed can cause a loss of important programs and data. If you're not sure, consult your computer dealer or some other person who is knowledgeable about your particular computer before you reinstall DOS.

Partitioning Your Hard Disk

If you are using a brand new hard disk (not floppy disks), chances are that it is already partitioned and formatted for use with DOS. If you are certain that the hard disk is not partitioned, you may need to partition the disk yourself.

This can be tricky business and is best left to people who are familiar with hardware. (This is particularly true if you unwittingly repartition a hard disk that has already been partitioned, because you're likely to lose all the programs and information stored on that disk!)

> NOTE: DOS 4 requires you use the SHARE command if you create a partition larger than 32MB; DOS 5 does not require you to use the program.

Partitioning is required in versions of DOS prior to Version 4 because DOS was incapable of accessing more than 32MB of data. The partitioning procedure allows you to divide a larger hard disk into several *logical* drives, none of which is larger than 32MB.

From DOS's perspective, each partition on a large fixed disk is, in essence, a separate hard disk. For example, if your computer has a 60MB fixed disk, you can partition it so that "drive C:" is 32MB and "drive D:" is 28MB.

One of these drives (usually C:) will be the *DOS partition*, in which DOS stores its own files. One partition will also be the *active partition*, in which DOS looks for instructions when you first turn on the computer. Assuming that you want to start your computer with DOS in control (which is always the case unless you've also installed another operating system), the active partition should be the same as the DOS partition (again, usually drive C:).

Any remaining partitions (logical drives) can be used for DOS, for an entirely different operating system, or for storing data. If you want to use the additional logical drives with DOS, use the FDISK program to convert the additional partitions into *Extended DOS partitions*. Optionally, you can format the extra partitions for use with another operating system (such as UNIX or OS/2), but to do this, you must follow the (entirely different) instructions that come with the other operating system.

If you decide to partition your hard disk yourself, refer to the documentation that came with your particular computer for specific information. Also check your DOS manual for information about the FDISK program, which you can use to partition your hard disk either before or after you install DOS.

Formatting the Fixed Disk

NOTE: DOS 5 includes the UNFORMAT command to let you recover from an accidental hard disk format. See the UNFORMAT entry in Appendix B for details.

After you complete the partitioning process, you might need to format the hard disk before installing DOS. Be forewarned that formatting the hard disk erases all information on the disk. Therefore, *do not format the hard disk if it already has any programs or data stored on it* unless you are absolutely certain that you no longer need any of those programs.

If you share a computer that others are currently using, you most certainly do not want to format the hard disk—doing so would destroy everybody else's programs and files, which will also wreak havoc on your popularity.

Even if your computer is fresh out of the box, the hard disk is probably already formatted. That's because, somewhere along the line, somebody should have fully tested your computer and its components. In most cases, this requires formatting the hard disk. If you are not sure that this has been done, ask your computer dealer.

After you are absolutely certain that the hard disk is not already formatted, follow these basic steps to format the hard disk:

1. If the computer is on, turn it off.

2. Insert the DOS Startup diskette (or the Install diskette with DOS 4 and DOS 5) in drive A: (as discussed in Chapters 1 and 2 of this book).

3. Turn on the computer.

4. If the screen asks for the current date, press the Enter key.

5. If the screen asks for the current time, press the Enter key again.

6. Type the command FORMAT C: /S. (Be sure to use blank spaces where shown; be sure to use the forward slash / rather than the backslash \ where indicated.)

7. Press Enter.

The formatting process might take many minutes to complete. When DOS finishes, it redisplays the A> prompt on the screen.

If you used the FDISK program discussed previously to create multiple DOS partitions, format these using DOS or another operating system if you prefer. If you want to use DOS, use the FORMAT command and specify the name of the extra drive, but do not use the /S switch. For example, if you created a partition named D:, you would type the command `FORMAT D:` and then press Enter. Wait until the A> prompt reappears before you type any more commands.

You can repeat this general procedure for any additional logical drives beyond D: (for example, `FORMAT E:` formats the next partition, `FORMAT F:` formats the next partition, and so on).

When you've finished formatting the entire fixed disk, you can start your computer without inserting a floppy disk in drive A:. To test the newly installed DOS, follow the steps in Chapter 2 for starting your computer with a hard disk.

Using DOS for the First Time

NOTE: If you are using DOS 5, see "Installing DOS 5" later in this Appendix.

If you are certain that neither DOS nor any other operating system is installed on your computer, you need to install DOS yourself. Unfortunately, it is impossible for this book to give you exact step-by-step instructions for installing DOS on your particular computer because different computers and different versions of DOS require different installation procedures.

To install DOS correctly on your computer, you should refer to the DOS documentation that came with your computer. However, certain aspects of these installation procedures are similar on most computers and with most versions of DOS, and those we can talk about in general.

Using DOS Version 3 Without a Hard Disk

If you are using a version of DOS prior to Version 4, and your computer does not have a hard disk, you can start your computer by inserting the DOS System Disk (also called the Startup Disk) in drive A: before turning on your computer.

However, the documentation will recommend (and provide instructions for) making copies of your original DOS diskettes. Follow those directions immediately. In the future, always insert the copy of your DOS Startup diskette in drive A: before you turn on the computer. That way, if your copy is damaged, you can recreate a new copy from the original diskette.

Using DOS 3 with a Hard Disk

If your computer has a hard (fixed) disk, and you are using a version of DOS prior to Version 4, you should be able to start your computer by removing any floppy disks from their drives and turning on the computer.

If DOS has not already been installed on the hard disk, try restarting the computer with the DOS Startup disk in drive A. If it works, you should see the A> prompt.

NOTE: All commands, including SYS and COPY, are referenced in Appendix B of this book.

In a nutshell, if you want to be able to boot up without the floppy disk in drive A, you can use the SYS command (for example, type SYS C: and press Enter) to copy system tracks to drive C and then use the COPY command to copy the files from the DOS floppy disks to your hard disk.

Your best bet, however, for information about preparing your fixed disk is to see the DOS documentation that came with your computer. That section tells you how to install DOS and copy it to your hard disk so that you can start your computer without inserting a floppy disk.

Installing DOS 4

If you are using Version 4 of DOS, you must complete the installation procedure whether or not your computer has a fixed disk. IBM computers that use PC DOS Version 4 offer this information in the manual titled *Getting Started with Disk Operating System Version 4.0*, which is included in the DOS package. Non-IBM computers that use MS-DOS Version 4 offer installation information in a similarly titled manual.

Although it is impossible to list the step-by-step instructions for installing DOS 4 on all computers, the following example lists some general questions that the installation might ask. This example assumes that you are installing MS-DOS Version 4 (for the first time) on a computer that has a hard disk.

First, if you have a printer attached to your computer, you should know what model it is and whether it is a parallel printer or serial printer. Refer to the manual that came with your printer for this information or ask your computer dealer.

Secondly, you need a blank diskette. This must be a new diskette (not one from your DOS package). Label this diskette SELECT COPY. The installation procedure will ask you to insert this diskette into drive A:. (It copies the information on the DOS Select diskette to the blank diskette.)

As the instructions in the manual state, first insert Disk 1 from your MS-DOS package into disk drive A:. Then either turn on the computer or, if the computer is already on, press Ctrl-Alt-Del (hold down the Ctrl key, hold down the Alt key, then press the Del key, and then release all three keys).

You might be asked to remove the Install disk and to replace it with the DOS Select disk that came with your DOS package. Do so if instructed and then carefully follow the instructions on the screen. You will have to enter

❏ How you want to install DOS, in terms of how much memory is allotted to DOS.

❏ The drive name on which you want to install DOS.

❏ The directory in which you want DOS installed. (Note that the installation program suggests a directory named DOS on hard disk drive C:.)

❏ Whether or not you want to copy the `system files` to the hard disk. If you have a hard disk, select option `1` by pressing Enter.

❏ How many and what type of printers you have connected to the current computer.

❏ Select a port for the printer.

When you've completed all the instructions on all screens, you'll see a message indicating that the installation is complete and successful.

Installing DOS 5

 The remainder of this Appendix focuses on installing DOS 5, both as a first operating system and as an upgrade to a previous version of DOS.

Installing DOS 5 on a Computer with No Previous DOS Version

In the unlikely event you are installing DOS 5 on a computer that does not currently use any version of DOS, you'll most likely need to refer to the documentation that came with your particular computer for detailed installation instructions. However, you may be able to install DOS 5 by following these steps:

1. Insert the DOS 5 Install disk in drive A.

2. Either turn on the computer or, if the computer is already on, press Ctrl-Alt-Del.

3. When the command prompt (A>) appears, type SETUP and press Enter.

The SETUP program automatically determines your system's current configuration and its available hardware devices (such as floppy and hard disk drives, video adapter(s), printers, and so on). Read each screen carefully and follow the instructions presented. You may want to browse through the following section on upgrading to DOS 5, because many operations in that section are identical to operations you'll perform when installing DOS 5 for the first time.

Upgrading to DOS 5

> NOTE: SETUP supplies additional help information whenever you press the F1 function key.

If DOS is already installed on your computer, upgrading your current version of DOS to DOS 5 is a pretty easy procedure. Microsoft's installation program, SETUP, has automated the process to such an extent that you might only need to press Enter a few times and insert disks as prompted. In addition, if you ever need clarification of what SETUP is telling (or asking) you, press F1 to call up the program's built-in context-sensitive help system.

Before You Upgrade to DOS 5

Your current system must meet two requirements (and should meet a third) before you can upgrade to DOS 5:

❏ Your computer must have at least 256KB of RAM.

❏ Your current version DOS must be version 2.11 or later.

❏ If you are installing DOS on a hard disk, the disk should have at least 3.3MB of free space.

If your hard disk drive does not have 3.3MB of available space, you must first upgrade your system files, then install the rest of DOS 5 onto floppy diskettes, and then copy selected programs to your hard disk. (For details about this process, see the following section "Handling Installation Problems.")

What SETUP Does

> NOTE: Most files on the DOS 5 distribution disks are compressed. The SETUP program automatically expands them into usable files.

Once you get the SETUP program started (as described in a few moments), it performs the following series of operations:

❏ Determines your system's hardware configuration.

❏ Backs up all of your existing files.

❏ Saves all of your current DOS's files in a directory called OLD_DOS.1.

❏ Stores your original system information (File Allocation Tables, root directory entries, AUTOEXEC.BAT, CONFIG.SYS, and so on) on an UNINSTALL diskette.

❏ Updates your current DOS partitions to be compatible with the new DOS 5 partitioning scheme.

❏ Expands compressed files on your DOS distribution disks and copies them to your DOS directory (usually \DOS).

❏ Creates a new CONFIG.SYS file that includes commands and installs device drivers that let DOS utilize available extended memory.

❏ Modifies your AUTOEXEC.BAT file to include a correct DOS PATH entry and, optionally, start the DOS Shell.

In addition, when you start SETUP, it determines your system's hardware configuration and then displays the results of its findings on a screen similar to the one in Figure A.1.

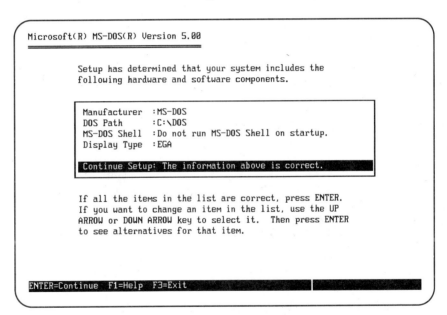

Figure A.1. The SETUP verification screen.

This screen gives you a chance to verify the following information:

❏ The manufacturer of your current version of DOS. (You can learn this information before you start SETUP by typing VER at the DOS prompt.)

❏ The directory in which DOS files will be stored. (SETUP suggests either your current DOS directory or the \DOS directory.)

❏ Whether or not the DOS Shell is run every time you boot your system. (By default, SETUP suggests that the Shell not be run.)

❏ Your type of video monitor. (You probably will need to change this only if your system includes two types of monitors.)

Try to determine how you want to respond to these entries before you start.

Also, if you have a third-party program that you use to back up your hard disk(s) (for example, Fastback Plus or Norton Backup), use it immediately before you upgrade your current version of DOS to DOS 5. Although you can use SETUP to back up your entire system, it uses the DOS BACKUP command, which is much slower and less efficient than most third-party programs.

Be sure to back up your hard disk(s). As reliable as most hardware and software is, accidents do happen—brownouts, power failures, and loose plugs can interrupt the installation process at critical times; hard drives can crash; and devices and plug-in boards can fail! Protect your data: A system-backup is an insurance policy that you cannot afford to be without.

One last thing before you begin installing DOS 5: You will need one blank 720KB, 1.2MB, or 1.44MB disk (or two blank 360KB disks); the disks may be formatted or unformatted. Label the disk(s) UNINSTALL (or UNINSTALL 1 and UNINSTALL 2).

Upgrading to DOS 5 on Floppy Diskettes

NOTE: Even if your computer has a hard disk, you should install DOS 5 on floppy diskettes.

In today's world, a computer without a hard disk drive is like a car with a one-pint gas tank—it's usable, but not very convenient. I assume, therefore, that you'll probably be upgrading DOS 5 on a hard disk. However, before you do so, I strongly suggest that you install DOS 5 on floppy diskettes.

Installing DOS 5 on floppy diskettes takes some additional time, and at first, you might think it unnecessary. However, this operation serves several important purposes:

❏ It gives you another backup of your DOS 5 files.

❏ It creates a Startup disk (a bootable system disk that you can use to start your computer if your hard drive fails).

❏ It gives you a convenient source of expanded (uncompressed) DOS 5 programs that you can copy to your hard disk if you ever need them (that is, you won't have to use the EXPAND command and your original DOS disks to retrieve a DOS file).

Although installing DOS 5 on floppy diskettes is a simple procedure, it is a little time-consuming. Take the time. You only need to do it once. After all, as I stressed before, you can never really take too many precautions with your computer, your programs, and your data.

If you are using 5 1/4-inch diskettes, SETUP installs DOS 5 on seven diskettes. Label them with the following names:

Startup
Support
Shell
Help
Basic/Edit
Utility
Supplemental

If you are using 3 1/2-inch diskettes, SETUP requires you to use only four diskettes:

Startup/Support
Shell/Help
Basic/Edit/Utility
Supplemental

These diskettes can be either formatted or unformatted. SETUP assumes that you will be using low-capacity (360KB or 720KB) diskettes. Although you can just as well use high-capacity diskettes, much of the space on those diskettes will not be used.

After you label your blank diskettes, use the following procedure to install DOS 5 on them:

1. Start your `computer` using your current version of DOS.

> NOTE: "Distribution disks" refer to the original DOS 5 disks, not the disks you label yourself.

---

2. Insert `Disk 1` of your DOS 5 distribution disks into drive A.

3. Type `A:SETUP /F` (the /F switch tells SETUP that this is a "floppy" installation).

4. Follow the `instructions` on your screen.

The installation process is nearly "bullet-proof"; that is, it's automated to the extent that all you need to do is press Enter, press Y, and then insert the various numbered distribution disks and your own labeled diskettes.

After programs are copied to the Supplemental diskette, SETUP will signal that the process is complete and suggest that you reboot with your new Startup diskette. If you have a floppy-only system, follow this advice; if you are now ready to install DOS 5 on your hard disk, press F3 to exit SETUP and return to the command prompt on your hard disk drive.

Upgrading a Hard Disk System to DOS 5

> NOTE: Even though your computer has a hard disk, you probably should install DOS 5 on floppy diskettes first (see the previous section for details).

If you are upgrading your current version of DOS to DOS 5, first label one blank diskette with the name UNINSTALL. (Note that if you use a 360KB diskette, you might need two diskettes; label them UNINSTALL 1 and UNINSTALL 2.) SETUP saves important files and system data on this diskette so that you can restore your system to its original state if the installation process is interrupted or if you later have difficulty using your programs with the new operating system.

SETUP creates the UNINSTALL diskette as another "insurance policy" to protect your system, programs, and data. However, if for some reason, the DOS 5 installation procedure is interrupted during the creation of the UNINSTALL disk, remove the disk from drive A, reboot your system, and then begin the upgrading procedure again from the start. No harm will be done to your system.

After the UNINSTALL disk has been created, however, it can be a lifesaver. For example, if the installation process is later interrupted (by a power failure, for example), you can reboot your computer with the UNINSTALL diskette in drive A and then continue the DOS 5 installation from exactly where you left off!

Most importantly, you can use UNINSTALL to restore your previous version of DOS and your original system files if you later determine that DOS 5 is incompatible with your current hardware or software. For details, see the later section "Restoring Your Previous Version of DOS."

To upgrade your previous version of DOS to Version 5, use the following steps:

1. Start your `computer` with your previous version of DOS (even if you've already created DOS 5 floppy diskettes).

2. Insert `Disk 1` of your DOS 5 distribution disks (not the disks you labeled yourself).

3. Type `A:SETUP`, which displays the screen shown in Figure A.2.

```
Microsoft(R) MS-DOS(R) Version 5.00
========================================================

        Welcome to Setup

        Setup installs Microsoft MS-DOS version 5.0 on your hard
        disk. During Setup, some of your current system files will
        be saved on one high-density or two low-density floppy disks
        that you provide and label as shown below:

            UNINSTALL #1
            UNINSTALL #2 (if needed )

        The disk(s), which can be unformatted or newly formatted,
        must be used in drive A.

        Setup copies some files onto the Uninstall disk(s), and
        others to a directory on your hard disk called OLD_DOS.
        Using these files, you can remove MS-DOS from your hard
        disk and reinstall your old DOS if you need to.


ENTER=Continue  F1=Help  F3=Exit
```

Figure A.2. The SETUP startup screen.

If SETUP refuses to install DOS 5 on your hard disk because of an incompatible hard-disk-manager program, read the instructions on the screen about getting additional information from the README.TXT file on the DOS 5 Distribution Disk #5. Then press F3 to exit SETUP and TYPE or PRINT that README.TXT file.

After carefully following whatever instructions in the README.TXT file best describe your particular hard disk manager, you'll probably be instructed to restart the SETUP program using the /U switch.

```
A:SETUP /U
```

If SETUP refuses to install DOS 5 on your hard disk because you don't have the required free space on the disk, press F3 to exit SETUP; then read the "minimal installation" discussion in the later section "Handling Installation Problems."

4. After you read the SETUP startup screen, press Enter, which displays the screen shown in Figure A.3. (Note that you can press F1 at any time for additional help information.)

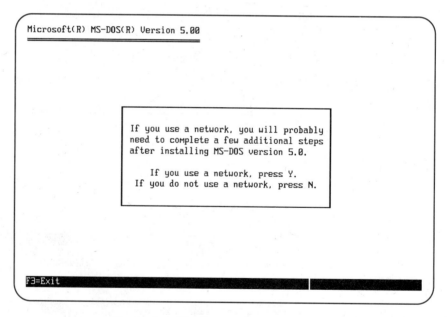

```
Microsoft(R) MS-DOS(R) Version 5.00



        If you use a network, you will probably
        need to complete a few additional steps
        after installing MS-DOS version 5.0.

            If you use a network, press Y.
         If you do not use a network, press N.



F3=Exit
```

Figure A.3. The "network query" screen.

5. If you are a user on a network, you might want to exit SETUP now and speak to your system administrator before you proceed with the DOS 5 upgrade. If you are responsible for installing DOS 5 on the network, be sure you read the

NETWORKS.TXT file on Disk 2 of your DOS distribution disks and study the "Upgrading Networks for MS-DOS Version 5.0" chapter in the Microsoft documentation before you proceed. Then press Y.

If you are not a user on a network, press N.

6. The next screen offers you the option of backing up all your hard disks. If you haven't yet backed up your system, do it now. If you choose to back up, SETUP displays a helpful screen similar to Figure A.4, which lists how many diskettes the backup procedure will require. You can use blank formatted or unformatted disks for the operation. Follow the instructions on the screen and be sure to insert the correct disks when SETUP asks for them.

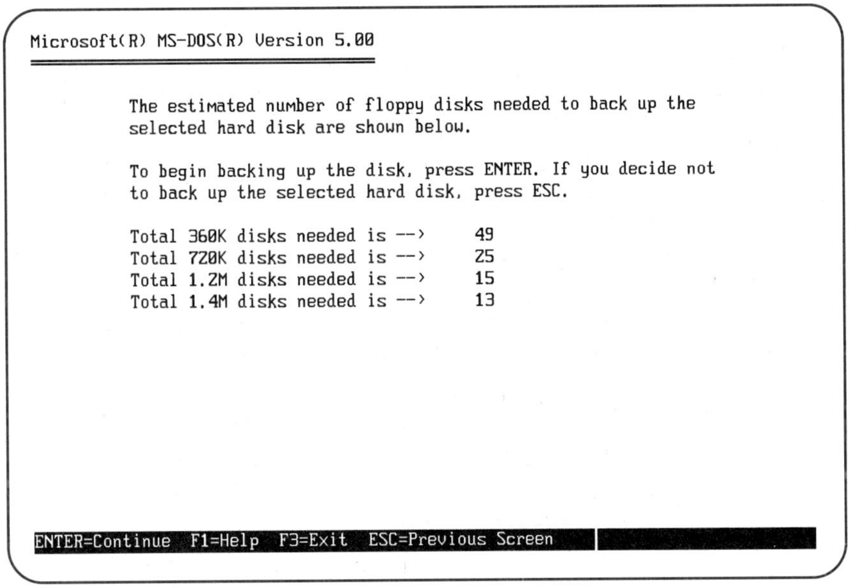

```
Microsoft(R) MS-DOS(R) Version 5.00
================================================

        The estimated number of floppy disks needed to back up the
        selected hard disk are shown below.

        To begin backing up the disk, press ENTER. If you decide not
        to back up the selected hard disk, press ESC.

        Total 360K disks needed is -->      49
        Total 720K disks needed is -->      25
        Total 1.2M disks needed is -->      15
        Total 1.4M disks needed is -->      13




ENTER=Continue  F1=Help  F3=Exit  ESC=Previous Screen
```

Figure A.4. The initial backup hard disks screen.

If you choose the option Do not back up hard disk(s), SETUP displays a verification screen similar to the one shown in Figure A.1. Change the information as required and then press Enter.

7. The next SETUP screen begins the installation process. Press Y to start the procedure; press F3 and then Y to exit the SETUP program.

8. Follow the instructions on each of the next screens. These will guide you through the process of creating an UNINSTALL diskette and upgrading your system to DOS 5. Actually, all you will have to do is swap diskettes and press Enter every once in a while. It's as simple and as painless a process as you'll find.

When the installation process is complete and successful, a screen prompt will inform you. You can reboot (press Ctrl-Alt-Del) to start using DOS 5.

Restoring Your Previous Version of DOS

In addition to your important system files and information, the UNINSTALL disk also contains a program called UNINSTAL.EXE. This program will let you restore your previous version of DOS if you encounter technical problems using DOS 5. (This is not likely, however, because DOS 5 is perhaps the most-tested program ever released.)

You can use the UNINSTALL disk to restore your system to its original state only if you have not performed certain operations with your computer. The following operations negate UNINSTAL's power to restore your system:

❏ Reformatting your hard disk.

❏ Repartitioning your hard disk.

❏ Deleting or moving one or both of the hidden DOS system files, IO.SYS and MSDOS.SYS.

❏ Using the DELOLDOS command (which deletes your original DOS files from your hard disk).

If you have performed one of the previous procedures, do not try to "uninstall" DOS 5! The UNINSTAL program will not function correctly and might even damage your data and hard-disk file structure.

To restore your previous version of DOS (or recover from an installation problem such as a power loss), insert the UNINSTALL disk in drive A (if you needed to use two 360KB diskettes, insert UNINSTALL 1). Then press Ctrl-Alt-Del to reboot your system. The UNINSTAL program immediately runs and displays easy-to-use instructions for restoring your original version of DOS. That's it; the process is very nearly automatic, and you will need to do little else than confirm that you actually want to proceed with the operation.

Because the UNINSTALL diskette is bootable (contains DOS 5 system files), you can also use it to restart your computer if your hard disk fails. Start your computer with the UNINSTALL diskette in drive A; press F3 and then Y to exit the UNINSTAL program. When the DOS prompt appears, you can again work with your system.

Although booting your system with the UNINSTALL diskette works fine, you should be more cautious with your data and create a specialized diskette for this purpose. That is, use either a Startup diskette (created during a floppy installation) or a "system" diskette (created by using the SYS command; see Appendix B for details).

Deleting Your Previous Operating System

When (and if) you are certain that DOS 5 will work fine on your system, you can delete your previous operating system, which is likely stored in a directory named OLD_DOS.1 (or something similar). At the command prompt (C>), type DELOLDOS (for DELete OLD Disk Operating System) and press Enter.

This command deletes all of the previous operating system files, the directory they were stored on, and itself (so this is a once-in-a-lifetime command!).

Handling Installation Problems

Several configurations of your current system may prevent SETUP from working correctly:

❏ The hard disk doesn't contain enough free space to perform a complete DOS 5 upgrade.

❏ The primary DOS partition (boot hard disk drive) is too small to accommodate all of DOS 5's files and programs.

❏ The hard disk drive has been partitioned by a third-party disk-manager program that is not compatible with DOS 5.

❏ The current DOS partition is no longer valid under DOS 5's new partitioning scheme.

The last three problems in this list need to be corrected by repartitioning your hard disk. For detailed instructions about this complex (and widely varying) procedure, see Chapter 4, "Trouble-shooting MS-DOS" in Microsoft's "Getting Started" manual. Note, also, that the README.TXT file on your DOS 5 distribution disks contains information about many third-party, hard-disk-manager programs; this information might help you install DOS 5 on a system that originally balks at the operation.

However, the first problem in the preceding list—insufficient hard disk space—can be easily overcome. The best way to eliminate the problem is to delete any old or unnecessary files on your boot drive. If you still don't have enough free space, you must perform a "minimal" installation.

A minimal installation updates your hard disk's "system" files (IO.SYS, MSDOS.SYS, and COMMAND.COM), creates an UNINSTALL diskette, and then creates new AUTOEXEC.BAT and CONFIG.SYS files. However, it does not expand and transfer to your hard disk any of the other DOS 5 programs. (To expand the DOS 5 files, you will need to perform a "floppy" installation with the SETUP /F command and then transfer the programs on those diskettes to your hard disk.)

To perform a minimal installation, follow these steps:

1. Perform a floppy `installation`; see the section "Upgrading to DOS 5 on Floppy Diskettes" for details.

2. Insert `Disk 1` of your DOS 5 distribution disks and type `SETUP /MIN`.

3. Make a `backup` of your system if you haven't already done so.

4. Follow the instructions to create an `UNINSTALL` diskette.

5. After SETUP copies the three DOS 5 system files to your hard disk, follow the instructions that tell you to reboot your computer: Press `Ctrl-Alt-Del`.

6. Copy to your hard disk drive as many essential DOS 5 `programs` from your expanded DOS 5 floppy diskettes as you can fit in the available space. (Normally, you will copy those files and programs into the `C:\DOS` directory.)

7. Rename your current AUTOEXEC.BAT and CONFIG.SYS files to `AUTOEXEC.OLD` and `CONFIG.OLD`.

8. Rename the AUTOEXEC.NEW and CONFIG.NEW files (which SETUP created) to `AUTOEXEC.BAT` and `CONFIG.SYS`.

9. Reboot your computer by pressing `Ctrl-Alt-Del`.

Alphabetical DOS Reference

This appendix provides a reference to all DOS commands and device drivers. For your convenience, there also is an instant reference guide inside the back cover of this book. This guide offers plain-English descriptions of commonly performed tasks, along with the commands required to perform those tasks.

Each entry in this appendix has the following format:

ENTRY

The command or device driver name, followed by a brief description, appears first.

Version   The versions of DOS in which the command or device driver is available are listed.

Type   **Command.** The type of command is described, as follows:

Internal: The command is always available from the command prompt.

External: The command uses a program that is stored on disk. Consequently, the command is only accessible if the appropriate program is available on the current disk, in the current directory, or in a directory included in the current PATH setting.

If a particular command requires an external program, that program's name is also included in this section. For example, the FORMAT command is listed as External (FORMAT.COM), which indicates that the FORMAT command requires that the file named FORMAT.COM be available on disk.

If an external DOS program is not available in the current directory and is not specified in the current PATH setting, you can precede the command with the location of the appropriate file directly at the command prompt.

For example, if FORMAT.COM is stored on the C:\DOS drive and directory, and C:\DOS is not in the current PATH setting, you can still activate the FORMAT command by entering the command

```
C:\DOS\FORMAT A:
```

Device Driver. Device drivers must be activated by a DEVICE or INSTALL command in the CONFIG.SYS file. Device drivers are special files that enable you to install and use optional devices, such as a mouse, RAM disk, or expanded memory.

The following box shows the DOS commands and device drivers discussed in this appendix, categorized as Internal, External, Batch File, or CONFIG.SYS commands. The categories, however, are somewhat general.

For example, FASTOPEN is a command that can be used directly at the command prompt, but generally it makes more sense to install FASTOPEN through the CONFIG.SYS file. All internal and external commands can be used in batch files, and many internal commands used in batch files can also be used at the command prompt. See the individual command or device driver entries in this appendix for more specific information.

Table B.1. Categories of DOS commands and device drivers.

Internal commands *(always accessible from the command prompt)*	
BREAK	PATH
CHDIR or CD	PROMPT
CLS	RENAME or REN
COPY	RMDIR or RD
DATE	SET
DEL	TIME
DIR	TYPE

ECHO	VER
ERASE	VERIFY
EXIT	VOL
MKDIR or MD	

External commands
(used primarily at the command prompt)

APPEND	JOIN
KEYB	LABEL
ASSIGN	MEM
ATTRIB	MIRROR
BACKUP	MODE
CHCP	MORE
CHKDSK	MSHERC
COMMAND	NLSFUNC
COMP	PRINT
DISKCOMP	DISKCOPY
DOSKEY	RECOVER
DOSSHELL	REPLACE
EDIT	RESTORE
EDLIN	SETVER
EXPAND	SORT
FC	SUBST
FIND	SYS
FORMAT	TREE
GRAFTABL	UNDELETE
GRAPHICS	UNFORMAT
HELP	XCOPY

Internal commands used solely (or primarily) in batch files

CALL	PAUSE
FOR	REM
GOTO	SHIFT
IF	

Commands and device drivers used solely (or primarily) in the CONFIG.SYS file

ANSI.SYS	FILES
BREAK	HIMEM.SYS
BUFFERS	INSTALL
COUNTRY	LASTDRIVE
CTTY	LOADHIGII

continues

Table B.1. *(continued)*

DEVICE	PRINTER.SYS
DEVICEHIGH	RAMDRIVE.SYS
DISPLAY.SYS	SHARE
EMM386.EXE	SHELL
DOS	SMARTDRV.SYS
DRIVER.SYS	STACKS
FASTOPEN	VDISK.SYS
FCBS	

DOS Shell Menu Access This section explains how to use commands from the DOS Shell. All DOS Shell operations can be activated from the keyboard or with a mouse, as discussed in the early chapters of this book.

If the command or device driver is not immediately accessible from a menu in the DOS 5 Shell, this section displays *None*. However, even if a command is not directly accessible from the DOS 5 Shell menus per se, you still can execute all DOS external commands from the Files List. Simply access the drive and directory that DOS is stored on (typically C:\DOS), highlight the command file name, and press Enter. Alternatively, double-click the file name with your mouse.

For example, suppose you want to use the MEM command from the Shell without using the command prompt. The entry for the MEM command in this appendix shows that it is an external command stored in the file MEM.EXE. (If you are using DOS 5, MEM.EXE is most likely located on the \DOS directory of your hard disk drive C:, as are all external DOS commands.)

First, using the Drives and Directory Tree areas of the Shell, select the drive and directory in which MEM.EXE is stored. Then, run the MEM.EXE program by highlighting its file name in the Files List and pressing Enter or move the mouse pointer to the MEM.EXE file name and double-click the mouse button. The screen displays report of memory usage (as described under MEM in this appendix). After you examine the display, press a key to return to the Shell.

As an alternative to using the Files List to run an external DOS program, you can add the program to any DOS 5 Shell group screen, as discussed in Chapter 11.

Syntax The syntax section describes the general format of the words and options used with the command. The command itself is shown in capital letters. Optional components are enclosed in square brackets

([]). (Do not include the square brackets in your own DOS command.) Variable components (for which you supply appropriate information) are displayed in *italics*. The symbol [...] indicates that you can enter multiple options, using the same format as the options immediately preceding.

The ¦ symbol in a syntax chart indicates that one option or the other (but not both) can be used in the command. For example, the syntax for the VERIFY command is

```
VERIFY [ON ¦ OFF]
```

The bracketed items are optional, and therefore you can omit them completely. Or, you can use either the ON or the OFF option (but not both simultaneously) with the command. Hence, all three of the following commands are valid:

```
VERIFY
```

```
VERIFY ON
```

```
VERIFY OFF
```

Clarification of the options and italicized variables used in the command section appears in the Usage section.

Usage   This section provides a general description of the command, what it does, and how to use it—including useful tips and warnings.

Examples   This section provides examples of how to use the command. Additional examples of most commands also appear throughout the book.

See Also   If there are related commands worth checking, this section either lists them or refers you to a chapter or section in the book that deals with the topic at hand.

ANSI.SYS

Controls the screen and keyboard by using standards set by the American National Standards Institute (ANSI). When installed via the CONFIG.SYS file, it allows you to customize screen displays and keyboard assignments (see Chapter 12).

Version   2 and later

Type   Device driver; valid only in the CONFIG.SYS file.

DOS Shell Menu Access   None

Syntax   `DEVICE = [drive][path] ANSI.SYS [/X][/L][/K][`
`/screensize:(rows,columns)`

in which *drive* and *path* specify the drive and directory path to the ANSI.SYS file (required only if ANSI.SYS is not stored in the root directory).

Usage   If your CONFIG.SYS file includes the command `DEVICE=ANSI.SYS`, you can use the PROMPT command to customize the screen and keyboard (see Chapter 12).

The following optional switches might be valid only on certain computers (see the DOS manual that came with your computer for the hardware-specific details of these features):

/X   Allows expanded keys to be remapped independently.

/L   Causes application programs to use a specific number of rows, as specified by the MODE command.

/K   In DOS 5, this switch is used only in the `SWITCHES=/K` command in CONFIG.SYS to access conventional keyboard functions with an enhanced keyboard.

`/screensize:`   In DOS 5, you set the size of the screen to the specified number of `(rows columns)` and `columns`.

Examples   If the ANSI.SYS file is stored in the root directory of the boot disk, then the following command, when included in the CONFIG.SYS file, activates the ANSI device driver at startup:

`DEVICE=ANSI.SYS`

If the ANSI.SYS file is stored in the \DOS directory of drive C:, the CONFIG.SYS file must contain the following command to activate the ANSI device driver at startup:

`DEVICE=C:\DOS\ANSI.SYS`

See Also   CONFIG.SYS, PROMPT, SWITCHES

APPEND

Sets a path for searching for files.

Version 3.3 and later

Type External (APPEND.EXE) becomes internal after being loaded.

DOS Shell Menu Access None

Syntax
```
APPEND [[drive:] path] [;[drive]path] [...] [;] [/
X:OFF] [/X:ON] [/PATH:ON] [/PATH:OFF] [/E]
```

in which *drive* is a disk drive name (such as C:), *path* is a directory path (such as \123), and . . . refers to any number of additional drives and paths separated by semicolons (*;*).

Usage When DOS is given instructions to locate a file, it usually searches only the current disk drive and directory. If the PATH command provides additional drives and directories to search, DOS searches those additional drives and directories only for program files (those with the extension .BAT, .COM, or .EXE).

APPEND tells DOS to search other drives and directories for data files. You use the APPEND command to allow program (.COM or .EXE) files to find their overlay files (see Chapter 17).

Do not use the APPEND command to allow programs to find data files on separate directories; this can create confusion. For example, suppose your word processing program locates a data file on one of the drives and/or directories specified in the APPEND command. Then, you change that data file and save it. Regardless of the APPEND command setting, the new version of the data file will be stored on the current drive and directory, leaving the original (and unchanged) file on its original drive and directory.

The /X and /Path switches are available in DOS 4 and 5 only. The APPEND command emulates the PATH command when you use the /X:ON (or /X) option. This option tells APPEND to search for and execute program and batch files. The default setting is /X:OFF.

The /PATH:OFF option prohibits the search for files when a drive and/or path is specified in the file name. The default setting, /PATH:ON allows APPEND to search for files, whether or not the file name includes a path.

The /E option stores the APPEND list of drives and directories in the environment. This allows batch files to access the drives and directories through the use of the %APPEND% variable name. The /E option is only valid the first time that APPEND is executed.

The command APPEND entered with no other information displays the currently appended drives and directories (or No Directory if none are defined). The command APPEND; cancels any previous APPEND settings, and limits searches to the current drive and directory.

Examples   Suppose you store all your program overlay files in a directory named \OVERLAYS on drive C:. Furthermore, you store spreadsheet files in a directory named \FINANCES, also on drive C:. If you enter the command APPEND C:\OVERLAYS;C:\FINANCES before using any programs, those programs automatically search the directories named \OVERLAYS and \FINANCES on drive C: for overlay and spreadsheet files. (Again, however, if you save an edited spreadsheet, it might not be stored back into the \FINANCES directory.)

To ensure that all files in the directory named \DOS are accessible from any other directory, and to store the APPEND setting in the environment, add the following commands to your AUTOEXEC.BAT file:

```
PATH C:\DOS
APPEND /E
APPEND C:\DOS
```

or to achieve the same result

```
APPEND /E
APPEND C:\DOS /X:ON
```

If you want to use both the APPEND and ASSIGN commands, be sure to use the APPEND command first. If you use the /X switch, you must disable the APPEND command by entering APPEND; before issuing a BACKUP or RESTORE command.

You can use the APPEND command in a network to access data files on a remote directory (including the file server).

See Also   ASSIGN, JOIN, PATH, SUBST

ASSIGN

Reassigns the default drive specified in a program to a new drive.

Version   2 and later

Type   External (ASSIGN.COM)

DOS Shell Menu Access	None
Syntax	`ASSIGN d1=d2 [...]` in which *d1* is the name of the drive that the program normally accesses, and *d2* is the name of the drive that you wish to use instead. The . . . refers to additional drive assignments, each using the *d1=d2* syntax.
Usage	The ASSIGN command need only be used with programs that are capable of accessing only a specific predefined disk drive. For example, suppose you have a spreadsheet program that insists on storing spreadsheet files on drive B: and offers no means for storing spreadsheet files on drive C:, where you want to store them. Entering the command `ASSIGN B=C` before using that spreadsheet program tricks the program into storing its files on drive C:. Note that, unlike many other commands, ASSIGN does not require colons with the drive names. For example, the command `ASSIGN B=C` is legal. However, you can also use the command `ASSIGN B:=C:` if you are in the habit of using colons. Also, be sure to use only disk drive names that are valid on your computer. For example, if your computer does not have a disk drive named F:, the command `ASSIGN C=F` displays the error message `Invalid Parameter` and ignores your request. The command ASSIGN alone reassigns drive letters to their originally designated drives. Be sure to use the ASSIGN command with no parameters before you use the BACKUP, RESTORE, LABEL, JOIN, SUBST, or PRINT commands. The commands FORMAT, SYS, DISKCOPY and DISKCOMP ignore any new drive assignments created by the ASSIGN command; they always use the original drive designations. Never use the ASSIGN command to assign your main working disk drive to a new drive. For example, suppose you have a blank RAM disk named drive D:, but all of your important files are stored on the hard disk drive C:. The command `ASSIGN C=D` makes drive C: "invisible," and any attempt to run programs or inspect drive C: is useless. From the computer's viewpoint, only the blank drive D: exists. In this case, you can't even use the ASSIGN command (without parameters) to restore the original drive settings, because the ASSIGN program is stored on the invisible drive C:. The only way to recover from this error is to reboot by typing Ctrl-Alt-Del.

To use a program that requires ASSIGN, but prevent it from disrupting other DOS commands and operations, you can create a batch file that executes, then disables, the ASSIGN command.

Examples Suppose you have a program named MYGAME.EXE that can only access disk drive B:, but you want to use it on your hard disk C:. You could create the following batch file, which activates ASSIGN, runs the MYGAME program, and then deactivates the ASSIGN automatically when you exit the MYGAME program:

```
REM **************** GAME.BAT
ASSIGN B=C
MYGAME
ASSIGN
```

To reroute all the files that a program usually stores on drives A: and B: to drive D:, use the command ASSIGN B=D A=D. Note the blank space between the two parameters.

See Also PATH, SUBST

ATTRIB

Changes the attributes of a file.

Version 3 and later

Type External (ATTRIB.EXE)

DOS Shell Menu Access Change Attributes... on the <u>F</u>ile pull-down menu.

Syntax
```
ATTRIB [+R|-R] [+A|-A] [+S|-S] [+H|-H] [drive:] [path]
file name [/S]
```

in which R determines the read/write status of the file, A determines the archive status of the file, S sets or clears a system file, and H sets or clears a hidden file, as shown in the following:

+R	changes a file's attribute to read-only.
-R	changes a file's attribute to read/write.
+A	activates the archive status of the file.
-A	deactivates the archive status of the file.
+S	sets the system attribute of the file.
-S	deactivates the system status of the file.
+H	sets the hidden attribute of the file.
-H	deactivates the hidden status of the file.

The *drive* and *path* parameters specify the location of the file; *file name* is the name of the file and can contain wild card characters.

Usage   The preceding syntax shows options for the ATTRIB command in Version 5 of DOS. Please be aware that Version 3.0 supports only the +R and –R switches, and does not support /S; nor does Version 3.0 display information about a files archive bit. Version 3.2 supports +R, –R, +A, –A, but not /S. Versions 3.3 and 4 do not support the +S, –S, +H, and –H switches.

ATTRIB lets you protect a file from accidental change or deletion. It also lets you determine whether or not a file is archived (copied) via backup commands such as BACKUP, RESTORE, and XCOPY. ATTRIB, without an A or R parameter, displays the current attributes of a file. The DOS 5 additions also let you create (or disable) system and hidden files, which cannot be "seen" by most DOS commands.

By default, any file can be altered or erased. To protect a file from accidental change or erasure, change its status to read-only using the +R option with the ATTRIB command. Any attempt to delete or change the file results in the error message `Access Denied`. To return a file to its normal read/write status, use the –R option with ATTRIB.

To prevent a file from being archived during a backup session, use the –A option with ATTRIB. To ensure that the file is archived during backup, use the +A option with ATTRIB.

To check the status of a file, use the ATTRIB command with only the file name. The file's status appears to the left of the file name. An `A` indicates that the file archive status is on and that the file has not been archived since it was last changed. An `R` indicates that the file currently has read-only status. Likewise, an `S` indicates a system file, and an `H` indicates a hidden file.

To include files in all subdirectories below the current directory, use the /S parameter at the end of the ATTRIB command.

The DOS 5 Shell also lets you change the hidden and system attributes. When one or both of these attributes are turned on, the file name is not displayed by the Command Prompt DIR command or in the Shell's Files List. (Note, however, that the Shell can display system and hidden file names if you choose the `File Display Options...` selection from the Options menu, and then toggle on the `Display hidden/system files` check box.)

To change file attributes using the DOS 5 Shell, go to the Files List and select a file (or files) by highlighting or by clicking once with the mouse. Then, pull down the File menu and select `Change Attributes....` You can change the attributes for selected files individually or as a group.

When the Change Attribute dialog box appears, attributes that are turned on are indicated by a right-pointing triangle. Toggle an attribute on or off by highlighting the attribute and pressing the Spacebar (or clicking the attribute once with the mouse).

Examples   Suppose you purchase a copy of the dBASE IV program and copy its files to a directory named \DBASE on your hard disk drive C:. You want to be sure that none of these files are accidentally changed or erased. Furthermore, you do not want to include these files in backup procedures, because you know they will never be changed on the hard disk.

First, you might check the current status of the files by entering the command

```
ATTRIB C:\DB\DBASE*.*
```

The resulting display shows that the files currently have read/write status (R is not displayed), and that the archive status is on (A is displayed), as shown here:

```
A                    C:\DBASE\DBASE3.OVL
A                    C:\DBASE\DBASE.EXE
A                    C:\DBASE\DBASE1.RES
A                    C:\DBASE\DBASE6.OVL
A                    C:\DBASE\DBASE1.OVL
A                    C:\DBASE\DBASE3.RES
A                    C:\DBASE\DBASE2.OVL
A                    C:\DBASE\DBASE1.HLP
A                    C:\DBASE\DBASE5.OVL
A                    C:\DBASE\DBASE4.OVL
A                    C:\DBASE\DBASE2.HLP
A                    C:\DBASE\DBASE2.RES
```

To change the program (.EXE), overlay (.OVL) and help (.HLP) files to read-only status, and to prevent them from being included in future BACKUP procedures, enter the following commands:

```
ATTRIB +R -A C:\DB\DBASE*.EXE
ATTRIB +R -A C:\DB\DBASE*.OVL
ATTRIB +R -A C:\DB\DBASE*.EXE
```

After making these changes, any attempt to erase the file named DBASE.EXE (for example) using the command

```
ERASE C:\DB\DBASE.EXE
```

results only in the error message `Access denied`, and DOS refuses to erase the file.

Suppose you want to protect all .COM and .EXE files on hard disk C: from erasure. To do so, change to the root directory and use the ATTRIB command with the +R option and /S switch.

```
ATTRIB +R C:\*.COM
ATTRIB -R C:\*.EXE
```

To print a list that details the status of all files on hard disk C:, enter the command

```
ATTRIB C:\*.* /S > PRN
```

Many programs create hidden and system files to store system information. Before DOS 5, if you wanted to delete those files and their directories, you had to use a third-party utility program to clear the attributes. Now, you can use the S and H switches following the ATTRIB command to clear all file attributes in the current directory so that you can delete all of the files there.

```
ATTRIB -H -R -S *.*
```

The DOS 5 Shell is particularly powerful—it lets you delete a read-only file without first clearing the file's read-only attribute! Although the Shell presents a Warning message, if you confirm the deletion, it immediately deletes the read-only file. This is potentially dangerous, so if you ever see the Read-only Warning message in the Shell, press Esc; then, check to see if you really want to delete that file.

See Also   BACKUP, RECOVER, XCOPY

BACKUP

Backs up files on the hard disk to floppy disks.

Version   2 and later

Type   External (BACKUP.COM)

DOS Shell
Menu Access   From the Program List, access the `Disk Utilities...` group and select `Backup Fixed Disk`.

Syntax   BACKUP [*source drive*] [*source path*] [*source file name*] [*destination drive*] [/F:*size*] [/S] [/M] [/A] [/D:*date*] [/T:*time*] [/L:*logfile*]

in which *source drive, source path,* and *source file name* identify the file(s) to be copied, and *destination drive* identifies the drive to which the files are to be copied. The various switches are discussed in the following section.

Usage   The BACKUP command is used to copy files from a hard disk to diskettes. Unlike the COPY command, BACKUP offers several options and features that make backing up the hard disk a little faster and easier. First, BACKUP can store a file that is larger than the capacity of a single floppy diskette by splitting the file among multiple floppy diskettes. Second, BACKUP automatically warns you when the floppy diskette to which you are copying files is full, and prompts you to insert a new disk.

In addition, BACKUP automatically formats a diskette (when the /F option is used), if the disk being copied to is not already formatted.

Files that are copied with the BACKUP command can *only* be retrieved with the RESTORE command. No other DOS command can access these copies.

You should label and number your backup diskettes with names such as Backup #1, Backup #2, and so on, so that you can use them in the same order during each backup session. During a BACKUP session, DOS displays the message

```
Backing up files to drive x: *** Diskette Number: nn
```

where *nn* is the disk number that you should write on the backup disk's label. (Later, if you ever need to recover files from these backups, DOS will ask you to insert them in the appropriate sequence.)

The various switches that are available for the BACKUP command are

`/F:size`	The /F switch tells DOS to format any unformatted target backup disks. See Table B.5 in the FORMAT entry for a list of acceptable values for `size`.
`/A`	By default, DOS erases all files on the target disk (the one being copied to) before copying any new files to it. If you specify the /A option, DOS adds new files to the target disk without first erasing the existing files. It is important to use the /A option if the diskette to which you are copying already contains backup files that you do not want to erase.
`/M`	The /M option tells BACKUP to copy only files that have been modified since the previous backup procedure.

/S	The /S switch tells BACKUP to include files in the subdirectories beneath the current directory.
/D:*date*	The /D switch tells BACKUP to copy only files that were created or changed on or after a specific date. The date must be entered in the format used by DOS (usually mm-dd-yy, unless modified by the COUNTRY.SYS device driver). Do not include any blank spaces in the switch.
/T:*time*	The /T switch tells BACKUP to copy only files that were created or changed on or after a specific time of day. Typically, this option is used with the /D switch to back up files that were created or changed on or after a certain time on a certain day. The time must be entered in the format used by DOS: hh:mm:ss, where *hh* is the hour (0–23), *mm* is the minutes (0–59), and *ss* is seconds (0–59). Do not include any blank spaces in the switch.
/L:*file name*	The /L option stores information about the backup in a log file on the source drive and directory, using the name you specify. The log file includes the date and time of the backup, the paths and names of the files that were backed up, and the number of the disk on which the files were stored. If you specify the /L switch without a file name, DOS automatically names the log file BACKUP.LOG. If you add your own file name, be sure to use a colon (:) between the /L and *file name*. Do not include blank spaces. DOS Versions 3.3 and 4 also let you specify a path for the log file.
/P	Used in DOS Versions 2.0 to 3.1 to specify the "pack" option, to store files in compacted form on the backup diskette.

The BACKUP command returns a code in the ERRORLEVEL variable, which can be detected by the IF ERRORLEVEL command in a batch file. The value of ERRORLEVEL is a number between 0 and 4, with the meaning of each value as follows:

0   Backup was completed successfully, no error.

1   No files were found to back up.

2   Some files were not backed up because of file-sharing problems (occurs only on networks).

3   Backup was aborted by Ctrl-Break or Ctrl-C.

4   Backup procedure was aborted because of a system error.

Never use BACKUP when an APPEND, ASSIGN, SUBST, or JOIN command is in effect. If you do, any attempted recovery in the future will likely damage the directory structure of the hard disk.

The BACKUP command must be able to find the FORMAT.COM file in order to work correctly. FORMAT.COM must be either in the current directory or in a directory specified by the current PATH command. In DOS Versions 3.3 and earlier, you must also use the /F switch in the BACKUP command if you want it to format the backup diskette.

Examples   To back up all files in the root directory to floppy diskettes, change to the root directory of that disk, also be sure that the BACKUP.COM program is available (either in the root directory or through a PATH command), and enter the command

```
BACKUP C:*.* A:
```

Note that if you do not specify a file name, BACKUP assumes that you mean all files on the current directory. Hence, a shortcut for entering the preceding command is simply `BACKUP C: A:`.

To back up all files on drive C:, including those in directories below the root directory, specify C:\ as the starting point and use the /S switch, as follows:

```
BACKUP C:\*.* A: /S
```

To back up all files with extensions .WKS, .WK1, .WK2, and .WKQ from the directory named \SSHEETS to the disk in drive A:, enter the command

```
BACKUP C:\SSHEETS\*.WK? A:
```

To back up all files with the extension .DBF, in the directory named \DBFILES, that were created on or after December 31, 1989, enter the following command:

```
BACKUP C:\DBFILES\*.DBF A: /D:12/31/89
```

If you wanted to limit the backup files in the preceding example to those created after 1:00 p.m. on December 31, 1989, you would add the /T switch to the command, as follows:

```
BACKUP C:\DBFILES\*.DBF A: /D:12/31/89 /T:13:00:00
```

You can combine as many parameters as you wish when using the BACKUP command. For example, the next command backs up every file on the hard disk, starting at the root directory C:\ and working down through all of the subdirectories (/S). The command stores information about the backup in a log file named BACKUP.LOG in the root directory of the hard disk (/L):

```
BACKUP C:\ A: /S /L
```

To repeat the preceding backup procedure more quickly in the future by backing up only files that have been changed, use the /A switch to add new files to the existing backup disks, and use the /M switch to limit backups to files that have changed since the previous backup procedure. The command now reads as follows:

```
BACKUP C:\ A: /S /A /M /L
```

Note that when you use the /A option with BACKUP, DOS "expects" to find the last diskette used in the previous backup in drive A:. If there is no disk in drive A:, you see the message `Insert last backup diskette in drive A:`. If you do not place the appropriate disk in drive A:, BACKUP aborts the operation.

See Also   COPY, RESTORE, XCOPY, and Chapter 11

BREAK

Determines when DOS checks the keyboard to see if the Break key (or Ctrl-C) has been pressed.

Version   2 and later

Type   Internal

DOS Shell Menu Access   None

Syntax
```
BREAK [=] [ON | OFF]
```

Usage   The BREAK command determines the frequency at which DOS checks to see if the Break (Ctrl-Break or Ctrl-C) key was pressed.

In its default configuration, in which BREAK is OFF, DOS only checks to see if Break was pressed when an operation accesses a standard device (that is, the keyboard, screen, printer, or communications port.) When BREAK is ON, DOS checks for a Break keypress before any system call, including reading or writing to the disk drives.

When BREAK is OFF, DOS can run at maximum speed. However, if you run a "calculation-intensive" program that never accesses a standard character device, and BREAK is OFF, there is no way to abort that running program.

If you set BREAK ON, DOS checks for a Break keypress more frequently, so you can interrupt a program that never accesses a standard character device. However, because DOS must check for Break keypresses more often, it runs a little slower (only about 1 or 2 percent in most cases).

The command `BREAK`, with no parameters, returns the current status of the Break setting.

When using the BREAK command in the CONFIG.SYS file, insert the = sign in the command. For example, including the command `BREAK=ON` in the CONFIG.SYS file ensures that frequent Break key scanning is installed during the startup procedure.

Examples   To make DOS check for a Ctrl-Break or Ctrl-C keypress before any system call, enter the command

`BREAK ON`

To limit Break key checking to standard character device operations, enter the command

`BREAK OFF`

To check the current status of the BREAK setting, enter the command

`BREAK`

This displays a message such as

`Break is off`

BUFFERS

Defines the number of disk buffers DOS uses.

Version   2 and later

Type   Configuration (used only in CONFIG.SYS)

DOS Shell Menu Access   None

Syntax   Versions 2 and 3:

`BUFFERS = number`

Version 4:

`BUFFERS = number[,sectors] [/X]`

Version 5:

`BUFFERS = number[,sectors]`

in which *number* is the number of disk buffers specified in the range of 1 to 99, and *sectors* is the maximum number of sectors that can be read or written in one disk transfer, in the range of 1 to 8.

Usage   The BUFFERS command is used to set the number of buffers used by your system. DOS 5 also allows you to specify a look-ahead buffer in the range of 1 to 8 sectors.

The default values for BUFFERS are generally

3   If any diskette drive is greater than 360KB.

5   If the computer system memory size is greater than 128KB.

10   If the computer system memory size is greater than 256KB.

15   If the computer system memory size is greater than 512KB.

Each disk buffer consumes 528 bytes (a little more than 1/2KB of RAM). Each look-ahead buffer consumes as much memory as one disk sector, usually 512 bytes. Application programs that take advantage of the DOS BUFFERS setting (most database managers and some spreadsheets) usually recommend an optimal number of buffers to use. Tape backup systems also might require more buffers than the default number. Check the manual that came with the application program or tape drive unit for further information.

The /X option (available only in DOS 4) tells DOS to use expanded memory. If the system does not have expanded memory or if the expanded memory is in use, the BUFFERS command is ignored and the default values are used. If expanded memory is available, then the largest number of buffers is 10,000 or the total amount of expanded memory, whichever is smaller. To use /X, the device driver for the expanded memory manager must be placed above the BUFFERS command in the CONFIG.SYS file.

If you use the PC DOS XMA2EMS.SYS device driver to install expanded memory, you must specify a page address for P255 in the `DEVICE=XMA2EMS.SYS` command before the line with the BUFFERS command in the CONFIG.SYS file. Otherwise, DOS ignores the /X switch.

Examples   To allocate about 11KB of RAM to 22 disk buffers, include the following command in your CONFIG.SYS file:

```
BUFFERS=22
```

To allocate about 25KB of expanded memory (rather than conventional RAM) to disk buffers, and about 4KB to look-ahead buffers, include the following two commands in your CONFIG.SYS file (in the order shown):

```
DEVICE=C:\DOS\CEMM.EXE 1024 ON
BUFFERS=50,8
```

See Also   FASTOPEN, FILES, SMARTDRV.SYS

CALL

Executes another batch file from within the current batch file.

Version   3.3 and later

Type   Internal (used in batch files and in DOSKEY macros)

DOS Shell Menu Access   None

Syntax   `CALL [drive][path] batch file name [parameters]`

in which *batch file name* is the name of the batch file that you wish to run, and *parameters* is a list of parameters that the called batch file can accept. The *drive* and *path* must be specified only if the batch file is not in the current directory or in a directory specified by the current PATH setting.

Usage   The CALL command is used within a batch file to execute another batch file. When the called batch file finishes its job, the calling batch file continues with its next command. If the batch file being called can accept command line parameters, you can include them in the CALL command.

When calling another batch file, you must specify the drive and directory location of that batch file if

1. The batch file is not in the current drive and directory.

   and

2. The batch file is not in a drive and directory specified in the current PATH.

To mimic the function of the CALL command using versions of DOS prior to 3.3, use the `COMMAND /C` command in place of CALL.

Examples   Suppose a batch file named TEST1.BAT contains the following commands:

```
@ECHO OFF
REM ------- TEST1.BAT
ECHO I'm in TEST1.BAT
CALL TEST2
ECHO I'm back in TEST1.BAT now
```

A batch file named TEST2.BAT contains the commands

```
2REM ------- TEST2.BAT
ECHO Now I'm in TEST2.BAT!
```

When you enter the command `TEST1`, the CALL command calls (executes) TEST2.BAT. After TEST2.BAT finishes its job, TEST1.BAT resumes its tasks. Your screen displays

```
I'm in TEST1.BAT
Now I'm in TEST2.BAT!
I'm back in TEST1.BAT now
```

The following TEST1.BAT batch file acts exactly the same as the previous TEST1.BAT; however, it can be used with versions 2 and later of DOS:

```
@ECHO OFF
REM ------- Test1.BAT
ECHO I'm in TEST1.BAT
COMMAND /C TEST2
ECHO I'm back in TEST1.BAT now
```

Note that although you can use CALL in a DOSKEY macro (with the previously described syntax and restrictions), when you call the batch file, you negate the advantages of the macro (speed, no worries about paths, and so on). Therefore, if you are creating a macro and you discover that you must call a batch file (for example, to use GOTO lines and labels), you are better off simply writing the entire command as a batch file.

See Also   GOTO

CHCP

Changes the code page (character set) for all possible devices.

Version   3.3 and later

Type   Internal (after installing NLSFUNC)

DOS Shell Menu Access	None
Syntax	`CHCP [code page number]`

in which `code page number` is a three-digit number that defines a foreign language character set.

Usage CHCP (an abbreviation for CHange Code Page) lets you select a character set for languages other than English for use with devices (such as the screen and a printer) that support code-page switching. Code-page options are listed in Table B.2.

Table B.2. Code page options.

Code Page Number	Alphabet
437	United States
850	Multilingual
860	Portuguese
861	Icelandic
863	French-Canadian
865	Nordic

Examples To change the code page to Portuguese, enter the command

`CHCP 860`

See Also MODE, NLSFUNC, COUNTRY.SYS

CHDIR or CD

Changes to a different directory or displays the name of the current directory.

Version	2 and later
Type	Internal
DOS Shell Menu Access	In the Directory Tree Area of the Shell, highlight the directory name and press Enter, or click once on the directory name with your mouse.
Syntax	`CHDIR [[drive][path]]`

or

`CD [.|..|\][drive][path]`

in which *drive* is the disk drive name and *path* is the directory (and, optionally, subdirectory) name. The \ symbol (alone) refers to the root directory. The .. symbol specifies the parent directory, which is one level higher than the current directory. The . symbol specifies the current directory.

Usage   Use CHDIR (or the abbreviated form, CD) to change the current, or working, directory on the current drive or on a separate drive. If you omit the drive specification, the current drive is assumed. If you include a drive name, the current directory of the specified drive is changed, but you remain on the current drive. If you omit the path name, the command displays the name of the current directory.

If you precede the path name with a backslash, DOS begins the search at the root directory. If you omit the initial backslash, DOS begins the search at the current directory.

Examples   Suppose you are currently in the root directory of drive C: and you wish to switch to the directory named WP, which is one level below the root directory. To do so, enter the command

```
CD \WP
```

To return to the root directory at any time, enter the command

```
CD\
```

To get to a subdirectory named DBFILES, which is stored "beneath" a directory named DBMS, enter the command

```
CD \DBMS\DBFILES
```

As an alternative to the preceding command, you could use two steps to access the \DBMS\DBFILES subdirectory. First, enter the command

```
CD \DBMS
```

to change to the DBMS directory. Then enter the command

```
CD DBFILES
```

Notice, in the second example, that the \ character was omitted, because DBFILES is only one level below the current directory DBMS and you do not want to start the search from the root directory.

If you want to switch from the DBMS\DBFILES directory to a directory named DBMS\DBTUTOR, you can use the double dot (..) symbol as an abbreviation for the parent directory. For example, you could enter the command

```
CD ..\DBTUTOR
```

After you are in the DBMS\DBTUTOR subdirectory, you could enter the following command to move up one directory (to the DBMS directory):

```
CD..
```

When the \DBMS directory is the current directory, entering the command `CD..` will move you up a level, to the root directory. Entering the command `CD..` from the root directory does nothing, because there is no higher level.

The following command makes the directory named JULY1991 on disk drive A: the current directory for that drive (regardless of which drive is the current drive at the moment):

```
CD A:\JULY1991
```

Any DOS commands (such as `DIR A:` or `COPY *.* A:`) issued after this command access the directory named JULY1991 on the disk in drive A:. If you were to enter the command

```
A:
```

at this point, to switch to the disk in drive A:, you would be accessing the JULY1991 directory of drive A:. When you enter the command

```
C:
```

to switch back to the hard disk, you would be in the same directory from which you left the hard disk.

To display the name of the current drive and directory, enter the command

```
CD
```

To display the current directory on another drive, specify the drive name, but not a path. For example, the following command displays the name of the current directory on the disk in drive A:

```
CD A:
```

NOTE: To display the name of the current directory at all times, enter the command `PROMPT $P$G`.

See Also   MKDIR, PROMPT

\

CHKDSK

Displays the status of a disk, checks for disk flaws, and optionally corrects some disk flaws.

Version   1 and later

Type   External (CHKDSK.COM)

DOS Shell Menu Access   None

Syntax   CHKDSK [*drive*] [*path*][*file*] [/F] [/V]

in which *drive* is the name of the disk drive of interest, *path* and *file* specify the location and name of the file to be checked, /F and /V are optional switches.

Usage   CHKDSK (pronounced *check disk*) is used to check the status of the disk and, optionally, to fix any errors on the disk. It produces a CHKDSK status report containing

Disk volume

Date the disk was formatted

Disk volume serial number (in DOS 5)

Total disk space in bytes

Number of hidden files and the amount of disk space they occupy

Number of directories and the amount of disk space they occupy

Number of user files and the amount of disk space they occupy

Total disk space available

Number of bytes in each allocation unit (in DOS 5)

Number of allocation units on disk (in DOS 5)

Number of available allocation units

Total amount of system memory (in DOS 5)

Amount of available system memory

Because files are not always saved contiguously on disk, the number of noncontiguous areas occupied by a file is reported when the file option is specified. (If files are fragmented, their processing time is slowed down.)

If the /F option is specified in the command, and CHKDSK finds any clusters in the file allocation table (FAT) that are not allocated to a file, CHKDSK displays the prompt

`Convert lost chains to file (Y/N)?`

If you type N in response, CHKDSK ignores the lost clusters (chains). If you answer Y, CHKDSK recovers the clusters, and places them in a file named FILE*nnnn*.CHK in the root directory of the disk (in which *nnnn* is a series of numbers beginning with 0000 and incremented sequentially with each .CHK file). After you check the files and retrieve any useful information, you can erase them.

The /V option is used to display the drive, path, and file name for all files on the disk.

You can redirect the output from CHKDSK to the printer (using > PRN) or a file (using > *filename.ext*). However, do not redirect output to a file when you use the /F switch with CHKDSK.

Examples   To produce a CHKDSK status report for drive C:, use

`CHKDSK C:`

To find (and optionally recover) lost clusters, use

`CHKDSK C: /F`

If you want to print a CHKDSK status report that contains the names of all files and fragmentation information, use

`CHKDSK C:*.* /V > PRN`

See Also   MEM, Chapter 17 (for information about defragmenting) programs.

CLS

Clears the screen.

Version   2 and later

Type   Internal

DOS Shell Menu Access   None

Syntax   `CLS`

Usage   CLS clears all information from the screen and places the prompt in the upper left-hand corner of the screen. CLS clears only the screen display, it has no effect on the contents of RAM or disk files.

Examples If, after you exit a program, the screen remains cluttered with irrelevant information, clear the screen by entering the command

CLS

COMMAND

Invokes a second copy of the command processor.

Version 1 and later

Type External (COMMAND.COM)

DOS Shell Menu Access Select the MS-DOS Command Prompt option from the Main Group of the Program List, or press Shift-F9.

Syntax COMMAND [drive] [path] [/P] [/C commands] [/E:size]

in which *drive* is the disk drive where COMMAND.COM is located, *path* is the name of the directory that contains COMMAND.COM, *commands* are optional commands, and *size* is a number between 160 and 32,768, which sets the size of the environment.

Usage COMMAND is generally used within programs to allow batch files (and other programs) to send commands directly to DOS, or to allow a temporary return to the command prompt.

If COMMAND is used without options in a batch file, it temporarily exits the program and displays the command prompt. You can interact with the COMMAND prompt in the usual manner. To return control to the batch file, enter the command EXIT

The /C option lets you include a series of DOS commands that are to be executed immediately. After processing these commands, control is returned to the batch file automatically, without the need to enter the EXIT command. The /C option can also be used within a batch file to process another batch file. (This mimics the action of the CALL command used in DOS Version 3.3 and later.)

The /P option disables the EXIT command so that the copy of the command processor remains in memory for the entire current session (that is, until you turn off the computer or reboot). If you attempt to use both the /C and /P options, the /P option is ignored.

The /E option (available in Versions 3.2 and later) lets you set the size of the DOS environment, within the range of 160 to 32,768 bytes. By default, the DOS environment size is set to 160 bytes.

Examples　The sample batch file that follows, when typed and executed, clears the screen and displays the messages `Going to DOS temporarily. Enter any DOS commands, then type EXIT to return`. You can use the DOS command prompt as you normally would. When you enter the EXIT command, control returns to the batch file and the screen displays the message `OK, I'm back to normal!`

```
@ECHO OFF
CLS
ECHO Going to DOS temporarily
ECHO Enter any DOS commands, then type EXIT to return
COMMAND
ECHO OK, I'm back to normal!
```

When you use the Shift-F9 key to exit the DOS Shell, the shell actually creates a secondary command processor, leaving the Shell "suspended" for the time being. Later, when you enter the EXIT command, the secondary command processor ends and control returns to the Shell.

See Also　CALL, SET, SHELL

COMP

Compares two or more files.

Version　1 and later

Type　External (COMP.COM)

DOS Shell Menu Access　None

Syntax
```
COMP [first drive][first path][first file name]
[second drive][second path][second file name][/D]
[/A] [/L] [/C ] [/N:number]
```

in which `first drive`, `first path` and `first file name` identify one set of files for comparison, and `second drive`, `second path` and `second file name` identify the second set of files.

Usage　COMP compares the contents of two files (or two sets of files) of identical size to determine whether or not there are any differences. If no differences are found, COMP returns the message `Files compare OK`. If any differences are found, COMP displays a maximum of 10 differences. After 10 differences are found, COMP displays the message `10 mismatches--ending compare` and stops comparing the two files. (COMP assumes that there is no need to compare the files any further, because there are already too many differences.)

When differences are found between the files being compared, COMP indicates the exact byte (character) location at which differences exist. By default, the location is displayed in hexadecimal notation. However, if you use the /D switch, differences are displayed as decimal numbers; if you use the /A switch, differences are displayed as ASCII characters.

The /L switch displays the line numbers in which any differences occur, and the /N switch limits the comparison of the files to a specified number of lines.

The /C switch makes the comparison "case-insensitive"; that is, COMP disregards the case of letters in the files. A file that contains the text `TEST` will match a file that contains `test` only if you specify the /C switch in the command.

If you omit file names from the command, COMP asks you for the names of files to be compared. You can use wild card characters in lieu of specific file names, to compare groups of files.

Do not use COMP to compare original files on the hard disk against files that were backed up onto diskettes with the BACKUP command. COMP will always find differences because BACKUP adds additional information to the diskette copies.

Note that when two versions of a file do not match, you can always tell which is the most recent version by using the DIR command to display the date and time.

When COMP finishes comparing files, it displays the message `Compare more files (Y/N)?`. Entering `Y` allows you to specify the names of other files to compare. Entering `N` returns you to the command prompt (or the DOS Shell).

Unlike DISKCOMP, which can only be used to compare diskettes, COMP can compare any two files or any two groups of files on any disk.

Examples   Assuming that the COMP.COM program is accessible through a predefined PATH command, enter the following command to begin a comparison:

```
COMP
```

The screen presents the prompt

```
Enter primary file name
```

Type a file name, such as TEST.TXT, and press Enter. Next, the screen asks

```
Enter 2nd file name or drive id
```

If the second file has the same name as the first, you need only enter the drive letter. You can also enter the entire file name with the drive letter. In this example, suppose you want to compare TEST.TXT with the file TEST2.TXT on drive A:. You would then enter the drive and file name at the second prompt as follows:

```
A:TEST2.TXT.
```

If no differences are found, COMP displays the following message:

```
C:TEST.TXT and A:TEST2.TXT
Files compare ok
```

If differences are found, COMP might display messages (to a maximum of 10), such as

```
Compare error at OFFSET 18
File 1 = 67                    File 2 = 78
```

If you don't want the information presented in hexadecimal (base 16) notation, you can have COMP translate to decimal (base 10) by using the /D switch. In the previous example, there is a difference between the two files at the 24th character (18 hex = 24 decimal). File 1 contains the letter "g" (ASCII hex code 67, or ASCII decimal code 103) at the 24th character position, while File 2 contains the letter "x" at that position (ASCII hex code 78, decimal code 120). No other differences are reported. (If you want to display the ASCII characters "g" and "x" directly, simply use the /A switch in the command.)

COMP then displays the message `Compare more files (Y/N)?` before returning to DOS. Type `N` to return to DOS, or `Y` to compare more files. You'll be prompted to enter the file names, exactly as when you first ran COMP.

The names of (or wild card characters for) files to be compared can be entered directly on the COMP command line. For example, to compare all .TXT files in the \WP directory on drive C: with all .TXT files in the \WP\WPFILES subdirectory, and to make the comparison case-insensitive, enter the command

```
COMP C:\WP\*.TXT C:\WP\WPFILES\*.TXT /C
```

If you attempt to compare two files that are different sizes, COMP displays the message `Files are different sizes.` COMP only attempts to compare files that are the same size, because it "knows" that two files of different sizes cannot possibly be identical.

See Also   FC, DISKCOMP

CONFIG.SYS

A file containing commands that tell DOS how to configure the computer.

Version   1 and later

Type   Modifiable ASCII text file.

DOS Shell   None
Menu Access

Usage   CONFIG.SYS is a special file that DOS automatically reads when you first turn on your computer. You cannot actually type the command CONFIG or CONFIG.SYS. Instead, you create a file named CONFIG.SYS in the root directory of your hard disk, or in the root directory of your Startup diskette.

You can use the EDIT or EDLIN editors (or any word processor or text editor capable of saving files in ASCII text format) to create and edit the CONFIG.SYS file.

Depending on your answers to prompts while installing DOS 5, the DOS 5 INSTALL program may create a CONFIG.SYS file or change your current CONFIG.SYS file.

The configuration commands that you can include in the CONFIG.SYS file include

BREAK=	Tells DOS how often to check for a Ctrl-C BREAK keypress.
BUFFERS=	Determines the number of buffers to be set aside for disk accessing.
COUNTRY=	Specifies the date, time, and currency format to be used.
DEVICE=	Identifies a device driver (a program that controls and configures an external device).
DEVICEHIGH=	Loads device drivers into reserved (upper) memory.

DOS=	Lets DOS access reserved memory and/or load itself into the High Memory Area (HMA) of extended memory; thus freeing more conventional memory for application programs.
FCBS=	Specifies the number of file control blocks that can be opened at any one time.
FILES=	Specifies the number of files that can be opened at one time.
INSTALL=	Loads memory-resident programs during startup.
LASTDRIVE=	Specifies the name of the highest named drive.
REM	Adds a blank line or a comment to a configuration file.
SHELL=	Specifies the name and location of the command processor (usually COMMAND.COM).
SWITCHES	Disables extended keyboard functions.
STACKS=	Specifies the number of stacks used by the system hardware interrupts.

The DEVICE, DEVICEHIGH, and INSTALL commands are used in the CONFIG.SYS file to install device drivers. Some device drivers that your version of DOS might include are ANSI.SYS, COUNTRY.SYS, RAMDRIVE.SYS, VDISK.SYS, PRINTER.SYS, and others discussed in this appendix. Your particular computer system might include additional device drivers for managing optional devices—for example, MOUSE.SYS or MOUSE.COM to control a mouse, or EMM386.EXE to manage expanded memory.

Examples   The following sample CONFIG.SYS file includes several DOS commands, as well as device drivers for both DOS and optional devices.

```
BREAK=ON
FILES=40
BUFFERS=20
DEVICE=C:\DOS\ANSI.SYS
DEVICE=C:\MOUSE1\MOUSE.SYS
DEVICE=C:\DOS\HIMEM.SYS
SHELL=C:\DOS\COMMAND.COM /P /E:256
LASTDRIVE=D
DEVICE=C:\DOS\RAMDRIVE.SYS 3072 128 64 /E
INSTALL=C:\DOS\FASTOPEN.EXE C:=(50) /X
```

The first command, `BREAK=ON`, activates frequent checking for a Break keypress. The command `FILES=40` specifies that a maximum of 40 files can be open simultaneously. The command `BUFFERS=20` specifies 20 disk buffers for conventional RAM.

The command `DEVICE=C:\DOS\ANSI.SYS` installs the DOS ANSI.SYS device driver for the screen and printer. The command `DEVICE=C:\MOUSE1\MOUSE.SYS` installs a mouse driver. (The MOUSE.SYS file, in this example, is stored in the \MOUSE1 directory of drive C:.)

The command `DEVICE=C:\DOS\HIMEM.SYS` activates the DOS 5 extended memory manager so that you can access memory above the 640KB limit.

The command `SHELL=C:\DOS\COMMAND.COM /P /E:256` specifies COMMAND.COM as the command processor. The /P switch makes the command processor permanent for the entire session, and /E:256 provides 256 bytes for the DOS environment.

The command `LASTDRIVE=D` provides for two hard disk (or RAM disk) names—C: and D:. The command `DEVICE=C:\DOS\RAMDRIVE.SYS 3072 128 64 /E` creates a 3MB RAM disk in extended memory. The command `INSTALL=C:\DOS\FASTOPEN.EXE C:=(50) /X` installs the DOS 5 disk caching program in expanded memory.

See Also   ANSI.SYS, BREAK, BUFFERS, COMMAND, DEVICE, DEVICEHIGH, DOS, FASTOPEN, FILES, INSTALL, RAMDRIVE.SYS, LASTDRIVE, SHELL

COPY

Copies a file or a group of files to or from a device.

Version   1 and later

Type   Internal

DOS Shell Menu Access   Select the drive and directory (if necessary) that contains the file to be copied. Next, select the file(s) that you want to copy by highlighting the file names. Press Alt or F10, highlight File, and press Enter. Then select `Copy....` Modify the To: prompt in the box to specify the drive, directory, and name of the copy (if different from the name of the original).

Press Enter after you fill in the dialog box. While copying is taking place, you see its progress on the screen. If, during the copy process,

DOS discovers that a specified file name already exists on the target drive and directory, it asks if it should skip copying the current file, or overwrite the contents of the identically named file on the target directory. You can select either option; then, DOS continues copying. For more information, see Chapter 8.

Syntax

```
COPY [source drive][source path][source file name] [/A]
[/B] [[+]][...] [destination drive][destination
path][destination file name] [/A] [/B] [/V]
```

in which *source drive, source path,* and *source file name* identify the location and name of the original file to be copied, and *destination drive, destination path,* and *destination file name* identify the target location and name of the copy. The symbol + indicates that you can combine several separate files to be copied to a single destination file.

Usage

COPY is one of the commands that you will probably use daily in your computer work. It allows you to make copies of files from one disk to another, from one directory to another directory on the same disk, or from one file to another file name on the same directory. It also allows you to copy information from one device to another; for example, from your screen to a disk or from a file to the printer. In addition, COPY lets you combine two or more files into a single file. When copying files, remember that the file being copied is referred to as the *source* file. The copy is referred to as the *destination* or *target* file. Whenever you use the COPY command, the source file is always listed before the target file. Hence, you can think of the syntax of the COPY command as being COPY *source file* TO *target file*. (The one exception is when only one file description is given; in this case, the syntax is more like COPY *source file* TO HERE). The Examples section demonstrates all of these permutations.

Another important point to keep in mind when copying files is that COPY automatically overwrites any file with the same name without warning (unless you use the DOS 5 Shell to copy files). For example, suppose you have a file named BACKUP.TXT, which contains a backup of your first quarter Income Statement. You create a second quarter income statement named SECQTR.TXT.

Then, you decide to make a backup copy of SECQTR.TXT and name that backup copy BACKUP.TXT. As soon as you complete the copy, BACKUP.TXT contains the second quarter statement, and the first quarter statement backup no longer exists.

To avoid overwriting an existing file when you use the COPY command, first use the DIR command to see if a file already exists.

For example, before naming your backup of the income statement file program BACKUP.TXT, enter the command DIR BACKUP.TXT. If DIR shows that such a file exists, simply use a different name for the new backup, such as BACKUP2.TXT.

Note that you cannot copy files to a write-protected diskette. If you attempt to do so, DOS replies with the message

```
Write protect error writing drive A
Abort, Retry, Fail?
```

(Versions of DOS prior to Version 3.3 display the options `Abort, Retry, Ignore`.) You can remove the disk from drive A:, remove its write-protect tab, and put it back in the drive (or put a different disk in drive A:) and type the letter `R` to try again. Or, type `A` to abort the command and return to the command prompt.

When you omit the destination, DOS "assumes" that the destination is the current drive and directory. For example, if your hard disk drive C: is the current drive and you enter the command `COPY A:LETTER.TXT`, COPY copies the LETTER.TXT file from the disk in drive A: to the current drive and directory.

This works only when the source refers to a drive or directory other than the current drive or directory. For example, if you enter the command COPY LETTER.TXT, DOS returns the message `File cannot be copied to itself`, because you specified the current drive and directory as both the source and destination of the copy. A single drive and directory cannot contain two files with the same name.

The various switches (/A, /B, and /V) are described in the following list. In general, you do not need to use any of these switches; however, when you use COPY to combine multiple files into a single new file, the /A and /B switches can be useful. Either option affects the preceding file name and all following file names until another switch is encountered.

/A   Treats the file as an ASCII text file.

With a source file: Copies all text up to (but excluding) the EOF (end-of-file) marker, Ctrl-Z.

With a destination file: Adds the EOF marker to the end of the destination file.

/B   Treats the file as binary format.

With a source file: Copies the entire file, including any and all embedded EOF markers.

With a destination file: Does not add the EOF marker to the end of the file.

/V   Verifies that the copy is accurate.

When DOS completes a successful copy, it displays the message `(n) file(s) copied`, where *n* is the number of files that were copied.

You also can include device names, such as PRN and CON, to copy text files to devices. For example, the command COPY LETTER.TXT CON displays the contents of the LETTER.TXT file on the screen (console). The command COPY LETTER.TXT PRN prints the contents of the LETTER.TXT file.

Examples   To copy all files from the current directory on the hard disk to a diskette in drive A:, enter the command

```
COPY *.* A:
```

This command works even though no drive or path for the source files is given, because COPY assumes the current drive and directory. The *.* symbol refers to all files (any "first name" and any extension). Because the destination specifies only A:, files are sent to whichever directory is current on the disk in drive A:.

Suppose that your current directory is \WP on your hard disk drive C:. The diskette in drive A: contains some files that you want to copy. Furthermore, the disk in drive A: is not divided into separate directories. To copy all of the files from the diskette in drive A: to the current C:\WP drive and location, enter the command

```
COPY A:*.*
```

The preceding command works although only one file name specification is given (that is, A:*.*), because COPY assumes that the destination for the copies is the current drive and directory (C:\WP in this example). The source is assumed to be all of the files on the diskette in drive A:.

You can make a copy of a file that has a different name than the original copy. This is useful for making two copies of the same file on the same disk and directory. For example, suppose you want to keep a backup copy of your spreadsheet, named DEC1991.WK3, on the same disk and directory. You decide to name this backup copy DEC1988.BAK. To make the copy, enter the command

```
COPY DEC1991.WK3 DEC1991.BAK
```

To make copies of all your spreadsheet files and assign the copies the extension .BAK, enter the command

```
COPY *.WK3 *.BAK
```

This command says "Copy all of the files with .WK3 as the extension to files with the same first name, but the extension .BAK."

Suppose that the root directory of drive C: (that is, C:\) is the current directory, and you want to copy a file named MOM.LET from the directory named \WP to the diskette in drive A:. To do so, enter the command

```
COPY C:\WP\MOM.LET A:
```

Suppose you want to perform the same operation, but you want to copy the file to a directory named \LETTERS on drive A:. Assuming that the diskette in drive A: already contains a directory named LETTERS, enter the command

```
COPY C:\WP\MOM.LET A:\LETTERS\MOM.LET
```

If you want to do the same operation, but you want to store MOM.LET with the file name MOMLET.BAK on the LETTERS directory of drive A:, enter the command

```
COPY C:\WP\MOM.LET A:\LETTERS\MOMLET.BAK
```

Suppose you have three ASCII text files named CHAPTER1.TXT, CHAPTER2.TXT, and CHAPTER3.TXT. You want to combine all three files into a single file named BOOK.TXT. (All of the source files and the destination file are on the same drive and directory.) To do so, enter the command

```
COPY CHAPTER1.TXT + CHAPTER2.TXT + CHAPTER3.TXT BOOK.TXT
```

Because all three source files in this example have very similar names, you could also perform the copy using the command

```
COPY Chapter?.TXT Book.TXT
```

Note that joining files with the + command in COPY works only with simple ASCII text files, combining word processing documents, spreadsheet files, database files, and other non-ASCII files in this manner is less likely to lead to unpredictable results. To combine these other types of files, refer to the manual for the program you originally used to create those files.

To get some practice using COPY as a means of copying information between devices, you might want to try the following examples. To copy the information you type on the screen into a file named SAMPLE.TRY, use the CON device name in the COPY command, as follows:

```
COPY CON SAMPLE.TRY
```

After you enter this command, the cursor waits on the screen on the next blank line. Type the following two lines (press Enter after typing in each line):

```
This is a test
This is a test
```

Next, type Ctrl-L (hold down the Ctrl key and press the letter L). It appears as ^L on the screen. (This will force the printer to do a form feed in a later example.)

Finally, either type Ctrl-Z or press the F6 key. This displays the end-of-file marker ^Z on the screen. After you press Enter, COPY assumes that, because you entered the end-of-file marker, you have finished typing the file. You are returned to the DOS prompt.

To verify that what you typed on the screen was stored in a file, enter the command

```
COPY SAMPLE.TRY CON
```

This displays the contents of the file (excluding the end-of-file marker, which COPY does not show).

Now, to copy the SAMPLE.TRY file from the disk to the printer, use the device name PRN as the destination for the copy, by entering the following command

```
COPY SAMPLE.TRY PRN
```

After your printer prints the file, it ejects the entire page from the printer (in response to the Ctrl-L "form feed" that you entered into the file).

See Also   BACKUP, DISKCOPY, XCOPY, PRINT, TYPE

COUNTRY

Configures the date format, currency symbols, and other local conventions for specific countries.

Version   3.0 (enhanced in Versions 3.3 and later)

Type   Device driver (COUNTRY.SYS) used in CONFIG.SYS.

DOS Shell Menu Access   None

Syntax   Versions 3.0 to 3.2:

`COUNTRY=`*nnn*

Versions 3.3 and later:

`COUNTRY=`*nnn*`[`*,codepage*`]` `[`*,drive:path*`\COUNTRY.SYS]`

in which *nnn* is the three-digit code for the country, *codepage* is a three-digit number for the code page (character set), and *drive* and *path* represent the drive and directory that contain COUNTRY.SYS.

Usage   Different countries use different formats for displaying dates, times and currency. Computers built in the United States show dates in the North American formats, as follows:

Date: 2-31-90

Time: 1:50:00p

The COUNTRY.SYS device driver lets you modify the format used to display and enter dates and times, to standards used in other countries. The COUNTRY.SYS driver was initially released with Version 3.0 of DOS, and it was revised and expanded in Version 3.3 and later versions.

To use COUNTRY.SYS to modify the date and time format, you generally include the COUNTRY driver in your CONFIG.SYS file, followed by an equal sign and a three-digit number, which in most cases is the same as the country's telephone dialing prefix. In Version 3.3 and later, you also can specify a code page, which reconfigures the character set to that of the foreign language (see the entry for NLSFUNC in this appendix). Table B.3 shows the available country codes and the default code page used by each. (Those that are available only in versions 3.3 and later are marked with an asterisk.)

Table B.3. Country codes
and code pages used with COUNTRY.SYS.

Country/Language	Country Code	Default Code Page
Arabic*	785	437
Belgium	032	437, 850
China**	086	437, 850, 936
Denmark	045	865, 850
English (Intrnatl.)*	061	437, 850
Finland	358	437, 850

continues

Table B.3. *(continued)*

Country/Language	Country Code	Default Code Page
France	033	437, 850
French-Canadian	002	863, 850
Israel	972	437
Italy	039	437, 850
Japan**	081	437, 850, 932
Korea**	082	437, 850, 934
Latin America*	003	437, 850
Netherlands	031	437, 850
Norway	047	865, 850
Portugal	351	860, 850
Spain	034	437, 850
Sweden	046	437, 850
Switzerland*	041	437, 850
Taiwan**	088	437, 850, 938
United Kingdom	044	437, 850
United States	001	437, 850

* Version 3.3 and later only.
** Version 5 only.

In Versions 3.3 and later of DOS, you can omit the three-digit country code and code page number (but you must still include the commas), in which case DOS uses the default country and code page.

Examples   Adding the following command to the CONFIG.SYS file:

```
COUNTRY=034
```

converts the date and time displays to those used in Spain. The equivalent CONFIG.SYS command, using DOS 3.3 and later versions and assuming that COUNTRY.SYS is stored on the \DOS directory of drive C:, would be

```
COUNTRY=034,,C:\DOS\COUNTRY.SYS
```

In the future, each time you start the computer, DOS will display the date in the format 31.12.1990 (for December 31, 1990), and the time in the format 12.50.00.00 (for 12:50 PM).

The following CONFIG.SYS command specifies the United States country code and code page and tells DOS that the COUNTRY.SYS file is on the root directory of drive C.

```
COUNTRY=001,437,C:\COUNTRY.SYS
```

The next time you reboot the computer, dates are displayed in
`mm/dd/yy` format, the time is displayed in `hh.mm.ss` format, the
decimal point is displayed as a period (.), and the currency symbol
is $. The standard American keyboard is also assumed.

See Also CHCP, NLSFUNC, KEYB, MODE

CTTY

Changes the standard input and output devices.

Version 2 and later

Type Internal

DOS Shell Menu Access None

Syntax `CTTY [CON | device name]`

in which `CON` resets the standard input and output devices to the
standard monitor and keyboard, and `device name` defines another
device—such as COM1, COM2, AUX, etc.—to be used as the
primary input and output device.

Usage The CTTY command is used to change the input and output devices
on a system to any character-oriented device having both input and
output capabilities, such as a teletype unit with both a keyboard and
printer, or a remote terminal with a CRT and a keyboard.

The CTTY command can only be used for application programs that
use DOS function calls. It cannot be used with BASIC and other
programs that do not use DOS function calls.

Examples To change the input and output device to a remote terminal
connected to COM1, enter the following command at the DOS
prompt:

```
CTTY COM1
```

To return to the standard console, use

```
CTTY CON
```

at the remote terminal.

See Also MODE

DATE

Displays and, optionally, lets you change the system date.

Version 1 and later

Type Internal

DOS Shell Menu Access None

Syntax `DATE [current date]`

in which `current date` is an optional date entered in the mm-dd-yy format, or the format specified by the current COUNTRY.SYS setting.

Usage Use the DATE command to check the current system date (the date your computer thinks is correct) and, optionally, to change the date. All programs that allow you to access the system date use the date defined by the DATE command.

The format of the date shown and the format you need to follow to enter a new date are determined by the COUNTRY setting in your CONFIG.SYS file. If you use United States formats for dates and times, the date is displayed in mm-dd-yy format, although you can enter it in either mm-dd-yy or mm/dd/yy format.

Examples To check the system date, enter the command

`DATE`

The screen displays the system date, and DOS gives you the opportunity to change it.

```
Current date is Thu 4-20-1991
  Enter new date (mm-dd-yy):
```

If the date shown is accurate, press the Enter key. To change the date, type it in the format shown on the second line (that is, mm-dd-yy in this example), and press the Enter key.

See Also TIME

DEL

DEL is identical to the command ERASE. See ERASE in this appendix.

DELOLDDOS

Delete Old Operating System is a DOS 5 command used to delete your old operating system after installing DOS 5 and determining you are satisfied with it.

Version	5
Type	External
DOS Shell Menu Access	None
Syntax	DELOLDOS
Usage	Deletes the previous version of DOS stored on the OLD_DOS.1 directory after you have installed DOS 5. Then, DELOLDOS deletes itself (sort of a once-in-a-lifetime command).

Use this command only after you are certain that DOS 5 works correctly on your system and that you no longer need your original version of DOS.

Example	You have been running DOS 5 for several weeks, and all your hardware options and programs are behaving properly. You decide to get rid of your old operating system. To do so, type

DELOLDDOS

and press Enter.

See Also	Appendix A

DEVICE

Used in CONFIG.SYS to install optional device drivers.

Version	1 and later
Type	Internal, Configuration (used only in the CONFIG.SYS file)
DOS Shell Menu Access	None
Syntax	DEVICE=[drive][path]file name[options]

in which *drive* and *path* indicate the drive and directory location of the device driver file, *file name* represents the complete file name and extension of the device driver, and *options* represents additional parameters and switches supported by the device driver.

Usage   The DEVICE command is used only in the CONFIG.SYS file to install drivers for optional devices, such as a mouse, RAM disk, extended memory, or other options.

DOS offers several of its own device drivers, discussed in this appendix, such as ANSI.SYS, DISPLAY.SYS, PRINTER.SYS, RAMDRIVE.SYS, and others. Your specific computer and any optional devices that you add, such as a mouse, provide their own device drivers.

Examples   When added to your computer's CONFIG.SYS file, the following commands install the ANSI.SYS device driver, which allows for customization of the screen display and keyboard and a 512KB RAM disk in extended memory.

```
DEVICE=C:\DOS\ANSI.SYS
DEVICE=C:\DOS\RAMDRIVE.SYS 512 /E
```

In the previous commands, the ANSI.SYS and RAMDRIVE.SYS drivers are located in the \DOS directory of hard disk drive C:.

See Also   ANSI.SYS, HIMEM.SYS, DISPLAY.SYS, PRINTER.SYS, RAMDRIVE.SYS, DRIVER.SYS, XMA2EMS.SYS, XMAEMS.SYS, DEVICEHIGH

DEVICEHIGH

Used in CONFIG.SYS to install optional device drivers into reserved memory of computers using the 80286, 80386, and 80486 microprocessors.

Version   5

Type   Internal, Configuration (used only in the CONFIG.SYS file)

DOS Shell Menu Access   None

Syntax   `DEVICEHIGH [SIZE] = [hexsize] [drive][path]device driver`

in which `SIZE = hexsize` is the minimum amount of reserved memory that must be available to load the specified device driver. You must enter the *hexsize* parameter as the number of bytes in hexadecimal notation.

Usage   The DEVICEHIGH command is used only in the CONFIG.SYS file to load device drivers (such as RAMDRIVE.SYS or VDISK.SYS) into the 384KB of reserved memory on 80286, 80386, and 80486 systems. This frees more of your 640KB of conventional memory for additional applications programs.

Before you can use a DEVICEHIGH command in your CONFIG.SYS file, you must activate an upper memory block manager. With an 80386 or 80486 computer, you can use the DOS 5 HIMEM, DOS =, and EMM386 commands (in that order) to activate upper memory blocks before using any DEVICEHIGH commands.

If your computer has a processor other than an 80386 or 80486, you can use DEVICEHIGH only if you have some other, third-party upper memory manager, such as a device driver for managing an expanded memory board.

Examples   In this sample AUTOEXEC.BAT file, which would require DOS 5 on an 80386 or 80486 computer, the first three commands after the leading REMark set up extended memory (via HIMEM.SYS) and upper memory blocks (via the UMB switch with DOS = and the EMM386 expanded memory manager). Then SETVER, ANSI, SMARTDRV, and RAMDRIVE device drivers are loaded into upper memory:

```
REM ************************** Sample CONFIG.SYS
DEVICE = C:\DOS\HIMEM.SYS
DOS = HIGH,UMB
DEVICE = C:\DOS\EMM386.EXE NOEMS
DEVICEHIGH=C:\DOS\SETVER.EXE
DEVICEHIGH=C:\DOS\ANSI.SYS
DEVICEHIGH=C:\DOS\SMARTDRV.SYS 1024
DEVICEHIGH=C:\DOS\RAMDRIVE.SYS 720 /E
```

When executing a DEVICEHIGH command, DOS estimates the amount of memory to allocate the driver based on its file size. If a device driver later attempts to allocate more than that amount of memory to a device, the entire system will likely hang.

To prevent this, you can use the SIZE=*hexsize* parameter to specify how much memory to allocate the driver. For example, the following command allocates 64K (which translates to 40 hex) to a device driver named MEMHOG.SYS

```
DEVICEHIGH SIZE = 40 C:\DOS\MEMHOG.SYS
```

See Also   DOS, LOADHIGH, EMM386, MEM

DIR

Displays a directory of file names.

Version   1 and later

Type   Internal

DOS Shell Menu Access   The Files List on the Shell shows the names of files in the current directory.

Syntax

```
DIR [drive][path][file name] [...] [/A:[-]attributes]
[/B] [/L] [/O:[-]order] [/P] [/S] [/W]
```

in which *drive* and *path* specify the disk drive and directory of interest, *file name* is an actual or ambiguous file name, *attributes* displays only those files having the specified attributes, and *order* controls the order in which DIR sorts and displays file names.

Usage   The DIR command is used to display the names of files on any disk drive or directory. By default, along with each file name it displays the size of the file (in bytes), and the date and time of the most recent change to the file.

If there are many files in the directory, they will scroll off the screen before you can read them all. To make the display more readable, use either the /P option, which pauses for a keypress after each "page" (screenful) of information, or use the /W option, which displays the file names in as many as five columns across the screen. (The /W switch, however, does not display file information such as size and date.) You can use both the /P and /W options to display many file names in multiple columns with screen breaks.

You can also press Ctrl-S or Pause at any time while DIR is displaying file names, to temporarily stop the display. To resume the display, press any character key or the Spacebar.

To increase the power and versatility of the DIR command, the following new switches have been added in DOS 5:

/A   *attributes* displays only names with the specified attribute(s). Used without an *attributes* value, the /A switch lists all file names, even system and hidden files. *attributes* can be any combination of the following values (do not separate values with spaces):

–	reverses the action of the *attributes* value
A	displays names of files that will be archived during the next backup
D	displays directory names
H	displays hidden file names
R	displays read-only file names
S	displays system file names

/B   Lists only the names of files and directories; no other information is displayed

/L   Displays all names in lowercase letters

/O: *sortorder* specifies the order in which DIR displays file and directory names. Used without an *order* value, the /O switch lists directories before files and sorts all names alphabetically. *order* can be any combination of the following values (do not separate values with spaces):

–	reverses the action of the *order* value
N	sorts alphabetically by name
E	sorts alphabetically by extension
D	sorts by date and time, earliest first
S	sorts by size, smallest first
G	sorts with directories grouped before files

/S   Displays the list of file and directory names in all subdirectories

As you will see in the "Examples" section, these switches let you completely control your directory listings. Coupled with these options, DOS 5 also lets you set a new environmental variable (`DIRCMD`) so that you can customize the *default* action of the DIR command; that is, what happens when you simply type DIR without adding any switches. All you need to do is add the following command to your AUTOEXEC.BAT file:

```
SET DIRCMD = switches
```

to specify exactly how you want the DIR command to operate. The next section discusses practical examples of how to use the new DIRCMD variable.

You can use wild card characters to search for specific types of files. However, if you have used ASSIGN or JOIN on a disk drive or directory, you should cancel the assignment before using the DIR command.

Examples   The command

```
DIR
```

displays all of the file names, sizes, dates, and times on the current disk drive and directory.

To view all the files on the current directory that have the .SYS file name extension, enter the command

```
DIR *.SYS
```

The command

```
DIR A:
```

shows all of the file names, sizes, dates, and times in the root directory of the diskette in drive A:.

To view the file information in the directory named \DBMS on the current disk drive, enter the command

```
DIR \DBMS
```

To view all files with the extension .DBF in the \DBMS directory on drive C:, enter the command

```
DIR C:\DBMS\*.DBF
```

To send a copy of the directory listing to the printer, follow the DIR command with the > (redirection symbol) and the PRN device name, as follows:

```
DIR > PRN
```

To store a copy of the directory listing in a text file, follow the DIR command with the > symbol and a file name. For example, the following command creates a text file named DBFFILES.TXT, which contains a list of the files in the \DBMS directory that have the extension .DAT.

```
DIR C:\DBMS\*.DAT > DBFILES.TXT
```

If you want to display all the directories and files in the current directory, sorted in alphabetical order, type

```
DIR /A /O
```

The new DOS 5 switches let you easily display directory listings that involve complex searches and sorts. For example, the following command lists all of the files on hard disk C: (one directory at a time, the most recent files first) that have not been saved since your last backup operation.

```
DIR C:\ /A:A /O:-D /S /W
```

Note that the minus sign (–) before the D option in the /O switch reversed its action; that is, latest date first, rather than earliest date first. All of the other options to the /A and /O switches work the same way. For example, the following command lists all of the directory names on drive D: in reverse alphabetical order (from Z to A).

```
DIR D:\ /A:D /O:-N /S
```

As you can see, you can create hundreds of useful customized directory listings. However, most of the time you simply want to display the files in a specified directory. DOS 5 lets you tailor the way the DIR command works to suit your own needs. For example, I don't like the way the default DIR command works; for me, the best DIR command would perform the following operations:

❏ Display all of the files in a directory, even hidden and system files

❏ Display all of the directory and file names in alphabetical order

❏ Pause after each screenful of information

To set the DIRCMD environmental variable so that it executes these options every time you type DIR, add the following line to your AUTOEXEC.BAT file. (Note that there is no blank space before the equal sign.)

```
SET DIRCMD= /A /O:N /P
```

In future sessions (or once AUTOEXEC.BAT is executed), every time you type DIR, DOS will check the DIRCMD variable first and then execute DIR with the options you specified.

If, in some special situation, you don't want to use one of the options you set in the DIRCMD variable, simply cancel the switch with a minus sign. For example, if you are using the previous DIRCMD variable, but you don't want names to be sorted alphabetically, type

```
DIR -/O
```

You still will see all file and directory names and the display will still pause. However, now the names will be displayed in the order in which you put them on the disk.

If the FIND.EXE program is available in the current directory or in your system search path, you can use it to locate files that were created on a particular date or at a particular time, or files that contain certain letters. For example, the following command locates all files that were created on September 12, 1988:

```
DIR | FIND "4-12-88"
```

The next command displays the names of all files on drive C: that have the extension .BAT and that were created or last changed on April 12, 1991. The file names are displayed in alphabetical order.

```
DIR C:\*.BAT /O /S | FIND "4-12-91"
```

See Also   FIND, SET

DISKCOMP

Compares two floppy disks.

Version   1 and later

Type   External (DISKCOMP.COM)

DOS Shell Menu Access   None

Syntax

```
DISKCOMP [first drive] [second drive] /1 /8
```

in which *first drive* and *second drive* are names of two different floppy disk drives (not a hard disk drive).

Usage   DISKCOMP compares two floppy disks to see if they are identical. (DISKCOMP cannot be used with a hard disk.) Both disks must be the same size and density (that is, you cannot compare a 3.5-inch disk to a 5.25-inch disk, or a high-density disk to a double-density disk).

DISKCOMP compares all the sectors on the disk on a byte-by-byte (character-by-character) basis. Therefore, it is best to use DISKCOMP to compare only disks that were created with the DISKCOPY command (discussed next). Because COPY has the ability to defragment files, it probably will store them differently than DISKCOPY does. Therefore, DISKCOMP might think that disks created with COPY commands are "different," even though they actually contain the exact same data.

If your computer has only one floppy disk drive, you can still use DISKCOMP to compare two diskettes. DISKCOMP prompts you to remove and insert the disks as necessary.

If DISKCOMP does not find any differences between the two diskettes, it displays the message `Diskettes compare OK`. If DISKCOMP does find differences, it displays the message `Compare error(s) on Track n, side y`, in which *n* and *y* are the track and side numbers.

When finished comparing disks, DISKCOMP displays the prompt `Compare more diskettes (Y/N)?` Type `N` to quit, or type `Y` to compare more diskettes.

Examples   Suppose you just used DISKCOPY to copy the diskette in drive A: to the diskette in drive B:. To verify that the two diskettes are identical, you enter the command

`DISKCOPY A: B:`

Suppose you have only one floppy disk drive, named A:, and you use DISKCOPY to make a copy of a disk. To compare the two diskettes using only the one drive, enter the command

`DISKCOMP A: A:`

the screen prompts you to insert and remove disks as necessary.

See Also   COMP, DISKCOPY

DISKCOPY

Makes an exact copy of a diskette onto another diskette.

Version   1 and later

Type   External (DISKCOPY.COM)

DOS Shell
Menu Access   Select `Disk Utilities...` from the Main group, then select `Disk Copy` from the `DOS Utilities...` group.

Syntax   `DISKCOPY [source drive][destination drive] [/1] [/V]`

in which `source drive` is the name of the drive containing the disk to be copied, and `destination drive` is the drive containing the disk that is to receive the copy. The /1 switch copies only the first side of a diskette. The /V switch verifies that the copy is correct.

Usage   DISKCOPY makes an exact duplicate of a diskette, using either one or two floppy disk drives. DISKCOPY cannot be used with a hard disk. If the disk receiving the copy is not already formatted,

DISKCOPY formats the disk automatically. DISKCOPY is easier than COPY or XCOPY when the diskette contains many directories because it automatically copies all files in all directories.

However, because DISKCOPY makes an exact byte-by-byte copy of a disk, it does not consolidate fragmented files.

If you've used the commands JOIN or SUBST in the current session, cancel them before using DISKCOPY. Similarly, a drive that is shared by other users in a network should not be used for DISKCOPY.

After you complete a DISKCOPY, the screen displays the message Copy another (Y/N)? Enter N to quit, or enter Y to perform another DISKCOPY operation.

You can use the DISKCOMP command (discussed previously) to verify that a DISKCOPY operation was accurate. However, the new /V switch lets you perform the verification during the copy itself. This operation slows the copy, but you no longer need to use the DISKCOMP command to verify that the copy is indeed exact.

The optional /1 switch, available in Versions 3.2 and later, copies only one side of the diskette, regardless of the type of drive or diskettes in use.

Examples   Suppose you have purchased an uncopy-protected program that is stored on a diskette, and you want to immediately make a backup copy of it. If you have two identical floppy disk drives named A: and B:, you can place the original disk in drive A: and a blank disk in drive B:, and then enter the command

```
DISKCOPY A: B: /V
```

To perform the same task, using only a single disk drive (named A:), insert the original diskette in drive A: and enter the command

```
DISKCOPY A: A: /V
```

The screen prompts you to remove and insert, the source (original) disk and destination (copy) disk as necessary.

See Also   CHKDSK, COPY, DISKCOMP, XCOPY

DISPLAY.SYS

Modifies the screen to display a non-English language character set.

Version   3.3 and later

Type   Device driver, loaded by a DEVICE command in the CONFIG.SYS file.

DOS Shell   None
Menu Access

Syntax
```
DEVICE=[drive][path]DISPLAY.SYS CON[:]=(type[,[hardware
code page][,additional codes]])
```

or . . .

```
DEVICE=[drive][path]DISPLAY.SYS CON[:]=(type[,[hardware
code page][,additional codes,sub-fonts]])
```

in which *DRIVE* and *path* are the drive and directory locations of the DISPLAY.SYS file, *type* is the display adapter type, *hardware code page* specifies the code page supported by the display device, *additional codes* represents a prepared code page, and *sub-fonts* specifies the number of sub-fonts supported for each code page (DOS 4 only).

Usage   Most computers built in the United States have the code page number 437, for the English language, built into the video display adapter. If you reside in the United States or in any other country that uses code page 437, then you should not install the DISPLAY.SYS device driver. However, if you reside in a country that uses a different code page, as listed in Table B.3 in the COUNTRY entry of this appendix, then you might need to use DISPLAY.SYS to reconfigure your screen to use a different character set.

You also must use the DISPLAY.SYS device driver if you want to use *code page switching*, which allows you to switch from one character set to another from the DOS command prompt. Note, however, that code page switching is not supported by MONO (monochrome) or CGA (Color Graphics Adapter) displays.

Many computers that support Versions 3.3 and later of DOS can help you modify your computer's character set without directly modifying your CONFIG.SYS file. However, because code page switching capabilities vary from one computer to the next, you should refer to the DOS manual that came with your computer for specific details and capabilities. In general, however, the following acceptable parameters can be used with the DISPLAY.SYS device driver:

type is either MONO (monochrome), CGA (Color Graphics Adapter), EGA (for Extended Graphics and VGA video adapters), or LCD (for liquid crystal display adapters).

hardware code page is the code page supported by the video adapter, typically 437 (English), 850 (multilingual), 860 (Portuguese), 863 (French-Canadian), and 865 (Norwegian).

additional codes can be a number between 0 and 12 to support multiple code pages. If a CGA or MONO display adapter is specified as the *type*, then this value must be 0. If the *type* specified is EGA or LCD, then this value should be 1 if 437 is specified as the *hardware code page*, or 2 if a different *hardware code page* is specified.

sub-fonts (available only in DOS 4) can be used only with display adapters that specifically support sub-fonts. For CGA and MONO adapters, *sub-fonts* must be omitted or set to 0. LCD display adapters support 1 additional sub-font. EGA adapters support as many as 2 sub-fonts.

Examples   The following commands, when included in the CONFIG.SYS file, set up the display adapter to use French-Canadian date and time formats, as well as the French-Canadian character set.

```
COUNTRY=002 863 C:\DOS\COUNTRY.SYS
DEVICE=C:\DOS\DISPLAY.SYS CON=(EGA,437,2)
```

Including the following commands in your AUTOEXEC.BAT file then prepares the French-Canadian character set and allows you to switch from one character set to another using the CHCP command.

```
MODE CON CP PREP=((863,850)C:\DOS\EGA.CPI)
MODE CON CP SEL = 863 KEYB US,863,C:\DOS\KEYBOARD.SYS
```

See Also   CHCP, COUNTRY, KEYB, MODE, PRINTER.SYS

DOS

Links conventional memory and reserved memory, and can load DOS into the high memory area (HMA).

Version   5

Type   Configuration, used only in the CONFIG.SYS file.

DOS Shell Menu Access	None
Syntax	`DOS = [HIGH ¦ LOW[,UMB ¦ NOUMB]]`

in which `HIGH` loads DOS into high memory, LOW keeps DOS in conventional memory (the default setting), `UMB` lets DOS use reserved memory as an extension of conventional memory (`UMB` refers to Upper Memory Blocks), and `NOUMB` maintains the distinction between conventional and reserved memory (the default setting).

Usage This new DOS 5 configuration command gives you access to most of your 640KB of conventional memory by storing the operating system in high memory and by letting you store device drivers and terminate-and-stay-resident (TSR) programs in reserved (upper) memory. With all of these programs moved out of conventional memory, your application programs can create and use larger data files.

Examples To link reserved and conventional memory and move the operating system into high memory, enter the following command in your CONFIG.SYS file:

`DOS = HIGH,UMB`

This command moves most of the COMMAND.COM program into reserved memory. Depending on how many other TSR programs and device drivers you have loaded, it can leave you more than 600KB of conventional memory for your applications programs and data files.

To free even more conventional memory, you can then enter

`DEVICEHIGH = C:\DOS\COUNTRY.SYS`

later in your CONFIG.SYS file to load, for example, the COUNTRY.SYS device driver into reserved memory.

After using the `DOS = HIGH,UMB` command in CONFIG.SYS, you now can also install the EMM386.EXE command in your AUTOEXEC.BAT file and then follow it with a LOADHIGH command, as in this example:

`LOADHIGH GRAPHICS.COM`

This line loads the TSR portion of the GRAPHICS program into reserved memory. (Note that you must install the EMM386.EXE driver before you can use the LOADHIGH command.)

See Also DEVICEHIGH, LOADHIGH

DOSKEY

Lets you display, edit, and run previously executed commands, and lets you create, run, and save macros.

Version 5

Type External (DOSKEY.COM)

DOS Shell Menu Access None

Syntax

```
DOSKEY [macro=commands ¦ /BUFSIZE=SIZE ¦ /HISTORY ¦
/MACROS ¦ /INSERT ¦ /OVERSTRIKE ¦ /REINSTALL]
```

in which *macro=commands* specifies a customized command named *macro* consisting of one or more DOS commands (and switches, if needed) except the batch command GOTO, and /BUFSIZE=*SIZE* determines the size of the buffer (in bytes) that stores the macros you create. The default size is 1024 bytes.

The following switches also may be used with the DOSKEY command; however, DOSKEY accepts only one switch at a time.

/HISTORY (or /H)	Displays all command lines stored in memory (so you can redirect the list to a file)
/MACROS (or /M)	Displays all current macros (so you can redirect the list to a file
/INSERT	Specifies "insert" mode as the default editing mode. Text that you enter is inserted into existing command-line text
/OVERSTRIKE	Specifies "overstrike" mode as the default editing mode. Text that you enter overwrites existing command-line text
/REINSTALL	Installs a new copy of DOSKEY into memory

Usage The DOS 5 DOSKEY program is a TSR command-line editor/macro generator that lets you recall, edit, and reuse previously executed commands. DOSKEY also enables you to create and run macros that act like small, fast batch files.

DOSKEY offers many advantages to DOS users. In fact, unless you use the DOS Shell exclusively, you probably should add the DOSKEY command to your AUTOEXEC.BAT file so that its features are always available. After you run DOSKEY, you have a remarkable array of convenient command-line tools at your disposal. For example, now you can

❑ Issue more than one command on a single line

❑ Display and use previously executed commands

❑ Edit and reuse previously executed commands

❑ Save and store a list of commands

❑ Create, use, and save *macros* (single-line, user-defined internal commands that act like batch files)

In fact, macros are so useful that many people will probably convert most of their simple, often-used batch files into macros, which run faster and are available in any directory as internal DOS commands. Table B.4 is a brief reference of DOSKEY's command-line editing options, and Table B.5 lists macro-creation codes and valid batch commands available for macros. For complete details about the program and tutorial for its use, see Chapter 15.

Table B.4. DOSKEY command-line keys.

Recalling command lines

Key	Action
↑	Recalls previous command
↓	Recalls following command
Pg Up	Recalls oldest command in buffer
Pg Dn	Recalls most recent command in buffer

Command-line editing

Key	Action
←	Moves the cursor one character left
→	Moves the cursor one character right
Ctrl-←	Moves the cursor one word left
Ctrl-→	Moves the cursor one word right
Home	Moves the cursor to beginning of line

continues

Table B.4. *(continued)*

Command-line editing

Key	Action
End	Moves the cursor to end of line
Esc	Clears the command line
F1	Copies one character from the previous command
F2*character*	Inserts previous command up to the character you type
F3	Copies any characters from previous command to the right of the current cursor location
F4*character*	Deletes previous command up to the character you type
F5	Copies current line into the buffer and clears the command line
F6	Inserts Ctrl-Z (the end-of-file marker) at end of the command line
F7	Displays all command lines in memory
Alt-F7	Deletes all command lines in memory
F8*text*	Displays the first command line that matches the text you enter
F9*line*	Selects the command specified by the line number (shown by pressing F7)
F10	Displays all macros in memory
Alt-F10	Deletes all macros in memory

Table B.5. DOSKEY macro keys.

Macro creation codes

Macro Symbol	Command Line Symbol
$G	> (Greater than symbol)
$L	< (Less than symbol)

Table B.5. *(continued)*

Macro creation codes

Macro Symbol	Command Line Symbol
$B	¦ (vertical bar symbol)
$T	Command separator
$$	$ (dollar sign symbol)
$1 ... $9	Replaceable variables
$*	Special variable that accepts all text on the command line after the macro name

Valid macro/batch commands

CALL

ECHO

FOR

IF

PAUSE

REM

SHIFT

Examples

After you execute the DOSKEY command (usually in your AUTOEXEC.BAT file), you have a multitude of command-line tools at your fingertips. For example, you now can type more than one command on a line; type a command, press Ctrl-T (which appears on the screen as the ¶ symbol), type another command, and so on. (Note that you can only type 127 characters per line.) This feature is handy when you need to change drives and directories and then start a program, as in the following command line, which changes to drive D: and starts the Harvard Graphics program in the \HG directory.

```
D:¶ CD\HG¶HG
```

DOS always stores your last command in a buffer so that you can quickly repeat the command by pressing the F3 key. When you use DOSKEY, however, DOS stores many of your previous commands (the number of which varies according to the size of the buffer you specify). You can recall previous commands by using the keys listed in the first part of Table B.4. The easiest way to recall the last command is to press ↑. For example, if you've issued the following three commands

```
D:¶CD\HG¶HG
C:
\WINDOWS\WINWORD
```

and you want to restart your Harvard Graphics program, you can recall the `D:¶CD\HG¶HG` command by pressing the ↑ key three times or by pressing the PgUp key (which displays the oldest command currently in the DOSKEY buffer).

You can move to a later command by reversing the commands—press the ↓ or PgDn keys. Note, however, that when you move past the oldest command, the display "wraps" to the most recent command; when you move past the last command, the display wraps to the oldest.

You also can easily edit a previously executed command. Suppose, for example, that you've just finished copying all your recent backup files to a floppy disk with a command such as

```
XCOPY *.BAK /A /S A:
```

and now you want to copy all your .TXT files to drive A:. You don't have to retype the entire command; simply use one of the methods listed in Table B.4 to quickly recall the command, and then edit it. For example, you could press → (or F3) to display the command, and then press the ← key until the cursor is under the "B". Because the command-line editor is in overstrike mode by default, type TXT to replace the original BAK characters, and then press Enter. (An even quicker method would be to press F2, type B, type TXT, and press F3 to complete the command.)

DOSKEY includes another feature that helps you edit a previously issued command. You can press the Ins key to change from "overstrike mode" to "insert mode"; this lets you add to a command line without changing the original. For example, if you recall the previous command and press the Ins key, you can add the /E and /V switches by simply typing them in the appropriate location. The characters to the right of the additions move to accommodate the new characters.

```
XCOPY *.BAK /E /V /A /S A:
```

To display a list of all the previous commands stored in the DOSKEY buffer, type the following command:

```
DOSKEY /HISTORY (or /H)
```

If you use many long commands or you want to save more commands than the default buffer holds, you can expand the DOSKEY buffer with a command similar to the following:

```
DOSKEY /BUFSIZE=2048
```

Note, however, that this doubles the size of the default buffer and uses another kilobyte of conventional memory. If you have the memory to spare, you might want to add this command to your AUTOEXEC.BAT file.

DOSKEY Macros

You also can use DOSKEY to create some very helpful macros. A macro, as the name implies, is a type of "big" command; that is, it can be either a single command that includes a complex set of options or a series of commands grouped together on one line.

One of the simplest—and most useful—macros you can create involves the TYPE command. When you use TYPE to display a long file, the text quickly scrolls off the screen unless you press Ctrl-S or use the MORE filter. The DOSKEY command lets you create the following macro, which pauses after each screenful of information:

```
DOSKEY TYPE=TYPE $1 $B MORE
```

Because DOS checks the current list of macros in the DOSKEY buffer before it checks its own commands, your new macro always executes when you type TYPE. Therefore, from now on, every time that you issue the TYPE command, DOS executes the command

```
TYPE FILENAME.EXT ¦ MORE
```

Note that you had to use the special symbol $B to enter the pipe (¦) character into the macro. Table B.5 lists all of the special symbols that you will need to use in your macros.

If you've created a macro that has the same name as another command or program, DOS always runs the macro first; thus, your macro executes much faster than a batch file and is available from any drive or directory, regardless of your current system PATH setting. However, if you want to execute a command that has the same name as a macro, simply precede the command with a space. Using the previous example, TYPE would execute your macro, but <space>TYPE would execute the original DOS command.

If you have created small batch files that you use often, you might want to convert them to macros. For example, if you are using a laser printer, you probably need to eject pages several times during the day. Rather than type the command `ECHO ^L > PRN`, you probably created a batch file called FF.BAT (form feed). You now can make this a macro by typing the following command:

```
DOSKEY FF=ECHO ^L $G PRN
```

(Note that you must use the $G notation to designate a > symbol in a macro.) Now, whenever you want to eject a page from the printer, simply type the FF command.

For all practical purposes, the previous macro is now an internal DOS command. To list all of your current macros, type

```
DOSKEY /MACROS (or /M)
```

Unfortunately, because all of your macros are stored in a RAM buffer, they are lost when you turn off your computer. However, if you save them in a batch file and then execute that batch file from AUTOEXEC.BAT, your computer will load your macros at the start of each session, thus creating your own "permanent" extensions to DOS. To create a batch file of your current macros, type

```
DOSKEY /M > C:\DOS\MACROS.BAT
```

This command sends a list of all your macros to the file MACROS.BAT, which might contain the following lines:

```
TYPE=TYPE $B MORE
FF=ECHO ^L $G PRN
```

Now all you have to do is edit the batch file to include the DOSKEY command at the start of each line

```
DOSKEY TYPE=TYPE $B MORE
DOSKEY FF=ECHO ^L $G PRN
```

and run the file from your AUTOEXEC.BAT file. If you use the examples in this section, your AUTOEXEC.BAT file might now contain the lines

```
C:\DOS\DOSKEY /BUFSIZE=2048
CALL C:\DOS\MACROS.BAT
```

Now the TYPE command will always work like you want it to, and you can always use the new DOS FF command whenever you need it.

See Also   Chapter 15

DOSSHELL

Activates the DOS Shell.

Version 5

Type External (DOSSHELL.EXE)

Syntax `DOSSHELL [/T[:L | M | H | V | S | U]]`

`[/G[:L | M | H | V | S | U]] [/B]`

in which

`/T:x` Runs the DOS Shell in text mode, with a resolution of Low, Medium, High, VGA, Super VGA, or 8514/A (U)

`/G:x` Runs the DOS Shell in graphics mode, with a resolution of Low, Medium, High, VGA, Super VGA, or 8514/A (U)

`/B` Lets the Shell sound warning beeps during operations

Usage Although the DOSSHELL command was introduced in DOS 4, the DOS 5.0 version of the Shell has been completely reworked and is much improved. It uses less memory, it's faster, and it contains several features found in Windows 3.0. The new DOS 5.0 Shell makes DOS easy to use for both beginners and advanced users.

The DOS 5.0 Shell lets you perform all of the essential DOS commands—copying files, creating directories, listing file names, and so on—from an easy-to-use graphical interface that includes pull-down menus, dialog boxes, an extensive context-sensitive help system, movable icons, mouse support, and enhanced DOS commands.

You also can perform many operations from the Shell that are not available from the command line, including "task switching," renaming directories, "associating" data files with executable files, moving files (through menu operations or by actually "dragging" file icons to other locations), viewing files in hexadecimal format, creating "groups" of related programs, and so on.

DOSSHELL.INI

The DOS 5 installation program creates an initialization file named DOSSHELL.INI, which configures the Shell to your particular computer and devices. If you install DOS 5 for use on a floppy-based system, DOSSHELL.INI is stored in the root directory of the Shell diskette. If you install DOS 5 for use on a hard disk, the DOSSHELL.INI file is created and stored in the \DOS directory of disk drive C:.

When you enter the command DOSSHELL at the command prompt, the DOSSHELL.COM program uses the settings stored in the DOSSHELL.INI file to configure the Shell with the initialization information stored there during previous sessions. On a hard disk system, the directory that contains DOSSHELL files (DOSSHELL.COM, DOSSHELL.EXE, DOSSHELL.INI, DOSSHELL.VID, DOSSHELL.GRB, and DOSSHELL.HLP) must be included in the current PATH setting. Otherwise, you will not be able to access the Shell unless its home directory is the current directory.

Because DOSSHELL.INI is an ASCII text file, you can edit it with a text editor, such as the DOS 5 Editor (for example, EDIT C:\DOS\DOSSHELL.INI from the command prompt.) However, it's rarely necessary to do so, because the DOS Shell itself manages most of the DOSSHELL.INI file.

Within the DOSSHELL.INI file, all the introductory text up to the first left bracket ([) is a comment (ignored by the computer). The first section beneath the comment is labeled [savestate]. This section records all the current settings in the Shell when you exit so that those same settings can be activated the next time you start the Shell.

screenmode	Text or Graphics for the screen mode
resolution	Low, Medium, or High resolution (depends on display type)
startup	Initial view
sortkey	Sort order of file names in Files list
pause	Enabled/Disabled pause when returning to Shell
swapmouse	Enabled/Disabled left-handed mouse
tasklist	Enabled/Disabled Task List
switching	Enabled/Disabled task swapping
sortorder	Ascending/Descending sort order of file names
displayhiddenfiles	Enabled/Disabled display of hidden files
replaceconfirm	Enabled/Disabled confirm on replace
deleteconfirm	Enabled/Disabled confirm on replace mouse

`confirm`	Enabled/Disabled confirm on mouse move/copy
`crossdirselection`	Enabled/Disabled select across directories

The second major section of the DOSSHELL.INI file is labeled `[programstarter]`. This section is updated automatically whenever you add, change, or delete groups or programs in the Program List area of the Shell; so there is rarely a need to alter this part of DOSSHELL.INI. Options you'll see listed include

`currentcolor`	Color selection at Shell startup
`filemanager`	Enabled/Disabled Files list
`command`	????????????? = enabled
`group`	Group definition between { and }
`program`	Program definition between { and }
`command`	Program command
`title`	Program title
`help`	Program help text
`pause`	Enabled/Disabled pause on return to Shell
`screenmode`	Graphics/Text screen mode for program
`alttab`	Enabled/Disabled switch with Alt+Tab
`altesc`	Enabled/Disabled switch with Alt+Esc
`ctrlesc`	Enabled/Disabled switch with Ctrl+Esc
`prevent association`	Enabled/Disabled prevent program switch

A third major section of the DOSSHELL.INI file begins with the command `color =`. This section lists every color scheme available in the Shell. This part of the file is an exception to the others in that, if you want to create a custom color scheme, you must do so by modifying this section of the DOSSHELL.INI file.

Each color scheme you create must start with a `selection =` command, end with two curly braces, and have the overall structure shown in the following example. When adding a new color scheme to DOSSHELL.INI, be sure to start the `selection =` command for the new color scheme beneath the second closing brace (}) that ends the color scheme above it.

```
selection =
{
    title = Basic Blue
    foreground =
    {
        base = black
        highlight = brightwhite
        selection = brightwhite
        alert = brightred
        menubar = black
        menu = black
        disabled = white
        accelerator = cyan
        dialog = black
        button = black
        elevator = white
        titlebar = black
        scrollbar = brightwhite
        borders = black
        drivebox = black
        driveicon = black
        cursor = black
    }
    background =
    {
        base = brightwhite
        highlight = blue
        selection = black
        alert = brightwhite
        menubar = white
        menu = brightwhite
        disabled = brightwhite
        accelerator = brightwhite
        dialog = brightwhite
        button = white
        elevator = white
        titlebar = white
        scrollbar = black
        borders = brightwhite
        drivebox = brightwhite
        driveicon = brightwhite
        cursor = brightblack
    }
}
```

The colors you can use in defining your color scheme are

black	brightblack
blue	brightblue
brown	brightyellow
cyan	brightcyan
green	brightgreen
magenta	brightmagenta
red	brightred
white	brightwhite

The last main section of the DOSSHELL.INI file begins with the `associations =` command that define associations between programs and data files. This part of the Shell is managed automatically when you set up associations via the Shell using the Association option on the File pull-down menu, so there is no need to edit this part of DOSSHELL.INI file yourself. Commands used in this part of the shell are

`program`	Name of program
`extension`	Associated file name extension

Normally, DOS expects to find the DOSSHELL.INI file in the same directory as the other DOSSHELL files (typically C:\DOS.) If you want to store that file elsewhere, you must use the DOSSHELL= command to indicate the path in the environment. For example, this command (best placed in the AUTOEXEC.BAT file) tells DOS that the DOSSHELL.INI file is located in C:\INIFILES:

```
SET DOSSHELL=C:\INIFILES
```

Examples   To run the DOS Shell from the command prompt, enter

```
DOSSHELL
```

To start the DOS Shell on a VGA monitor in high resolution graphics mode (60 lines) with warning beeps, enter this command

```
DOSSHELL /G:H2 /B
```

To run the Shell in upper memory (assuming you've already activated upper memory blocks), enter

```
LOADHIGH DOSSHELL
```

See Also   Chapter 3

DRIVER.SYS

Assigns logical names to disk drives.

Version   3.2 and later

Type   Device driver, activated by a DEVICE command in CONFIG.SYS

**DOS Shell
Menu Access**   None

Syntax   `DEVICE=[drive:][path\]DRIVER.SYS /D:ddd[/T:ttt] [/S:ss] [/H:hh] [/C] [/F:f]`

in which *drive* and *path* are the location of the DRIVER.SYS file, *ddd* specifies the drive number, *ttt* specifies the number of tracks per side, *ss* specifies the number of sectors per track, *hh* specifies the maximum number of heads, and *f* specifies the form factor.

Usage   DRIVER.SYS is generally required only when you add a new external disk drive to your computer and that disk drive does not offer its own device driver. Any computer can support a maximum of twenty-six disk drives, named A: to Z:. Each partition on a single hard disk represents a drive. (For example, a 60MB hard disk that is partitioned into two drives, C: and D:, counts as two disk drives.)

Of the available switches, only /D is mandatory. You must specify a number in the range of 0 to 127 with /D. Note that floppy drive A: is referred to as drive 0 and is assumed to be internal. Floppy drive B: is already numbered 1, even if the computer does not actually have a second floppy disk drive. Therefore, you should avoid using both the number 0 and 1 with the /D option. A value of 2 represents a third floppy drive, which must be external.

The first fixed (hard) disk, usually named C:, is numbered 128. This may be either an existing internal drive or a new external drive. The second fixed disk drive is numbered 129; the third fixed disk drive is numbered 130; and so on.

The optional /T switch specifies the number of tracks per side on the disk. If omitted, the number defaults to 80. The optional /S switch specifies the number of tracks per sector, in the range of 1 to 99. If omitted, 9 is assumed. The optional /H switch specifies the maximum head number for the drive, in the range of 1 to 99. If omitted, 2 is assumed.

The optional /C switch activates the *changeline support* feature available on some disk drives. This allows the drive to detect whether or not the drive door has been opened since the last disk access. If omitted, DOS assumes that this feature is not available on the drive. Note that computers based on the earlier 8086 and 8088 microprocessors generally cannot support this feature.

The optional /F switch specifies the *form type* for an external floppy disk drive.

Table B.6 shows examples of the DRIVER.SYS switches for commonly used external floppy disk drives.

Table B.6. DRIVER.SYS settings used with floppy disk drives.

Drive Capacity	Disk Size	Tracks (/T)	Sectors (/S)	Heads (/H)	Form (/F)
160KB/180KB	5.25	40	9	1	0
320KB/360KB	5.25	40	9	2	0
1.2MB	5.25	80	15	2	1
720KB	3.5	80	9	2	2
1.44MB	3.5	80	18	2	7

DOS automatically names external drives using alphabetical sequencing. For example, suppose your computer already has two floppy drives, named A: and B:, and one hard disk named C:. The first time DOS encounters a DEVICE=DRIVER.SYS command in the CONFIG.SYS file, the newly specified drive is named D:.

To assign the highest letter names to RAM disks rather than to external disk drives, place the preceding DEVICE=DRIVER.SYS command(s) the DEVICE=RAMDRIVE.SYS commands in your CONFIG.SYS file. In this way, external drives are assigned names before the RAM disk.

Remember that any changes you make to the CONFIG.SYS file are not activated until the next time you reboot. Also, be sure to check the documentation that came with your external disk drive to determine its specific requirements and whether it offers a device driver that can be used in lieu of DRIVER.SYS. Also, adding new disk drives to a computer often requires changing dip switch settings inside the computer. Again, only the documentation that comes with a new disk drive can provide specific information.

Examples   Suppose you have an AT-type computer with a 1.2MB disk drive
named A: and a hard disk partitioned into two drives named C: and
D:. The following command, when entered into your CONFIG.SYS
file, adds a 720KB, 3.5-inch disk drive named E: to the computer
(assuming the drive is properly connected and the DRIVER.SYS file
is stored in the directory named DOS of hard disk drive C:).

```
DEVICE=C:\DOS\DRIVER.SYS /D:2 /T:80 /S:9 /H:2 /F:2
```

See Also   CONFIG.SYS, DEVICE

DRIVPARM

Defines the parameters of disk or tape drive.

Version   3.2 and later

Type   External (executed in CONFIG.SYS)

**DOS Shell
Menu Access**   None

Syntax
```
DRIVPARM = /D:number [/C] [/F:type] [/H:heads] [/I] [/N]
[/S:sectors] [/T:tracks]
```

where

/D:*number*   Specifies the drive number to be modified, and can
be any value in the range 0 through 255, where
0 = drive A:, 1 = drive B:, and so forth

/C   Specifies a drive that can determine whether or not
the drive door is closed

/F:*type*   Specifies the type of drive from the following list:

    0   160/180/320/360KB (5.25-inch) floppy disk

    1   1.2MB (5.25-inch) floppy disk

    2   720KB (3.5-inch) floppy disk (the default)

    5   Hard disk drive

    6   Tape drive

    7   1.44MB (3.5-inch) floppy disk

/H:*heads*   Specifies the maximum number of heads for the
drive (from 1 to 99)

/I	Specifies a 3.5-inch floppy disk drive that your system would not normally support
/N	Specifies a nonremovable device
/S:*sectors*	Specifies the number of sectors per track (from 1 to 99)
/T:*tracks*	Specifies the number of tracks per side (from 1 to 999)

Usage   Whenever a drive performs an I/O (input/output) operation, DOS checks an internal table that lists the characteristics of that drive. The DRIVPARM command modifies that table for an existing drive.

The /I switch is not available in version 3 of DOS. Some manufacturer specific versions of DOS, such as IBM PC-DOS, may not include DRIVPARM.

Example   Suppose your drive E: is an internal tape drive that writes 10 tracks of 99 sectors each. You can change the way DOS stores data on that drive by using the DRIVPARM command in your CONFIG.SYS file to alter the internal DOS table entry for drive E: (or rather, drive #4), as shown:

```
DRIVPARM = /D:4 /F:6 /H:1 /S:40 /T:20
```

This command tells DOS that drive E: is a tape drive (/F:6) that has one head (/H:1), writes 40 sectors (/S:40) per track, and 20 tracks (/T:20).

See Also   DRIVER.SYS

ECHO

Turns ECHO mode on or off, and sends characters to the screen or printer.

Version   1 and later

Type   Internal (generally used in batch files)

DOS Shell Menu Access   None

Syntax
```
ECHO [ON | OFF] [message]
```

in which *message* is text or characters that you want the batch file to display.

Usage   Normally when a batch file executes its commands, it first displays the entire command on the screen. However, if you turn the ECHO off, the batch file will execute its commands without displaying them on the screen. ECHO remains off until the batch file finishes executing or the file encounters an ECHO ON command.

Regardless of whether ECHO is on or off, text to the right of an ECHO command is always displayed on the screen. When ECHO is ON, however, the command itself and the message are displayed. For example, if ECHO is OFF, the following command

```
ECHO Hello friend
```

displays

```
Hello friend
```

But when ECHO is ON, the same command displays

```
ECHO Hello friend
Hello friend
```

As an alternative to setting ECHO OFF, you can precede commands in a batch file with an @ character (Versions 3.3 and later). For example, the command @ECHO Hello friend displays only `Hello friend`, whether ECHO is on or off. To prevent the first ECHO OFF command in a batch file from appearing on the screen, use @ECHO OFF instead.

Entering the command ECHO directly at the DOS prompt displays the current status of the ECHO option. Entering the command ECHO OFF directly at the DOS prompt turns off the display of the prompt. Enter the command ECHO ON to recall the prompt.

ECHO affects only the display of commands within the batch file; it does not affect information messages such as `1 file(s) copied`, at the end of a COPY command. To hide such messages, redirect them to the NUL device. For example, the command `COPY *.BAK A: > NUL` copies all .BAK files from the current drive and directory to the disk in drive A:, but does not display any message during or after the copy procedure.

To redirect echoed characters to the printer, use the `> PRN` redirection symbol and device name. For example, to send a form feed (to eject a page) to the printer, use the command `ECHO ^L > PRN`, where `^L` is typed by pressing Ctrl-L (hold down the Ctrl key and type the letter L). This command works the same whether it is included in a batch file or typed at the command prompt.

Examples   The following batch file, named GREET.BAT, clears the screen, presents a couple of greeting lines, and customizes the DOS prompt:

```
REM -------------- GREET.BAT
CLS
ECHO Welcome to DOS
ECHO Here is the prompt...
PROMPT $P$G
```

Because this batch file does not turn off ECHO, it displays the following cluttered screen when executed:

```
C:>ECHO Welcome to DOS
Welcome to DOS
C:>ECHO Here is the prompt
Here is the prompt
C:>PROMPT $P$G
C:\>
```

The improved version of GREET.BAT includes an ECHO OFF command as the first line.

```
@ECHO OFF
REM -------------- GREET.BAT
CLS
ECHO Welcome to DOS
ECHO Here is the prompt...
PROMPT $P$G
```

When this batch file is executed, it presents this much neater display:

```
Welcome to DOS
Here is the prompt
C:\>
```

Note that you can also use ECHO to display a message from a DOSKEY macro; however, DOS always displays the command along with the message. In other words, the @ symbol and the OFF switch have no effect on any ECHO commands used in a macro.

See Also   DOSKEY, REM

EDIT

Creates or edits a text file with the new full-screen DOS editor.

Version   5

Type   External (EDIT.COM)

DOS Shell   Select the `MS-DOS Editor` option from the Main
Menu Access   Group of the Program List.

Syntax   `EDIT [drive:][path]file name [/B] [/G] [/H] [/NOHI]`

in which *drive*, *path*, and *file name* provide the location and name of the file you want to create or edit, and the following switches let you change default display settings:

/B	Displays EDIT in monochrome on a color monitor.
/G	Provides fast updates for CGA monitors. If your monitor flickers, it doesn't support this option; restart EDIT without /G.
/H	Displays the maximum number of lines permitted by your display adapter.
/NOHI	Lets you use a monitor that doesn't support high intensity (do not use with COMPAQ laptop computers).

Usage   EDIT, the new DOS full-screen text editor, is a long overdue addition to the operating system. Its menus, mouse support, cut-and-paste options, and search-and-replace feature let you create and edit ASCII files much more easily than you could with the archaic EDLIN line editor. As a bonus, EDIT's full-screen display also lets you browse through text files more easily than you can with the DOS TYPE command.

EDIT lets you quickly and easily perform the following operations:

❏ Create new text (ASCII) files

❏ Read or edit existing text files on a full-screen editor

❏ Print a file

❏ Move, delete, and copy blocks of text

❏ Merge two files

❏ Search an entire file for a text string

❏ Replace some or all occurrences of a text string

Note that EDIT and the QBASIC programming environment share common code in DOS 5, and they use the same initialization file—QBASIC.INI. Any color or configuration changes that you make to EDIT automatically take effect when you start QBASIC, and vice versa.

As with most Microsoft products, EDIT includes a *context-sensitive* help system that provides instant on-line help. Context-sensitive means that the position of the cursor determines the type of help that is displayed when you press F1 or select Help from the Menu Bar. For example, if the highlight is on the Print command in the File menu when you press F1, a window displays information about how to use that option.

EDIT lets you use two sets of keyboard commands for most actions— a Microsoft set and a WordStar-compatible set. If you already know the WordStar editing commands, you can immediately begin using most of the functions of EDIT.

As a handy reference, Table B.7 lists all of the help commands you can use in the EDIT program and Table B.8 shows you how to access all of the program's features. However, for a complete discussion of EDIT and a tutorial of its use, see Chapter 10.

Table B.7. Help keys.

Actions	Keystrokes
View EDIT Help	F1 (or click the right mouse button)
Exit Help	Esc
View "Getting Started"	Shift-F1
Pull down the Help menu	Alt-H
Move to next topic	Tab
Move to previous topic	Shift-Tab
Move to next topic starting with *char*	*char*
Move to previous topic starting with *char*	Shift-*char*
View previous topic	Alt-F1 (or double-click the Back button)
View next Help topic	Ctrl-F1
View previous Help topic	Shift-Ctrl-F1

Table B.8. EDIT actions and keystrokes.

Cursor movement

Actions	Microsoft Keystrokes	WordStar-Compatible Keystrokes
Left one character	←	Ctrl-S
Right one character	→	Ctrl-D
Left one word	Ctrl-←	Ctrl-A
Right one word	Ctrl-→	Ctrl-F
Up one line	↑	Ctrl-E
Down one line	↓	Ctrl-X
First indention of current line	Home	
Beginning of current line		Ctrl-Q,S
Beginning of next line	Ctrl-Enter	Ctrl-J
End of line	End	Ctrl-Q,D
Top of window		Ctrl-Q,E
Bottom of window		Ctrl-Q,X

Text-scrolling keys

Actions	Microsoft Keystrokes	WordStar-Compatible Keystrokes
Up one line	Ctrl-↑	Ctrl-W
Down one line	Ctrl-↓	Ctrl-Z
Up one page	PgUp	Ctrl-R
Down one page	PgDn	Ctrl-C
Left one window	Ctrl-PgUp	
Right one window	Ctrl-PgDn	
Set bookmarks (maximum of 4)		Ctrl-K,0-3
Access set bookmarks		Ctrl-Q,0-3

Text-selection keys

Actions	Microsoft Keystrokes	WordStar-Compatible Keystrokes
Left one character	Shift-←	
Right one character	Shift-→	
Left one word	Shift-Ctrl-←	
Right one word	Shift-Ctrl-→	
Current line	Shift-↓	
Line above	Shift-↑	
Screen up	Shift-PgUp	
Screen down	Shift-PgDn	
To beginning of file	Shift-Ctrl-Home	
To end of file	Shift-Ctrl-End	

Insert and copy keys

Actions	Microsoft Keystrokes	WordStar-Compatible Keystrokes
Toggle Insert and Overstrike modes	Ins	Ctrl-V
Copy selected text to Clipboard	Ctrl-Ins	
Move selected text to Clipboard	Shift-Del	
Move current line to Clipboard		Ctrl-Y
Move text to end of line to Clipboard		Ctrl-Q,Y
Paste contents of Clipboard	Shift-Ins	
Insert blank line below cursor position	End-Enter	
Insert blank line above cursor position	Home,Ctrl-N	

continues

Table B.8. *(continued)*
Delete keys

Actions	Microsoft Keystrokes	WordStar-Compatible Keystrokes
Delete character left of cursor	Backspace	Ctrl-H
Delete character at cursor	Del	Ctrl-G
Delete from cursor to end of word		Ctrl-T
Delete selected text	Del	Ctrl-G
Delete leading spaces from selected lines	Shift-Tab	

Find and change keys

Actions	Microsoft Keystrokes	WordStar-Compatible Keystrokes
Repeat; find same text	F3	Ctrl-L
Search for text		Ctrl-Q,F
Change text		Ctrl-Q,A

Examples The command

```
EDIT C:\CONFIG.SYS
```

brings a copy of the CONFIG.SYS file into the editor so you can make changes. The command

```
EDIT C:\DOS\DOSSHELL.INI /H
```

brings the DOSSHELL.INI file into the editor, with the maximum number of lines available for your monitor displayed.

See Also Chapter 10

EDLIN

Creates or edits a text file.

Version 1 and later

Type External (EDLIN.COM)

DOS Shell Menu Access	None

Syntax

```
EDLIN [drive] [path] file name
```

in which *drive*, *path* and *file name* provide the location and name of the file you want to create or edit.

Usage

The EDLIN command is used to activate a line editor that can create and edit text files by deleting, inserting, editing, and displaying lines of text, and by searching for, deleting, or replacing text within one or more lines. In addition, EDLIN automatically creates a backup file of the original file, with the extension .BAK.

If the *file name* specified in the EDLIN command doesn't exist, it is created in the current directory unless the optional drive and path parameters are specified. After a new file is created, your screen displays the following message and EDLIN prompt:

```
New file
*
```

If the named file exists, it is opened and loaded into the editor and the following message and EDLIN prompt are displayed:

```
End of input file
*
```

After the file is opened, EDLIN uses 14 commands to create and edit lines of text. These commands, used at the EDLIN prompt, can be used together to form a multiple command line.

*n*A (Append) is used to append *n* number of lines from the disk file, when the file being edited is too large to fit into the 64KB of memory used by EDLIN. For example, if the file LARGE.TXT is being edited, only those lines that fit into 64KB of memory are loaded into the editor; the rest remain stored on disk. To load the next 20 lines of text, use the command 20A at the EDLIN prompt. Remember, however, that memory is limited. You must have room for the appended lines of text. Therefore, you should use the *n*S command to save 20 lines of text before appending 20 lines of text. If you attempt to append more lines of text than are stored on disk, EDLIN displays a message telling you that the end of the file has been reached.

first line, last line, to line [,count] C (Copy) is used to copy lines of text from one place in the file to another, in which *first line* is the first line to be copied, *last line* is the last line to be copied, and *to line* defines where the text will be inserted into the file. A line number can be any integer from 1 to

65,529. To specify the line after the last line in storage, use #. To specify the current line, use a period (.). Use the ⌐count option to define the number of times you want the text to be copied. If ⌐count is not used, the text is copied once.

[from line][,to line] D (Delete) is used to delete one or more lines of text from the file. If the command is used without the optional *from line* and *to line* parameters (for example, just D), only the current line of text is deleted. If only one first line number is specified (for example, 5D), only the specified line is deleted. When only the second line number is used (for example ,4D) text lines between the current line and the specified line are deleted.

n is used to edit a single line of text, in which *n* is the number of the line you want to edit. By entering a line number and pressing Enter at the EDLIN prompt, the line number and line of text are displayed. As with the D command, a line number (*n*) can be any integer from 1 to 65,529, # specifies the line after the last line in storage, and a period (.) specifies the current line. When editing a line

→ displays and skips over characters you do not want to change.

← erases the last character in the line.

F3 displays the remainder of the line.

F2, followed by a character, displays all characters up to but not including the character.

Ctrl-Break or Esc, followed by Enter, cancels all changes to the line and returns you to the EDLIN prompt.

Enter accepts any changes made to the line and returns you to the EDLIN prompt. If you press Enter when the cursor is in any position other than the first character position in the line, all remaining characters on the line are erased.

E is used to Exit the EDLIN editor and save all changes to disk. If you are editing an existing file, the original file is renamed and given the extension .BAK, thus preserving it for future use. Any previously saved file with the same file name and the .BAK extension is deleted from disk. If there is not enough room on your disk to store the new file, the original file is not renamed, only the portion of the new file that fits on the disk is saved, with the extension .$$$, and all unsaved text is lost.

[n] I (Insert) is used to insert lines of text in a file, in which the optional *n* specifies the number of the first line to be inserted. For example, 5I inserts the new text lines after line 4. If you specify # as

the line number, the new text is inserted after the last line in storage. To end the insert mode and return to the EDLIN prompt, press Ctrl-Break.

[*first line*][*,last line*] L (List) is used to list or display a maximum of 24 lines of text on your screen. If you use L without specifying line numbers, EDLIN displays 11 lines before the current line, the current line, and 12 lines after the current line. If there aren't 11 lines before the current line, EDLIN displays all of the lines before the current line and adds extra lines after the current line—for a maximum of 24 displayed lines of text.

If you specify the last line without specifying the first line (you must include the comma, as in ,22L), EDLIN displays 11 lines before the current line, the current line, and ends with line 22. If you only specify the first line (as in 10L), EDLIN displays a maximum of 24 lines beginning with line 10.

[*first line*] [*,last line*] [*,to line*] M] (Move) is used to move lines to a new location in the text file. All lines between (and including) the *first line* number and *last line* number are moved to the *to line* number position. If you omit the *first line* and *last line* parameters, the current line (marked with an asterisk) is the only line moved. For example, the command 10,12,30M moves lines 10, 11, and 12 to line 30.

[*start line*] [*,end line*] P (Page) displays lines in the text file one page (screenful) at a time. After each page is displayed, the prompt Continue (Y/N)? appears. Type Y to view the next page, or N to return to the * prompt. For example, the command 1,200P displays the first 200 lines in the file being edited, pausing after each screenful of text is displayed.

Q (Quit) displays the prompt Abort edit (Y/N)?. If you type Y, all changes made to the text file in the current editing session are abandoned, and you are returned to the command prompt. If you type N, you are returned to the command prompt. If you type N, you are returned to the EDLIN * prompt.

[*from line*] [*,to line*] [*?*] R old string^Z[new string] (Replace) replaces the *old string* with the *new string* in all lines between the *from line* and the *to line*. If ? is included, EDLIN asks for permission before replacing text in each line. To type the ^Z character, press Ctrl-Z or the F6 key. For example, the command 1,200RJane^ZMarsha searches the first 200 lines of the file for the name Jane, and replaces the name with Marsha.

[*from line*] [*,to line*] [?] S *string* (Search) searches the file, from the line number specified in *from line* to the line number specified in *to line* for the specified *string* of characters. If you do not use the optional ? parameter, the search is stopped after the first matching string is found. If you include the ? parameter, EDLIN displays O.K.? when it finds a matching string and waits for a keypress, and then proceeds to search remaining lines. For example, the command 1,200SBanana searches the first 200 lines of the file for the word Banana.

[*line*] T [*drive*] [*file name*] (Transfer) merges lines from a separate text file into the file being edited, above the *line* number specified. For example, the command 20 T C:MOVEIT.BAT merges the entire file named MOVEIT.BAT from the current directory of drive C: into the file being edited, and places all incoming text above line 20.

[*lines*] W (Write) writes the number of *lines* specified out to a disk file with the .BAK extension, starting at the first line. Generally used to add more lines of text after running out of memory.

The command

EDLIN C:\AUTOEXEC.BAT

brings a copy of the AUTOEXEC.BAT file into the EDLIN editor for making changes.

See Also   EDIT

EMM386.EXE

Transforms part of extended memory into expanded memory, and also lets DOS access upper memory.

Version   5

Type   External (used in CONFIG.SYS or the command line)

DOS Shell Menu Access   None

Syntax   For CONFIG.SYS

[*drive*][*path*]EMM386.EXE [*memory*] [*mem options*]

in which *drive* and *path* identify the location of the EMM386 program, *memory* specifies the amount of memory (in KB) to be allocated as expanded memory, and *mem options* consists of several optional parameters that control how memory is used.

For the command line

`[drive][path]EMM386 [ON | OFF | AUTO] [W=ON | W=OFF]`

in which *drive* and *path* identify the location of the EMM386 program.

Usage   For CONFIG.SYS

The EMM386 program is a memory manager that can be used only by computers running the 80386 or 80486 microprocessors. It lets DOS

❏ Simulate expanded memory in extended memory (use EMM386 if your computer has only extended memory available, but your applications nccd to usc cxpanded memory).

❏ Access your system's reserved memory (use EMM386 if you want to store device drivers and TSRs there rather than in conventional memory).

The default values of the *memory options* that can be used with EMM386 usually don't need to be changed for normal operations. However, if you need to manually control how EMM386 controls memory, you can use one or more of the following options:

`W=ON	OFF`	Enables (ON) or disables (OFF) support for the Weitek math coprocessor. (The default is OFF.)
`Mcode`	Specifies the segment base address. Values of *code* are 1 through 14, which represent the following addresses, respectively: C000H, C400H, C800H, CC00H, D000H, D400H, D800H, DC00H, E000H, 8000H, 8400H, 8800H, 8C00H, 9000H.
`FRAME=address`	Establishes the segment base at a specific address
`/Paddress`	The same as `FRAME=`
`/Pnumber=address`	Establishes the segment address for a specific page. *number* is the number of the page, and *address* is its location.
`X=address range`	Excludes a range of addresses from being affected by the EMM386 command

B=*address*	Specifies the lowest address for expanded memory banking. (The default is 4000H.)
L=*minXMS*	Specifies that at least *minXMS* extended memory will still be available after EMM386 is loaded.
A=*altregs*	Sets the number of "fast alternate registers" that are alloted to ERMM386. (The default is 7; values can range from 0 through 254.)
H=*handles*	Specifies the number of handles that EMM386 can use. (The default is 64; values can range from 2 through 255.)
ram	Activates upper memory blocks and sets aside a 16K page frame for swapping data into and out of expanded memory.
noems	Activates upper memory blocks, without setting aside a 16K page frame, and without using any extended memory to simulate expanded memory.
/y=*path*	Specifies the location of EMM386.EXE after bootup.

Even though EMM386 can be used to simulate expanded memory in extended memory, EMM386 is probably more widely used as a tool for using upper memory. Every 80386 and 80486 computer has 384K of reserved (also called upper) memory between the 640 RAM mark and the 1MB mark. (Memory above 1MB is extended memory.)

Historically, this 384K has been used for code that manages the system hardware, such as the video display. However, a great deal of it has been unused and wasted. That memory has been called reserved memory in the past, because it was inaccessible to the user. DOS 5, however, makes that memory available to you and calls it upper memory blocks.

You need to use a combination of the HIMEM.SYS, DOS=UMB, and EMM386 programs and drivers to prepare the upper memory blocks. Once you've done so, you can use the DEVICEHIGH and LOADHIGH commands to load device drivers and TSR programs into upper memory, thereby conserving a substantial amount of conventional memory (RAM) for other programs, such as spreadsheets and word processors.

Examples **For CONFIG.SYS**

The following DOS 5 commands, in the CONFIG.SYS file of an 80386 or 80486 computer 1) activate extended memory (HIMEM.SYS), 2) load DOS into the high memory area and set up a link between conventional and upper memory, (DOS=HIGH,UMB) and 3) activate upper memory without using any extended memory to simulate expanded memory.

```
DEVICE = C:\DOS\HIMEM.SYS

DOS = HIGH,UMB

DEVICE = C:\DOS\EMM386.EXE NOEMS
```

You can then use DEVICEHIGH commands beneath these commands in CONFIG.SYS to load device drivers into upper memory. You may also use the LOADHIGH command in the AUTOEXEC.BAT file, and at the command prompt, to load TSR programs into upper memory.

If you wanted to simulate 1MB of expanded memory in extended memory in the previous example and still have access to your upper memory blocks, you'd need to use the RAM option, rather than the NOEMS options, in the third line:

```
DEVICE = C:\DOS\EMM386.EXE 1024 RAM
```

To verify your memory setup, you can use the MEM /C command which lists available conventional, upper, expanded (EMS), and extended (XMS) memory (if any).

For diskless workstations and remote-boot machines, you can use the /Y switch to specify a location of EMM386 after bootup is complete. For example, when you run Windows 3 in enhanced mode, it looks for EMM386.EXE at whatever drive and directory you specify in the DEVICE= command that starts EMM386. If, for whatever reason, that location changes after bootup, you need to specify that location with the Y switch. For example,

```
DEVICE = C:\DOS\EMM386 NOEMS /Y=N:\NETDRIVE
```

Usage **For the command line**

Before you can use EMM386 from the command line, you must first install the driver (with the appropriate options) in your CONFIG.SYS file (see the preceding section). Used from the command line, EMM386 performs the following functions:

❏ Displays the status of the EMM386 driver

❑ Enables or disables expanded memory

❑ Enables and disables support for the Weitek math coprocessor

If you are simulating expanded memory with the EMM386 driver because one of your applications requires expanded memory, you can return that expanded memory to the extended memory pool by disabling the EMM386 command. If you have installed the Weitek coprocessor on your system, you should use EMM386 to enable support for the chip.

Examples   **For the command line**

To determine the current state of your expanded memory simulation, simply type EMM386 at the command line. To disable expanded memory emulation, type

```
EMM386 OFF
```

If you have installed the Wietek math coprocessor, you can either permanently turn on expanded memory support for it with the EMM386 W=ON command, or you can use the command EMM386 AUTO to turn on support only when a program requests the coprocessor.

See Also   DEVICEHIGH, DOS, HIMEM.SYS, LOADHIGH

ERASE

Removes a file from the disk.

Version   1 and later

Type   Internal

DOS Shell Menu Access   Use the mouse or keyboard to select the file(s) from the Files List to be deleted. Then select `Delete...` from the File pull-down menu.

Syntax   `ERASE [drive][path][file name] [/P]`

in which *drive* and *path* identify the disk drive and directory of the file to erase, and *file name* is the name of the file (or group of files) to erase.

Usage   The ERASE command "erases" a file from the disk. (The ERASE and DEL commands are identical.) In all versions of DOS prior to DOS 5, after you erase a file, it is impossible to retrieve without a utility program that can "unerase" files. (See the discussion of the ERASE command in Chapter 8 for more information.)

However, in DOS 5, the action of ERASE is no longer irreversible within DOS. The new UNDELETE command can now recover a file that you remove with ERASE.

You can retrieve a deleted file because DOS doesn't actually erase the *data* in a file when it deletes a file—it simply removes references to that file on the disk. If you mistakenly delete a file, you can restore this information by using the UNDELETE command—but you must use the command immediately (see the UNDELETE entry later in this appendix).

If you attempt to erase a file that is designated as read-only, DOS refuses your request and returns the message `Access denied.` (Use the `ATTRIB -R` file name command to change the file back to read/write; then, use the `ERASE` command to erase it.) On a network, you might get the `Access denied` message if you attempt to erase a file that is being used by another user.

Note that the Delete option in the File menu of the DOS Shell does allow you to delete read-only, system, or hidden files without first changing their attributes. The Shell displays a Warning dialog box and asks you to confirm the deletion, and then it carries out the deletion. If you are deleting files from the Shell and you see a dialog box warning you that you are about to delete a read-only file, you would be prudent to cancel the operation, make sure that you indeed want to erase that file, and only then proceed with the deletion.

If you attempt to erase a file on a diskette that has a write-protect tab on it, DOS returns the message `Write protect error writing drive` *x*, in which *x* is the name of the drive containing the diskette. To erase the file, first remove the write-protect tab.

If you attempt to erase all of the files on a disk or directory using the command `ERASE *.*`, DOS asks for further confirmation by presenting the prompt `Are you sure (Y/N)?`. Type `Y` to proceed with the deletion, or `N` to prevent the deletion. (Note that DOS presents this warning message only when you attempt to delete all of the files on a disk or directory.)

The /P switch is available only in DOS Versions 4 and 5. If specified, DOS asks for permission before erasing each file. For example, if you enter the command `ERASE *.BAK /P`, DOS individually presents each file on the current drive and directory that has the *.BAK extension, and displays the prompt `Delete (Y/N)?` If you answer `Y`, the file is erased. If you answer `N`, the file is not erased.

Examples To erase a file named LETTER.BAK from the current drive and directory, enter the command:

```
ERASE LETTER.BAK
```

To erase all of the files with the extension .BAK from the current drive and directory, enter the command:

```
ERASE *.BAK
```

To erase a file named LETTER.BAK on the directory named \WORDS\LETTERS on drive C:, enter the command:

```
ERASE C:\WORDS\LETTERS\LETTER.BAK
```

If you have DOS 4 or 5, and you want to selectively erase files that have the .BAK extension from a directory named \WP\WPFILES, enter the command

```
ERASE C:\WP\WPFILES\*.BAK /P
```

See Also UNDELETE, MIRROR

EXIT

Exits a secondary command processor and returns to the original.

Version 1 and later

Type Internal

DOS Shell Menu Access None

Syntax EXIT

Usage Returns control to the original command processor after you create a secondary command processor using COMMAND. EXIT also is used to return to the DOS Shell, if the DOS Shell is exited with the Shift-F9 key combination.

If the secondary command processor was created with the /P switch to make that processor permanent, EXIT will not be able to leave the secondary processor.

If no secondary processor is currently active, the EXIT command just redisplays the command prompt and does nothing.

Examples After pressing Shift-F9 (or selecting the `Command Prompt` option from the Main Group of the Program List) to exit the DOS Shell, enter the command

```
EXIT
```

to return to the Shell.

See Also   COMMAND

EXPAND

Expands a compressed file into a usable file.

Version   5

Type   External

**DOS Shell
Menu Access**   None

Syntax
```
EXPAND [source drive:][source path]source file name
[target drive:][target path]target file name
```

in which *source drive*, *source path*, and *source file
name* specify the location of the compressed file, and *target
drive*, *target path*, and *target file name* specify the
location of the uncompressed version of the named file.

Usage   The EXPAND command is new in DOS 5. Many DOS 5.0 files are
stored on your distribution disks in compressed form to save space.
EXPAND was added to DOS to uncompress these files and copy
them to your hard disk or floppy disks.

Because the DOS SETUP program calls EXPAND automatically, you
won't need to use this command to uncompress files when you
initially install DOS. However, you might need to use EXPAND to
copy a DOS program from your distribution disks if that program
was accidentally deleted or corrupted on your hard disk.

Examples   Let's assume that your ANSI.SYS device driver is stored in a location
on your hard disk that has become defective. When you try to use
the DOS commands that require that driver, they return error
messages. You can't simply copy ANSI.SYS from a DOS disk
because it is stored in compressed format and is therefore unusable
in its current state. The EXPAND command lets you retrieve this
compressed file without having to go through the entire DOS setup
procedure again.

To replace the file, place Disk 2 of your DOS distribution disks in
drive A: and change to that drive. The file you are looking for is
ANSI.SY_ (all compressed DOS files end with an underscore (_)

character). Use the DIR command to be sure that you are using the correct disk. To uncompress the file and store it in the DOS directory of drive C:, issue the following command:

```
EXPAND ANSI.SY_ C:\DOS\ANSI.SYS
```

FASTOPEN

Installs a disk caching system that speeds disk accessing.

Version	4
Type	External (FASTOPEN.EXE)
DOS Shell Menu Access	None
Syntax	`FASTOPEN drive[=n][...][/X]`

in which *drive* specifies the drive to be accessed with FASTOPEN and *n* is the number of directory or file locations to be maintained in memory.

Usage FASTOPEN installs a disk caching system in your computer's memory, to speed operations that involve disk accessing. FASTOPEN keeps track of the locations of files and directories on the disk in memory, unlike the BUFFERS command, which maintains a copy of the file allocation table (FAT). FASTOPEN actually speeds access to the FAT stored in the disk buffers, and therefore should be used in addition to, rather than in lieu of, the BUFFERS command in CONFIG.SYS.

The *drive2* parameter can be any valid disk drive name. However, using FASTOPEN with a RAM disk generally does not speed disk accessing. Also, the *drive2* parameter must not refer to remote drives on a network nor to any drives defined by an ASSIGN, JOIN, or SUBST command.

The *n* parameter specifies the maximum number of files or directories that FASTOPEN will maintain. The acceptable range is 10 to 999. The default value for PC DOS is 34; the default value for MS-DOS is 10. Each file or directory location maintained in memory requires 48 bytes. Therefore, an *n* setting of 34 uses 306 (9 (x) 34) bytes, or approximately 1/3KB.

If multiple drives are specified in a single FASTOPEN command, the *sum* of all *n* parameters must not exceed 999.

The optimal setting for FASTOPEN varies from one system to the next. A good rule of thumb, however, is to use neither exceptionally large nor exceptionally small numbers for *n*. The *n* value should be at least 10, or should reflect the number of levels of directories on your hard disk. For example, if the "deepest" subdirectory on your hard disk is named \DBASE\DBTUTOR\ALBERT, which extends down three levels, you would still want to use 10, rather than 3, as the *n* value.

After FASTOPEN is activated, it remains in memory for the remainder of the session and cannot be modified or deactivated. Therefore, all drives that will use FASTOPEN should be specified in a single FASTOPEN command.

The /X option tells DOS to use expanded memory rather than conventional RAM for all FASTOPEN operations. This conserves conventional RAM space; however, the /X option can only be used when a preceding command in the CONFIG.SYS file has already activated expanded memory, such as DEVICE=HIMEM.SYS in DOS 5. If expanded memory is used for FASTOPEN, the total number of bytes used by FASTOPEN may not exceed a single 16KB page of memory. Depending on the expanded memory manager you use, you might need to include P254 as a page in the command that activates expanded memory (see the "Examples" section).

Note that the version of FASTOPEN with DOS 4 supports an additional *look-ahead buffers* parameter. Also, the DOS 3.3 version doesn't support the /X switch.

You can enter the FASTOPEN command directly at the command prompt or with a command in your AUTOEXEC.BAT file. Optionally, in Versions 4 and later of DOS, you can activate FASTOPEN via your CONFIG.SYS file by preceding the command with `INSTALL=`.

Once FASTOPEN is activated, it keeps track of the name and location of every file you open so that if you reopen that same file later, DOS can find it much more quickly. Each file entry in the FASTOPEN cache uses about 48 bytes of memory.

Examples   Typing the following command at the command prompt, or placing it in your AUTOEXEC.BAT file, starts FASTOPEN with the capability of tracking 20 file names on drives C: through F:,

```
FASTOPEN C:=20 D:=20 E:=20 F:=20
```

If upper memory blocks have been made available on the computer, this command can be used instead to use upper memory rather than conventional memory for the cache.

```
LOADHIGH C:\DOS\FASTOPEN C:=20 D:=20 E:=20 F:=20
```

In each of the examples that follow, the commands are presumed to be contained in the CONFIG.SYS file.

The following command assumes that the FASTOPEN.EXE file is stored in the directory named DOS on disk drive C:. Only disk drive C: is managed through FASTOPEN, and the default value of 34 is used for the *n* parameter.

```
INSTALL=C:\DOS\FASTOPEN.EXE C:
```

The next command activates FASTOPEN for two hard disk drives, named C: and D:, assigning 450 directory and file buffers to each. Note that because 450[+]450 equals 900, the 999 maximum sum of the *n* parameters is not exceeded. In this example, the FASTOPEN.EXE file is assumed to be stored in the root directory:

```
INSTALL=FASTOPEN.EXE C:=(450) D:=(450)
```

See Also   BUFFERS, HIMEM.SYS, INSTALL, XMA2EMS.SYS

FC

Compares two files.

Version   5

Type   External (FC.EXE)

DOS Shell Menu Access   None (unless you add it to a program group).

Syntax   **For ASCII files:**

```
FC [/A] [/C] [/L] [/Lb n] [/N] [/T] [/W] [/nnnn]
[drive:] [path\] file name1 [drive:] [path\] file
name2
```

For binary comparisons:

```
FC [/B] [drive:] [path\] [file name1] [drive:]
[path\] [file name2]
```

where

/A   Abbreviates the output of the ASCII comparison.

/B   Forces binary (byte by byte) comparison with no attempt to resynchronize characters after a mismatch.

/C   Ignores upper/lowercase distinctions.

/L Forces ASCII comparison, where FC attempts to resynchronize characters after a mismatch. Sets the line buffer to *n* lines, the default being 100. Files that differ in length by more than this amount will not be compared.

/N Displays line number in ASCII comparisons.

/T Does not expand tabs to spaces.

/W Deletes white space (tab and spaces) before comparing files.

/nnnn Specifies the number of lines that must match after a difference is found. The default is 2. If fewer matching lines are found, FC displays the matching lines as differences.

Usage Unlike DISKCOMP, which can compare only two entire matching diskettes, FC can be used to compare any two individual files, regardless of where they are stored. For example, you can use FC to compare a file on a hard disk to one on a floppy.

FC displays its findings as follows:

- ❏ The name of the first file.
- ❏ Lines from the first file that differ in the two files.
- ❏ The first line to match in both files.
- ❏ The name of the second file.
- ❏ Lines from the second file that differ in the two files.
- ❏ First line in the second file to match.

For example, in the following output from the command FC FIRST.TXT SECOND.TXT, the first lines that differ in the two files are "Apples" (FIRST.TXT) and "Artichokes" (SECOND.TXT). The first lines that do match are "Bananas" and "Bananas" in both files.

```
FC FIRST.TXT SECOND.TXT
Comparing files FIRST.TXT and SECOND.TXT
***** FIRST.TXT
Apples
Bananas
***** SECOND.TXT
Artichokes
Bananas
*****
```

If you compare binary files using the /B switch, FC displays the unmatched byte and their relative addresses. If the files being compared are identical, FC displays the message

```
fc: no difference encountered
```

Examples If the files are not on the same drive and directory, be sure to specify the path. For example, the following command compares the file named CHAP1.WP on the C:\WP51 directory of drive C to a file with the same name on the floppy in disk drive A.

```
FC  C:\WP51\CHAP1.WP  A:\CHAP1.WP
```

If you wanted to compare the binary file named APPEND.EXE on the C:\DOS directory with the copy on the XDOS directory, and print the results, you would use this command:

```
FC  C:\DOS\APPEND.EXE  C:\XDOS\APPEND.EXE  >  PRN
```

Note that when comparing binary files (.EXE, .COM, .SYS, .OBJ, .LIB, .BIN), binary comparisons are the default, so the /B switch is unnecessary.

FCBS

Specifies the maximum number of file control blocks that can be open simultaneously.

Version 3.0 and later

Type Internal (used only in CONFIG.SYS)

DOS Shell Menu Access None

Syntax
```
FCBS = max,permanent
```

in which *max* is the total number of file control blocks that can be open simultaneously, and *permanent* is the number of file control blocks that are protected from automatic closure.

Usage This rarely used CONFIG.SYS command is required only when you need to run DOS Version 1 application programs with later versions of DOS. It allows DOS to use the old-fashioned *file control blocks* (FCBS) method of managing files, in addition to the newer *file handles* approach of Version 2 and later.

The default value for *max* is 0, but any value in the range of 0 to 255 is acceptable. The value of the *permanent* parameter must be equal to or less than the value of *max*.

If you attempt to use a program that requires the older FCBS method of managing files, with a newer version of DOS, the program will simply stop running at some point, or (if you're lucky) display DOS's error message *FCB unavailable*. Either way, the solution is to use the FCBS command in your CONFIG.SYS file, and to experiment with different values.

The default setting for FCBS is 4,0 (four file control blocks, none permanent), unless the DOS SHARE program is installed, which increases the default value of FCBS to 16,8. Use these values as starting points when experimenting with larger values in the FCBS command in your own CONFIG.SYS file.

And don't forget that the FCBS command in the CONFIG.SYS file is not activated until the next time you start your computer, or reboot by pressing Ctrl-Alt-Del.

Examples   The following command, when included in your CONFIG.SYS file, provides for a maximum of ten simultaneously open file control blocks, five of which are protected from automatic closure.

```
FCBS=10,5
```

See Also   SHARE

FILES

Specifies the maximum number of open files that a program can manage simultaneously.

Version   2 and later

Type   Internal (used only in CONFIG.SYS)

DOS Shell Menu Access   None

Syntax   `FILES=max`

in which `max` is the maximum number of files that can be open simultaneously.

Usage   The FILES option in the CONFIG.SYS file specifies the maximum number of file handles that DOS can simultaneously manage. DOS defaults to a maximum of eight active file handles. Five of these file handles are used by the standard input and output devices: the screen, keyboard, printer, communications devices, and the DOS error handler. (Technically, these devices are not "files" per se; however, DOS still must use file handles to manage their input and output.) This leaves three available file handles for open disk files.

Most modern programs, particularly database management and multisheet spreadsheet programs, can handle more than three simultaneously open files. Therefore, to use the programs (without getting a `Too many files are open` error message), you probably need to use a FILES command in your CONFIG.SYS file to manage more than eight file handles. (The manual that comes with a program that manages multiple files will specify the minimum setting.)

The minimum setting for FILES= is 8; the maximum is 255. Each file handle (above the default of 8) uses approximately 39 bytes of memory. Even the most sophisticated database management programs rarely require that you set FILES= to a number greater than 50.

Examples   The following command, when placed in the CONFIG.SYS file, lets your computer run programs that can manage as many as 40 simultaneously open files; the other five file handles are used by the input and output devices.

`FILES=45`

See Also   BUFFERS

FIND

Searches multiple files for specific text.

Version   2 and later

Type   External (FIND.EXE)

DOS Shell Menu Access   None

Syntax   `FIND [/V] [/C] [/N] [/I] "text" [[drive][path][file name] [...]]`

in which *text* is the text to search for (enclosed in quotation marks), *drive* and *path* are the names of the drive and directory to be searched, and *file name* is the name of a specific file to be searched. You can specify more than one file to be searched (each separated by a blank space), but you cannot use ambiguous file names.

Usage   FIND searches specified files for a particular character string (that is, a letter, number, word, or group of words). The string being searched for must be enclosed in quotation marks. To search for a quotation mark, place three quotation marks in the string.

FIND searches only the files listed at the end of the command. These files should contain only text. Command files (such as those with

.EXE, .COM, or .BIN extensions) cannot be searched. Similarly, many files created by word processing systems cannot be reliably searched, because they might contain special formatting codes.

By default, FIND is case sensitive, which means that it considers upper- and lowercase letters as unequal. Therefore, if a file contains the word *Hello*, and you attempt to find *HELLO*, FIND will not "see" the match. However, if you use the DOS 5 /I switch, FIND becomes insensitive to case, and the words *HELLO*, *Hello*, and *hello* all will match.

FIND does not limit its search to whole words, unless spaces are included within the quotation marks. For example, a search for *"dog"* will find *dog*, *hotdog*, *doggie*, and *antidogmatic*. However, a search for *" dog "* will find only the word *dog*.

You can use the following four options with FIND:

/ I   Makes the search case insensitive.

/ V   Finds lines that do not contain the string.

/ C   Counts the number of times that the string occurs within the file, but does not display the lines.

/ N   Displays the number of each line that contains the string.

The /N and /C options are incompatible, because /C displays only a total count, rather than individual lines. If you include both /N and /C in a FIND command, the /N is ignored. Note that, unlike most other DOS commands, the / options in FIND are placed before the string and file names, rather than at the end of the entire command.

FIND can accept input from any source. If you do not specify a file name with FIND, it waits for input from the keyboard. It continues accepting text until you press F6 or Ctrl-Z and Enter. You can pipe information into FIND using the | character. You also can redirect the output from FIND to a separate device, such as to a file or the printer, using the > redirection symbol. FIND is also useful in many macros that you can create with the new DOSKEY command. Examples in the next section demonstrate these techniques.

Examples   Suppose you have three files, named LETTER1.TXT, LETTER2.TXT, and LETTER3.TXT, and you want to know which one is the letter to Bob. Assuming that all three .TXT files are on the current directory and that FIND.EXE is accessible through a predefined PATH command, the following command searches all three files for the string *"Bob"*:

```
FIND "Bob" LETTER1.TXT LETTER2.TXT LETTER3.TXT
```

Assuming that LETTER2.TXT is the only file that contains the name Bob, the result of the FIND command looks something like this:

```
---------- LETTER1.TXT
---------- LETTER2.TXT
Dear Bob:
---------- LETTER3.TXT
```

If you include the /N option in the FIND command, the line number (corresponding to the EDLIN line number) is displayed in square brackets to the left of the matching line, as follows:

```
FIND /N "Bob" LETTER1.TXT LETTER2.TXT LETTER3.TXT
---------- LETTER1.TXT
---------- LETTER2.TXT
[1]Dear Bob
---------- LETTER3.TXT
```

If you use the /C option, only the total number of lines that contain the search string is displayed, as follows:

```
FIND /C "Bob" LETTER1.TXT LETTER2.TXT LETTER3.TXT
---------- LETTER1.TXT: 0
---------- LETTER2.TXT: 1
---------- LETTER3.TXT: 0
```

If you use the /V option, as follows, all lines that do not contain the search string are displayed.

```
FIND /V "Bob" LETTER1.TXT LETTER2.TXT LETTER3.TXT
```

The output of this command would include all of the text in the LETTER1.TXT, LETTER2.TXT, and LETTER3.TXT files, except the *Dear Bob* line.

The next command searches for the text *"Don't go!" she cried* (including the quotation marks) in the files named CHAPTER1.DOC and CHAPTER2.DOC (note that upper- and lowercase characters don't need to match).

```
FIND /I """Don't go!"" she cried" CHAPTER1.DOC CHAPTER2.DOC
```

The following command does the same, but displays its output on the printer, because of the > PRN symbol.

```
FIND /I """Don't go!"" she cried" CHAPTER1.DOC CHAPTER2.DOC > PRN
```

The next command displays file names in the current directory that contain the number *1991*. Note how the output of the DIR command is used as input into the FIND command through the use of the pipe character (|).

```
DIR ¦ FIND "1991"
```

The resulting output might look something like this:

```
Directory of C:\
FIN1991
<DIR>     12-29-87    5:43a
1991EST   TXT     10240    1-18-91     8:32p
1991ACT   TXT     62976   12-22-91    12:45p
1991TAX   DBF     77184   12-22-91    12:34p
QTR1991   WKS      1024    4-12-91    11:11p
```

The following command displays the names of files in the directory named \BUSINESS that were created on August 1, 1991:

```
DIR ¦ FIND "8-01-91"
```

To exclude messages displayed by the DIR command, such as Volume in drive C has no label, use FIND to exclude lines that have a lowercase letter *e*, as in the following example:

```
DIR ¦ FIND /V "e"
```

To hide messages and directory names in a DIR command, use two FIND commands, as in this example:

```
DIR ¦ FIND /V "e" ¦ FIND /V "<DIR>"
```

FIND is also useful in DOS 5 DOSKEY macros. For example, FIND is limited because you can't use wild cards in the *file name* parameter. To search all of the files in a directory, you'd have to type in every name! The following macro enables you to search for a single word in every file of a directory:

```
DOSKEY FINDTXT=FOR %A IN ($1) DO FIND /I /N "$2" %A
```

The FOR loop cycles through any wild card file specification that you use as the first parameter ($1) after the macro name. The FIND command looks for the specified string ($2), disregards case (/I), and displays the line number of each occurrence (/N). If you are looking for the name *Davis* in your letters (which all use the .DOC extension), you would simply type

```
FINDTXT *.DOC davis
```

See Also   DIR, DOSKEY, FOR, TYPE

FOR

Sets up a loop to repeat a command.

Version 2 and later

Type Internal

DOS Shell Menu Access None

Syntax At the command prompt and in DOSKEY macros, the syntax is

FOR `%variable` IN `(set)` `DO command`

In batch files, including batch files that create macros, the syntax is

FOR `%%variable` IN `(item list)` `DO command`

in which `variable` is a single character (a–z), `item list` is a list of items to process (separated by blank spaces), and `command` is the command to be repeated.

Usage FOR repeats a command until it processes all of the items in a list. The `%` or `%% variable` (represented by a letter) assumes the value of the next item in the list with each pass through the loop. That variable then becomes part of the DO command. Examples that follow demonstrate this concept.

Examples In the following batch file command `%%a` is the variable and (LETTER1.TXT LETTER2.TXT LETTER3.TXT) is the item list. The command to be executed is `TYPE %%a`.

```
FOR %%a IN (LETTER1.TXT LETTER2.TXT LETTER3.TXT) DO TYPE %%a
```

When the command is first executed, the `%%a` variable is assigned the value LETTER1.TXT; therefore, the DO section of the command expands to become `TYPE LETTER1.TXT`. On the second pass through the loop, `%%a` is assigned the value LETTER2.TXT, so the command executed is `TYPE LETTER2.TXT`. On the third pass through the loop, `%%a` assumes the value LETTER3.TXT, so the command executed is `TYPE LETTER3.TXT`.

Because there are only three items in the item list, the FOR command stops after the third loop. The net result of the command, of course, is that it displays the contents of three different files: LETTER1.TXT, LETTER2.TXT, and LETTER3.TXT.

To enter this sample command directly at the DOS prompt, type the following:

```
FOR %a IN (LETTER1.TXT LETTER2.TXT LETTER3.TXT) DO TYPE %a
```

The same basic rule of thumb works for macros. The following
HUNT macro searches all the directories on drives C:, D:, E:, and F:
for a file name or pattern (for example, HUNT *.BAT). If you were
entering the macros at the command prompt, you'd type it

```
DOSKEY HUNT=FOR %x IN (C: D: E: F:) DO DIR %x\$1 /S/B
```

If, on the other hand, you were creating a batch file that creates
macros for you (perhaps automatically at startup), you'd enter this
command into that batch file:

```
DOSKEY HUNT=FOR %%x IN (C: D: E: F:) DO DIR %%x\$1 /S/B
```

See Also   SHIFT

FORMAT

Formats a blank disk.

Version   1 and later

Type   External (FORMAT.COM)

DOS Shell   Select `Disk Utilities` from the Main Group screen of the
Menu Access   Program List, and then select `Format` from the next screen.

Syntax   `FORMAT drive [/1] [/4] [/8] [/0] [/B] [/Fsize] [/T:tracks] [/N:sectors] [/S] [/V:label] [/Q] [/U]`

in which `drive` is the name of the drive containing the disk to be
formatted, `tracks` is the number of tracks per side, `sectors` is the
number of sectors per track, and `label` is the optional volume label.
The `size` parameter specifies the amount of storage in kilobytes
(KB).

Usage   Use FORMAT to prepare blank (empty and unformatted) disks for
use with your computer. The FORMAT command has been
overhauled in DOS 5 so that it is a lot safer than it was in previous
versions of DOS. In DOS 1 through 4, when you formatted a hard
disk or diskette that already had information on it, the information
was completely erased. Even write-protected files (protected with
the ATTRIB +R command) were irretrievably erased by the
FORMAT command. Therefore, if you are using one of those
versions of DOS, be very careful when you use the FORMAT
command.

Until DOS 5, the data on an accidentally formatted hard or floppy disk could only be recovered by an "unformat" program from a product such as the *Norton Utilities* or *PC Tools Deluxe*. In DOS 5, the FORMAT command (by default) performs a "safe format" on hard disks and diskettes—data is not destroyed during the format; only the FAT tables and directory information are deleted. If you do mistakenly format your hard drive or a diskette that contains information, the new UNFORMAT command lets you restore the original FAT and recover most of your files.

Although the default operation of FORMAT doesn't actually erase any data on your disks, it still checks the disk media itself for bad sectors. Thus, the new DOS 5 format and older versions of FORMAT take approximately the same amount of time.

The /Q switch performs a "quick" format on already formatted disks. It cancels DOS's screening for bad sectors and simply deletes the FAT tables and directory information. As you can imagine, this type of format takes only a few seconds.

The /U switch cancels the new DOS 5 "safe format" and performs the same destructive format on your disks that earlier versions of DOS did.

Attempting to use a disk that has not been formatted usually produces the error message `General Failure error reading drive x` in which x is the name of the drive containing the unformatted disk.

Before you format a disk, the screen prompts you to insert a disk into the appropriate drive and press Enter to proceed.

If you attempt to format a hard disk that has already been formatted and has a volume label, DOS asks that you `Enter current Volume label for drive x:` (in which x refers to the appropriate drive). If you enter the appropriate label, FORMAT proceeds. If you do not enter the appropriate label, FORMAT cancels the operation. (Enter the DIR or VOL command at the command prompt to view the current volume label.)

If you are formatting a hard disk that has no label, the screen displays the message

```
WARNING, ALL DATA ON NON-REMOVABLE DISK DRIVE x: WILL BE LOST!
Proceed with Format (Y/N)?
```

If you are absolutely certain that you want to totally erase everything on the hard disk, answer Y. If you do not want to lose this information, enter N. Even if you mistakenly continue at this last level of warning, DOS 5 includes the UNFORMAT command to let you reconstruct most (often all) of you files from the formatted hard disk (see the UNFORMAT entry in this appendix for details).

You cannot format a diskette that has a write-protect tab on it. Nor can you format any "virtual" disk, such as a RAM disk, or a network disk. You also can't format a disk affected by the ASSIGN, JOIN, or SUBST commands.

After the formatting procedure is completed, FORMAT displays the number of bytes available on the disk. If there are any flaws on the disk, these are marked as bad sectors, which are not usable. The total amount of available disk space is equal to the total space minus the bad sectors. A sample output from a FORMAT command on a 1.2MB floppy disk is

```
Format complete

1213952 bytes total disk space

353280 bytes in bad sectors
860672 bytes available on disk

Format another (Y/N)?
```

If you enter the FORMAT command, but DOS cannot find the FORMAT.COM file on the current drive and directory, or in a directory specified in the current PATH, DOS displays the message `Bad command or file name` and returns you to the command prompt (or the DOS 5 Shell).

In most cases, you only need to use the FORMAT command followed by the name of the drive containing the disk to be formatted. However, in addition to the /Q and /U switches, you can use several other options with FORMAT.

/0   Formats a PC DOS Version 1 compatible disk (available in MS-DOS Versions 2 to 3.2).

/1   Formats one side of the diskette only, even if the diskette and drive are double-sided (Version 1, and Versions 3.2 and later).

/S   Makes the formatted disk a system disk that can be used to boot the computer. (If you use this option, it must be the last switch on the line.)

/ V   Lets you assign a volume label (name) to the disk, which appears whenever you use the DIR command. The label can have as many as 11 characters.

/ 4   Formats a 5.25-inch diskette in a high-capacity drive as a low-capacity (360KB) diskette. (PC DOS Versions 3.0 and later, MS-DOS Versions 3.2 and later.)

/ 8   Specifies eight sectors per track (Versions 1 and 3.2 and later).

/ T   Lets you specify the number of tracks to place on the disk. Usually, you don't need to use this parameter, because FORMAT automatically generates the appropriate number of tracks for a disk. If you need to use the /T option, place the number of tracks you want to produce after the /T: symbol. Cannot be used with a hard disk. (MS-DOS Versions 3.2 and later.)

/ N   Lets you specify the number of sectors per track on the disk being formatted. (MS-DOS Versions 3.2 and later, PC DOS Versions 3.3 and later.)

/ B   Formats a diskette, and sets aside space so that system tracks can later be copied to the diskette using the SYS command. (Unlike /S, however, this command does not automatically copy the system tracks.) Cannot be used with either /S or /V.

/ F   (DOS 4 and 5 only) Specifies the capacity of the diskette being formatted.

The number of tracks per side and sectors per track of various floppy diskettes are given in Table B.6 in the DRIVER entry of this appendix. If you omit the /T and /N switches from the FORMAT command, DOS automatically formats the disk with the usual number of tracks and sectors.

The /F parameter is valid only in DOS Versions 4 and 5. You can use /F in lieu of /T and /N to format a diskette designed for use in drives other than the current drive. The value of /F, however, must be equal to or less than the capacity of the drive. Table B.9 lists possible values for the /F switch.

Table B.9. Acceptable values for the DOS 5 /F switch.

Disk Size	Drive Capacity	Acceptable /F Values
5.25-inch	160KB	160
5.25-inch	180KB	160, 180
5.25-inch	320KB	160, 180, 320
5.25-inch	360KB	160, 180, 320, 360
5.25-inch	1.2MB	160, 180, 320, 360, 1200, 1.2
3.5-inch	720KB	720
3.5-inch	1.44MB	720, 1440, 1.44

Although DOS provides flexibility in formatting diskettes for use in lower capacity drives, the diskettes themselves do not always offer the same flexibility. For example, you cannot format a 1.2MB high-density diskette in a low-capacity drive. You can, however, format a 360KB diskette in a high-capacity drive, for use in a 360KB drive. Similarly, you will find it impossible to format a 3.5-inch, 1.44MB disk in a 720KB drive.

Some optional switches are mutually exclusive or invalid for certain types of drives. In summary

❏ You cannot use /V or /S with /B.

❏ You cannot use both /8 and /V.

❏ You cannot use /N or /T with 320KB or 360KB diskettes.

❏ You cannot use /1, /4, /8, /B, /N, /O or /T with a fixed (hard) disk.

Versions 4 and 5 of DOS request a volume label after formatting a disk, even if you do not use the /V switch in the FORMAT command. In earlier versions, you must use the /V switch to enter a volume label when formatting is complete. DOS displays the message `Volume label (11 characters, ENTER for none)?`. Type a volume label with as many as 11 characters (including blank spaces), and then press Enter. Alternatively, press Enter if you do not want to add a volume label.

If you use FORMAT within a batch file, you can use the IF ERRORLEVEL command to check the results of the format. The codes returned by FORMAT are as follows:

0   Format successful

3   Format aborted by user (Ctrl-Break or Ctrl-C)

4   Format aborted due to error

5   Format aborted by user answering N to the prompt concerning a fixed disk drive

Examples   Suppose you have a new box of blank, unformatted diskettes that you want to format for use in your computer. Change to the hard disk directory that contains the FORMAT.EXE file. Then, place one of the unformatted diskettes in drive A: and enter the command

```
FORMAT A:
```

Follow the instructions that appear on the screen.

To make the diskette in drive A: bootable (one that you can use to start your computer), enter the following command:

```
FORMAT A: /S
```

Note that this command copies only the system tracks and COMMAND.COM to the new diskette. It does not copy your current CONFIG.SYS or AUTOEXEC.BAT files to the bootable diskette.

Suppose you want to format a 720KB, 3.5-inch disk in drive B: which is a 1.44MB, 3.5-inch drive. Using DOS 5, enter this command:

```
FORMAT B: /F:720
```

To accomplish the same result using an earlier version of DOS, enter this command:

```
FORMAT B: /T:80 /N:9
```

Suppose your computer has a 5.25-inch, high-capacity drive (named A:), but you want to format a 360KB diskette in that drive. Using DOS 5, enter this command:

```
FORMAT A: /F:360
```

Using an earlier version of DOS, enter this command:

```
FORMAT B: /4
```

If you want to use the DOS 5 FORMAT command to reformat an already formatted diskette in drive A:, you have three options:

❑ You can simply issue the FORMAT A: command, which checks for bad sectors on the disk, erases the file allocation tables and directory information, creates a hidden file that lets UNFORMAT recover this information if necessary, and does not delete any data on the disk.

❏ You can issue the FORMAT A: /Q command, which skips the check for bad sectors, erases the file allocation tables and directory information, creates the hidden recovery file, and also doesn't actually delete any data.

❏ You can issue the FORMAT A: /U command, which checks for bad sectors and completely erases the disk so that any data on the disk is irretrievably lost.

See Also GOTO, UNFORMAT, MIRROR

GOTO

Transfers control to a new command in a batch file.

Version 1 and later

Type Internal (used only in batch files)

DOS Shell Menu Access None

Syntax GOTO *label*

in which *label* is the name of a line, preceded by a colon, in the current batch file.

Usage Normally, the commands in a batch file are processed sequentially from top to bottom. The GOTO command lets you alter this sequential processing by passing control to a new part of the batch file. The section to which you pass control must have a name (called a label) that is preceded by a colon (:). However, when referencing the label in the GOTO command, you omit the colon. For example, you might use the label :End in a batch file, but you pass control to that label with the command GOTO End.

GOTO is usually used in conjunction with the IF command. Be careful that your GOTO commands do not set up infinite loops. For example, the following batch file repeatedly executes the DIR command:

```
:ShowDir
DIR
GOTO ShowDir
```

The loop, in this example, is infinite, because it doesn't contain an IF command that can pass control to a command outside the loop. After a batch file begins an infinite loop, you can regain control of the system only with a Ctrl-C or Ctrl-Break keystroke, or by rebooting or shutting off the computer.

Examples   The following batch file, named NEWDISK.BAT, attempts to format the disk in drive A:. If no error occurs during formatting, the GOTO command passes control to the label named :End. If an error does occur, the batch file displays an error message:

```
@ECHO OFF
REM -------------- NEWDISK.BAT
FORMAT A:
IF ERRORLEVEL = 0 GOTO End
ECHO WARNING! The disk in drive A: cannot be formatted!
:End
```

See Also   IF, CALL

GRAFTABL

Activates the graphics characters set.

Version   3 and later (modified in Version 3.3)

Type   External (GRAFTABL.COM)

DOS Shell Menu Access   None

Syntax   `GRAFTABL [code page| /STA]`

in which `code page` is a number identifying the character set to be used, and /STA shows the current status of GRAFTABL.

Usage   The Color Graphics Adapter (CGA) display often distorts the images of graphics and non-English language characters that have ASCII values greater than 127. The GRAFTABL command provides an additional 1,360 bytes of memory in which "clearer" versions of these characters are stored.

The following code page values can be used in the GRAFTABL command:

437   USA Graphic Character Set (default)

850   Multilingual Graphic Character Set

860   Portugese Graphic Character Set

863   Canadian-French Graphic Character Set

865   Nordic Graphic Character Set

GRAFTABL is not needed for systems using EGA or VGA video adapters.

If GRAFTABL is used in a batch file, you can use the IF ERRORLEVEL command to check for an error. Error codes returned by GRAFTABL are

0   Successful operation, new graphics character set is loaded.

1   Successful operation, but new graphics character set has replaced an existing graphics character set.

2   No new graphics character table loaded; previous graphics character set is still active.

3   Invalid parameter was entered with command; no action was taken.

4   Incorrect DOS version in use; must use DOS Versions 3.3 or 4.

Examples   The following examples assume that GRAFTABL.COM is stored on the current drive or directory, or in a directory specified in the current PATH setting. The command

```
GRAFTABL /STA
```

displays only the current graphics character set, as in the following example:

```
USA version of Graphic Character Set Table is already loaded.
```

The next command activates the graphic character set for the United States:

```
GRAFTABL 437
```

See Also   NLSFUNC

GRAPHICS

Allows graphics to be printed by pressing Shift-PrintScreen.

Version   2 and later

Type   External (GRAPHICS.COM)

DOS Shell Menu Access   None

Syntax   Versions 2 through 3.1:

```
GRAPHICS printer [/R] [/B]
```

MS-DOS Versions 3.2 to 3.3:

```
GRAPHICS printer [/R] [/B] [/LCD] [/C] [/F] [/
P=port]
```

Versions 4 and 5:

```
GRAPHICS [printer] [[drive][path]file name]
[/R][/B][/PB:id]
```

in which *printer* is a valid printer type. In Versions 4 and 5, *drive*, *path*, and *file name* represent the location and name of the *Graphics Profile* file (usually C:\DOS\GRAPHICS.PRO), *id* represents the print box size, and *port* is a valid DOS device name.

Usage GRAPHICS is required only when you want to print graphics by pressing Shift-PrintScreen, rather than using your graphics program to do the printing. When loaded, GRAPHICS uses approximately 6KB of conventional memory (RAM).

The first parameter after the GRAPHICS command (which is optional) must be a valid printer name. Valid printer names vary from one computer to the next. In versions 4 and 5 of DOS, the GRAPHICS.PRO file includes valid printer names (and additional information). You can use the command TYPE GRAPHICS.PRO > PRN to print this list.

The basic printer types supported by GRAPHICS are as follows:

COLOR1	IBM PC color printer with a black ribbon.
COLOR4	IBM PC color printer with an RGB (red, green, blue, and black) ribbon.
COLOR8	IBM PC color printer with a CMY (cyan, magenta, yellow, and black) ribbon.
DEFAULT	Any Hewlett-Packard PCC printer.
DESKJET	A Hewlett-Packard DeskJet printer.
GRAPHICS	IBM PC Graphics printer, IBM PC ProPrinter, and IBM Quietwriter printer, and compatibles (the default if no parameters are listed).
GRAPHICSWIDE	IBM PC Graphics Printer with a 13.5-inch wide carriage.
LASERJETII	A Hewlett-Packard LaserJet II printer.

PAINTJET	A Hewlett-Packard PaintJet printer.
QUIETJET	A Hewlett-Packard QuietJet printer.
QUIETJET PLUS	A Hewlett-Packard QuietJet Plus printer.
RUGGED WRITER	A Hewlett-Packard Rugged Writer printer.
RUGGED WRITERWIDE	A Hewlett-Packard Rugged Writer wide printer.
THERMAL	IBM PC Convertible printer.
THINKJET	A Hewlett-Packard ThinkJet printer.

The /R option reverses the colors of black-and-white images. It usually is used to print graphics as black on a white background, as opposed to a monitor's white characters on a black background.

The /B switch prints a background color; however, it is only valid if the printer type is COLOR4, COLOR8, or some other printer that prints in color.

The /C switch, available in Versions 3.2 and 3.3 of MS-DOS, centers the printout on the paper. The /F switch, also available only in Versions 3.2 and 3.3 of MS-DOS, rotates the printed image by 90 degrees, so that it is printed sideways on the page. The /P= option in MS-DOS Versions 3.2 and 3.3 specifies a printer port, which can be 1 (for LPT1), 2 (for LPT2), or 3 (for LPT3). If omitted, LPT1 is assumed.

The options /PB switch, available in DOS 3, specifies a *print box*, the dimensions of the printed area on a page. The /PB switch should be followed by a colon, and a print box identifier:

/PB:STD   Specifies the standard size print box, with dimensions resembling a standard display monitor. (If the /PB switch is omitted, STD is assumed.)

/PB:LCD   Specifies a print area that matches the dimension of liquid crystal display (LCD) monitors. Use this switch when you want the printed image to have the same dimensions as the LCD screen.

You can use /PRINTBOX instead of the abbreviation /PB in a GRAPHICS command if you prefer. Information about print boxes and other display and printer features is listed in a file named GRAPHICS.PRO that comes with DOS Versions 4 and 5.

GRAPHICS.PRO is an ASCII text file that you can view or print using the DOS TYPE and PRINT commands.

Using the GRAPHICS command and the PrintScreen key will not print graphs more quickly than a graphics program does; the delay before printing even begins can take as long as three minutes.

Note that on many enhanced keyboards you can print the contents of the screen simply by pressing the PrintScreen key, rather than pressing Shift-PrintScreen.

Examples

To print black and white graphics images, using the PrintScreen key, first enter the command

```
GRAPHICS
```

at the DOS command prompt.

To print color graphics from the screen on a color printer, using the colors that most closely match those on the screen, first enter this command at the command prompt:

```
GRAPHICS COLOR8 /R /B
```

See Also

GRAFTABL

HELP

Provides on-line help at the command prompt.

Version

5

Type

External

DOS Shell Menu Access

None (the Shell has its own help system)

Syntax

```
HELP [command]
```

where *command* is the command you need help with. Omitting a *command* presents a lists of commands.

Usage

Use HELP to get a quick reminder of the syntax and options of DOS commands entered at the command prompt. Instead of using HELP, you can also follow any command with the /? switch.

Examples

The command

```
HELP DIR
```

displays help about the DIR command. This command does also

```
HELP /?
```

For a list of all the DOS commands that have available help, enter

```
HELP
```

HIMEM.SYS

Device driver that manages the use of extended memory.

Version	5
Type	External (used only in CONFIG.SYS)
DOS Shell Menu Access	None
Syntax	`[drive][path]HIMEM.SYS [memory options]`

in which `drive` and `path` specify the location of the HIMEM.SYS driver and `memory options` includes the following switches:

`/HMAMIN=memory`	Specifies the amount of memory (in KB) that a program must use before HIMEM.SYS assigns it to the High Memory Area. (The default is 0; values range from 0 to 63.)
`/NUMHANDLES=number`	Specifies the number of *extended memory block* handles that are available at one time. (The default is 32; values range from 1 to 128.)
`/INT15=extmem`	Specifies the amount of extended memory (in KB) to be allocated to the INT15 interface.
`/MACHINE:name or code`	Specifies which A20 handler should be used to provide access to the High Memory Area (HMA)—the first 64K of extended memory. You can use either the name or code listed in Table B.10.
`/A20CONTROL:ON ¦ OFF`	ON tells HIMEM to always use A20 lines; OFF tells HIMEM to use A20 lines only if the A20 line was off when HIMEM.SYS was loaded.
`SHADOWRAM:ON ¦ OFF`	OFF tries to disable *shadow RAM* (RAM that is used to store ROM routines to speed execution) and

return that RAM to the pool of memory available to DOS and applications.

/CPUCLOCK:ON | OFF   Determines whether HIMEM.SYS alters the clock speed of your computer. If your computer's speed changes after installing HIMEM.SYS, try using /CPUCLOCK:ON at the end of your DEVICE=HIMEM.SYS command to give control back to the CPU clock.

Table B.10. Names and codes used with the /MACHINE switch.

Name	Code	Type of Handler
at	1	IBM PC/AT (the default value)
ps2	2	IBM PS/2
pt1cascade	3	Phoenix Cascade BIOS
hpvectra	4	HP "Classic" Vectra (A and AT)
att6300plus	5	AT&T 6300 Plus
acer1100	6	Acer 1100
toshiba	7	Toshiba 1600 and 1200XE
wyse	8	Wyse 12.5 MHz 286 M/C
tulip	9	Tulip SX
zenith	10	Zenith ZBIOS
at1	11	IBM PC/AT
at2	12	IBM PC/AT with alternative delay
css	12	[CSS Labs]
at3	13	Philips
fasthp	14	HPVectra

In most cases, HIMEM.SYS detects the correct A20 handler automatically, so you should only need to use /MACHINE switch in the event that DOS reports problems or can't access the High Memory Area. Check the README.TXT file on your C:\DOS directory or DOS 5 Distribution disk #5 for any late-breaking A20 handlers.

Usage   HIMEM.SYS is DOS's extended memory manager: It makes extended memory available to applications, and it oversees that memory to prevent programs from trying to use the same memory simultaneously. If you have an 80286, 80386, or 80486 computer that contains extended memory, you should always install HIMEM.SYS or some other memory manager that uses the XMS Extended Memory Specification.

HIMEM.SYS also lets you move much of DOS into extended memory, thus freeing a large block of conventional memory for your application programs. For details, see the DOS entry in this appendix.

To access the unused portion of reserved memory on a 386 or 486 computer, you must use HIMEM.SYS before using the EMM386.EXE driver and the DOS command. For details and examples, see the EMM386 entry in this appendix.

Examples

Only one application can use the High Memory Area at a time. If you omit the /HMAMIN switch or set it to 0, HIMEM.SYS allocates HMA to the first application that asks for it. To ensure the most efficient use of high memory, set /HMAMIN to the value of the largest application that needs to use that area. For example, to restrict the use of HMA memory to applications that require more than 32KB of memory, use the following command in your CONFIG.SYS file:

```
DEVICE=C:\DOS\HIMEM.SYS /HMAMIN=32
```

The DOS 5 Installation program attempts to determine the type of computer that you are using and insert the proper setting for the /MACHINE switch. However, if you install the Phoenix Cascade BIOS chip in an existing AT compatible computer, you would change the previous DEVICE command to the following:

```
DEVICE=C:\DOS\HIMEM.SYS /HMAMIN=32 /MACHINE:3
```

Many fast 386 and 486 computers include a *shadow RAM* feature, by which slow ROM routines are moved into faster RAM to speed system execution. The SHADOWRAM: option tries to disable that shadow RAM so system memory is made available to DOS and applications.

```
DEVICE=C:\DOS\HIMEM.SYS /HMAMIN=32 SHADOWRAM:OFF
```

See Also

DOS, EMM386

IF

Makes a decision in a batch file by determining whether a condition is true.

Version

1 and later

Type

Internal (used in batch files and DOSKEY macros)

DOS Shell Menu Access   None

Syntax

```
IF [NOT] ERRORLEVEL number command
IF [NOT] "string1" == "string2" command
IF [NOT] EXIST file name command
```

in which *number* is a number corresponding to an ERRORLEVEL value, *string1* and *string2* are text, *file name* is the name of a file, and *command* is a DOS command.

Usage

The IF command lets a batch file "decide" which task to perform next. If the condition on which the decision is based proves "true," then the command to the right of the IF statement is executed. If the condition proves "false," the command is not executed and processing continues normally at the next command. (Although IF can be used in DOSKEY macros, its use is limited because macros will not accept GOTO, which increases the decision-making power of the IF command.)

The decision can be based on a DOS error (using ERRORLEVEL), a user's entry (string1 == string2), or the existence of a file (EXIST). The NOT option is used in the same way it is used in English. For example, IF a condition does NOT occur, then do (something).

When using ERRORLEVEL, a value of 0 always indicates that no error occurred. A value of 1 or greater indicates that an error did occur. IF ERRORLEVEL returns "true" if the ERRORLEVEL value is greater than or equal to the compared value. For example, if the BACKUP command returns an ERRORLEVEL value of 1, 2, 3, 4, or 5, then the command IF ERRORLEVEL 1 GOTO End passes control to the :End label, because each of those values is greater than or equal to 1. However, if BACKUP returns a 0 ERRORLEVEL value in the previous example, the GOTO End command is completely ignored, and processing continues at the next line in the batch file.

Note that very few DOS commands return a value in ERRORLEVEL. If you use an IF ERRORLEVEL command beneath a command that does not return an ERRORLEVEL value, the batch file assumes there was no error (even if there was).

When comparing text strings, you typically use a parameter passed from the command line. For example, suppose you create a batch file named ME.BAT, and the user enters a command such as ME Fred. The command

```
IF "%1" == "Fred" GOTO HimAgain
```

passes control to a label called `:HimAgain`. If the user enters any other name, such as `ME Jane`, the `GOTO HimAgain` command is ignored and processing continues at the next line.

If either string in an IF command is null (empty), the IF command presents a `Syntax Error` message. To avoid this message, use a period at the end of each string. For example, to see if a parameter was omitted from the command line, compare the parameter followed by a period to a period. For example, using the ME.BAT example again, if the user enters `ME` without a name, the following line passes control to a label named `:NoName`:

```
IF "%1." == "." GOTO NoName
```

The EXIST option checks to see if a file exists. For example, the command `IF NOT EXIST LOGON.BAT GOTO MakeFile` passes control to the `MakeFile` label if a file named LOGON.BAT does not exist on the current drive and directory.

If the named file contains a wild card character, then any file that matches the pattern determines a "true" result. For example, the command `IF EXIST C:\DBASE\*.DBF GOTO Done` passes control to the `:Done` label if any file in the C:\DBASE directory has the extension .DBF.

Examples   See Chapters 14 and 15 for practical examples of using IF in batch files and a DOSKEY macro.

See Also   DOSKEY, GOTO

INSTALL

Installs DOS memory-resident programs by way of the CONFIG.SYS file.

Version   4 and later

Type   Internal (used only in CONFIG.SYS)

DOS Shell Menu Access   None

Syntax   `INSTALL=[drive][path]file name[options]`

in which *drive*, *path*, and *file name* are the location and file name of the memory-resident program to be installed, and *options* represents options supported by the program.

Usage	INSTALL is used to install four terminate-and-stay-resident (TSR) programs in DOS 4 and 5. The only DOS 4 and 5 programs that can be used with INSTALL are FASTOPEN.EXE, KEYB.COM, NLSFUNC.EXE, and SHARE.EXE.
	If INSTALL is used in CONFIG.SYS to load a TSR program, the AUTOEXEC.BAT file doesn't need to include a command to execute that program. Furthermore, because the CONFIG.SYS file is executed before AUTOEXEC.BAT, the AUTOEXEC file can contain commands that make use of the already installed and active program.
Examples	The following command, when placed in your CONFIG.SYS file, loads and activates the DOS 5 FASTOPEN disk caching system:
	`INSTALL=C:\DOS\FASTOPEN.EXE C:50`
See Also	DEVICE, CONFIG.SYS, FASTOPEN, KEYB, NLSFUNC, SHARE

JOIN

Joins a disk drive to a directory path.

Version	3.1 and later
Type	External (JOIN.EXE)
DOS Shell Menu Access	None
Syntax	`JOIN [original drive] [new drive\path][/D]`
	in which *original drive* is the name of the drive that you wish to "hide," and *new drive\path* is the location of the new drive and directory to be used for storing data.
Usage	JOIN is commonly used to substitute a hard disk drive or RAM drive for a floppy disk drive. Generally, you only want to do this if you are using an older program that is not designed to run on a hard disk. By using JOIN, you can "trick" the old program into storing and accessing files on a hard disk or RAM disk rather than a floppy disk drive.
	There are quite a few rules involved in using JOIN. These concern both the guest disk drive (the one being connected—that is, the floppy disk drive) and the host disk drive and directory (the one being connected to—that is, the hard disk or RAM disk). The host directory name must be included in the command, and it must refer to a level-1 directory. That is, the directory being joined to must not

be a child to another directory. Hence, you can JOIN to the directory C:\TEMPFILE, but not to the subdirectory C:\TEMPFILE\TEMP2. If you specify a directory on the host drive that does not exist, JOIN automatically creates the directory.

The host directory must be empty. Attempting to use a nonempty directory on the host drive produces the error message `Directory not Empty`, and cancels the JOIN procedure.

Neither the host nor the guest drives can be virtual drives created by the ASSIGN or SUBST commands. Furthermore, neither can be network drives.

After the drives are joined, the entire guest disk, including all directories and subdirectories, becomes a part of the host directory. The guest root directory becomes the equivalent of the named host drive directory, and any subdirectories of the guest drive become subdirectories of the host directory. The guest disk drive and directory become "invisible" to DOS; any command that refers to that drive and directory returns an error message, such as `Invalid drive specification`.

After the join has taken effect, you can access files only through the new host directory. Therefore, if you join drive A: to C:\TEMPFILE, the command DIR A: would be invalid. Instead, you would use the command DIR C:\TEMPFILE.

After you've issued a JOIN command, avoid using the commands ASSIGN, BACKUP, CHKDSK, DISKCOMP, FDISK, DISKCOPY, FORMAT, LABEL, RECOVER, RESTORE, SUBST and SVS. To view the current status of any JOIN commands, enter the command JOIN with no parameters. To disengage an existing JOIN, enter the JOIN command with the /D option.

Examples   Suppose you want to treat a directory named \TEMP on drive C: as though it were disk drive B:, because you really don't have a disk B:. First, enter the command DIR C:\TEMP to make sure that the \TEMP directory is empty (shows only the . and .. entries). Or, if \TEMP does not exist, enter the command MD \TEMP at the command prompt to create the new directory.

Next, enter the command

`JOIN B: C:\TEMP`

to have DOS treat the \TEMP directory as though it were disk drive B:. Now you can run your "old" DOS program, which insists on accessing drive B: for data files. However, the program will "think" that the C:\TEMP directory is drive B:, and that's where it will store, and search for, files.

When you have finished using the old DOS program, enter the command JOIN B: /D to disable the JOIN.

See Also   ASSIGN, SUBST

KEYB

Selects a keyboard layout.

Version   1 and later

Type   External (KEYB.COM)

DOS Shell   None
Menu Access

Syntax   Syntax for KEYB varies considerably among computers and some versions of DOS. The syntax for Version 3.3., at the command prompt or in a batch file, is

```
KEYB [country code[,[code page]
[,[drive][path]file name]]]
```

If you are using DOS 4 or 5, you can use the previous syntax or, alternatively, activate KEYB in the CONFIG.SYS file using the syntax

```
INSTALL=KEYB [country code[,[code
page][,[drive][path]file name]]][ID:xxx]
```

in which *country code* is a two-letter abbreviation for a country, *code page* is a three-digit code page number, and *drive*, *path*, *file name* represent the location and name of the keyboard definitions file (usually C:\DOS\KEYBOARD.SYS). The *xxx* option specifies a three-digit keyboard code.

Usage   KEYB changes the United States layout of your keyboard to match that of another country. Unlike earlier versions of DOS, which use commands such as KEYBUK (for United Kingdom), KEYBFR (for France), and so on, Versions 3.3, 4, and 5 of DOS use a space between the KEYB command and country abbreviation (that is, KEYB UK or KEYB FR).

Because KEYB is an external command, it must be on the current drive and directory, or in a directory specified in the current PATH setting, in order to be accessible.

The two-letter abbreviation used in the KEYB command must be one of those listed in the leftmost column of Table B.11. The optional three-digit code page must be one that is available for the country, as listed in the third column of the table. (If omitted, the current code page is used.)

The optional /ID: switch in DOS 5 selects a keyboard layout using the Keyboard ID number listed in Table B.11. This is used only for the countries that support more than one keyboard: France, Italy, and the United Kingdom. If /ID: is omitted, the default (first-listed) keyboard code is assumed.

Table B.11. Two-letter abbreviations and code pages for KEYB.

Two-Letter Abbreviation	Country	Acceptable Code Pages	DOS 5 Keyboard ID #
BE	Belgium	850	120
CF	Canadian (French)	850, 863	058
DK	Denmark	850, 865	159
FR	France	437, 850	189 or 120
GR	Germany	437, 850	129
IT	Italy	437, 850	141 or 142
LA	Latin America	437, 850	171
NL	Netherlands	437, 850	143
NO	Norway	850, 865	155
PO	Portugal	850, 860	163
SF	Switzerland (French)	850	150
SG	Switzerland (German)	850	000
SP	Spain	437, 850	172
SU	Finland	437, 850	153
SV	Sweden	437, 850	153
UK	United Kingdom	437, 850	166 or 168
US	U.S.A., Australia	437, 850	103

Be sure to provide the complete location and file name of the keyboard file (usually C:\DOS\KEYBOARD.SYS) as the third argument in the KEYB command.

After you activate KEYB, you use *dead keys* to type accented characters. Dead keys, when initially pressed, display nothing. However, when you press a certain letter key after pressing a dead key, the typed character appears with its appropriate accent mark. For specific maps to code pages and dead keys for your country's keyboard, refer to the DOS manual that came with your computer.

Entering the command KEYB with no parameters displays the two-letter country code and code page currently in use.

After you install KEYB, the following keys let you switch keyboard styles:

Ctrl-Alt-F1   Switches to the standard U.S. keyboard.

Ctrl-Alt-F2   Switches to the keyboard driver specified in the KEYB command

Examples   To configure your computer for the French-Canadian language, first add the following commands to your CONFIG.SYS file (assuming that your computer has an EGA or VGA display adapter):

```
COUNTRY=002 863 C:\DOS\COUNTRY.SYS
DEVICE=C:\DOS\DISPLAY.SYS CON=(EGA,437,2)
```

Then, add these commands to your AUTOEXEC.BAT file:

```
MODE CON CP PREP=((863,850)C:\DOS\EGA.CPI)
MODE CON CP SEL = 863
KEYB US,863,C:\DOS\KEYBOARD.SYS
```

After completing the installation, you can press Ctrl-Alt-F1 to use the U.S.A. keyboard, or Ctrl-Alt-F2 to use the French-Canadian keyboard.

See Also   COUNTRY, DISPLAY.SYS, MODE, PRINTER.SYS

LABEL

Assigns or changes a label to a hard disk or a floppy diskette.

Version   3 and later (PC DOS); 3.1 and later (MS-DOS)

Type   External (LABEL.COM)

DOS Shell Menu Access   None

Syntax   `LABEL [drive] [label]`

in which *drive* is the name of the disk drive containing the disk to which you want to assign a label, and *label* is the label (name) you want to assign.

Usage   The LABEL command lets you assign, view, change, or delete a disk volume label. The term *volume* refers to the collection of files on the disk. The label is basically a name and is entirely optional. If you choose to assign a label to a disk, that label appears as the first line of the display whenever you use the DIR, TREE, VOL, and CHKDSK commands.

The label you assign can be as long as 11 characters and can include spaces and underline characters. The label should not, however, include any of the following characters: * ? / \ or | .

You should include the disk drive name to the right of the LABEL command. (If no disk drive is specified, then the current disk drive is assumed.) If you use the LABEL command to assign a name to a disk, the new label overwrites any existing name. If you do not include a label with the LABEL command, DOS displays the existing label (if any), and prompts you to type a new label. If you press Enter without typing a new label, you'll be asked whether or not you want to delete the label. Answer `Yes` (Y) or `No` (N) and press Enter.

You cannot assign a label to a network drive. Similarly, you should avoid using LABEL with disk drives that are currently affected by ASSIGN, JOIN, or SUBST commands.

Note that you also can use the /V option with the FORMAT command to assign a label to a disk. The VOL command lets you view the current label, if any.

Examples   The following scenario demonstrates the ways in which you can use LABEL. To start, suppose you place a blank formatted diskette in drive A: and enter the DIR command. The first line of the output informs you that `Volume in drive A: has no label`.

Next, you decide to assign the name WPFILES to that disk. To do so, enter the command

```
LABEL A:WPFILES
```

The disk in drive A: is now labeled WPFILES. To verify this, enter the command

```
LABEL A:
```

and the screen displays the following information:

```
Volume in drive A is WPFILES
Volume label (11 characters, ENTER for none)?
```

As the screen explains, you now can enter a new volume label and then press Enter. (At this point, if you were to type in a new label, the new label would replace the existing one.) If you do not want to change the existing label, just press the Enter key.

If you press the Enter key, the screen then displays the prompt

```
Delete current volume label (Y/N)?
```

If you type Y and press Enter, the existing label is removed. If you type N and press Enter, the current label is retained.

See Also   FORMAT, VOL

LASTDRIVE

Sets the maximum number of accessible disk drives.

Version   3 and later

Type   Internal (used only in CONFIG.SYS)

DOS Shell Menu Access   None

Syntax   LASTDRIVE=x

in which *x* is a drive name specified by a letter from A to Z.

Usage   LASTDRIVE is used only in the CONFIG.SYS file. In most situations, this command is not required, because DOS can detect as many as five disk drives (drives A: through E:, including a RAM disk) after reading the CONFIG.SYS file. Three exceptions when you would want to use LASTDRIVE in your CONFIG.SYS file are

❑ When you have created more than one RAM disk.

❑ When you plan to use the SUBST command to create an artificial disk drive.

❑ When you will have drives with names higher than the letter E:.

Examples   Suppose your computer has a floppy disk drive named A: and one hard disk named C:. Your CONFIG.SYS file also contains two DEVICE=RAMDRIVE.SYS commands, which create two RAM disks. Furthermore, you occasionally use the SUBST command to create an artificial drive. Given this situation, you should include the command

LASTDRIVE=F

in your CONFIG.SYS file. That way, DOS will be prepared to manage the two RAM disks, which automatically are named D: and E: by the DEVICE=RAMDRIVE.SYS commands in CONFIG.SYS, as well as your artificial drive F:, when you enter a SUBST command at the command prompt.

See Also   SUBST

LOADFIX

Loads a program above the first 64KB of conventional memory.

Version — 5

Type — External (LOADFIX.COM)

DOS Shell Menu Access — None

Syntax

`LOADFIX [drive:][path]file name`

where *drive:*, *path*, and *file name* identify the location and name of the program you want to run.

Usage — DOS 5 uses a new memory-management scheme that releases much of the conventional memory that earlier versions of DOS used for themselves. Some programs may have trouble running if loaded into this now freed area of memory. When this happens, the error message `Packed file corrupt` appears.

To get around this, use the LOADFIX command to run the program in more "traditional" areas of memory above 64KB.

Examples — A game program named ZANDOO displays the error message `Packed file corrupt` when you try to run it under DOS 5. The program is stored on C:\GAMES with the file name ZANDOO.COM. To run the program, type `LOADFIX C:\GAMES\ZANDOO.COM` at the command prompt, and press Enter.

See Also — SETVER

LOADHIGH

Loads programs into the 384KB of upper memory above 640KB, freeing space in conventional memory.

Version — 5

Type — Internal

DOS Shell Menu Access — None

Syntax

`LOADHIGH [drive][path]filename` or
`LH [drive][path]filename`

in which *drive:path\filename* specifies the location and name of the program you want to load.

Usage   LOADHIGH is one of the new DOS 5 commands that are designed to free as much conventional memory as possible for your application programs. Before you can use LOADHIGH, you need to run an upper memory block manager program. On an 80386 or 80486 computer with DOS 5, you can use this series of commands in your CONFIG.SYS file:

```
DEVICE=C:\DOS\HIMEM.SYS DOS =HIGH,UMB
DEVICE=C:\DOS\EMM386.EXE NOEMS
```

On an 80286 computer, you need to use a third-party, upper memory manager; most likely the device driver program that came with your expanded memory board (see its documentation).

LOADHIGH (or the equivalent LH) can be used either at the command prompt or in the AUTOEXEC.BAT file. However, LOADHIGH is probably most effective as a command in your AUTOEXEC.BAT file. After you establish that a program fits into upper memory, use AUTOEXEC.BAT to load the TSR into upper memory every time you start the computer.

Unfortunately, DOS does not let you know if the loading operation is successful. If a program cannot fit into upper memory, DOS just moves it into conventional memory without a warning or message. You can, however, check the status of both conventional and upper memory using the MEM /C command.

Examples   The following AUTOEXEC.BAT file commands load a mouse driver, some common DOS memory resident programs, and a third-party TSR program (a pop-up alarm, appointment book, etc.) into upper memory rather than conventional memory (assuming CONFIG.SYS has already prepared the upper memory):

```
LOADHIGH C:\MOUSE1\MOUSE

LOADHIGH C:\DOS\MODE COM1:9600,n,8,1,b
LOADHIGH C:\DOS\LPT1:,,b
LOADHIGH C:\DOS\PRINT.EXE /D:LPT1
LOADHIGH C:\DOS\DOSKEY
LOADHIGH C:\DOS\FASTOPEN.EXE C:=10 D:=10

LOADHIGH C:\UTILS\SYSCTRL.COM
```

In all preceding seven commands, LOADHIGH could have been abbreviated LH.

See Also   DEVICE, DEVICEHIGH, DOS, EMM386

MEM

Displays the amount of used and available memory.

Version 4 and later

Type External (MEM.EXE)

**DOS Shell
Menu Access** None

Syntax `MEM [/PROGRAM | /DEBUG | CLASSIFY]`

where /PROGRAM can be abbreviated as `/P`, `/DEBUG` can be abbreviated as /D, and CLASSIFY can be abbreviated as /C.

Usage MEM displays all currently used and unused conventional memory (RAM) and extended or expanded memory if available. Because MEM is external, it must be on the current drive and directory or in a directory specified in the current PATH setting when you enter the MEM command at the DOS command prompt.

Used with no switches, MEM displays only basic memory usage. The /PROGRAM option displays programs and device drivers currently loaded into memory. The /DEBUG option presents more detailed information about programs, internal device drivers, and installed drivers in memory. Both options display memory locations and sizes in hexadecimal.

You cannot use both the /PROGRAM and /DEBUG options in a single MEM command.

The /C Switch shows the contents of conventional memory and upper (reserved) memory in decimal format.

As with all DOS commands that display information, you can use > PRN to print the report (though you may need to eject the page yourself) or use | MORE to page through the report on the screen.

Examples Assume that a COMPAQ 386 computer running MS-DOS 5 uses the following CONFIG.SYS file commands:

```
files=40
break=off
device=c:\dos\himem.sys
dos=high, umb
device=c:\dos\emm386.exe noems
devicehigh=c:\dos\ramdrive.sys 360 /e
device=c:\dos\smartdrv.sys 512
shell=c:\dos\command.com c:\dos\ /p
```

The AUTOEXEC.BAT file for this same computer contains the commands

```
rem
*********************************AUTOEXEC.BAT
c:\dos\mode com1:9600,n,8,1,r
c:\dos\mode lpt1:,,b
prompt $p$g
path c:\dos;d:\pdox35
loadhigh f:\mouse1\mouse
loadhigh c:\dos\print.exe /d:lpt1
loadhigh c:\dos\doskey.com
c:\dos\mirror c: /tc /td /te /tf
md h:\temps
set temp=h:\temps
path
h:\temps;c:\dos;c:\wp51;d:\utils;d:\dbase;f:\fontware
rem set dtl_lblopt=on
call macros
```

Entering the command MEM immediately after startup might show (approximately) the following memory usage:

```
 655360 bytes total conventional memory
 655360 bytes available to MS-DOS
 604448 largest executable program size
4194304 bytes total contiguous extended memory
      0 bytes available contiguous extended memory
3247104 bytes available XMS memory
        MS-DOS resident in High Memory Area
```

Here's a summary of what this tells you:

655360 bytes (640KB) of RAM are installed in this computer.

655360 (all of that RAM) have been made available to DOS.

604448 bytes RAM remain after loading DOS, device drivers, and so forth.

4194304 bytes extended memory are installed in this computer.

0 of those bytes are unused (that is, not under control of HIMEM.SYS)

3247104 bytes of "usable" extended memory are available (after installing parts of DOS, the RAM disk, etc., in that area).

MS-DOS resident in High Memory Area tells that DOS is in high memory.

The command MEM /C (or MEM /C > PRN or MEM /C ¦ MORE
would display a more detailed report showing every program loaded
into conventional and upper memory, the space they occupy, and
the remaining available space:

```
Conventional Memory:Name          Size in Decimal      Size in Hex
-----------------------------      -----------------    -----------
MSDOS              15856           (  15.5K)            3DF0
HIMEM               1184           (   1.2K)             4A0
EMM386              8208           (   8.0K)            2010
SMARTDRV           22016           (  21.5K)            5600
COMMAND             2624           (   2.6K)             A40
MODE                 480           (   0.5K)             1E0
FREE                  64           (   0.1K)              40
FREE                  64           (   0.1K)              40
FREE              604608           ( 590.4K)           939C0

Total  FREE :         604736       (590.6K)

Upper Memory :

    Name             Size in Decimal      Size in Hex
 ----------          ---------------      -----------
SYSTEM             163840           (160.0K)            28000
RAMDRIVE            1184            (  1.2K)              4A0
MOUSE              12784           ( 12.5K)             31F0
PRINT               5760           (  5.6K)             1680
DOSKEY              4064           (  4.0K)              FE0
MIRROR              6544           (  6.4K)             1990
FREE                  96           (  0.1K)               60
FREE              133264           (130.1K)            20890

Total  FREE :         133360       (130.2K)

Total bytes available to programs (Conventional+Upper) :   738096   (720.8K)
Largest executable program size :                          604448   (590.3K)
Largest available upper memory block :                     133264   (130.1K)

    4194304 bytes total contiguous extended memory
          0 bytes available contiguous extended memory
    3247104 bytes available XMS memory
            MS-DOS resident in High Memory Area
```

Notice that even with the resident portions of RAMDRIVE, MOUSE,
PRINT, DOSKEY, and MIRROR loaded into upper memory, 130.2KB
of upper memory is available, which underscores how much
memory earlier versions of DOS wasted.

For a more detailed report with hexadecimal memory addresses,
use the command MEM /PROGRAM which would print something
like this:

Address	Name	Size	Type
000000		000400	Interrupt Vector
000400		000100	ROM Communication Area
000500		000200	DOS Communication Area
000700	IO	000C10	System Data
001310	MSDOS	001570	System Data
002880	IO	009050	System Data
	HIMEM	0004A0	DEVICE=
	EMM386	002010	DEVICE=
	SMARTDRV	005600	DEVICE=
		000820	FILES=
		000100	FCBS=
		000200	BUFFERS=
		0002C0	LASTDRIVE=
		000740	STACKS=
00B8E0	MSDOS	000040	System Program
00B930	COMMAND	000940	Program
00C280	MSDOS	000040	-- Free --
00C2D0	COMMAND	000100	Environment
00C3E0	MSDOS	000040	-- Free --
00C430	MODE	0001E0	Program
00C620	MEM	000090	Environment
00C6C0	MEM	0135A0	Program
01FC70	MSDOS	080370	-- Free --
09FFF0	MSDOS	028010	System Program
0C8010	IO	0004B0	System Data
	RAMDRIVE	0004A0	DEVICE=
0C84D0	MSDOS	000060	-- Free --
0C8540	MOUSE	0031F0	Program
0CB740	PRINT	001680	Program
0CCDD0	DOSKEY	000FE0	Program
0CDDC0	MIRROR	001990	Program
0CF760	MSDOS	020890	-- Free --

```
    655360 bytes total conventional memory
    655360 bytes available to MS-DOS
    604448 largest executable program size
   4194304 bytes total contiguous extended memory
         0 bytes available contiguous extended memory
   3247104 bytes available XMS memory
           MS-DOS resident in High Memory Area
```

or use MEM /DEBUG to print an even more detailed listing.

See Also   CHKDSK, DIR

MKDIR or **MD**

Creates a directory or subdirectory.

Version	2 and later
Type	Internal
DOS Shell Menu Access	Position the highlight on parent directory of the directory you want to create. (Use the root directory if you want to create a directory that is one level beneath root.) Press F10 or Alt and then select `Create Directory...` from the File pull-down menu.

Syntax

`MKDIR [drive][path]directory name`

or

`MD [drive][path]directory name`

in which *drive* is the name of the disk drive, *path* is the path (if any), and *directory name* is the name of the new directory that you want to create.

Usage

MKDIR (and its abbreviated form, MD) allows you to create a new directory or subdirectory on a disk. The directory you create can be either one level beneath the root (such as \UTILS) or a child directory of one or more other directories (such as \UTILS\DATA). A single directory name can consist of no more than eight characters and can include a three-letter extension preceded by a period (exactly the same format as a file name). An entire path name, consisting of several subdirectory names (such as WP\BOOKS\CHAPTERS), can contain a maximum of 63 characters.

The directory name that you assign cannot be the same as any other directory name on the disk, nor can it be the same as any file on the parent directory.

If you use the \ character in front of the first directory name, the directory is created in reference to the root directory. If you omit the first \ character, the directory is created in reference to the current directory (that is, as a child to the current directory). Examples in the following section demonstrate these principles.

You probably should not use the MKDIR command when using drives affected by the ASSIGN, JOIN, or SUBST commands. DOS allows you to create subdirectories when these commands are in effect, but the actual location of the directory might not be where you think it is. For example, if you enter the command `ASSIGN A = C` and then enter the command `MKDIR A:\TEMP`, the \TEMP directory is actually created on drive C:, not drive A: as the MKDIR command implies.

If you attempt to create a directory, but you get the error message `Unable to create directory`, one of five things is wrong.

1. The directory already exists.
2. A file that has the same name as the directory already exists.
3. You specified a parent directory that does not exist (for example, \UTILS\DATA, but \UTILS does not exist).
4. The disk is full.
5. The root directory already contains the maximum number of files.

Examples   To create a directory named WP one level beneath the root directory, enter the following command:

```
MD \WP
```

To create a subdirectory named WPFILES beneath the \WP directory, you could use one of two techniques. If any directory other than \WP is the current directory, you must enter the command

```
MD \WP\WPFILES
```

If on the other hand, \WP is the current directory, you can use a shortcut and enter the simpler command

```
MD WPFILES
```

The following example demonstrates the importance of using the leading \ character with MKDIR. Suppose that you change to the \WP\WPFILES subdirectory by entering the command

```
CD WP\WPFILES
```

If you then enter the command

```
MD TEXT
```

the TEXT subdirectory is created as a child to the current directory, because the command doesn't begin with the \ character, which symbolizes the root directory. Therefore, the actual path name for the new subdirectory is WP\WPFILES\TEXT.

However, if you include the leading backslash in the command, as follows:

```
MD \TEXT
```

the new directory is created as a child to the root directory only (even though your current directory is WP\WPFILES). That is, its path name is simply \TEXT, rather than \WP\WPFILES\TEXT.

Suppose that you try to create a directory named \TEMP by entering the command MD TEMP, and DOS displays the error message Unable to create the Directory. Usually, this error occurs because a directory or file named TEMP already exists. To safeguard against this error, enter the TREE command to see whether a directory named TEMP already exists on your hard disk. If not, enter the command DIR TEMP to see whether a file named TEMP already exists in the current directory.

See Also   CHDIR or CD, RMDIR or RD

MIRROR

Records system information (the root directory, boot record, file allocation tables, and partition table) so that you can recover from accidental formats and deletions.

Version   5

Type   External (MIRROR.COM)

DOS Shell Menu Access   None

Syntax   MIRROR [*drive* ...] [/T*drive*[-*entries*]] [/U] [/ PARTN] [/1]

in which *drive* ... specifies the drive or drives whose system information is to be saved and the following switches determine how the information is saved:

/T*drive*[-*entries*]	Installs a memory-resident program that tracks which files are deleted on the specified drive(s). The optional *entries* parameter specifies the maximum number of files to be tracked (1-999)
/U	Uninstalls the memory-resident file-tracking program from memory
/PARTN	Saves the partition tables of a hard disk onto a floppy disk
/1	Saves only the latest system information.

Usage   The MIRROR command is one of the important file recovery utilities
that has been added to DOS 5; UNDELETE and UNFORMAT are the
others. When DOS reformats a hard disk or an already formatted
floppy diskette, it doesn't actually erase the data in the disk, it
simply clears the root directory and deletes the file allocation tables
(FATs). The MIRROR command saves that system data so that the
UNFORMAT command can use it to restore the file and directory
structure of your disks. The information in the MIRROR.FIL file can
also help the UNFORMAT command restore deleted directories that
branch off the root directory.

By default, MIRROR creates two system information files
MIRROR.FIL (the most recent data) and MIRROR.BAK (the previous
MIRROR.FIL file renamed). To ensure that this system data is as
accurate (current) as possible, you probably should specify
all of your hard disk drives in a MIRROR command in your
AUTOEXEC.BAT file. This lets you recover the files and directories
on your hard disk up to the current session.

The "delete tracking" option loads a memory resident program that
creates a file called PCTRACKR.DEL, which records the locations of
deleted files on the specified drive. DOS places the file in the root
directory of the affected drive so that the UNDELETE program can
use it to recover accidentally deleted files. Note, however, that the
PCTRACKR.DEL file can only keep track of a limited number of files:
When the limit is reached, the oldest file is replaced by the newest,
the second-oldest by the next, and so on (this keeps PCTRACKR.DEL
from growing too large). Table B.12 shows the default number of
entries that PCTRACKR.DEL can hold for different sizes of drives:

Table B.12. Default entries.

Disk Size	Number of Entries
360KB	25
720KB	50
1.2MB	75
1.44MB	75
20MB	101
32MB	202
More than 32MB	303

Note that the size of the file increases proportionately with the
number of entries that it holds. For example, the size of

PCTRACKR.DEL file for a 360KB disk is only 5KB, but the file for a drive of greater than 32 megabytes is 55KB.

Examples   The new MIRROR command is actually a stand-alone version of the same utility offered by the PC Tools package (as are the new DOS UNFORMAT and UNDELETE commands). If you are familiar with the PC Tools versions of these programs, you can use the DOS 5 programs in exactly the same way.

If you have two hard disk drives on your system (C: and D:) or if you have one drive partitioned into two drives, you can insert the following command into your AUTOEXEC.BAT file to protect your system information:

```
MIRROR C: D:
```

If you want to use the additional safety feature of having MIRROR track deleted files on those drives, use the following command:

```
MIRROR /TC /TD
```

If, for example, you use programs on your 20MB drive D: to generate daily reports and actively create and delete many files on that drive, you might want to track more than 101 files (the default). To use the default number of entries on drive C: but increase the number of entries held by the PCTRACKR.DEL file on drive D:, use the following command:

```
MIRROR /TC /TD-300
```

The partition table of your hard drive contains vital system information. You should save a copy of the partition table on a floppy disk so that UNFORMAT can use the information to reconstruct the directories and files on your hard disk after a catastrophe. To save partition table information for drive C: on a floppy disk, type

```
MIRROR /PARTN
```

and then type C when you see the prompt What drive?.

MODE

Prepares devices for use.

Version   1 and later (varies among DOS versions and specific computers)

Type   External (MODE.COM)

DOS Shell Menu Access   None

Syntax The syntax for the MODE command depends partly on the particular device you are installing and partly on the specific features offered by your computer. The command is generally used to alter the manner in which your computer uses devices (such as the printer, screen, and keyboard) to adjust to your particular work needs. The sections that follow provide the syntax for commonly used devices.

Usage The sections that follow present some general MODE command techniques and options. To take full advantage of the features offered by your computer, refer to the DOS manual that came with your computer or to the user's manual for your specific computer.

MODE **Monitors**

MODE lets you define the adapter used for your monitor and the width of the screen (in characters). It can also be used to realign text on the screen.

Syntax **Monitors**

MODE can use several different syntaxes to adjust your monitor:

```
MODE display
MODE display,lines
MODE [display],shift[,test]
MODE CON [:] COLS=cols LINES=lines|
```

in which

display specifies the display mode as 40, 80, BW40, BW80, CO40, CO80, or MONO; *shift* can be either R (to shift right) or L (to shift left); *test* is specified by the letter T, which allows you to repeat the specified *shift* until alignment is accurate; *cols* specifies the number of columns to display, either 40 or 80; and *lines* specifies the number of lines to display, either 25, 43, or 50.

Usage **Monitors**

Valid options for the *display* parameter of the MODE command include

40	Sets the display width to 40 characters.
80	Sets the display width to 80 characters.
CO40	Enables color and sets the display width to 40 characters.
CO80	Enables color and sets the display width to 80 characters.
MONO	Activates a monochrome monitor.

(See Chapter 12 for examples of these options.)

Note that defining the monitor type as color (CO) does not immediately change the color of the screen. It does ensure, however, that any programs that can use color will do so.

EGA and VGA display adapters allow monitors to display more than 25 lines of text. The *lines* parameter in the MODE command lets you change the number of lines from the default value of 25 to either 43 or 50.

The *R* and *L* options work only with a Color Graphics Adapter. If an 80-character width is used, R and L shift text two columns. If a 40-character width is used, R and L shift text one column. The *T* option should be used to help you determine when text is properly aligned.

Examples   **Monitors**

To double the size of the characters on your monitor, enter the command

```
MODE 40
```

To realign your color (CGA) monitor to compensate for letters that are scrolled past the left edge of the screen, adjust the right margin by entering the command

```
MODE CO80,R,T
```

To realign your color (CGA) monitor to view letters that are chopped off at the right edge of the screen, adjust the left margin by entering the command

```
MODE CO80,L,T
```

Note that the last two commands display a test pattern on the screen and then question your ability to view certain characters. Answer N until the requested characters are visible on the screen; then enter Y

If you have an EGA or VGA adapter, or any other adapter that can display more than 25 lines of text on the screen, enter the command

```
MODE CON LINES=43 COLS=80
```

to permit 43 lines of text to be displayed on your screen. Note that DOS commands (such as DIR) take advantage of the new line spacing and character size, but some application programs might not.

To return to the default number of lines, enter the command

```
MODE CON LINES=25
```

MODE   **Parallel Printers**

MODE also allows you to configure printers attached to the parallel port. In most cases, you don't need to do this, because most programs, including DOS, take care of the printer automatically. (If you have problems with a printer, refer to the manual that came with that printer.)

Syntax   **Parallel Printers**

The general syntax for preparing a parallel printer for DOS Versions 1 to 3.3 is

```
MODE printer port [COLS][,lines][,P]
```

in Versions 4 and 5, the syntax is

```
MODE printer port [COLS=cols][,LINES=lines][,RETRY=
retry attempts]
```

in which *lines* is the number of lines per printed page, *cols* is the number of characters printed per line, and *retry attempts* determines how DOS interacts with the parallel printer.

Usage   **Parallel Printers**

You must specify LPT and a port number—LPT1, LPT2, or LPT3— when using MODE to configure a parallel printer. Other options and valid settings are summarized as follows:

cols   80 for printers with 8-inch carriages, or 132 for wide-carriage printers or compressed print on 8-inch printers.

lines   Either 6 lines or 8 lines to the inch.

retry   Usually E for network parallel printers, B for "infinite
attempts   retry" (similar to specifying P in earlier versions of DOS—not recommended for network printers), or R to send text only when the printer is ready. This is the default setting and is recommended for most printers.

Not all printers are able to accept different characters-per-line or lines-per-inch settings. Many insist on using the default values: 80 characters per line and 6 lines per inch. (Your printer manual explains how to use special features independently of the MODE command.)

If you use the MODE command to configure a parallel port, be sure that you include exactly two commas. If you omit an optional parameter, include the comma as a placeholder.

The P option used in Versions 1 through 3.3 of DOS specifies infinite retries on a parallel printer. For example, the command `MODE LPT1 ,,P` uses the default column spacing and line widths, but tells DOS to wait indefinitely for the printer to be ready, should it find the printer not ready when initially sending data.

Examples **Parallel Printers**

Several Epson, IBM, and other dot-matrix printers are capable of printing in densities other than the standard modes of 10 characters per horizontal inch and 6 lines per vertical inch. These printers respond to the MODE command for parallel printers.

For example, assuming that you have a compatible printer with a wide (13.5-inch) carriage and that the printer is attached to the LPT1 (also called the PRN) port, you can enter this command to print the full width of the paper, at 8 lines to the inch:

`MODE LPT1 COLS=132 LINES=8`

To adjust the column width without adjusting the number of lines per inch, use this command instead:

`MODE LPT1 COLS=80`

MODE **Serial Port**

If you use a modem, you probably use some type of communications software. This software allows you to configure your communications settings. Similarly, if you use a FAX board, it, too, automatically adjusts the settings for the communications (serial) port. Both of these optional devices completely override any communications port settings that you specify with the MODE command. In fact, you should avoid using MODE altogether when using a modem or FAX board (unless instructed otherwise by the documentation that came with your modem or FAX board).

On the other hand, serial printers often rely on DOS to set the communications settings. Specifically, they rely on the MODE command.

Syntax **Communications Port**

The general syntax for using the MODE command to configure a serial port for a serial printer is

`MODE port[:]rate[,parity[,`

or in DOS 4 and 5

```
databits[,stopbits[,P]]]]
MODE port BAUD=rate [DATA=databits] [STOP=stop bits]
[PARITY=parity] [RETRY=retry attempts]
```

in which

port is the name of a serial communications port: COM1 or COM2 in DOS Version 3.2 and earlier; COM1, COM2, COM3, or COM4 in DOS Versions 3.3 or later; *rate* is the baud rate: 110, 150, 300, 600, 1200, 2400, 4800, 9600, or 19200; *databits* is the number of bits per transmitted character: either 5, 6, 7, or 8. (Only DOS 5 supports the 5 and 6 options.) If omitted, the default is 7; *stopbits* is the number of bits between characters: either 1, 1.5, or 2, where 1 is the default, if omitted for all baud rates except 110, which defaults to 2. (Only DOS 5 supports the 1.5 option.) *parity* is either NONE, ODD, EVEN, SPACE, or MARK; and *retry attempts* is either E, B, R, or none (as discussed in the previous section pertaining to parallel communications).

Usage   **Serial Port**

If you omit any of the preceding settings, placing only the comma in its place, the default values are used for that setting (except for baud rate, which you must specify). Default values are even parity, 7 data bits, 1 stop bit (or 2 stop bits for 110 baud).

Examples   **Serial Port**

Assume that you have a serial printer attached to the second serial communications port (COM2). To set that port to a baud rate of 1200 with 8 data bits, 1 stop bit, no parity, and infinite retry attempts, enter the command

```
MODE COM2: 1200,N,8,1,P
```

or using DOS 4 or 5 syntax

```
MODE COM2 BAUD=1200 DATA=8 STOP=1 PARITY=NONE RETRY=B
```

at the command prompt (or in your AUTOEXEC.BAT file).

MODE   **Redirecting Parallel Output**

You can use MODE to tell DOS to send output that would normally go to the parallel port (usually PRN) to the serial port instead. Before doing so, be sure that the communications parameters for the serial port are ready, as described in the preceding section, "MODE for the Serial Port."

Syntax	**Redirecting Parallel Output**

The general syntax for redirecting parallel port output to the serial port is

```
MODE printer[:]=port[:]
```

in which *printer* is the name of the printer port (LPT1, LPT2, or LPT3) and *port* is the name of the serial communications port (COM1 or COM2 in DOS Versions 3.2 or earlier; COM1, COM2, COM3, or COM4 in DOS Versions 3.3 or 4).

To cancel the redirection, use only the printer parameter in the MODE command.

Examples	**Redirecting Parallel Output**

To redirect printed output originally intended for a parallel printer to a serial printer attached to the COM2 port, first enter the MODE command required to set up the communications parameters for the serial printer. Then enter the command

```
MODE LPT1:=COM2:
```

Any output to LPT1 (or PRN device, in this example) is rerouted to the COM2 port. To cancel this redirection, enter the command

```
MODE LPT1:
```

MODE	**Preparing a Code Page**

You can use the MODE command to prepare a non-English code page or several code pages for use with a particular device.

Syntax	**Preparing a Code Page**

The general syntax for preparing a hardware device for a specific DOS code page is

```
MODE device CP PREP= ((code page list) drive\path\file name)
```

in which

device is a DOS device name—either CON, PRN, LPT1, LPT2, or LPT3; *code page list* is one code page or a list of code pages, including 437, 850, 860, 863, 865, or any other that is supported by your hardware; and *drive path\file name* specifies the location and name of the Code Page Information (.CPI) file.

Usage	**Preparing a Code Page**

You can use CODEPAGE rather than the abbreviation CP in the MODE command. You can also use PREPARE rather than the abbreviation PREP.

Valid code page information files for most computers include

EGA.CPI   Code Page Information file for EGA and VGA video display adapters

LCD.CPI   Code Page Information file for liquid crystal display (LCD) screens

4201.CPI   Code Page Information file for the IBM Proprinter II, Model 4201

4208.CPI   Code Page Information file for the IBM Proprinter II, Model 4208

5202.CPI   Code Page Information file for the IBM Quietwriter III Printer, Model 5202

Check the user manual that came with your computer for other possible code page information files.

You can use the MODE command to prepare a code page for a device only after the DEVICE=DISPLAY.SYS or DEVICE=PRINTER.SYS command in the CONFIG.SYS file has installed the appropriate device driver for the code page.

You can list one or more code pages in the MODE CP PREPARE command. Separate each three-digit code page number with a space.

Examples   **Preparing a Code Page**

Assuming that your CONFIG.SYS file already contains a command such as DEVICE=C:\DOS\DISPLAY.SYS CON=(EGA,437,3), the following command prepares three code pages—850, 437, and 865—for use on the screen console.

```
MODE CON CP PREP=((863,437,850)C:\DOS\EGA.CPI)
```

The command can be included in your AUTOEXEC.BAT file or can be typed at the command prompt.

Another command, which would probably be entered at the command prompt, changes the initial MODE CON CP PREPARE command. In this example, the command changes the code pages to 850, 437, and 865. The double commas indicate that the second code page (437 in this example) remains unchanged.

```
MODE CON CP PREP=((850,,865)C:\DOS\EGA.CPI)
```

MODE   **Selecting a Code Page**

After you have used the DEVICE command to install a device driver for a code page, and you have used the MODE CP PREPARE command to prepare a code page, you can use the MODE CODEPAGE SELECT (abbreviated MODE CP SEL) command to select a code page to be used.

Syntax

Selecting a Code Page

To use the MODE command to select a code page, use the general syntax

```
MODE device CP SEL code page
```

in which *device* is the device name of an installed device, either CON, PRN, LPT1, LPT2, or LPT3, and *code page* is a valid code page number, usually 437, 850, 860, 863, 865, or any other number that is supported by your hardware.

Usage

Selecting a Code Page

To select a code page for the screen, the CONFIG.SYS file must already contain the proper DEVICE=DISPLAY.SYS command, and the MODE CON CP PREP command must have already prepared the code page. Similarly, to select a code page for the printer, the CONFIG.SYS file must already contain the proper DEVICE=PRINTER.SYS command, and the MODE PRN (or LPT#) CP PREP command must have already prepared the code page for the printer.

You can also use the MODE command to restore a code page or check the status of the current code page. To display the currently active code page (in DOS 4 or 5), use the syntax

```
MODE [device] [CODEPAGE] /STATUS
```

If you lose a code page because the printer or some other device is temporarily turned off and then turned back on, you can reinstall the current code page without rebooting. Use the MODE command with the syntax

```
MODE device CODEPAGE REFRESH
```

Examples

Selecting a Code Page

Assuming that the CONFIG.SYS file already contains a DEVICE=DISPLAY.SYS command to install the code page device driver for your monitor, the following commands prepare code pages 863 and 850 and select code page 863 as the current code page:

```
MODE CON CP PREP=((863,850)C:\DOS\EGA.CPI)
MODE CON CP SEL = 863
```

The next command installs code page 863 into the keyboard:

```
KEYB US,863,C:\DOS\KEYBOARD.SYS
```

The following command displays the currently active code page for the display monitor:

```
MODE CON CODEPAGE /REFRESH
```

The following command reactivates the current code page for the printer connected to port LPT1:

```
MODE LPT1 REFRESH
```

The following DOS 5 command displays the current status of all devices:

```
MODE /STATUS
```

MODE   **Setting Typematic Rate**

The MODE command also lets you set the *typematic rate* of your keyboard. The typematic rate is the speed that DOS repeats characters when you press and hold down a key; it also adjusts the delay that DOS waits before it begins repeating the characters.

Syntax   **Setting Typematic Rate**

The syntax for setting the keyboard's typematic rate is

```
MODE CON: RATE=rate DELAY=delay
```

in which *rate* specifies the typematic rate as a value from 1 (2 characters per second) to 32 (30 characters per second), and *delay* is a number from 1 through 4 that specifies the wait period (in quarters of a second; 1 = .25 second) from the time you press the key to the time the character begins repeating.

Usage   **Setting Typematic Rate**

This MODE command lets you change your keyboard configuration so that it is more or less responsive to keypresses. By default, the keyboard repeats characters slowly—at about 11 characters per second. Although this is usually adequate for typing at the command line, when you use a word processor or spreadsheet in which you must move through pages of text or figures, the movement of the cursor generated by your arrow keys might seem sluggish. This MODE command lets you correct this situation.

Examples   **Setting Typematic Rate**

To speed cursor movement to its fastest response time, insert the following command into your AUTOEXEC.BAT file:

```
MODE CON RATE=32 DELAY=1
```

Note that you must always specify both parameters in this command, even if you are changing the setting of only one.

The previous command speeds your keyboard typematic rate to its fastest time. If you type with a heavy touch, you might need to use a higher number for the DELAY parameter (maybe a 3 or 4). However, the highest RATE speed is usually the best; when you use the arrow keys or draw a line after changing this setting, you'll probably never use the default settings again.

In many versions of DOS, you can see the current status of MODE settings by entering one of these commands:

```
MODE
MODE ¦ MORE
MODE /STATUS
MODE /STATUS ¦ MORE
```

In addition, you may be able to check the status of an individual device by following the MODE command with the device name. For example, the following command displays the status of the first serial port (COM1):

```
MODE COM1:
```

See Also   KEYB, DISPLAY.SYS, PRINTER.SYS

Because MODE may vary with different dealer versions of DOS, check the DOS manual that came with your computer (if any) for additional options or differences.

Note that in DOS 5, the `retry=b` option for configuring parallel and serial printer ports replaces (is the same as) the `retry=p` option used in earlier versions of DOS.

MORE

Pauses the screen scrolling.

Version   2 and later

Type   External (MORE.COM)

DOS Shell Menu Access   None

Syntax   `MORE`

Usage   Normally when you use a command that displays a great deal of information, such as TYPE or TREE, that information quickly scrolls off the screen. You can start and stop scrolling by pressing Ctrl-S or (on some computers) the Pause key. However, it is much easier to use the MORE filter to force the display to pause automatically at the end of each screenful. You can even use MORE in your DOSKEY macros to create your own pausing "DOS commands."

When MORE is activated, scrolling pauses automatically after every 23 lines of text (24 lines in DOS 5), and the prompt -- `more` -- appears at the bottom of the screen. At that point, you can press any key to view the next screenful of information. (Optionally, you can type Ctrl-Break or Ctrl-C to return to the DOS prompt.)

MORE acts as a filter, and it must have information piped or redirected into it. There are two ways to do so. Either type a command and follow it with ¦ `MORE` or enter the MORE command followed by a < symbol and the name of the file you want to view. The following examples demonstrate these techniques.

Examples   Suppose that a software package that you purchased includes a file named READ.ME that you wish to read. To pause between filled screens, enter the command

```
MORE < READ.ME
```

You could accomplish exactly the same result by using MORE as a filter to the TYPE command, as follows:

```
TYPE READ.ME ¦ MORE
```

If you enter the MORE command with no parameters, as follows:

```
MORE
```

it waits for input from the keyboard. To return to the DOS prompt, press the F6 key or Ctrl-Z.

When you use the TYPE command to view text files, you almost always want the screen to pause after each screenful of information. However, because the TYPE command offers no "pause" switch (such as the /P in DIR), you might want to use the DOSKEY command to create a macro that always pauses after each screenful of text. To do so, enter the following command:

```
DOSKEY TYPE=TYPE $1 $B C:\DOS\MORE
```

Now, whenever you enter the TYPE command followed by a file name, DOS automatically runs the MORE filter for you. You can use this same procedure to create other "pausing" macros.

See Also   DOSKEY, TYPE

MSHERC

Lets you run programs using graphics requiring a Hercules graphics card.

Version   5

Type   External (MSHERC.COM)

DOS Shell Menu Access   None

Syntax   `MSHERC [/HALF]`

in which the /HALF switch must be added if a color adapter is also installed in your system.

Usage   You need to install the MSHERC device driver if you will be running a program that uses graphics modes of the Hercules display adapter. This driver lets DOS display the proper characters on your screen. If your system also includes a color display adapter (CGA, EGA, or VGA), you need to specify /HALF in your command line.

Examples   If you frequently use programs that require a Hercules graphics card (and your DOS programs are located in the \DOS directory of drive C), add the following line to your AUTOEXEC.BAT file so that MSHERC is always active:

`C:\DOS\MSHERC.COM`

Note that if your computer has an 80286, 80386, or 80386 microprocessor, you can load MSHERC into reserved memory to save conventional memory. To do so, first install the EMM386.EXE device driver and then include the DOS=UMB command in CONFIG.SYS. Finally, use the LOADHIGH command to load MSHERC into reserved memory.

If you rarely use programs that require the Hercules graphics adapter, run MSHERC from the command line whenever you need it. That way, no memory is wasted by storing a device driver that you rarely use.

See Also   DOS, EMM386, LOADHIGH

NLSFUNC

Provides support for country information and the CHCP command.

Version   3.3 and later

Type   External (NLSFUNC.EXE)

DOS Shell Menu Access   None

Syntax   NLSFUNC [[*drive*][*path*]\ *file name*]

in which *drive*, *path*, and *file name* represent the location and name of the country information file (usually C:\DOS\COUNTRY.SYS).

Usage   The NLSFUNC command loads the extended country information from the country information file and then allows you to use the CHCP command to select a code page. NLSFUNC must be executed before the CHCP command can be used.

You can include the NLSFUNC command in your AUTOEXEC.BAT file, or you can type the command directly at the command prompt. Optionally, you can have your CONFIG.SYS file install the NLSFUNC command using the syntax INSTALL=NLSFUNC.EXE (or INSTALL=C:\DOS\NLSFUNC.EXE). If you use the INSTALL option, be sure to specify the complete path and file name, including the .EXE extension.

You can use the NLSFUNC command only once during a DOS session. For this reason, it is often best to place the command in your AUTOEXEC.BAT or CONFIG.SYS file. If you attempt to load NLSFUNC more than once during a session, DOS displays the message NLSFUNC already installed.

Examples   The following command, entered at the command prompt or included in an AUTOEXEC.BAT file, installs the NLSFUNC program using the usual COUNTRY.SYS country information file, which is stored on the C:\DOS directory:

NLSFUNC C:\DOS\COUNTRY.SYS

As an alternative to installing NLSFUNC through the AUTOEXEC.BAT file or from the command prompt, you can instead include this command in your CONFIG.SYS file:

INSTALL=NLSFUNC C:\DOS\COUNTRY.SYS

See Also   CHCP

PATH

Specifies multiple directories to be searched for programs.

Version   2.0 and later

Type   Internal

DOS Shell Menu Access   None

Syntax   `PATH [drive][path][;][...]`

in which *drive* is the name of the drive to search, and *path* is a directory name or directory/subdirectory sequence. Multiple drive and directory specifications must be separated by semicolons, with no blank spaces.

Usage   PATH sets up a series of disk drives and directories that DOS will search for program files if those files are not on the current drive or directory. This is a valuable capability, because it allows you to access DOS external programs, such as ATTRIB, CHKDSK, FIND, PRINT, and others, from any drive and subdirectory. Note, however, that PATH only searches for executable program files (including batch files) that have the extensions .BAT, .COM, and .EXE. (The APPEND command searches for other types of files.)

Whenever you attempt to run a program, DOS searches the current drive and directory for the appropriate file. If the file cannot be found on the current drive and directory, DOS checks the PATH setting and searches the specified directories and subdirectories in the order in which they are listed. As soon as the file is located, it is loaded into memory and the program (or batch file) is executed.

It's a good idea always to include in your PATH command the drive and directory that contain your word processor or text editor. That way, you can use it at any time, on any drive or directory, to create or change files. Because PATH is such an important and frequently used command, it is nearly always included in the AUTOEXEC.BAT file.

The current PATH setting is always stored in the DOS environment. It can be accessed from a batch file using the variable name %PATH%, or it can be displayed by entering the command SET at the command prompt.

Examples   Suppose that you have stored all your DOS programs—such as CHKDSK.COM, FIND.COM, and so forth—in a directory named

\DOS on drive C:. You've stored some additional utility programs in a directory named \UTILS on drive C:. Finally, you've stored your word processor in a directory named \WP.

To ensure that all of the DOS commands, your utility programs, and your word processor are accessible at all times from any drive or subdirectory, enter the command

```
PATH C:\DOS;C:\UTILS;C:\WP
```

Note that each directory specification is separated by a semicolon, without any blank spaces.

To include the root directory in a PATH command, specify its name simply as the drive name followed by a backslash (\). For example, the following command adds the root directory to the previous PATH command example:

```
PATH C:\;C:\DOS;C:\UTILS;C:\WP
```

To view the current PATH setting at any time, enter the command

```
PATH
```

without parameters. To cancel a previously defined path, enter the command

```
PATH ;
```

See Also   APPEND, Chapter 11

PAUSE

Pauses a batch file or macro and waits for a keypress.

Version   1 and later

Type   Internal (used in batch files, macros, and the DOS Shell)

DOS Shell Menu Access   None

Syntax   PAUSE

Usage   The PAUSE command temporarily halts a batch file and presents the message `Strike a key when ready....` or `Press any key to continue...` in DOS 4 and 5. When you press a key, processing continues normally at the next line in the batch file. However, if you press Ctrl-Break or Ctrl-C, the batch file immediately terminates.

You can use an ECHO command above a PAUSE command to present a more descriptive error. For example, if the batch file needs to wait for the user to insert a diskette in drive A:, you can use an ECHO command to present the message `Insert diskette into drive A:`.

To hide the message that PAUSE normally displays, redirect the output to the NUL device. Precede the PAUSE command with your own descriptive messages, as in the example that follows.

Examples   The following batch file uses two ECHO commands to display messages and a PAUSE command to temporarily halt processing:

```
@ECHO OFF
ECHO Place a diskette in drive A:.
ECHO Then press any key to copy
ECHO (or press Ctrl-Break to cancel the operation).
PAUSE > NUL
COPY %1 A:
```

When executed, the batch file displays the messages

```
Place a diskette in drive A:
Then press any key to copy.
(or press Ctrl-Break to cancel the operation)
```

The PAUSE > NUL command then interrupts command execution and waits for a keypress. (PAUSE does not display its own message in this example, because its output is redirected to the NUL device.)

If the user presses Ctrl-Break or Ctrl-C during the pause, DOS displays the message `Terminate batch job (Y/N)?`. Enter `Y` to terminate the batch file or `N` to proceed. If you press any other key during the pause, the COPY command proceeds normally.

Note that the PAUSE command can be used in exactly the same way in a DOSKEY macro. For example, you could shorten the previous batch file and use it as the following macro:

```
DOSKEY COPY=ECHO Place a diskette in drive A: and press a key $B
ECHO Or press Ctrl-Break to cancel the operation $B PAUSE $B COPY $1 A:
```

Unfortunately, because you cannot turn off the command display in a macro, this macro doesn't look good on the screen; however, it functions exactly as the batch file did, with the PAUSE command performing the same operation.

See Also   DOSKEY, ECHO

PRINT

Activates background printing.

Version | 2 and later

Type | External (PRINT.COM)

DOS Shell Menu Access | Select a file (or files) to print. Then select Print from the File pull-down menu. Note that you must first load the resident portion of the PRINT program before you start the DOS Shell; otherwise, the Print option in File menu is unavailable.

Syntax | The syntax for initializing the PRINT command is

```
PRINT [[/D:printer port] [/Q:queue size] [/
B:buffer size] [/U:busytick] [/M:max ticks] [/
S:time slice]]
```

The syntax for using the PRINT command after it has been installed is

```
PRINT [[drive][path][file name] [...]] [/C] [/T] [/P]
```

in which *drive*, *path*, and *file name* identify the file (or files) to be printed.

Usage | PRINT lets you print files "in the background," thus allowing you to use your computer while the printer is active. PRINT allows you to specify several files to be printed and then it places all the files in a queue (in which they await their turn to be sent to the printer). When PRINT finishes printing one file, it automatically begins printing the next file in the queue.

PRINT can only be used to print ASCII text files (files that do not contain "strange" graphics characters when displayed with the TYPE command). It cannot print files created by spreadsheet, database management, or word processing programs, unless those files have already been converted to ASCII text format. PRINT cannot print executable program files, such as those with the extensions .BIN, .COM, or .EXE.

A portion of the PRINT command (called the *resident portion*) must be loaded into RAM before you can use the command. To load the resident portion from your AUTOEXEC.BAT file without actually printing a file, use the /D option. (Failure to do so when using DOS 5 makes the Print option inaccessible from the DOS Shell File menu.)

If you are working at the command line and do not load PRINT into memory before using the command, DOS asks you to specify a print device and suggests PRN. Usually, this is the correct device (it represents LPT1 or the first parallel printer port), so you can just press Enter.

You can use wildcard characters in file names. For example, the command PRINT *.BAT prints a copy of all batch files in the current directory. However, unless you use the /Q option to extend the length of the queue, the PRINT command prints only the first ten batch files accessed.

The optional switches used with PRINT during initialization are described in more detail in the list that follows. These options can be used only once during a session—when you initialize the PRINT command. You can use any of these switches in the PRINT command in your AUTOEXEC.BAT file.

/D:*device*	Must be the first listed switch if several are used. The *device* name can be any valid DOS device name, such as LPT1, LPT2, LPT3, PRN, COM1, COM2, COM3, COM4, or AUX.
/Q:*queue size*	Specifies the maximum number of file names that can be stored in the queue. *Queue size* can be any number in the range of 4 to 32. If omitted, DOS uses the default of 10.
/B:*buffer size*	Sets the size of the internal buffer used to store text to be printed. *Buffer size* can be any number in the range of 512 bytes to 16KB. If omitted, the default of 512 is used.

The other options require an understanding of how the PRINT command works. Basically, your computer contains a clock that "ticks" about 18.2 times per second (with most computers). Each "tick" is called a *time slice*. When DOS simultaneously performs multiple operations, such as printing in the background while running a spreadsheet program, it allocates a certain percentage of time slices to each operation.

Because the clock ticks so quickly, it appears that DOS is doing both jobs simultaneously, although in reality it's switching back and forth (very quickly) from one job to the other.

The PRINT command uses a certain percentage of clock ticks to manage background printing. You can use the default percentage by omitting the following optional switches, or you can customize PRINT by using these switches in your initial PRINT command.

/S:*time slice*	Specifies the number of time slices that PRINT allocates to other operations. The *time slice* parameter can be any value between 1 and 255. If omitted, DOS uses a default value of 8. A higher time slice value slows the background printing and speeds the foreground task.
[/M:*max ticks*]	Specifies the maximum number of time slices that PRINT can use to pass characters to the printer. *Max ticks* can be any value in the range of 1 to 255. If a value is omitted, DOS uses the default value of 2. A higher *Max ticks* number means faster background printing but slower execution of the foreground task.
/U:*busytick*	Specifies the number of clock ticks that PRINT will wait for the printer to become available. This option is called into play only if the printer is busy (unable to accept text) when PRINT is ready to send some characters. *Busytick* can be any value in the range of 1 to 255. If a value is omitted, DOS uses the default value of 1. If PRINT waits for the printer longer than the number of time slices specified in *busytick*, it surrenders its current time slice to the foreground operation.

To calculate the actual percentage of time that is allocated to PRINT, use the formula

$$\frac{max\ ticks}{(time\ slice + busytick)}\ (x)\ 100$$

By default, PRINT uses a /M:max ticks value of 2, a /S:time slice value of 8, and a /U:busytick setting of 1. Therefore, PRINT actually gets (2/(8+1))*100, or 22 percent, of all time slices. Because the printer is usually the slowest device on the computer, 22 percent of the time slices is usually sufficient to keep it running at top speed. (The foreground operation runs at 78 percent of its normal speed.)

If the /U (busytick) setting is too high, PRINT spends a lot of time waiting for the printer to become available, and the foreground task does nothing. Generally, the default setting of 1, or perhaps a small value such as 2 or 3, is the best setting for the /U option, unless your printer is extraordinarily fast and you want your background print operations to have top priority.

Ideally, getting the maximum performance from the PRINT command is a matter of allocating exactly the right amount of time to PRINT to make your printer run at full speed without allocating more time than the printer can actually use. However, experimenting with these options is a laborious and time-consuming task, and unless your printer or foreground task is unbearably slow, you should probably use the default settings.

After PRINT has been installed and is currently printing files, switches that you can use include

/T   Terminates the entire print queue, including the current file

/C   Removes specified files from the print queue

/P   Adds specified file names to the print queue

Entering the command PRINT with no options or file names displays the names of files currently in the queue.

While PRINT is in control of the printer, attempting to use another program to print a file causes the display of an error message such as `Device not ready` or `Printer out of paper`. You must either wait until PRINT finishes or use `PRINT /T` to cancel the background printing.

Never use MODE PREPARE or MODE SELECT to switch printer code pages while PRINT is printing text.

PRINT cannot be used in a network.

Examples   Suppose that you want to be able to use the PRINT command from within the Shell and want to be able to line up as many as 20 print jobs for your parallel printer. To do so, you'd need to add this command to your AUTOEXEC.BAT file:

```
PRINT /D:LPT1 /Q:20
```

Adding this command to your AUTOEXEC.BAT file consumes about 6.3KB of conventional memory. If you're using DOS 5 and upper memory blocks, you can use the following command in your AUTOEXEC.BAT file instead, which places the resident portion of PRINT in upper, rather than conventional memory:

```
LOADHIGH PRINT /D:LPT1 /Q:20
```

When you boot up your computer, you'll briefly see a message like this on your screen, as DOS loads the memory-resident portion of PRINT into conventional or upper memory:

```
Resident portion of PRINT loaded
PRINT queue is empty
```

Assuming that PRINT.COM is available on the current disk and directory or in a directory specified in the PATH setting, the following command places in the queue as many as 20 files with the extension .DOC, from the current directory, and starts printing the first listed file:

```
PRINT *.DOC
```

After printing starts, the command prompt reappears. You can now use your computer to run any program you want. (However, you cannot access the printer while PRINT is printing in the background.)

To see a list of the file names currently in the queue (in the order in which they will be printed), enter the command

```
PRINT
```

The next command removes the file CHAP11.DOC from the print queue and inserts the file CHAP11.TXT into the queue:

```
PRINT CHAP11.DOC /C CHAP11.TXT/P
```

To stop all background printing and empty the queue, use the command

```
PRINT /T
```

See Also   TYPE

PRINTER.SYS

Allows code page switching with printers that support the capability.

Version   4 and later

Type   External device driver (PRINTER.SYS) activated by DEVICE in the CONFIG.SYS file.

**DOS Shell
Menu Access**   None

Syntax
```
DEVICE=[drive][path]PRINTER.SYS
port=(type[,(hardware code page list][,max pages)]
```

in which *drive* and *path* indicate the location of the PRINTER.SYS file. Other options are described in the following section.

Usage   PRINTER.SYS can be used only with printers that support code page switching. Users in the United States do not need to use the PRINTER.SYS device driver unless they want to print text written in a foreign language.

Parameters used in the DEVICE=PRINTER.SYS command include

port	Specifies the port to which the printer is connected: either LPT1, LPT2, LPT3, or PRN (same as LPT1).
type	Specifies the model number of the printer. Most versions of DOS support the following printer models, but your computer might support others (see either the DOS manual that came with your computer or your printer manual):

4201	IBM 4201 Proprinter family
	IBM 4202 Proprinter XL
4208	IBM 4207 Proprinter X24
	IBM 4208 Proprinter XL24
5202	IBM 5202 Quietwriter III

hardware code page list	Specifies one or more code pages that are supported by the printer (usually 437, 850, or both).
max pages	Specifies the maximum number of code pages that can be prepared with the MODE PREPARE command. The maximum value is 12, although most printers can support only 1 or 2.

Examples   The following command, when added to the CONFIG.SYS file, prepares an IBM model 4201 printer, connected to parallel port LPT1, for use with the 437 (English language) code page and one code page that can be installed by the MODE command. The command assumes that the PRINTER.SYS file is stored in the \DOS directory of disk drive C:.

```
DEVICE=C:\DOS\PRINTER.SYS LPT1=(4201,437,1)
```

The next command, entered at the command prompt or stored in the AUTOEXEC.BAT file, copies the fonts for the 850 (multilingual) code page from the 4201.CPI file to the device driver for the printer.

```
MODE LPT1 CP PREP=((850) C:\DOS\4201.CPI)
```

The following command then selects code page 850 for current use with the printer:

```
MODE LPT1 CP SEL=850
```

See Also   DRIVER.SYS, KEYB, MODE, your printer or computer manual

---

PROMPT

Changes the system prompt and activates ANSI features.

Version   2 and later

Type   Internal

DOS Shell Menu Access   None

Syntax
```
PROMPT codes
```

in which codes are special codes preceded by the $ symbol that define the system prompt and optionally configure the screen and keyboard.

Usage   Many versions of DOS display the command prompt as simply the current drive followed by a greater than sign:

```
C>
```

You can change the prompts to include any text by typing the text after the PROMPT command. In addition, you can use the codes listed in Table B.13 to display special features in the prompt.

Table B.13. Command prompt codes used with the PROMPT command to display special features.

Code	Displays
$D	Current date
$T	Current time
$N	Current drive
$P	Current drive and directory
$V	Version of DOS in use
$_	Carriage Return/Line Feed
$e	Escape character
$H	Backspace
$Q	= symbol
$G	> symbol
$L	< symbol

Code	Displays
$B	¦ character
$$	$ symbol
$C	(character
$F	) character
$A	& character
$S	Blank space

Note in the table that the $_ code, which displays a Carriage Return/ Line Feed combination, actually breaks the prompt into two lines.

The $H character is a backspace that erases the preceding character. For example, $T displays the system time in the format 12:29:03.25. However, THHH erases the last three characters and displays 12:29:03 instead.

If you use the $P option to display the current drive and directory, the current drive must always be ready. If you attempt to switch to an empty floppy disk drive when the PROMPT command uses $P, the screen displays the message

```
Not ready reading drive
Abort, Retry, Fail?
```

To return to the command prompt, type F.

The $e character, which represents the Esc key, can be used with display control codes offered by ANSI.SYS to control the screen colors and to customize function keys. These work only if your CONFIG.SYS file contains the command DEVICE=ANSI.SYS. Note that the e must always be lowercase. See Chapter 12 for additional information.

Examples Entering the following command from the DOS directory of your hard disk:

```
PROMPT Current location - $P -$G
```

changes the system prompt to display

```
Current location - C:\DOS ->
```

Entering the command

```
PROMPT $D $T$H$H$H $B
```

displays a prompt containing the current date, the current time (erasing the hundredths of a second), and a trailing ¦ character, as follows:

```
Mon   4-25-1988 22:29:56 ¦
```

Entering the PROMPT command

```
PROMPT $D$H$H$H$H$H$_$T$H$H$H$_$V$P:
```

displays the system prompt with the current date, time, version of DOS, and drive and directory broken into four separate lines, as follows

```
Mon   4-25
12:35:00
MS-DOS Version 5.00
C:\DOS:
```

The command

```
PROMPT Say the magic word $G
```

changes the system prompt to display

```
Say the magic word >
```

Entering the command

```
PROMPT
```

with no parameters cancels the newest PROMPT setting and redisplays the default prompt.

See Also   Chapter 12

RAMDRIVE.SYS

Creates a RAM disk. (Called VDISK.SYS in some versions of PC DOS).

Version   3.2 and later

Type   Device driver (installed with a DEVICE command in CONFIG.SYS)

DOS Shell Menu Access   None

Syntax   DOS Version 3.2:

```
DEVICE=[drive][path]RAMDRIVE.SYS [size] [sectors]
[entries] [/E]
```

DOS Versions 3.3, 4, and 5:

```
DEVICE=[drive][path]RAMDRIVE.SYS [size]
[sectors][entries] [/E] [/A:]
```

Usage   RAMDRIVE.SYS creates a RAM disk, or virtual disk, in memory. Check your computer's DOS manual, or the root directory or DOS directory on disk, to determine whether RAMDRIVE.SYS or VDISK.SYS is available on your computer. This section focuses on the more common RAMDRIVE.SYS device driver, most of which is directly relevant to VDISK.SYS as well. Any important differences are noted.

A RAM disk formats memory—either conventional RAM, extended memory, or expanded memory—as though it were a disk drive. DOS treats the RAM disk as though it were a real (physical) disk; all the operations that you normally use to manage disk files work with the RAM disk as well.

The major differences between a RAM disk and a physical disk are

1. The RAM disk is 10 to 20 times faster than a physical disk.

2. Everything is erased from the RAM disk as soon as the power is cut off.

The first optional parameter, *size*, specifies the size of the RAM disk in kilobytes. If this parameter is omitted, the default value of 64KB is used. The range of acceptable values is 1 to the maximum amount of available memory on your computer. If you specify a size that leaves less than 64KB of conventional memory available, RAMDRIVE automatically adjusts the size of the RAM disk so that it leaves 100KB of conventional RAM for programs.

Because part of the RAM disk is used for the boot record, file allocation table (FAT), and directory (exactly as on a physical disk), the actual amount of available storage on the RAM disk is somewhat less than the *size* specified in the DEVICE command.

The second optional parameter, *sectors*, specifies the sector size in bytes. Acceptable values are 128, 256, and 512. If you omit this option or specify an invalid sector size, DOS uses the default value of 128.

In general, the larger the sector size, the faster the performance of the RAM disk. However, because files are stored in entire sectors and never in parts of sectors, a large sector size wastes disk space if you want to use the RAM disk to store many small files.

The third optional parameter, *entries*, specifies the maximum number of files that can be stored on the RAM disk. Any number in the range of 2 to 512 is acceptable. If omitted, the default value of 64 is used.

Each directory entry uses 32 bytes of the RAM disk (including empty entries). If the value you specify in the *entries* parameter is not a multiple of the sector size, RAMDRIVE adjusts your entry parameter upward. For example, if you specify 9 directory entries and a 128-byte sector size, DOS adjusts the parameter upward to allow 12 directory entries. The reason is that 9 (x) 32 = 288 which is not evenly divisible by 128. However, 12 (x) 32 = 384 which is evenly divisible by 128.

If the size of the RAM disk is too small to hold the boot record, FAT, directory, and two additional sectors, the number of *entries* specified in your DEVICE command is rounded down until these conditions can be met. If RAMDRIVE cannot round down far enough to meet these conditions, DOS displays an error message and the RAM disk is not installed.

DOS Version 5 also offers the /E switch, which installs the RAM disk in expanded memory. The optional /A switch installs the RAM disk in expanded rather than extended memory.

Storing a RAM disk in extended or expanded memory conserves conventional RAM for program execution. However, each RAM disk created in expanded or extended memory uses about 800 bytes of conventional RAM to manage the RAM disk. You can use as much as 16MB of extended or expanded memory for one (or several) RAM disks.

In PC DOS Version 4, you can specify the maximum number of sectors that can be passed in each access by using /X (or /A), followed by a colon and a value between 1 and 8. If you omit this value, DOS uses the largest (and fastest) setting of 8.

Each DEVICE=RAMDRIVE.SYS or DEVICE=VDISK.SYS command in your CONFIG.SYS file creates a separate RAM disk. DOS automatically names each one in alphabetical order, starting with the first available disk drive name. For example, if you have one hard disk, named C:, and your CONFIG.SYS contains two DEVICE commands that install RAM disks, the RAM disks are automatically named D: and E:.

If your RAM disk (or disks) extends beyond the name E:, you must include the LASTDRIVE directive in your CONFIG.SYS file to specify a drive name beyond the last RAM disk. For example, if your computer has a drive C:, and you plan to create three RAM disks, named D:, E:, and F:, your CONFIG.SYS file must contain the command LASTDRIVE=G.

If you are using DOS 5 upper memory blocks, you can load the RAM disk driver into upper memory and use either extended or expanded memory for the RAM disk itself, thereby conserving conventional memory.

For example, the command

```
DEVICEHIGH=C:\DOS\RAMDRIVE.SYS 750 /E
```

creates a 750K RAM drive in extended memory and puts the driver for managing that RAM disk (which occupies about 1.2K) into upper memory. The DEVICEHIGH command for activating the RAM disk must be placed in the CONFIG.SYS file, beneath the commands that activate HIMEM.SYS, DOS=UMB and the EMM36.EXE driver that activates upper memory blocks.

Examples The following command, when included in the CONFIG.SYS file, creates a 64KB RAM disk in conventional memory. It assumes that the RAM disk device driver, named RAMDRIVE.SYS, is stored in the \DOS directory of drive C:. Assuming that the computer has a single hard disk, named C:, the RAM disk is named D:

```
DEVICE=C:\DOS\RAMDRIVE.SYS
```

If your computer uses VDISK.SYS rather than RAMDRIVE.SYS, and the RAMDRIVE.SYS file is stored in the \DOS directory of drive C:, the following CONFIG.SYS command performs the same installation as the previous command:

```
DEVICE=C:\DOS\VDISK.SYS
```

The next command creates a 730KB RAM disk in extended memory with 512KB sectors and a maximum of 128 directory entries:

```
DEVICE=C:\DOS\RAMDRIVE.SYS 720 512 128 /E
```

The equivalent command using most versions of VDISK.SYS is

```
DEVICE=C:\DOS\VDISK.SYS 720 512 128 /E
```

If your computer has expanded memory and your CONFIG.SYS file contains a device driver to activate expanded memory, you can use the /A switch to use all or some of the expanded memory for the RAM disk. The DEVICE command that activates the expanded memory in your CONFIG.SYS file must precede the DEVICE command that creates the RAM disk so that expanded memory is already active when the RAM disk is installed.

The following command assumes that at least 1MB of expanded memory is installed and active and that the RAMDRIVE.SYS device driver is stored in the root directory of drive C:. The command then creates a 1MB RAM disk in expanded memory, with 512-byte sectors and a maximum of 128 directory entries:

```
DEVICE=RAMDRIVE.SYS 1024 512 128 /A
```

The equivalent command using VDISK.SYS, which is assumed to be stored in the root directory of drive C:, is

```
DEVICE=RAMDRIVE.SYS 1024 512 128 /A
```

The following commands divide 4MB of extended memory into four 1MB RAM disks. If the computer already has physical disks named D: and E:, these four RAM disks are named F:, G:, H:, and I:. The LASTDRIVE command, also included in the CONFIG.SYS file, prepares DOS to handle at least this many drives:

```
LASTDRIVE=J
DEVICE=C:\DOS\RAMDRIVE.SYS 1024 512 64 /E
DEVICE=C:\DOS\RAMDRIVE.SYS 1024 512 64 /E
DEVICE=C:\DOS\RAMDRIVE.SYS 1024 512 64 /E
DEVICE=C:\DOS\RAMDRIVE.SYS 1024 512 64 /E
```

One of the best uses of a RAM disk is for storing the temporary files that some programs create on the fly. Those programs will run faster because they will use the faster RAM disk. Because most programs automatically erase their own temporary files anyway, there's no harm in storing them on the volatile RAM disk.

Most modern programs will check the environment for a variable named TEMP. If they find that variable, they will store their temporary files on whatever drive and directory TEMP indicates.

Suppose that your CONFIG.SYS file contains the following commands, the HIMEM.SYS driver activates extended memory, and the RAMDRIVE.SYS driver creates a 512K RAM drive which, for example, is drive H:.

```
DEVICE = C:\DOS\HIMEM.SYS
DEVICE = C:\DOS\RAMDRIVE.SYS 500 /E*
```

Now, in your AUTOEXEC.BAT file, you could add these commands to create a directory named TMP on the RAM disk (drive H:) and then tell all programs (that check) to use that for their temporary files:

```
MD H:\TMP
SET TEMP = H:\TMP
```

Although it's not imperative to create a directory on the RAM disk, it is useful because a root directory is limited to storing 512 files, whereas a subdirectory has no limits.

See Also   Chapter 17, LASTDRIVE

RECOVER

Attempts to recover files from a disk with damaged sectors.

Version   2 and later

Type   External (RECOVER.EXE)

DOS Shell Menu Access   None

Syntax

```
RECOVER [drive][path][file name]
```

in which *drive*, *path*, and *file name* specify the location and name of the file to be recovered or

```
RECOVER disk drive
```

in which *drive* is the name of an entire disk drive to recover.

Usage   Occasionally, a disk sector goes bad and loses some information. The effect of this loss can be anything from a nuisance to a catastrophe. For example, if the bad sector wipes out your Christmas card list of 10 people, you probably will survive. However, if the bad sector wipes out the file allocation table (FAT, the "map" that tells DOS where to find all the files on the disk), you could lose everything on the disk and that is indeed unpleasant.

The RECOVER command attempts to recover as much of a lost file as possible. However, it can only recover portions of simple text files that were stored in the bad sector. Never use RECOVER to attempt to recover program files (that is, those with .COM or .EXE extensions). If you recover one of these programs and run it, there is no telling what the recovered program might do. (Murphy's Law dictates that the recovered program probably will make matters worse.)

RECOVER is a drastic measure that should only be used as an absolute last resort. If you make backups of your files regularly, you probably will never need to use the RECOVER command. If a bad sector wipes out a file or directory, you can just copy the backup files back onto the disk.

Never use RECOVER on a networked disk drive nor on a drive that is affected by an ASSIGN, JOIN, or SUBST command. Don't try to use RECOVER to retrieve a file that was accidentally deleted with the DEL or ERASE command, it won't work. In general, only use RECOVER when all else fails!

Examples   Suppose that you attempt to access your only copy of the file FORMLET.TXT, which is an ASCII text file. However, the disk drive whirs and buzzes for a moment and then finally stops to report that it cannot access the file because of a bad sector. A few experiments with DIR and TYPE indicate that most files seem OK, so the damage is isolated to FORMLET.TXT. To recover FORMLET.TXT, enter the command

```
RECOVER FORMLET.TXT
```

If RECOVER is successful, you should be able to access the information in FORMLET.TXT in the newly created file FILE0001.REC. However, any information that was stored in the disk sector that went bad will not be in the file.

In a more drastic situation, you attempt to use a disk and cannot access any information. Even the DIR command tells you that it cannot display file names because of a bad sector. Don't panic (yet).

First, try to find someone who knows a lot about computers and ask for help. This person might be able to diagnose the problem and fix it without using the drastic RECOVER command.

If you can use XCOPY to copy files off the damaged disk, do so. Save any files that can be saved. After you've copied files to good diskettes, erase them from the damaged disk. Check to see whether you have backups of the files that you cannot copy from the damaged disk.

After you've salvaged what you can from the damaged disk, enter the RECOVER command with only a drive specification (for example, RECOVER C:). RECOVER attempts to recover as much information as it can from the disk. Unfortunately, it places the recovered information in files named FILEnnnn.REC, in which nnnn is a number starting at 0001; you won't have access to the original file names.

Next, you need to figure out exactly what RECOVER did to your files. Use a word processor or text editor to examine the files. When you see data that you recognize, save it under an appropriate file name on a different disk. You might have to spend quite a long time untangling the mess that RECOVER has created, so be prepared for some unpleasant work.

When you finish recovering whatever information you can, remember how unpleasant the experience was and make backups frequently in the future.

REM

Identifies a remark in a batch file.

Version 1 and later

Type Used only in batch files and in CONFIG.SYS.

DOS Shell Menu Access None

Syntax
```
REM comment
```
in which *comment* is a line of text.

Usage REM is generally used to write remarks (notes to yourself) within a batch file that remind you of what various commands do. If ECHO is on, any text to the right of the command appears on the screen while the batch file is running. If ECHO is off, the text is not displayed while the batch file is running.

DOS version 4 and 5 also let you use REM in the CONFIG.SYS file.

Examples The AUTOEXEC.BAT file shown in Listing B.1 includes several comments used to describe the purpose of various commands.

Listing B.1. Sample batch file with comments.

```
@ECHO OFF
REM *********************** AUTOEXEC.BAT
REM --- Put COMSPEC in the environment.
SET COMSPEC=C\DOS\COMMAND.COM

REM --- Set up the PATH.
PATH C:\WS4;C:\DOS;C:\UTILS;C:\DBASE

REM --- Turn off verification to speed processing.
VERIFY OFF

REM --- Install the mouse driver.
C:\MOUSE1\MOUSE

REM --- Make all DOS 4 files accessible.
APPEND /E
APPEND C:\DOS
```

```
REM --- Initialize PRINT.COM and design the command prompt.
PRINT /D:LPT1 /Q:20
PROMPT $P$G

REM --- go straight to the DOS Shell.
DOSSHELL
```

In DOS versions 4 and 5, REM is also useful in CONFIG.SYS files for "cancelling" complex commands. For example, if you occasionally need to use a one-megabyte RAM disk, but you don't want to tie up your extended memory all the time, you can enter the following line in your CONFIG.SYS file:

```
REM DEVICE = C:\DOS\RAMDRIVE.SYS 1024 512   /E
```

This keeps the command in the file but makes it a "remark," a nonexecuting line. To activate your RAM drive, delete the REM command and reboot your computer.

See Also   ECHO

RENAME or REN

Changes the name of a file.

Version   1 and later

Type   Internal

DOS Shell Menu Access   Highlight the file (or files) to be renamed. Then press F10 or Alt, pull down the File menu and select `Rename....`

Syntax   `RENAME [drive][path] currentfilename newfilename`

in which *drive* and *path* specify the location of the file you want to rename, *currentfilename* is the name of the file you want to rename, and *newfilename* is the new name for the file.

Usage   RENAME (and its abbreviated form REN) allows you to change the name of a file or group of files. It has no effect on the contents of the file. RENAME cannot be used to change the location of a file (that is, you cannot rename C:\UTILS\RESQ.COM to A:\RESQ.COM). RENAME always assumes that the file will still be stored on the same disk and subdirectory.

You cannot rename a file to a name that already exists on the specified drive or directory. For example, if you have a file named LEDGER.TXT and a file named LEDGER.DOC, the command `RENAME LEDGER.TXT LEDGER.DOC` returns the error message `Duplicate file name or File not found`. Both

LEDGER.TXT and LEDGER.DOC remain unchanged. (The same error message appears if you attempt to rename a file that does not exist on the specified drive and directory.)

You can also use wildcard characters in the file names. For example, entering the command `RENAME CHAPTER?.TXT CHAPTER?.DOC` attempts to rename all files that begin with CHAPTER and one other character, followed by the extension .TXT, to the same file name, but with the extension .DOC. However, if a duplicate file name is encountered during the renaming process, DOS displays the error message `Duplicate filename or File not found`, and no other files are renamed. You need to enter the commands `DIR *.TXT` and `DIR *.DOC` to figure out which files were renamed and which were not.

Note that the existing file name is always listed first, and the new name is listed second. Hence, the "English" syntax for the RENAME command is `RENAME <existing file name> TO <new file name>`. If the file being renamed is not on the current drive and directory, you need only specify the drive and directory for the original file name. RENAME assumes that you intend the same drive and directory for the new file name.

Examples   To change the name of the file named FORMLET.TXT to FORMLET.DOC in the current directory, enter the command

`RENAME FORMLET.TXT FORMLET.DOC`

To change the extension of all files in the current directory from .TXT to .DOC, enter the command

`REN *.TXT *.DOC`

To change the name of the file TEMP.TXT to JUNK.OLD in the directory named \LETTERS on drive C:, enter the command

`RENAME C:\LETTERS\TEMP.TXT JUNK.OLD`

The JUNK.OLD file is automatically stored on the C:\LETTERS drive and directory.

Entering the command

`RENAME TEMP.TXT`

generates the error message `Invalid number of parameters`, because no new name for the file is specified. TEMP.TXT remains unchanged.

If a command such as

`REN INTRO.TXT INTRO.DOC`

returns the error message `Duplicate filename or File not found`, either there is no file named INTRO.TXT in the current directory, or there is already a file named INTRO.DOC in the current directory. The command DIR INTRO.* would show you which problem was causing the error message.

See Also   COPY, XCOPY

REPLACE

Replaces files on a disk or adds new files.

Version   3.2 and later

Type   External (REPLACE.EXE)

DOS Shell Menu Access   None

Syntax   REPLACE [source drive] [source path] [source file name] [destination drive] [destination path] [destination file name] [/S] [/A] [/P] [/R] [/W]

in which source drive, source path, and source file name indicate the location and names of new files, and destination drive, destination path, and destination file name are the location and name of files to be replaced.

Usage   The REPLACE command replaces existing files with new files of the same name. It is generally used to update existing files, typically replacing old versions of programs with new ones. However, it can be used to add new files to a disk without replacing any files. REPLACE can also search directories on a destination disk for files that need to be replaced.

The syntax of REPLACE might seem backward from what the English equivalent of the command might be. The actual English syntax would be REPLACE <new files> OVER <old files>

The various options that you can use to control REPLACE include

/A   Adds source files that do not already exist on the destination disk, to the destination disk. Cannot be used with /S or /U.

/P   Prompts you before replacing or adding each file; lets you select whether or not to replace or add the file.

/R   Replaces read-only files as well as read/write files.

/S   Searches all subdirectories beneath the destination directory for matching file names.

/W   Tells REPLACE to pause before transferring files, so that you can change diskettes.

/U   (DOS 4 only) Replaces files on the target directory that have a more recent date.

You can combine switches at the end of the REPLACE command.

When REPLACE finishes its job, it returns a value in the ERRORLEVEL variable so that you can build batch files that make decisions based on an IF ERRORLEVEL or IF NOT ERRORLEVEL statement to respond to possible errors. The ERRORLEVEL values returned by REPLACE are

0   REPLACE completed normally.

1   REPLACE was aborted because of an error in the command line.

2   No source files were found.

3   A nonexistent source or destination path was given.

5   A read-only file was encountered on the destination drive, and no /R option was provided to permit an overwrite.

8   Not enough memory exists to perform the REPLACE.

11   An invalid command was entered—too few or too many parameters.

15   An invalid drive name was specified in the command.

22   An incorrect version of DOS is in use.

Examples   Suppose that drive A: contains a diskette with files named LETTER1.TXT, LETTER2.TXT, LETTER3.TXT, and NEWFILE.TXT. The directory named \WPFILES on drive C: contains the files LETTER1.TXT, LETTER2.TXT, and LETTER3.TXT. To replace the files in C:\WPFILES with files of the same name on the disk in drive A:, enter the following command while the \WPFILES directory of drive C: is current:

```
REPLACE A:*.* C:
```

In response to the command, DOS shows the following information:

```
REPLACE Version x.xx (C) Copyright 19xx
Replacing C:\WPFILES\LETTER1.TXT
Replacing C:\WPFILES\LETTER2.TXT
Replacing C:\WPFILES\LETTER3.TXT
3 file(s) replaced
```

Note that only the LETTER1.TXT, LETTER2.TXT, and
LETTER3.TXT files on drive C: are replaced. The NEWFILE.TXT file
on drive A: is not copied or replaced because there is no file by
that name on the destination directory (that is, there is no
C:\WPFILES\NEWFILE.TXT to replace).

You could use the /P option in the previous example to have DOS
ask you for permission before each replacement. For example, if you
entered the command

```
REPLACE A:*.* C: /P
```

you would see a prompt such as

```
Replace C:\WPFILES\LETTER1.TXT? (Y/N)
```

Type Y to replace the file; type N to cancel the replacement. After
you answer Y or N, REPLACE asks for permission before replacing
any other files.

If you want to add new files from drive A: to drive C: without
replacing any existing files, use the /A option as follows:

```
REPLACE A:*.* C: /A
```

This command displays the message

```
Adding C:\WPFILES\NEWFILE.TXT
1 file(s) added
```

In this case, LETTER1.TXT, LETTER2.TXT, and LETTER3.TXT
remain unchanged on both drives A: and C:. However, because drive
C: does not contain a file named NEWFILE.TXT, that file is copied
from the source drive A: to the destination drive C:.

You can use the /A and /P options together. For example, the
command

```
REPLACE A:*.* C: /A/P
```

asks for permission before copying any files from drive A: to
drive C:.

Suppose that you copy several files from several different directories
on your computer at work. You take the files home for the weekend
and make some changes. When you get back to work on Monday,
you need to replace all the old files with your new copies. Rather
than individually copying each file to the appropriate subdirectory,
you can use the /S option with REPLACE to have it automatically
locate the appropriate subdirectories and replace the files.

To ensure that REPLACE has access to all the subdirectories on the destination disk, you must run the REPLACE command from the root directory. For example, assuming you want to replace old files on drive C: with new copies of those files stored in drive A:, enter the following command:

```
CD\
REPLACE A:*.* C: /S
```

Note that unless you use the /R switch at the end of the command, REPLACE will not overwrite files that are marked read-only by an ATTRIB +R command. Therefore, the command

```
REPLACE A:*.COM C: /R
```

replaces all files on drive C: that have the extension .COM with copies of files (with the same name) from drive A:. Even files defined as read-only are replaced.

If you use the /W switch, REPLACE pauses to allow you to place a source diskette in the disk drive. For example, if you enter the command

```
REPLACE A:*.* C: /W
```

REPLACE displays the prompt `Press any key to begin replacing file(s)` before going to work. You can insert a new disk and press any key to begin the replacement.

See Also   COPY, XCOPY

RESTORE

Restores backup files from floppy disks.

Version   2 and later

Type   External (RESTORE.COM)

DOS Shell Menu Access   Select `Disk Utilities...` from the Main Group screen, and `Restore Fixed Disk` from the Disk Utilities group screen.

Syntax
```
RESTORE backup drive [destination drive]
[destination path][destination files] [/S] [/P]
[/B:date] [/A:date] [/E:time] [/L:time] [/M] [/N]
```

in which `backup drive` is the name of the drive containing the backup diskettes; `destination drive`, `destination path`, and `destination files` identify the location and names of the files to be restored and `date` and `time` represent dates and times when files were created or last changed.

Usage RESTORE retrieves from diskettes to the hard disk files created with
the BACKUP command. (RESTORE cannot access files that were
copied or created with any command other than BACKUP.) You can
use RESTORE to recover a single file, a group of files, or all the files
on a disk.

When you use RESTORE, it requests that you insert backup diskettes
into a floppy disk drive in the same order in which they were
created during BACKUP. For this reason, you must clearly number
your BACKUP diskettes as you create them. If you insert a disk out
of order, DOS displays the prompt `Warning! Diskette is out
of sequence` and prompts you to remove that diskette and replace
it with the appropriate one.

RESTORE provides several options to help you specify the exact files
that you want to restore. Note that options which use the date and
time parameters require you to specify a date or time in valid DOS
format. For example, if you are using the default United States
settings, the valid format for dates is mm-dd-yy (for example,
12-31-88), and the valid format for times is hh:mm:ss (for example,
13:30:00 for 1:30 in the afternoon). The options for RESTORE are as
follows:

/A:*date*	Restores all files that were created or modified on or after the specified *date*.
/B:*date*	Restores all files that were created or modified on or before the specified *date*.
/L:*time*	Restores all files that were created or modified on or later than the specified *time*.
/E:*time*	Restores all files that were created or modified on or earlier than the specified *time*.
/S	Restores all files in the specified directory and in all subdirectories.
/P	Causes RESTORE to display a prompt requesting permission to restore read-only files, hidden files, or files that have been modified since the last BACKUP.
/M	Restores only files that have been modified or deleted since the last BACKUP.
/N	Restores only files that no longer exist on the destination disk.

When using either /L or /E to specify a time, be sure to also use /A or /B to specify a date.

Never attempt to use RESTORE when an ASSIGN, JOIN, or SUBST command is active. Doing so might damage the directory structure of your hard disk and cause a loss of data.

When RESTORE is finished, it sets the ERRORLEVEL variable to one of the following values:

0   RESTORE completed successfully.

1   No files to restore were found.

2   Some files were not restored because they were in use by others (on a network).

3   RESTORE procedure was canceled because the user typed Ctrl-Break or Ctrl-C.

4   RESTORE was aborted due to a system error.

You can use the IF ERRORLEVEL command in a batch file to determine whether a RESTORE command was successful.

PC DOS Versions 2 to 3.2 support only the /S and /P switches. Versions 3.3, 4, and 5 do not restore the system files nor COMMAND.COM. These must be copied using the SYS command. In PC DOS, the system files are named IBMBIO.COM and IBMDOS.COM. In MS-DOS, these are named MSDOS.SYS and IO.SYS.

Examples   Suppose that you regularly use BACKUP to back up all the files on your hard disk. Then you make many erroneous changes in all of the files in the C:\UTILS directory. To restore those files to their original contents, first delete the incorrect files. Then insert your first BACKUP diskette into drive A:, and from the drive C: prompt. enter the command

```
RESTORE A: C:\UTILS\*.*
```

DOS presents the instructions

```
Insert backup diskette nn in drive A:
Strike any key when ready
```

in which *nn* represents the backup disk number that you are to insert in drive A:. After you insert the disk and press Enter, DOS displays the following prompts and proceeds with the restoration:

```
*** Files were backed up 09/26/1991 *** ***
Restoring files from drive A: *** Diskette: nn
```

In a variation of the preceding situation, suppose that you mistakenly changed only some of the files that were on the \UTILS subdirectory. In that case, use the /P switch so that you can limit the restoration of files in the \UTILS directory to only those that you specify. Enter the command

```
RESTORE A: C:\UTILS\*.* /P
```

See Also   BACKUP

RMDIR or **RD**

Removes an empty directory.

Version   2 and later

Type   Internal

DOS Shell Menu Access   The Delete option on the File pull-down menu when an empty directory is selected in the Directory Tree area.

Syntax   `RMDIR [drive] path`

The command can be abbreviated as

`RD [drive] path`

in which *drive* is the name of the disk drive containing the directory, and *path* is the name of the directory (or subdirectory) that you wish to remove.

Usage   RMDIR (and its abbreviated equivalent, RD) lets you remove a directory from a disk. You cannot remove the root directory, the current directory, or a directory that contains files. Attempting to remove any such directories displays the error message `Invalid path, not directory, or directory not empty` and leaves the directory intact.

To delete a directory, first switch to that directory using the CHDIR or CD command. Then use DIR to see whether it contains any files. COPY any files that you want to keep to another directory or a diskette. Then use ERASE *.* to erase all files. Enter DIR again to be sure that all files have been erased. Any files that DOS refuses to erase are probably set to read-only, hidden, or system status. Use the command ATTRIB -R -S -H *.* to set the files to read/write status and then enter the ERASE *.* command again.

After the DIR command indicates that there are no files left in the subdirectory (except for . and ..), use the CD or CHDIR command to change to another directory. Then enter the RMDIR or RD command with the appropriate directory name to remove the subdirectory.

Examples	This example offers a typical scenario that demonstrates how to remove a directory. Suppose that you need to free some storage space on your hard disk, so you decide to remove a directory named \TEMP that you have not used in a long time.

First, change to that directory using the command CD \TEMP. Then enter the command DIR to display the files in that directory

You decide that only one file, named IMPORTNT.TXT, is worth saving, so you enter the command COPY IMPORTNT.TXT C:\WP\WPFILES to copy the file to the \WP\WPFILES directory, for example.

Then enter the command ERASE *.* to erase all files on the directory. When you enter DIR again, you discover that not all the files have been erased. Therefore, enter the command ATTRIB -R -S -H *.* to set all remaining files to read/write status. After you enter the ERASE *.* and DIR commands, you see that the only files remaining on the subdirectory are . and ...

Now you are ready to remove the subdirectory. First, enter the command

```
CD\
```

to move to the root directory. Then enter the command

```
RD \TEMP
```

to remove the directory.

When you enter the TREE command or return to the DOS Shell, note that the \TEMP directory no longer exists.

See Also	MKDIR, CHDIR

SET

Enters and displays environment settings.

Version	2 and later
Type	Internal
DOS Shell Menu Access	None
Syntax	```SET [variable[=setting]]```

in which *variable* is a variable name and *setting* is the value you want to store in that variable.

Usage   The environment is an area in RAM reserved for storing certain settings, such as the drive and directory location of the command processor (COMMAND.COM), the customized PROMPT in use (if any), and the current search PATH.

Parameters defined in the environment can be accessed from within batch files. To do so, use a variable name surrounded by percent signs (no blank spaces) as follows:

%COMPSEC%   Returns the location of the command processor.

%PROMPT%   Returns the current customized prompt setting.

%PATH%   Returns the path used to search for program files.

%APPEND%   Returns the path used to search for nonprogram files, assuming that an APPEND /E command stored the APPEND setting in the environment.

To view the environment settings from the DOS prompt, enter the command SET with no parameters.

You can also use SET to store your own information in the environment, which is sometimes handy with batch files. Be careful not to use the variable names COMSPEC, PROMPT, PATH, or APPEND for your own variables, because these are already used by DOS. The variable name also may not contain spaces. Because the size of the environment is limited, try to use short variable names.

By default, DOS sets aside 127 bytes for the environment. You can use the COMMAND command to increase the size of the environment; however, you should do so early in your CONFIG.SYS file, using the SHELL command, because as soon as DOS loads a memory-resident program, you can no longer expand the size of the environment.

The named variable can be accessed from any batch file using the syntax *%variablename%*. Examples are provided in the discussion of the SHIFT command in this appendix and in Chapter 14.

Examples   To store the name *Janice* in an environmental variable named `Name`, enter the command

```
SET NAME=Janice
```

To view the current status of the environment, enter the command

```
SET
```

See Also   PATH, PROMPT, SHIFT, COMMAND

SETVER

Tricks a program into believing that it is running under a version of DOS other than DOS 5.

Version   5

Type   External (SETVER.EXE)

DOS Shell Menu Access   None

Syntax   Initially installed in the CONFIG.SYS file with the syntax

```
DEVICE=[drive] [path] SETVER.EXE
```

Once SETVER is installed, you can use this syntax at the command prompt to view the current version table

```
[drive] [path] SETVER
```

or use the following syntax to add a program to the version table:

```
[drive] [path] SETVER filename n.nn
```

or use this syntax to delete a program from the current version table:

```
[drive] [path] SETVER filename /DELETE [/QUIET]
```

where

`[drive] [path]` indicate the location of the SETVER.EXE file (if not in the current path.); `filename` indicates the file name of the program that you want to add to or delete from the version table so that program will "think" it's running under an earlier version of DOS; `n.nn` indicates the version of DOS you want the program to "think" it's running under; `/DELETE` (or `/D`) deletes the named program from the version table so that it will resume running under DOS 5; and `/QUIET` (or `/Q`) is used in conjunction with /DELETE to suppress the message normally displayed when using /DELETE.

Usage   The SETVER command lets you use older programs with DOS 5. In versions before DOS 5, when you updated to the new operating system, you sometimes had to wait until your favorite programs were updated before you could use them with the new DOS. Even more unfortunately, if you used older programs that were no longer being supported by their makers, you couldn't use them with the new DOS at all. SETVER lets you trick software into believing it is actually running under a previous version of DOS, say 3.3 or 4.01, for example.

As convenient as this command might be, SETVER is not foolproof. You might have problems with the old software anyway; for example it could inexplicably lock up or it could consistently lose data files. Therefore, before you use SETVER, always be sure to back up the specified program, its auxiliary files, and any data files you have created to this point.

SETVER must be initialized in the CONFIG.SYS file, using either the DEVICE= or DEVICEHIGH= command, before you can use it at the command prompt or in AUTOEXEC.BAT. If SETVER is not initialized, an attempt to use it at the command prompt seems successful, but is followed by a note reminding you that SETVER is inactive at the moment because it wasn't activated in the CONFIG.SYS file.

If you try to run a program with DOS 5 and see the error message `Packed File Corrupt`, refer to LOADFIX in this appendix for a solution.

Examples　In a CONFIG.SYS file, the following command loads SETVER into conventional memory during bootup (which occupies about 0.4K):

```
DEVICE=C:\DOS\SETVER.EXE
```

The following command loads SETVER into upper memory, provided that all the CONFIG.SYS commands required to activate upper memory precede this command:

```
DEVICEHIGH=C:\DOS\SETVER.EXE
```

The following command prints the current version table. (You can use ¦ MORE to slow output, or >PRN to print it.)

SETVER

The next command adds a program named XBASE to the SETVER table and assigns version 3.30 of DOS to that program:

```
SETVER XBASE.EXE 3.33
```

The screen will display a warning message (which you should read carefully), followed by a message like

```
Version table successfully updated
The version change will take effect the next time you restart your system
```

Note that if you attempt to run the XBASE program now, it will still try to run under DOS 5. However, once you reboot, XBASE.EXE will be added to the SETVER table, and every time you run XBASE in the future, DOS will "trick" it into thinking it's running under DOS 3.30.

If at some point in the future, you get an updated version of your XBASE program, which runs fine under DOS 5, you'll want to remove XBASE from the SETVER table, using the following command:

```
SETVER XBASE.EXE /DELETE
```

See Also LOADFIX

SHARE

Provides support for file sharing and diskette change protection.

Version 3 and later

Type External (SHARE.EXE)

DOS Shell Menu Access None

Syntax
```
SHARE [/F:filespace] [/L:locks]
```

in which *filespace* sets the amount of memory space to be used for file sharing, and *locks* sets the maximum number of file and record locks.

Usage SHARE allows two or more programs that are running simultaneously on one computer to share files. (This is different from a network, in which multiple computers share files and other resources.)

After SHARE is loaded, all programs that support SHARE must check to see whether a file is in use by another program before modifying data in that file. If another program has exclusive use of the file (that is, the file is locked), the current program is denied access. If the other program has a record or several records locked, the current program can view but not change the locked records. (However, a particular program that uses SHARE might impose other rules.)

SHARE is also used with Version 4 of DOS to support hard disk partitions larger than 32MB. If you use partitions larger than 32MB with DOS 4, the SHARE.EXE file must be in the root directory of the hard disk or in the directory specified by the SHELL command in your CONFIG.SYS file. In DOS 5, however, you no longer need to use the SHARE command to create large partitions; simply specify the size of the partition with the FDISK program.

Some floppy disk drives can keep track of whether the disk in the drive has changed since the last access. DOS does not take advantage of this feature until you load the SHARE program.

You can load the SHARE program in your CONFIG.SYS file using the INSTALL (not DEVICE) command. Optionally, you can load SHARE directly from the command prompt.

If you do not use the /F: switch in the SHARE command, DOS sets aside 2,048 bytes of memory to manage file sharing. If you do not use the /L: switch, DOS defaults to a maximum of 20 locks.

Specifying /F: and /L: values larger than the default values increases the amount of memory usage proportionately.

Examples

To install SHARE (using the default settings) directly from the command prompt, enter the command

SHARE

To install SHARE during system startup (specifying 4,096 bytes of RAM for file sharing management and specifying a maximum of 40 locks), include the following command in your CONFIG.SYS file (assuming that the SHARE.EXE file is stored in a directory named \DOS):

INSTALL=C:\DOS\SHARE.EXE /F:4096 /L:40

See Also

DRIVER.SYS

SHELL

Installs the command processor.

Version

3 and later

Type

Internal (used in the CONFIG.SYS file)

DOS Shell Menu Access

None

Syntax

SHELL=[*drive*][*path*]*file name options*

in which *drive*, *path*, and *file name* identify the location and name of the command processor, and **options** are options provided by the command processor.

Usage

SHELL installs the DOS *command processor*; the program that takes commands from the command prompt and executes them. By default, the DOS command processor is the COMMAND.COM file.

There are three main reasons for using SHELL:

❏ To specify the location of the command processor (COMMAND.COM).

❏ To use a command processor other than COMMAND.COM (perhaps one you created yourself if you're a programmer.)

❏ To increase the size of the DOS environment, where SET variables are stored.

Normally, DOS searches the root directory of the startup drive for the command processor and assumes its name is COMMAND.COM. If COMMAND.COM is not in the root directory of drive C: (for example, in DOS versions 4 and 5, it's typically in C:\DOS), you must use the SHELL command to specify the location of COMMAND.COM.

Similarly, if you are using a custom command interpreter, such as one you've created on your own, you must use the SHELL command to indicate the location and file name of that command processor.

The SHELL command does not support any switches of its own. However, you can use whatever parameters and switches the command interpreter normally uses to the right of the command interpreter's file name in the SHELL command.

When using the SHELL command to alter the size of the DOS environment, be aware that the minimum size of the environment is 160 bytes, the maximum size is 32,768 bytes, with the default size being 256 bytes.

Examples   The following CONFIG.SYS command:

```
SHELL=C:\DOS\COMMAND.COM C:\DOS /P
```

specifies that the command processor to be used is COMMAND.COM, which is located on the C:\DOS directory. Note that the parameter and switch at the end of the command, C:\DOS and /P, are part of COMMAND.COM, not the SHELL command; \DOS sets the COMSPEC environmental variable to C:\DOS, and /P makes the command interpreter permanent so that another command interpreter cannot be executed during the current session.

Suppose that you want to increase the size of the DOS environment from 256 bytes to 512 bytes because there is currently not enough room for all your SET variables. To do so, you would alter the previous CONFIG.SYS command example to look like this:

```
SHELL=C:\DOS\COMMAND.COM C:\DOS /E:512 /P
```

Here again, the /E:512 is actually a COMMAND.COM switch, not a SHELL switch.

See Also   COMMAND, EXIT

SHIFT

Shifts parameters in a batch file.

Version   2.0 and later

Type   Internal (batch files and DOSKEY macros only)

DOS Shell   None
Menu Access

Syntax   `SHIFT`

Usage   SHIFT moves the parameters passed to a batch file one position to the left. That is, if %1 is LETTER1.TXT and %2 is LETTER2.TXT, then after the SHIFT command, %1 becomes LETTER.TXT and %2 no longer has a value. SHIFT is used mainly to create batch files that can accept more than the usual limit of nine parameters (or an unknown number of parameters).

Examples   The following sample batch file, which I'll assume is named TEST.BAT, can be used to demonstrate how SHIFT works on your computer.

```
ECHO OFF
 :Top
ECHO 1= %1
ECHO 2= %2
ECHO 3= %3
ECHO 4= %4
ECHO 5= %5
ECHO Shifting now[elp]
ECHO.
SHIFT
IF NOT .%0 -- . GOTO Top
ECHO Demo over
```

If you create this batch file, you should then execute it, passing at least two parameters to it. For example, the following command

```
TEST Dog Cat Mouse Fish
```

passes four parameters.

After you enter the command, the screen shows

```
1= Dog
2= Cat
3= Mouse
4= Fish
5=
Shifting now...
```

Then the SHIFT command shifts the parameters' values, and the batch file shows the contents again.

```
1= Cat
2= Mouse
3= Fish
4=
5=
Shifting now...
```

After the next SHIFT, the batch file shows

```
1= Mouse
2= Fish
3=
4=
5=
Shifting now...
```

This process continues until all the parameters are empty.

The SHIFT command works in exactly the same manner in DOSKEY macros. For a complete discussion of SHIFT, see the section titled "Passing More than Nine Parameters" in Chapter 14.

See Also   FOR, SET

SMARTDRV

Enables a disk cache in extended or expanded memory.

Version   5

Type   External (SMARTDRV.SYS)

DOS Shell
Menu Access   None

Syntax   [*drive*][*path*]SMARTDRV.SYS [*initial size*] [*minimum size*] [/A]

in which *drive* and *path* specify the location of the SMARTDRV.SYS file, *initial size* determines the size (in KB) of the cache, and *minimum size* determines the minimum size of the cache during operations.

Usage   Microsoft's SMARTDrive (SMARTDRV.SYS) was originally packaged with Windows; now DOS 5 can use this disk cache to improve system performance. However, because of its roots with Windows, you probably should choose SMARTDrive over other caches if your system is also running Windows. Remember, do not use SMARTDrive in conjunction with another disk cache program— it's a waste of memory and can cause memory conflicts.

Disk *caches* speed system operations by storing recently accessed information in extended or expanded memory so that your program can use the data directly from RAM rather than accessing the disk again. Reading from RAM is almost instantaneous; reading from a disk (especially a floppy diskette) is much slower. In general, large caches let you store more data in RAM and lead to more efficient disk I/O operations. However, if you create too large a cache, some application programs that require extended or expanded memory might not have enough memory to run properly. (Windows 3.0 is the exception here; when it needs more memory, it simply "shrinks" the SMARTDrive cache . . . no matter how large a cache you set!)

As a rule of thumb, use SMARTDrive on your system if you have at least 512KB of extended memory or 256KB of expanded memory. (If you must use expanded memory, be sure to add the /A switch to your SMARTDRV.SYS command line.) If your system includes both extended and expanded memory, simply use the largest area; SMARTDrive works well in both types of memory. Remember, however, that your CONFIG.SYS file must contain command lines that set up extended or expanded memory *before* you use the SMARTDRV.SYS command.

If you can spare the memory, you can use a cache as large as 2MB. However, you won't need a cache this size unless you are working with a program that performs constant disk accesses. In general, database and spreadsheet programs benefit from large caches, but word processors do not.

A couple of interesting notes:

❑ You can improve SMARTDrive's performance by regularly running a defragmentation program on your hard disks.

❑ If you are using an 80286 or 80386 computer, SMARTDrive will run better in extended memory.

❑ If you specify a cache that is larger than the available extended or expanded memory, the program simply uses all available memory.

Examples   You must use the DEVICE command to install the SMARTDrive disk cache from your CONFIG.SYS file. However, the SMARTDRV.SYS command line must be placed *after* the appropriate memory manager. For example, if you want to locate a 512KB cache in extended memory, a line similar to the following must be placed after the `DEVICE = HIMEM.SYS` (or other memory manager) command:

`DEVICE = C:\DOS\SMARTDRV.SYS 512`

If you want to locate the cache in expanded memory on a 386 or 486 computer, you must insert the following command *after* the `DEVICE = C:\DOS\HIMEM.SYS` and `DEVICE = C:\DOS\EMM386.EXE` command lines:

`DEVICE = C:\DOS\SMARTDRV.SYS 512 /A`

If you are also running Windows 3.0 on your computer, you probably should specify the *minimum size* parameter of SMARTDrive. If Windows needs more memory, it will shrink the size of the cache to gain additional memory for its own programs. If you don't specify a minimum cache size, Windows can actually shrink the cache to 0, thus eliminating its usefulness. A typical SMARTDrive command line for a system running Windows 3.0 might be

`DEVICE = C:\DOS\SMARTDRV.SYS 1024 25`

See Also   FASTOPEN

SORT

Sorts lines of text that are input from a command, device, or file, and outputs the sorted text to a file or device.

Version   2 and later

Type   External (SORT.EXE)

DOS Shell Menu Access   None (although in the Files List, you can select a sort order for file names by selecting `File Display Options...` from the Options pull-down menu)

Syntax   `SORT [/R] [/+start column]`

in which `start column` is the column on which the sort is based.

Usage   SORT can act both as a command and as a filter for other commands. Because it is an external program, it must be accessible for use. Typically, SORT.EXE is stored in a directory that is included in your PATH command, so that you always have access to it.

As a filter, you can use SORT to the right of a command and | character. For example, the command SETVER C: | SORT displays the DOS version table sorted alphabetically by file name. As a command, SORT can be used to sort an ASCII text file. For example, the command SORT ASCII.TXT sorts the rows in a file named ASCII.TXT into alphabetical or numerical format.

The /R option causes a file to be sorted in reverse order (that is, Z to A). The /+ option specifies that the sort begin at a certain column in the file or display.

Note that SORT performs its sort in a very "literal" manner; it does not "process" the information that it is sorting. For example, when sorting dates, SORT considers 12/31/87 to be later than 1/1/88, because 12 is larger than 1 (it does not take the year into consideration). When sorting times, 5:00 p.m. is considered earlier than 8:00 a.m., because 5 is smaller than 8.

Numbers are sorted properly only if they are correctly aligned. For example, the following column of numbers would be sorted properly:

```
   1.0
  99.0
 223.3
1234.5
```

But the next column of numbers would not be sorted properly because it is not right-aligned:

```
1.0
2346.11
3
99
```

SORT provides only a rudimentary sorting capability. For more realistic sorts (and sorts within sorts) you need a more powerful program, such as a database management system, a spreadsheet, or a word processor.

Examples   The DOS 5 DIR command contains several new switches that let you sort directory listing information. With earlier versions of DOS, however, you have to use the SORT command to control the output of DIR. The following examples show you how to mimic the actions of a few of the new DOS 5 DIR switches.

The output from a DIR command displays the file name, extension, size, and date and time of creation of the most recent change. The information is consistently displayed in the following columns:

Section of DIR	Column
File name	1
Extension	10
Size	15
Date	24
Time	34

To display the files in a directory in alphabetical order, enter the command

```
DIR ¦ SORT
```

To display the files sorted by size (smallest to largest), enter the command

```
DIR ¦ SORT /+15
```

To display the files sorted by date, and to display the output on the printer, enter the command

```
DIR ¦ SORT /+24 > PRN
```

Consider another use of the SORT command. Suppose you have a file named NAMELST.TXT, which contains the following information:

```
Zorro    Albert    123 A St.
Moore    Renee     P.O. Box 2800
Adams    Arthur    988 Grape St.
```

Entering the command

```
SORT < NAMELST.TXT
```

displays the names in alphabetical order, as follows:

```
Adams    Arthur    988 Grape St.
Moore    Renee     P.O. Box 2800
Zorro    Albert    123 A St.
```

Entering the command

```
SORT < NAMELST.TXT /R
```

displays the contents of the file sorted in reverse order (Z to A), as follows:

```
Zorro    Albert    123 A St.
Moore    Renee     P.O. Box 2800
Adams    Arthur    988 Grape St.
```

The following command displays the contents of the NAMELST.TXT file sorted by street address (which begins in the sixteenth column in the file):

```
SORT < NAMELST.TXT /+16
```

The resulting display from this command is

```
Zorro   Albert   123 A St.
Adams   Arthur   988 Grape St.
Moore   Renee    P.O. Box 2800
```

Note that when sorting a column that contains both numbers and letters, as in the previous example, the numbers are listed before the letters (that is, 988 comes before P.O. Box).

To actually sort a file, as opposed to just displaying its contents in sorted order, use an output redirection symbol and a new file name. For example, the following command creates a new copy of the NAMELST.TXT file, sorted by last name, in a file called NEWLIST.TXT:

```
SORT < NAMELST.TXT > NEWLIST.TXT
```

If you were to enter the command `TYPE NAMELST.TXT` after entering this command, you would see that the file does indeed contain the same information as NAMELST.TXT, but in sorted order, as follows:

```
Adams   Arthur   988 Grape St.
Moore   Renee    P.O. Box 2800
Zorro   Albert   123 A St.
```

To replace the contents of NAMELST.TXT with the contents of NEWLIST.TXT, and then erase NEWLIST.TXT, enter the command

```
COPY NEWLIST.TXT NAMELST.TXT
```

and then the command

```
ERASE NEWLIST.TXT
```

See Also   DIR

STACKS

Changes the number of stacks used by hardware interrupts.

Version   3.2 and later

Type   Internal (used only in CONFIG.SYS)

DOS Shell Menu Access   None

Syntax	`STACKS=number,size`

in which *number* specifies the number of stacks (in the range of 8 to 64), and *size* specifies the size (in bytes) of each stack (in the range of 32 to 512).

Usage Very few computers need to use the STACKS directive. It is only required when a particular program brings the entire system to a halt, displaying the message `Fatal: Internal Stack Failure, System Halted`. You must turn off the computer at this point (you cannot do anything else).

When you turn on the computer again, do not run the problem program. Instead, examine your CONFIG.SYS file to see if it already contains a STACKS command.

If your CONFIG.SYS file contains the command `STACKS=0,0`, then the computer might not support dynamic stacks. You should not change the STACKS setting (and, therefore, you cannot use the program that caused the Fatal error).

If no STACKS command is listed, then your system is using the default of 9 stacks with 128 bytes each. Try increasing the number of stacks, rather than the size; then, reboot (press Ctrl-Alt-Del) and try running the program that halted the system. You might need to experiment, raising the number of stacks a little each time, until the program runs successfully.

Examples The following command, when included in the CONFIG.SYS file, sets the number of stacks to 12, each using the default of 128 bytes:

`STACKS=12,128`

SUBST

Substitutes a subdirectory for a disk drive.

Version 3.1 and later

Type External (SUBST.EXE)

DOS Shell Menu Access None

Syntax `SUBST [original drive new drive new path] [/D]`

in which *original drive* is the drive that you wish to "hide," and *new drive* and *new path* specify the drive and path that are to replace the drive being hidden.

Usage   SUBST lets you use a directory in place of a disk drive. It is generally used to "trick" programs that are incapable of using directories into using them. For example, suppose you have an old accounting package that can only store its data on a diskette in drive B:. You prefer that the program store its data on the subdirectory named \ACCT\DATA on your hard disk drive C:. The SUBST command allows you to "trick" the accounting program into doing just that.

The original drive specified in the SUBST command does not have to actually exist on your computer. For example, if your accounting package insists on storing data on drive B:, and your computer does not even have a drive B:, SUBST still allows you to substitute a directory for drive B:.

The original drive that you are attempting to substitute cannot be the current drive. For example, if you want to use subdirectory C:\ACCT/DATA as a substitute for drive B:, drive B: cannot be the current directory when you enter the SUBST command.

The new drive can be any drive from A: to E:, or higher if you've used the LASTDRIVE option in your CONFIG.SYS file to specify a larger highest-drive name (see the LASTDRIVE entry in this appendix).

When a substitution is in effect, it influences all DOS commands, which can make things a bit confusing. For example, if you set up drive and path C:\TEMP as the substitute for drive D:, then a command such as DIR D: will actually show you the files stored on C:\TEMP.

SUBST cannot be used with a network disk drive. When a substitution is in effect, do not use the ASSIGN, BACKUP, CHDIR, CHKDSK, DISKCOMP, DISKCOPY, FDISK, FORMAT, JOIN, LABEL, MKDIR, PATH, RESTORE, or RMDIR commands. Before using any of these commands, cancel the substitution. To do so, use the syntax

SUBST *original drive* /D

To see if a substitution is in effect at any time, enter the SUBST command without any parameters.

Examples   The following series of steps shows how to set up, use, and then delete a substitution. Suppose your computer does not have a drive B:, and you want to use a program that can only use a drive B:. You decide to create a directory named \FAKE_B on your hard disk drive C: to store the information that the program usually stores on drive B:.

First, be sure the hard disk is the current drive, and enter the command

```
MD \FAKE_B
```

to create the new directory (if it does not already exist).

Next, use the SUBST command to substitute C:\FAKE_B for drive B: by entering the command

```
SUBST B: C:\FAKE_B
```

As a test, enter the following commands at the command prompt to store a simple file on this phony drive B: (the [^]Z character is entered by pressing the F6 key or by typing Ctrl-Z):

```
COPY CON B:TEST.TXT
This is a test
[^]Z
```

To verify that the file TEST.TXT is stored on "drive B," enter the following commands at the command prompt:

```
DIR B:
TYPE B:TEST.TXT
```

You can see from the results of these commands that the TEST.TXT file actually exists on the fake drive B:. If you enter the command

```
SUBST
```

the screen shows you that C:\FAKE_B is being used to act as drive B:, as follows:

```
B: => C:\FAKE_B
```

You now can run the old program that stores and reads files only on disk drive B:. When you finish using that program, return things to normal. To cancel the substitution, enter the command

```
SUBST B: /D
```

Now if you enter the command

```
DIR B:
```

you receive only the error message `Invalid drive specification`, because there is no longer a fake drive B:. Where are the files that were being stored on this fake drive B:? They are on the substitution drive and directory, C:\FAKE_B. To verify this, enter the command

```
DIR C:\FAKE_B
```

and display the files in the directory.

For added safety, you can create a batch file that sets up the substitution, runs the "old" program, and then automatically cancels the SUBST command. That way, you don't have to worry about inadvertently leaving the SUBST command active when you've finished using the program that requires the fake drive. The following batch file presents an example that runs a program named OLDACCT:

```
REM *************** FAKEIT.BAT C:
IF NOT EXIST C:\FAKE_B\*.*: MD \FAKE_B
SUBST B: C:\FAKE_B CD \OLDACCT
OLDACCT
SUBST B: /D
```

See Also   ASSIGN, JOIN

SWITCHES

Disables extended keyboard function.

Version   4 and 5

Type   Internal (used only in CONFIG.SYS)

Syntax   `SWITCHES = /K`

Usage   Disables extended keyboard functions on the enhanced keyboard, to provide compatibility with programs designed for use on conventional keyboards. Note that this command is available only in DOS 4.

Example   To mimic a conventional keyboard, even though an enhanced keyboard is attached to the computer, include the command

`SWITCHES=/K`

in your CONFIG.SYS file. This disables extended keys, like F11 and F12, thereby providing compatibility with programs that "expect" a conventional keyboard.

If you use the `SWITCHES=/K` command in your CONFIG.SYS file, and you also want to load ANSI.SYS, you must include the /K switch with ANSI.SYS (that is, `DEVICE = C:\DOS\ANSI.SYS /K`).

See Also   CONFIG.SYS

SYS

Makes a bootable DOS system disk.

Version	1 and later
Type	External (SYS.COM)
DOS Shell Menu Access	None

Syntax

SYS *drive*

in which *drive* is the name of the drive that contains the diskette to which you copy the DOS system tracks.

Usage

Whenever you start your computer, it automatically reads the DOS system files from the disk to "pull itself up by its bootstraps" (or *boot* for short). If the computer cannot find the system files that it needs, DOS displays the error message `Non-system disk or disk error` and waits for you to insert a diskette that contains the system files (also called the system tracks).

If your computer has a hard disk, it most likely boots from the root directory of the hard disk. You only see the `Non-system disk` error if you turn on your computer without first opening the drive door or removing the disk from drive A:.

If your computer does not have a hard disk, drive A: must contain a bootable diskette when you turn on the computer; otherwise the `Non-system disk` error message is displayed. To make additional bootable diskettes for your computer, you can use either the FORMAT /S command, or the SYS command.

Generally, you use the SYS command to make a bootable diskette from a diskette that is already formatted and already contains files. If you use the alternative FORMAT /S command, it erases all files on the disk!

There are several rules that you must follow before using SYS:

❑ The diskette in the current drive must be a system (bootable) diskette.

❑ The diskette to which you are copying the system tracks must already be formatted.

❏ The diskette to which you are copying the system tracks must have sufficient space to store the system tracks, otherwise DOS displays the error message `No room for system on destination disk.`

In all versions of DOS, the SYS command copies to the diskette the files that are necessary to start the computer, which are usually hidden. In DOS 5, SYS also copies the COMMAND.COM file to the new disk. No version of DOS, however, copies your CONFIG.SYS or AUTOEXEC.BAT files, so the new bootable disk might not behave exactly as your original Startup diskette (unless you copy CONFIG.SYS and AUTOEXEC.BAT to the new Startup diskette yourself).

You cannot use the SYS command to write on a network drive, nor on a pseudo-drive created with the ASSIGN or SUBST commands.

When formatting your own diskettes, you can use the /S switch with the FORMAT command to perform the same operations that the SYS command does. Optionally, you can use the /B switch with the FORMAT command to reserve enough space so that SYS can be used later to store the system tracks.

Examples   Suppose you purchase a new word processing program for use on your laptop computer, which does not have a hard disk. However, you want to be able to boot from the word processing program's disk.

To do so, start your computer with your usual Startup diskette in drive A:. Then, put the new word processing disk in drive B:, and enter the command

`SYS B:`

at the command prompt. If there is sufficient room on the word processing disk, DOS displays the message `System transferred.`

Actually, a better (and more reliable) technique would be to make a bootable diskette, and then copy the word processing programs to the new disk. That way, you can store the original word processing diskette in a safe place, in case the copy becomes lost or damaged.

To use this technique, start your computer in the usual manner, with your Startup diskette in drive A:. Then put a new, blank, unformatted diskette (*not* the word processing diskette!) in drive B:, and enter the command

`FORMAT B: /S`

at the command prompt.

After DOS finishes formatting the new diskette, and the command prompt reappears, you can enter the following commands to copy your CONFIG.SYS and AUTOEXEC.BAT files to the new bootable diskette:

```
COPY CONFIG.SYS B:
COPY AUTOEXEC.BAT B:
```

Then, remove the DOS diskette from drive A: and put the original word processing diskette in its place (in drive A:). Enter the command

```
COPY *.* B:
```

When copying is complete, remove all diskettes, and label the new disk something like *Bootable Word Processing Diskette*. To test the new diskette, turn off the computer, and then use the new Bootable Word Processing Diskette in drive A: to start the computer. Your computer should start correctly.

You can use the DIR command to verify that the diskette contains all the word processing programs, or enter the command required to start your word processing program.

It's always a good idea to keep an extra bootup disk around, even if you have a hard disk, in case a hard disk problem prevents the system from starting at some time in the future.

When creating such a disk, be sure to copy your COMMAND, CONFIG, and AUTOEXEC files to that disk. Starting with a blank unformatted disk in drive A, and the C> prompt showing, here's the exact sequence of steps to follow to create this spare boot-up disk:

```
FORMAT A: /S
COPY C:\DOS\COMMAND.COM A:
COPY C:\CONFIG.SYS A:
COPY C:\AUTOEXEC.BAT A:
```

See Also FORMAT

TIME

View or change the system time.

Version 1 and later

Type External in Version 1.0; Internal in all later versions

DOS Shell Menu Access None

Syntax   TIME [*hh:mm:ss.hn*][A|P]

in which *hh* is the hour (0 to 24), *mm* is minutes (0 to 59), *ss* is seconds (0 to 59), and *hn* is hundredths of seconds.

Usage   TIME lets you view or change the system time. The time is expressed on a 24-hour clock, where 0 is midnight, 12 is 12:00 noon, 13 is 1:00 in the afternoon, and 23 is 11:00 p.m. Hence, the time 23:59:59.99 is one hundredth of a second before midnight, and 00:00:00.00 is exactly midnight.

On most computers, a small internal clock keeps the time accurate and runs even when the computer is turned off. The clock, however, isn't perfect, and it sometimes can lose track of time. The TIME command lets you see what time the computer "thinks" it is, and, optionally, lets you change that time.

DOS 4 and 5 support the A and P options; which can be used to specify A.M. or P.M.

Examples   To check the current system time on your computer, enter the command

TIME

The screen replies with a message such as

Current time is 13:47:58.68
Enter new time:

If you press the Enter key at this point, the time remains unchanged. Optionally, you can type a new time, using the hh:mm:ss.hh format. (Actually, you need to enter only hh:mm.) For example, to change the current time to 1:50 p.m., type 13:50 at the Enter new time: prompt and press Enter.

To enter the current time as 1:50 in the afternoon, using DOS 4, you could enter the command.

TIME 1:50p

See Also   DATE

TREE

Displays the directory structure.

Version   2 and later

Type   External (TREE.COM)

DOS Shell Menu Access	None (DOS displays the directory tree whenever you view a File List)
Syntax	Versions 2 through 3.3 use

TREE [*drive*] [/F]

Versions 4 and 5 use

TREE [*drive*][*path*] [/F] [/A]

in which *drive* is the name of the drive whose directory structure you want to display, and *path* is the starting directory for the TREE display.

Usage	TREE displays the names of all directories on a disk. If you include the /F option, TREE also shows the names of all the files on each directory and subdirectory. If you do not specify a drive name in the command, the current drive is assumed.

All versions of DOS prior to 4 display all directories on the disk, regardless of which directory is current. In DOS 4 and 5, only the current directory and directories beneath are displayed, unless you specify the root directory as the starting directory.

DOS 4 and 5 display the directory in a vertical tree structure, similar to the way it appears on the Shell screen. In these versions, you can also specify the /A option to use only ASCII characters in the display, which provides for universal code page acceptance, and speeds printing slightly.

Examples	To view the names of all directories on the current drive, enter the command

TREE

or if you are using DOS 4 or 5, enter the command

TREE \

To view the names of all files on each directory, enter the command

TREE /F

or in DOS 4 or 5

TREE \ /F

To pause the information displayed by the TREE command, use the MORE filter as follows:

TREE | MORE

or

TREE /F ¦ MORE

To sort the list of directory names and pause the display (using DOS 3.3 or earlier), enter the command

```
TREE | SORT | MORE
```

To print a copy of the directory tree, enter the command

```
TREE > PRN
```

or in DOS 4 or 5

```
TREE \ > PRN
```

To print a list of all files in all directories, using DOS version 3.3 or earlier, enter the command

```
TREE /F > PRN
```

or in DOS 4 or 5

```
TREE \ /F > PRN
```

In DOS Versions 3.3 and earlier, you can display a summarized TREE structure—without all the blank lines and redundant subdirectory listings—and limit the display to lines that contain the word "Path" by entering the following command

```
TREE | FIND "Path"
```

or to control scrolling

```
TREE | FIND "Path" | MORE
```

See Also   DIR, MKDIR, FIND, MORE

TYPE

Displays the contents of a file.

Version   1 and later

Type   Internal

DOS Shell Menu Access   The View option on the File pull-down menu when a single file is selected in the Files List of the Shell

Syntax   TYPE [*drive*][*path*]*file name*

in which *drive* and *path* specify the location, and *file name* is the name of the file you want to view.

Usage   TYPE provides a quick and easy way to look at the contents of a file. If the file that you display contains only ASCII text characters, the output is quite readable. However, if you use TYPE with a program, spreadsheet, database, or some word processing files, the contents seem to consist of strange graphics characters (such as happy faces) and the computer might even occasionally beep.

If you need to stop the TYPE command before it is finished, press Ctrl-Break (or Ctrl-C).

Examples   To view the contents of a file named READ.ME on the current drive and directory, enter the command

```
TYPE READ.ME
```

To pause the TYPE command so that it displays only a single screenful of information at a time, use the | MORE filter, as follows:

```
TYPE READ.ME | MORE
```

To send the output of the TYPE command to the printer, use the > PRN symbol and device name, as follows:

```
TYPE READ.ME > PRN
```

Before printing a file, use the TYPE command without > PRN to preview the file's contents on the screen. If the file contains strange characters, don't use > PRN to print it.

If the file that you want to view is not on the current drive and/or directory, specify the drive and directory before the file name, as follows:

```
TYPE C:\NEWWARE\READ.ME
```

If you are using DOS 5, you might want to create a macro version of TYPE that *always* pauses after each screenful of text. If you call the macro TYPE, DOS will always execute the macro—not the DOS command. For example, if you put the following command in your AUTOEXEC.BAT file, every time you enter the TYPE command, it will pause at each screenful of information:

```
DOSKEY TYPE=TYPE $1 $B MORE
```

See Also   DOSKEY, MORE, PRINT

UNDELETE

Restores files deleted with the DEL or ERASE commands.

Version   5

Type   External (UNDELETE.EXE)

DOS Shell   In the Disk Utilities group in the Program list.
Menu Access

Syntax   `UNDELETE [drive][path][file name] [/DT | /DOS | /ALL]`
               `[/LIST] [/HELP | /?]`

in which *drive* contains the file(s) you want to recover, *path* specifies the location of the file(s) you want to recover, and *file name* is the name of the file(s) to be recovered.

Usage   DOS wild cards can be used to recover groups of files. If you omit the filespec, UNDELETE attempts to recover all files in the specified location.

`/DT`	Recovers only those files listed in the *delete tracking* file produced by the MIRROR /T command. UNDELETE prompts you to type the first letter of each file you want to recover.
`/DOS`	Recovers files that DOS lists as deleted. This switch causes UNDELETE to ignore any existing *delete tracking* file. UNDELETE prompts you to type the first letter of each file you want to recover.
`/ALL`	Undeletes all specified files without prompting you first. UNDELETE uses the *delete tracking* file if one exists; otherwise, it recovers the files that DOS lists as deleted. It automatically supplies a character (#%&-), number (01234567890), or letter (A–Z), in that order, to complete the file name and create a unique name.
`/LIST`	Lists all of the deleted files in the specified path that can be recovered, as determined by other switches.
`/HELP` or `/?`	Displays a help message.

> NOTE: If you do not specify a switch, UNDELETE uses the *delete tracking* file (if available); otherwise, it uses the DOS list of deleted files.

NOTE for DOS 5.0 users: The new UNDELETE command is an excellent file recovery utility and a long-awaited addition to DOS. When DOS deletes a file, it doesn't actually erase the data in that file, it simply deletes references to the file in the file allocation tables and in the root directory listing. The UNDELETE command lets you restore those references (if you have not yet stored new data over the old files). The most important aspect of using this command is to use it as soon as possible after an accidental deletion, especially before you save any new data to the affected disk; otherwise, the data you are trying to recover might be overwritten by new data.

No matter how advanced a DOS user you are, you will invariably delete a file accidentally or delete a file intentionally, but later discover that you need it after all. Several utility programs, such as *Norton Utilities, Mace Utilities,* and *PC Tools Deluxe,* became major products primarily because they offered this undeleting capability. In fact, the new DOS 5.0 UNDELETE command is actually a stand-alone version of the same utility offered by the PC Tools package (as are the new UNFORMAT and MIRROR commands). If you are familiar with the PC Tools versions of these programs, you can use the DOS 5.0 programs in exactly the same way.

When you run UNDELETE, it shows the current directory, file specification, and information about deleted files, as in the following example

```
Directory: C:\
File Specifications: *.*
Delete-tracking file contains        2 deleted files
Of those,        files have all clusters available
                 1 files have some clusters available
                 0 files have no clusters available

MS-DOS directory contains 428 deleted files
Of those,        159 files may be recovered
```

In this example, only two files on C:\ have been deleted since DOS 5 was installed on this machine and MIRROR activated. There are, however, 428 deleted files on C:\, 159 of which are still recoverable.

If you do not use the /LIST or /ALL switch, the screen will also provide information about each deleted file, including file name, extension, size, date and time created, and date and time deleted (if using delete tracking) and ask whether you want to undelete it, as in the following example:

```
Using the delete-tracking file.

MYFILE  EXT  8128  8/27/90 5:00p Deleted 6/30/91 1:40p
All of the clusters for this file are available. Undelete (Y/N)?
```

If you want to undelete the file MYFILE.EXE in the preceding example, press Y. If you do not want to undelete the file, press N. If you want UNDELETE to stop displaying names of deleted files, press Ctrl-C or Ctrl-Break, then Enter.

Note that when undeleting a file without the delete-tracking file, its first character is always displayed as a question mark, and no information about the deletion date or time is given, as in the next example:

```
Using the MS-DOS directory
?YFILE  EXT  8128  8/27/90 5:00p ... Undelete (Y/N)?
```

If you press Y to answer Yes, you'll also be prompted to provide the missing character shown as ? in the file name. In this example, you'd press the letter M to change ?YFAVE.EXT to MYFAVE.EXT.

Example

The command

```
UNDELETE /DT /LIST
```

lists the deleted files on the current drive and directory in the delete-tracking file. The command

```
UNDELETE /DOS /LIST
```

lists all the files in the DOS Directory that have been deleted, whether or not the deletion was listed in the delete-tracking file.

The command

```
UNDELETE F:\HSG\*.SCR
```

tells DOS to attempt to undelete deleted files with the extension .SCR in the HSG directory of drive F:. (Omitting the drive, directory, and filename pattern tells DOS to check all files on the current drive and directory.)

The command

```
UNDELETE /?
```

provides a quick reminder of UNDELETE syntax and switches.

See Also:

DEL (ERASE), MIRROR, UNFORMAT

UNFORMAT

Recovers files and directories from an accidentally formatted disk and can restore some deleted directories.

Version 5

Type External (UNFORMAT.COM)

DOS Shell Menu Access None

Syntax

```
UNFORMAT drive: [/J | /L[ /PARTN | /TEST]]
```

in which *drive* specifies the drive that contains the disk from which you want to recover directories and files

Usage The UNFORMAT command is one of the new DOS 5 file recovery utilities (MIRROR and UNDELETE are the others). When DOS reformats a hard disk, it doesn't actually delete the data in that hard disk (unless you specify the /U switch), it simply clears the root directory and deletes the file allocation tables (FATs). The UNFORMAT command uses the information in the MIRROR.FIL file (created by the MIRROR command) to restore those system areas, thus UNFORMATing the directory structure of the hard disk and the references to your individual files. The information in the MIRROR.FIL file can also help the UNFORMAT command restore deleted directories and files that branch directly off the root directory.

By default, UNFORMAT uses a file created by the MIRROR command to reconstruct directories and files on your hard disk. If you have never used the MIRROR command or if you haven't used it recently, UNFORMAT can still restore your disk; however, the process is much slower and might not be completely accurate.

Note that if your hard disk requires a device driver (such as ONTRACK's DMDRVR.BIN), you can use UNFORMAT to recover an accidentally formatted disk only if you first boot your system from a floppy diskette that includes that driver. The floppy diskette must be a bootable (system) disk that contains the needed driver (and support files, if any) and also includes a CONFIG.SYS file with the appropriate entries. To protect your hard disks, create this recovery diskette whenever you add a new hard drive that requires a device driver.

You can use the following switches to control the operation of UNFORMAT:

/J	Checks to see whether files have been created by the MIRROR command, and lets you choose which of the files you want to use. (Press Esc to cancel this operation.)
/L	Lists all files and subdirectories found by UNFORMAT
/P	Prints the information displayed by the /L switch
/PARTN	Restores the partition table information that you saved on a floppy disk with the MIRROR /PARTN command.
/TEST	Simulates the UNFORMATing operation without actually writing any data to your disk

UNFORMAT also has another important use. If you've used the MIRROR /PARTN command to save partition table information to a floppy diskette, you can use UNFORMAT to reconstruct a damaged partition table. See the last part of the "Examples" section for a complete discussion of this procedure.

Examples   The UNFORMAT command is actually a stand-alone version of the utility offered in the PC Tools package (as are the new MIRROR and UNDELETE commands). If you are familiar with the PC Tools versions of these programs, you can use the DOS 5 programs in exactly the same way.

If you accidentally format hard disk drive D: and your DOS commands are on drive C:, you can restore drive D: by typing the following command:

```
UNFORMAT D: /J
```

The /J switch tells UNFORMAT to restore the drive by using the hidden file created by the MIRROR command. However, if you haven't used MIRROR recently (or ever), you probably should make a trial run first. Type the command

```
UNFORMAT D: /L /TEST
```

to see exactly what the UNFORMAT command will do before you actually use it; that is, files might need to be deleted or truncated while UNFORMAT is restoring drive D:.

You can also restore an accidentally formatted floppy disk. The following command uses the hidden MIRROR file (if it exists) to unformat the floppy disk in drive A:

```
UNFORMAT A:
```

If the MIRROR file doesn't exist, the command tries to restore the disk anyway.

If your system has `logical` drives (for example, your physical drive has been partitioned into logical drives C:, D:, and E:) and you see the error message `Invalid drive specification` when you try to access drive D:, you've just stepped into the Twilight Zone of computing disasters. This unremarkable error message actually means "Drive D: no longer exists!" DOS can't find the definition for that drive in the partition table.

To restore the partition table for hard disk drive D: (if you've previously used the MIRROR /PARTN command to save the information to a floppy diskette), type

`UNFORMAT /PARTN`

Next, enter the letter of the floppy drive you want to use and insert the diskette with the partition table information into the drive. UNFORMAT then compares the data saved in the MIRROR file (PARTNSAV.FIL) to the actual hard disk drive. If the data doesn't match, the procedure ends immediately. If the data matches, UNFORMAT restores the partition table and tells you to reboot with the Startup DOS diskette. Finally, after your system boots, you must now run UNFORMAT again (without the /PARTN switch) to restore your file allocation tables and root directory.

See Also   MIRROR, UNDELETE

VDISK.SYS

See RAMDRIVE.SYS

VER

Displays the version of DOS in use.

Version   3 and later

Type   Internal

DOS Shell Menu Access   None

Syntax   `VER`

Usage   The VER command displays the version number of DOS that is currently running on your computer.

Examples   Suppose you call a software dealer to get some help, and they ask you which version of DOS you are using. To find out, enter the command

VER

at the command prompt.

If you see the message `Bad command or file name`, you either spelled the command incorrectly or you are using a version of DOS prior to 3.0.

VERIFY

Displays or sets file-writing verification.

Version   2 or later

Type   Internal

DOS Shell Menu Access   None

Syntax   VERIFY [ON | OFF]

Usage   Commands that store data on disks do not normally double-check to ensure that the correct information is written. Because disk-writing errors are quite rare, double-checking every character that is stored on disk is counterproductive—it takes time and needlessly slows DOS.

However, there might be cases in which you want to be sure crucial information or large programs are stored correctly. When such circumstances arise, you can set the VERIFY status ON. Doing so slows DOS operations, but it gives you piece of mind.

To view the current status of the verification option, enter the VERIFY command with no parameters. To turn on verification, use the command VERIFY ON. To turn off verification, use the command VERIFY OFF.

Note that turning on the verification feature is the same as using the /V option in COPY and DISKCOPY commands.

Examples   Suppose you are preparing to send some important information, stored on diskettes, to a company in Istanbul. It isn't easy to get information to and from Istanbul, so you want to be sure that the data you send is accurate the first time.

First, check the status of the verification feature by entering the command

```
VERIFY
```

The screen informs you that VERIFY is off. Therefore, enter the command

```
VERIFY ON
```

Now you can use COPY, or some other program, to store the necessary information on the diskette in drive A:. Because verification is on, the copy takes a little longer than usual.

When you finish making the copy, enter the command

```
VERIFY OFF
```

to turn off verification and permit DOS to run at top speed.

See Also   COPY

VOL

Displays a volume (disk) label.

Version   2 and later

Type   Internal

DOS Shell Menu Access   Pull down the Options menu and select `Show Information....` The disk's volume label, if any, is shown as the Disk Name.

Syntax

```
VOL [drive]
```

in which *drive* is the name of the drive whose label you want to see.

Usage   You can use the LABEL command (or the /V option with the FORMAT command) to assign a name (label) to a disk. This name can be as many as 11 characters and is displayed whenever you view the directory of the disk with a DIR command or use the TREE or CHKDSK commands.

The VOL command also displays the label assigned to the disk. Unlike other commands, however, VOL displays only the label and none of the other information.

Examples   Suppose you place a diskette in drive A: to see if it has been assigned a label. Enter the command

```
VOL A:
```

If there is no label assigned to the disk, DOS displays the message `Volume in drive A has no label`. If there is a label assigned to the disk, DOS displays the message `Volume in drive A is` *name*, in which *name* is the volume label.

See Also   LABEL, FORMAT

XCOPY

Copies files.

Version   3.2 and later

Type   External (XCOPY.EXE)

DOS Shell Menu Access   None

Syntax   `XCOPY [source drive] [source path] [source file name] [destination drive] [destination path] [destination file] [/S] [/E] [/P] [/V] [/A] [/M] [/D:date] [/W]`

in which `source drive`, `source path`, and `source file name` identify the file (or files) to be copied, and `destination drive`, `destination path`, and `destination file` identify the destination of the copy. The `date` option is a date in mm/dd/yy format (or the appropriate format for a foreign country).

Usage   XCOPY is an extended version of the COPY command, offering many additional features and options. It allows you to automatically copy only files that have been changed since the last XCOPY command or only files that have been changed since a particular date. XCOPY also can copy files from subdirectories beneath the current directory (creating subdirectories as needed on the destination disk). The features that XCOPY offers are available as the following switches:

`/A`   Copies only files that have been changed (that is, files with the archive bit on), but does not turn off the archive bit.

`/D:date`   Copies files that were created or modified on or after a specified date.

`/E`   Copies subdirectories, creating the subdirectories on the destination disk if they do not already exist.

`/M`   Copies modified files (that is, files with the archive bit on) and turns off the archive bit.

/P	Prompts you for permission before copying each file.
/S	Copies files from the current directory and from all subdirectories beneath the current directory.
/V	Verifies that the copy was 100 percent successful.
/W	Waits for a source disk to be inserted.

When using the /D option, be sure to enter the date in the appropriate format, as specified by your computer's COUNTRY setting. In the United States, you can use either the mm/dd/yy format, or the mm-dd-yy format. For example, both 12/31/91 and 12-31-91 are valid dates.

The /A and /M options both limit copying to files whose archive bit is set to ON. The archive bit is ON whenever a file is first created, or changed. The /A option leaves the bit set on after the copy takes place. The /M option turns off the archive bit after copying the file. Therefore, the /M option is similar to the BACKUP command, which copies only files that have the archive bit set, and then turns off the archive bit.

The /S option copies all files in all subdirectories that are children of the current directory on the source drive. Therefore, if you are copying from the root directory, XCOPY copies all disk files, creating subdirectories on the destination disk as necessary. However, empty subdirectories are not created on the destination disk unless you specify the /E option. You can only use /E if you've already specified the /S option.

Examples   To copy all of your spreadsheet files with the extension .WK?, from all directories on hard disk drive C: to the diskette in drive A:, first switch to the root directory of drive C:; then enter the XCOPY command as shown:

```
CD\
XCOPY *.WK? A:\ /S
```

Because the /S option is used and the copy was initiated from the root directory, all files with the .WK? extension are copied, regardless of the directory on which they are stored.

To repeat this XCOPY command in the future, but to include only spreadsheet files that have been changed since the last XCOPY or BACKUP command, use the /M parameter, as follows:

```
XCOPY *.WK? AZ:\ /S /M
```

To copy all files with the extension .DBF, which were created or modified on or after December 1, 1990, from the directory named \DBASE on drive C: and all subdirectories beneath \DBASE, to drive A:, enter the command

```
XCOPY C:\DBASE\*.DBF A:\ /S /D:12/1/90
```

To copy all files and the directory structure (including empty sub-directories) from the diskette in drive A: to the diskette in drive B:, enter the command

```
XCOPY A:\*.* B:\ /S /E
```

In this example, the \ characters are included after the drive names to ensure that all subdirectories are referenced from the root directory. Note that, in this case, the *.* is optional. If you do not specify a file name after a drive and directory specification in an XCOPY, *.* is assumed. Therefore, the following command performs exactly the same operation as the previous one:

```
XCOPY A:\ B:\ /S /E
```

To force XCOPY to pause for a disk change before beginning the copy process, to ask permission before copying each file, and also to verify the accuracy of each copy, use the /P, /W, and /V options as follows:

```
XCOPY *.TXT A: /P /W /V
```

See Also COPY, BACKUP

XMAEM.SYS

Emulates the expanded memory on IBM 80386 computers using IBM PC DOS Version 4 (see EMM386 for DOS 5 equivalent).

Version IBM PC DOS 4

Type Device driver activated by a DEVICE command in CONFIG.SYS

DOS Shell Menu Access None

Syntax
```
DEVICE=[.drive][path]XMAEMSYS size
```

in which *drive* and *path* specify the location of the XMAEM.SYS file, and *size* specifies the amount of expanded memory to allocate.

Usage All computers that use the 80386 microprocessor support *virtual memory*, which enables any type of memory (including disk storage) to "act like" extra RAM (or expanded memory). IBM computers that use the 80386 microprocessor (such as the PS/2 Model 80) and DOS 4 include the XMAEM.SYS device driver that uses extended memory to emulate expanded memory.

Non-IBM 80386 computers offer the same capabilities as IBM 80386 computers, but the device driver for emulating expanded memory usually has a different name. Furthermore, the device driver is described in the computer's manual—not the DOS manual—and probably exists on a separate diskette (often labeled "Supplemental Programs" or "Device Drivers") that came with your computer.

For example, the COMPAQ computer provides the CEMM.SYS device driver, which emulates expanded memory. CEMM.SYS is stored both on the COMPAQ Supplemental Programs disk and in the COMPAQ MS-DOS4 disks. If you have two copies of the device driver for emulating expanded memory, use the one on the DOS diskettes to ensure that you are using the correct device driver for your version of DOS. Otherwise, when the computer attempts to install the device driver, DOS might display the error message `Incorrect DOS version`.

The XMAEM.SYS device driver specifically emulates the IBM Personal System/2 80286 Expanded Memory Adapter/A, which conforms to the LIM EMS standard 4.0 and uses extended memory to do so. The `DEVICE=XMAEM.SYS` command must precede the `DEVICE=XMA2EMS.SYS` command in your CONFIG.SYS file, so that the expanded memory is emulated before the XMA2EMS.SYS device driver activates it.

If you do not use the optional *size* parameter in the DEVICE=XMAEM.SYS command, all extended memory is converted to expanded memory. If you use the *size* parameter, it must specify the size of expanded memory in 16KB pages. For example, 1MB of expanded memory is 1,024 kilobytes. Furthermore, 1,024 divided by 16 is 64. Therefore, to emulate 1MB of expanded memory in extended memory, you must specify 64 as the *size* parameter.

Examples   If the XMAEM.SYS file is stored in the \DOS directory of drive C:, and you want to use all the extended memory as expanded memory, include this command in your CONFIG.SYS file (above the DEVICE=XMA2EMS.SYS command):

```
DEVICE=C:\DOS\XMAEM.SYS
```

If you want to use 1MB of extended memory for expanded memory, include this command in your CONFIG.SYS file (above the DEVICE=XMA2EMS.SYS command):

```
DEVICE=C:\DOS\XMAEM.SYS 64
```

If you are using a COMPAQ 386 computer and you want to use 2MB of extended memory as expanded memory, be sure the CEMM.SYS file is stored in the \DOS directory of drive C:, and include this command in your CONFIG.SYS file:

```
DEVICE=C:\DOS\CEMM.SYS 2048 ON
```

With the CEMM.SYS device driver, you do not need to use a second DEVICE command to activate the expanded memory. The ON option in the DEVICE command activates the expanded memory immediately.

See Also   Chapters 15 and 16, XMA2EMS.SYS

XMA2EMS.SYS

Installs expanded memory in IBM PC DOS Version 4.

Version   IBM PC DOS Version 4

Type   Device driver (activated by a DEVICE command in CONFIG.SYS)

DOS Shell Menu Access   None

Syntax
```
DEVICE=[drive][path]XMA2EMS.SYS [FRAME=hex
address] [Pxxx=hex address [...] [/X:size]
```

in which *drive* and *path* specify the location of the XMA2EMS.SYS file, *hex address* is a memory address specified in hexadecimal notation, *xxx* is a page number, and *size* specifies the amount of expanded memory in 16KB pages.

Usage   The XMA2EMS.SYS device driver is included with IBM PC DOS Version 4. Other computers and versions of DOS usually offer similar device drivers. For example, the COMPAQ CEMMP.SYS device driver installs expanded memory on COMPAQ 80286-based microcomputers.

The XMA2EMS.SYS device driver can be used to install expanded memory on an IBM 80286 or 80386 computer that has one of the following EMS adapters installed:

❏ IBM 2MB Expanded Memory Adapter

❏ IBM Personal System/2 80286 Expanded Memory Adapter/A

❏ IBM Personal System/2 80286 Memory Expansion Option

❏ An IBM Model 80 or other IBM 80386-based computer with the XMAEM.SYS device driver already loaded

The optional parameters that you can use with the XMA2EMS.SYS device driver include

hex address   When used with the FRAME= option, the **hex address** must refer to a starting address that specifies four contiguous 16KB page frames. Acceptable values are in the hex range of A000 through E000 (although a range of C000 to E000 is safer because it avoids conflicts with video memory).

xxx   Refers to a page frame number, in which **xxx** can be 0, 1, 2, or 3 for expanded memory switching, or 254 or 255 for DOS functions. The **hex address** specified with the **Pxxx=** option must refer to the starting point of a 16KB page frame, in the hexadecimal range A000 through E000 (although a range of C000 through E000 is safer because it avoids conflicts with video memory).

size   Represents the size of expanded memory to install in 16KB chunks. The minimum is 4 (4 x 16KB = 64KB of expanded memory). If you specify a **size** in the **DEVICE=XMAEMS.SYS** command when emulating expanded memory in extended memory on an 80386 computer, the **/X:size** parameter in the **DEVICE=XMA2EMS.SYS** command is ignored.

If you use the FRAME= option to specify four contiguous 16KB page frames, you cannot individually set pages P0 through P3. However, you can still set pages P254 and P255 individually, as long as you use memory locations that are not already in use by the FRAME= option.

If you want to install a RAM disk (using the RAMDRIVE.SYS device driver) or the FASTOPEN disk caching system in expanded memory (using the /X option with these device drivers), you must specify a 16KB page block of memory in the DEVICE=XMA2EMS.SYS command for P254. If you use the /X option with the BUFFERS command in CONFIG.SYS to install the disk buffers in expanded memory, you must specify a starting address for P255 in your DEVICE=XMA2EMS.SYS command.

The memory addresses for P254 and P255 must not conflict with the 64KB page frame specified in the FRAME= option, or with the 16KB blocks of memory that have been assigned individually to P0, P1, P2, and P3.

To see which memory addresses are available for a page frame or individual pages, use the DEVICE=XMA2EMS.SYS command in your CONFIG.SYS file, but do not include the FRAME= or Pxxx= options. DOS displays available frames and pages when you reboot (but it does not install the expanded memory). Write down or print these suggested frame and page addresses; then, modify the DEVICE=XMA2EMS.SYS command in your CONFIG.SYS to use the available frames and pages.

Examples   Suppose you want to activate all of your expanded memory, and you also want to use expanded memory for the disk buffers and FASTOPEN disk caching program in order to conserve conventional RAM. If your XMA2EMS.SYS file is stored on the \DOS directory of drive C:, and if you have an expanded memory adapter installed in your computer, your CONFIG.SYS file should contain commands similar to the following (in the order shown):

```
DEVICE=C:\DOS\XMA2EMS.SYS FRAME=D000 P254=C000 P255=C400 BUFFERS=15,2 /X
INSTALL=C:\DOS\FASTOPEN.EXE C:=(50,25) /X
```

In this example, the FRAME=D000 option allocates memory addresses from D000 to one byte beneath E000 for expanded memory switching. Therefore, pages 254 and 255 are installed at the non-conflicting addresses C000 and C400.

If your computer does not have an expanded memory adapter, but does use the 80386 microprocessor, you can achieve the same results by including these commands (in the order shown) in your CONFIG.SYS file:

```
DEVICE=C:\DOS\XMAEM.SYS
DEVICE=C:\DOS\XMA2EMS.SYS FRAME=D000 P254=C000 P255=C400
BUFFERS=15,2 /X INSTALL=C:\DOS\FASTOPEN.EXE C:=(50,25) /X
```

If you are using a non-IBM computer, you must use other device drivers to activate and emulate expanded memory. For example, suppose you have a COMPAQ 386 computer with 4MB of extended memory. You want to use 2MB of that memory as expanded memory, part of which is used to manage the disk buffers and FASTOPEN disk caching program. You also want to use 1MB of extended memory as a RAM disk and reserve the remaining 1MB of extended memory for programs that can use it directly (such as Lotus 1-2-3 Version 3).

Assuming that all of your device drivers are stored in the \DOS directory of drive C:, include the following commands in your CONFIG.SYS file (in the order shown):

```
DEVICE=C:\DOS\CEMM.EXE 2048 ON
BUFFERS=15,2 /X
INSTALL=C:\DOS\FASTOPEN.EXE C:=(50,25) D:=(50,25) /X
DEVICE=C:\DOS\RAMDRIVE.SYS 1024 512 128 /E
```

For specific information about using extended and expanded memory adapters designed for your computer, see the DOS manual that came with your computer, or see your computer's Technical Reference Guide.

See Also   BUFFERS, FASTOPEN, RAMDRIVE.SYS, XMAEM.SYS, Chapters 15 and 16

ASCII Code Character Set

(including IBM extended character codes)

ASCII Value		ASCII Character	ASCII Value		ASCII Character
Dec	Hex		Dec	Hex	
000	00	null	016	10	►
001	01	☺	017	11	◄
002	02	☻	018	12	↕
003	03	♥	019	13	‼
004	04	♦	020	14	¶
005	05	♣	021	15	§
006	06	♠	022	16	▬
007	07	●	023	17	↨
008	08	◘	024	18	↑
009	09	○	025	19	↓
010	0A	◼	026	1A	→
011	0B	♂	027	1B	←
012	0C	♀	028	1C	FS
013	0D	♪	029	1D	GS
014	0E	♪♪	030	1E	RS
015	0F	☼	031	1F	US

| ASCII Value | | ASCII Character | ASCII Value | | ASCII Character |
Dec	Hex		Dec	Hex	
032	20	SP	073	49	I
033	21	!	074	4A	J
034	22	"	075	4B	K
035	23	#	076	4C	L
036	24	$	077	4D	M
037	25	%	078	4E	N
038	26	&	079	4F	O
039	27	'	080	50	P
040	28	(	081	51	Q
041	29	)	082	52	R
042	2A	*	083	53	S
043	2B	+	084	54	T
044	2C	,	085	55	U
045	2D	-	086	56	V
046	2E	.	087	57	W
047	2F	/	088	58	X
048	30	0	089	59	Y
049	31	1	090	5A	Z
050	32	2	091	5B	[
051	33	3	092	5C	\
052	34	4	093	5D	]
053	35	5	094	5E	^
054	36	6	095	5F	_
055	37	7	096	60	`
056	38	8	097	61	a
057	39	9	098	62	b
058	3A	:	099	63	c
059	3B	;	100	64	d
060	3C	<	101	65	e
061	3D	=	102	66	f
062	3E	>	103	67	g
063	3F	?	104	68	h
064	40	@	105	69	i
065	41	A	106	6A	j
066	42	B	107	6B	k
067	43	C	108	6C	l
068	44	D	109	6D	m
069	45	E	110	6E	n
070	46	F	111	6F	o
071	47	G	112	70	p
072	48	H			

ASCII Value Dec	Hex	ASCII Character	ASCII Value Dec	Hex	ASCII Character
113	71	q	148	94	ö
114	72	r	149	95	ò
115	73	s	150	96	û
116	74	t	151	97	ù
117	75	u	152	98	ÿ
118	76	v	153	99	Ö
119	77	w	154	9A	Ü
120	78	x	155	9B	¢
121	79	y	156	9C	£
122	7A	z	157	9D	¥
123	7B	{	158	9E	Pt
124	7C	¦	159	9F	ƒ
125	7D	}	160	A0	á
126	7E	~	161	A1	í
127	7F	DEL	162	A2	ó
128	80	Ç	163	A3	ú
129	81	ü	164	A4	ñ
130	82	é	165	A5	Ñ
131	83	â	166	A6	ª
132	84	ä	167	A7	º
133	85	à	168	A8	¿
134	86	å	169	A9	⌐
135	87	ç	170	AA	¬
136	88	ê	171	AB	½
137	89	ë	172	AC	¼
138	8A	è	173	AD	¡
139	8B	ï	174	AE	«
140	8C	î	175	AF	»
141	8D	ì	176	B0	░
142	8E	Ä	177	B1	▒
143	8F	Å	178	B2	▓
144	90	É	179	B3	│
145	91	æ	180	B4	┤
146	92	Æ	181	B5	╡
147	93	ô	182	B6	╢

| ASCII Value | | ASCII Character | ASCII Value | | ASCII Character |
Dec	Hex		Dec	Hex	
183	B7	⊓	217	D9	⌐
184	B8	⌐	218	DA	⌐
185	B9	╢	219	DB	█
186	BA	║	220	DC	▄
187	BB	╗	221	DD	▌
188	BC	╝	222	DE	▐
189	BD	╜	223	DF	▀
190	BE	╛	224	E0	α
191	BF	┐	225	E1	β
192	C0	└	226	E2	Γ
193	C1	┴	227	E3	π
194	C2	┬	228	E4	Σ
195	C3	├	229	E5	σ
196	C4	─	230	E6	μ
197	C5	┼	231	E7	τ
198	C6	╞	232	E8	Φ
199	C7	╟	233	E9	θ
200	C8	╚	234	EA	Ω
201	C9	╔	235	EB	δ
202	CA	╩	236	EC	∞
203	CB	╦	237	ED	ø
204	CC	╠	238	EE	∈
205	CD	═	239	EF	∩
206	CE	╬	240	F0	≡
207	CF	╧	241	F1	±
208	D0	╨	242	F2	≥
209	D1	╤	243	F3	≤
210	D2	╥	244	F4	⌠
211	D3	╙	245	F5	⌡
212	D4	╘	246	F6	÷
213	D5	╒	247	F7	≈
214	D6	╓	248	F8	°
215	D7	╫	249	F9	•
216	D8	╪	250	FA	·

| ASCII Value | | ASCII Character | ASCII Value | | ASCII Character |
Dec	Hex		Dec	Hex	
251	FB	√	254	FE	∎
252	FC	η	255	FF	
253	FD	$_2$			

Index

specifications, 238-239
storing on backup diskettes,
    337-338
text
    background printing, 368-371
    creating and naming, 283
treating as devices, 374-375
troubleshooting, 210-213, 249
viewing contents, 167-170
XCOPY.EXE, 244
files area, DOS Shell, 38
FILES command, 595-596,
    711-712
Files List Shell, running DOS
    programs, 95
filter programs, 239-240
Find (Search menu) option,
    278-279
FIND command, 241-244, 712-715
    /C switch, 713-714
    /I switch, 713
    /N switch, 713-714
    /V switch, 713-714
FIND.EXE file, 241
fixed disks, *see* hard disks
floppy disks, *see* diskettes
Flu-Shot + program, 587
FOR command, 433-434, 716-717
foreign language alphabets, 597
form-feed (^L) character, 363
Format (Disk Utilities menu)
    option, 129
FORMAT command, 717-723
    /1 switch, 719-721
    /4 switch, 720-722
    /8 switch, 720-721
    /B switch, 720-721
    /F:size switch, 720-722
    /N:sectors switch, 720-722
    /O switch, 719-721
    /Q switch, 718, 723
    /S switch, 719-722
    /T:tracks switch, 720-722

/U switch, 718
/V:label switch, 720-721
`Format complete` message, 127
Format dialog box, 126
formatting
    disk incompatibility problems,
        573-577
    diskettes, 122-129
    hard disks, 601-602
    high-level, 519-522
    invisible characters, 256-257
    low-level, 518-519
fragmentation of files, 583-585
FS keys
    edits commands, 246
function keys
    see also keys
    assigning commands to (creating
        batch file), 414-416
    assigning multiple commands
        to, 377
    resetting to original defini-
        tions, 379
    using to type text, 377-379

G

$G macro code, 473
/G switch
    EDIT command, 287, 690
/G:x switch
    DOSSHELL command, 679
`General failure reading drive x` message, 90, 125,
    300, 341, 718
$GG macro code, 473
GOTO command, 423, 723-724
GRAFTABL command, 597,
    724-725
    /STA switch, 724
graphical user interfaces
    (GUI), 515
graphics, printing, 366-367

Sams—Covering The Latest In Computer And Technical Topics!

Audio

Audio Production Techniques for Video	$29.95
Audio Systems Design and Installation	$59.95
Audio Technology Fundamentals	$24.95
Compact Disc Troubleshooting and Repair	$24.95
Handbook for Sound Engineers:	
The New Audio Cyclopedia	$79.95
Introduction to Professional Recording Techniques	$29.95
Modern Recording Techniques, 3rd Ed.	$29.95
Principles of Digital Audio, 2nd Ed.	$29.95
Sound Recording Handbook	$49.95
Sound System Engineering, 2nd Ed.	$49.95

Electricity/Electronics

Basic AC Circuits	$29.95
Electricity 1, Revised 2nd Ed.	$14.95
Electricity 1-7, Revised 2nd Ed.	$49.95
Electricity 2, Revised 2nd Ed.	$14.95
Electricity 3, Revised 2nd Ed.	$14.95
Electricity 4, Revised 2nd Ed.	$14.95
Electricity 5, Revised 2nd Ed.	$14.95
Electricity 6, Revised 2nd Ed.	$14.95
Electricity 7, Revised 2nd Ed.	$14.95
Electronics 1-7, Revised 2nd Ed.	$49.95

Electronics Technical

Active-Filter Cookbook	$19.95
Camcorder Survival Guide	$9.95
CMOS Cookbook, 2nd Ed.	$24.95
Design of OP-AMP Circuits with Experiments	$19.95
Design of Phase-Locked Loop Circuits	
with Experiments	$19.95
Electrical Test Equipment	$19.95
Electrical Wiring	$19.95
How to Read Schematics, 4th Ed.	$19.95
IC Op-Amp Cookbook, 3rd Ed.	$24.95
IC Timer Cookbook, 2nd Ed.	$19.95
IC User's Casebook	$19.95
Radio Handbook, 23rd Ed.	$39.95
Radio Operator's License Q&A Manual, 11th Ed.	$24.95
RF Circuit Design	$24.95
Transformers and Motors	$24.95
TTL Cookbook	$19.95
Undergrounding Electric Lines	$14.95
Understanding Telephone Electronics, 2nd Ed.	$19.95
VCR Troubleshooting & Repair Guide	$19.95
Video Scrambling & Descrambling	
for Satellite & Cable TV	$19.95

Games

Beyond the Nintendo Masters	$9.95
Mastering Nintendo Video Games II	$9.95
Tricks of the Nintendo Masters	$9.95
VideoGames & Computer Entertainment	
Complete Guide to Nintendo Video Games	$9.50
Winner's Guide to Nintendo Game Boy	$9.95
Winner's Guide to Sega Genesis	$9.95

Hardware/Technical

Hard Disk Power with the Jamsa Disk Utilities	$39.95
IBM PC Advanced Troubleshooting & Repair	$24.95
IBM Personal Computer	
Troubleshooting & Repair	$24.95
IBM Personal Computer Upgrade Guide	$24.95
Microcomputer Troubleshooting & Repair	$24.95
Understanding Communications Systems, 2nd Ed.	$19.95
Understanding Data Communications, 2nd Ed.	$19.95
Understanding FAX and Electronic Mail	$19.95
Understanding Fiber Optics	$19.95

IBM: Business

Best Book of Microsoft Works for the PC, 2nd Ed.	$24.95
Best Book of PFS: First Choice	$24.95
Best Book of Professional Write and File	$22.95
First Book of Fastback Plus	$16.95
First Book of Norton Utilities	$16.95
First Book of Personal Computing	$16.95
First Book of PROCOMM PLUS	$16.95

IBM: Database

Best Book of Paradox 3	$27.95
dBASE III Plus Programmer's Reference Guide	$24.95
dBASE IV Programmer's Reference Guide	$24.95
First Book of Paradox 3	$16.95
Mastering ORACLE	
Featuring ORACLE's SQL Standard	$24.95

IBM: Graphics/Desktop Publishing

Best Book of Autodesk Animator	$29.95
Best Book of Harvard Graphics	$24.95
First Book of DrawPerfect	$16.95
First Book of Harvard Graphics	$16.95
First Book of PC Paintbrush	$16.95
First Book of PFS: First Publisher	$16.95

IBM: Spreadsheets/Financial

Best Book of Lotus 1-2-3 Release 3.1	$27.95
Best Book of Lotus 1-2-3, Release 2.2, 3rd Ed.	$26.95
Best Book of Peachtree Complete III	$24.95
First Book of Lotus 1-2-3, Release 2.2	$16.95
First Book of Lotus 1-2-3/G	$16.95
First Book of Microsoft Excel for the PC	$16.95
Lotus 1-2-3: Step-by-Step	$24.95

IBM: Word Processing

Best Book of Microsoft Word 5	$24.95
Best Book of Microsoft Word for Windows	$24.95
Best Book of WordPerfect 5.1	$26.95
Best Book of WordPerfect Version 5.0	$24.95
First Book of PC Write	$16.95
First Book of WordPerfect 5.1	$16.95
WordPerfect 5.1: Step-by-Step	$24.95

Macintosh/Apple

Best Book of AppleWorks	$24.95
Best Book of MacWrite II	$24.95
Best Book of Microsoft Word for the Macintosh	$24.95
Macintosh Printer Secrets	$34.95
Macintosh Repair & Upgrade Secrets	$34.95
Macintosh Revealed, Expanding the Toolbox,	
Vol. 4	$29.95
Macintosh Revealed, Mastering the Toolbox,	
Vol. 3	$29.95
Macintosh Revealed, Programming with the Toolbox,	
Vol. 2, 2nd Ed.	$29.95
Macintosh Revealed, Unlocking the Toolbox,	
Vol. 1, 2nd Ed.	$29.95
Using ORACLE with HyperCard	$24.95

Operating Systems/Networking

Best Book of DESQview	$24.95
Best Book of DOS	$24.95
Best Book of Microsoft Windows 3	$24.95
Business Guide to Local Area Networks	$24.95
Exploring the UNIX System, 2nd Ed.	$29.95
First Book of DeskMate	$16.95
First Book of Microsoft QuickPascal	$16.95
First Book of MS-DOS	$16.95
First Book of UNIX	$16.95
Interfacing to the IBM Personal Computer,	
2nd Ed.	$24.95
Mastering NetWare	$29.95
The Waite Group's Discovering MS-DOS	$19.95
The Waite Group's Inside XENIX	$29.95
The Waite Group's MS-DOS Bible, 3rd Ed.	$24.95
The Waite Group's MS-DOS Developer's Guide,	
2nd Ed.	$29.95
The Waite Group's Tricks of the MS-DOS Masters,	
2nd Ed.	$29.95
The Waite Group's Tricks of the UNIX Masters	$29.95
The Waite Group's Understanding MS-DOS,	
2nd Ed.	$19.95
The Waite Group's UNIX Primer Plus, 2nd Ed.	$29.95
The Waite Group's UNIX System V Bible	$29.95
The Waite Group's UNIX System V Primer,	
Revised Ed.	$29.95
Understanding Local Area Networks, 2nd Ed.	$24.95

Understanding NetWare	$24.95
UNIX Applications Programming:	
Mastering the Shell	$29.95
UNIX Networking	$29.95
UNIX Shell Programming, Revised Ed.	$29.95
UNIX System Administration	$29.95
UNIX System Security	$34.95
UNIX Text Processing	$29.95
UNIX: Step-by-Step	$29.95

Professional/Reference

Data Communications, Networks, and Systems	$39.95
Gallium Arsenide Technology, Volume II	$69.95
Handbook of Computer-Communications Standards,	
Vol. 1, 2nd Ed.	$39.95
Handbook of Computer-Communications Standards,	
Vol. 2, 2nd Ed.	$39.95
Handbook of Computer-Communications Standards,	
Vol. 3, 2nd Ed.	$39.95
Handbook of Electronics Tables and Formulas,	
6th Ed.	$24.95
ISDN, DECnet, and SNA Communications	$44.95
Modern Dictionary of Electronics, 6th Ed.	$39.95
Programmable Logic Designer's Guide	$29.95
Reference Data for Engineers: Radio, Electronics,	
Computer, and Communications, 7th Ed.	$99.95
Surface-Mount Technology for PC Board Design	$49.95
World Satellite Almanac, 2nd Ed.	$39.95

Programming

Advanced C: Tips and Techniques	$29.95
C Programmer's Guide to NetBIOS	$29.95
C Programmer's Guide to Serial Communications	$29.95
Commodore 64 Programmer's Reference Guide	$19.95
DOS Batch File Power	$39.95
First Book of GW-BASIC	$16.95
How to Write Macintosh Software, 2nd Ed.	$29.95
Mastering Turbo Assembler	$29.95
Mastering Turbo Debugger	$29.95
Mastering Turbo Pascal 5.5, 3rd Ed.	$29.95
Microsoft QuickBASIC Programmer's Reference	$29.95
Programming in ANSI C	$29.95
Programming in C, Revised Ed.	$29.95
QuickC Programming	$29.95
The Waite Group's BASIC Programming	
Primer, 2nd Ed.	$24.95
The Waite Group's C Programming	
Using Turbo C++	$29.95
The Waite Group's C++ Programming	$24.95
The Waite Group's C: Step-by-Step	$29.95
The Waite Group's GW-BASIC Primer Plus	$24.95
The Waite Group's Microsoft C Bible, 2nd Ed.	$29.95
The Waite Group's Microsoft C Programming	
for the PC, 2nd Ed.	$29.95
The Waite Group's Microsoft Macro	
Assembler Bible	$29.95
The Waite Group's New C Primer Plus	$29.95
The Waite Group's QuickC Bible	$29.95
The Waite Group's Turbo Assembler Bible	$29.95
The Waite Group's Turbo C Bible	$29.95
The Waite Group's Turbo C Programming	
for the PC, Revised Ed.	$29.95
The Waite Group's TWG Turbo C++Bible	$29.95
X Window System Programming	$29.95

For More Information, Call Toll Free

1-800-257-5755

All prices are subject to change without notice.
Non-U.S. prices may be higher. Printed in the U.S.A.

DOS 5 Shell Survival Guide

	Action	Option(s)	See pages
	Activate Shell	Type EXIT and press Enter or type DOSSHELL and press Enter	679-683
1.	Move highlight bar	Press Tab to move from area to area; ↑, ↓, ←, → moves within area	38
2.	Move mouse pointer	Roll your mouse	198-200
3.	Pull down a menu	Hold down Alt and press underlined letter or click desired option	42-44
4.	Select a drive	Highlight and press Enter or click drive	37
5.	Select a directory	Highlight and press Enter or click directory name	74
6.	Expand/contract directory	Highlight directory name and press + or – or click directory icon	74-75
7.	Select file for operation	Press Add (Shift+F8), highlight, and press the Spacebar or hold down Ctrl and click file name	229-231

	Action	Option(s)	See pages
8.	Run a program (file with .EXE, .COM, or .BAT extension)	Highlight and press Enter or double-click	385, 508
9.	Get help	Select an option from Help pull-down menu or press F1	49
10.	Run program or select program group	Highlight and press Enter or double-click	108-109
11.	Activate or deactivate task swapper	Select Enable Task Swapper from the Options pull-down menu	110-115
	Change overall view	Select an option from the View pull-down menu	45
	Exit the Shell	Select Exit from the File pull-down menu, or press F3	54-55

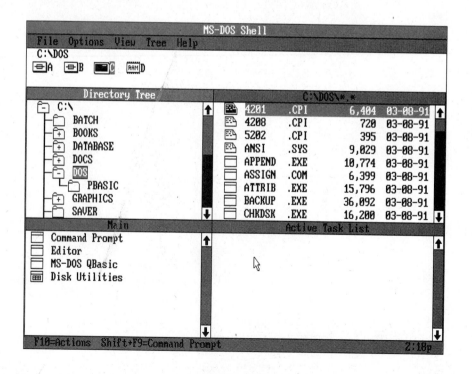